Protecting Privacy in

Surveillance Societies

Protecting Privacy in Surveillance Societies

THE FEDERAL REPUBLIC OF GERMANY,
SWEDEN, FRANCE, CANADA,
AND THE UNITED STATES

DAVID H. FLAHERTY

The University of North Carolina Press

CHAPEL HILL AND LONDON

Library of Congress Cataloging-in-Publication Data

Flaherty, David H.
     Protecting privacy in surveillance societies : the Federal Republic
of Germany, Sweden, France, Canada, and the United States / by
David H. Flaherty.
     p.   cm.
     ISBN 0-8078-1871-2 (alk. paper)
     1. Data protection—Europe. 2. Privacy, Right of—Europe.
3. Data protection—Canada. 4. Privacy, Right of—Canada. 5. Data
protection—United States. 6. Privacy, Right of—United States.
I. Title.
K3264.C65F56   1989
342'.0858—dc19
[342.2858]   89-4762
                         CIP

The paper in this book meets the guidelines for permanence
and durability of the Committee on Production Guidelines for
Book Longevity of the Council on Library Resources.

Printed in the United States of America

93 92 91 90 89   5 4 3 2 1

Selected material in this book has appeared in somewhat different form in
the following articles and is reproduced with permission of the JAI Press, Inc.:
David H. Flaherty, "The Need for an American Privacy Protection Commission,"
Government Information Quarterly 1 (1984): 235–58, and David H. Flaherty, "The
Emergence of Surveillance Societies in the Western World: Towards the Year 2000,"
Government Information Quarterly 5 (1988): 377–87.

For Michael

Contents

Part 3: France

Part 4: Canada

Tables

Preface

Concern for the protection of personal privacy in the face of the massive surveillance capacities of governments and corporations is a leading issue in all Western industrialized societies. Individuals want to be left alone and to exercise some control over how information about them is used. Legislators have responded to widespread fears about the impact of computers on personal privacy by enacting protective laws. These measures seek to control the government's collection, use, and dissemination of personal information by means of codes of fair information practices. The issue is whether such data protection laws and the agencies created to implement them have been effective watchdogs in limiting governmental surveillance of the population and in promoting bureaucratic accountability in data use.

This book is a comparative examination of the passage, revision, and, especially, implementation of data protection laws at the national and state levels in five countries. The focus is an evaluation of the accomplishments in controlling surveillance by the officials charged with protecting certain aspects of personal privacy in the Federal Republic of Germany, Sweden, France, Canada, and the United States. Although data protectors in Sweden and France also regulate the private sector, the emphasis in the volume is on activities in the public sector. Since I am persuaded that data protection laws and agencies are necessary, I want them to be as effective as possible in achieving their objectives—hence this book.

The countries selected for treatment illustrate the leading approaches to data protection. Despite having the oldest national data protection law, Sweden is presented here as the prototype of the surveillance society. The West German state of Hesse has the oldest state law, and West Germany itself has had the most successful national system of data protection to date. As a federal political system, it offers valuable comparisons with North America. Canada has the most developed system of data protection in North America, because the United States does not have a single agency that concentrates on the oversight of data protection under its Privacy Act of 1974. France is of intrinsic interest because of its expansive 1978 law.

There is an important distinction between privacy protection and data protection. "Privacy" is a broad, all-encompassing concept that envelops a whole host of human concerns about various forms of intrusive behavior, including wiretapping, surreptitious physical surveillance, and mail interception. Individuals claim a right to privacy for an enormously wide range of issues from the right to practice contraception or have an abortion to the right to keep bank records confidential. I am particularly concerned with "data protection," an aspect of privacy protection that is especially involved with control of the collection, use, and dissemination of personal information. Data protection is implemented to limit this type of surveillance by other persons and organizations and thus to preserve individual privacy. It is at present the most critical component of privacy protection, because of the ongoing automation of data bases.

References to "surveillance" in this volume primarily denote supervision, observation, or oversight of individual behavior through the use of personal data rather than through such mediums as a camera or a private detective. Electronic surveillance by computers is treated as the central problem of data protection, because it depends on the collection and linkage of personal information.

At one level this volume is a foreigner's perspective on data protection in various countries, written primarily for foreigners. Yet each case study sheds comparative light on data protection in other countries. Although there are problems of understanding the workings of data protection in any country, an effort was made to reach an appropriate level of comprehension of evolving systems that, in fact, tend to undergo periodic modification through statutory revision or changes in personnel and administrative practices. My research in the 1980s has been continuous in order to avoid superficial and erroneous impressions, although the final product necessarily reflects my own views on a relatively complex subject. The different data protection agencies had an opportunity to review and comment on what I had written about them, but I made all decisions on the final text.

This volume is consciously critical, because data protection agencies have not attracted meaningful scrutiny by independent observers. With few exceptions, the limited secondary literature on data protection adopts a celebratory tone or produces broad general overviews primarily listing national laws in a descriptive format. Data protectors themselves are occupied with the practical and political aspects of running their offices. As one of them wrote to me in 1988, they need to be reminded of how much remains to be done. One purpose of this volume is to explain the various systems of data protection in order to promote intelligent responses by them to usual and unusual problems. This goal is especially problematic given the myopic nationalism of some members of the data protection community.

In assessing particular agencies one becomes aware of the varying personalities at play and of some of the personal clashes that occur. My interest has been in the intellectual character of the debates over how to control surveillance, and there is clearly no intention, for example, to pick sides in internal agency disputes. I made my judgments after due consideration of varying opinions and facts. The process of interviewing as many different people as possible, inside and outside of government, promoted understanding of particular problems and issues, even though one never has the time or resources to do enough research.

The facts and general ideas developed in hundreds of interviews have greatly shaped the findings of this volume. Since a high percentage of my interviews have been with the staff who actually do the detailed work of data protection, the views analyzed in this volume reflect as closely as possible the reality of implementing data protection as opposed to elite managerial perceptions of what is or should be occurring. I have interviewed many of the professional staff members of data protection agencies on several occasions. They were always responsive to my questions about their current problems with implementation, thereby contributing enormously to the substance of this volume. Statements based on interviews are not attributed in the text itself, because I promised confidentiality to respondents.

Except for a few years' hiatus in France, I have enjoyed unrestricted access to data protection personnel in the various countries. I regret that I was unable to spend more time with the many members of the governing boards of the agencies in Sweden and France. In Sweden and West Germany, my linguistic deficiencies led me to depend on translations into English of documents prepared by government agencies or by colleagues and research assistants; fortunately, the vast majority of my interviews were in English.

Whenever possible, I have interviewed civil servants, lawyers, journalists, academic specialists, and civil libertarians outside the data protection agency. I have attended annual meetings of the data protection commissioners on various occasions, a large number of academic and professional meetings of privacy advocates, and staff meetings of the data protection agencies in France and West Germany. My research has also relied on a large number of published and unpublished sources, especially annual reports of federal and state data protection commissioners.

My approach to writing this book has been empirical and functional. I have sought to understand reality as opposed to the language of the relevant statutes. I have returned many times to each agency, so as to overcome the usual superficiality of tourist visits. I was in fact flattered when a West German respondent characterized me as "an international inspector of data protectors." (Less flattering was another inquiry in France as to whether I worked for the CIA.)

A word about my objectivity as a writer, since it is not possible to achieve strict neutrality in these matters and, at the same time, anyone in my position runs a significant risk of being co-opted. I have had only slight hesitation in asking sensitive questions at data protection agencies, because of my ultimate responsibility to readers. But I naturally sought to have cordial relations with the data protectors I was writing about, even though I have not always been successful. On one occasion, review of a draft case study led the head of an agency to order me to leave the premises. This necessitated fence-mending exercises with his successors and some subsequent restrictions on my access to the staff for interviews. I am deeply grateful to those colleagues who eventually persuaded me that my career as a social scientist was not at an end. Fortunately as well, every other data protection agency proved most hospitable to the goals of public policy research. Yet I recognize the inherent conflict of trying to be constructively critical of privacy protection efforts, while dependent on data protectors as my prime sources.

Because of an introduction to Professor Alan F. Westin at Columbia University in September 1964, I have devoted a significant part of my academic career to the study of privacy issues. This book, and the accompanying volume, *Privacy and Data Protection: An International Bibliography* (London, U.K., and White Plains, N.Y., 1984), are based on a conviction that data protection should be subject to academic inquiry and objective criticism. I am also a privacy advocate, in the sense that I seek to raise the consciousness of governments and individuals to the human values and interests that are at stake when surveillance practices are uncontrolled. Creating, implementing, and improving privacy and data protection laws and practices is a matter of pressing public concern in the Western world. The major burden is being carried by dedicated and talented government officials in the several countries. In a spirit of constructive criticism, this volume seeks to assist in the process of regulating government information systems in the interests of preventing unnecessary intrusions into the lives of individuals. Although I recognize the risk that my critical comments about data protection may be misused by opponents of data protection in a particular country, I hope that the advantage of being a foreigner (except in Canada) permits me to claim some objectivity in addressing these matters.

January 1989
London, Canada

Acknowledgments

As a research project ends, one recognizes the enormous amount of assistance and support received from other institutions and individuals. I start with the essential financial support of the Ford Foundation, the Social Sciences and Humanities Research Council of Canada, and the Academic Development Fund of the University of Western Ontario. At Western, I have also had important intellectual and personal support from faculty and students of the History Department, the Faculty of Social Science, and the Faculty of Law. As always, I remain deeply indebted to the staff of the reference department of the D. B. Weldon Library at the University of Western Ontario, especially George Robinson, and to Marianne Welch of the Law Library. I would also like to acknowledge the support for publication received from the University of Western Ontario's J. B. Smallman Research Fund.

This research has enjoyed the essential support of a small, dedicated staff. Frances Kyle was the secretary and administrative assistant from the fall of 1981 to January 1983. Lizbeth Carruthers ably succeeded her through the end of 1984, when Penelope Lister took her place. I cannot exaggerate the critical importance of their respective contributions. Marnie Cudmore returned to the scene of an earlier Privacy Project and rendered valuable assistance in the summer of 1983.

I have had two outstanding student research assistants from the Faculty of Law. Terence J. Donohue worked with me from 1981 to 1983. His skills in the German language were of particular value, as were those of my colleague Erich Hahn. From 1983 to 1985 Peter Harte brought his excellent critical capacity to bear on my case studies.

Cecilia Magnusson of the Law and Informatics Research Institute of Stockholm University rendered valuable research assistance with Swedish sources, and Agneta Dolman helped with Swedish translations.

I have done research in at least ten countries in connection with this book and conducted literally hundreds of interviews. Since it is impossible to identify by name everyone that I have ever consulted, I have listed below the persons whose assistance was of the most value in each country. I regret that this impersonal listing cannot be supplemented by a running commentary on the stimulating exchanges and good times we have had together.

Because I have primarily studied specific institutions in each country, I have benefited most from the excellent cooperation of the successive heads of the several data protection agencies. It has been especially generous of the leadership and professional staff of data protection offices to be willing to cooperate with an academic trying to understand how they do their work. I trust that my general admiration for their achievements is not lost from sight in the following pages.

In West Germany I am most grateful to the following people: Dr. Reinhold Baumann, Professor Dr. Hans Peter Bull, Herr Herbert Burkert, Dr. Ulrich Dammann, Dr. H.-J. Kerkau, Dr. Ruth Leuze, Herr Ottermann, Dr. Reinhard Riegel, Dr. Werner Ruckriegel, Dr. Rudolf Schomerus, Frau Helga Schumacher, Dr. W. Schmidt, Professor Dr. Spiros Simitis, Herr Jürgen Werner, Dr. Heinrich Weyer, and Dr. Walter Wiese.

I would like in particular to thank the following for valued assistance in Scandinavia: Jon Bing, Mats Börjesson, Hans Corell, Simon Corell, Jens Danielsson, Arve Føyen, Jan Freese, Carl-Gunnar Janson, Sten Markgren, Thomas Osvald, Jørgen Paulsen, Edmund Rapaport, Nils Rydén, Helge Seip, Peter Seipel, Knut Selmer, Hans Wranghult, and Rabbe Wrede.

In France I wish to acknowledge the generous hospitality of the Commission Nationale de l'Informatique et des Libertés and especially the staff of its Centre de la Documentation. I am also grateful to the following persons: Maître Alain Bensoussan, Mlle M. Boisnard, Mme M. Briat, Mme F. Chamoux, M. Jean Pierre Chamoux, Mme M. Delcamp, M. Daniel Duthil, M. Jacques Fauvet, Dr. H. P. Gassmann, M. Gervais, Mlle F. Hamdi, Mme M. C. Hoffsaes, M. Louis Joinet, Mme N. Lenoir, M. Herbert Maisl, M. A. Pezé, M. Jean Rosenwald, and Senator Jacques Thyraud. Mme Chamoux gave me the particular benefit of her careful reading of the French case study, as did Anne Laberge of the Quebec Commission d'Accès à l'Information.

For Canada, I am especially grateful to: Barry Baker; the Hon. Perrin Beatty; Gerry Bethell; Dr. Peter Gillis; Ann Goldsmith; Dr. John W. Grace; George Hamelin; Holly Harris; Inger Hansen, Q.C.; Robert Jelking; the Hon. Bob Kaplan; William Kaplan; Jake Knoppers; T. Murray Rankin; Thomas B. Riley; Dr. Peter Robinson; Philip Rosen; Stephen J. Skelly, Q.C.; J. Kenneth Strang; Blaine Thacker; William Ward Sulston; Gerard Van Berkel and Jill Wallace. I must also thank several Quebec experts for allowing me to review the findings of their forays into European data protection: Thérèse Giroux, Caroline Pestieau, Maria Sauer, and Lucy Wells.

The following persons in the United States have greatly assisted me: Lois A. Alexander, Robert P. Bedell, Robert Belair, William T. Cavaney, John P. Fanning, Robert M. Gellman, Evan Hendricks, David Nemecek, Hugh V. O'Neill, G. Russell Pipe, Ronald L. Plesser, Priscilla M. Regan, Harold C. Relyea, Robert Ellis Smith, Robert Veeder, Fred W. Weingarten, and Alan F. Westin.

Finally, many events and activities helped to sharpen my thinking about data protection. I want to acknowledge the opportunity afforded me to write a draft of the conclusions to this volume, when I was a guest of the Rockefeller

Foundation as a resident scholar at the Villa Serbelloni in Bellagio, Italy, for a month in 1983. The opportunity to reflect on the directions of my research findings was invaluable.

The Rockefeller Foundation allowed me to organize a five-day conference in Bellagio in April 1984. Twenty-three specialists in data protection from nine countries gathered together for informative discussions. They offered valuable comments on my draft conclusions to the present volume. The Ford Foundation also furnished financial support for this conference.

In 1984 I prepared a report on foreign privacy and data protection laws and policies for the Office of Technology Assessment of the U.S. Congress. In addition to strengthening my judgment about the necessity of oversight mechanisms to make data protection effective, the drafting of the report permitted me to focus on certain specific applications of technology, such as computer matching and machine-readable identity cards. I have relied on this report at several points in this volume (David H. Flaherty, *Data Protection and Privacy: Comparative Policies,* A Report to the Government Information Technology Project, Office of Technology Assessment, U. S. Congress [U. S. Department of Commerce, National Technical Information Service, 1986, PB86–205689]). I was also a member in 1984–85 of the oversight panel for the Office of Technology Assessment's study of federal government information technology and civil liberties.

One of the problems of studying data protection is that it is a new aspect of public policy that does not fit neatly into any single academic discipline. The European Consortium for Political Research sponsored a week-long workshop on privacy and data protection in Barcelona in March 1985, primarily involving political scientists, lawyers, and sociologists from Western Europe. This was an instructive and helpful opportunity to discuss our respective interests in an academic context, and I am grateful to Charles Raab of the University of Edinburgh for inviting me to participate.

During the academic year 1985–86, I was a visiting scholar at the Stanford Law School, which allowed me an uninterrupted period of research and writing. I am deeply grateful to Dean John Hart Ely and his colleagues, especially Thomas F. McBride and Lawrence M. Friedman, for making this opportunity possible.

In 1985–87, I served as staff consultant to the Canadian House of Commons's Standing Committee on Justice and Solicitor General for its three-year review of the operation of Canada's Privacy Act and Access to Information Act. Since I drafted the privacy portions of the committee's report, I have at least tried to contain my enthusiasm for quoting it as an authoritative source.

In 1987 Marcel Pepin, then the director of the Quebec Commission d'Accès à l'Information, invited me to give the keynote address to the annual meeting in Quebec of privacy and data protection commissioners from twenty countries. This experience was truly seminal for me in refocusing my attention on the theme of surveillance societies. I am grateful for discussions at a Statistics Sweden conference in June 1987 that helped me to shape my views about Sweden as a surveillance society.

Several people read the entire manuscript at a critical juncture and greatly shaped further revisions. Even if I did not follow all of their good advice, I am deeply grateful to Sid Noel of the Department of Political Science at the University of Western Ontario and Kenneth L. Kraemer of the Public Policy Research Organization, University of California, Irvine.

In the summer of 1987, Deidre Smith, a law student at the University of Western Ontario, assisted me with editing of the case studies. She proved to be a brilliant editor, and I am most grateful to her. I want to acknowledge as well the careful editing of Margaret Morse at the University of North Carolina Press, where it was also my privilege to benefit from the supportive editorial guidance of Iris Tillman Hill.

Abbreviations

ASAP	American Society of Access Professionals
BDSG	West German Federal Data Protection Act, 1977
BfD	Office of the Federal Data Protection Commissioner, West Germany
BKA	Federal Criminal Investigation Office, West Germany
BMI	Federal Ministry of the Interior, West Germany
CEIC	Employment and Immigration Canada
CFDT	Democratic Confederation of Labor, France
CGT	General Confederation of Labor, France
CIA	Central Intelligence Agency, United States
CIII	Center for Information and Initiatives on Computerization, France
CISI	Compagnie Internationale de Services en Informatique, France
CNIL	National Commission on Informatics and Freedoms, France
CPIC	Canadian Police Information Centre
CSIS	Canadian Security Intelligence Service
DALK	Parliamentary Commission on Revision of the Data Act, 1976–84, Sweden
DDASS	Agency for Health and Social Assistance, France
DHHS	Department of Health and Human Services, United States (formerly HEW)
DIB	Data Inspection Board, Sweden
DOMI	Data Processing Methods Division, Ministry of Health, France
DPC	Data Protection Commissioner, West Germany
ENA	National School of Administration, France
FBI	Federal Bureau of Investigation, United States
FDP	Free Democratic Party, West Germany
FOIA	Freedom of Information Act, United States
GAO	General Accounting Office, United States
HEW	Department of Health, Education, and Welfare, United States (now DHHS)

HUD   Department of Housing and Urban Development, United States

INSEE   National Institute of Statistics and Economic Studies, France

LMI   State Ministry of the Interior, West Germany

NIR   National Identification Register, France (formerly RNIPP)

NRW   North Rhine–Westphalia, West Germany

NTIA   National Telecommunications and Information Administration, United States

OECD   Organization for Economic Co-operation and Development, Paris

OIRA   Office of Information and Regulatory Affairs, OMB, United States

OMB   Office of Management and Budget, United States

OPM   Office of Personnel Management, United States

OTA   Office of Technology Assessment, United States Congress

PCIE   President's Council on Integrity and Efficiency, United States

PIN   Personal Identification Number

PMI   Agency for the Protection of Mothers and Children, France

RCMP   Royal Canadian Mounted Police, Canada

RNIPP   National Identification Register, France (now NIR)

SARB   Commission on the Vulnerability of Swedish Society

SCB   Statistics Sweden

SDECE   Service for External Documentation and Counterespionage, France

SIN   Social Insurance Number, Canada

SIRC   Security Intelligence Review Committee, Canada

SPAR   National Register of Names and Addresses, Sweden

SPD   Social Democratic Party, West Germany

Protecting Privacy in

Surveillance Societies

Introduction

The Emergence of Surveillance Societies

The central theme of this volume is that individuals in the Western world are increasingly subject to surveillance through the use of data bases in the public and private sectors, and that these developments have negative implications for the quality of life in our societies and for the protection of human rights. Moreover, despite the advent of privacy and data protection laws in response to such concerns, there is some evidence that we have created only the illusion of data protection.

Western industrial societies run the increasing risk of becoming—or may already be—surveillance societies, as one component of being information societies.[1] Various automated data bases now in existence facilitate surveillance of individuals. The threat to the right to be left alone is serious, since only partial regulatory solutions have yet been achieved, especially for the private sector in North America.[2] The data base of the Credit Bureau of Greater Toronto, for example, monitors credit information of six million residents of Ontario. Approximately 10 percent of the adult population appears in the national police computer known as the Canadian Police Information Centre.[3] The five largest consumer credit companies in the United States each maintain records on an average of 120 million consumers.[4] In every country, federal and state governments maintain large numbers of data bases that keep different segments of the population under observation. Some of these forms of surveillance are of course quite legitimate in a democratic society, but their cumulative impact on individual privacy is negative.

In this age of automation, detailed surveillance can be initiated when individuals apply for benefits from or interact with agencies, or it can occur on an ex post facto basis. The personal histories of individuals are available for scrutiny at any time, and aspiring bureaucrats are constantly inventing new ways to use existing data for other administrative purposes, whether to enforce an agency's mandate, to respond to new governmental or legislative directives, or for law enforcement. For instance, during continued Palestinian unrest in 1988, the Israeli government ordered 400,000 adult Gazans to replace their old identity cards. When Gazans came to comply, secretaries punched their identity numbers into computers that instantly displayed outstanding tax obligations, arrest records, and other data.[5] This episode illustrates the capacities of mass surveillance in today's world.

Credit card companies maintain on-line data bases that not only profile the day-to-day activities of millions of users, but also make it possible to locate their whereabouts at specific times as on-line card verification occurs. Credit card companies watch what people purchase. For example, an American lawyer returning from a vacation in Paris was informed by her bank that someone (in fact, herself) had been purchasing clothes abroad with her credit card. She was upset by what she perceived as surveillance of her own activities.[6] Banks have similar monitoring capacities through the build-up of personal profiles for various purposes and the increased use of automated teller machines.

Other examples of technological innovations with implications for governmental surveillance are more exotic but nevertheless representative of the scale and pace of innovation. The Hong Kong government, for example, has plans to monitor the movements of 230,000 local automobiles by means of uniquely identifiable emitting devices attached to each car, which will monitor use of the roads and assign variable fees.[7] Such a computerized information system could easily be employed as well to monitor and store data on the physical movements of the population; even in its current mode, the data produced for the control of road use should be segregated from other administrative uses. In a similar development, various correctional agencies want misdemeanor offenders serving sentences at home to wear an electronic bracelet, which emits a digital code enabling the authorities to monitor their movements. Such electronic monitoring devices are becoming common in North America.[8]

Consider as well the invention of optical storage devices for mainframe computers that permit the use of laser beams to store massive amounts of personal data in digital form. A single optical disk can store four billion characters, comparable to forty reels of magnetic tape. These data can be transferred to a host computer at the rate of thirty million characters per second. Similar devices for personal computers, known as magneto-optical disk drives, can store 250 million to one billion characters that can be altered at will.[9]

The huge storage capacities of the newest computers facilitate surveillance, since it is so easy and relatively cheap to store and access large amounts of personal data. IBM has announced a four-megabit memory chip that is capable of storing more than four million pieces of data on a chip that is about one-quarter by one-half inch. Sixteen full pages of the *New York Times* can be stored in an area about the size of the period at the end of this sentence and can be read from the chip in about a quarter of a second.[10] Each day brings announcements of major developments in data storage that make it possible, for example, to purchase the names, addresses, and telephone numbers of 93 percent of Canadian telephone subscribers on a single disk; such data can be organized, enriched, linked, and retrieved with considerable ease in order to build profiles of individuals, who correctly sense that such activities pose serious risks to their interests.[11]

In the 1960s, when large computers first became common, the major apprehension, most notably in the United States, was the creation of one great national data bank. The avoidance of this scenario in the West has nevertheless resulted in a series of discrete data banks that are not yet fully integrated, yet have tremendous potential for active and passive surveillance of individuals by governments and corporations. The U.S. Congress's Office of Technology Assessment remarked in 1988 that "a *de facto* national database is actively being created, although in a piecemeal fashion."[12] It is the proliferation of information banks, rather than the existence of any single one of them, that poses the fundamental challenge to privacy interests. When personal data exist, they will be used, not always to the benefit of the individual. Several American sociologists concluded that "mass surveillance through personal documentation feeds on itself. The more important events in life entail production or consumption of personal documentation, the more feasible it is to institute effective surveillance through direct checking based on such data. Imaginative administrators of surveillance organizations are constantly seeking new uses for personal data in these ways." Perhaps a book published in 1974 announcing the end of private life was simply premature, since the technical feasibility of a world without much privacy is fast approaching.[13]

The increasing automation of the work place also makes possible insidious and effective electronic monitoring of the work force, especially of those employees representing the less powerful segments of society, such as non-unionized, temporary, or part-time laborers and job applicants, who often are members of the less advantaged socioeconomic strata.[14] Profiles of work output are produced daily for such persons as airline reservation clerks and clerical personnel who handle large amounts of information in large data bases. Research is uncovering considerable resistance to monitoring in the work place because it leads to stress and the erosion of human values.

Another aspect of the development of surveillance societies is the widespread effort to introduce such intrusive technologies as the polygraph (for lie detection) and urinalysis (for drug testing). These typify both the entrepreneurial search for an application of newly developed technology and the naive quest for technical solutions to such serious social problems as low productivity, employee theft, and drug and alcohol abuse. Rather than management identifying an important issue and then turning to the technocrats for a solution, technological advances are driving the process of problem identification. The Californian inventors of a urinalysis machine, appropriately called EMIT, naturally sought a market for their error-prone product, which, one need hardly add, was first tested and used on prisoners, a classic example of a powerless group in society whose claims to the most elemental forms of human dignity are frequently ignored. Scientists are also developing machines that will track people through how their brains recognize complex patterns of light and sound and through the pattern of the genetic information in their DNA molecules.[15]

To counter suggestions that the idea of surveillance societies is farfetched, it is worth reflecting on the known surveillance capacities of national intelligence agencies. The key achievements are physical observation by satellite cameras and electronic interception of communications by a wide variety of devices. Any person can be the target of such surveillance, if the political will exists to do so. The United States has long intercepted the conversations of Soviet leaders as they drive about Moscow in limousines. During the *Achille Lauro* hijacking episode in 1985, the National Security Administration provided the Reagan administration with almost instant access to the telephone communications of the Egyptian president. All telephone conversations routed through microwave towers in Washington, D.C., are routinely received by the Soviets (who permit the Americans similar free range in Moscow) in what Bob Woodward refers to as a massive invasion of the privacy of citizens. Such tapes are fed directly into computers for keyword analysis. The United States has developed a capacity to tap Soviet undersea communication cables by the use of submarines and an electronic pod that is almost impossible to detect.[16] These extraordinary revelations are no doubt only the tip of the iceberg of current capacities.

Other intelligence studies indicate that surveillance and noncompliance with basic controlling laws is not a recent phenomenon. In *Spycatcher,* Peter Wright reveals that MI5, the British domestic intelligence service, long had undercover officers posted in the Newcastle headquarters of the National Insurance office of the Department of Health and Social Security in order to supply data on demand on almost the total population of Britain. When the decision to automate was finally made around 1970, MI5's main concern was to try to establish a linkage to the proposed Newcastle computer. The most surprising result would be that they were hindered in their desire for continued access to information, since the 1984 Data Protection Act has a major exemption for national security interests.[17]

Massive surveillance capacity already exists through data banks, and surveillance activities are almost completely unregulated. For example, eight of the ten provinces in Canada do not have data protection legislation for the public sector; Ontario, the largest province, belatedly enacted such a law in 1987, after more than a decade of discussion.[18] The record at the state level in the United States is similarly deficient. In North America, information technology is galloping ahead of regulation and control, especially in the private sector, where the public must largely rely on self-regulation by the companies involved. European examples of surveillance are also common, as the example of Sweden, the prototype of a surveillance society, illustrates.

For reasons that are more fully developed below, Sweden is the model surveillance society in the Western world, because of its high degree of automation, the pervasiveness of Personal Identification Numbers (PINs) to facilitate record linkages, and the extent of data transfers between the public and private sectors.[19] Further, a complex legal structure, dominated by the principle of openness expressed in its famous Freedom of the Press Act, makes available to third parties a wide range of identifiable personal data that are normally kept confidential in other countries.

In Swedish society only a limited amount of space—physical, mental, and behavioral—is left for the individual in his or her relations with the government and with other persons. There is less privacy available for an individual to enjoy than in other Western societies (outside Scandinavia). Again, the wealth and wide-open spaces of Sweden mean that the physical aspects of personal privacy are less at risk than those elements that limit opportunities for intimacy, anonymity, and reserve.[20] Individuals do not function well without real opportunities to withdraw from the public sphere on a regular basis in order to enjoy and cultivate a sense of personal autonomy.

A central national data bank, known as SPAR, is in effect a national population register, containing for each person such varied data as name, PIN, address, citizenship, marital status, assessed income, taxable capital, and possession of real property.[21] None of these items, it should be realized, can be kept confidential in Sweden. A person's income and net worth, for example, are regularly published commercially at the county level from public records; such data have practical applications, such as in checking credit worthiness, but they can also serve to satisfy a large dose of individual curiosity.

In practice, there is relatively little personal information that one can keep secret from the government or other individuals in Sweden. To demonstrate the ready accessibility of data, the press regularly publishes all of the information it has collected from public registers concerning the director of Statistics Sweden.[22] In fact, the various state administrative agencies know more about the lives of citizens than almost anyone except a compulsive diarist or record keeper, a condition rapidly being approached in other countries. This situation is especially threatening for administrative information used to make decisions about individuals.

The critical issue is the purpose for collecting and using data. In 1987 the Swedish government and legislature decided to create a register on the more than one million boats in the society, because of the belief that such assets represent, in some way, the fruits of tax avoidance or evasion. The Social Democrats, in power since 1982 and for most of the last half century, believe that there should be no free riders in the society, that is, everyone should pay their fair share of taxes. However admirable this sentiment in any democratic society, the reality is that such data bases are the further development of a surveillance state, in a country already widely acknowledged, in the compelling words of data protector Jan Freese, to be a paradise for data banks.[23]

Sweden is not making social policy choices based on a careful balancing of conflicting values and goals, but is rushing headlong into cumulative technological applications without sufficient consideration of privacy interests. Perhaps it should simply be said that collective interests are achieving paramountcy over the individual good. Good intentions prevail. A senior official of the National Tax Board once said, when his agency's apparently insatiable demand for personal data was under attack, that "coming under surveillance is a privilege."[24] Data protection requires close scrutiny of various technological imperatives to ensure that the thrust toward the Information Age is an intelligent, informed process, one that is mindful of its consequences for the lives of everyone, yet governments and legislators in all Western countries seem largely incapable of such systemic considerations.

Sweden is an especially important example of a surveillance society because of the two large-scale public debates about privacy that broke out in the 1980s as a form of instinctive resistance to the Big Brother tendencies of its government. The major eruptions concerned a register-based census of population that was proposed in 1983, known as FOBALT, and also Project Metropolitan in 1986.[25] Both controversies represent the public's outraged expression of fundamental concerns about the prospects for preserving individual privacy. These outbreaks can only be expected to multiply, not least by contagion across national boundaries, as the rate of incorporation of new surveillance technologies continues to quicken in the last decade of this century. The pace of innovation is such that we have all been too sanguine about the preservation of a right to individual privacy in the years to come.

Sweden illustrates the technical possibility of creating a superbly efficient surveillance society in which, for example, private activity of many kinds can be monitored with relative ease. In the waning years of the twentieth century, our technocratic societies can accomplish what George Orwell could only fantasize about in the aftermath of the Second World War. Electronic surveillance, telecommunications devices, and integrated relational data bases of personal information are only beginning to have an impact on individual privacy, but (to use marketing language) their prospects are enormous.

Our capacity to create surveillance societies should force us to confront fundamental questions about their desirability, but often the pressure for economic efficiency and effectiveness overpowers any pause to consider the human values that are being trampled, especially by governments and legislatures. Does anyone want to live in a country where the "underground economy" could not survive because of governmental regimentation and control? That is a choice increasingly facing individuals, governments, and, in particular, data protectors, who should be the front-line troops in resisting such fundamental encroachments on private life.

Protecting Privacy in Surveillance Societies

The extent of contemporary concern over the protection of personal privacy in advanced industrial countries is now well documented. Casual perusal of any newspaper indicates the extent to which problems of personal privacy of the most pressing sort remain in the public eye. People sense that they have lost control over the protection of their own privacy in a world dominated by computers, even if most individuals are as yet only vaguely aware of the real social cost and implications of dossiers on each of us.[26]

Public opinion polls continue to suggest that the protection of personal privacy is among the most important issues in every Western nation. In the United States the polling firm of Louis Harris and Associates has regularly asked the same question since 1976 about the extent of public "concern" about privacy; this has revealed an increase in a positive response rate (very concerned and somewhat concerned) from 47 percent in 1976 to 76 percent in 1979 and 1983.[27] In a 1982 local interview survey, 90 percent of respondents in London, Ontario, a city which is sufficiently representative of the Canadian population to be a leading place for marketing firms to test their products, said protecting privacy was important or very important. In comparison to six other social and economic issues, protection of privacy was rated as only somewhat less important than controlling inflation, unemployment, and crime, but more important than stopping the spread of nuclear weapons and ending strikes. Sixty-two percent of the sample was very concerned or somewhat concerned about current threats to their personal privacy. Eighty-four percent agreed or somewhat agreed that storage of personal information on computers poses a danger to personal privacy.[28] These survey results are strong evidence of continuing concern for the protection of privacy.

Table 1 lists the kinds of privacy interests for which individuals ought to be able to claim protection with respect to information about themselves. This is an inventory of the ultimate values that should serve as the premise for the more detailed information-control principles and practices included in data protection activities. The specific terms and other efforts at definition in the table are an addition to the general working definition of privacy for this volume, what Alan F. Westin defined in *Privacy and Freedom* as the desire of persons to choose freely under what circumstances and to what extent they will expose themselves, their attitudes, and their behavior to others. For purposes of data protection, individuals (and/or data protectors as their surrogates) want to exercise as much control as possible over information about themselves, because of the risks of unnecessary or unauthorized surveillance.[29]

In order best to limit surveillance, one may envision individuals as having certain attributes that are fixed and others that are variable over the course of their lives. Among the fixed attributes are race, sex, date of birth, and, at any given point, a past history (whether it be of financial transactions, employment, medical treatment, religious and political affiliations, criminal behavior, etc.) Among variable attributes one may list beliefs, behaviors, and relationships with others, which all may persist for long periods but are not immutable. Individuals should have the right to control access to information about either type of attribute, including the right of refusal to provide such information. Additionally, if individuals divulge information, they may compel confidentiality; even when freely given, individuals should consent to the use

Table 1. Privacy Interests of Individuals in Information about Themselves

---

- The right to individual autonomy
- The right to be left alone
- The right to a private life
- The right to control information about oneself
- The right to limit accessibility
- The right of exclusive control of access to private realms
- The right to minimize intrusiveness
- The right to expect confidentiality
- The right to enjoy solitude
- The right to enjoy intimacy
- The right to enjoy anonymity
- The right to enjoy reserve
- The right to secrecy

---

made of the information provided. They should also have the expectation that such information as they provide will be recorded accurately. With regard to the immutable events of their history, individuals should expect amnesty after a longer or shorter period of time—for instance, juvenile misdemeanors should not necessarily affect an individual's life permanently. Finally, those who collect data should envisage a prospective amnesty and set a "statute of limitations" on the information gathered, in recognition that what might have been true of the subject at the time of collection—particularly with regard to beliefs and behaviors—may not be true at a later time.

Other careful attempts to define privacy are directly relevant to the concerns of individuals. After discussing various American efforts at definition and seeking a neutral concept, Ruth Gavison concluded that "in its most suggestive sense, privacy is a limitation of others' access to an individual."[30] This definition is again most relevant to data protection as a limit on surveillance.

In a valuable overview, Arnold Simmel argued that "privacy is a concept related to solitude, secrecy, and autonomy, but it is not synonymous with these terms; for beyond the purely descriptive aspects of privacy as isolation from the company, the curiosity, and the influence of others, privacy implies a normative element: the right to exclusive control to access to private realms." In his view, "the right to privacy asserts the sacredness of the person" and "any invasion of privacy constitutes an offense against the rights of the personality—against individuality, dignity, and freedom." Thus Simmel agrees with Edward J. Bloustein's elegant argument for privacy as an aspect of human dignity.[31]

Simmel makes two other definitional points that are especially relevant for understanding the reasons for wanting privacy and the character of its invasion: "Many of the claims to the right to privacy are difficult to distinguish from other claims to rights of the personality, from claims to respect for personal integrity, and from claims against interference by government and other external agents." The emphasis on integrity resonates with Swedish concerns. Perhaps even more importantly, Simmel recognized twenty years ago that "violations of privacy often are injuries inflicted by relatively large and powerful forces upon the smallest and weakest element in society, the individual, who may be poor, uneducated, and a member of a minority group."[32] Such trends have been especially evident in the practice of computer matching in the United States, which is discussed in Chapter 29.

Concern for the protection of privacy is of course an element in the national and international movement for human rights and freedoms. The preamble to the United Nations Charter, for example, seeks "to reaffirm faith in fundamental human rights, in the dignity and worth of the human person." Such concern for the individual underlies the historical and philosophical origins of claims to personal privacy. In West Germany and France, these are often based upon the constitutional protection of "the dignity of man."

Vital personal interests are at stake in the use of personal data by governments and other organizations. Whether in computerized or manual form, such activities threaten the personal integrity and autonomy of individuals, who traditionally have lacked control over how others use information about them in decision making. The storage of personal data can be used to limit opportunity and to encourage conformity, especially when associated with a process of social control through surveillance.[33] The existence of dossiers containing personal information collected over a long period of time can have a limiting effect on behavior; knowing that participation in an ordinary political activity may lead to surveillance can have a chilling effect on the conduct of a particular individual.[34] Data collection on individuals also leads to an increase in the power of governments and other large institutions. At the same time, as Sweden illustrates, the general public may perceive data collection coupled with surveillance activities as being in the public interest or at least as not threatening their own interests, when the process promises to accomplish such goals as the saving of tax money in welfare payments and the prevention of fraud. Such surveillance in fact threatens all of us.

Thus, as discussed and illustrated throughout this volume, the protection of privacy requires the balancing of competing values. Techniques available for legitimate purposes have the secondary effect of being invasive of individuals' perceived right to control their own lives. Most persons have difficulty seeing how a program, for example, to link personal records in order to prevent overpayments to physicians has potentially negative ramifications for those whose records may be processed for the linkages, especially if it occurs without external controls. This requires the intervention of persons concerned with the preservation of privacy, but the forces promoting surveillance are so powerful that the playing field is hardly level.

The protection of privacy is neither a liberal nor a conservative political issue. Except perhaps for some social democrats who regard concern for personal privacy as inimical to the best interests of the state—at least under certain circumstances—the privacy issue should attract political support from both the left and the right. As David Burnham wrote, "The gradual erosion of privacy is not just the unimportant imaginings of fastidious liberals. Rather, the loss of privacy is a key symptom of one of the fundamental social problems of our age: the growing power of large public and private institutions in relation to the individual citizen."[35] Defending the right of an individual to privacy has become more than a simple insistence on the need for solitude or the right to be left alone; it has become one of the fundamental rallying points of persons concerned to restrict the intrusion of governments and of the great private-sector concerns in the lives of every human being.

Recent U.S. presidential politics have illustrated the failure to recognize the potential unifying role of sensitivity to privacy. In part because President Jimmy Carter's privacy initiative proved to be a dismal failure in political terms, the Reagan administration made no positive moves in this area. This default has been especially serious because of the deficiencies in overall implementation of the Privacy Act of 1974, which are discussed below in the case study on the United States. When David Burnham raised a public outcry in 1983 with a front-page story in the *New York Times,* alleging that there were plans to share census and tax data throughout the United States government (it was in fact a plan for statistical data sharing under controlled conditions), the Reagan administration killed the plans for such a law, asserting that it was committed to the protection of privacy.[36] Such a commitment has in fact been nearly invisible during the Reagan era, especially in the face of public concern over the extensive use of computer-matching programs. It has reached the point where privacy advocates, including an unusual mixture of professional, business, and civil liberties groups, are persuaded that the 1974 Privacy Act needs to be revised substantially to respond to the realities of today's technology.[37] Even during the Reagan era, this coalition has successfully achieved several important pieces of sectoral protection for privacy and, equally importantly, made constitutional recognition of a right to privacy a major issue during the confirmation hearings of Robert Bork in 1987. In contrast to the rejected Bork, the successful nominee to the Supreme Court, Anthony Kennedy, acknowledged a right of privacy: "There is a zone of liberty, a zone of protection, a line that's drawn where the individual can tell the Government, 'Beyond this line you may not go.'"[38]

The protection of personal privacy will clearly remain a major societal issue for the foreseeable future. Around it reverberate such sensitive concerns as protecting national sovereignty, limiting big government, controlling record linkages, the loss of personal identity, the uses of unique Personal Identification Numbers, and the risks of various types of governmental and private data banks.

The Role of Data Protection Agencies

Concern about surveillance societies necessitates consideration of the legislative efforts to date to regulate such novel developments from the perspective of protecting individual rights. Since 1970, the passage of general data protection laws has been the primary response of national and state governments to the perceived demand for the protection of personal privacy. Every Western industrial nation either has a data protection law in place or has one under active consideration. Laws that primarily regulate the public sector are sometimes extended to private sector personal information systems as well. In federal countries, provinces and states have joined or are joining this movement toward data protection for the public sector. The Organization for Economic Co-operation and Development and the Council of Europe's initiatives on data protection have encouraged this process of emulation among advanced industrial nations.[39] Data protection agencies seek to regulate all stages of surveillance by promoting accountability and fair information practices.

The case studies below offer a broad overview of what these developments in data protection mean for surveillance practices in advanced Western industrial societies. Such an effort is intended to serve as an antidote to the perspective that accepts these reforms uncritically and assumes that individual privacy is permanently safe because data protection exists. It is naive to believe that surveillance societies will not flourish by reason of the existence of data protectors; in fact, one unintended consequence of their presence is the prospering of surveillance societies, because the public has a false sense of security, and the data protectors themselves have, or have used, limited power.

Under the broad rubric of ensuring privacy, the primary purpose of data protection is the control of surveillance of the public, whether this monitoring uses the data bases of governments or of the private sector. Although a discussion of what constitutes privacy is compelling, it is more pragmatic to approach an evaluation of data protection agencies by focusing on what is being done to limit surveillance. We may accept initially as a given that surveillance, carried out for whatever presumed benevolent purpose, has the potential to hinder our liberty and erode democracy. The effectiveness of data protection is measured by the extent to which it prevents surveillance from having these detrimental consequences.

Manual record keeping has always facilitated efforts at social control, although it is and has been ultimately inefficient for large populations in comparison to what computers and telecommunications make possible. People and organizations have always watched one another, but the level of efficiency that computers make possible poses fundamental problems for the individual, because governments and the private sector have an extraordinarily enhanced ability to collect and use personal data. One of the conclusions of this volume is that we need to reframe data protection laws to permit data protectors to confront surveillance practices more directly.

Given traditions of surveillance since time immemorial, how does an individual, an organization, or a society establish the acceptable limits on such intrusiveness? In simple terms, surveillance can be good or bad, depending on who does it, why it is being done, and how it is carried out. On the positive side, we encourage programs to observe suicidal persons carefully, we want national security risks kept under democratic control, and we expect governments to ensure that expenditures on social programs are in compliance with statutory requirements. We want people to obey the criminal laws and to pay their fair share of taxes. The real issue is how far we are prepared to venture in a democratic society to accomplish these legitimate goals, since all personal information systems are surveillance systems of one kind or another.

There appears to be a consensus against a totalitarian society or a police state, because of regrettable precedents for each. All of us shudder at living in the fictional worlds of George Orwell's *Nineteen Eighty-Four* or Margaret Atwood's *The Handmaid's Tale* (1985). At what point does surveillance become unacceptable, whether by private detectives, the police, or welfare and taxation authorities? At what point does surveillance actually take place, when data are collected or when they are used? The shaping of appropriate answers to these questions is a concern of this entire volume. Official privacy protectors have a basic role to play in crafting society's answers to these questions, in part because governments created their agencies in order "to protect privacy," but also because since data protectors were first established, problems of surveillance have become much more severe owing to the exponential growth in automation. The questions do not admit a one-time solution.

The problem of controlling surveillance is rife with ambivalences. Governments are the worst offenders against privacy, at least in terms of demonstrable abuses against individuals and groups, yet they are charged with promoting such basic societal goals as efficiency and cost controls. They also make the rules by which social programs, for example, are to be operated, many of which incorporate highly intrusive practices. Who is to control the government? One ultimate, but weak, answer, of course, is the electorate, which can itself display great tolerance for surveillance, depending upon the popularity of the perceived targets.

The politics of surveillance are fascinating. Governments ostensibly need to promote surveillance for legitimate purposes but also want to preserve individual privacy. It is highly unlikely, however, that a government or a legislature will take an antisurveillance tack or refrain from intrusive measures without considerable prodding, if surveillance can be perceived or justified as being in the public interest. Nevertheless, there is little possibility that a Western society will decide that total information surveillance is both desirable and practical. But a real dividing line has to be established between what is and is not acceptable, something that governments have little inclination, or sometimes capacity, to do for themselves. The only hope is that governments can be shamed or pressured into forsaking practices that data protectors and other defenders of civil liberties identify as unacceptable, because the authorities have the ultimate power to engage in surveillance for whatever purposes.

Nonetheless, along the way, governments have somewhat blindly and haltingly assigned a fundamental role to data protectors as watchdogs over surveillance practices. Their job, in brief, has essentially become one of serving as the conscience of the government, and sometimes the private sector, with respect to acceptable levels of data surveillance. To this end, they do and should continue to play the leading role in articulating and applying the language of data protection legislation and in trying to fashion protective and investigative measures to ensure that the appropriate rules to minimize unnecessary observation are followed. However, one of the fundamental contradictions this volume also examines is that data protectors are watching the governments and the legislatures that appoint and fund them. We are left to question the adequacy of the mechanisms created to date in our respective societies to preserve privacy and limit governmental surveillance.

This volume asks how effectively the data protectors are doing their jobs. The essential question is whether data protection laws and agencies, as currently constituted, are an effective antidote to the emergence and installation of surveillance societies. Are they providing only the illusion of data protection at present? Are they in fact legitimizers of the application of new technology, although they appear to be ensuring data protection? The case studies offer some unsettling answers to these questions.

The emphasis of this volume is on what data protectors are actually doing in the public sector and the problems they are encountering. The goal is to contribute to an understanding of, and solutions to, the basic problems that have emerged in the process of formulating and implementing laws and practices for data protection, since they are of such vital importance for the preservation of individual rights in the face of massive surveillance capacity.

Promoting bureaucratic accountability in data use is at the heart of the functions of data protection agencies. Accountability means that bureaucrats must, in one way or another, answer to the data protection agency when making decisions about information collection and use.[40] This issue is critical, because aspiring civil servants seek data on individuals to design and evaluate programs, to augment their prestige and power, and, as a product of a supposed technological imperative, to enable them to use the latest hardware and software programs. Bureaucrats are thus a major source of government initiatives for information collection, because of the standard delusion that more data will solve problems. Although surveillance cannot always be limited directly, data protection agencies can promote bureaucratic accountability in four ways: by direct regulation, by reports to the legislature, by ensuring that individuals obtain access to their own data, and by appeals to the public. Data laws can also mean that courts will back the legal rights of citizens to an accounting.

A fundamental pessimism about the deterioration of regulatory agencies over time also inspires this discussion. Unless a deity has endowed data protectors with some form of special status to insulate them from historical forces, there is every expectation, based on comparable performances by other such specialized bureaucracies, that the quality and effectiveness of their performance will deteriorate and become debased over time. This phenomenon is not only the result of a lack of appropriate diligence, but a natural developmental process, a life cycle, that appears to be systemic to public administration. Thus, the public is faced with increasing threats to privacy coupled with a projected weakening of the protective apparatus developed to date.

This volume analyzes a series of fundamental policy problems of data protection, primarily from the perspective of those charged with the duty of limiting surveillance. The study includes a number of issues and questions intrinsic to the development of data protection in comparative perspective, including an analysis of the introduction of data protection laws and the legislative process to date, the characteristics of public policy making in this area, and administrative problems that have developed in the process of enforcement. A central concern is the effectiveness of existing and proposed data protection laws in the several countries. Contentious issues in data protection are emphasized. The final conclusions, based on an analysis of both successes and failures of efforts to control governmental surveillance, are ultimately prescriptive about the future of data protection.

All of the countries studied here had similar problems with invasions of privacy that triggered the enactment of their data protection laws. I have been concerned with understanding just how congruent these problems really were and, relatedly, why similar statutory solutions were sought and enacted. Identifying the opponents of data protection has not been an easy task, since there has been virtual legislative unanimity in its favor, but I have tried to discover the countervailing pressures and the attempts to sidetrack the process, especially during the implementation phase. How has the bureaucracy resisted the introduction of data protection? I have also inquired about the individual and collective rewards available to the staff of data protection agencies for their efforts to make the legislation effective.

The general analysis of current issues in surveillance control in this volume emphasizes particularly the process of enforcement, whether on a sector-by-sector basis, as in the United States, or by means of licensing, registration, or advising, as in the European and Canadian models. The experience of implementation is especially important, because data protectors receive insufficient critical attention once laws are enacted. As the data protection initiative confronts entrenched political and bureaucratic centers of power, it has encountered resistance. The relative stringency of enforcement and the seeming reluctance of certain data protectors to tackle the most sensitive types of government information-handling activities are related areas of concern. Both the environment in which data protection has arisen and the political climate in which it is being applied are of concern. Attitudes of politicians have also evolved in a comparable manner, so that initial enthusiasms for data protection are now sometimes tempered by actual experience and by the emergence of such competing interests as reducing the costs of government, locating terrorists, or discouraging fraudulent activities in the welfare and taxation systems. The process of controlling enforcement has also highlighted the importance as solutions to challenges to personal privacy of such practices as limiting the collection and storage of personal data and the destruction and anonymization of data.

The regulation of specific types of government administrative information systems processing personal data is a leading concern of this book.[41] In the face of difficult choices, the preference has been for especially sensitive and controversial data banks, since they highlight issues of surveillance. These are areas of primary concern to data protectors and sources of stigmatizing information for purposes of social control.

Monitoring the impact of regulation in various areas of data collection has not proven to be an easy task. Computerized police records are a sensitive issue in most Western countries, and data protectors have generally tended to tread lightly in such areas. The political problems encountered in regulating a national statistical agency, for example, are substantially fewer than those involved in regulation of the information-handling practices of the police. Welfare record keeping raises the prospect of over surveillance versus the freedom to cheat, and the prospect of changing or reducing qualifying criteria for programs in order to minimize data collection. Similarly, the problems of confidentiality associated with medical and health records held by government agencies directly illustrate the issue of balancing the interests of citizens during the process of data protection. For all of these information-handling areas, the volume illustrates the need to ensure effective implementation of data protection.

Two facets of data protection in the public sector receive particular attention. One continued focus is the use of administrative data for record linkages or computer matching, which has been the prime privacy issue of the 1980s. Unfortunately, the major concern of the custodians of data is the efficiency of administrative operations, not the protection of privacy, whereas the general public fears the unnecessary surveillance that such concentrations of information facilitate. A second focus concerns the implications of controversies over the use of personal identification numbers and similar unique identifiers in most countries. There is a rational fear, based on the Swedish experience, of the record linkages that the introduction or perpetuation of a numbering scheme makes possible. The public wisely suspects the effectiveness of controls over the exchange of data among government computers. There are significant advantages for data protection in limiting the spread of national numbering schemes and in placing strict controls on government and private sector uses of such numbers, as the Canadian federal government did in 1988 for its Social Insurance Numbers.

Certain common themes arise throughout the volume in addition to the central motif of the control of surveillance. There is a sustained concern with the relationship between citizens and the state in the late twentieth century. On the one hand, the political world is shaped by the introduction and use of powerful computer technology in public administration, the promotion of effective and efficient government, and the broad reach of a society's information policy. On the other hand, individuals want a transparent, open government that is not a prime challenger of such highly valued interests as personal privacy. In short, the public wishes to continue to enjoy a private life by ensuring bureaucratic accountability. The ultimate challenge is to create and foster an informed trust between the individual and the state with respect to the collection and use of personal information.

The Structure of the Case Studies

Because of the complexity of understanding national systems of data protection and surveillance, a series of case studies comprise the core of this volume. They follow a standard format in order to facilitate explicit and implicit comparisons. This approach permits persons interested in a single issue to follow it from one case study to the next by focusing on a specific chapter or subsection. Various subthemes are highlighted and reviewed as they arise in a case study, but it is only in the conclusions to the volume that a final statement is made on each one, as a form of reflective summation of the experience of various countries and actors.

The first issue is why nation-states require data protection laws in this Information Age. The second major question is how best to protect personal data, once a decision is made to have an appropriate general law. More than any other part of the volume, the conclusions present the personal views of the author, based on observations of efforts to reduce surveillance. They also reflect the contrasting points of view of other experts in data protection and, moreover, are the end result of exposing the main ideas in the conclusions to continued debate and revision, most notably at a conference on Privacy and Data Protection held at Bellagio in Italy in 1984.[42] The conclusions also discuss the points of comparison that are particularly significant, revealing, or problematic among the countries dealt with in the case studies.

The differences in the structure of each case study reflect the contrasts between nations with federal and unitary systems of government and the occasional irrelevance of a particular issue in a country. The first chapter in each part discusses the model of data protection adopted in a country and the organization of the data protection agency. The Federal Republic of Germany and Canada use an advisory model, while Sweden and France have regulatory and licensing approaches. The second describes the goals of data protection as set forth in the legislation. The third chapter analyzes the characteristics of the regulatory agency created to implement data protection, focusing in particular on its independence, its powers of intervention in the activities of governmental agencies, and its use of power. Because the most important national differences in controlling surveillance arise from the process of implementation, the fourth chapter describes the staffing and basic approach to implementation of the data protection agency, its detailed activities in supervising data protection, and the evolution of controlling principles in practice. The fifth chapter focuses on how sensitive problems of data protection are being met in various types of information-handling activities. Each case study selects for detailed analysis one or several of the most important or controversial personal information systems in each society. In effect, this chapter constitutes a case study of data protection in different types of information systems. The final chapter looks more generally at how each country has responded to privacy and surveillance problems.

Part 1

The Federal Republic of Germany

Chapter *1*

The West German Model

Introduction

West Germany is the only federal system of government that has introduced comprehensive data protection legislation. The Federal Data Protection Act (BDSG) became law for the public and private sectors on January 27, 1977.[1] Each state that did not already have general laws passed a similar law covering its public sector soon after the federal initiative. The detailed principles of both federal and state laws for the control of surveillance incorporate the fair information practices common in such legislation in other countries. As is the case elsewhere, implementation is decentralized; the heads of all federal and state agencies have primary responsibility to ensure that the statutory requirements are followed.

The federal law creates an independent Data Protection Commissioner (DPC), who, by advising the federal government and individual ministers, ensures that the Data Protection Act is implemented. If the commissioner discovers infringements of the law in the processing of personal data, he or she can submit a complaint to the competent authority.

The federal Data Protection Commissioner's office has counterparts in each of the eleven states, which, under the federal constitution, implement both the federal law and their complementary state laws. While this case study concentrates on the federal system of data protection, it will also examine the experiences of the state systems of Hesse and North Rhine–Westphalia (NRW). The actions of the state Data Protection Offices are especially important, because as much as 80 to 90 percent of personal information from the public sector is held at the state level. States have primary responsibility for education, police, and health, whereas the federal government dominates security, defense, insurance, and social security.

Since 1969 Germans have produced a mature and well-developed system of data protection, which can serve as a very important model elsewhere. The impressive advances made by the Germans are especially relevant to the North American experience; Canada and the United States operate under similar federal systems, and West Germany's large population of 61 million makes it a more useful example than the smaller Scandinavian countries.

This case study permits an introductory discussion of a number of the major themes of this volume. It provides the opportunity for an initial assessment of the relative success of the federal and state offices in controlling governmental surveillance of the public. Implementation of data protection in Germany benefits from a complementary system of data protection and from a very legalistic system that reflects the country's political culture. Data protection in the Federal Republic also has a stronger constitutional base than in any other country. Perhaps most importantly, the experience of German data protection agencies during the last decade shows a fully functioning, advisory model of data protection that has won considerable victories in protecting individual rights, because of strong leadership, talented staff, an emphasis on mediation and auditing, and a capacity to learn from experience. Finally, the West German example allows discussion of the problem of independent exercise of power by data protectors—an issue in every country committed to effective implementation.

The Development of Legislation

In 1970 the state of Hesse was the first jurisdiction anywhere to enact a general data protection law in response to concern about the social implications of automated data processing in the public administration. Although the debate over privacy and computers began in the late 1960s, at about the same time as the emergence of similar concerns in other advanced industrial democracies, it took almost ten years for a federal law to emerge. The federal Ministry of the Interior (BMI) presented the Bundestag (the lower house of the legislature) with a draft law in 1973.

Several troublesome issues explain the long gestation period. The first problem was the regulation of data transfers within the federal government. The computer industry then won an extension of the law to manual files on individuals that are readily accessible for repeated uses. A third reason for delay was the contention from a variety of sectors that provisions in various special laws already offered a great deal of data protection and that no further external regulation or supervision was required. Finally, the need for an independent supervisory agent was at issue.

Although the law enacted in Hesse provided for a Data Protection Commissioner, there were no plans for a comparable post in the draft federal legislation. Officials of the Ministry of the Interior anticipated that individual ministers would be responsible for the implementation of data protection, on the assumption that leading politicians and civil servants were in the best position to know what to do in their respective spheres and to determine what particular exemptions were needed in the special laws regulating ministerial activities. Because of a strong societal commitment to the rule of law, West Germans do not share North American cynicism about the behavior of civil servants under such circumstances.

The West German media did become increasingly involved in discussions of the proposed law. The leading weekly, *Der Spiegel,* published an article on the eve of the passage of the BDSG under the title: "Data Protection: 1984 is no longer far away."[2] It paid particular attention to the views of certain experts that the proposed law was inadequate in light of articles 1 and 2 of the West German federal constitution or the Basic Law of 1949, which provide the constitutional underpinnings for the right to privacy. Article 1(1) provides that "the dignity of man shall be inviolable. To respect and protect it shall be the duty of all state authorities." Article 2 states: "Everyone shall have the right to the free development of his personality in so far as it does not infringe the rights of others or offend against the constitutional order or the moral code."[3] Such public

Table 2. Chronology of West German Data Protection Legislation

1969	Social Democratic party holds national power.
1970	State of Hesse enacts a Data Protection Act.
1973	Federal Ministry of the Interior presents a draft bill on data protection to the Bundestag.
1975	Spiros Simitis becomes Data Protection Commissioner for the state of Hesse.
January 27, 1977	Federal Data Protection Act (BDSG) enacted.
1978	Hans Peter Bull becomes federal Data Protection Commissioner.
1979	Heinrich Weyer becomes Data Protection Commissioner for the state of North Rhine–Westphalia (until September 1987).
October 1, 1982	Helmut Kohl, a Christian Democrat, replaces Social Democrat Helmut Schmidt as chancellor.
1983	Major controversy over the census of population.
	Reinhold Baumann becomes federal Data Protection Commissioner.
March 6, 1983	Formation of a coalition government of the Christian Democratic party and the Free Democratic party.
December 15, 1983	Federal Constitutional Court's decision in the census case creates a constitutional right to informational self-determination.
November 11, 1986	Hesse revises its Data Protection Act.
1987	Controversy over the census of population.
January 27, 1987	Reelection of the coalition government.
1988	North Rhine–Westphalia revises its Data Protection Act.
	Alfred Einwag becomes federal Data Protection Commissioner.

discussion was especially inspired by a fear that the government's proposals on data protection, personal identification numbers, and population registration were being inappropriately linked together as a package. In fact, these constitutional articles have provided essential underpinning for the effort to control governmental surveillance. The BDSG can be strengthened or reinforced by recourse to the principle of the right to a private personality founded in the constitution.

The legislature played a crucial role, here as elsewhere, in the enactment of strong data protection legislation. During the 1970s, there were no major differences over data protection among the political parties, and the changes proposed were not made along party lines. Popular debate in West Germany was low key in comparison to discussions of the U.S. Privacy Act in the circumstances surrounding Watergate. The impetus for the inclusion in the federal legislation of a commissioner came from the Interior Committee of the Bundestag. The first federal commissioner, Professor Hans Peter Bull, wrote of the controversy that it was obvious that the administration itself would hesitate to implement new rules for data processing, at least if it appeared they would cause inconvenient alterations in method and style of administration: "One of the main reasons for creating an independent external supervisory authority was that a special ombudsman would be necessary to whom people could address their complaints about inadequate processing, and this should be a trustworthy person (or commissioner) not too much involved in administration itself."[4] Bull's point about the advantages of a supervisory authority not involved in other administrative activities is strongly supported by evidence from other countries.

Formative Influences

West Germany's historical experience has in fact produced two somewhat contradictory social imperatives. The experience with Nazis, Communists, and repressive governments inspires a need for checks on the power of the state to monitor personal activity, so as to preserve individual autonomy. Concurrently, order is characteristic of the German mentality, leading to a regimented society in which it is normally considered desirable for the state to manage without the direct participation of the citizens.

Another characteristic of West Germany, going beyond the general specificity of European Civil Law—compared to the common-law heritage of English-speaking countries—is the tradition, especially since the end of the Nazi era, of very detailed laws controlling governmental activity. In a fashion comparable to contemporary France, but differing from North America or Britain, West Germany is overtly preoccupied with issues of power, which results in considerable emphasis on the rule of law in what is essentially a law-driven society. Its constitution requires a legal rationale for every administrative act of the government. Public administration involves the continuing development and revision of specialized laws and regulations to govern all public services, in contrast to the North American practice of enacting very general legislation and leaving decisions on implementation to the civil service. Surprisingly, this preoccupation with the rule of law extends as well to the security agencies and the police. In a very significant way, this legalism, by ensuring the specific and elaborate enumeration of individual rights, protects personal freedom by seeking to limit governmental surveillance.[5]

Exacting legalism is complemented by a traditional belief in the trustworthiness of the civil service, which helps to explain the type of data protection system adopted. The assumption is that civil servants will obey the law and are worthy of trust by one another and by the public they serve. A 1976 survey showed that the general public was much more afraid of the abuse of personal data by the private rather than the public sector. Sixty-two percent of those then surveyed believed that the state should know as much as possible about the individual citizen. A 1983 survey revealed that, while the public still fears abuse by the private more than the public sector, 60 percent felt that computers have given the state too many opportunities for control, and 65 percent felt that as little information as possible should be given to the state, marking a growing lack of confidence in the government since the enactment of data protection.[6]

The experiences of other countries have also influenced the development of West German data protection. The rejection of administrative licensing in favor of an advisory system was a conscious decision. As Bull explains, while every government minister is responsible to the Bundestag for his or her own department, including data protection, the constitution provides that no one in government has the ultimate power to order a ministry to do anything, except the minister who implements a law in his or her own agency.[7] Such ministerial autonomy is consistent with the traditions of legalism and trust in the civil service, while giving direct powers of intervention to the DPC would have required constitutional changes.

In supporting a federal Data Protection Commissioner rather than a commission, West Germany also rejected the more decentralized decision-making model implemented in Sweden and France. There is no commission with the final power to make decisions, nor does the federal DPC have an advisory board. It is an open question if such a board (whether executive or advisory) promotes data protection, especially in the public sector, or whether it simply facilitates political compromises over surveillance within a miniparliament, thus weakening the consistent defense of privacy interests that data protectors must undertake. It has been suggested that the creation of such a board would be contrary to West German tradition, wherein such boards are mainly used for self-governing administrations, but apparently the precedents are not determinative. Civil servants in particular do not regard themselves as needing an additional reference group beyond the directions they receive from a minister and the Bundestag, which again reflects the legalistic character of society.

Experimentation with the commission model has occurred at the state level; however, most data protection specialists continue to favor the more centralized scheme. An eleven-person committee exists in Bavaria as an advisory body to the commissioner. As an academic expert, Bull initially advocated such a device, but by the end of his term in office he was not as certain of its merits. The Bavarian committee, which has broad representation, can help the state DPC in difficult decisions, but there is also a predictable tendency to encourage internal compromises at the expense of data protection interests before releasing advice and to tie the hands of the commissioner.

Rhineland-Palatinate has a commission made up of members of the state parliament and representatives of the Landtag and the Ministry of the Interior. It has the same advisory powers as a single Data Protection Commissioner. Bull has observed that although the system does function, progressive decisions are difficult under such a regime. Professor Spiros Simitis of the University of Frankfurt, who has been the Hesse Data Protection Commissioner since 1975, is similarly skeptical of the utility of collecting the varied interests in society together in such an advisory commission, whether in West Germany or elsewhere. Other observers describe data protection in Rhineland-Palatinate as ineffective and superficial, largely due to the burden of developing the appropriate expertise. One positive side effect may be that the commission system helps to attract the interest of members of the legislature, some of whom serve on it. Since the legislature often tries to promote enhanced surveillance, it is valuable to have some members working at least part-time as watchdogs over it.

The Organization of Data Protection

The BDSG could not have been effective without the creation of the office of the federal Data Protection Commissioner. Given the enormous range of successful activities undertaken by the office, as described below, its invention seems essential. The system of data protection has also worked reasonably well without giving the commissioner the actual power to direct a ministry or public body. The Swedish Data Inspection Board has such a direct power of intervention through its licensing responsibility, but its impact on the public sector has not been as pervasive or profound as the federal DPC's, which also inspects systems to ensure compliance with the law. In 1975 Simitis wondered if this model of nonintervention would continue to work in his state, since administrators might develop ways to resist the office. He suspected that he might eventually have to seek the regulatory powers of the Swedish model, but he has not yet had to do so.

The advisory responsibilities of the federal commissioner are spelled out in the legislation. The incumbent may make "recommendations for the improvement of data protection" in order to ensure observance of the law. In addition, and more importantly, he or she may advise the federal government, individual ministers, and other public authorities in matters of data protection. The commissioner is also required to respond to certain requests from the government or legislature for investigations, opinions, and reports.[8] A leading commentary on the BDSG states that this investigatory power is reserved for very serious matters, so that it is not weakened through overuse.[9] The commissioner also has the right to consult the Bundestag at any time. Bull often took the initiative of giving statements to legislative committees of the Bundestag.

The commissioner's advisory function, especially in terms of encouraging the inclusion of provisions for data protection in other types of special legislation and regulations, is particularly well developed. Bull has argued that these advisory or "preventive" services are almost more important than the audits.[10] Yet the investigative actions of the commissioner also have a valuable preventive effect. It is difficult to reorganize administrative processes once they are fixed, and it is easier and more effective to avoid unnecessary infringements of the individual's privacy by demanding protective measures in the planning phase.

The primary task of the various commissioners is to supervise the development of data processing in the public sector from the perspective of concern for personal privacy. Except in four small states, their only responsibility for the private sector is to keep informed of developments. Section 19 of the BDSG establishes core responsibilities for supervising, advising, and acting as an ombudsman for complaints from individuals.

The existence of Data Protection Commissioners highlights a number of dilemmas for making data protection effective. A non-German looking at the position is struck by the pervasiveness of the commissioner's influence. However, there are practical problems of implementation, various types of resistance by the West German civil service, the broad range of data-processing applications in the federal public sector, and the advent of new technology in continuing waves, all of which tend to promote extensions of governmental surveillance. These problems are examined in greater detail below.

In speaking to an English audience, Bull made the classic understatement that the system of data protection in the Federal Republic is "complicated."[11] There is a national data protection office and eleven state commissioners or commissions, which are not responsible to the national commissioner; thus each office can interpret and apply the relevant law as seems fit. Neither federal nor state commissioners can impose their advice on the bureaucracy. Government agencies are directly responsible to the legislature to ensure that the data protection statute is observed within their domain, a type of self-administration also characteristic of U.S. and Canadian government agencies.

At the most basic level, responsibility for data protection is shared between any DPC and the public administration. In practice, the impetus inevitably comes from a specialized bureaucracy, the Office of the Data Protection Commissioner, which has data protection as its particular mandate, with different agency officials acting as facilitators. Most public agencies have a data protection officer who is the first line of approach in implementing the legislation. However, unlike the United States, a DPC exists to ensure that the data law is in fact obeyed. Although Bull has pointed out that the various authorities for data protection "are obliged to cooperate," the process of coordination of regulation is not simple, especially since competing interests are at stake.[12]

The policy field is made more complex by the role of Ministries of the Interior at both the federal and state levels. They not only developed the original data protection laws, but they also continue to consult on interpretation of the law and coordinate revisions on behalf of the legislature. Further, they are responsible for internal implementation within their own ministries, which includes supervision of police activities and general developments in data processing. State Ministries of the Interior (LMIs) also oversee implementation of data protection in the private sector. Thus, not only is responsibility for the implementation of data protection shared between levels of government, and between the commissioners' offices and the public service, but also between the commissioners' offices and the Ministries of the Interior. Although the DPC has supervisory and advisory responsibilities to ensure that the federal Ministry of the Interior observes the federal data protection law, the latter has a similar obligation. Just as the Ministries of the Interior played a prominent role in developing data protection laws, they retain ultimate responsibility within their important domestic jurisdiction for observance of the law.[13]

Under the West German constitution of 1949, the states exercise substantial powers. In contrast with North American federal systems, they have a direct responsibility to execute federal laws as if they were enactments of their own legislatures. For example, the BDSG has direct application to a state in the execution of federal responsibilities. The supplementary data protection law passed in each state only applies to state activities, which excludes the private sector. Thus a state DPC is in charge of data protection in the public sector under the BDSG rather than its counterpart state statute.

The largest West German state, North Rhine–Westphalia, with a population of more than seventeen million persons, has its own Data Protection Commissioner. Ultimately the state Ministry of the Interior in NRW can decide whether to follow the advice given by the state DPC on matters lying within its assigned jurisdiction. This division of power and its final disposition depends upon the constitution. The same condition holds true for advice about data protection given by the state DPC to any other ministries of the government, which themselves decide whether to follow such advice. Furthermore, the various Ministries of the Interior coordinate the development and revision of data protection laws for all of the government ministries. The LMI is also the supervisory authority in North Rhine–Westphalia for data protection in the private sector. The ordinance in NRW under the BDSG states that the LMI should handle the private sector, so the DPC has no direct role in this domain, although he may express opinions.[14]

A further characteristic of data protection in the Federal Republic is the extent to which special laws either modify, annul, or strengthen the BDSG. Section 45 contains a long list of federal statutes that take precedence over the data protection law, including those dealing with the confidentiality of federal statistics and tax information. These do not water down the principles of data protection but are examples of data protection statutes that were already in place in existing law. Nevertheless, the fact remains that none of the Data Protection Commissioners have explicit jurisdiction if the appropriate legislature has passed a specific law dealing with a particular type of information-handling activity. Yet the Federal Constitutional Court could intervene, if there were claims that such sectoral legislation weakened the data protection principles of the BDSG. One of the primary tasks of any commissioner is to shape the development of appropriate data protection for a particular sector. Such principles need to be applied to a wide variety of personal information in order to limit surveillance.

Chapter 2

The Goals of Data Protection

What do data protection laws and data protection agencies seek to accomplish for the control of governmental surveillance? This chapter evaluates the purposes of the West German legislation in order to assess their relevance for confronting governmental surveillance directly and for giving data protectors a clear and specific mandate. It also describes the kinds of conflicts over the scope of the legislation that have emerged in recent years and the impact they have had on the control of surveillance practices.

Statutory Objectives

Although the general inspiration for the development of data protection laws is apparent, the goals are rarely spelled out in satisfactory detail. The Federal Data Protection Act (BDSG) is an act "on Protection against the Misuse of Personal Data in Data Processing," the stated purpose being, according to section 1, "to ensure against the misuse of personal data during storage, communication, modification and erasure (data processing) and thereby to prevent harm to any personal interests of the person concerned that warrant protection."[1] The interconnections between data processing and the personal interests of the individual, which are not defined, are neither totally apparent nor explicit.

That the statutory history of the development of a law serves as an aid to its interpretation, or at least as an additional argument to support findings based on the law itself, to some degree compensates for the weakness of the statement of goals.[2] Thus the overall purposes of the BDSG are well known, even if they are not spelled out in the legislation. Spiros Simitis restates the goal as "to protect the personal interests of the individuals affected by the storage and retrieval of their data and thus to ensure the free development of their personality."[3] Although one group of experts argues that it would be impolitic and counterproductive to attempt to spell out the goals of data protection in detail, more explicit legislation would facilitate, guide, and indeed stimulate efforts to control surveillance.

Section 3 stipulates that data processing in the public sector can only occur as permitted by the BDSG, a provision in another law, or with the consent of the individual. Section 9 prescribes that "the storage and modification of personal data shall be permissible where necessary for the legitimate accomplishment of the tasks for which the storage unit is competent." Although the

30

definition of "necessary" is open to debate, section 9 is an initial guide to questioning the legitimacy of a particular surveillance practice. In addition, the coverage of the BDSG, in contrast to the Swedish Data Act of 1973, is not limited to automated personal data files.[4] However, the statute's language has led to some controversy over just what types of information are covered. Most data banks using either automated or semiautomated methods of data processing fall within the scope of the BDSG.[5] Section 4 establishes a number of standard rights: persons must be informed about the existence of data and be given the right of correction and placing restrictions on their use; they may even compel the deletion of data under certain circumstances.

The legislation emphasizes the control of data processing. At a Council of Europe conference in 1982, Dr. H. Auernhammer of the federal Ministry of the Interior (BMI) emphasized that the objective was to control the handling and processing of personal data and not primarily their content. The developers of the BDSG decided that the stages of data processing requiring regulation "were the input of data into a data processing system, their transmission and their alteration and obliteration while inside the system." Thus under the BDSG "the right to process personal data depends on the purpose of the processing, i.e., it is related to the practical task to be performed with the aid of data processing."[6]

However, Hans Peter Bull, the first federal Data Protection Commissioner (DPC), shifted the emphasis of the law by identifying data protection "as a kind of human rights protection in a technological society." This interesting idea reveals his own approach: "Technological progress has caused a lot of social problems. . . . People feel uneasy about data banks and information systems storing and transmitting an enormous amount of personal data within the shortest time. They know that automated data processing is done nearly everywhere—in public administration as well as in private companies and associations. People even know that by using these instruments others can win more influence and power and become able to suppress or injure their opponents."[7]

One emphasis of Dr. R. Baumann, Bull's successor, was to clarify how information would be used. In his view, his job was "not only protecting people from excessive probing by the State. It was also to help the maintenance of administrative efficiency and of even increasing it through the use of computer systems."[8] This opinion worries some data protection advocates because the pressure for surveillance in the name of efficiency is so great that it is risky for data protectors to ally themselves too closely with such forces.

Some observers believe that the 1983 census controversy was the first time that many West Germans became worried about the processing of personal information by their government. The results of a survey made in 1983 by Klaus Lange of the Society for Mathematics and Data Processing highlighted ambivalent attitudes toward the electronic revolution with fears outweighing hopes; 81 percent of those interviewed feared an invasion of privacy.[9] The other concerns expressed in the survey supported Bull's view that persons are opposing data processing for reasons of privacy and also because of deficiencies of the computerization process, such as mistakes and delays. He wisely emphasized the need for accuracy as a goal of data protection; if surveillance is determined to be in the public interest, the targets should at least be correctly identified.

As is apparent, conflicts over the appropriate scope of data protection begin with the legislation and, in certain cases, spread within the data protection agency itself. The vagueness and imprecision of the law's language results in frequent differences of opinion. Traditionally, the agency itself determines what general terms mean, then applies them to a variety of situations, but given the German propensity to draft specific legislation to govern practically every activity of a public agency, there are numerous opportunities for interested parties to disagree about interpretation.

The traditional suspicion of the bureaucracy's expansionist tendencies applies even to the public servants involved in the virtuous activity of data protection. Opponents of the federal DPC's office use the limited definition of section 1(1) of the data law to try to restrict its scope. The DPC has countered that one must interpret the law in its entirety, in particular the general language in section 3 on the permissibility of data processing; data protection is not simply an issue of preventing "misuse" of information.[10]

One of the enduring conflicts involves the meaning of the word *"datein"* or "files," as defined in section 2 of the BDSG and in the state laws. It is argued that the laws are only intended to apply to "datein," which is in some ways a synonym for automated as opposed to manual data. The legislators in fact wanted to include some manual files under data protection, but the problem is to distinguish among notebooks, paper files, manual files, and "datein."

The definition of the appropriate scope of data protection is critical; a narrow limit could restrict the DPCs' control functions. The latter argue that they are not limited to "datein" but can audit any personal data.[11] The census decision of the Federal Constitutional Court, which is discussed in Chapter 3, supported the DPC's position, stating that any personal information can be sensitive regardless of its means of storage. This 1983 ruling silenced those critics who contended that effective public administration was being undermined.

Conflicts about the appropriate scope of data protection, either on substantive or methodological grounds, also occur within the staff of a Data Protection Commissioner. Disagreements about approaches arise: to use a mediating approach, emphasizing good relations or, alternately, to be conflict-oriented, taking a strong stance on data protection. The question is ultimately one of style, springing from different interpretations of the legislation.

Some of the staff think they should be attempting to expand their scope by interpreting the BDSG broadly, in part because they are so aware of the risks of surveillance systems. However, the federal DPC's office did not find cases of intentional misuse of personal data during its first years of operation, leaving its opponents to argue that the BDSG has been very successful and, perhaps, the DPC's office should be cutting back on its activities.[12]

The statutory objectives of the data law are open to interpretation and, consequently, the personal philosophies and ideologies of the DPC's staff influence their determination of the scope of data protection, although this is obviously a very sensitive matter to evaluate. For example, Bull, the first federal DPC, is an active member of the Social Democratic party. During his term of office, he tried to act in a nonpartisan manner, and he restricted his own political activities. However, his political ideology is reflected in his belief that the dimensions of social organizations have become too large. In his view, it may become necessary to limit the size of some large organizations in order to give the individuals working in them a sense of what they are doing, what they know, and what they need to know. Bull argues that it would be better to break up some large organizations in the public sector into smaller units in order to promote effectiveness and to restrain the spread of depersonalization and alienation. He also thinks that government agencies need to become more aware of the civil rights of citizens. Although it is difficult to find support for such positions in the text of the BDSG, Bull was in a position to advance his personal perspective in the course of his work in data protection. There are of course those within the office who are concerned that the scope of data protection should be kept within fairly restricted grounds. The point is not to suggest substantial conflict on this issue but rather to indicate that different opinions exist within the same small agency.

Debate about the appropriate scope of the law has not been confined to the federal DPC's staff or to data protection specialists. Those being regulated often find themselves disagreeing with the DPC's interpretation. Government agencies have traditionally been left alone to accomplish their assigned tasks, and civil servants naturally convinced of the importance of their functions do not like to have their traditional practices questioned. Some may have anticipated that data protection would be focused on such sensitive agencies as the police and security rather than on agencies of the federal government engaged in the ordinary processing of personal information, without realizing that the preservation of privacy is at issue there as well.

Philosophical Objectives

The BDSG covers restrictions on data processing but does not explicitly define personal privacy or its relation to data processing. In a speech in 1981, Bull linked the two themes to focus on surveillance: "My task as Federal Commissioner for data protection is only to protect the privacy of individuals against the risks of illegitimate or unfair collection, storage and processing of personal data."[13] He noted that "men are anxious whether they will become 'transparent' for others and therefore subject to all kinds of social pressure.

They want to continue living as individuals, with all their personal characteristics and attitudes and, if they like, to be left alone."[14] A publication by Bull's office also emphasized that the protection of privacy was at the heart of the law:

> The Federal Law on Data Protection . . . is not a law to protect data. Rather, its aim is to protect the citizen. This fact is not made sufficiently clear in the title of the law. That, in turn, is because the realm of the personality—which is to be protected—is not sufficiently subject to definition. When are the individual's rights in regard to personality, as stipulated in the Constitution, infringed upon? The answer cannot come from general regulations; such infringement always depends on the special circumstances of the individual. In view of this fact, the German legislators decided to guard individual rights in regard to personality by protecting data that relates to persons.[15]

The BDSG emphasizes the obligation of individuals to determine for themselves exactly which of their interests in privacy are threatened. A pamphlet on data protection that appeared in 1978, for example, went so far as to state that "you as the person concerned in this law, have the opportunity to apply your own interpretation of the law with regard to which interests [in the data] are justified and which items [of the data base] are to be [exempt] and protected. The progressive application of the law will essentially depend on the interest and involvement of the parties and organizations concerned."[16] The pamphlet specifically stated that "the personal sphere is a term hard to define; there is an area of special value which needs protection by law."[17]

At the Council of Europe's Conference on Data Protection in 1982, Professor Simitis contended that it was not possible to state clearly the privacy interests to be protected in a particular piece of legislation. In his view, which the conclusions to this volume contest, it was not possible in 1970 or today to define the appropriate privacy interests very precisely. He argued that under the Swedish Data Act, for example, the legislature simply recognized the need for action and set up a control institution, and that the Swedish and Hessian data protectors were only now in a position to identify the conflicting interests. Simitis argues, more persuasively, that special data protection laws for particular sectors are now possible. He is essentially advancing the attractive legal solution of a system of general principles for data protection, coupled with special laws to govern particular applications.

Although the protection of privacy is not an explicitly stated goal of the data protection law, it is an underlying objective. Privacy is not an absolute value; like most fundamental rights, its scope depends on context. Fortunately, the 1983 decision of the Federal Constitutional Court has drawn upon the principles of private personality and human dignity in the Basic Law to adopt a definition of privacy that is close to Alan Westin's classic effort.[18] The Court's definition, and indeed that of the DPC, have not gone unchallenged.

The relationship of the Data Protection Commissioners with their respective legislatures has the potential to be a source of conflict and also of significant support. Nearly all committees of the Bundestag have data protection and the work of the DPC on their agenda at one time or another. Staff members accompany the federal commissioner to these committee meetings and may also answer questions. No member of the legislature is currently asking the DPC's office to expand its role, although the issue will likely arise in the context of future revisions of the BDSG. Conservative members of the Bundestag, on the other hand, have argued for less interference with the police and national security agencies.

Some critics outside the DPC's office suggest that the office needs a stronger link to the legislature as a source of support for its watchdog activities. Bull did not believe this to be the case, and Baumann was satisfied with the current arrangements. Bull made it a practice to attempt to meet with his legislative critics to respond to their inquiries directly.[19] However, not all concerns originating from the legislature are dealt with so privately. When the federal attorney general openly criticized the DPC's handling of security issues in 1982, Bull responded publicly.

Hesse is unique in that its legislature has a standing committee on data protection, which in effect furnishes Simitis with an advisory group. He also addresses the legislature in person at least once a year. His views and reports are sent to this committee and then to the Interior Committee. Simitis in effect spends a good deal of time lobbying with the four political parties concerning his reports, budgets, and amendments to the law. This approach facilitates a better link to the legislature than is available to the federal DPC.

Information Management Objectives

The final goal of data protection pertains to control over the collection and use of personal information. The BDSG specifies that the storage, modification, and dissemination of personal data is permissible, "where necessary for the legitimate accomplishment of the tasks for which the storage unit is competent."[20] This appears to be the only legal basis upon which the DPC can question the right of a public agency to collect particular personal information. The DPC has adopted the "informational separation of powers" theory; the state need not know everything about an individual, and its agencies must limit their information to only that which is necessary to fulfill their tasks.[21] Bull simply believes that organizations collect too much information, and he fears that if data are stored, they will be used, perhaps for unforeseen purposes.

One of the important goals of the BDSG and the federal DPC is to make data processing in the Federal Republic open, accessible, reviewable, and susceptible to supervision and auditing. Bull has stated:

> Administrative agencies as well as industrial companies often do not make any efforts to explain to people what is going on with information

collected about them. So even legitimate and reasonable forms of data processing seem to be mysterious and incomprehensible. People do not believe that the fantastic technical devices suitable for so many purposes as a matter of fact are only used for legal purposes and in a correct way. Distrust also arises from the fact that some special branches of public administration have established data nets without public control: the police agencies and security services. People normally have no contacts with them; but from time to time they read that some of these services are supposed to have acted illegally, e.g., observing groups of political opponents, conscientious objectors, etc. Thus, a general feeling of uneasiness can arise, and indeed has developed in some countries, including the Federal Republic of Germany.[22]

Sections 10 and 11 of the BDSG repeat the vague language of section 1, which restricts the dissemination of personal data within the public sector and to outside bodies. In general, this is "permissible where it is necessary for the legitimate accomplishment of the tasks for which the dissemination unit or the recipient is competent."[23] The control on dissemination outside the public sector adds the following statement to the language just quoted: "or where the recipient can demonstrate convincingly that his interest in the data to be disseminated is justified and the dissemination of the data does not harm interests of the person concerned that warrant protection."[24] This is not only an expansive provision by the standards of other countries, but the vague language is an obvious source of controversy. Moreover, the data protection law does not include the standard principle of forbidding the use of personal data for purposes other than those for which they were collected.

Critics recognize that the various Data Protection Commissioners want to restrict the transfer and interconnection of personal information among ministries at the various levels of government. Bull noted that in the security field almost every step in the processing of personal data is an encumbrance on the rights of the persons concerned, so that these types of exchanges require careful supervision.[25] In the critics' view, the tendency to deny such transfers produces an extremism in data protection that is not in the best interests of the goals of the legislation. The result of such initiatives on the part of the DPCs would be that each separate ministry would have to collect all the data it wanted, which would ultimately be an additional burden on the population in time and money. Data protectors generally argue that the police and security agencies do not need access to all available information, so that controls should exist on the permissible extent of collection and communication of personal information. The current strong criteria are whether a particular data transfer conflicts with the constitutional rights of individuals, and whether a proposed transfer is legal under existing statutory law. Although various statues regulate government and judicial access to data, one gains the impression that in practice there are very few controls on such access to personal information, so long as the data seem necessary for some purpose.

A fundamental goal of data protection should be questioning the initial proposal to collect data, so as to further the general aim of reducing surveillance. This is facilitated by applying the principle of necessity; increased use of erasure, destruction, and anonymization of personal information is also important. As Chapter 5 demonstrates, the federal DPC's office has in fact engaged in such questioning in certain areas. Because of its advisory responsibilities, it is already in a position to comment on the proposed impact of any new legislation on the collection of information; normally this is a routinized activity at the DPC's office, except when ministries do not forward early drafts.[26]

Worthwhile as these information management objectives may be, conflict remains inherent to the implementation of any public policy. This is particularly the case if it intrudes into a previously unregulated field, such as data processing, or an area that is difficult to define, such as privacy. Such conflicts over the appropriate scope of a novel statute are inevitable during the implementation phase. Conflicts of personality and substance are even inevitable among the eleven Data Protection Commissioners and one commission charged with related responsibilities in the Federal Republic.

The DPC has encountered differences of opinion over the appropriate scope of data protection as it has tried to control certain surveillance systems in the public sector. One example will illustrate the point. At least in its early phases the relationship between the DPC and the Federal Criminal Investigation Office (BKA) was stormy; it is now more harmonious in practice, if not in principle. At a conference in 1979 Bull and Dr. Horst Herold, the then head of the BKA, clashed over the appropriate scope of data protection. When Bull suggested that some uses of the most important data banks of the BKA and certain data collected for them lacked a legal basis, Herold accused him of engaging in data protection for its own sake, claiming that such extreme views would make the "very essence of police work infinitely more difficult, if not preventing it altogether."[27] Such reactions are predictable when data protectors challenge prevailing surveillance practices. The general point is that those engaged in law enforcement generally resist the introduction and then the implementation of data protection for the kinds of reasons just discussed.

The DPC is also in a position of occasional conflict with the federal Ministry of the Interior, whose outlook generally reflects government policy and inclinations on surveillance. Some members of the DPC's office have realistically suggested that regular conflicts on matters of substance with this ministry are unavoidable and that there are certain points on which no compromise is possible. For example, the timing of external events and various political considerations sometimes affect the Ministry of the Interior's agreement or disagreement with the DPC's recommendations. Likewise, the presentation of the DPC's annual report early in the new year tends to provoke action before it is discussed in the Bundestag. In practice, it is very rare for the federal ministry to attempt to use an exemption, even in the security fields, to keep the DPC's office from supervising specific data processing. The DPC's office has largely avoided being at loggerheads on a regular basis with the ministry and has also avoided being overwhelmed by its large "parent" agency. Nonetheless, it is difficult for an outsider to judge whether such peaceful relations have been won at the expense of individual rights.

State data protectors also meet some organizational resistance in the state Ministries of the Interior (LMIs). The LMIs also have a fundamental obligation to see that data protection principles are enforced in several areas. The problems emerge when a commissioner reaches a different interpretation of the law than the data protectors who work for the LMI (who can also be in conflict with other parts of their own ministry). Often the source of discord is the belief on the part of the LMI officers that they have a better understanding of the realities of public administration than the commissioners. In addition, they believe themselves to be in a better position to evaluate in advance the risk of conflicts in implementing certain recommendations for data protection. Various examples of such problems are discussed in other sections of this study.

Because West Germany is a federal state, information management conflicts, which affect the practice of surveillance, are further intensified by jurisdictional wrangling. Fundamental conflicts over the scope of data protection have emerged in Baden-Württemberg and in North Rhine–Westphalia (NRW). In the case of these conflicts, developments in NRW are a microcosm of the federal scene and perhaps for other states.

Dr. H. Weyer, the Data Protection Commissioner for NRW until 1987, had fairly strong views on the scope of data protection, especially in light of the explicit provision in article 4 of the state constitution, guaranteeing data protection as a constitutional right. He believes, therefore, that his office is responsible for supervising the observance of constitutional rights and of all the data protection rules.[28] Nevertheless, the state Ministry of the Interior is ultimately responsible for the implementation of data protection in NRW, and this has led to significant conflicts between the LMI and the state DPC.

It is clear that the jurisdiction of the data protection office does compete with LMI's supervisory role. LMI staff members feel that both the federal and state Data Protection Commissioners are unnecessarily expanding the scope of their activities, and they regard the state DPC as an ombudsman with a limited advisory responsibility. This contrast in views quickly led to disagreement over a broad or narrow interpretation of the meaning of the relevant laws. The LMI staff feels a strong urge to resist what it perceives to be the expansionist tendencies of the state commissioners (a problem that is less noticeable at the federal level).

The jurisdictional debate extends even to local government. Weyer had differences of opinion with communities over the extent to which they should be subject to data protection. The federal DPC is not responsible for implementation at the municipal level, but some of the state DPCs have adopted this duty. Weyer regarded regulating more than 400 communities as a central and difficult part of his job. Each municipality functions as a single unit in the exercise of its responsibilities, which leads to a great deal of local interchange of personal information. Despite some instances of cooperation, municipalities resist the efforts of the state DPC's office as an agency of the state government to supervise and inspect them. Even the Cabinet in NRW cannot order local municipalities to answer Weyer's questions about their information systems.

The state legislatures often are not supportive of data protection, because the members, elected at the local level, usually favor the government and municipalities' interests on every issue. In many ways the state legislators view data protection as an obstacle to effective public administration. As in other countries, they did not anticipate the real consequences of such legislation. Weyer agrees that data protection may be a hindrance to the efficient operation of the state government, but he regards protecting the rights of citizens as a higher priority. Although the final resolution of these jurisdictional questions may only occur through revision of the law, Weyer was confident that the legislature would give him the powers he thought he needed. This result becomes less likely as legislatures recognize that these powers may be used to control their recurrent enthusiasm for more surveillance of the population.

The major source of conflict about the objectives and scope of the data law has been the legislature. Comments in the Bundestag over the appropriate scope of data protection are particularly important, because in most countries the legislature generally has the final responsibility to determine the proper scope of data protection. More importantly, in difficult cases the legislature must decide whether a surveillance program is acceptable and necessary. However, legislative changes are hard to accomplish, not least because of the pattern of slight legislative attention after the enactment of legislation. The Bundestag, especially through its Interior Committee, made the final determination on the shaping of the BDSG in 1976. If the goals of data protection are now to be refashioned, then at least some commentators believe that careful definitions are required and concrete realities must be explored. Technological assessments of surveillance capabilities need to be carefully executed.

Chapter 3

The Power of Data Protection Commissioners

In order to be effective in limiting governmental surveillance, data protectors require independence, powers of intervention, and the willingness to use them. This chapter begins the evaluation of how well Data Protection Commissioners (DPCs) have been able to function in this regard.

Independence

Under the Federal Data Protection Act (BDSG), the government rather than the Bundestag selects the Data Protection Commissioner, because of the doctrine of ministerial responsibility. The incumbent is independent in the performance of his duties and subject only to the law. The commissioner's office exists within the federal Ministry of the Interior (BMI), and the commissioner is subject to the supervision of the minister of the interior, who must provide the personnel and material resources necessary for the accomplishment of the tasks of the DPC's office.[1]

Professor Hans Peter Bull, the first Data Protection Commissioner, characterized the office as an independent authority within the executive framework of the federal government rather than as an organ of the legislature. Bull further explained that the DPC's "public law relationship" with the government means that he is comparable in personal status to a government minister but otherwise like a professional civil servant. This relative independence means that the federal government only has the power of supervision concerning his or her obedience to law.[2]

The federal commissioner is a part of the Ministry of the Interior for administrative purposes only; it cannot directly instruct the DPC, whatever the politics of the current minister or the momentary enthusiasms or concerns of a particular government about the need for surveillance. Bull explained that the DPC's "competence to give evidence or to make statements on secret facts is subject to permission by the minister of the interior. But this does not impede the Commissioner from giving his opinion publicly on general questions, legal problems, or draft prescriptions as long as no personal data of people concerned or official secrets (classified material) are included."[3] The DPC's salary (and thus by implication his rank) is that of a high-ranking director of an underdepartment in the federal ministry. Some critics have argued that Bull should have earned as much as a state secretary, the highest civil servant appointment, because of the importance of the position.[4] The commissioner's staff members are officers of the Ministry of the Interior and are primarily recruited from there because of government restrictions on hiring. This does make possible the secondment and rotation of civil servants and further helps guarantee their personal independence.

Despite the emphasis on the independence of the DPC and his office, their administrative attachment to the BMI creates some division of loyalties and interests. In theory, the staff is responsible only to the commissioner but, in effect, an ambitious person must pay attention to his or her career prospects within the ministry. The first generation of senior staff members at the DPC's office was not overtly concerned about such personal considerations, as the record of their activities in data protection demonstrates. However, the BMI is the final arbiter on salaries, pensions, the ranking of jobs, and promotions. Since promotion to the higher ranks within the BMI generally requires experience in several different areas, someone who remains too long in data protection may lose his or her prospects for promotion. Ambitious staff members at the DPC's office also sense that antagonizing their superiors in the ministry may not help their careers.[5]

This problem of the relationship between the DPC's office and the BMI for purposes of career paths surfaced in 1986 in the Riegel affair. Dr. Reinhard Riegel, a forceful figure, was responsible for data protection for the security services and the police. After the failure to reappoint Bull in 1983, the new conservative minister of the interior, Friedrich Zimmermann, became less and less enamored of Riegel's efforts to limit surveillance. In order not to lose his future prospects, Riegel was forced to accept a "promotion" within the BMI, ending his career at the DPC's office. Since this was a clear case of muzzling an effective watchdog, the press turned the issue into a minor cause célèbre. More importantly, the staff of the DPC's office interpreted the experience as threatening their independence and that of the office; the episode contributed to their demoralization. Finally, the Social Democrats publicly questioned the DPC's independence, because of the Interior Ministry's control over his personnel. Without parliamentary debate, the government rejected such suspicions, a judgment with which Dr. R. Baumann, the incumbent DPC, simply concurred.[6]

Budgets are another aspect of governmental control. The DPC negotiates for his budget with the Ministry of the Interior, which then bargains with the Ministry of Finance and ultimately the legislature.[7] Simitis has stated that the question of who furnishes the budget for a data protection agency is crucial to its independence. He emphasizes the central importance of ensuring "not an absolute independence . . . but the largest possible degree of independence."[8] During periods of budgetary restrictions, the BMI can use funding as a form of control. When the commissioner, supported by the opposition parties, sought four new staff members in 1986, the government replied that the increase in work was the temporary result of the 1983 census decision. In the interim, agencies that the DPC's office had to control grew quickly in both staff and complexity of information systems. Toward the end of his term, Baumann called on the Bundestag to fund his office adequately, noting that the federal budget for electronic data processing was more than one hundred times that of his office.[9]

Finally, changes in ruling party often determine the political persuasion of the minister of the interior. This, in turn, can affect the selection of the federal DPC, as happened in 1982. In that year, the government led by the Social Democrats was defeated. Minister of the Interior Gerhard Baum, of the liberal Free Democratic party (FDP)—a party traditionally associated with the protection of individual rights against the state—and his state secretary had been strongly supportive of data protection. This was important, as always, in creating a favorable climate for Bull to exercise a considerable degree of independence and aggressiveness. The new chancellor, Helmut Kohl, of the Christian Democrats, made the controversial appointment of Friedrich Zimmermann as minister of the interior.[10]

Rumors spread that Zimmermann did not plan to reappoint Bull when his five-year term expired. A conservative newspaper claimed, on the basis of information from Zimmermann's office, that "Bull is accused of having a one-track mind on data protection and of being neglectful of security interests."[11] Zimmermann wanted data protection to pose fewer hindrances to police and security work. Furthermore, he viewed Bull as a member of the Social Democratic party (SPD) and saw no reason to keep him in office when his term expired. Politicians in the Bundestag, especially members of the SPD, interpreted the failure to reappoint Bull as a political act against a person who had acted independently. Bull's demise speaks volumes about the ability of a government to control the implementation of data protection by striking at its leadership when an opportunity arises.[12]

Bull's experiences indicate the continuing problem of the federal appointment process: the government can appoint public administrators sympathetic to the prevailing ideology. The decision not to reappoint Bull was obviously due more to the minister's politics than to the commissioner's competence, but the warning for independent-minded DPCs in any Western country is clear. Yet this mixing of public duties and private ideology is inevitable to an extent in any Western democracy. One (unattractive) alternative is to make such postings lifetime appointments. The increasing consequence of such a policy is the coopting of a comfortable senior civil servant, who will not challenge fundamental government interests.

A different model for the relationship between the Data Protection Office and the state bureaucracies is found in Hesse, whose Data Protection Act makes stronger provisions for independence. The legislature elects the commissioner on the proposal of the government, and the incumbent serves during its electoral life. When a Christian Democrat–Liberal coalition succeeded the long-ruling Social Democrats in 1987, Spiros Simitis was nevertheless reelected because, as a government spokesman indicated, "an *independent commissioner* is seen to be of particular interest for our citizens." Simitis emphasizes the importance of the public perceiving his office as being attached to the legislature and not as part of the public administration.[13] He believes the DPCs elsewhere should not be treated as normal civil servants and integrated into the public administration, as is the case at present. They should be located outside the normal hierarchy in order to ensure maximum independence.

The issue of independence as affected by structural controls will continue to be pursued throughout this volume. Choices always have to be made. If the federal DPC were in fact attached to the Bundestag, the office would have no direct access to public administrations (which they have now). The benefit for the federal DPC's office might be a public image of more independence, and it could also rotate staff within the Bundestag.

Powers of Intervention

As has been discussed, the DPC's role is primarily that of adviser; he or she has the power to investigate and persuade but not the authority to issue binding instructions. However, when the commissioner discovers or alleges infringements of the BDSG or any other data protection laws or regulations, article 20(1) of the law empowers him or her to submit a formal complaint to the competent body, which must respond within a time fixed by the DPC: "Should the Commissioner hold that the answer is not satisfactory, he can only report the case to the Parliament so that the deputies or the public media would be able to admonish or attack the Government."[14] Bull regularly used this significant power to admonish an agency for illegal acts, regarding it as a valuable supplement to his advisory power. On the basis of several investigations, he successfully objected privately to the impermissible storage and dissemination of personal data.[15] In numerous instances, however, the agencies took the position that such processing was lawful. An agency cannot substitute its own interpretation of the BDSG for that of the commissioner. In a strictly legal sense, disagreements about data protection in the public sector are ultimately settled by the minister in charge at either the federal or state level. Fortunately, the DPC can appeal to the media and to the legislature, if his objections are not taken into account. The Interior Committee is the main link between the legislature and the agency.

Simitis believes that his independence as Hesse DPC is more protected than that of his federal counterpart. In his view federal or state agencies can make it difficult for the data protection staff to gain access to their premises and records, whereas his close relationship with the state parliament reduces this prospect. The Hesse DPC has the explicit right to obtain information from public administrations, making them fully transparent to him. If a minister does not take his advice, Simitis can make a report to the legislature to get necessary action, and he can also appeal to the media. This dual process is so persuasive that Simitis is unaware of any case in which a minister has failed to respond on an issue.[16]

The various commissioners do enjoy considerable powers of persuasion, although this is a variable situation. That they have no final mandate to issue regulations is a limitation, but it has not proven to be a significant hindrance.[17] In Hesse the ultimate resort to public opinion has worked very well to date, and the commissioners have used the media effectively to shape public opinion on specific issues.

The Use of Power

Both because of the significance of the emerging surveillance societies and the oversight role inherent in data protection legislation, the various Data Protection Commissioners are inevitably involved in questions of the relative distribution of power. Initially intended as watchdogs over the application of surveillance technology, they have become adjudicators in seeking the appropriate balance between personal privacy and state efficiency. Their role involves a meaningful accumulation of power, as their activities build upon and reinforce one another. Herbert Burkert sees at least some risk of the commissioners becoming a new estate in society.[18] Such a peril is intensified by the theory that as the power and scope of data protection increases, its proponents inevitably become overzealous in the exercise of their responsibilities.

Although data protectors tend to dismiss such speculations, in part because of a government's residual power to amend any legislation, the issue demands continued wary attention. Bull directly acknowledged the issue: "To date, there is a broad consensus that collecting, evaluating and transmitting data is an aspect of the balance of power in society and state, and that fair solutions for these problems must be elaborated in many areas of politics and economy."[19] To ignore these issues of power is to tread a dangerous path.

Although an outsider may be struck at first glance by the amount of power delegated to the commissioners, Dr. H. Weyer in North Rhine–Westphalia took a pessimistic view of his own power and that of his fellow regulators. He emphasized that as DPC he had no power to order, to fine, or to sue. Weyer believes that the ultimate enforcement of data protection depends on citizens suing the government or a public agency in the courts. Such an approach approximates that of federal data protection in the United States. A few such lawsuits have occurred, some at his instigation, but too few for his liking.

The appointment of Dr. Baumann to succeed Bull in 1983 renewed fears about the continued independence and power of the federal DPC, since he was a senior official of the federal Ministry of the Interior. Baumann emphasized that he was not a member of a political party, but an independent, and that he would be due for mandatory retirement at the end of his first term (as occurred in 1988). He had not known Zimmermann before the appointment, thus lending credence to the view that the minister was trying to free a senior job at the BMI and remove Bull, the overly enthusiastic watchdog, at the same time. Baumann could also point to other commissioners, such as Ruth Leuze in Baden-Württemberg, who had come to their posts from ministries of the interior yet displayed considerable independence. In 1987 she was in fact reappointed to a second eight-year term.

In terms of power, the initial goals of data protection are difficult to oppose, especially during election campaigns. But after several years of enforcement activities in West Germany, there were indications of a growing discontent within the political arena, which has continued to the present day. Data protection affects different activities in different ways, yet the power of certain groups, including the police and the security agencies, makes it possible to resist a stronger enforcement in critical sectors of society. Such attitudes are epitomized in the comment of the government of Baden-Württemberg on Dr. Leuze's third annual report as DPC: "The personal rights of the citizens are protected in data processing as far as this is compatible with accomplishing the task of administration."[20]

In 1986 Baumann used the Interior Committee of the Bundestag to solve a problem with the guidelines on security clearances of the Federal Agency for the Protection of the Constitution. He had already unsuccessfully tried to persuade the secretariat of the BMI. The Interior Committee instructed his office and the BMI to settle the issue together and to report the result. In Baumann's view, the government was more cooperative under the pressure of the Interior Committee, and a precedent now exists for this committee to ask for a matter to be resolved in this fashion. Thus the legislature is always the federal DPC's last resort, after persuasion with the agency in question has failed.

Resistance to data protection is inevitable in every country, as it begins to intrude on the surveillance practices of powerful domains by seeking basic changes in their information-handling behavior. The commissioners are, by definition, always critical of government legislative proposals. In this sense, the 1983 census debate was very important for promoting the health of data protection, since the climate for data protection in the winter of 1982–83 was poor, given the public discussion of the demise of Bull. The Constitutional Court postponed an expensive census because of concern for privacy interests. Members of the new ruling coalition, especially including Minister of the Interior Zimmermann, and all members of the Bundestag, who had unanimously supported the census law, had their consciousness raised (again) about the centrality of data protection to public concerns. Although a small cadre of detractors viewed the decision as increasing the risk of data protectors roaming unchecked through society, there is almost no evidence of any tendency in this direction. Nor has the government any lack of power to cope with such a hypothetical problem. The sheer force of numbers easily permits government lawyers, for example, to outlast the commissioners on many issues.

Despite statutory independence, data protection agencies in West Germany and elsewhere can only venture so far in the exercise of power, just as the regulated can only go so far in resisting their supervision and advice. At least until the 1983 census decision, the political climate for implementation also varied from time to time. The Social Democrats and Green parties clearly remain more sympathetic to data protection than do the conservative parties at the federal and state levels. After the court's decision, some Christian Democratic politicians even discussed the creation of a board to advise the federal DPC, which could be construed as an attempt to control the activities of the office, now that it has become an important intervener against state surveillance practices.

The Decision of the Federal Constitutional Court

The real issue is how to protect the independence of a data protection agency once it becomes an effective watchdog over various ministries. Claims of hard economic times may cloak an attempt to muzzle a data protection agency by restricting the growth of its budget or by cutting it back, as has happened in Sweden.[21] The ultimate, difficult consideration is that any government will only tolerate so much opposition to its proposals for surveillance from a data protection agency, whatever its statutory degree of independence, hence the benefit of establishing data protection as a constitutional right of the individual, so that courts may intervene.

The great controversy in 1983 over the census of population, which is discussed in detail in Chapter 5, subjected the adequacies of data protection itself to public and judicial scrutiny and led the Constitutional Court in Karlsruhe to confirm a new basis for data protection as a constitutional right. The establishment of such a basis for data protection is an exceptional support for the watchdogs, since the legislatures now have to be more mindful of the Constitutional Court.

On December 15, 1983, the Court ruled unanimously that West Germans have a constitutional right to self-determination about the use of their own personal information on the basis of articles 1 and 2 of the Constitution. An individual is now free, in theory, to decide whether to give out information, and any government agency, whether federal or state, collecting personal data has to do so in accordance with specific legal procedures. The court stated that the "free development of personality under modern conditions of data processing implies the protection of the individual against unlimited collection, storage, use, and transmission of his/her personal data."[22] Furthermore, the court insisted "that the institution of an independent data protection commission is an indispensable requirement for the effective protection of the individual's right to determine the use of his personal data, the so-called 'fundamental right of informational self-determination.'"[23] Such a right—if it is meaningfully used—may be the ultimate antidote to governmental surveillance.

The court ruled that although this right is not absolute in the face of competing societal values, information collection and use have to occur on the basis of established laws and in response to the overwhelming public interests of the community. The decision does not make clear what claims the individual can make, which leads to broad and narrow views of the law's application: the legitimacy of any use of personal data depends on the specific context. According to the court, "these restrictions require . . . a [constitutional] *legal basis* which delineates, in a way clearly perceptible to the citizen, the prerequisites for, and extent of, the restrictions; and which fulfills the demands contained in the rule of law of *precision of legal norms*. . . . The legislator, in law making, further has to observe the principle of *due proportion*."[24]

The Federal Constitutional Court has in effect given constitutional standing to data protection agencies by insisting that their existence is essential for data collection to occur. Data protectors and legislators are still preoccupied with interpretation of the implications of this revolutionary decision for their work, since the court has left it to others to apply the language of the decision. The legislatures have to develop procedures for individuals to control their own data, which is gradually leading to strong laws for specific information systems; the need for sectoral laws has been reinforced. The constitutionality of any such law can be challenged on the basis of the Constitutional Court's decision. Others initially feared that the need for laws for all data-processing activities could bring the public administration and the legislative process to a grinding halt. A flood of new laws and regulations to control the flow of personal information would be much too bureaucratic a form of data protection in the opinion of some, but this has not occurred. One narrow solution is to interpret the decision as only applying to automated data, but those arguing for its universal application have the upper hand, especially since the decision follows the views of Simitis.[25]

The activities of data protectors in seeking to limit governmental surveillance have been given strong reinforcement in the public sector by the Court's decision, which has confirmed the goals of data protection and also routed the (few) critics and opponents of data protection activities. One important implication for independence is that it would prevent the Bundestag from ever abolishing the federal DPC or withdrawing the BDSG. In fact, the federal and state legislatures have to respond to the decision, or more cases will go to the Constitutional Court in future years. Regrettably, this process is moving very slowly.

Chapter 4

The Implementation of Data Protection

Since effective implementation is a key factor in the successful conduct of data protection, this chapter pays extended attention to what has happened since West Germany introduced the Federal Data Protection Law (BDSG) in 1977. The particular focus is the activities of data protection agencies at the federal level and in the states of North Rhine–Westphalia (NRW) and Hesse, to identify what approaches they have used in trying to limit governmental surveillance practices and with what success. Special attention is paid to staffing, since the choice of employees has proved to be so critical to this effort. There is also extensive discussion of the various activities of data protectors as they seek to accomplish their statutory tasks. Finally, the chapter treats the evolution in practice of data protection principles.

Data Protection Commissioners and Their Staffs

The Commissioners

The qualifications and achievements of Professor Hans Peter Bull, the first federal Data Protection Commissioner (DPC) from 1978 to 1983, inevitably become one benchmark against which his successors can be measured. He was one of the first German lawyers to be actively involved with the topic of data protection and was closely involved in the formulation of the federal legislation. As mentioned in Chapter 3, Bull's membership in the Social Democratic party (SPD) was publicly known and shaped to some extent his philosophy in performing his duties.[1] While the federal DPC must not be directly involved in partisan political activities, for Bull to be a member of the SPD connotes a stronger adherence to the ideological tenets of his party than would be the case of a comparable official in a typical political party in North America. Bull, for example, has remained strongly worried about the effects on society of the growing reliance on computers, and he generally gives priority to human interests over technological potential. He also believes that public administrations lack confidence in individual self-determination and that bureaucracies perceive the state as the master and not the servant of the public, which further helps to explain the positions he took as DPC and the tenacity with which he pursued his tasks.

When the issue of Bull's reappointment arose, Minister of the Interior Friedrich Zimmermann argued that data protection should not take priority over such other interests as the security of the state. Bull strongly denies that this was his view and asserts that he aimed at an equilibrium of interests affecting surveillance. He did not seek conflicts, nor did he avoid them, recognizing that they were often stepping stones to better understanding and desirable practices.[2]

Although the selection of a Data Protection Commissioner from outside the federal civil service was initially thought to be desirable, following the experience with Bull, there was a shift in the Ministry of the Interior's definition of desirable qualifications. Rather than a private citizen, a public servant was chosen to succeed Bull. Dr. Reinhold Baumann, who held the post from 1983 to 1988, had thirty years' experience as a lawyer in the public administration, primarily with the federal Ministry of the Interior itself. Seemingly, the ministry had wearied of the "informed advocate" model, preferring Baumann's intended "good management" approach. Baumann did not solicit the new position but regarded it as an attractive opportunity at the end of his career.

Baumann's successor in 1988, Dr. Alfred Einwag, has also spent his public service career since 1956 in the federal Ministry of the Interior, most recently as a senior official in the department overseeing the domestic security service. Both the opposition Social Democrats and the junior coalition partner Free Democrats voiced misgivings about the appointment, because this government lawyer had spent most of his career "on the other side of the data protection fence" and because he could be reviewing decisions made in his earlier posts. Like his predecessor, Einwag will reach retirement age at the end of one term as federal DPC.[3]

While the federal appointment process is politically sensitive, selection at the state level can be openly partisan. In North Rhine–Westphalia political affiliation was an important qualification. Heinrich Weyer, the commissioner for NRW from 1979 to 1987, obtained his position as the first DPC when the Free Democratic party (FDP) was in control of the Ministry of the Interior in NRW.[4] The FDP minister simply asked Weyer, a lifetime member of the party, if he wanted the job and then recommended him to the cabinet. The Landtag appointed him for a renewable eight-year term. Although the appointment appears to be "political," Weyer protests that it was not, since he could not be removed from office, had no superior, and remained a civil servant.[5] Yet he also remained a party member, and his term was not renewed after another party took control of the state.

For the first DPCs it seems that it made little difference whether they were drawn from private life, the civil service, or political patronage, in that the posts were filled by highly qualified people who took an activist approach. Any appointment process may produce competent individuals, provided that each has sufficient capacity to handle a fast developing and highly politicized policy field. Regardless of how a commissioner is appointed, his or her qualifications are a crucial issue. An inadequate background in the sensitive issues associated with surveillance and data protection may lead a commissioner into difficulties with the media, the public, the legislature, and often all three. Without the support of these partners in the policy process, data protection can become virtually impossible, since the commissioner has no real authority to compel observation of the laws but depends on cooperation and accommodation.

The Hessian appointment process may be the only system that recognizes this need for continued support. The term of office is coincidental with the electoral life of the legislature, and the commissioner is elected by its members.[6] Spiros Simitis, a professor of law at the University of Frankfurt, has been the Hessian commissioner since 1975. He continues to be reelected to the post by overwhelming majorities, despite the vicissitudes of state electoral politics. Simitis has now outlasted Jan Freese of Sweden as the major international influence on the conduct of data protection.

The Staff

The problems surrounding the hiring, training, retention, and rotation of staff are significant for data protection agencies, since small numbers are being asked to bear heavy burdens as watchdogs over surveillance. The commissioners have the power in theory to recruit and appoint their own staff but, perhaps as a consequence of the fact that data protection jobs are classified as civil service positions, the federal DPC initially advertised and filled positions on the basis of open competitions. There is in fact no requirement for open competitions, especially for heads of sections. Selecting officials is a bit like a chess game for the federal commissioner, since it involves attracting relatively senior personnel from within the federal Ministry of the Interior. However, if a civil servant moves from the Ministry of the Interior to the DPC and then becomes qualified for promotion, the only real option is to return him or her to the ministry at a later date. The lack of room for promotion of senior staff within the federal DPC's office, which for these purposes is part of a grade-oriented Ministry of the Interior, presents real difficulties, since the most experienced staff members have a natural inclination to pursue their career prospects.

The related problem of staleness due to a lack of promotion opportunities is not limited to the federal level. The staff in Hesse are generally new, young, and talented. In theory, they expect to spend five or six years working for the state DPC but do not plan to make a permanent career in the office. The problem is that this model of recruiting young staff and then transferring them to other government departments as they advance in rank has rarely worked in practice. Most of Simitis's staff members have been with him for significant periods of time and have not found an opportunity to go elsewhere, in part because of their relatively high rank.

There have been suggestions in the last few years that some of the state DPCs lack sufficiently experienced personnel to implement the law competently. However, the field was new to many people and, as experience is accumulating, the seriousness of the problem declines. There are no appointments to the staffs of the federal or state DPCs made for political reasons. The high percentage of lawyers and jurists in the civil service is reflected even more in a field like data protection, which itself has a significant legal component. Especially at the federal DPC's office, some staff members have multiple qualifications for their roles, such as being both jurists and having data protection or data-processing experience. Those with previous involvement in data protection play a significant role in the initial training of newcomers to the field.

Most of the people working in North Rhine–Westphalia are lawyers, which reflected Weyer's characterization of the issues as primarily legal questions. As Weyer himself was not an expert, he could not recruit from an established personal network. Consequently, he hired most of his staff from state agencies. One insight into the training process that he offered was that all of the staff, including himself, had to shift their personal values from the central goal of pursuing efficiency toward protecting the rights of citizens.

The office of the federal Data Protection Commissioner in Bonn is organized in a series of five units, which are responsible for various administrative divisions of the federal government. This system of staff specialization by type of information system is a major reason for the effectiveness of data protection at the federal level. Staff members develop the specialized competence that permits them to understand the surveillance implications of a system. The prior experience and personalities of senior staff members also shape the approach that each takes to data protection. For example, Dr. R. Riegel, who headed the unit concerned with the police and intelligence service until 1986, is a jurist who originally started to work as a public prosecutor in Bavaria. He later worked for the Ministry of the Interior on harmonization of jurisdiction between the police laws and the penal laws. Bull invited Riegel to the federal office because of his experience with the police and security field. All of this shaped a very aggressive and persistent approach to his work.

Nonetheless, there is some reason for concern about staff qualifications in information technology. For instance, Weyer had only one data-processing expert on staff, which is typical of the situation in most countries and better than some. The lack of such expertise presents a risk that a wide gap will develop between the staff's legal and technological knowledge. The problem may become more serious, due to the difficulties of recruiting and retaining data-processing and auditing specialists. While the staff do acquire considerable understanding over time of the intricacies of automation, financial resources to facilitate the continued upgrading of such skills are inadequate.

Attitudes and Approaches to Implementation

Although each of the sections in the federal DPC has responsibility for a particular range of activities under the general guidance of the commissioner, a number of significant differences have emerged in the way they approach their respective tasks, although, as in other countries, the emphasis is on mediation, conciliation, and education.

Activities in the sensitive area of police records are a useful example of the conciliatory or collegial model. Initially, there was strong resistance from the police to the DPC's supervisory activities, but gradually they developed confidence in Riegel and his associates. The police anticipated interference in their work by persons who did not understand their problems, but in fact found the data protection staff had undertaken prior research so as to understand the intricacies of the police situation. As a result, the federal DPC's office gradually won the confidence of the staff of the federal police.

The public stance of the federal and state police still is that the BDSG has hurt their activities, but there is now more practical interest in data protection among them. In its work with the police, which probably is typical, the staff of the DPC's office has gone from studying theory to studying actual surveillance practices, so that it is now difficult for the police to make decisions that will bewilder the DPCs. It has also become more difficult for the police to try to misinform the DPCs about the necessity for certain data-processing and data retention practices. The approach of Riegel and his associates is to try to convince the police authorities of the appropriateness of certain practices, to attempt to find agreement, to agree on occasion to disagree, and to avoid conflict (but not at any cost). Despite his own aggressive character, Riegel did not see much benefit in alienating the persons and organizations he was attempting to supervise, although his unit did issue formal complaints when necessary.

It is Riegel's view that resistance to data protection has largely come from the presidents of the police and security agencies, not from the civil servants. He regards the relationship between the data protectors and those being regulated as very cooperative: they do not always agree, but they do negotiate compromises and incremental improvements. Riegel was also of the opinion that his work was not particularly a function of the incumbent commissioner or of the governing political coalition. His experiences after the change of coalition government in 1982 initially persuaded him that the DPC's ongoing work would be unaffected. He carried out an inspection at a counterespionage agency and made a number of recommendations for change in a document submitted to the appropriate government ministry. The ministry indicated that it would accept most of Riegel's recommendations for data protection. Moreover, he had a friendly discussion with the counterespionage agency about the timing of his next inspection, so that he could report on any progress in the annual report. Finally, Riegel was optimistic that the change of commissioner would not hinder or change the activities of his unit, which indeed proved to be the case until Minister of the Interior Zimmermann removed him from the office in 1986.

Collegiality in implementation is promoted because civil servants are regulating other civil servants, who traditionally share positive attitudes toward their respective roles. A well-developed system to implement any new law exists, and the BDSG was simply put in place. Tensions over compliance are more likely to exist between managers and data processors within a particular organization. Furthermore, the law mandates that officials of public agencies help the DPCs with implementation.[7] One can contrast this commitment to compliance with the tortuous efforts in the United States from the time of the Carter administration to justify the transfer of personal data among federal agencies for computer-matching programs, even though it requires a strained interpretation of the Privacy Act of 1974 to justify such exchanges.[8]

This collegiality among civil servants is further supported by the virtual monopoly of lawyers or jurists in the higher civil service ranks: they tend to know one another, and they "speak the same language." In addition to shared legal training, most of the staff of the federal DPC have previous experience as administrators. This situation is somewhat comparable to the existence of the small, integrated elite of civil servants at the head of the many agencies implementing government policy in Sweden. One can contrast this process of elite accommodation with the situation in English-speaking countries, where laws on a subject like data protection are written in a highly legalistic vein, yet implementation is in the hands of civil servants who normally have little experience in interpreting the actual language of legislation or in working with lawyers. English-speaking civil servants also seem more likely than their European counterparts to regard laws and lawyers with considerable suspicion.

Nevertheless, within the federal office there is a significant difference of opinion about the appropriateness of collegiality. One section, which has a markedly different "mental attitude" toward data protection, believes that the process of confrontation with the custodians of personal data inspires mutual respect. This section's leader under Bull was prepared to contrast the amount of progress he achieved with that of his associates, and after three years in his position he concluded that confrontation was the most productive approach to surveillance control.

The approach of this group has its basis both in ideology and experience. Despite changes in personnel, members of this section continue to bring a strong philosophical basis to their thinking about data protection. They tend to be adherents of the left-wing Green party. They believe that data protection provides a very fundamental service in attempting to restrict the collection of personal information and unlicensed data processing. After environmental protection, they believe data protection is the second most important societal issue and a part of an appropriate concern with human and civil rights. During Bull's tenure, this unit contributed a valuable perspective to internal debates over limiting surveillance.

There are those inside and outside the federal DPC's office who much admire the accomplishments of this unusual group, and there are those inside the agency who believe that its confrontational approach has hindered the activities of the office as a whole. The criticism within the DPC's office is that the preoccupation of any one section with fundamental questions, and the accompanying clashes of personality, produce negativism among those regulated, which hurts future good relations between the commissioner and the agencies.

It is almost inevitable that the DPCs should adopt a mediating and conciliatory role in the application of the principles of data protection in practice. The tendency to search for an appropriate compromise is understandable in human terms and in terms of the realities of the exercise of power in public administration. Determining acceptable and legal levels of surveillance requires finding a satisfactory balance at any point in time.

Bull's recruitment of a high-quality staff helped to ensure continuity in data protection after Baumann replaced him in 1983. Since his departure brought the staff closer together, it would have been difficult for the new commissioner to impose dramatic alterations in the direction of staff work without significant changes in personnel. The same conditions should prevail since Baumann's term ended in 1988.

Simitis has had the most extensive experience of running a West German data protection office and of fashioning approaches to controlling surveillance. He strongly believes in having a young staff, since they are more willing to question the commissioner and public administrations. Simitis runs his office on the basis of cooperation and a search for consensus with those being regulated. The staff tries to specialize by field, but its small size has made this difficult. The Hesse office concentrates on furnishing views on relevant matters to the legislature, although the burdened staff finds it hard to choose among such competing goals as commenting on draft legislation, giving advice, and carrying out inspections. Its members do try to find general solutions for data protection problems. Some observers suggest that the contrasting approach in North Rhine–Westphalia is the traditional legal method of finding solutions to specific cases.

Simitis makes the point that data protectors have to be good politicians and not simply good judges. This is an important perspective on what are, after all, civil service positions. Other informed observers of the role of the federal Data Protection Commissioner also regard it as a political position and suggest that Bull was especially political in connection with his views on the police and security agencies. Simitis's handling of the problem of computer linkages illustrates his approach. He is concerned not to appear totally hostile to all forms of such matching activities, with the consequent risk of being dismissed as a Luddite, yet to find concrete ways of resisting excessive surveillance practices.

Bureaucratic Tendencies

There has been some criticism and concern in Germany and elsewhere about the bureaucratic aspects of the development of data protection, especially the size of staffs and their cost. This concern is essentially misguided, since the real risk is of inadequate resources being dedicated to the control of governmental surveillance. The federal DPC's office in 1982 had a staff totaling thirty-five persons, including the commissioner. By 1987 the total was thirty-one. Seventy-five percent of the staff are professionals directly involved in data protection. The offices of the state Data Protection Commissioners also vary widely in size. For example, the DPC for the city-state of Hamburg (pop. 1.75 million) is expected to function with the assistance of two persons in addition to himself.

Nevertheless, some of the smaller offices are very active. Simitis has been the leading proponent of small staffs in order to avoid bureaucracy. In his view the ideal is for a DPC to employ six or eight people with direct responsibility for various sectors of the public administration.[9] The size of his office remained stable (with eight professional positions) for at least a half-dozen years. Simitis eventually recognized, with the encouragement of his staff, that he needed as many as twelve professionals and a total staff of twenty-five to do the job properly. There was criticism that Simitis, with his tiny staff, was giving only the illusion of data protection.

Since critics of data protection are quick to suggest that the enforcement agencies have the typical expansionist tendencies of bureaucracies, it should be noted that the staff sizes of the federal and state agencies seem eminently reasonable. When Weyer was criticized about the size of his staff (which is comparable to that of the federal DPC), he noted that the state Ministry of the Interior had set the size of his office prior to his appointment. The growth of all the offices appears to have stabilized, and some have even decreased in size. The number of staff members recruited over time does raise issues of bureaucratic growth and the thrust for increased power, but probably in just the reverse direction from what critics have suggested. As in all countries, the real risk is that staff sizes and expenditures are inadequate for the control of surveillance.

Evaluating the actual cost and size of data protection offices is very difficult. For example, each ministry of the federal and state governments in West Germany has its own data protection officers, who serve as contacts for the DPC's office, but who also have other tasks. Consequently, they are an additional, indirect cost of data protection. As a result of difficult economic times in the 1980s, some downward adjustment in staff sizes occurred. There is little room for growth and, apparently, little perception of a need for it. In response to occasional criticism, Bull concluded that there is hardly any area of public administration that can achieve such a relatively large effect with so few means. For example, the entire cost of his office in 1980 was less than the cost of printing and distributing the legislature's budget statement.[10]

One final bureaucratic issue is the question of whether data protection agencies, like other supervisory agencies before them, will tend to become coopted over time by adopting the mentality of those they regulate. This suspicion is associated with the findings of Ralph Nader and his researchers in monitoring the work of American regulatory agencies.[11] Herbert Burkert has perceptively noted that, in the immediate future, the issue of information control and regulation will not disappear as an important concern of the general public, since information technology is a growth industry and an increasingly powerful economic sector. Whenever power collects, there is an inevitable urge to harness and control it. The ability of a data protection agency to renew itself, so as to prevent being coopted, will also be encouraged by the limited terms of office of the DPCs themselves; a newcomer will likely want to incorporate new ideas and personnel.

Data Protection Activities

Supervision, Investigation, and Auditing

Supervision and auditing of surveillance practices, advising on specific situations, and investigation of complaints cover all aspects of the federal public administration. The federal office prepares an annual plan for its multiple activities, but this cannot always be fulfilled because of the impact of external events, such as the 1983 census controversy. Unlike the burdens placed on the Swedish and French agencies by the licensing aspects of their empowering legislation, the office is free to set its own priorities and create its own agenda, enabling it to be more responsive to current affairs. Various units proportion their activities differently, perhaps spending more time reviewing pending regulations from government agencies than doing inspections. The key roles of consultant/adviser and inspector are in fact difficult to keep distinct and may result in a data protector taking a closer look at arrangements that he or she had a role in shaping.

The staff holds weekly meetings to receive reports from each section and to review significant developments. The commissioner thereby promotes collegial dialogue with his associates. For example, after the census decision of the Federal Constitutional Court, all of the senior staff produced internal papers on its implications for their work. Bull encouraged considerable private debate among his staff but sought to present a united external front in favor of data protection, since under the BDSG his was the ultimate decision on action.[12]

The several units of the federal DPC's office carry out investigations of various types of information systems, based upon citizens' complaints or a suspicion that a particular area requires detailed examination. Systematic audits are planned over a several-year period, thus increasing the scope and range of data protection activities. Cautious federal agencies seek to work out their arrangements for data processing with the DPC's office in advance; the data protectors then must remain vigilant that these institutions do not revert to old ideas and practices. In regulating a particular agency, the DPC's office presses its inquiries but is usually content to let the responsible organization make the final determination on the appropriateness of data processing, except when very sensitive issues of surveillance are involved.[13]

At the state level, using Hesse as an example, about 40 percent of the activity of the DPC's office is taken on its own initiative, 40 percent in response to inquiries from the state administration, and perhaps 15 to 20 percent in response to complaints from individual citizens. In general the office is now doing more of its work in response to inquiries and less on its own initiative than it did previously, reflecting the view of Simitis that data protectors have an "essentially consultative task" concerning new initiatives, policies, and measures.[14] The office has developed guidelines for various specific types of information, such as that used in research, education, health, hospitals, and cancer registries. The staff members would like to spend more time auditing, which is neglected because they are kept busy drafting specialized data protection laws for short-staffed government departments, thus in part becoming victims of their own skills. One is of course inclined to view this as just another implementation game on the part of the regulated.

The staff members of the DPCs' offices have become experts in both data processing and information flows. Not only do they emerge from their supervisory and inspection activities with a good understanding of the work of the agency under review, but they can also serve as informal consultants when problems arise. The informed sentiment within the federal office is that data protection need not impose more costs and more complexity on data-processing activities, since the goals of data protection and data processing are complementary and not antagonistic. This assessment slights the reality that controlling mass surveillance systems raises more sensitive issues than complementarity and expenditures.

Inevitably, as already noted in Chapter 3, some conflicts occur during the course of the DPCs' supervisory activities. The federal commissioner had to remind agencies that he has the power to check adherence to the BDSG and other regulations on data protection. There was conflict with the Finance Department over the relationship between the secrecy of tax records and the federal DPC's power of investigation. The Federal Chancellor's Office, which is the supervisory authority for the federal intelligence service, for the first time made use of the security proviso of the BDSG, whereby a competent federal authority can decide in certain circumstances "that the inspection of documents and files would jeopardize the security of the Federal Republic and of the Land."[15]

The data protection agencies also assist in the development of new laws on data protection, modification of existing laws, and establishment of new guidelines. The federal office advises federal ministries and individual committees of the Bundestag on the implications for surveillance of a great many different legislative proposals. This work has been particularly influential in the development of new rules and regulations for police and social security data.[16] The pattern involves persistent pursuit of the goals of data protection, even if the results are not always immediately positive.

The auditing unit in the federal office participates in the regulatory work for each type of information system. Its members have backgrounds in data processing rather than law. They often take part in planned inspections and have visited most types of information systems within federal jurisdiction. Frequency of audits can range from more than twice a year to every few years. There are a few organizations that have not yet been audited, and some small, nonsensitive information systems that recur widely in the society are being excluded. Despite the infrequency of audits, the DPC's office believes that its recommendations on security and related matters have a ripple effect in other organizations with similar tasks.

An inspection team consists mostly of members of the unit responsible for the agency being inspected and one or two specialized auditors. Its members check the legality of the data processing, while the specialized auditors review written plans and actual practices, physical and electronic security in data-processing activities, and the environment of the information system. In practice, these tasks cannot be separated, because knowledge about organization and material content of a task are interdependent. The audit team attempts to point out security weaknesses in an information system and to evaluate local controls for data protection. They also try to learn whether data are being processed illegally or stored too long.[17]

One auditor has a specific responsibility to accompany Riegel—and now accompanies his successor, Ulrich Dammann—to the various security agencies. This person requires fairly specialized expertise about security operations in order to be effective. For example, he asks technical questions concerning strategies of defense against various intrusive measures. The DPC can then ask for the strengthening of a security practice, such as in a transmission system.

An audit of a given information system takes approximately a week if the system is not too large, but the time may range from two to six weeks. In advance of a visit to a site, the unit reads all of the laws and regulations concerning the tasks of the organization, examines the organization chart, and studies the data-processing system and the distribution of responsibility for information handling. In order to understand the data flow in the entire system being audited, charts are prepared to trace personal information from its source to a particular agency and its subsequent dissemination. As part of their examination of the "communication process," the auditors are interested not only in where the data are processed, but also where they come from and where they are transmitted.[18] They seek a full awareness of the surveillance capabilities of any system.

The audit team usually meets the head of the organization, the chiefs of various sections, the data protection officer, and the head of the internal employees' association. They are especially concerned with various aspects of protective security for personal information. The audit team believes they are given accurate information during their site visits if they ask the right questions. In part, this is a product of the elite accommodation discussed in the last section. Their success is also a function of their techniques to learn relevant information. For example, they may ask similar questions of several on-line operators in a given institution.

The DPC's office is accustomed to temporary resistance to its audit activities, which can then lead to negotiations at the site or consultations with the Interior Committee of the Bundestag. Occasional problems are usually settled after negotiations with the commissioner himself. The Federal Agency for the Protection of the Constitution tested Baumann in 1983 by refusing to produce certain documentation on the grounds that it was not of interest; the issue was in effect a legal debate over article 19 of the BDSG concerning the power of the commissioner.

When he released his first annual report in 1984, Baumann noted that he and his staff "did not come across any scandalous goings-on in the information processing of the federal administration; there were, however, many cases of questionable or incorrect handling of personal data. These are not due to intentions to misuse these data, though, but rather on negligence or erroneous interpretation of the law." The DPC does not assign specific blame for a problem if assurances of correction are received. Follow-up audits are also conducted to check on compliance, and negative reports can have detrimental effects on the career of the person responsible.

The most powerful sanction that the audit group can recommend is a complaint by the commissioner to the appropriate authority in an administration. The DPC has made such complaints about inadequate security.[19] The team has rarely found real disasters during audits. In one instance, which demonstrated an insufficient awareness of data protection, the organization lacked the funds to do the job appropriately. Audit results are more likely to be adopted if the recommendations are not too expensive, or too complicated to be understood and implemented.

Data Registers

Section 19(4) of the BDSG requires the federal commissioner to keep a register of automated data banks containing personal information, which the public may consult. Public authorities (except for national security agencies) are required to report all of their automated data files. There are between 1,200 and 1,500 data banks registered at the federal level, but requests to consult the register are rare. This may be a result of its not being published or automated. The DPC is able to provide extracts from the collected material to the public but not complete copies, because of the costs involved.

Under section 12(1) of the BDSG, government agencies at the federal and state levels are further required to publish annual listings of their own data banks of personal information. The notices are placed in the *Bundesanzeiger,* but no one in authority reviews the accuracy of the details. Bull wanted the public notifications to pass through his office to ensure that the information given is accurate and complete. He sought to combine this information with the details his own office keeps on its own register, because the current systems offered neither a complete, nor understandable, picture of the data processing within a particular agency either for the use of the DPC or an individual.[20]

The state data protection agencies also maintain registers comparable to the federal effort. Section 26 of the 1986 Hessian act provides for regular publication of the register maintained by the state DPC and improves the quality of detail supplied by government agencies. In North Rhine–Westphalia the DPC has received more than 20,000 declarations for his unpublished register.

Dr. Dammann of the federal DPC's office indicated that his office regards its register of data banks in the public sector as a tool for gaining a first impression of the scope of existing information systems, but that such a form of registration is only useful as a part of the learning process in the early stages of data protection. Simitis agreed that the register of public registers is the basis for his office's supervision and that its existence permits understanding and rationalization of the public administration. More importantly, however, the register allows reflection on the bureaucratic development of public administration by identifying the reasons for the existence and use of certain data bases.[21] Nevertheless, the West German system of publicizing data banks is deficient for purposes of alerting the population to surveillance practices.

Access to Data and Complaints from Individuals

In its various publications the federal DPC's office—like its French counterpart, the National Commission on Informatics and Freedoms—has insisted that the exercise of control by means of individual requests for access to personal data is the ultimate means of insuring that data protection is implemented. The DPC asserts that interested citizens are the most important guarantee for the proper application of data protection; an individual must exercise the right to be informed.[22]

An individual may approach a government agency by letter, in person, or occasionally by telephone. There is no obligation for the agency to respond within a stated time, nor is there any specification as to how much detail needs to be furnished in advance about the information requested. The information conveyed must be easily read and understood, and an individual may insist on further explanations.[23]

Section 13 of the BDSG allows certain limitations of the obligation to release information, particularly in the areas of tax information, national security, and criminal files. As in France, however, the DPC can examine police and security files on behalf of individuals and can reveal selected information but not the complete records. If an individual is refused access to state police files, the DPC's office can check them to determine, in particular, the "legality" of the data being collected. All of the Data Protection Commissioners favor this right of indirect access. On the other hand, section 13 of the BDSG further stipulates that requests for access cannot hinder the "legitimate accomplishment" of the tasks of the agency in question, but this phrase is not further defined. Refusals of individual requests for access to information can be appealed to the DPC, but his power is limited to efforts at persuasion. Unlike the Canadian Privacy Act, the BDSG contains no provision for a further appeal to the courts. In practice, there are no charges to the individual for access to federal files, because the system of accounting is too difficult and expensive to administer.

Simitis actually favors a scheme whereby the government would be required to notify each person annually of the data banks in which he or she is included.[24] Continuing technological developments may soon make such a proposal less burdensome to the officials involved, but no administration in any country is likely to want to inform the public, in any systematic, overt way, about the extent of governmental surveillance. Nonetheless, the 1986 Hesse act strengthens the individual's right of access in important ways. Subjects must be notified when data are first stored in an automated data base and, for data stored prior to January 1, 1987, public agencies are given a two-year grace period to make such notifications. Corrections to existing data must be sent to all bodies that have received the inaccurate information. Moreover, if any data subject "suffers any prejudice to his rights" by illegal data processing, the parent body of the agency processing the data shall be liable for damages.[25]

Given the West German and French data protectors' emphasis on the importance of individual access, the results to date are very discouraging. Generally speaking, the number of requests for access has been very low. One explanation is that existing labor laws govern access to personnel files, and that the most interesting files, held by the various police and security agencies, are never fully accessible to the individual. The inadequate guides available to the public also fail to promote the use of access rights. Individuals appear to be relying on the data protectors, or perhaps even the administrations, to protect their interests. There is even some suggestion that people are reluctant to exercise their right of access for fear of being labeled as troublemakers and then attracting even more surveillance.

Like his state counterparts, the federal DPC functions as a very specialized type of ombudsman for data-processing activities, since the federal law also provides that an individual may complain "if he believes that his rights have been violated as a result of his personal data being processed by the public authorities or other public bodies of the Federal Republic."[26] As is true of other parts of the BDSG, these grounds for complaint to the federal DPC are very vague.

There have been few formal complaints to the DPC, but there are certainly a number of inquiries. In his last year in office, Bull received about 1,000 written submissions from citizens, including requests for information and material, questions, and comments. Despite their small numbers, complaints furnish leads to problems that require further investigation.[27] The incidence of complaints usually coincides with a report in the press. Many concern national security, especially the very sophisticated systems of the Federal Criminal Police.

The kinds of appeals to the commissioners demonstrate some public concern about surveillance practices. Individuals complain that government records contain false and unclear information or obsolete medical or psychological statements, that criminal history records are being used that should have been erased in the central registry of criminal records, and that government inquiries are an invasion of privacy.[28] Other citizens have complained about unsolicited advertising, the wording of specific provisions in data protection laws, and the costs imposed to obtain their own data.

Bull has interpreted the fact that the number of complaints is not very high to indicate that "there is no mass movement for privacy protection. On the other hand, one must take into account that many facts and risks in the field of data processing are unknown to the public and cannot be familiar to it. So people underestimate the risks or believe that affairs are mostly handled in a correct manner even if information is disseminated incorrectly." He has also argued that data protection currently involves the protection of rights and interests in a situation where individuals have not yet realized the disadvantages of data processing.[29] In sum, people unaware of the extent of governmental surveillance do not react to it by exercising their rights of access and complaint, and the government itself has no incentives to engage in extensive publicity on this score.

Annual Reports

The best single source for understanding the work of the various Data Protection Commissioners is their detailed annual reports. The federal report is delivered to the president of the Bundestag and then published as an official document of the legislature. Normally, a spokesman for each party comments publicly in the legislature on the annual report of the DPC.[30] Unusual in other countries, such an event helps to legitimate the work of data protectors and to maintain their vital links with the legislature. Moreover, the party spokesmen have kept their posts for long periods, thus becoming legislative experts on data protection, a condition not duplicated in most other countries. Baumann attributed the failure of the Bundestag to discuss his 1985 and 1986 reports to the press of business, but his argument for a two-year reporting period, to prevent a certain "tiredness" and "depreciation" of the subject of data protection, seems in fact to show the negative federal climate for data protection then prevalent.

Bull devoted considerable time to preparing his annual reports, and his last effort for 1982 cast a retrospective look over his term of office. Baumann was inclined to rely on staff preparation and to reduce the amount of detail treated. However, the office does tend to repeat concerns about issues until someone pays attention to them. Bull pointed out that his critics on occasion seemed not to have read what he had written or to have misunderstood his observations. Secrecy restraints also limited what he could reveal about his evaluations of the security agencies, although he did review these materials in confidential sessions of the Interior Committee. Like his successor, Bull made specific reports to the Bundestag, especially on such a matter as the census case, and issued official statements on various themes, such as the association between research and data protection.[31] The working relationship between the DPC and the Bundestag makes the reporting and consultative requirements burdensome but very important.

At the state level, the Hesse Data Protection Commissioner makes annual or interim reports to the legislature, after which the minister of the interior is required to present the government's comments to parliament.[32] Simitis has expressed great confidence that the power of publicity enjoyed by any Data Protection Commissioner, including the right to make annual reports to the legislature and to speak there, is of considerable assistance in achieving the goals of data protection.

Public Relations

The federal DPC, like other national data protection agencies, faces significant problems in informing the public of its activities and of their rights. Burkert says that one of the main functions of data protectors is to transmit their knowledge to their clientele and adapt their experience during revision and review of the law.[33] The annual report on the state of surveillance contributes significantly to this goal. Nevertheless, the conduct of public relations is one of the most important weapons available for making data protection effective in the public sector. A primary form of public relations for the federal DPC has been the preparation and publication of information brochures and citizens' guides.[34] In an imaginative effort to publicize data protection, the Berlin DPC issued a booklet containing postcards addressed to institutions from which individuals can make requests for access to their own data. The several editions of this booklet have been a very practical way of publicizing data protection.

It is difficult to measure public opinion or public awareness of data protection, given the lack of relevant surveys. The available figures on the number of requests for access to individual data and the number of complaints to Data Protection Commissioners suggest that the level of public awareness of data protection was relatively low, at least prior to the 1983 census controversy. Perhaps it is more important for the control of surveillance that awareness of data protection has sunk relatively deeply into the minds of those running the activities of government in all sectors. As in so many comparable areas, such as control of the environment, a specialized interest group, data protectors, pursues goals that are very much in the public interest. Bull suggests that the DPC has obtained a higher profile than similar agencies and that there is a general abstract awareness of the existence of mechanisms for data protection.

The media are the most powerful source of pressure on government agencies. Successful contact with them is critical to the conduct of data protection in any country, and a fundamental guarantee of the independence of any Data Protection Commissioner. Media criticisms of the objectives of data protection have been few, although the usual concerns about the costs and expansionist tendencies of a new program arise from time to time. Bull responded to one critic that he knew of no one who regarded data protection as the highest goal or the main political task and challenged his data on the costs of implementation.[35]

One can hardly expect the daily media in any country to be well-informed critics of data protection once a national law has been enacted, unless disputes arise that can be sensationalized. Even the serious media tend to react predictably, in accordance with their political allegiances. Thus the conservative press, such as *Die Welt* or the *Frankfurter Allgemeine Zeitung*, are more likely to support the security or police agencies against the forays of data protectors than the leading left-wing newspaper, *Frankfurter Rundschau*.

Reaction to controversial events is an important vehicle for heightening public awareness. The enormous debate over the census of population in 1983 and the decision of the Federal Constitutional Court brought data protection forcefully to public attention and ensured that almost no one in the country could be unaware of its benefits. All of the leading commissioners had featured roles as the controversy continued to boil. Bull, who was in the process of being replaced, found that he was perceived as defending the minister of the interior's census, even though his primary argument was that persons did not have reason to be anxious about the confidentiality of statistical data. He did not focus on the value or necessity of the census itself: "I came into opposition to people who expressed distrust in all public agencies and claimed that the Minister of the Interior would be able to instruct the statistical offices to communicate the data to police and security or financial agencies, etc."[36] Bull issued several press releases concerning the DPC's position on the census itself. The media were in constant contact with the agency.

Data protection retained some of this visibility in the immediate aftermath of the census fight, but it is not much in the news in the late 1980s. In early 1984, there were two hundred reporters present when the federal office released its sixth report, which received front-page coverage for the first time. For a time, the topic of ensuring controls on surveillance systems attracted high prestige.

After the murder of a Foreign Office official by terrorists in 1986, Minister of the Interior Zimmermann suggested in an interview that the oversight role of data protectors hindered efforts to protect such officials. The *Frankfurter Allgemeine Zeitung* followed up with a story implying that data protection was a sacred cow that needed to be slaughtered in order to allow full use of computers to capture terrorists. Baumann replied that data protection is a basic constitutional requirement to preserve individual rights. The belief that terrorists could be caught if computers were fully mobilized reveals a naive faith in the computer and a failure to appreciate the risks of excessive surveillance.[37]

The utility of a commissioner with a gift for media relations is inestimable; often the public profile of the agency will be a function of this talent. At the state level, Weyer in NRW made an effort to keep in contact with the press, but reflected that it only prints what it determines to be interesting. In a novel twist on the usual approach to public relations, he suggested that his conflicts with the state government furthered the goals of data protection by making it better known, since the press lives on bad news. In Hesse, Simitis is especially talented at handling contacts with the media. In Baden-Württemberg, Dr. Ruth Leuze attracts a great deal of attention because of her outspokenness on surveillance issues.[38]

Bull's standard approach, similar to that of Simitis, was to attempt to achieve consensus by private negotiation and reserve appeals to the public for situations when an agency was not complying with his recommendations. Nevertheless, the federal Ministry of the Interior was critical of his regular appearances in public, even before the census debate made him especially visible. When Baumann succeeded Bull in the heat of the census fight, he announced that he would not appeal unnecessarily to the public but would deal privately with public authorities, the Bundestag, and its committees about problem areas. It now seems that Baumann was unwise, not least because the census case forced him into the limelight in any event. This experience indicates that the process of data protection is truly a public area of policymaking, impossible to practice solely in private.

The actual control of surveillance is a very specialized matter, despite its central importance for society. The public need not be interested in its intricate details. Burkert concludes that a subconscious layer of concern about privacy exists among the general public, as the census debates demonstrated. In his view, the general public has a high level of expectations about the impact of data protection, and some are very quick to question why data should even be collected in certain sensitive areas of information practice. The argument about the subconscious level of concern about privacy has a bearing on a related argument about the importance of the press in keeping alive a level of public concern for privacy. Thus questions of privacy, public relations, and the media are inextricably intertwined in the continuing effort to limit governmental intrusiveness.

Data Protection in Practice

Shaping New Laws and Regulations

Section 19(5) of the BDSG states that the Federal Commissioner shall strive to achieve cooperation with the public authorities and other public establishments responsible for ensuring that the provisions on data protection are observed in the states and also with the supervisory authorities established by the states for the private sector. This stipulation requires cooperation among data protection agencies themselves and relationships among the various DPCs and the federal and state Ministries of the Interior.

The federal and state Data Protection Commissioners meet at least several times a year to discuss data protection problems.[39] In addition, there are special working groups on selected issues. The consultative groups seek to harmonize legal opinions on pending legislation and on the practices of the various types of agencies. A minor barrier to cooperation is that DPCs are legally independent and ultimately responsible for data protection only in their jurisdictions. Moreover, the customary federal-state conflicts extend to data protection as well.

Because of varying personalities and philosophies, the data protection offices display a great diversity in styles of operation and attitudes to cooperation. Yet, for a federal system, West Germany has the advantage of relatively integrated federal and state data protection laws. The prospects for coherent application of these laws are very good, since detailed solutions can be followed at both levels.

The BDSG serves as an umbrella statute; supplementary laws and administrative regulations are necessary to ensure that the goals of controlling excessive surveillance are fully implemented throughout the public administration. The Data Protection Commissioners devote considerable efforts, alone and together, to influencing such developments at the federal and state levels.[40] All of the commissioners provided briefs for the Federal Constitutional Court in the census case, and seven appeared as experts, the only ones invited to testify.

The basic point for limiting surveillance is that any legislative or administrative initiatives concerning personal information must take account of the views of the Data Protection Commissioners in a society which requires detailed legal authorization for most forms of data collection. Since it is at least somewhat difficult for legislative committees to act contrary to the advice rendered, the commissioners are a factor in political decision making.[41] Yet such advice is not always followed, as Weyer in North Rhine–Westphalia frequently noted. In the press release accompanying his fourth report on May 2, 1983, he stated that although legislatures had acknowledged the need to regulate the use of personal data in specific areas, the trend is to permit public offices greater access to sensitive data. Weyer regretted that more of his recommendations were not followed in the 1982 Population Registration Act for his state.[42] This situation reflects one of the dilemmas of the advisory versus licensing approach to data protection. While West German or Canadian data protectors run the risk of having their advice ignored or spurned, their Swedish and French counterparts, whose powers of compulsion are much greater, are often reluctant to take strong stands against surveillance practices for fear of offending the government and other powerful interests.

There is recurrent concern in the Federal Republic and elsewhere that hard economic times may continue to pose a significant hindrance to the inclusion of provisions for data protection in relevant laws, since such conditions encourage the proliferation of surveillance practices. For example, when unemployment is high, politicians try to limit payments to the unemployed. A recent law against illegal employment requires employers to notify the social security agency about any work done by an individual, thus encouraging the establishment and use of new data banks. There was inadequate last-minute contact with Data Protection Commissioners before the enactment of this law. Nevertheless, some additional protections were added during passage. Efforts to limit surveillance often depend on such piecemeal changes.

Decisions of the Data Protection Agency

One of the goals of this volume is to investigate the general principles that data protection agencies have been developing in the course of implementing their respective laws. The aim is to understand the basic principles for the control of surveillance that underlie decisions of a particular data protection agency, which, in theory, should be clear in its judgments and advice.

The federal DPC's office itself does not have a standard format for its decisions on any given matter. The federal commissioner simply lodges with the appropriate federal authorities complaints that often involve very precise legal interpretations of the application of the BDSG.[43] The complexity of decisions appears to match the level of sophistication achieved in the process of implementation. Nevertheless, this power of complaint is not comparable to the licensing power of the Data Inspection Board in Sweden. The German commissioners could benefit from some regulatory power for specific, sensitive surveillance practices, where their advice can be too easily ignored.

The DPC may find that not enough data are being erased or that data are being stored which are no longer necessary, or that dissemination is taking place from incomplete or inaccurate records.[44] On other occasions, the DPC finds it necessary to enter complaints about inadequate concern for security. The latest annual reports note that there are a number of federal offices which still do not engage in appropriate supervision of data processing. There have also been failures to ensure that the destruction of data is carried out according to the appropriate regulations.[45] In his first year, Baumann filed formal objections against seven offices out of thirty-one visited. Some concerned numerous and serious flaws in substantive law, such as lengthy storage of data by the security authorities and technical and organizational problems in data security.[46] Baumann is persuaded that over 80 percent of the problems thus identified are corrected or at least minimized.

Much more might have been learned for purposes of this volume about litigation under the data protection acts, appeals to other authorities from the decisions of data protection agencies, and the imposition of civil and criminal sanctions for breach of the various laws. But there has been very little activity under any of these categories, except for appeals to political and administrative authorities within a particular ministry.[47] The criminal sanctions in the BDSG, which apply only to illegal dissemination, modification, or obtaining of personal information, have been applied several dozen times.[48] There are no penalties for the illegal collection of personal information.

Except in Baden-Württemberg, a Data Protection Commissioner unhappy about a particular aspect of data protection cannot go to court. Under standard West German law, the right of appeal to the courts can only be used by individuals or organizations aggrieved by a finding of the data protection agency. The Austrian Data Protection Law allows greater use of the courts, and its commission can assist a litigant in court. Burkert raises the interesting question of whether the courts should have a larger role in the implementation of data protection, or whether they in fact can be sensitive enough to this particular type of issue.[49] For the most part, the primary issues of data protection can be handled without recourse to the courts. Fortunately, the 1983 decision of the Federal Constitutional Court provided data protectors with essential constitutional support in their fights to limit surveillance.

Chapter 5

The Regulation of Surveillance Systems

This chapter examines in detail the impact that data protection has had on various types of national and state information systems in the public sector in West Germany, specifically social security, the police, security services, and personal identification systems, in order to facilitate comparative analysis of similar information systems among the various countries treated in this volume. The ultimate goal is to assess the relative success of national data protectors in controlling governmental surveillance. As discussed further in Chapter 6, the Federal Constitutional Court's 1983 census decision necessitates the enactment of specific legislation for each type of information system, a process in which the commissioners have a critical role to play. This chapter illustrates the limited achievements to date in achieving compliance with these constitutional principles.

Social Security

There are approximately 150 automated personal information systems for social security, which is the most important part of the social welfare system.[1] In social security there are four major systems, which are interlinked through central computers. These include insurance for unemployment, sickness, and accidents, as well as income support for older people. All four of these social security information systems are moving from manual to electronic data processing, involving many local terminals. The organizations for unemployment insurance and old age income support, in Berlin and Nuremberg respectively, have large central systems previously used for batch processing but now becoming interactive. Regulation of these agencies is made more complex because of the number of subsidiary systems used in each area. For instance, in the area of old age insurance five federal corporations and seventeen state public corporations maintain data bases used in administering programs. The system of unemployment insurance in Nuremberg, which employs a staff of approximately 3,000, illustrates the complexities of controlling data surveillance in this field. The agency has seven to ten subsidiaries in the states and approximately 350 local outlets in cities and towns. Persons looking for work contact the agency locally. If no work is available, the central computer in Nuremberg is alerted by means of a letter to an individual allocating funds to him. At the local level, unemployment insurance information is kept on a card index file; there are plans to automate the entire system.

A major restatement, codification, and development of the laws on social security has resulted in a series of achievements for data protectors in limiting surveillance. Now all issues related to social security are treated under special laws that comprise the Social Code, the tenth book of which became law in 1980. The federal and state data protectors played a significant role in its development. These special regulations contain requirements on the use of information at the federal and state levels that are stronger than those of the Federal Data Protection Law (BDSG). Provisions for data protection were inserted when the Social Code was actually being drafted. In a number of meetings between the Data Protection Commissioner (DPC) and the leaders of the main organizations concerned with social insurance, there was considerable discussion of how much information an individual applicant had to furnish to a social insurance organization under the "duty to cooperate" of those receiving benefits.[2] The new provisions restrict the amount of individual data that a person has to provide. The DPCs' offices try to make sure that information is being exchanged correctly and for necessary purposes. One of the reasons that there is limited enthusiasm for computer matching is that the new special legislation in Book 10 fully protects the social security field from such intrusions. In addition, access to tax data for matching purposes is controlled by a very strong tradition of secrecy.[3]

Book 10 of the Social Code provides a series of new arrangements for the protection of social data, including the duty to protect them as a part of social secrecy.[4] The responsibility to maintain secrecy is vastly expanded to a larger number of offices. The circumstances under which data can be disseminated are also regulated. Unless dissemination is specifically permitted, the various social insurance offices have no duty to inform, to give testimony, or to present or distribute personal data. Data transfers have to be for a legitimate reason. Thus the parameters of governmental surveillance in social security have been established with the help of data protectors.

The annual reports of the federal DPC contain extensive information about its complex and continuing work in social security, including the considerable problems of coordination with the states. For instance, in 1981 the DPC's office conducted a comprehensive investigation at the Federal Insurance Institute for white collar employees and concluded that it had suitably incorporated data protection requirements into appropriate administrative practice.[5] The institute has not fallen into the temptation in determining rehabilitation benefits of taking any data imaginable into its already highly sensitive data base, and has, for example, stopped collecting information on psychological handicaps and drinking and smoking habits. The DPC's office continues to monitor any further developments in the linkage of data bases on the state of health of those insured.

The Federal Institute of Labor has also made a considerable and successful effort to implement data protection.[6] Initially, the registration of the data banks of the Labor Institute was incomplete, because manual data banks in the labor administration were not included.[7] There were also additional problems with the way in which certain information, such as medical opinions, was not being given to individuals who asked to examine their files. At the urging of the DPC, the Labor Institute solved this problem in a way that the office recommends to other organizations for certain purposes. It now treats all information on a person, in whatever form, as a single file contained in a data base.

The Police and Criminal Information Systems

The most important federal police agencies are the Federal Border Police and the Federal Criminal Investigation Office (BKA). The BKA has many of the same national functions as the Federal Bureau of Investigation in the United States. It prosecutes especially serious crimes, cooperates with the state police, and maintains several systems of criminal records; it is also the central police agency for the electronic data network maintained jointly by the federation and the states.[8] Despite its intended role as a coordinating agency for the state police, there is a natural tendency, as in all police activities, to centralize more and more data with the BKA.

The primary task of policing is the responsibility of the states, whose police forces are subject to the supervision of the state data protection agencies. The state police constitute 90 percent of all the police in the Federal Republic, and most states have major police computers with terminals in various towns. These are covered by special laws and data protection regulations.

The BKA in Wiesbaden is the central agency for the joint electronic information network known as INPOL, to which a number of law enforcement agencies at the federal and state level have access. This computer-matching system contains a central index of persons, information on wanted persons and wanted property, and an offender/offense file. At least nine states have police-owned or regional administrative.computer centers linking them to the INPOL network, which has 4,000 terminals. The entire surveillance system, containing more than three million names, is subject to the relevant provisions of the federal and state data protection acts.[9]

INPOL also contains a fact retrieval system for important and complex crimes, known as PIOS, which was created "to provide a method enabling the electronic acquisition, and documentation, of facts extracted from voluminous files in complex investigations."[10] The system is used against terrorism, drug trafficking, and organized crime and can search information systems in an intelligent manner. It contains various registers. The BKA, which is in charge of PIOS, wants to use it for ordinary police purposes. The DPC's office, which has inspected the system, regards it as dangerous because it uses so much soft data. The office views its application to minor crimes as inappropriate and insists that the new security laws require a clear limitation of the use of PIOS to defined areas of important and serious crimes, limitations of data storage on nonsuspects, specific responsibilities for the federal and state police, accountability for data-processing activities, and internal review procedures to eliminate mistakes and control time limits.

The federal DPC's office has succeeded in reducing the central storage of personal data by the BKA to such national information as concerns serious criminal offenses.[11] It has not encountered any restrictions on its right of access to police data for purposes of investigation, nor have the police tried to hide behind the possible exemptions from the BDSG offered by section 19(3). The DPC's office does not blindly accept the notion that the police need certain information but exercises external control over the kind of information they use. It evaluates the jurisdictional rights and assigned tasks of the police, particularly under special laws. To a certain extent it queries the collection and storage of certain types of information but does not try to be better at criminology than such authorities. Yet, to limit police surveillance, the DPC does have the power to assert that a form of information collected or held by the authorities is against the relevant laws or rules. Certain unclear situations have led to impasses over the discretionary power of the police.

Nevertheless, the BKA gradually recognized that it held too many personal data, making them hard to work with. The DPC's recommendations have led to the deletion of some stored information. The police have been persuaded to destroy some fingerprints, 1.25 million paper files, and related names in their computers. Although there have been conflicts with the state Ministries of the Interior (LMIs) and the BKA involving the appropriate collection and use of such information, the police are now tending to follow the DPC's guidelines on the amounts of information stored and the length of storage.[12]

One of the major accomplishments of data protection agencies was the development by 1981 of guidelines and rules for the collection of data, which the various ministers of the interior also played a significant role in fashioning.[13] These guidelines control such matters as when a dossier on an individual can be commenced, how long personal data can be stored, and such matters as access to and inspection of police records. Formerly, such practices remained largely informal and varied from one police office to the other. A second set of guidelines concerns how names and addresses can be put into police dossiers in manual or automated form for each type of police information system.

At the state level, North Rhine–Westphalia (NRW) provides an example of a conflict over police use of information. The police were in the habit of privately checking local population registers at night to verify the identities of suspicious individuals. The state DPC wanted to deny such access to the register. Although the Interior Ministry agreed that this was an appropriate position to take, it did not want people being held in jail overnight. One proposed solution was that the police could obtain partial printouts of everyone included in such a local registry. The state DPC said that the police could not have a list of every inhabitant. The ministry proposed putting a terminal in each police station, but the data protection law for NRW is unclear on whether this is permissible. The police in NRW are subject to the final controlling authority of the data protection department of the LMI in terms of their need for information. Thus in 1983 the minister of the interior settled this issue by a regulation contrary to the wishes of Dr. Weyer, the DPC. Article 7 specifies that each county police authority may have online access to the local population register. Until terminals are obtained, each office can also have a printout of everyone in these local data bases. These rules bind all parties concerned, including the DPC for NRW, and can only be overturned if the courts decide that it is contrary to the population register law, which Weyer regards as unlikely.

The various data protection agencies have been especially concerned with record linkages among the various police information systems. This is particularly important as integration of state and federal police data banks occurs. For example, the federal and state Data Protection Commissioners in a controversial decision approved a sophisticated file-matching procedure of the BKA known as *Rasterfahndung.* It is essentially a pattern-search recognition technique. The process involves a search of private-sector information systems by the BKA for security purposes in order to identify certain patterns. In one episode the BKA suspected that a known terrorist in Hamburg lived in an apartment for which the landlord paid the electricity bill on behalf of the tenants. The BKA used the records of the local Electricity Board in order to discover the names and addresses of persons who had unusually large consumption rates for their homes, on the assumption that such persons might be paying the bill for the suspected terrorist. By a process of elimination, the police narrowed the field to 2,000 suspects, who were interrogated and the terrorist discovered. Obviously, this surveillance technique of pattern recognition involves searching massive amounts of personal information, which can only be done by computer.

At a 1980 conference, the several Data Protection Commissioners agreed that the Rasterfahndung technique was not contrary to data protection regulations and provisions, and that section 24 of the BDSG, dealing with the permissibility of the dissemination of personal data by private bodies in the public interest, permitted this practice. The data protectors did recommend a concrete framework of regulations for pattern-recognition search techniques. More recently, Dr. R. Baumann, the federal commissioner, questioned the utility of such practices, because the terrorists are well acquainted with police methods and leave few traces in data banks.[14]

Professor Hans Peter Bull continues to have a great many concerns about shaping appropriate data protection controls to surround the use of Rasterfahndung, especially by the BKA: "The matching of entire data banks or important parts thereof with data banks that are not maintained by federal or state police may only be conducted when the legal prerequisites in the individual case have been complied with and sufficient factual clauses warrant acceptance that this practice is necessary for the solution or prevention of complicated crimes, for the capture or arrest of wanted persons, or for averting a present and serious danger in an individual case. A data match for the purpose of prosecuting crimes requires the prior approval of the Department of Public Prosecution."[15] Such concerns are examples of how data protectors seek to impose controls on data surveillance.

Moreover, the statutes governing police activities grant the police access to various registers for any concrete danger. The DPC tries to establish rationales for conditions under which access can occur. Although there are draft guidelines on the subject, the various federal ministries have not yet given the legislature a chance to consider the subject.

The conflicts between the data protectors and the BKA have been intense. This is in part explained by the fact that police and intelligence agencies are accustomed to only a minimum amount of oversight of their surveillance practices. The former head of the BKA, Dr. Horst Herold, was particularly enthusiastic about the use of computers, which led to clashes with Bull in particular. Quarrels continue among politicians in the states over the control and use of police data.[16] There is a natural tendency for the police to argue that their work is paramount among the interests of society. Bull in particular reminded the police and the security forces that they too are regulated by the Constitution.[17] In 1986 Baumann noted the failure of the authorities to follow the collective advice of the commissioners on the need for limits to the broad police investigative powers in personal data under the new article 163d of the Code of Criminal Procedure. He wanted a comprehensive agreement in place on how law enforcers use personal information.

The Security Agencies

There are three national security agencies: the Federal Agency for the Protection of the Constitution, for internal security; the Federal Intelligence Agency, for foreign security; and the Military Counterintelligence Service, for military security. The surveillance practices of these agencies, with certain exceptions, are generally subject to the data protection laws.

It has been suggested that because of the Third Reich the power of the DPC's office to scrutinize the work of security agencies was essential for public acceptance of the BDSG. The law does exempt security agencies from publishing notices of their information systems and from granting individuals access to their own files.[18] These exceptions do not, however, affect the DPC's overall responsibilities for supervision and inspection. The security agencies can only escape supervision if the competent federal authorities decide "in the case concerned that the inspection of documents and files would jeopardize the security of the Federal Republic or of a state."[19] Such an exemption has very rarely been made.

Because individuals do not have a right of access to their own data held by a security agency, the DPC's office believes that it has to be particularly vigilant to protect personal interests in this area. In some instances and under certain new regulations for the security authorities, access can be given to an individual, if the interests of the person concerned prevail against the security interests of the state.[20] Such privileged access, even through the mediation of the DPC, is also rare.

The federal DPC's office sometimes acts in response to complaints about data processing by the intelligence services—a field where, as Bull noted, legal problems of collecting and storing data are extremely difficult and political disputes have been very hot for more than a decade.[21] A select unit of the DPC's office, whose members are given special security clearances, visit the data processing rooms of the security agencies to conduct inspections. Only the commissioner and the head of this section can look at individual files of the Federal Intelligence Agency. Dr. R. Riegel, who directed this unit until 1986, was allowed to see every individual file he asked to examine, except for the names of sources. In 1980 the DPC's office randomly selected five cases of espionage and terrorism to investigate the methods of the police and the data exchanges taking place among the security agencies, including the BKA. This inspection revealed no procedures contrary to the BDSG.[22]

Despite its impact on the security agencies, the DPC's office believes that a great deal remains to be done. In its view, much activity of security agencies can in fact be openly described. The office is particularly concerned to reduce the enormous amount of data stored and to control data transfers, even though a significant amount of data has already been destroyed. In other instances the office has agreed that certain information can continue to be stored for a brief period.[23]

At the end of 1981, Bull noted that the office's intensive supervision of these agencies had revealed a series of practices contrary to data protection regulations, such as storage of data that were no longer necessary, dissemination from incomplete or inaccurate records, and "data bank inquiries" at the Federal Agency for the Protection of the Constitution for anticipated security checks made without the knowledge of the person concerned. He also noted that the provisions for the filing of data in the information systems of the police and the security authorities are often being construed too "generously."[24] Baumann's first annual report noted the successful completion of a comprehensive audit at the Federal Office for the Protection of the Constitution, which concluded that it had made a considerable effort to clean up its data files and had cooperated fully in granting the office access to its records.

The DPC's office is especially concerned to encourage more specific legislation to control the exchange of personal data among the security authorities. This particularly includes a desire to restrict the traditional role of federal agencies in assisting one another through data transfers. Bull regards data transfers under this customary practice as no longer tolerable.[25] He argues that in the security field almost every step in the processing of personal data is an encumbrance on the rights of the persons concerned.[26] Section 10 of the BDSG is inadequate to correct the situation, and special regulations are required. Because there are three security agencies, plus the BKA and the Federal Border Police, the constitutional and legal provisions regulating data transfers are very complex. Baumann concluded in 1988 that the government's proposals to revise the BDSG to control such exchanges were too lenient.[27]

Naturally, a number of critics have alleged, at least on occasion, that the work of the federal DPC's office is interfering with the important responsibilities of the security agencies, especially in the field of controlling terrorism.[28] Although the office insists that it is not in fact hostile to the security agencies, such accusations raise key issues, especially when they originate with Minister of the Interior F. Zimmermann. Although the Federal Agency for the Protection of the Constitution tried to hinder Baumann's access to certain data in 1986, he won his point in the Interior Committee of the Bundestag, when he took the issue there. Such an agency attempts to exploit what it perceives as changes in the political climate to resist data protection. From its perspective, the BDSG is a strange object that is hard to learn how to handle.

Bull believes that the security forces pose a real threat to the interests of individuals and that they have not been subjected to adequate scrutiny. When representatives of the security agencies insist that data protection laws impede their work, he points out, in a telling phrase, that "optimal efficiency is only possible within the framework of justice and the law."[29] Bull further argues that police and intelligence activity unrestricted by law is unthinkable for a constitutional state. The Bundestag must engage in a concrete weighing of the conflicting interests in order to lead to appropriate resolutions under applicable law. In his view the executive cannot exempt itself from the constitution and the laws.

The politicians involved in oversight of security operations are usually too busy to pay much attention to the details of activities and are reluctant to tolerate criticisms of the police and security forces. Thus oversight of security forces has not been very effective, and new antiterrorism laws continually increase their surveillance powers. The police and security forces are so powerful that their irritation does have continuing negative repercussions for some of the DPC's other work, including the possible encouragement of opposition to data protection during revision of the 1977 law.

Fortunately, the police and security agencies are also sensitive to public criticism by data protectors. Greater progress will occur when these agencies recognize some of the benefits of cooperation to promote acceptable limits on data surveillance. In the interim, diplomacy remains an essential tool of effective data protection.

Data protectors have, in fact, had impressive successes in achieving data protection in the police and security fields; their counterparts in other countries have had a tendency to steer clear of these two powerful sets of interests.[30] Yet these very successes have attracted some unfavorable publicity from the press, the public, and leading politicians, mostly because of the mistaken notion that data protection has somehow unnecessarily hindered such important activities. West Germans do not have a lot of confidence in their ability to maintain public order, in part because of recurrent terrorist outbreaks. In contrast to the situation in other countries, the police and security agencies are almost always subject to detailed laws and regulations. Thus security issues come to public attention regularly as legal questions about the extent of compliance with the relevant rules.

The decision of the Federal Constitutional Court gives new authority to data protectors in their work with police and security agencies.[31] It is now difficult for anyone to resist their right to inspect paper files and other data bases for national security. The DPC's office staff continues to work at data protection for the police and security forces. Data protectors do research to frame appropriate questions, conduct audits, and expect their decisions and recommendations on specific points to have a cumulative effect in other aspects of an agency's work. They also understand that in practice they cannot audit every dossier maintained by such administrations. Guidelines now exist on all aspects of the collection, use, transfer, linkage, and erasure of personal data, but the process of translating these guidelines into statutory controls presents complex problems of balancing interests. Significant differences of opinion even exist among the parties in the governing federal coalition.

Population Registration, PINs, and Identity Cards

There are approximately 25,000 local population registers maintained by communities.[32] They are used by municipal, state, and federal authorities for a variety of administrative purposes and are gradually becoming more and more automated. In the 1970s West Germans resisted efforts to introduce a twelve-digit Personal Identification Number (PIN) for each inhabitant.[33] Critics argued that PINs were a fundamental threat to the principle of privacy incorporated in the constitution. Parliamentarians agreed that no system of data processing based on a unique personal identifier should be created without a corresponding system of data protection. The idea of assigning PINs has not been raised again since a legislative committee rejected it in 1976, which, at least for the present, keeps an important facilitative tool for surveillance out of the hands of the authorities.

The 1983 census decision of the Federal Constitutional Court further impeded the development of PINs, since the court made negative comments about them in discussing the possibilities of carrying out a census of the population solely on the basis of administrative data bases (as is done in Denmark). The Karlsruhe decision correctly suggested that such a form of census would require PINs, which it described as even harder on the people than the present format for taking a census.

In 1978 Bull responded to a request from the Ministry of the Interior for comments on the draft law on population registration.[34] He made a number of suggestions to safeguard the privacy of citizens under basic constitutional principles. He suggested that multiple usages of collected information should be avoided and that the citizen should give identical information to the various interested offices. The citizen should also have the traditional rights of fair information practices in connection with local population registers. The personal information stored should be limited to what is essential and not sensitive. Sensitive information might include reasons for the denial of the right to vote, for example. Bull agreed that basic information such as name, sex, birthdate, and address can be distributed fairly liberally to public administrations: "Transmission of data going beyond the basic information is permitted only in exceptional cases and under certain conditions regulated by law."[35] Individual names and addresses can be provided to private individuals.

In 1980 the Bundestag passed the Registration Act, which outlines rules for the establishment and use of local population registers, but does not include provisions for PINs. The duties of the registration authorities are "to register the inhabitants in their area of jurisdiction in order to be able to establish and prove their identities and places of residence." The registration offices are also permitted to use their information to prepare for elections; to issue income tax cards, personal identification cards, and passports; and to assist in military and civil service surveillance. To fulfill these duties, the population registers are permitted to share nineteen types of data.[36] Through their own laws, states can expand the list of the information permitted to be stored. The principle of necessity to fulfill legal tasks governs what information can be released to an agency.[37] The federal Ministry of the Interior has also been preparing a statute on local population registration in order to promote appropriate and consistent rules for data protection from state to state.[38]

Bull participated in extensive debates that succeeded in creating a level of data protection for the registration system. He concluded that the Registration Act constituted a considerable step forward in data protection, although more data are still being stored than are really necessary to fulfill the functions of the registration authorities, and various releases may still need to be more strictly regulated. Bull was also unhappy about the permissible dissemination of personal data to religious associations and about possible uses of the data by police authorities.[39]

The current system of numeration is one in which separate government agencies develop and use their own systems for particular purposes. For example, there is a pension insurance number for use in the social insurance system, but it is not used as a general personal identifier, unlike the Social Security Number in the United States.[40] This Renten number combines both alphabetic and numeric digits, which reveal birthdates and other personal information. Such numbers can only be used for old age insurance purposes, although there is a current fear that they will be used as an identification key in all four major social security systems and thus inadvertently become a national identification number. The DPC's office will try to prevent this development.

The data protectors suffered a serious setback in 1986, when the Bundestag approved legislation for a machine-readable identity card as one component of new security laws. Although the government planned such cards only to control frontier crossings, the number of applications increased considerably, especially for security dragnets.[41] The motivations included the need for a card that was hard to counterfeit. Data protectors wanted the cards to be used solely for border crossings and recommended against storage of data on the travels of specific individuals. The 1983 census controversy postponed their introduction, and the Karlsruhe decision provoked the Interior Committee of the Bundestag to ask for the advice of the Data Protection Commissioners, who used this opportunity to seek stronger and more precise provisions for the law, although to limited effect. They asked the Ministry of the Interior to explain the need for a new automated card, especially because of the risks of the development of multiple uses and of the storage of data to produce profiles of individuals.

The issue was very political. The Green party did not want any identification cards, the Social Democrats are opposed to automated cards, while the coalition government accepted them. The Social Democratic Minister of the Interior for Hesse asserted that the cards made possible total control of citizens. Chancellor Kohl denied that the country was becoming "a night-watchman state."[42]

The law on identity cards defines to whom and under what conditions data from the registers of cardholders maintained by the states may be disclosed. The border authorities are allowed to use the registers to check certain matters, but no permanent record will be maintained of entrances and departures from the country. There are some circumstances where police and security agencies may store information gathered during security checks. Citizens may use the cards as a means of identification in the private sector, although, as in France, people are not obliged to carry them.

A fully automated system of identity cards makes it easier to create profiles of individuals. The data protection authorities recognize that new uses for the cards are bound to emerge and will be difficult to control, especially for security purposes. For his part, Baumann lamented the creation of such an infrastructure for surveillance that these cards represent, because it will be easy to extend their use to other purposes. He felt that there had been inadequate justification of the need for the cards and no satisfactory analysis of the associated benefits and risks. Nonetheless, in his 1987 report he continued to warn the government of shortcomings in the law, while praising the data protectors for their vigilance.[43]

Census and Statistics

Enormous public controversies broke out in 1983 and 1987 over the scheduled censuses of population. A 1983 public opinion poll indicated that 52 percent of the population mistrusted the census questions and that 25 percent of the 25 million households would not complete the form.[44] It was not enough for the minister of the interior to argue that people should trust the new government, since the German people were clearly not in a frame of mind to do so. The 1983 controversy illustrates the continued public anxiety about surveillance practices and the failure of the Federal Statistical Office to take adequate account of public sensibilities about data protection in carrying out its preparations for the census.

The Federal Statistical Office was unprepared for the extent of public resistance that began in February 1983, despite the number of warnings it had received about potential problems. It had paid little attention to the concerns of its own internal data protection official. The office had conducted the 1970 census without any difficulty, and it already had a law for the 1983 effort, using the same procedures as 1970 in order to save money.

Two Hamburg lawyers challenged the constitutionality of the census law on the grounds that it constituted an invasion of privacy, especially with respect to the use of the data. The Federal Constitutional Court heard from the representatives of statisticians and from the leading data protectors. Statisticians advanced their usual arguments for carrying out their traditional activities. Certain of the commissioners used the first court hearing to explain their remaining concerns about the census law, especially the continuation of the dubious practice of using the data for correcting local population registers.[45]

Continued public anxieties about such a socially useful activity as a census are a reminder of how much people continue to worry about the erosion of their personal privacy. Spiros Simitis, the Hesse Data Protection Commissioner, described the controversy as the first mass movement for data protection in West German history and as an example of how data protectors cannot always pick their issues. Segments of the population became aroused about the proposed census, because of their general fears about the use of computers in data processing and the need to set limits on governmental data collection. There were literally hundreds of phone calls to the Hesse office demanding limits on government information collection. Simitis reported to the Hessian parliament that the census law was unconstitutional, a position upheld by the Federal Constitutional Court.

Even though the case for any society's need for a population census can be made successfully, even though the strong tradition of confidentiality at statistical agencies can be demonstrated, and even though political considerations and irrationality motivate some of the resistance to the census, it provides a recurrent opportunity in every country for people to oppose the collection of personal information by government agencies. The census, as one of the very few universal and compulsory data collection activities, generates some basic hostilities. Censuses between 1969 and 1971 in North America and Western Europe had helped to spark the original data protection movement.

The Federal Statistical Office was relatively unreceptive to representations from the staff of the federal Data Protection Commissioner about potential problems with data protection. At an early date, the DPC's office indicated that it did not like the use of the census to correct local population registers, even though there is a legitimate problem of too many persons being registered locally versus the actual numbers living there.[46] The law permitted correction of specific data, but no action could be taken against individual respondents. The fundamental problem with the planned census was the failure to maintain an absolute functional separation between statistical and administrative uses of personal data.[47]

The census controversy placed the DPC in a very awkward situation, since he appeared to be defending the plans for the census. Bull's main theme was that the census posed far smaller risks to the citizen than many other forms of data collection; nevertheless, he insisted that census information must only be used for statistical purposes. The DPC concluded on behalf of the federal and state Data Protection Commissioners in a March 1983 press release that people's fears about the census were unfounded, and that adequate safeguards were in place.[48]

In December 1983 the Federal Constitutional Court in effect postponed the census on grounds of potential invasion of privacy, despite the passage of the special census law by a unanimous legislature and the general support of major data protection officials for the census.[49] The court found that some of the provisions of the census law were unconstitutional, such as the use of census data to correct local population registers or to give information to certain government ministries for planning purposes.[50] Some of the measures for data protection in the census law were also not clear enough for the general public to understand.

In 1984 the federal minister of justice announced a comprehensive overhaul of both the federal Data Protection Law and the 1983 census law. The Cabinet agreed on a draft bill for a new national census law, which was enacted at the end of 1985. Zimmermann stated that the bill took full account of the Karlsruhe decision and that it had a positive rating from the federal and state Data Protection Commissioners. The Social Democrats and the Green party declared their opposition to the proposed 1987 census. The Greens viewed the census as a step toward a total state. Both parties questioned the need for such an all-encompassing survey addressed to every resident of the country, a point of view supported by Simitis. The Hesse DPC insisted in 1988 that future censuses would have to rely on voluntary compliance and that statisticians would have to devise new creative procedures for collecting data.[51]

Statisticians now have to separate the collection of data for statistical purposes from the collection of information used for administrative purposes, a lesson that it seems rather late in the day to have to learn, especially given prior experience in other Western countries. Cities and towns have to separate statistical and administrative uses of personal information. There will also have to be more rules on data security, improvements in obtaining informed consent from respondents, and the furnishing of more information to the public about the intended uses of census information. The statisticians expect to rely more heavily on voluntary surveys, because of the court's insistence on the principle of proportionality, requiring the least possible interference in the lives of citizens, which is a significant victory against governmental surveillance. There are also changes in how the 600,000 local enumerators are recruited.[52]

Statisticians at both the state and federal level now have all the more reason to pay very careful attention to the formal and informal advice of data protection officials, even though they have already functioned for years on the basis of special data protection laws. Although a citizen may have an absolute obligation to furnish data for the census, this can only occur for purposes specified by law and with adequate measures to protect against the unlimited collection, storage, use, and transfer of personal data. In other words, statisticians have learned, at substantial cost, that data protection responds to meaningful individual concerns about surveillance. To their dismay, they have also learned that the existence of data protection and data protectors is not sufficient to calm public anxieties about preservation of their privacy.

Both Baumann and Bull, perhaps in part because they were somewhat embarrassed that their public statements did not quiet the census storm, agreed in 1984 that the public reaction to the proposed population census was based on irrational fears and misinformation. Baumann wrote that "the impression was given regarding some of the participants that, with their boycott, some of those opposed to the population census did not give priority to data protection interests but were following other political goals." At the same time, the controversy made it quite clear that certain segments of the populace did not trust the state.[53] Bull concluded that the data protection risks of the 1983 census were in fact minimal:

> The clash over the population census has shown me how easily many citizens are taken in by horrific news, how impaired is the perceptive faculty of the bureaucracy—even though everyone has experience with agencies, both negative and positive—and how uncertain is the power of decision of many people. My concern was and is that the energies that in this case were applied against a state action are missing for more important problems. But those who should have worked against the irrational elements of the protest movement out of their official responsibility, restricted themselves to spirited appeals and overall demands for confidentiality, instead of taking upon themselves the thankless task of promoting privacy through detailed information.[54]

One firm conclusion is that the census controversy in 1983 was in no way a highly rational activity, nor one that was devoid of partisan politics.

In 1986 the legislature approved a new Federal Statistics Act, which stipulates under what circumstances and in what form statistical offices may disseminate personal data. Although the conference of federal and state Data Protection Commissioners has studied the application of data protection principles to statistics over the years, much of their considerable input was not accepted in framing the law.[55] It is at least somewhat responsive to the Karlsruhe decision, although it is not a data protection act. The government has permitted the enactment of strong, prostatistics legislation, and in principle, legislators do not want to hear about statistics and data protection again.

The 1987 census, the first in seventeen years, was extremely controversial and provoked extraordinary resistance, even though it was ultimately successful. Many elements of the 1983 debate were repeated. The Federal Statistical Office spent 45 million DM on public relations, which is many times the annual budget of the federal DPC's office, in the largest such effort by the state in German history. The office minimized the intrusiveness of the census inquiries and, in fact, asked few questions. Individual responses were quickly anonymized. Public resistance was inspired by exaggerated fears of information technology and record linkages, lack of public confidence in the practice of strict separation of statistical and administrative uses of data, fears of the abuse of census data, mistrust of the Christian Democratic government, and a general rejection of the state in a symbolic boycott.[56] Two discrete episodes reinforced public anxiety and encouraged the Green party's attack on the census: the introduction of the machine-readable identity card and the fact that the central traffic register (ZEVIS) is now accessible to the police, despite expectations that it would not be. Such fears of a surveillance state are abroad in every advanced industrial society, so that it is almost impossible for data protectors or statisticians to calm such anxieties by rational means.

The 1987 West German census controversy is a further indication of why at least some statistical agencies are in continuing trouble with the public. The specific surveillance issues are largely symbolic and based on a nonexistent or inadequate public awareness of the true nature of statistical work and of the protective measures for confidentiality that are already in place. The taking of a census offers the best opportunity for a vociferous minority to resist all forms of governmental surveillance. To be precise, the census is one of the best available vehicles for an opposition group like the Green party to mobilize public opinion against an incumbent government for political purposes. What is evident, and at the same time unfair, is that a census law in West Germany that has passed all the necessary legislative stages and benefited from the good advice of data protectors—even if not all of that advice has been accepted—can still encounter vigorous and even violent public reactions. Such manipulation of public opinion for political advantage is possible, in part, because the strong data protection laws and statistical laws currently in place are not well enough known to the general public, and because public anxieties about surveillance practices using administrative data are so great.

Chapter 6

Responding to Privacy and Surveillance Problems

This chapter summarizes various problems that West German data protectors have had with the process of implementation of data protection and reviews how the laws might be revised to meet contemporary realities of power relationships and governmental surveillance.

The Adequacies of Implementation

Since 1978 the basic framework of data protection laws has been well established in West Germany, the work of data protection has become more routine, and the results less spectacular. The first decade of implementation at both the federal and state levels has been very successful, and efforts at the respective levels have complemented one another. Halfway through his term as federal commissioner, Professor Hans Peter Bull made a very important general statement about the early record of his office: "What has been achieved is a change in the general understanding of data protection. . . . More and more, data protection is respected and regarded as a constituent part of fair administration."[1] Achieving such understanding on the part of the regulated agencies is a critical goal for data protectors in every country.

No sensational examples of flagrant abuse of surveillance measures have been discovered in the public sector in Germany or, indeed, elsewhere. Although Bull admits that more intensive investigative activity in the computer centers of the federal administration might uncover additional instances of prohibited uses of personal data, the probability is not great enough to justify the creation of an extensive data protection bureaucracy.[2] He found that unmistakable infractions of clear data protection regulations were, as a whole, rare. The main problem was and is the low priority given to the rights of individuals by government agencies, not deliberate disregard for those rights. As Bull reported:

> Every administration has a tendency to overrate its interest in the best possible way to fulfill its tasks, equating this with the interests of the person concerned—so it happens, for example, that systems for the settlement of accounts (for example, the Telephone Service) are adjusted so that priority is given to improving the ability to recover payments, while

the point of view that we should avoid the possible formation of large stores of sensitive data is underrated; or it happens that the dangers from the central collection of documents relating to criminal records are given too little weight.[3]

This is a well-informed reminder that in any country individuals may have legal rights to data protection, but what counts is how they are weighed in the balance by the operators of data systems; hence the need for data protectors as watchdogs over surveillance practices.

Despite inevitable conflicts with certain public administrations, especially those unused to oversight, the Data Protection Commissioner's office in particular has done its work without any major breakdown in its relationships with the subjects of regulation. In many ways this is surprising, given the contentious character of some of the specific matters in dispute in the police and security fields in particular. Apparently the police in the states, where such activities are concentrated, still feel that data protection interferes with their work. The annual reports of the Data Protection Commissioner (DPC) are full of illustrations of progress achieved, even if many problems continue to exist. In many ways the various levels of data protectors have successfully engaged in a very active program of consciousness raising in the public administration, and the general public has supported their efforts. The routine level of commitment to data protection is high: what remains are controversies in working out the details of implementation.

Various sources of opposition to data protection include concern over the distribution of power, intellectual or emotional issues, and sociological factors. Some federal ministries believe that the DPC's office has been pushing them a bit too far in the interests of restricting surveillance, since they perceive themselves as trying to serve the public interest. The DPC's office regularly questions whether it is necessary for these ministries to collect, store, or use such large amounts of personal information. In this sense, the federal civil service regards the DPC's office as restrictive. Officials are predictably uncomfortable with cross-cutting laws such as the Federal Data Protection Act (BDSG), which have wide application, and they are inclined to refuse information and to hinder implementation. Conflicts seem inevitable for anyone attempting to regulate data processing for whatever purpose, since computers are still sometimes perceived as powerful tools with only positive benefits— only Luddites would want to diminish their use.

The various data protection agencies have been very successful in attracting talented individuals to their staffs. That the transition from Bull to Baumann as DPC did not initially lessen the effectiveness of data protection testified to the skills and commitment of the federal staff. More recently some difficulty in recruitment of employees of the same caliber is occurring as data protection becomes more routinized, which is a problem in every country.

Spiros Simitis has made the important point that data protection needs to be constantly adapted to experience, including learning from the mistakes of data protection. He favors a functional rather than a formalist approach to data protection, emphasizing observation and inspection of government agencies rather than accepting the information they are willing to divulge. One of the critical achievements of data protection efforts in the Federal Republic, in his view, has been the development of an understanding of how government agencies use their data, despite the fact that they have contested this process, allowing the creation of specific data protection rules to govern appropriate uses of personal information.[4]

The control of surveillance in West Germany, as elsewhere, is an unfinished business. Some staff members feel they cannot assure the general public that data protection in their domain is truly adequate, because they have not visited or audited many state institutions, such as hospitals. There is general agreement on the importance of trying to make data protection more effective in local administrations and in the far-flung parts of large public administrations.

More so than in other countries, data protection in Germany is a highly legalistic activity, because of the law-driven character of the society and the new constitutional basis for data protection; thus the approach to the control of surveillance tends to be more legalistic than technical and organizational. Such concern for sectoral legislation is admirable, although Simitis has described its achievement as "an irksome and often long-drawn-out process."[5]

The technical specialists in data protection believe that they should know more about electronic data processing and the organization of information systems and data flows. On the other hand, some data processors believe that data protectors are not accepting the practical and technical realities of what can be accomplished. Simitis concludes that even though data protection is now recognized as "vital to the functioning of every democratic society," it is heading for its worst crisis, because of the problems of adequately relating it to technological developments in data processing and related processes.[6] The current laws, in his view, may be too linked to a particular technology. Again, such problems exist in other countries.

Revision of the Data Protection Laws

The Federal Data Protection Act was hardly in place before proposals for its revision began to surface.[7] From the beginning the general consensus has been that the BDSG should only be changed marginally; it may only be the legislators who seek to "improve" this law, but there is now a better sense that the law needs strengthening to further curtail governmental surveillance.

One important, continuing inspiration for changes in the BDSG is the successful innovations that have been tested in state laws. The latest version of the Hessian Data Protection Act is a model legislative effort to comply with the Karlsruhe decision and to respond to the changing technological environment. It is perceived as heavily favoring data protection and as a great improvement on existing German legislation. Two main improvements apply the Hessian law to personal data held in all forms of files and records and mandate improved notifications to citizens of the purposes of data collection. Most of Simitis's suggestions were adopted at some point in the process. The parliament significantly improved the government's draft of the new law, which is a reminder of the key continued role for legislators in strengthening such legislation.

Simitis concludes that the new act, "more closely than was ever done before, links processing of personal data to the obligation—laid down in the Constitution and confirmed by the Federal Constitutional Court—to permit processing only under such conditions as will guarantee the citizen's right to know and to decide for himself as to who should use his personal data at what time and for what purposes."[8] This key goal in the revision of all West German legislation can contribute significantly to limiting governmental surveillance. The legislature in Hesse further accepts that improving the general law is only an intermediate step; it now has to act on draft regulations for statistics, the police, and hospitals in order to comply with constitutional standards.

North Rhine–Westphalia (NRW) included some initial improvements in its original data protection law. The state act of March 15, 1988, designed to comply with the Karlsruhe decision, is about the same as the 1986 Hesse law.[9] Weyer proposed sixty improvements but only about one-third were accepted by the state Ministry of the Interior, leaving him to try to persuade the Interior Committee in private sessions.

The process of revision at the state level has featured alternative scenarios. One especially negative sign was that in 1982 the Baden-Württemberg legislature, dominated by the Christian Democrats, revised its state data protection law, because of dissatisfaction with some of the vigorous enforcement activities of Commissioner Ruth Leuze. The legislators weakened her jurisdiction and independence and the statute itself. In her report for 1987, Leuze criticized the resistance of the state government to passing a new general law. In a state like North Rhine–Westphalia, where there have been controversies over the work of the DPC's office, the argument is that the legislature did not dare to reduce the functions of the agency, fearing a hostile reaction from the press.

In 1982 the federal government published a set of proposals for the revision of the BDSG that did not change any of the structure or fundamentals. Another set of draft proposals from the federal minister of the interior appeared in 1983. In both cases there was some criticism of the specific ideas about revising the BDSG, which include clarification of the definitions of a "file" and of the "personal interests which warrant protection" under the law.[10] Although any legislative process of statutory revision is not always controllable, there was general acceptance in 1982–83, at least at the federal level prior to the census decision, that the fundamental principles of data protection should not be changed. In his first annual report Baumann rejected the 1983 proposals as falling far short not only of the 1982 draft but also of some essential aspects of the law now in force.

The events of 1983 resulted in a complete reopening of the revision process, because of the December decision of the Federal Constitutional Court in connection with the census controversy. Its recognition of the principle of individual self-determination of information use as a fundamental right now has to be central to all general and sectoral data protection enactments. In the view of Baumann, "it will in particular have to be examined if the fundamental right to informational self-determination calls for more transparence in data processing and a stricter limitation on data use. The scope of application of the Federal Data Protection Act and the citizen's right to obtain information must be extended."[11]

The decision of the Karlsruhe court has revolutionary implications for data protection, since its proponents now have legitimacy for views that were previously dismissed or disregarded by legislators.[12] In April 1984 the federal minister of justice, Hans Engelhard of the Free Democratic party, called for a comprehensive overhaul of the BDSG and criticized the federal Ministry of the Interior (BMI) for attempting to solve the problem with small changes. The BMI still tends to resist the need for substantial changes, in part because of its basic sympathy for the needs of data processors in public administration. Even the internal proponents of data protection at the BMI fear the imposition of additional bureaucratic burdens. It is taking some time to sort out these conflicting interests among the specialists and the legislators to produce a reasonable interpretation of the census decision; there are even suggestions that this will extend until the life of the current Bundestag expires in 1991.

It is not proving easy to find a middle ground between maximum and minimum views of the Karlsruhe decision. There has been no legislative product yet, but going slow has some benefits. In the interim, the various DPCs' offices try to shape new or revised laws by the standards of the decision. It is hard for the legislatures to process all of the proposed new laws, because there are so many of them.[13] The development of specific amendments to laws for distinct fields is very tedious, and the federal structure further complicates matters.

Unfortunately, the failure to revise the BDSG to date permits both the government and public administrations to continue old practices, increases the pressure on data protectors to accept de facto practices, and lessens the pressure to respond to the Constitutional Court's decision. Because a general constitutional principle allows an agency to do its work for a period of time without a law, the delay also encourages use of transitional rules for continuing old surveillance practices. The federal office is hearing arguments that the transitional rules could last another four years, i.e., through the next legislative period. It is not clear what the courts think about such transition rules. German constitutional law gives the legislature the responsibility to adapt to its decisions. The court does not have the final say, nor can the DPCs' offices ignore existing laws. There is no transitional period in general for compliance, but legislators have to weigh the consequences for the government. There are differences of opinion concerning the period of time that is required or available to comply with the decision. Simitis wants to be tougher with the police and the archives about the time necessary to update the data protection aspects of their laws.

The Federal Data Protection Act continues to play a vital role in the co-ordination of data protection activities with the states. The problem is some-what complicated by the fact that parties in opposition at the federal level appear to want to strengthen the BDSG, yet their ideas about data protection are not always being implemented in states that they govern, which is of course understandable, but does lead to problems in trying to predict the course of legislative changes. The prospect of different political perspectives on the appropriate role and scope of data protection means that different states could ultimately have varying standards for data protection, which could pose prob-lems for the regulation of interstate transfers of personal information in such systems as those maintained by the police. Moreover, revisions of data protec-tion laws proceed at both levels of government with some evident competition over progress and innovation. The state DPCs are not docile followers of their federal counterpart and seek to shape the revision of their own laws based on their own experiences and desires. Yet a process of constitutional centralization goes forward, as in most federal systems.

At the federal level the several political parties have developed different strategies for revising the BDSG, which are usually set forth in annual debates over the reports of the DPC and in party platforms. Revision of the BDSG thus remains to some extent a partisan issue. Agreeing on the exact nature of the detailed changes is the real problem. The conservative parties could no longer attempt to return the DPC to a status similar to that of the auditor general, as they originally favored during the enactment of the law. Because of the law-driven character of the society, proposals for revision of the BDSG are excep-tionally complex. There are often attempts to change legal definitions and to specify even more precisely the regulation of data transfers and dissemination by a particular government department.

The need to compensate individuals for damages suffered by a breach of the data protection act is being debated with respect to a revised BDSG, even if no test case has yet been brought forward, giving the argument at least sym-bolic importance. Both NRW and Hesse have provisions for the payment of restitution or damages to individuals for breaches of personal privacy through abuses of data processing. The federal DPC also wants formally to remove all costs for individual access to data. There is continued discussion of the NRW innovation of creating a constitutional right to data protection; resistance centers on the rigidity of such a scheme and the fact that it might promote too much focus on individual rights.

All data protectors have advised their respective legislatures concerning the implications of the Karlsruhe decision. There is general agreement that section 10 of the BDSG, which permits the transfer of data to meet administrative needs, is much too broadly defined and that specific sectoral laws will have to be developed, as has been done for social security data. Some data protectors even discuss the need to introduce licensing systems in certain parts of the public sector in order to combat surveillance effectively.

The hands of the commissioners will really be tied, however, if the legislature does not act to pass sectoral measures in compliance with the 1983 decision. They are only consultants on revision; a solution that would enhance their real role would be difficult to fashion in the existing constitutional system. It is hard to settle competing interests inside the government in order to produce adequate draft legislation for the Bundestag, because of the number of internal experts on specific problems and the variety of competing interests. The process further involves the various political parties. The fate of data protection's revision is problematic, since the Christian Socialist Union, key members of the governing coalition, are so concerned with security.

At the end of 1987, the government published a draft bill to completely overhaul the BDSG rather than to try to amend the current law. The government claims that it will then be in compliance with the Karlsruhe decision, a view rejected by opposition parties. The bill does strengthen individual access rights and contains a measure by which individuals can claim damages for illegal data processing.[14] Baumann disputed the claim that his powers would be strengthened and lamented the lack of progress on general revision of the BDSG. He insisted that the commissioner must be vested with sufficient authority, including the right to conduct systematic inspections. Baumann argues that "new legislation must not be limited to codifying existing practices. . . . The guiding principles . . . should rather be the necessity of data processing and its reasonableness and commensurability as compared with the interference with the individual's right of self-determination."[15] In his last annual report, he specifically criticized the proposed revisions for their weakness in addressing new technological developments and in controlling information storage and data exchanges by security agencies.[16] He also wanted automated and manual data processing to be covered in the same law.

In essence, the continuing debates over revision of the BDSG demonstrate the difficulty of persuading any government to restrict its surveillance practices, since all regimes believe that they always act in the best interests of the citizens. Once again, the legislature will have to insist on stronger preventive measures.

Part 2

Sweden

Chapter 7

The Swedish Model

Introduction

The Data Act of 1973, the first national law on data protection, has had a considerable influence on the development of statutes in other Western European countries. Its goal is to prevent "undue encroachment" on individual privacy. In judging this risk, the statute instructs the Data Inspection Board (DIB) to pay special attention to the nature and quantity of the personal data being collected, how and from whom the data are being acquired, and the attitudes of the data subjects. It is unlawful to start or maintain a data base of personal information (Swedes use the term "personal file" or "register") in machine-readable form without applying for and obtaining a license from, and in certain sensitive cases the permission of, the DIB, unless the Cabinet or Riksdag (legislature) creates it.[1] The original statute mandated DIB licensing in advance, but the 1982 revision of the Data Act introduced a more permissive system, focusing more on controlling sensitive uses of personal data as a means of restricting surveillance.

The DIB exercises a great deal of control over the collection and dissemination of personal data, regulating the usages of the resulting register, and enforcing a system of responsible keepers for computerized data banks. The law itself establishes a detailed set of duties for such keepers. There are also various civil and criminal penalties for breach of the Data Act.[2]

The power of the Cabinet or legislature to create a personal file outside the jurisdiction of the DIB permits the government to circumvent its prior review and also limits the authority of the agency.[3] Its decisions can also be appealed to the government (meaning in effect the minister of justice), but this happens infrequently. Even though this appellate process furnishes an excellent structural mechanism for balancing competing interests, it makes it difficult for the DIB itself to prevent certain instances of increased surveillance.

Jan Freese, who was a senior staff member of the DIB from its inception and director general from 1977 to 1986, played a critical role as a publicist and activist for data protection. He appeared regularly in the media to warn about the consequences of record linkages for increased surveillance in an automated society. Since high-quality, articulate, and activist leadership is essential to the success of data protection, Freese exemplifies one path to success.[4] In April 1986 he was succeeded by Mats Börjesson, who had been director general of the National Court Administration since 1975. As a highly experienced professional administrator, he can be expected to understand the pressing issues of data protection and to use common sense in solving them.

In terms of the themes of this volume, Sweden illustrates the disadvantages of a highly regulatory and bureaucratic approach to controlling surveillance, such as also exists in France, Norway, and the United Kingdom. Freese's strong leadership also contributed to his departure from the DIB, when conflicts of ideology and practice with the elected government became counterproductive. He consistently resisted more surveillance of the public through data collection. The highly automated character of Swedish society, the existence of universal Personal Identification Numbers, and the principle of openness necessitate strict data protection, but they also facilitate extensive efforts at social control. Sweden illustrates the kind of surveillance society that results when record linkages are so easy to accomplish that the power holders cannot resist using them to try to solve real and alleged social problems.

The Development of Legislation

Sweden has an established system of Commissions of Inquiry to ensure that problems of public policy are evaluated seriously; this process facilitates a swift response by the enactment of legislation. The debate over privacy and computers began in the mid-1960s, about the same time as in the United States, but the Swedish population census of 1970 raised a large number of concerns about governmental surveillance. In part, Swedes became excited about privacy protection because they were involved earlier than other countries in large automated information systems, Personal Identification Numbers, and record linkages. The historic Freedom of the Press Act also makes a great deal of government information publicly available. Freese has suggested that the computerization of society threatened this principle of freedom of information, so the use of computers was carefully monitored from an early date.[5]

A Parliamentary Commission on Publicity and Secrecy of Official Documents was first set up in 1969; its 1972 report on "Computers and Privacy" proposed a special statute on data protection. The 1973 law created the Data Inspection Board to regulate the collection, storage, and dissemination of identifiable personal data held in computerized form by either the public or private sectors. The critical innovation was the establishment of a mandatory licensing system for all such information systems, except for those created at the direction of the government (meaning the Cabinet) and the Riksdag. Freese, one of the secretaries of the commission that proposed the Data Act, argues that licensing was essential to determine the actual state of data processing.[6]

The Swedish model of data protection has had an enormous and direct influence on the development of data protection in Western European countries, even though the exact details of the Swedish model have not been widely imitated. The French law of 1978 is perhaps the clearest example (outside Scandinavia) of the adoption of its basic characteristics. The British Data

Protection Act of 1984 was also heavily influenced by this model, since it employs a universal registration scheme for computers processing personal data in the public and private sectors.[7]

The Data Act of 1973 has been amended twice. The changes that took effect in 1981 and 1982 marked a fundamental retreat from a licensing requirement to a more permissive system of simple registration with the DIB, except for sensitive data. After filing a request to maintain a personal data file, most custodians can proceed without the explicit permission of the board. The 1982 Act had the goal of reducing the bureaucratic burden and costs of data protection and of making the system of selective licensing self-supporting.[8]

The DIB emphasizes that it originated these amendments because it better understood the situation in data processing and wanted to concentrate on the most critical and complicated issues of privacy. The revisions were a change in emphasis about what was needed in terms of efficient implementation. In many ways, the amendments simply codified the simplified procedures and actual practices that the DIB had been following since 1974.[9]

Hans Corell, a senior official of the Ministry of Justice, described licensing as "too bureaucratic. It is not possible, we found out, to grant a license to every file."[10] In his opinion, "it has become necessary, not only in Sweden, to abandon the idea of a general requirement for licences to operate data files." He believes licensing requires too many continuing intrusions into both the public and private sectors, the grant of exceptional powers to the licensing agency, too large a staff, and an impossible burden of inspections to ensure adequate observance of licenses.[11] Thus, in his view, the 1982 changes "aimed at rationalisation of the Data Inspection's activities so as to ensure concentration of its resources on such personal data files as are particularly sensitive with regard to privacy."[12]

While increased efficiency in the use of governmental resources may be a popular political goal, the amendments nonetheless sparked debate, passing by only one vote. The Social Democrats and Communists, then in opposition, suspected that the proposed amendments were a means of weakening the system of data protection. They favored giving increased resources to the DIB. In part, this merely reflected opposition politicians playing a customary role; the Social Democrats adopted a diametrically opposed position when they formed the government later that year. Incumbents are less enthusiastic about having vigorous watchdogs over their surveillance practices. In Sweden, more so than in other countries, data protection has remained a political football, in part because of Freese's outspokenness as director general.

The DIB further acts as the licensing and supervisory agency for the Credit Information Act of 1973 and the Debt Recovery Act of 1974. Freese stated that "these two Acts add some extra power to the Data Act when it regulates computerized credit information etc."[13] The problems of data protection in these two areas were also under study in the early 1970s. A government committee, separate from the one that recommended the Data Act, simply suggested that the Data Inspection Board was the logical agency to implement these two laws.[14] Freese claims that the Freedom of the Press Act, the Data Act, and the Credit Information Act permitted the legislature to shape future developments in computer technology from what is technically possible to what is humanly acceptable.[15]

The Debt Recovery Act creates a system of licensing for credit collection agencies, so as "not to cause a debtor unnecessary harm or inconvenience or subject him to improper pressure or other improper debt-collecting measures."[16] The Credit Information Act and Debt Recovery Act regulate both manual and automated personal files, although the information systems of the regulated agencies are now in fact almost wholly automated. The Credit Act defines credit information as data assessment or advice provided as guidance for judgments concerning another person's credit worthiness or economic trustworthiness. The DIB in effect licenses credit agencies. The criteria are that their activities have to be in the public interest and conducted in an expert and sound manner: "Particulars concerning the person's political or religious beliefs, race or skin colour must not be collected, stored or transmitted in credit information activities."[17]

Formative Influences

In order to understand the interplay of data protection and public surveillance, a number of shaping influences require discussion. In comparison with the other countries treated in this volume, Sweden has a small population of approximately 8.4 million. In the twentieth century it has been very homogeneous, oriented toward the search for consensus, and strongly committed to rationalist, egalitarian, secular, and empirical values, although there are signs of change in recent years.[18] The existence of a unitary state means that the system created for data protection is relatively simple and straightforward. Creating a control agency like the Data Inspection Board fits in well with the traditional model of government, where departments that actually make policy are minuscule in size, and separate administrative agencies carry out most government activities.

The small population, coupled with a commitment to a very high standard of living (with associated high labor costs) meant that Swedes early foresaw the productivity gains available through automation. Sweden is thus one of the most computerized countries in the world, especially in public administration, and this high degree of automation is generally well accepted.[19] Consequently, Sweden is "a paradise for registers," the DIB having established the existence of 50,000 personal information systems. Freese estimates that a well-brought-up, well-behaved, unmarried adult probably appears in about one hundred systems; a married person might appear in twice as many.[20]

The paternalistic state collects a great deal of personal information about its residents, probably more than citizens know about themselves, according to

Table 3. Chronology of Swedish Data Protection Legislation

1969	Parliamentary Commission on Publicity and Secrecy of Official Documents established.
1970	Controversy over the census of population.
1972	Parliamentary Commission on Publicity and Secrecy of Official Documents issues its report on *Computers and Privacy*.
1973	Data Act enacted.
	Credit Information Act enacted.
July 1, 1973	Data Inspection Board (DIB) begins operations with Claes-Goran Källner as director general.
1974	Debt Recovery Act enacted.
1976	After forty-four years, Social Democrats lose power in national elections to a nonsocialist coalition.
	Parliamentary Commission on Revision of the Data Act (DALK) created.
1977	Jan Freese becomes director general of the DIB.
1978	Parliamentary Commission on Revision of the Data Act issues a major report.
March 20, 1980	Secrecy Act amended.
1981	Credit Information Act and Debt Recovery Act amended.
1982	Major amendments to the Data Act.
September 19, 1982	Social Democrats return to power.
1983	Controversy over the census of population.
July 1, 1983	Major amendments to the Data Act enter into effect.
1984	Parliamentary Commission on Revision of the Data Act ceases to exist.
September 15, 1985	Re-election of the Social Democrats.
1986	Public controversy about Project Metropolitan.
April 1986	Mats Börjesson becomes director general of the DIB.
September 18, 1988	Re-election of the Social Democrats.

some DIB members.[21] The "information gluttony" of the 1960s has not been sated. Liberal exchanges of data between the public and private sectors are customary; there is much more cooperative information handling of this type than in the other countries covered in this volume. Freese argues that computerization has "contributed to a massive flow of data between the state, municipal and private sectors of Swedish society. It is no longer a case of two-way communication but of multi-way communication."[22] The principle of openness reinforces this tendency of data flow among various authorities. A technical adviser to the DIB pointed out that the cost of introducing American computers promoted multiple uses of the same machine and data linkages to promote efficiency and to reduce the costs of automation. Despite the efforts of the DIB, such tendencies from the 1960s have not yet been rethought; in fact, the Social Democrats would like to create an even more managed society.

In short, Sweden is already more of a surveillance society than its Western counterparts, a condition closely associated with the introduction of a system of national identification numbers (PINs) in 1947. Every individual is identified by a unique ten-digit Personal Identification Number, which includes full information on date of birth and sex. The numbers are routinely available and widely used, creating a very dangerous capacity for surveillance and abusive personality profiling. The use of the PIN as the standard identifier for individuals in all public and private information systems facilitates the linkage of personal information. University students are registered by their PIN, and it appears on all telephone bills. A universal system of Personal Identification Numbers, coupled with sophisticated automation and telecommunications, is the key to a successful surveillance society.

The principles of general data protection are relatively new in Sweden and are in seemingly direct conflict with the long-established commitment to open government. In the United States, France, and Canada, there was a less dramatic time lapse between the introduction of freedom of information and data protection legislation, although similar tensions exist. The Freedom of the Press Act, perhaps the most famous Swedish law, embodies the principle of freedom of information or publicity. In Freese's view, the publicity or openness of public documents creates an information society, since all information collected by public authorities is in principle open to everybody.[23] In contrast to most other nations, most official (public) governmental information is readily available to citizens, including computerized data. The principle of public access to official records means, for example, that it is customary for companies to purchase address lists and other personal data from official government bodies.[24]

Thus the principle of accessible government information prevails over the principle of personal privacy; the Data Act is subordinate to the constitutional right of access to information.[25] Despite the fact that the Freedom of the Press Act is not a guarantee of total openness, the principle of publicity creates inevitable problems for the protection of personal information, especially in automated systems. In essence, the Data Act was a qualification of the principle of freedom of information, made in recognition of the threat to personal privacy posed by the age of computers.

The Swedish commitment to open government seems based upon a paternalistic view of the state; the North American approach is more clearly confrontational. Swedes tend to trust their government and to regard it as a benign force. The government has not engaged in any great breach of public trust or confidence, as in the Watergate episode in the United States or comparable activities involving the Royal Canadian Mounted Police Security Services in Canada in the 1970s, although the recent scandals about arms sales abroad and the failure to solve the murder of Olaf Palme may change attitudes. A substantial segment of the population regards the state as beneficent and protective of the individual rather than threatening. The public expects the government and civil service to handle problems in a pragmatic fashion and to subordinate individual rights to the collective needs of society in certain cases. This derives from "the deeply held Swedish belief, transcending ideological differences, . . . that the ills of a free society can be cured, that injustice is intolerable." Marquis Childs called this approach the middle way, "a conviction that reason can prevail in righting the wrongs of a troubled world."[26]

The faith in government combined with an acceptance of the primacy of collective interests creates a serious dilemma for the DIB, since it means that citizens are not a particularly loyal constituency for data protection when it appears to conflict with specific surveillance initiatives of the Social Democratic government. The DIB, especially under Freese, saw itself as an advocate for individual rights in a highly regulated and regimented society, where there is less room for the individual to maneuver than in North America. Some argue that Swedes need to fight for their freedom, and that other nations should regard it as an example of what might happen if they are not careful.

The DIB under Freese perceived its role as preventing regimentation by the state, whereas other Swedes do not believe their society is excessively controlled. The DIB's problem lies in the fact that Swedes themselves are not especially interested in protecting or developing their personal rights. There is no tradition of concern for privacy and other individual rights. The Social Democrats, who are the exponents and beneficiaries of this mainstream opinion, were strong supporters of the Data Act, even opposing its alleged "weakening" in 1982. But since they were returned to power, this majority party has clashed with data protection interests. They regard the collection of detailed information on the population as normal, whereas the minority liberal and conservative parties resist such surveillance tendencies. Hans Corell in part explains this ideological clash by reminding us that the Data Act originated in prosperous times. In the more austere economic climate of the 1980s, the government is concerned about the cost-effectiveness of data protection and wants new ways to enforce the tax laws and to prosecute welfare fraud through surveillance. Corell concluded in 1984 that not only were such demands at odds with the protection of privacy, but many appeared willing to give up some data protection in order to punish abusers of the system.[27] While such sentiments have not disappeared, continued public debates about the diminution of privacy may have made them more of a minority view.

The prevailing system of public consultation further promotes confidence in government. The normal assumption is that an agency such as the Data Inspection Board will simply carry out the statutory tasks assigned to it, and that those being regulated, including both the public and private sectors, will naturally cooperate. The types of antagonisms expected in North American society are notably absent in Sweden and West Germany. The basic tendency in both countries, at least in the civil service, is to comply with the law rather than to seek ways around it.

The Data Act was obviously not the first provision for the protection of personal privacy. As in most other Western legal systems, the general development of legal protections for personal privacy has occurred in a very haphazard fashion. Nevertheless, preexisting regulations for data protection continue to have some significance, such as elements of the penal code and administrative laws.[28] Principles for data protection were already incorporated in such statutes as the Police Record Act and the Criminal Record Act, just as they now are set in place in new or revised sectoral legislation.

Another formative influence on the conduct of data protection is the relatively ambiguous relationship between concern for privacy and the practice of surveillance in the society. Given a list of ten issues in 1976 and 1984 surveys, about 12 percent of the sample ranked protection of personal privacy as the most important issue; overall, it ranked third or fourth on this score, behind issues like unemployment, inflation, and environmental protection.[29] Respondents underestimated the number of personal files kept on them, yet more than half of the respondents in 1984, as against 34 percent in 1976, agreed entirely with the statement that "government agencies keep an unnecessary number of computerized files." Even more surprisingly, 38 percent of respondents regarded the storage in public files of data about age and income as an invasion of privacy; an equal number were not at all bothered by what is in fact customary practice. More than 75 percent agreed or partly agreed that government agencies should have the proper means to check that people do not cheat on their taxes (which means more record linkages).

It seems surprising, especially after the 1983 debate over the census, that only 24 percent of respondents had followed the public discussion of computerized files either closely or rather closely. Only one-third had mainly positive opinions concerning the increased use of computers. It is therefore hardly unexpected that 40 percent thought their own privacy was less well protected today than it was five years ago.

A catalogue of formative influences on the development of data protection cannot avoid emphasizing the uniqueness of Scandinavian society and raise questions about the relevance of its experience for the non-Scandinavian world. The potential for abusive record linkages is especially serious for the powerless in society, since they are more subject to an assumption of guilt/fraud than the powerholders, because the benefits received by the powerless can be checked and their statements verified through their PINs. By any standard of comparison in the Western world, Swedes live in a heavily regulated and controlled society that significantly reduces the scope for privacy in individual relations with the state. The Data Inspection Board struggles to accomplish its statutory tasks in such a special world.

The Organization of the Data Inspection Board

The DIB is an independent authority with a Board of Directors, appointed for fixed terms, representing various political parties and interest groups. The board establishes basic policy, but most decisions are made by the professional staff, headed by a director general, who is also a member of the board.

The board is a directorate with decision-making powers under the Data Act. Except for the director general, its members, who are selected by the Cabinet for four-year terms, represent the legislature, the major trade unions, industry, the public administration, and the research community. Although this is much broader representation than on the French National Commission on Informatics and Freedoms (CNIL), almost three-quarters of the latter have the advantage, in terms of independence, of not being selected by the government or the legislature. Four members of the Swedish board represent the several political parties in the Riksdag. There are also representatives of white- and blue-collar labor unions, of data processing, of industry, and one editor of a newspaper and one medical professor. Representation of each of these interests is standard practice for such a policy-making body as the DIB.[30]

The presence of a significant number of legislators on the board means that it contains a wide variety of political opinions without one party dominating. In some ways, this allows the board to function as a miniparliament, and the conflicting points of view on the appropriate scope of data protection are often reflected within the board itself. Its members debate issues until consensus is reached, allowing it to act unanimously on most occasions. The overt political input into such decisions is an attractive aspect of Swedish and French data protection, because it sensitizes a few politicians to surveillance problems.

There has been impressive continuity in the membership of the board, with the leading members serving several terms. To date, prominent persons have been willing to oblige simply because they are interested in the subject, and they appear to wield considerable power. Such a sense of public service is highly developed among the elite.

For the first ten years, the DIB had departments of licensing and of inspection, each directed by a head of department.[31] In light of the revised Data Act, the DIB introduced a new organization in 1983, featuring three departments. The licensing and supervisory functions are now united in separate departments for public authorities and for the private sector. This means that staff perform both licensing and auditing duties, which reflects the new goal of enhancing the supervisory role in implementation. A small third unit, which handled the credit and debt areas, is now part of the private sector department. As in West Germany, the staff tends to specialize in types of information systems in order to cope with the complexities of each area.

Almost since it began operations on July 1, 1973, the DIB has had a stable staff of approximately thirty people, of whom twenty are professionals with decision-making responsibilities. At present, there are thirty-five staff members. It has consciously remained a small organization. Freese regarded this size as adequate to protect privacy.[32] Without the simplified licensing procedures, the DIB would have needed more staff.

The actual decision-making process of the DIB is complex, reflecting the relationship between the professional staff, the director general, and the appointed board. The staff takes decisions on a great many routine licensing matters, especially under the simplified licensing procedures. In general, only specific cases go forward to the director general, and if necessary, to the board, in contrast to the situation of the CNIL, where both in theory and practice the commissioners make routine decisions themselves. Freese contended that the staff, not the director general, decided what issues went to the board. He stated that most decisions are taken by the head of the licensing division, a smaller number by the director general, and the most important ones, perhaps some forty a year, by the board.[33]

Under Freese, the board claimed to make the important policy decisions on individual cases and also the initial decisions that served as models in a particular sector. It seemed to be generally agreed, at least within the DIB, that the board was not simply rubber stamping staff decisions but was very active in examining certain issues in great detail. Börjesson regards the board as advisers rather than decision makers. He reviews annual plans on budgets and priorities with them and gives them progress reports, but the basic decisions, in most instances, are for him and his staff. In a delicate situation, however, the board's advice would force reconsideration of a pending decision. Yet in almost all instances, Börjesson and his board are in complete consensus.

Because the staff controls the flow of information, it influences the board's perspective on a given subject; however, this is true of most public administration models. Members of staff are permitted to attend meetings of the board in order to follow discussions and to respond to queries; generally as many attend as have time to do so. In Freese's last years, the staff was more individualistic in orientation, resulting in increased conflict between the staff and the board. Perhaps the staff's increased willingness to adopt strong privacy stances is a by-product of the security achieved by making all staff positions tenured. This may be particularly true, if one also considers that the board gradually changes over time, meaning that if conflicts of opinion develop, the staff anticipates that eventually new members with different viewpoints will replace the resistant ones.

The major policy decisions are presented in written form and made publicly available for examination. When Börjesson arrived at the DIB, he found that documentation of its decisions was sparse, so he set about improving the situation in order to promote consistency in its rulings. The office's first-published annual report outlines both its own decisions and those of the government on appeals from the agency since 1973.

It is possible for a member of the board to issue a written dissent, but this is very rare. The directors general have strenuously argued that they are not in a position to influence the board's decisions, and that decisions taken by themselves or members of staff closely follow earlier board guidance.[34] In theory, the board sets precedents and ultimately formulates broad policy guidelines. However, there are several problems with this presumption; Freese certainly dominated his board. Moreover, the board's decisions lack consistency.

Students of DIB decision making have found it difficult to establish patterns in the process. Political scientist Sten Markgren interviewed board members about the meaning of preventing "undue encroachment upon personal privacy" and found great variances among them. In her study of the board, Annette Kavaleff, a Finnish lawyer, found that the board itself had taken only 150 to 160 decisions from 1973 to 1981, which is a very small percentage of total licensing and supervisory activities. Moreover, there were substantial differences in the decisions taken at various levels within the DIB. Decisions taken below the level of the board were much more interesting than those she was studying. She also found the board's decisions were inconsistent. One decision might favor new technology, for example, while the next opposed it. In attempting to analyze the jurisprudential thinking at work in various types of decisions and the interests being protected, Kavaleff had great difficulties in identifying major trends and concluded that they did not exist. On the positive side, Kavaleff found that the board was promoting such standard practices under administrative law as the right to control information about oneself and the right to be informed; these derive from the principle of publicity and openness. She also found considerable emphasis on good record-keeping practices and a concern with the decentralization of information systems.[35]

Chapter 8

The Goals of Data Protection

What do data protection laws and data protection agencies seek to accomplish for the control of governmental surveillance? This chapter evaluates the purposes of the Swedish Data Act in order to evaluate its relevance for confronting surveillance problems directly and for giving data protectors a clear and specific mandate. It also describes the kinds of conflicts over the scope of the legislation that have occurred in recent years.

Data Processing

As has been true in other countries, the processing of personal information by computers inspired the original movement for data protection. The scope of the Data Act is thus restricted to files, lists, or other notes kept in automated and identifiable form.[1] Manual files are not regulated, which was an issue during the recent revision of the statute. Jan Freese claimed not to be worried about the exclusion of manual records, since the trend to automation is clear, but he wanted responsible keepers to flag the separate existence of manual files by notations in automated records.

Section 5 of the Data Act provides that "in conjunction with the granting of permission to set up and keep a personal file, the Data Inspection Board (DIB) shall issue regulations concerning the *purpose* of the file." As revised in 1982, this section governs the purpose but not the contents of files, because certain "free" data, such as names and addresses, can be stored in files under Swedish law. Since a responsible keeper has to identify the purposes of a particular system, defining the meaning of "purpose" is one of the key problems in implementation.

Although a main task of the Data Inspection Board is to monitor automated data processing, it emphasizes that it is not inherently antagonistic to computerization. Freese suggested that "data processing has already meant a fantastic development in most fields of society. Usually the benefits do exceed the cost, but it depends very much on how, when and where we use this new tool."[2] In his view, society would come to a halt without the use of computers. Yet Freese drew an analogy to the complex regulations that now apply to the use of automobiles: "We do need some traffic rules."[3]

Privacy Considerations

Preventing the occurrence of "undue encroachment upon the privacy of the registered person" is the primary concern of the Data Act.[4] However, the law contains only limited indications about how the DIB should define "personal privacy" or measure "undue encroachment."

The definition of personal privacy is especially problematic. The Swedish language does not have a word for privacy but refers instead to *integritet,* which is sometimes translated as personal integrity. Freese regularly defined privacy in the classic American language of Samuel Warren and Louis Brandeis as "the individual's right to be left alone."[5] However, this is a personal interpretation; the term privacy is not suitably defined within the statute, nor even in the 1982 revisions.[6] Freese remains adamant that further definition of privacy would create an inflexible situation, any precise definition being either too rigid or too vague, necessitating frequent changes or requiring too many exceptions.[7]

Others involved in the enactment or revision of the Data Act are more sensitive on this point. They cite the problems of preparing such a legal definition and the lack of preparatory material available to them. Even granted the merit of these points, academic and civil service critics still believe that the effort at definition could have been, and still should be, made. The 1982 revisions might have at least encapsulated eight years of experience in a working definition, which could have been included in the act to assist both the DIB and data custodians in its application.

In a pamphlet on the Data Act published in 1973, P. G. Vinge, who was a member of the governing board of the DIB from 1983 to 1987, noted that it was not considered possible in the Data Act to make clear distinctions about key concepts and that the responsibility for their definition lay with the DIB. Such a formulation needed to be a dynamic, on-going process; "our ideas on privacy are not permanent, but are affected by social and technological development. In addition, these ideas are different in different age groups and population groups, and also vary depending on the type of information concerned."[8] As the conclusions to this volume will argue, such a subjective, mutable conception of privacy is unsatisfactory. Protection of the individual from unwarranted surveillance is a more important and fundamental human right than Vinge suggested. Even though specific individuals vary greatly in their own conception and valuation of privacy, depending in particular on age and levels of education, a core element of concern for privacy remains in place.[9]

Similar problems of definition occur in connection with the meaning of "undue encroachment" upon personal privacy. The Data Act states that "in judging whether undue encroachment may occur, special attention shall be paid to the nature and quantity of the personal data to be recorded in the file, to how and from whom the data are to be collected, and to the attitude to the file held by, or which may be assumed to be held by, the persons who may be registered. . . . No other data nor other persons may be registered than in accordance with the purpose of the file."[10] Such general directions entrust a great deal of discretionary power to the board. The suspicion is that, as with the definition of privacy itself, the DIB has simply let its policy evolve rather than building a body of evident rules based on first principles.[11] Freese states that "a person must be prepared to accept some encroachment as a member of a society. The protection of privacy is therefore restricted to such encroachment as can be regarded as undue."[12] Such circular reasoning results in the DIB having responsibility, in most cases, for balancing the competing social interests of the individual against the collective.

In its efforts to understand the meaning of undue encroachment upon personal privacy, the DIB uses the exemptions to protect privacy in the Secrecy Act, which is discussed below, as a guide to concern for privacy in the public sector. Secondly, the board seeks the opinions of persons or organizations affected by an information system. For example, a local union or special interest group may be asked to comment. This is a very desirable practice, despite the inherent difficulties of knowing whether the responses are motivated solely by concern for privacy as opposed to, for example, concern for job security or hostility to new technology. On occasion, the DIB has had to choose between a local union willing to allow data collection, while the national organization was opposed. Further difficulties occur when there are no organizations for persons such as patients. In theory, the board need only consider "undue encroachment" without any reference to the benefits of data collection. However, in practice it recognizes the benefit side of the interest involved. In this way the Data Act gives rise to a trial and error process of determination, which seems inherent in any detailed process of implementation.

The DIB has made a number of general statements in connection with its effort to define undue encroachment upon personal privacy that illustrate how much discretion it has in practice. Freese focuses on the threat of surveillance when attempting to explain or define the dangers of encroachments. He refers to the need "to avoid the spider net, the control society."[13] A 1978 report of the Parliamentary Commission on Revision of the Data Act (DALK) also concluded that the basic aim of data protection "should, as hitherto, be to prevent a more or less wild growth of personal registers for more or less unspecified purposes. It must therefore be required that reasonable grounds exist for the registered contents in relation to the object of the register."[14]

The possibility exists that opinions of interested parties will differ sharply about the meaning of undue encroachment upon personal privacy, especially if the protection of privacy challenges economic interests. Surveys indicate that concern for the protection of personal privacy remains a significant issue.[15] Yet the condition of the economy has been an even more central matter in the 1980s. It is suggested that individuals have an inclination to give up a certain amount of privacy in order to promote economic development or efficiency. There is a preference for reducing welfare costs by catching cheaters over protecting the privacy of the indigent. The socioeconomically disfranchised sectors face the greatest risk of surveillance in all countries.

Defining the weight to be attached to the protection of privacy is also an issue among political parties. The Social Democrats and the trade unions tend to view questions with implications for privacy in a broader societal context.

They want to collect information in order to know how well welfare programs are working, for example. The issue of weighing privacy interests also arises when the Data Act is used to restrict the use of word processing or telecommunications, but the real motivation is protecting against the loss of jobs. Freese was insistent that the Data Act (and the DIB) should only be concerned with data protection, but his critics were not as sanguine about what was actually happening.

Despite the powerful and beneficial influence of the DIB since 1974, data protection remains a critical need; it is a very fundamental issue concerning the appropriate balance of individual rights vis-à-vis the state and society in the 1980s. The DIB faces continuing problems in determining the appropriate weight to grant to competing interests, unless, as should be the case, it places primary emphasis on the articulation and defense of privacy interests.

Information Management Objectives

The Data Act contains a number of detailed provisions for information management. The DIB can examine the nature and quantity of personal data to be recorded, how and from whom the data are to be collected, and the attitudes of the persons registered to the information system.[16] Unless special reasons exist, a personal file can only be established on "members, employees or customers of the responsible keeper of the file, or persons in similar relationship with the latter."[17] Like the equivalent French law, the Data Act also defines certain data as especially sensitive. Except in a case where "specially cogent reasons exist," only a public authority responsible for keeping a record of such particulars can maintain a personal file containing information about a person's criminal, health, psychiatric, or social welfare records; sexual history; race; or political or religious beliefs.[18]

These restrictions are much stronger and more precise than those of most other nations, with the exception of legislation directly influenced by the Data Act, such as that of Norway and France. These rules reflect a society in which the availability in public files of information on age and general income is not considered very irksome by a majority of the population, but considerable sensitivity exists about personal data on criminality, health, political opinions, or family problems.[19]

The Data Act also contains the customary code of fair information practices. Information on individuals must be accurate: "If there is reason to suspect that personal data in a personal file are incorrect, the responsible keeper of the file shall without delay take reasonable measures to ascertain the correctness of the data and, if reason exists, to correct them or delete them from the file."[20] Acceptable levels of accuracy depend on the potential uses of the data. The DIB accepts a lower level of reliability for information used for statistical as opposed to administrative purposes. Moreover, measures taken to insure the accuracy of data and its subsequent correction are to be "reasonable."[21]

There is a strong provision in section 9 concerning the completeness of personal information: "If a personal file contains personal data which, in view of the purpose of the file, must be considered incomplete, or if a personal file which constitutes a list of persons omits anyone who, in view of the purpose of the file, must be expected to be recorded in it, the responsible keeper of the file should make the necessary addition. Such an addition must always be made if the omission may be assumed to involve undue encroachment upon personal privacy or a risk of loss of rights." This section of the Data Act strays explicitly away from the initial preoccupation with the protection of personal privacy as a negative right (freedom from interference) in its reference to the question of the risk of loss of unspecified rights, to the imposition of a positive obligation. In practice, however, the DIB has not enforced this requirement. In his commentary on the data law, Freese suggests this remedy would be available to a person seeking an apartment from a housing authority, if it failed to keep a name on file. This is an example of how Swedish data protection touches on matters irrelevant to the preservation of privacy in a possibly undesirable manner.

Section 11 of the Data Act prohibits the disclosure of personal data "if there is reason to assume that the data will be used for automatic data processing contrary to this Act." Presumably the latter phrase means that the data might be used to further undue encroachment on personal privacy. Such a control on dissemination would not apply to public-sector data banks created by the government or the Riksdag, unless the DIB's recommendations had been accepted. Another control on dissemination occurs in section 13, which provides that the responsible keeper of a file, or any other person concerned with a personal file or with data collected for inclusion in it, "may not without authorization reveal what he has learned from it concerning the personal circumstances of an individual."[22] In this instance files kept by public authorities are subject to the provisions of the Official Secrets Act. There are similar restrictions against passing on information that has been lawfully disseminated.[23]

The final provision on the storage of personal information also helps to limit surveillance. Section 14 ensures accessibility by determining that automated data used by public authorities in judicial or administrative proceedings shall be added to the documents in the case in a readable form, unless special reasons (such as economic costs) dictate otherwise. As in the French data protection law, the purpose may simply be to ensure that persons can access the data used in making decisions affecting them. The Riksdag decided that such a matter should be within the goals of data protection.

Conflicts Inherent in the Data Act

The discussion in this chapter has identified a number of areas of inherent conflict within the Data Act, particularly in connection with the problem of identifying an intrusion on privacy, of defining the concept of privacy itself, and determining at what point the protection of the individual's right outweighs the state's collective interest. With respect to both the public and private sectors, the Data Act generally leaves such issues to the DIB with the possibility of an appeal to the government from its decision. The belief of the DALK committee in 1978 that the board could only make such determinations on a case-by-case basis further increased the potential for decisions hostile to surveillance by responsible keepers: "The basic idea should . . . be that all registration of personal data may in itself involve a risk of encroachment upon personal privacy, but that it is the form of the register—in a wide sense, in each particular case that decides whether this encroachment should be judged to be undue or not. . . . In DALK's opinion, data collected for a specific purpose should in principle not be used for other and later arising purposes, even if this means that the advantages of data processing cannot be fully and wholly utilized."[24] The latter statement in particular is very strong on a fundamental issue of linking data that were never intended for the proposed surveillance.

The DIB has the responsibility to determine the necessary balance of interests. Detailed regulations concerning every aspect of a particular license are required in so far as necessary to prevent invasion of privacy; however, the DIB is instructed to exercise its supervision so that "it does not cause greater costs or inconvenience than is necessary."[25] Thus, the law itself explicitly recognizes the need to balance interests. In fact, the Data Act insists essentially on a case-by-case determination of competing interests; a sector-by-sector approach to various categories of information might be more desirable and efficient and probably occurs in practice.

In a number of instances the Data Act is subordinate to the Freedom of the Press Act, which was discussed in Chapter 7, and the Secrecy Act. The dissemination of data in files kept by public authorities is subject to the provisions of the Official Secrets Act.[26] At the same time "regulations regarding dissemination of personal data may not restrict the duties of public authorities under the Freedom of the Press Act."[27] There is no absolute secrecy under the Secrecy Act because of the Freedom of the Press Act.

The relationship between the Data Act and the Secrecy Act is complex, yet the latter reinforces the principles of data protection for many types and forms of personal information, including manual records. One of the interests protected by the Secrecy Act is the personal privacy of individuals, as in the case of hospital, medical, or financial information.[28] The data must be kept confidential, "unless it is evident that the information can be disclosed without the individual or any person closely related to him being harmed." This test obviously covers broad interests in limiting surveillance. Section 16 of chapter 7 of the Secrecy Act specifically applies to individual information contained in a register covered by the Data Act, "if it can be assumed that the information, if disclosed, would be used for automatic data processing in violation of the provisions of the Data Act."

The Secrecy Act also regulates the transfer of personal information among government authorities. The revised law of 1980 stipulates that secrecy should be maintained between authorities; "a general exception is that information may be communicated to another authority if it is evident that the receiving authority's interest in getting the information is superior to the interest protected by the secrecy rule."[29] This appears to permit a great deal of leeway. Moreover, "there is no general rule that information which is secret with one authority will remain secret if transmitted to another authority."[30] The obvious problem is balancing the interests involved in a society which is committed to openness, opposed to absolute secrecy, yet trying to protect privacy. Fortunately, various laws at least attempt to create conditions under which such interests can be suitably balanced in individual cases, stimulated in practice by the oversight role of the DIB.

From the perspective of many years of operation, the DIB has largely managed to avoid major conflicts with government agencies over the scope of data protection. There are a variety of explanations for this situation, not the least of which is the ultimately conciliatory approach that the board has taken to its work. From an early stage it also recognized that the complex issues of data protection necessitated political decisions by legislators to balance conflicting factors, such as the need for privacy, balanced budgets, and the costs of ensuring security.

The DIB further benefits from the fact that the fifteen or so ministries that formulate government policy are generally small, averaging several hundred persons in total. The Cabinet issues guidelines on policy and regulations with the advice of these ministries, which then decentralize administration to various independent authorities. With a total staff of approximately thirty, the size of the DIB is not completely disparate in comparison to those being regulated, at least at the policy-making level; however, some of the independent agencies that implement policy, such as the Ministry of Employment, have as many as 10,000 employees. In contrast to West Germany or France, Sweden does not have a large, powerful Ministry of the Interior to oppose the DIB. Of course, it can be argued that in focusing attention in its early years on Statistics Sweden and the research community, the DIB was consciously avoiding entanglements with strong vested interests in more important administrative agencies. More recently, as Chapter 11 will indicate, the DIB has not been reluctant to tackle major issues.

Another explanation for lack of significant public conflicts between the DIB and government agencies is the provision for exempt data banks. Although the DIB argues that in practice its views are taken into consideration for information systems created directly by the government or Riksdag, there is a natural tendency to tread lightly in prescribing detailed regulations when government intentions have been clearly indicated. The DIB is of course not "a state within a state" and has to accept the authority of parliament, the ultimate arbiter of this surveillance society.

As will be noted in Chapter 9, the DIB has regularly found itself in conflict with government ministries in recent years over the issue of linking information from several ministries for a particular purpose, because hard economic times encouraged governments to attempt to control expenditures by matching records. Labor unions favored such activities in order to improve the economic situation.[31]

Informed observers seem to agree that there has been little public conflict over the activities of the Data Inspection Board in the public sector. The primary critics are the government authorities who run afoul of the DIB in the course of implementing legislation and public policy. There is no continued, significant media or legislative criticism of DIB decisions. The press tends to side with the DIB. This situation contrasts with West Germany or France and indicates that criticism of data protection is more likely during the first few years, rather than after a statute like the Data Act has been more fully accepted (or ignored).

The most significant group of nongovernmental critics has been the academic research community. Researchers were surprised to discover that they require licenses for their personal registers like any other user.[32] As in the case of Statistics Sweden, academic critics suspected that the DIB was attacking a weaker segment of society rather than dealing with the larger and more sensitive data bases of the police and intelligence services. While a professor at the University of Stockholm, Social Democrat Sten Johansson, now head of Statistics Sweden, publicly accused Freese of using data protection to provide a haven for tax evaders.

On the whole, the Data Act has been implemented by the DIB without arousing a great deal of criticism and antagonism from among the regulated. One academic critic suggests that this lack of conflict exhibits a very high level of Swedish conformity to law once it has been enacted. The systematic mode of consultation with all the interests in society in advance of legislation reinforces this climate. This condition also suggests that the DIB has not been powerful enough to limit governmental surveillance.

Chapter 9

The Power of the Data Inspection Board

In order to be effective in limiting governmental surveillance, data protectors require independence, powers of intervention, and the willingness to use them. This chapter begins the evaluation of how well the Data Inspection Board (DIB) has been functioning in this regard, particularly with respect to controlling record linkages in a hostile political climate.

Independence

The independence of the Data Inspection Board is established by standard constitutional practice rather than by any specific provision of the Data Act. Jan Freese described the agency as "an autonomous authority which administers the Data Act independently." Although the DIB is an organ of government, such agencies are autonomous: "Compared with its counterparts in many other countries, the typical government agency in Sweden has more the character of an administrative tribunal, stressing its independence towards other institutions."[1] The constitution forbids a member of the government or Cabinet, meaning the minister of justice, from intervening in the day-to-day affairs of the DIB.

The Cabinet (through the staff of the Ministry of Justice) selects or accepts members of the Data Inspection Board because they come from various constituencies. Freese's theory was that board members should be present as individuals and not as spokespersons for industry, unions, or political parties. This is less true for the four members of the legislature, who tend to vote in accordance with party policy on a major issue. Thus Social Democrat Kurt Hugosson, who served for nine years, sided with his party in 1982 to oppose the revisions to the Data Act. But it is rare for Social Democrats on the board to dissent from decisions that are against the blue-collar trade unions and the civil service unions. The politicians have not dominated the decision-making process at the DIB as much as their French counterparts, although one member claims that they have tried to do so. Freese's strong leadership was the vital difference.

It is surprising that the governments in power have not tried harder to influence the direction of the DIB by utilizing their power to select its members. Perhaps it is inconvenient for such purposes that DIB terms are four years, elections occur every three years, and basic changes of governments actually occurred in 1976 and 1982. But once the Social Democrats returned to power, they tried to influence the DIB's position on such things as record linkages by choosing members sympathetic to their goals. Freese regarded this as politicizing the board. The continued presence of a strong director general was the government's greatest obstacle to shaping the board's approach, and Freese's departure left some questions about its future role.

While the DIB may be independent in terms of its structural arrangement within the constitution, in other countries the persons charged with implementing data protection are sometimes unwilling to utilize their full degree of independence because of concerns for future career options. The data protector who is too forceful a critic of government practices may find that his or her term is not renewed, as was the case with Professor Bull in West Germany. The Swedish model provides for this concern by using the civil service hierarchy. Until 1986, the status of the directors general was equivalent to that of a judge, because of their career paths. Both Claes-Goran Källner, the first director general, and Freese, his successor, began their careers as judges in the administrative courts. They then served in various parts of the public administration, as is customary. The fact that they could at any time at least attempt to return to judicial duties provided career security, which reinforced their position of independence.

However, the most important guarantee of independence until 1986 was that the director general received a life-time appointment, which was a departure from standard practice of appointing directors of such agencies for a renewable six-year term.[2] The government ended this pattern for several inspection agencies in 1986; Freese regards this as a disaster in constitutional terms. The DIB's special situation worked well, because Freese in particular was an enthusiastic data protector, but control of the appointment by the minister of justice could become a liability if a weak person were named.

Mats Börjesson's term will end with his retirement. A more systemic protection for his independence is that any director general receives an 80 percent pension if removed after a single term. Such a person can also resign at his or her own volition after a total of twelve years as a director general without giving any reasons and with a pension.

The DIB has an administrative association with the Ministry of Justice, somewhat akin to the relationship of the federal Data Protection Commissioner in Germany with the Ministry of the Interior. The minister of justice has no supervisory role over the implementation of the Data Act by the DIB, but his staff have a separate responsibility for revisions to the Data Act, for processing appeals to the government against the DIB, and for the budget of the agency. The DIB's budget appears under its own heading in the budget of the ministry. The ministers visit the DIB on occasion to inform themselves about the current situation, including finances, so budgetary control is critical. Since he previously directed an administration within the purview of this ministry, Mats Börjesson has had considerable experience in functioning within it, without allowing the ministry to interpret his mandate for him. Since he is governed only by the Data Act in reaching decisions, these are not discussed with the ministry.

The attitude of any minister of justice toward data protection can make a difference for the DIB, but there were a half-dozen different ministers during Freese's tenure as director general, so that no minister was very likely to challenge his views about implementation, at least until the last incumbent stayed in office for several years. The more significant issue is the influence that such a minister is able to wield in negotiations over the DIB's budget with the minister of finance. Although the Social Democrats opposed the 1982 revisions to the Data Act that sought to make the DIB self-financing, they have other reasons to differ with the agency over its application of the Data Act to record linkages in particular.

In his 1987 book, Freese recalls an incident when a representative of the Social Democratic majority, who was a member of the Parliamentary Commission on Revision of the Data Act (DALK), privately threatened to turn the DIB into a department within the Ministry of Justice should Freese not be willing to consider supporting a considerable "loosening" of the Data Law. Subsequently the chairman of DALK reported to the government that there was no consensus regarding the idea of weakening the Data Act.[3]

In practice, the government can limit the effective independence of the DIB by control over its budget. Between 1982 and 1986 the annual budget of the DIB amounted to approximately 7.5 million Swedish kronor (Skr), divided almost equally between the permission and inspection functions.[4] Inflation was primarily responsible for annual increases. The annual budget for 1987–88 was almost 13 million Skr, because of expensive new quarters and office automation. The goal of the 1982 law, subsequently reinforced when the Social Democrats returned to power, was to make the DIB self-supporting and without a regular budget. The DIB charges annual fees to the responsible keepers of personal registers to cover licensing and permission costs. These proceeds are meant to finance its licensing, inspection, and supervisory functions, but it resisted the government on this point for a number of years. A minority of the DALK Commission opposed these proposed changes, arguing that the agency's financial resources should be increased in recognition that the protection of privacy must have some costs.

In fact, the DIB's revenue has made up less than 10 percent of its budget. For the 1983–84 budget year, the DIB hoped to raise almost three-quarters of its budget from standard licensing fees of 240 Skr and from extra permissions. The problem of projecting revenues is that the DIB did not know the total number of responsible keepers that would require a standard license, and only one annual license can be required for a whole series of personal registers held by an authority. The fact that Statistics Sweden (SCB) and a small boat club pay the same amount leads to obvious resistance from the smaller users, who also regard the fee as a tax on data processing. It is hardly surprising that the DIB's goal of being self-supporting remains elusive, and the government continues to cover budgetary deficits.

The DIB has had to overcome staff resistance to being a debt collection agency. Some staff members were unaware of the obligation to charge a fee; others billed as little as 20 percent of the payable time, illustrating the staff's aversion to such a system. The auditing staff had to develop strategies to identify nonregistrants. The burden of such an effort and of giving advice about filling out the licensing form has had the ironic effect of further reducing the amount of time the staff could spend on inspections. Prior to 1982, the DIB knew there were unlicensed users but did not have the time to find them, testimony to the bureaucratic burden of this model of data protection. The goal of self-financing detracts from the implementation of data protection and, in the minds of some staff members, hurts the DIB's good working relationships with responsible keepers. Moreover, staff demoralization over money disputes with the Ministry of Justice led to a massive loss of the most experienced staff members in 1985–86. Börjesson's view is that self-financing in the form of cost recovery, which is expected of other inspection boards, will ensure the DIB's independence. Although recent budget increases make it even less likely that cost recovery will be fully successful, the current effort to do so seems to satisfy the Ministry of Justice.

Swedish observers point out that all public authorities face a harsh financial climate and find it hard to believe that the agency is not able to be self-supporting. The problem is further complicated by the tight budget for implementation. The funds available for public relations, including the promotion of security measures, are very modest. Careful audits necessitate an adequate travel budget, as the German practice illustrates, yet the DIB's travel funds are very limited. Audits done on the basis of documentation supplied by informants or licensees are hardly an adequate substitute for on-site inspections. The solution may come if self-financing proves workable over time (which seems unlikely at the moment), and the DIB obtains full control over its own financing and expenditures.

The budgetary situation raises real questions about the ability and independence of the DIB to carry out its statutory duties in the public and private sectors. Even with the 1982 changes to the Data Act, there are genuine questions about the ability of the DIB to meet its goals on the basis of its current budget and staff size. Since no other data protection agency has been under such pressure to become self-financing, the government's efforts in this realm look like an unsubtle effort to undermine data protection.

Powers of Intervention

When the Data Inspection Board was first created, some foreign critics suggested that it had enough licensing power in the public and private sectors to take over every aspect of society. Despite the hyperbole of this assertion, the DIB does wield considerable powers. In essence, anyone seeking to maintain a personal file has to apply to the Data Inspection Board to be licensed.[5] The Data Act broadly defines a "personal file" as "any file, list or other notes kept by automatic data processing and containing personal data referable to the individual concerned."

The 1982 act significantly turned away from the system of universal, advance licensing of all personal information systems to become primarily a registration system. The act now requires explicit permission and a license from the DIB only for files containing information on sensitive topics, judgments or appraisals of a person, or on persons with no established relationship with the responsible keeper. Permission is also necessary if the file in question is derived from any other personal files, subject to certain qualifications.[6] In practice, most responsible keepers from the public and private sectors now simply announce their intentions to the DIB before starting to keep personal files.[7] All such registrants, however, are subject to detailed regulation by the DIB.

This broad licensing and supervisory power is significantly restricted by the stipulation that permission is not required for personal files set up by the government or Riksdag. Prior to such a decision, however, the opinion of the Data Inspection Board must be sought for a file which is to contain personal information that normally would require the permission of the DIB.[8] The government (meaning the elected majority party/Cabinet) or the Riksdag have established approximately 600 data banks. At least thirty-five of the data bases of Statistics Sweden are thereby exempt from the need to obtain licenses from the DIB.[9] The government and the legislature thus retain ultimate power to create data banks exempt from DIB supervision. A few government decisions of this type can create very large information systems, because of the size of existing tax and welfare schemes. The current director general of the DIB points out that these government decisions regulate "the most sensitive personal files kept in the administration."[10] The DIB, for example, failed to influence a new tax law, so that it does not contain data protection principles that would regulate the tax register in a clear way. Senior staff members believe that this piece of legislation demonstrates the inflexibility of a statute for purposes of data protection, as opposed to licensing and advising by the DIB.

One important control on the government's power to create exempt data banks is the requirement that the DIB must be consulted in advance in cases involving the sensitive personal information covered in section 2 of the Data Act. Moreover, section 4 of the Data Ordinance of 1973, as amended in 1979, provides that in expressing an opinion on such a proposed government or Riksdag data bank, the DIB should employ the same grounds for judgment used in examining an application for a license. In fact, the DIB claims to treat each such request as a normal licensing case. Its power to issue detailed regulations for data protection also applies to data banks that are exempt under section 2a, unless the government or Riksdag have issued regulations on the matter.[11] Under similar conditions, the DIB also has the power to alter such regulations or issue new ones for exempt banks, if the circumstances affecting personal privacy change.[12]

The government's power to create data banks facilitates surveillance projects, although the DIB claims that the government has not used this provision to avoid data protection. The constitutional theory is that any authority, such as the DIB, always has to be under the ultimate jurisdiction of the government and Riksdag, reflecting the strong societal commitment to legislative supremacy. A similar situation exists with respect to the independence of the federal Data Protection Commissioner in West Germany. The problem facing the designers of the Data Act was to create a DIB with sufficient independence. The original committee proposed this exemption in the law as a practical solution to a constitutional problem.

Nevertheless, the exemption from compulsory licensing under section 2a has been a central topic of debate. The DALK Commission noted that some have considered "that the exemption implies a serious and unjustified departure from the basic idea of the Data Act, since the information in such registers has a breadth and depth which lacks any equivalent in the private sector." DALK nevertheless concluded that "experience has not shown that decisive objections can be raised against this arrangement from the privacy aspect."[13] It decided that the exemption had limited practical scope owing to the rules to be observed under the Data Act. The Data Inspection Board also pointed out that the difference in handling of government or Riksdag proposals and of licensing cases is mainly formal. Because great weight is attached to its opinion, it has supervision over the use of such registers and can issue special regulations concerning them. For this reason, but also for constitutional reasons and to avoid jurisdictional conflicts, DALK concluded that the present state of affairs should continue.[14]

In times of economic difficulties, the exemption in section 2a provides an escape from the rigors of data protection. Presumably the government in power has more inclination to use it than the Riksdag, but large public information systems are normally created or at least approved by the legislature. The DIB can only render its advice and finds it difficult to alter extant plans for any such system, like the recently announced register for all boats. In terms of ultimate power, this exemption from licensing does provide a solution when the interests of the DIB and a large government ministry conflict and means that the government makes the final decisions on acceptable limits of public surveillance.

A further restriction on the powers of intervention of the DIB is that under section 25 of the Data Act its decisions in specific cases can be appealed to the government by the attorney general on behalf of the general public in order to safeguard its interests. Such a responsibility is a normal part of the mandate of the attorney general. Responsible keepers may themselves launch an appeal. For two cases that occurred in 1987, the Ministry of Justice reversed the DIB.

Such appeals to the government are standard procedure under the general rules of administrative law, and, in effect, restrain excessive application of data protection principles as opposed to competing interests.[15] The government receives as many as 8,000 such appeals each year on a very broad range of issues. A reversal of a DIB decision does not result in the resignation of its leadership, nor does it necessarily establish a precedent with respect to future decisions. Under administrative law, the DIB should adjust to a government decision on an appeal, but it is hard to set precedents for the kinds of decisions it makes. The system tends to regard such appeals as a form of safety valve against the abuse of power and favors a balance between too few and too many. Thus one component of DIB thinking on any decision is to discourage an appeal to the government; at the same time, it is not a great blow for the DIB to be reversed, because of the apparent difficulty of reconciling competing interests in data protection.

Although the Cabinet can play a role in deciding a direct appeal to the government by responsible keepers against the DIB, in practice the minister of justice exercises the decisive influence in an informal procedure. His division for general administrative affairs seeks opinions on the matter from the appellant, the DIB, and the attorney general as a representative of the public interest. The staff then presents the issue in the case to the minister in an objective fashion. They may make a recommendation, or the minister may ask for their opinion.

The minister of justice makes decisions on appeals against the DIB in the name of the Cabinet. If an appeal raises an important issue, the minister may ask for a Cabinet discussion; otherwise, the minister simply mentions his decision in the course of a regular meeting. Thus the most sensitive issues in data protection are ultimately settled by politicians, as is the case in most countries studied in this volume. However democratic, this condition tends to favor the installation of surveillance societies.

Freese is proud of the fact that during its first ten years there were only 100 or so appeals to the government out of 40,000 cases handled by the DIB. In his view this does not indicate the agency's whole-hearted acceptance of whatever responsible keepers want, but its search for solutions in the process of decision making: "The DIB suggests constructive alternatives intended primarily to satisfy the demands for privacy but also the demands of responsible keepers for rational and economically sound data processing."[16] Freese also emphasizes that the low rate of appeal at about ten cases a year continued through changes in governing parties. However, the rate of appeals doubled to about twenty cases a year after the Social Democrats returned to power in 1982, which was primarily a reflection of sharply competing goals in an era of financial restraint.[17]

Appeals to the government nevertheless involve important and controversial cases. Appeals are more likely to occur from the public sector, as it presents the biggest threat to privacy, deals with more complicated issues, and does more record linkages. When Statistics Sweden and the DIB had major conflicts in the

1970s over a statistical practice known as imputing and the character of a particular survey, the government took decisions generally favorable to the SCB.[18] The government can also take political considerations into account; it tends to seek a compromise in such situations. For example, the minister of construction and building authorized the Association of Communes to link data on those receiving special subsidies for apartment rentals with data from government social security records in order to try to stop the underreporting of incomes. The DIB turned down the proposal on grounds of concern for privacy, but the minister simply proposed to permit the linkages in a manner satisfactory to the DIB.[19] The conservative *Svenska Dagbladet* reported on March 3, 1983, that the DIB was anxious about the new government's record of approving record linkages. Freese did not draw too negative conclusions from the fact that they had been overruled. The minister of justice for his part wanted to lessen the importance of the differences of opinion. In his view, the DIB is expected to be restrictive, since it is its obligation to protect privacy. He added that the right of appeal to the government would be of no value if the decisions of the DIB always prevailed.

Finally, with respect to the DIB's powers of intervention, the Data Act contains a series of penalties and damages for breach of the statute. For example, under section 20 it is a criminal offense punishable by fine or imprisonment not exceeding one year to "willfully or by negligence" set up or keep a personal file without permission, to infringe a regulation issued under the act, or to disseminate personal data in violation of the act. Section 21 introduces the innovative concept of "data trespass," whereby any person who unlawfully procures access to automated information or who unlawfully alters, obliterates, or enters automated information in a file shall be sentenced to a fine or to imprisonment not exceeding two years, unless the offense is punishable under the Penal Code.[20] This regulation covers all forms of data processing. An individual may complain to a public prosecutor or the DIB may initiate a prosecution. The board made a conscious decision in 1982 to start more prosecutions of keepers who refuse to register, and at least ten cases for prosecution were identified in the next half year. It has also resorted to prosecution, rather than continued argumentation, for operators of data banks in the private sector who do not want to pay for licenses.

During the election period in 1982 the DIB threatened to prosecute the committee supervising the elections for planning to allow a committee on immigration to write to immigrants in order to increase the rate of participation. Automated data were available on the 50 percent who had not voted in the 1979 communal elections, and the plan was to send out political information from various parties. This required linkages of commune data in order to secure correct addresses, and the election committee failed to apply for permission. The committee chairman responded that urgent action was necessary. The DIB decided to wait to receive the committee's explanation before deciding whether to prosecute.[21] After receiving the committee's explanation, the DIB prosecuted its chairman. Although three levels of courts agreed that a crime had been committed, the chairman was acquitted, because he had reason to believe that an official of his committee had secured the necessary authorization from the DIB.

Section 23 of the Data Act provides civil damages to an individual about whom a responsible keeper has kept incorrect information.[22] Damages can be claimed for both pecuniary and nonpecuniary injury. Moreover, the responsible keeper in question faces strict liability. The plaintiff only needs to sue the last responsible keeper in the chain (who has a right of recourse against prior keepers) and does not have to search to find out where the error was made.[23] The chancellor of justice, an independent official concerned with the conduct of officials, receives demands for compensation against the government. Each year he receives a few claims for liability for errors in personal registers. The compensation is relatively modest.[24]

The Control of Record Linkages

Because Sweden has so many data banks in both the public and private sectors, and because each citizen is uniquely identified by a Personal Identification Number, record linkages for large and small forms of surveillance are proliferating, and their treatment for purposes of data protection well illustrates the exercise of power. Under section 2 of the Data Act, the DIB has to give specific permission for the linkage of files that are to contain "personal data procured from any other personal file, unless the data are recorded or disseminated by virtue of a statute, a decision of the Data Inspection Board, or by permission of the person registered."

Freese was the most ardent foe of record linkages among data protectors in Western countries. Because Sweden already had so many automated data banks, he strongly resisted various linkages proposed by government agencies in particular. There have even been plans to link all important computer files of personal data. Freese and other members of the board are concerned about the real prospects of creating a surveillance society based on computers. He warns that a society that could develop a workable scheme to end all tax frauds would be an impossible place for persons to live. He is also very emphatic about the risks of linking for decision-making purposes records that are in fact of questionable quality in terms of erroneous data; this is a very telling objection.

There are more substantial flows of personal data that can be matched among the state, municipal governments, and the private sector than in other countries, a point also acknowledged by Börjesson. Freese noted that "in few other countries, if any, can, for example, the insurance companies be linked computer-to-computer with the Motor-Car Registry, or even with a centrally run population file. It is even possible for a private car dealer to link up via a terminal with the Motor-Car Registry, or for a state authority to 'plug in' in the same way to the files of a private credit information company."[25] The actual practice in these cases illustrates a response to the public's need for credit information; the system operates under the supervision of the DIB. Yet there are serious risks that such computer profiling, if based on inaccurate data, could lead to unjust treatment of individuals.

Freese and his colleagues at the DIB emphasize that they are not hostile to all forms of record linkages. One estimate is that 80 to 90 percent of the linkages proposed to the DIB are approved. However, it resists linkages in which the users do not know why the personal information was collected or are seeking to link very sensitive information, such as data on alcoholics and drug addicts. An activity is considered risky if it is carried out to exercise surveillance over the population or to avoid direct collection of information from individuals.[26] Freese has no problems with linkages for the purpose of updating a file, such as changing the address of an individual. Börjesson told *Privacy Times* that the DIB is supportive of data linkages to keep administrative records accurate, "but we are very restrictive with our permits when the purpose of the match is to control the individual."[27]

Freese's main concern, and it seems most sensible, is with the quality of the data used in record linkages. One has to know when, why, and how the data were collected before any linkages should be attempted. He points out that one can hardly conduct effective record linkages on the basis of poor medical diagnoses, for example: "Unless one knows from whom, when, how and why the data were compiled, the linked processing will be misleading. Unfortunately, the DIB has only too often come across instances where linking of various data submitted at various times for various purposes has made the most honest of persons look like a crook."[28] In his view, a complex system of linkages will not work, because it is impossible to assure the quality of the data and to inform citizens of their rights.

The DIB points out that the pressure for more record linkages comes from general administrators and not data processing specialists, who tend to be more aware of the problems of data quality. One example used is that persons planning linkages need to be aware of the actual meaning of a net income figure for a person before using the data elsewhere. The net income figures for tax purposes may not be relevant or have a suitable meaning for another use. There seem to be no problems in linking hard facts about an individual, such as a birth date, but it should be impossible to link soft information, which has to be turned into hard "facts" for purposes of linkage. It is a hard fact that a person drinks a quart of alcohol a day, but it is a soft fact to classify someone as an alcoholic. This illustration is useful in explaining the resistance of the DIB to record linkages for surveillance purposes.

The important point is that almost all record linkages are subject to regulation by the DIB. The social welfare agencies have pressed for linkages in order to compare the income that individuals have declared for tax purposes and to be eligible for welfare benefits. Freese took a strong stand against the linking of these two files, even for socially useful purposes such as catching welfare cheaters.[29] This is not to suggest the DIB is always successful. For example, the taxation authorities are seeking all available automated data held by banks on income from interest and on dividends received by individuals. When the banks asked the DIB if this was possible under their license from the DIB, the latter said no, but the banks gave the personal information to the tax authorities anyway. The DIB sought to prosecute the banks under the Data Act, but the case was dropped by the prosecutor assigned to the case. The highest level of state prosecutor is now deciding whether this was a legitimate decision. The tax authorities would like to create a taxation system based on automated access to existing administrative data bases in the private sector. They want to avoid licensing by the DIB, which resists the creation of a society in which individuals are even more controlled.

In the Swedish system of data protection, the ultimate resolution of such a clash of interests has to be made by the government; but, like most of the other countries treated in this volume, Sweden has a system in which the privacy interests of individuals are articulated by the Data Inspection Board during such a process. Thus debates about record linkages are not likely to cease, because of administrative enthusiasm for enhanced surveillance.

The Political Climate and the Use of Power

The exercise of its jurisdiction naturally involves the DIB in the use of power, but there are contrasting points of view about how well it has exercised this function. The research community has argued that the DIB is too powerful and interfering. Foreign observers also tend to regard the powers of the DIB as quite extraordinary. Kerstin Aner, a member of the Liberal party in the Riksdag, replies that "Americans don't understand how we can give so much power to an agency. . . . But to us, it is still quite natural to trust government." She added that, in any event, "everything has to be licensed in Sweden, even the shooting of elks."[30]

In contrast to assertions of the great power of the DIB is the view that it has no real power beyond its advisory functions and what the government allows it to do. Although the staff of the DIB believes that it needs power to protect ordinary citizens in a highly regulated society, some argue that it is simply a tiny outfit that can only send out minor challenges toward a variety of targets. Much more so than Freese, the staff was inclined to the view that the DIB is relatively weak, especially in the face of evolving technology. One can point to its seeming reluctance to confront the most politically entrenched agencies of government, such as the police, the welfare authorities, or the national tax agency, at least during the 1970s.[31]

A technical adviser to the DIB is of the opinion that lawyers who write laws like the Data Act do not understand information systems. Thus the statute is outdated in terms of technical reality. In his view, data protection acts can only furnish data processors with guidelines and new ways of thinking about the need for data protection, and it is impossible for the DIB to control what is really happening. Although overstated, this argument has considerable relevance to any overall evaluation of the capacity of all data protectors to limit surveillance.

Freese rejected assertions of weakness out of hand. In his view, the evidence is that the DIB does its job well, even if a dark sector exists that generally escapes regulation. Freese certainly acted in an independent manner. He was fearless about criticizing the government or a particular ministry about government decisions on proposed record linkages that went against the recommendations of the DIB. He appeared unconcerned about his enemies at the highest political levels or the risks of being overturned on appeal. He cultivated his own friends in the legislature and in the ministries. He tended to take the optimistic view, contrary to that of his staff (which in his view needed encouragement), that the hostile political climate was not a real problem. By way of illustration, he correctly viewed the concern with economic crime as a cyclical matter.

The difficulty in writing about the DIB is to describe its function in implementing the principles of data protection without exaggerating its power. As an agency with broad oversight responsibilities for information-handling activities in both the public and private sectors, in a society where the two are subtly and directly intertwined, the DIB is much in the public eye, influential and powerful. Contrary to many other Swedish boards, but very much like its counterparts in other countries, its work touches every segment of public administration. The DIB under Freese played a heady role for more than a decade but, under new leadership, it now treads somewhat more carefully to avoid major conflicts with the Cabinet and the Social Democratic members of the Riksdag. As in France, some of the novelty of data protection has worn off, even if the society has succeeded in creating an oversight mechanism for ensuring that privacy interests are publicly identified and debated. The Social Democrats have reestablished their traditional dominance over political life and are unlikely to tolerate what may be perceived as continued obstructionism by the DIB of major government initiatives. The departure of Freese in 1986 had something to do with this general political situation. The Social Democrats created the DIB, but the agency has less influence with the current government than its conservative predecessor, because of the individualistic advocacy role it has adopted in the face of massive surveillance. Börjesson's view is that conflict is not good for the DIB in the long run and that it is contrary to the Swedish way of doing business; yet conflict may be an integral part of successful data protection.

Fortunately, the government's options for controlling the DIB are somewhat limited. It could not actually remove Freese, nor alter the core budget of the DIB, so long as it attempts to become self-financing as required by the revised Data Act. Budget shortfalls at the end of Freese's term strengthened the government's hand over such matters as financing a new computer system for the office and renting new premises, which in fact led him and many of his senior staff to seek new careers. The government could also change the members of the board itself. It could also revise the Data Act again or, more likely, continue to overturn specific DIB decisions on appeal. Since Freese remains an effective publicist with ready access to the press, and the public remains concerned about the social impact of automation, none of these options is very palatable for the government.

Since 1982, data protection has been in a more perilous political position in Sweden than in any of the other countries treated in this volume, but the DIB is managing to do its work. It is well enough known that the government does not want to risk an ongoing confrontation. The government was also relatively careful on data protection issues, because of the risk of having privacy protection become an election issue in 1985. Thus public opinion is in fact forcing the government to act somewhat prudently in its surveillance practices.

The changing political climate is the primary issue affecting the exercise of power by the DIB, as in all of the countries examined in this volume. As noted earlier, the argument is that the political climate in the 1980s has swung away from an interest in data protection to concern about other societal problems. All political parties supported data protection during the 1970s, but this consensus began to break up even before the return of the Social Democrats to power in 1982, because of hard economic times. In the 1980s the Social Democrats and Conservatives have spent more time discussing deregulation, decentralization, and freedom.

At issue is whether the DIB must adjust to the changing political climate. Does it only have the power that the government grants it? Can data protection only be strong when the government and the legislature are strongly supportive? Freese's departure made these concerns even more compelling.

The best illustration of how the changing political climate can affect data protection was the major concern of the Social Democrats with what is called "economic crime."[32] It was one of two major issues targeted for action, the other being control of narcotics. A three-member Commission against Economic Crime, appointed after the 1982 elections, reported in 1984. Hans Corell of the Ministry of Justice pointed out that such concern with tax evasion and economic crime leads to "an increasing need for society to control citizens" and "a somewhat different attitude towards privacy protection."[33] This has resulted in the government's demand for more and more data on personnel, clients, and related matters, so that surveillance could be carried out. The commission proposed more than thirty changes to legislation to combat economic criminality and sought to promote cooperation among authorities for enforcement. Since the goal was increased control of behavior, it had clear negative implications for data protection, but the thrust was short-lived.

Although much of the debate over economic crime dealt with rhetoric rather than current practices, the DIB has continued to take a strong stand against the record linkages that it disapproves. Freese especially singled out linkages for purposes of controlling economic crime, which made him unpopular with Social Democrats; he fears an even more regimented society. At least certain members of the board of the DIB and leading staff members are of the opinion that the climate for the implementation of data protection had become negative, because of these Social Democratic initiatives and because the government tended to rule against the DIB's position in appeals based on issues of record linkage.

Hans Corell gave an insightful overview of the problems of data protection in 1984 in language that linked him to Freese's positions. He described the pressures to engage in file matching for purposes of control and the accompanying risks to the interests of individuals, because of problems with data quality, when information is used for purposes for which it was not collected: "There is an urgent need to try in every way possible to avoid the dangers to privacy inherent in this technique. In my opinion, it is doubtful whether the method should be allowed to the extent now practised."[34] He noted a proposal in Sweden to ban all matches not specifically sanctioned by law.

Corell commented that, given the current economic and political climate, the trend toward more matching of divergent files will be difficult to resist: "The decision is of a political nature, and in the discussion it is always more difficult to attract an interest for the elusive concept of protection of privacy against the declarations by administrators and technicians that large gains in rationality will be made, if this method is used." He emphasized the need for routines to allow individuals to correct files. Corell seems to favor a system of requiring permission from some kind of authority, such as the DIB, for each data match, because this allows a productive exchange between the user and the regulator. On the other hand, he recognizes that this authority "may be entrusted with issues of discretion that really should be solved politically."[35]

The real problem illustrated in this statement and in the general Swedish experience is that the government and the legislature in any country do not have the expertise or the time to make the detailed decisions required for effective data protection; their instinctive predilection is for more surveillance. Corell's informed judgment is that conflict between a data protection agency and the government should simply be viewed as part of the system of balancing competing values. In his view, domestic data protection authorities constitute a "balancing element in a debate which would otherwise perhaps deal too much with efficiency and rationality only."[36]

Chapter *10*

The Implementation of Data Protection

Effective implementation is a key factor in the successful conduct of data protection. Thus this chapter pays considerable attention to the activities of the Data Inspection Board (DIB) since the enactment of the Data Act in 1973. What approaches has it used in trying to limit governmental surveillance practices and with what success? Special notice is paid to staffing, since the choice of people is so critical to this effort. There is also extensive discussion of the various activities of data protectors as they seek to accomplish their statutory tasks. Finally, the chapter treats how data protection principles have evolved in practice.

The Staff of the Data Inspection Board

The Director General

The director general is both the administrative head of the DIB and the chair of the eleven-member board. He or she is expected to have a legal and judicial background, as was the case with the first two incumbents. The position is not designed for a political appointment, as is the practice in comparable top positions. The director general is classified as a civil servant. The director general is well paid in order to reduce the financial incentive to change positions within government and to increase stability in the position. Yet senior management positions in the private sector continue to be more lucrative, as evidenced by Claes-Goran Källner's departure in 1977 and Jan Freese's in 1986.

The approach of the director general significantly influences the operation of the DIB. In particular, his or her political ideology and career experience affects the definition of appropriate balance between individual rights and societal surveillance. Although he was accustomed to downplaying his role, Freese has clearly been the most important single influence on the development and implementation of data protection. He exercised a significant personal and intellectual influence on the work of the board and the staff because of the force of his personality, his understanding of the subject matter, and his energetic conception of the position. Freese is very willing to take strong public positions on matters affecting data protection.

Although it is difficult to define Freese's political views in terms of an ideological spectrum, he appears to hold strongly conservative views, at least in the context of a prevailing commitment to social democracy, although, from an international perspective, it might be more meaningful to describe his political views as libertarian in character. As such, he is strongly opposed to the centralization of information systems, either in terms of their location in Stockholm or in terms of building up single, large data banks.[1]

Freese claims that his political views are known to no one else, a position echoed by his successor. Although he regularly states his opinions publicly on issues that have political implications, as director general of the DIB he regarded himself as not involved in politics. Politicians and the general public had some trouble in making such subtle distinctions about a man who remained very much in the public eye and who articulated a philosophy of individualism in a highly ordered society.

Freese further tends to be a considerable alarmist about the challenges to personal privacy, which shaped his approach to implementation: "Few things are eternal. Privacy can easily be lost, and one does not really miss it before it has been abolished."[2] In a 1981 speech Freese better explained the need for controlling surveillance: "An individual is usually looked upon as a free prey, whom the authorities may register because of social reasons as he is a citizen, or whom private business wants to register because he may be a client. . . . The information is moved from one end of society to another and lots of files are linked to each other [creating new information] without giving citizens a fair chance to find out: who knows what about me, when and why! And remember that one of the important differences between man and computer is that the computer never forgets."[3] Freese has been quoted as saying that "as a member of a community, one must be prepared to accept a certain amount of intrusion. . . . The protection of personal privacy is therefore restricted to what can be considered improper."[4] Thus he publicly stated his unwillingness to allow expansive record linkages, even if the purpose was catching welfare cheaters: "The road to 1984 is paved with good intentions. Besides that, you can't compare apples and pears—two data banks could have different rules for collection, and that can affect the quality of information."[5]

Freese's high-profile approach was important for attracting public support and discouraging certain bureaucrats and politicians from challenging him. His ideas on data protection and on the impact of computers on society regularly appeared in the media, and he is well known among the general public for these activities, much more so than his counterparts in other large countries. His position as director general did not limit his freedom to express himself on all kinds of issues. He is well informed about the latest technological developments in computers, informatics, and data communications. One of his favorite themes, which exemplifies his expansive view of relevant issues, is the need to simplify bureaucracy, because "information athletes" unconsciously use computers to abuse citizens. Freese argues with a beguiling simplicity, which his critics call vagueness: in his view, for example, there is simply no conflict between efficiency and privacy; as rational goals, they are not always in collision.

Freese's DIB was a data protection agency dominated by one person. He is articulate, thoughtful, self-assured, persuasive, and calm in the face of controversy; he can even be demagogic and something of a guru in his pronouncements on the world around him.[6] His simple style of communication makes him very appealing for the media. He handled all of the most interesting problems that surfaced at the board. Yet Freese is also an insider and political fixer who knows how to operate in the intimate corridors of power in Stockholm. For all of these reasons, Freese anticipates one of the major conclusions of this volume in illustrating the importance of personality and a capacity for public relations in trying to make data protection effective. The process has been much better for his continued presence, and the effort to control surveillance could become much weaker in his absence.

Freese's successor, Mats Börjesson, is quite a different person. Like Baumann in Germany, he took the appointment as director general as the final step in a long government career. Imposing administrative order on the DIB, including the reduction of backlogs in licensing decisions, is his forte. He recruited three specialists in data processing and upgraded staff positions to attract persons with more experience. Despite introducing a series of radical administrative changes at the DIB, Börjesson favors a low-key, cooperative approach to the control of surveillance, quite comparable to Baumann in West Germany. For example, as a watchdog, he prefers to guide government agencies rather than to bark and bite. His view is that the task of the DIB is to produce some acceptable solutions to surveillance problems, and he is optimistic about finding them.

Staff Training and Approaches

All of the staff members of the DIB are in effect civil servants with typical lifetime tenure, unless the government were to abolish the agency or reduce its numbers. The staff are employed by the DIB as an independent entity. Thus, in contrast with one view of the West German situation, their futures are not directly at stake as they actively implement the Data Act. A problematic consequence is that the original staff was together too long; there has been less job mobility than in the other countries studied in this volume. One purpose of the 1983 office reorganization was to reinvigorate the staff, but this only occurred in 1985–86 with wholesale departures.

Except for the departure of the first director general in 1977, the group of senior executives responsible for the daily operation of the DIB largely remained intact from the beginnings in 1974 until Freese and Nils Rydén, the deputy director, left in 1986. The lack of new blood from outside appointments, coupled with promotion from within, contributed to the routinization of implementation and an absence of fresh perspectives. This core group included Freese, Rydén, and Thomas Osvald, who specializes in supervision and security issues. Rydén, a jurist, formerly worked on information systems for the police and for the Criminal Board. Osvald originally was a systems representative for IBM and a systems expert with the Swedish Agency for Administrative Development, which furnished him with a background in data processing.

The latter point is important, given the ongoing concern that the DIB lacks personnel with adequate technical understanding of electronic data processing. The lack of training to converse with technocrats is the critical issue. Although it is difficult to recruit such specialists for an agency like the DIB, Börjesson now has two staff members with technical training.

Most of the professional staff of the DIB continue to be persons trained initially in law. Their on-the-job training has focused on data protection and information technology, with some exposure to computers, on the assumption that implementation of the Data Act requires persons trained in regulatory activities. They attempt to control the free hand that technicians and technologists have enjoyed for so long in designing information systems. Nevertheless, the lack of high-level staff training in data processing may become more significant under the 1982 revisions to the Data Act, which were designed to increase the amount of time devoted to supervision and inspection.

An important characteristic of the DIB staff is the sharing of expertise. Although the organization plan is typically hierarchical and rigid, such a design is primarily meant for outsiders, so that they will know whom to approach in a particular case. In practice, the experts in the different sections offer advice to one another according to their areas of training or current specialization.[7] The degree of continuity in the staff meant that employees developed considerable collective and personal expertise in various facets of data protection.

The shared concern for the interests at stake also stimulates a strong staff commitment to the control of surveillance. At least under Freese, the staff perceived themselves as the guardians of privacy; other interests in society should be protected and represented in other ways. Despite Freese's emphasis on the constructive approach to regulation, there is perhaps less of a tendency in Sweden than in West Germany to try to balance competing interests internally. The staff defend their approach by suggesting that for too long technocrats have been controlling society, because no one understood what they were doing. Consequently, it is now appropriate for lawyers to implement data protection through the DIB.

The staff of the DIB take a very collegial and low-key approach to their work. The process of consensus building begins by each section of each department, and each department as a whole, meeting weekly to discuss progress on various matters and new problems that have arisen. Freese claimed to encourage dissent among his professional staff, but, in fact, this occurred very rarely, perhaps indicating the influence of an aggressive director general, and perhaps reflecting the esprit de corps that developed from stable, long-term professional associations.

Some staff debates do occur over the place of a person's politics and ideology in the work of the DIB. The consensus model works better for the private sector than the public sector, where more competing interests are at work. There are adherents of sole reliance upon the language, inadequate as it is, of the Data Act. But there is also a highly developed strain of individualism as opposed to collectivism. Even more so than in other countries, Swedish data protectors view themselves as defending the rights of the individual against big government. Only a tiny minority at the DIB under Freese held the view that privacy should give way to collective interest as articulated by the government. Data protection is thus a central component of concern for individual rights in a controlled society.

Bureaucratic Tendencies

In terms of its size and costs, the DIB has avoided expansionist tendencies. This is a matter of pride and a result of conscious effort. As Freese stated, "We have tried to avoid bureaucracy—and I have reason to believe that we have been rather successful. We have tried to concentrate on advising and there are rather a lot of responsible keepers of personal files who have been able to use cheaper and better routines in spite of our demands for privacy protection. It is important to see that privacy must not always cost very much."[8] Critics did not accuse Freese of an overexpansion of the work of the DIB, because it tried to stick to its original task of protecting privacy.

The antibureaucratic tendencies of the DIB are evident in the 1982 revisions to the Data Act. Prior to then, amendments proposed by the DIB, intended to reduce the amount of ritualistic and formalistic licensing, were hesitantly received, in fear that it would appear to be an effort to weaken data protection. The Swedish and Norwegian experience with systems of universal licensing of personal registers has shown that an enormous burden of routine work often results. The revisions, which streamline the licensing scheme, had the direct benefit of reducing the burden on the bureaucrats themselves.

The report of the Parliamentary Commission on Revision of the Data Act (DALK) attempted to indicate what an appropriate level of involvement was, while emphasizing the importance of avoiding excessive bureaucratization; any revised legislation "should involve no greater interference in public or private activities than is clearly warranted, with regard to the desire to defend the personal privacy of the citizen."[9] Even this wording, however, indicates that the final determination of the appropriate level of regulation was largely left to the decision of the DIB until the 1982 revisions. Yet, unlike the situation in West Germany, the DIB does have an advisory board to provide guidance on such matters from outside the bureaucratic perspective.

Even with the recent revisions, the DIB remains highly bureaucratic in practice. The amount of routine work imposed on the small staff has created serious impediments to effective controls on surveillance. Other problems tending toward routinization include low salaries in comparison to the private sector (which affects the quality of staff that can be recruited), lack of funds for staff education and to carry out audits, and the requirement to act as a debt collection agency in order to become self-financing. All these factors led to the demoralization of Freese's staff, which in turn deadened initiative and aggressive activism. Börjesson has been tackling these problems directly.

Since data protection agencies have usually been the first of the defense measures erected by national governments in the rush toward an information society, there is an inevitable risk that a data protection agency will ultimately become involved in every aspect of this process. The tendency is toward an expansion of data protection activities. Freese himself does not want the DIB to be engrossed in all aspects of computers and informatics; he regards it as an alarm signal and forecaster of future trends but inappropriate to deal with everything.

The DIB's Operational Tools

Statutory Duties

Licensing has traditionally been the main activity of the DIB. The forecast in the early 1970s was that it would have to license a total of 5,000 personal registers and that some 800 new registers would be created each year. By 1981 the DIB in fact had licensed 33,000 personal registers, and there were 4,000 requests each year for new or amended licenses.[10] Although there were some initial delays in the issuance of licenses, by 1982 all of the major information systems had been regulated.

The burden of licensing has been such that the DIB quickly moved toward the adoption of a "standard operating procedure" and, eventually, a four-page application form. The private sector welcomed this simplification. The DIB's finding that more than 80 percent of the applications concerned registers having only marginal implications for the protection of personal privacy encouraged the development of simplified licensing procedures. Nevertheless, the 1978 DALK report noted that even with the simplified procedures, the time-consuming licensing process detracted from the DIB's work on supervision and inspection.[11] The report discussed a reporting procedure to replace the requirement of a formal license: "This should apply to such registers as admittedly exist in large numbers but which manifestly cannot be assumed to involve a risk of undue encroachment on privacy."[12]

The DALK recommendations led to the 1982 revisions. The DIB endorsed this proposal, arguing that the reporting procedure would allow for concentration on surveillance issues.[13] The changes distinguish between a license and permission. All responsible keepers still need to apply for a single license for all of their registers but its receipt is usually automatic with the application. The DIB does not even screen in advance the accuracy of the detailed applications.[14] Certain classes of sensitive information or sensitive uses of data (health, criminality, religious affiliation, and political opinions) require permission prior to establishment of the system. Such permission is also necessary to collect data on individuals without any direct link to the responsible keeper, such as follows from employment, or for procuring data from any other personal file.

Under the Data Act a responsible keeper is anyone for whose purposes a personal file is kept, if the file is at his or her disposal.[15] In the public sector this means that the ministry or agency is the responsible keeper; a particular individual serves only as the contact person with the DIB.[16] Responsible keepers have to ensure that the provisions of the Data Act and their license are implemented.[17] If they cease to keep a file, there is an obligation to notify the DIB, which "shall . . . prescribe what is to be done with the file." Destruction of public records is governed by the National Archives, with whom the DIB acts in consultation. Thus, there is a very important element of self-enforcement in the Data Act.

The quantity of detail required in applications furnishes some sense of the burden data protection imposes on both users and regulators, just as it requires a responsible keeper to consider the implications of any use of data for the privacy interests of individuals. The DIB issues regulations concerning these requests to ensure that the protection of personal privacy is maintained. It can also issue regulations for exempt data banks, if the Cabinet or parliament has not done so.[18] In practice, such precise directives are issued regularly, because the higher authorities only establish the need for an exempt register, wisely relying on the expertise of the DIB to spell out the necessary provisions for data protection. These regulations are issued either at the time of granting a permission (if such a step is necessary) or after an inspection. Because the details of applications for licenses are readily available, the DIB is able to shape its directives to the sensitivity of the data in question.[19]

The DIB thus has substantial power to obtain information about data processing activities. The responsible keeper has to deliver to the DIB "the information concerning the automatic data processing that the board requests for its supervision."[20] The board does not encounter any resistance to this provision, even though proper documentation of information systems is often lacking.

Detailed regulation is also evident in the guidelines on security and documentation of information systems, which the DIB prepared to supplement the general language of the Data Act. Regulations determine that responsible keepers have a duty to protect "the file against unauthorized access, alteration or destruction."[21] Before data processing, keepers have to check that legal authorization exists to order or commission the processing. The responsibility of any person receiving output of such data processing also has to be clear. Over any six-month period, responsible keepers have to be able to furnish an account of the data processing to which a file has been subjected, the identities of the person asking for such data processing, of those who did the programming and who delivered the results to the person who ordered them, and of those receiving the product. These records are "intended to facilitate an exact reconstruction of the data processing which occurred on a particular occasion."[22] This audit trail can be used to identify attempts at unauthorized access to a data base. Requiring such a detailed audit trail is impressive by the standards of any country, but the extent of compliance by data users is uncertain, as the DIB has done little auditing.

The legislature has endowed the DIB with very strong powers to carry out inspections, including "the right of admission to any premises where automatic data processing is carried out or where a computer or equipment or recordings for automatic data processing are kept. The board also has the right of access to documents relating to automatic data processing and may make arrangements for [ordering the] operation of a computer."[23] The DIB initiates inspections in response to complaints from individuals or from staff members doing the licensing, either in the course of processing a request for one, or to verify if the conditions of a license are being met. The DIB sometimes selects a particular sector for intensive inspections. The inspection department also acts upon material it has noticed in the press or reports from friends in data processing and associations of interest groups. Finally, the DIB initiates inspections on a geographic basis in order to affirm its existence and presence. The auditors can check the details of a license application, issue new detailed regulations for the register in question, or alter existing ones.

In almost every instance, the DIB advises the subjects of the investigation in advance. Otherwise the inspectors find that it is a great waste of time while persons in a system look for documentation and information. Sometimes the DIB learns that appropriate documentation does not exist; even less frequently, the responsible personnel are not on the premises, despite advance notice from the DIB. In response to a suggestion that advance notification might lead to quick changes in approach by the keepers, the inspection department notes that the goal of inspection is to change routines in any event. In contrast to the practice in West Germany, the DIB usually seeks to examine a specific point, such as the form of authorizations or logging routines, and does not conduct an overall inspection, unless time permits.

The inspection department of the DIB has conducted up to one hundred inspections each year, but perhaps only one-half of them involved actual visits. Prior to 1982, only three people were doing inspections for the DIB, but, under the 1982 revisions, the organization has increased this number by broadening the responsibility. Most of the effort of inspection has involved public administrations, such as the taxation and police authorities. Generally speaking, the DIB inspectors have encountered frank cooperation. Those being inspected often regard the DIB personnel as individuals committed to improving a system from the point of view of confidentiality and not as menacing agents of a powerful institution.[24]

Media reporting of the results of major DIB inspections has a beneficial effect on compliance. For example, the DIB found that a social service authority in the commune of Stockholm was keeping an illegal data bank concerning the dealings of 300,000 welfare recipients with the authority. In 1979 the DIB had directed it to maintain an audit trail of every transaction for six-month periods; in October 1982 it discovered that no such log was being kept and threatened to remove the permission for maintaining the data base, if a forthcoming inspection did not discover compliance. The press soon carried reports from an official of the DIB that the welfare administration had indeed complied in full with their requirement.[25]

The actual utility of DIB inspections for the control of surveillance is more difficult to assess, not least because they tend to be so infrequent. People question how much it actually knows about what is happening in the processing of personal data. The agency expected to issue 25,000 licenses in the first year under the new Data Act in order to collect the annual licensing fee, but the actual number did not reach 10,000. This lends credence to the view that the DIB is not able to find out in detail if the Data Act is being obeyed. Some observers claim knowledge of data users who have not registered; others point out the impossibility of searching the desks of individuals for small, powerful microcomputers.[26] Yet, for the public sector in particular, there is considerable confidence in the commitment of data processors to compliance with the Data Act. As the earlier comments on Swedish culture indicated, the society as a whole and the civil service in particular are inclined to be law-abiding.

Mats Börjesson, the current director general, is strongly committed to strengthening the DIB's inspections. Using complaints from individuals and information in the media as his prime guides, he contemplates a range of responses to problems that includes reminders or admonitions, regulations, and even reports to the police. Börjesson acknowledges that regularly inspecting 27,000 licenses covering 100,000 files requires new methods of supervision. He also contemplates publishing the results of broad investigations of how the Data Act is working in various sectors in order to inform the public and to improve the DIB's advice on privacy protection.[27]

Section 15 of the Data Act states that the supervision by the DIB "shall be so exercised that it does not cause greater costs or inconvenience than is necessary." Thus the law emphasizes a constructive, pragmatic approach to regulation. The inspection division contends that in a small society the principles of data protection are well understood. It has found few cases of willful noncompliance with the Data Act. If "data criminals" are found, their motive is usually economic and not the invasion of privacy. Penalties have only rarely been imposed after an inspection. Freese emphasized that "the inspection right is limited to making sure that EDP [electronic data processing] does not lead to undue infringement of personal privacy." Nevertheless, "if the DIB is refused admission to premises or access to documents, the responsible keeper may be ordered to pay a fine."[28]

As noted earlier, the inspection function of the DIB has been impeded by limited resources, the continued burden of existing work, and the need to collect unpaid license fees. Some critics have charged that supervision is minimal and that the DIB does not want to find certain breaches of the licensing requirement of the Data Act, since the number of pending applications was always large during the 1970s. The 1982 amendments have not yet made the inspection duties more effective.

Data Registers

Sweden is an exception from the general practice of maintaining a central register of existing data banks. The DIB simply publishes a small booklet, which offers some general information about the Data Act, subject access, and brief information about the most important registers, primarily in the public sector.[29] Unlike Canadian practice, this guide does not attempt to describe the 50,000 extant registers. The DIB is generally skeptical about the utility of actually publishing an inventory or catalog of data bases, because it becomes outdated so quickly. Due to the paperwork involved, the Riksdag rejected the creation of such a register of registers in 1982.[30] The legislature may also be reluctant to document the extent of surveillance that actually takes place.

The DIB's address register of all responsible keepers, however, does provide the index to a comprehensive directory, because data custodians have to keep an up-to-date list of the personal files for which they are responsible.[31] Since an outsider looking for such information can contact the DIB for assistance, the agency should perhaps publicize more fully the availability of its register of responsible keepers and make it available at various locations in the form of printouts. One suspects that few are presently aware that the DIB has such a resource.

The problem of updating information about extant data bases is a serious issue for those countries with licensing or registration schemes. One solution would be an on-line register of data bases that could be updated regularly. The Canadian solution is to provide annual updates. The need is to reduce the resources devoted to what is intended to be an interim goal but not an end in itself. An oversight system requiring notification of each minute change in a register is too bureaucratic.

Individual Access to Data and Complaints

Under section 10 of the Data Act, persons making a written request to a responsible keeper have the right to receive a printout of their data from a file. Such information is free of charge to the individual, unless the DIB allows a fee for "special reasons." In two cases so far, charges were imposed by the Cabinet, and a person requesting printouts more often than once a year may also be charged. These conditions illustrate a desire to reduce the burden on responsible keepers, which is an issue in every country. Yet a citizen has the right to require that a correction be made in a personal register, the responsible keeper has to provide assistance to ensure the changes are made, and the DIB can revoke a particular license if this is not done.[32] An amendment effective January 1, 1988, requires the correction of "misleading" information as well, which is expected to cause trouble for credit information companies. Failure to comply can lead to a suit for personal damages.

The right of access does not apply to exempt registers governed by the Secrecy Act, such as those for police records and, in some individually considered cases, social and medical records.[33] There is no access to criminal history files, but the DIB, like the German federal Data Protection Commissioner, will act as intermediary and check the accuracy of information. Surprisingly, this service has been rarely used. The whole issue of sensitive exempt registers raises serious questions about the utility of subject access as a means of protection for the individual. The DIB can also exempt a particular register if there is no manifest risk of encroachment on privacy.[34] In practice, it has rarely done so.

In 1976 only 20 percent of respondents were aware of their right of access under the Data Act, although by 1984 the number jumped to two-thirds, 10 percent of whom had in fact requested a printout. Those with more education and those under the age of fifty were much more aware of their right and were more likely to have exercised it than those with a primary or secondary school education or aged over fifty.[35]

In general, most organizations have received very few requests from individuals for access to information about them. Freese thinks that people only use these important rights when it appears necessary. They also obtain a great deal of informal access, while others adopt a survivor mentality and do nothing. His perspective suggests that subject access is not used more often because the population sees no need to do so, which has largely proven to be the case in Norway as well. Nevertheless, Freese believes that the right of citizens to see the information in their files has led to improvements in the quality of record keeping, in part because of the penalties for noncompliance imposed by section 20 of the Data Act, and in part because the civil service and the government know that ultimately everything they do is subject to public scrutiny under the principle of openness. All government officials know that public scrutiny is also possible in retrospect.[36] In Freese's view, access rights are simply a part of individual rights in a democratic system.

An aggrieved citizen can complain to the DIB about information handling. The DIB continues to receive more than 500 complaints each year, one-third for each of the three acts it administers. Most are very specific in character and can be solved by a phone call or a letter to the record keeper.[37] Debtors and creditors in particular learn quickly if problems exist in registers affecting them. The staff of the DIB manages such a heavy load, because experienced personnel know who can readily handle the issue in question without extensive background preparation.

Thus the DIB acts as a "data ombudsman," a role that Freese claims is its most important function. In his view "the celebrated 'man on the street' not infrequently runs into difficulties whenever something goes wrong, in which case he may need all the help he can get to achieve that rectification which the services of a 'data ombudsman' can provide. The erroneous information may have spread like ripples on the water to other data processing systems, of whose existence the aggrieved person may not even be aware."[38] Most complaints about information-handling activities, particularly those of public administrations, are now brought to the DIB, which, in describing its handling of complaints, has referred to itself as a "wailing wall" for the general public.[39] Since Börjesson also regards complaints as an important measure of actual invasions of personal privacy, he is surprised that there are more grievances against companies than public authorities, given the tone of the public debate over privacy.

A significant judgment delivered by the Ängelholm district court on December 4, 1981, demonstrates the risks that a responsible keeper runs in maintaining inaccurate information about a person. The issue in the case revolved around section 23 of the Data Act, which permits a person who suffers harm because of incorrect information to sue the responsible keeper. The Housing Department of the municipality of Åstorp determined in 1977 that a couple should receive a housing allowance of a certain amount per month. Based on subsequent tax information, it reduced their housing allowance, demanded compensation for surplus payments, and began a fraud investigation. In 1979 the local taxation authority did a reassessment, and the Housing Department repaid the amount in question in 1980.

The plaintiffs subsequently filed a claim for damages "for mental pain and suffering" and for loss of interest. Evidently the Housing Department had failed to update its records based on the local reassessment. The court concluded, in holding the municipality responsible for damages to the plaintiffs for injuries due to the incorrect information in the file, that "it was incumbent upon the Municipality, as responsible keeper of the file, to give careful consideration to measures taken on the basis of computerized information." According to the court, the plaintiffs were not only very much shocked by the investigation, but they suffered "worry, insomnia and a feeling of disgrace."[40] Although the plaintiffs sought 4,000 Skr in damages, they received only one-sixth of that amount from the court.[41] The case illustrates that the Data Act even seeks to prevent what might be called inaccurate surveillance.

The ultimate problem with subject access is the consequences of exercising this right. A senior official of the Ministry of Justice concluded in 1984 that many persons still experienced difficulties in exercising their rights, because of a reluctance to make necessary corrections in the public administration and a tendency to blame the computer. The individual has to expend a lot of effort to achieve corrections. Hans Corell also believes that increases in the complexity of systems and in the linkage of external files heighten the risks of errors and make it difficult for an individual to detect them.[42]

Public Relations

In arguing for revisions to the Data Act in 1982, the DIB noted that its function of furnishing information to the public had been very much neglected, presumably because of the crush of licensing activities.[43] In the early years the DIB initiated a standard public relations campaign to increase public awareness. A manual on the application of the Data Act, which had several editions, included instructions and recommendations on how to fill out requests for licenses.[44]

Public awareness has been further enhanced by the DIB's policy of making its working records (including investigations) open for public consultation, except for documents declared confidential at the request of the licensee with the agreement of the director general.[45] Copies of the results of the deliberations of the board are also available to the public. Even the salaries of its employees are publicly posted at the DIB, thus giving local evidence of the extent of surveillance of individuals.

Senior staff of the DIB also attempt to raise the consciousness of experts and academics by regularly publishing articles, primarily in data-processing journals. They report on major decisions of the DIB and contribute to the discussions stimulated by study commissions and seminars or by the utilization of certain data.[46]

Although the DIB prepares an annual report of its activities, until 1987 it was not designed or intended for public distribution. This brief report, dealing primarily with finances, has normally been made for budgeting purposes to the Ministry of Justice, of which the DIB is nominally a part. The DIB under Freese was deficient in the kind of annual reporting that has proven to be so useful in promoting implementation and policy review in other countries.[47] Freese finally acknowledged that such a document would improve public awareness, but none appeared until 1987, when Mats Börjesson recognized its utility.[48] He is especially concerned about the public's lack of understanding of the facts of data processing today, which is an implicit criticism of Freese's alarmism: critics accuse him of unnecessarily frightening the public about the use of computers.

Unfortunately, the DIB has not pursued public information services systematically, especially in terms of relations with the media. Yet whatever its institutional deficiencies, it benefited greatly from Freese's particular talents as a publicist. He spent most of his time handling external relations for the DIB, remaining in touch, in person or by telephone, with seventy or eighty other directors general in the public sector, while his deputy ran the daily operations. In a society based overwhelmingly in one central city, Freese has a broad network of contacts. He works well with the media and writes on his own initiative. Freese made no secret of his willingness to appeal to the media when problems arose in data protection, which is a key to successful implementation.

The Cabinet had to be especially aware of this prospect in deciding on appeals from decisions of the DIB.

Data Protection in Practice

From Principles to Practices

As has been suggested, the Data Act devotes more space to spelling out detailed practices and procedures than to enunciating clearly defined, underlying principles. Moreover, since the DIB has primarily made licensing decisions in response to specific applications, it has not paid much attention to broad general principles either, although it is relatively easy to identify the practices that dominate implementation, especially in connection with the public sector.

As noted in Chapter 9, the DIB is generally hostile to linkages of data bases, even within the same information system. One control mechanism to ensure that data are used solely for the purposes for which they were collected is informed consent. For example, early in 1983 the DIB approved an application from an insurance company to use certain files on members of an electrical trade union for linkage purposes, but the decision (which was not unanimous) was in effect negative, since each person registered in the data base would have had to consent to the linkages.[49]

The DIB is further aware of the tendency to develop new uses for licensed information systems. Thus it is wary of authorizing a system of information as such, as opposed to permitting a particular use. The DIB wants to authorize a particular purpose for the file in question, but it is not managing to achieve this, especially in connection with data bases created by the government.

The DIB also pays careful attention to the actual data collected in any single information system. The staff glances at the actual information collected in every application for licensing and identifies "unnatural" details. Since a government agency has to adhere to its statutory mandate, the DIB can question and even prohibit information collection. In its view, the issue of collecting unauthorized information has become less of a problem over time.

Another identifiable DIB practice favors the decentralization of personal registers. This in part explains the extraordinary attention paid to Statistics Sweden during the 1970s. It also accounts for why the DIB would resist a scheme to end all tax frauds, because it would create impossible conditions for people. A number of the staff prefer the development of segregated data bases but recognize that the new distributed and relational data bases counter this wish.

In its 1978 report, DALK identified three areas that are relevant to understanding the practice of data protection by the DIB. It first discussed the question of the examination of the need for a particular register during the licensing procedure.[50] DALK noted that "no guidance is given in the Data Act as to the significance to be ascribed, in examining a license application, to the need for an intended register," except that certain very delicate personal information may only be collected if called for by a strong societal or other public interest. DALK thought that the question of the need for an intended register should be discussed in terms of the "public interest." Although the practice of leaving such decisions to the DIB is flexible, DALK noted that "as regards the balancing of different interests, the Data Inspection Board has powers of decision which, according to the terms of reference, should properly accrue to the legislative assembly."[51] Thus it acknowledged the problems created by the failure to define principles for controlling surveillance adequately in the Data Act.

However, DALK determined that the present system functioned well and should be continued. The result is to leave the DIB as the determiner of "the public interest" in most cases. In one significant area, DALK wished to restrict the power of the DIB by concluding "that decisions concerning the establishment and use of such public personal registers as give a deeper insight into the private circumstances of individual citizens should be made by Parliament or the Government and not left to the public authorities which are to use the registers in their administrative work."[52] Leaving the decision to the parliament or Cabinet should apply to the creation of new registers or to the adaptation of existing registers for new purposes. Again according to DALK, the government and parliament should listen to the DIB's advice, but the final decision should rest with the legislature. The relevant sections of the Data Act were not altered in the 1982 revisions. The fact remains, as DALK recognized, that the significance of the public interest is not closely defined or regulated in the Data Act, leaving the DIB with significant power to control surveillance practices that it disapproves.

A second area of concern about the work of the DIB identified by the DALK Commission involves the definition of "soft data" and other sensitive information. It accepted the definition of soft data as "appraisals of people's family conditions, behaviour, social adjustment, psychic status, educational performance, job performance, etc."[53] DALK correctly concluded that determination of sensitivity must be judged on a case-by-case basis, including not only the kind of information but also the manner of its collection, the purpose of the register, and who has access to the data.[54] It decided that a general definition of soft data, or a general rule as to when sensitive data should be collected, could not be appropriately embodied in the Data Act. DALK approved the "very restrictive attitude" of the DIB toward soft and sensitive data.

Finally, DALK considered the participation of employees in the examination of proposed personal registers.[55] A new Act on Joint Regulation of Working Life required employers and employees in the public and private sectors to negotiate together on various items. DALK concluded that the creation of personal registers could usefully form a part of such negotiations and that the DIB should take account of what the varying parties had con-cluded. The results should not be binding on the DIB, since, for example, different trade union organizations might have contrasting views on the same register: "It must also be the Board's responsibility to ensure that the application of the Data Act is as uniform as possible throughout the country. The Board should thus have the final right of decision on the question as to whether the risk of undue encroachment upon personal privacy exists."[56] Thus one is left with a situation in which the application of the Data Act for the control of surveillance very much depends on the specific practices that the DIB chooses to pursue.

Shaping New Laws and Regulations

The staff members of the DIB are recognized as experts on data protection and related information policy and as such serve regularly as expert consultants on government commissions of inquiry on major issues. In many cases, the DIB does not try to make the final determination by itself (or is not allowed to) but engages in constructive consultations and the writing of government reports. The well-established consultative mechanism guarantees that the DIB has an opportunity to express itself on surveillance practices. From July 1, 1987, to June 30, 1988, the DIB commented on forty-eight legislative proposals that were referred to it. In this sense, it is in a better position to influence data protection at the formative stages of policy-making than its counterparts in other countries, which lack a helpful mechanism for keeping informed. Although mandated by section 2a of the Data Act, politicians' reluctance to take a public stand against data protection interests also motivates such consultations. Moreover, the government must ask the DIB for its opinion before creating new personal registers.

It is indicative of the role of the DIB in shaping new laws and regulations that several senior members of the staff have drawn particular attention to the problem of having a principle of openness that is not adapted to the age of computerized registers and that often conflicts with data protection recommendations. Their sense is that special legislation will be required to restrict openness in certain circumstances. Freese pressed the government to define exactly when an official document is regarded as received, drawn up, or dispatched and thus accessible to the public: "Today there are so many people saying that all information retrievable from a data bank ought to be public, which is going too far." In his (correct) view, Sweden has not yet adjusted the principle of openness to the new information society.

Relations with the Regulated

In small countries such as Sweden, the leading public policymakers are often in contact, congregating in the key city, for one purpose or another.

Geographical and cultural factors facilitate elite accommodation between senior persons involved in data protection and data processing; cooperation and consultation is simply one aspect of professional life. The numerous commissions of inquiry mean that talented individuals often begin their civil service careers as secretaries or consultants to these commissions. Regular encounters continue thereafter as they ascend the hierarchy. For example, the initial DIB foray into the field of police information systems began with a lunch involving the director general of the DIB, the head of the licensing department, and their police contact. Differences of opinion arose, because the law is unclear on certain matters, but the cordial beginning to the relationship meant that problems were sorted out. Because the DIB was also a new authority, its role vis-à-vis the police had to be clarified, leading to very good cooperation, the success of which can be attributed at least in part to elite accommodation.

As protectors of the public interest, the DIB, from another perspective, feels a particular obligation to represent a complaining party on any point and consequently is often in confrontation with large authorities over surveillance practices. Moreover, the inspection specialists consciously try to avoid any suspicion of being involved in a "buddy system" with major authorities or private-sector companies. There will no doubt be some transitional problems now that licensing and inspection are being done, in principle, by the same staff.

The conclusion that emerges from an investigation of the relationships between the DIB and those being regulated is that the actual people concerned in any particular activity, whether licensing or inspection, have a great deal to do with the successful outcome of the endeavor. Experience indicates that the aggressiveness of the DIB's activities is a function of the individuals representing the data protection agency.

However, not all interactions between the DIB and public authorities are inherently confrontational. Each large public agency in Sweden, as in other countries studied in this volume, has at least one contact person on matters affecting data protection. In effect, this person serves as an internal lightning rod for an agency and facilitates cooperation with the DIB by trying to ensure compliance with the Data Act.

Interaction with the DIB has proven to be very useful for some large public systems. The police, for example, have found it very beneficial to have the support of the Data Act, especially in contacts with the mass media. A license from the DIB serves in effect as a seal of approval. In this sense a data protection agency has the indirect effect of legitimizing and expediting the introduction of new technology and new uses for information; ideally, it also plays a central role in trying to limit governmental surveillance.

Chapter *11*

The Regulation of Surveillance Systems

This chapter reviews the impact that the Data Inspection Board (DIB) has had on controlling the practices of certain significant holders of personal data in the public sector and in so doing assesses the relative success of the DIB in controlling governmental surveillance. A central theme is that the preparation of detailed data on each personal register for licensing purposes stimulates responsible keepers to implement fair information practices and hence to reduce unauthorized surveillance. A related argument is the extent to which the DIB, because of powerful competing interests, has been unable to achieve effective control over surveillance in a number of sensitive areas. The following treatment is not comprehensive, because of the complexity of governmental arrangements in some fields, the lack of readily available data, and a redundancy of experience that arises from the DIB's mandatory licensing activities in the public sector from 1973 to 1982. Since these activities have been discussed in some detail in previous chapters, it is only necessary to review the selective results of implementation in order to illustrate various aspects of data protection in practice and to illuminate the problems of actually reducing mass surveillance.

The Police and Criminal Information Systems

The National Swedish Police Board handles the centralized police registers for police information systems in 118 police districts, of which Stockholm is the largest. There are national data bases on police work and criminals, including registers on sentences, arrests, and criminal intelligence. The National Prison Board has similar registers. The National Police Board also maintains a large automated system known as the Judicial Information System, which is used by courts and prosecutors. The other half of the police information systems deals with operational matters.

As in other countries, police data protection began well before the enactment of the Data Act. Two important statutes from the early 1960s incorporate important principles of data protection. The Criminal Record Act regulates a register of inmates that is automated and used by the courts.[1] The Police Record Act governs all police registers. Like the German system, this statute specifies what information the police can collect and who can use it. Some of the police registers share the same information systems but are controlled in terms of who can take information from a particular register. There is no subject access to police registers, in part to protect against third party use of the information. Since no individuals can have access to their criminal records, employers cannot force potential employees to obtain a printout as a condition for getting a job.

Because of these other statutes, the actual impact of the Data Act on police information systems has not been very important, since less needed to be done than in other areas. The DIB has evidently influenced the revision of the relevant police laws. Moreover, the police do discuss plans for new information systems with the DIB. In order to secure standard licenses, they also had to improve the documentation of their own information systems to find out what they were really doing, which had a beneficial impact on their own planning for security. The computer and legal experts of the police now know more about what is happening in their own information systems, which is a normal result of the implementation of data protection. The problem for the DIB has not been lack of access to information concerning the various police systems, but the complexities of the issues involved in their regulation.

The DIB communicates with the police through a specific individual with data protection responsibility at the National Swedish Police Board. From the initiation of the Data Act until late 1981, this person was Hans Wranghult, who subsequently became head of the criminal police for Stockholm. In 1970, when police computer systems were first being set up, the government wanted a legal expert to head the division, especially because of the need to work in compliance with the special police laws. Thus Wranghult was in an excellent position to understand the privacy aspects of the Data Act. He and his associates discussed privacy problems internally before approaching the DIB in order to try to anticipate what might be accepted as reasonable practices.

The DIB has separately licensed approximately twenty-five to thirty police registers. Although it has not been able to control certain police information systems, because they were created by the government, the DIB claims that it has nevertheless exercised significant influence by expressing its views in advance and by retaining the power to supervise and inspect. But since the DIB has done so little auditing, one may question its actual impact on the surveillance aspects of such registers.

The DIB has been willing to question the police carefully, especially when representing a complaining party. It has on occasion asked about the purpose of information kept in police files. It also pursues complaints by individuals concerning information they think the police have about them. Freese said that the DIB could enter police headquarters and check to see that records were being handled properly.[2] The National Police Board lost its challenge to the DIB's right to inspect a district police office without advance notice to the central authority. The DIB regards it as perfectly natural that the police and taxation authorities, for example, are not fully cooperative with the auditing required under the Data Act.[3] Yet Mats Börjesson, the current director general, regards it as perfectly clear that there are no restrictions on the DIB's checking of police records. Indeed, he was planning a major audit of the National Police Board at the end of 1988.

Some of the staff at the DIB believe that the police have been difficult to work with, at least in times past, in part because it is almost impossible to tell them what personal information they should be collecting. It is also suggested that the Secrecy Act makes it difficult to control the contents of police registers. As in other countries, the police were under some initial apprehension about the actual impact of the DIB on law enforcement activities. In general, the DIB and the police seem to have developed a working relationship over time, which in part reflects a positive societal attitude toward policing.[4] However, critics from the mass media argue the need to watch the police in order to avoid the risks of a police state.

There has been recent discussion of police methods of investigation because of some problems with wiretapping. So at least in the media, certain questions are now raised about whether the Swedes can really trust their police. In 1984 an off-duty policeman in a provincial town checked police data files to see whether a prospective lodger in his mother's flat had a criminal record. He was found guilty of a violation of the Data Act and his obligation of professional secrecy as a policeman. The Court of Criminal Appeals upheld his conviction and fine.[5]

The National Tax Board

In the early 1980s Freese had a number of public conflicts with the tax authorities about the methods of preventing so-called economic crime. In his view, bureaucracy in the tax system must be simplified, since it is the complexity of the laws that encourages evasion. The Swedish Enforcement Service, a unit of the National Tax Board, has a staff of 3,000 persons operating out of 81 local offices, which offers some sense of the magnitude of the task facing the DIB in attempting to supervise this single activity. Furthermore, Eric Hallman, deputy director of the Tax Board, has offered useful insights into the climate for data protection in this field. His premise is that individuals today care more for their rights than their obligations to society: "That's why the representatives of the Society have to use control, coercive measures and sometimes penalties. From this background I understand that the individual can feel the threat of undue infringement of personal integrity."[6] The pressures for broad surveillance are thus clearly stated.

The automated register for the Enforcement Service has already converted manual files for more than 50 percent of the population. Not all of the manual files could be converted, because, Hallman explained, "there were too many notes which without doubt were of such a kind that they could cause undue infringement of privacy. It could be remarks like 'alcoholic,' 'work shy,' 'welfare case,' etc." In this instance automation has purged some soft data, because the DIB had to approve each item for inclusion in the new register and also issued directions about the purposes for which it could be used. While Hallman acknowledged the advantages of automation for controlling the contents and uses of files, he also remarked on an inclination to keep additional comments on people in paper files, which are not subject to the jurisdiction of the DIB. This type of surveillance problem is of serious concern in countries that exempt manual records from data protection.

Hallman's presentation revealed the extraordinary range of registers accessible, sometimes on-line, to the local tax enforcement offices.[7] In his view, such indirect collection facilitates accuracy and should occur as much as possible in an on-line mode in order to facilitate the exchange of needed information among authorities. Thus tax enforcers do their investigative work in other data banks, because they are so readily available, far more so than in any other country studied in this volume. In drawing up a balance of competing interests, Hallman strongly articulated the case for enforcing the tax laws by using all available personal data. Tax returns can be audited by linking together various registers, and persons that evade or avoid taxes can be located. Such conditions allow Sweden to be characterized as a surveillance society. The public's tolerant attitude is influenced by the fact that everyone's net income and tax deductions are public information; thus there is not even a tradition of secrecy for most tax data, which other countries treat as confidential.

The DIB has real problems in trying to control the flow of data from banks to the tax enforcers. As mentioned previously, when it ruled that the banks' licenses forbade such data transfers, banks provided the information anyway. The DIB tried to prosecute, but a prosecutor dropped the case, a decision confirmed by the attorney general, because the tax laws were unclear. Börjesson acknowledges that public prosecutors find it difficult to prosecute for crimes against the Data Act, because they have little experience with computers and need to be educated. He has not yet had enough experience to know whether this unwillingness to prosecute will prove to be a problem for the DIB.

For its part, the National Tax Board wants to rely increasingly on automated access to other registers to operate a tax system depending primarily upon extant data bases rather than self-reporting. The tax authorities sometimes see no reason why they should be licensed or supervised by the DIB. Freese, for his part, could not rely solely upon his data quality argument to resist such linkages and has to talk, in what can only be described as realistic terms, about the risks of a "controlled society."

More recently, the minister of finance proposed an amendment to the Tax Assessment Act, whereby his auditors, using computers, would have unrestricted access to automated personal data at an organization or company. The DIB, under Mats Börjesson, secured a special act to cover such tax audits, which specifies that the "scrutiny of personal registers may not lead to unauthorised encroachment on the personal privacy of a registered individual."[8] This brief law effectively asserts the primacy of the Data Act over a specialized form of computer surveillance of individuals and, moreover, authorizes the DIB to issue detailed regulations on compliance (which it did on August 25, 1988). These required the balancing of some strongly competing interests, including restrictions on the right to use information obtained on third parties for further audits. Börjesson has secured a significant victory for data protection of the sort that his West German colleagues have been finding difficult to achieve in recent years.

The divergent perspectives on privacy protection of the DIB and the Tax Board create serious problems in balancing their respective interests. Hallman ultimately takes refuge in the fact that the legislature imposes the burden on enforcement offices of carrying out detailed investigations in different registers and, of course, it is the legislature that sets the ultimate balance. This creates serious problems for the DIB, since its ability to influence the Riksdag against surveillance is often much less than that of a large administrative body like the Tax Board.

The Social Democrats' announcement of major tax reforms at the end of 1988 could be a two-edged sword for data protection. Although abolition of state income taxes for all but the top 10 percent of wage earners would remove most taxpayers from these rolls, they will still be subject to municipal income taxes, which the National Tax Board administers in cooperation with local tax authorities. An even more careful surveillance system will also have to be in place to monitor the well-to-do, since the government wants to outlaw methods that individuals and corporations use to beat the existing tax system.[9]

Personal Identification Numbers

As discussed in Chapter 7, Personal Identification Numbers (PINs) serve as unique identifiers for all residents. Because of the extent to which PINs facilitate record linkages and because "people should not be thought of as numbers," Freese sought to restrict their use.[10] The real dilemma is deciding whether the benefits of the numbers offset the extent to which they facilitate extensive surveillance. PINs are in fact critical to the success of a surveillance society.

In 1978 the Parliamentary Commission on Revision of the Data Act (DALK) focused on "the risks of undue encroachment upon personal privacy through data, originally collected for one purpose, being later used for other purposes which were not planned from the outset."[11] DALK finally rejected the view that the use of PIN should be restricted in order to limit the possibilities of record linkages, since this would only temporarily restrict the linking of registers. The difficulties of working without PINs would soon be overcome. DALK recognized the need to be able to identify each registered individual and to link registers. In fact, DALK emphasized the practical difficulties and transitional costs that would arise if PINs were abolished. In its view, the problem of unique identification would itself pose increased risks for personal privacy.[12] Since other countries have vigorously opposed the introduction of PINs on grounds of concern for personal privacy, it is unusual, to say the least, to find PINs being advocated as a protective measure.

DALK proposed restrictions on the circumstances under which an identity number should be required. It recommended the vague standard to the DIB that an individual should only be asked to provide his identity number when needed. DALK noted further that both the public and private sectors were using the PIN to link registers "in order to check the correctness of particulars submitted by the individual in a different context."[13] In this statement DALK itself came very close to advocating the kind of record matching that has aroused considerable anxieties in the United States.

Although DALK realized that questions concerning the use of PINs and the rights of the individual involved a number of conflicting interests, both the government and the Riksdag had emphasized the need for uniformity and justice concerning means-tested benefits: "With the need for control there follows inevitably the corresponding renunciation of the demand for protection of personal privacy. But everybody would appear to agree that the need for control cannot justify taking this renunciation to undue lengths. On the other hand, the defense of personal privacy must not assume such forms that, rightly or unrightly, it is looked upon as striving to prevent the control which most citizens, especially in their capacity as taxpayers, feel to be urgent and necessary."[14] Such language is a classic Social Democratic justification for the creation of a surveillance state in Sweden.

DALK concluded that a final balancing of conflicting interests could not be established solely through a rule in the Data Act. Parliament, not the DIB, should determine the types of controls on individuals that should exist for taxation and means-tested benefits: "Otherwise it may be foreseen that, on account of the constantly growing computerization, the [Data Inspection] Board will increasingly have to decide on requests, on economic grounds among others, for permission to use registers for various other rational purposes than those for which they were originally set up."[15] This statement flew in the face of the DIB's aspirations and, indeed, its statutory obligations. A significant conflict exists between asking parliament to make continuing determinations on such matters and the role of the DIB under the Data Act.

While the Data Act does not even mention the Personal Identification Number, the DIB continues to receive complaints about its use.[16] There is no information system in which PINs are not used as unique identifiers, since there is no incentive requirement, as in North America, for organizations to develop their own filing numbers for persons. The PIN is always being adapted for new uses, such as a recent introduction of the encoded number on each person's driver's license. This occurred as all such licenses, which are valid for ten years, were being renewed. The motor vehicle bureau claims that the government approved the practice, but it was not cleared with the DIB in advance. The latter held its fire on this particular point, until the Riksdag had finished its work on this specific measure. This illustrates how important it is for the DIB, and its counterparts in other countries, to know when to intervene in the case of a new application of surveillance in order to be effective. Given the burden of daily work, being able to choose its current target is both a necessity and a political opportunity; it is also a sign of ultimate weakness.

The DIB also has to accept the fact that PINs are already pervasive in important systems in the private sector. Bank checks, for example, have PINs on them. At the same time, the DIB realizes that it will only be a matter of time before someone dreams up new uses for the PINs on drivers' licenses. It is very difficult for a data protection agency to try to limit the uses of unique personal identifiers once they exist in a society.

The use of the Personal Identification Number remains a partisan political issue. In 1984, a leader of the Moderate party gave a speech about the need to reduce the use of the PIN as part of his party's call for more freedom in society. This led to renewed media attention to PINs and illustrates how opposition politicians searching for an issue regularly stimulate the privacy debate in various countries. In what was effectively a way to postpone decision making until after the national elections in 1985, the government appointed a Commission on Data Protection and the Principle of Publicity to consider the possibility of restricting the uses of the PIN. In 1987 it made proposals to limit unauthorized uses of the numbers, either by an act forbidding the use of PINs or by an amendment to the Data Act to restrict their use. At the beginning of 1989, the minister of justice had not yet announced a decision. Realistically, there seems little likelihood that the use of the PIN will be cut back dramatically, because of the significant costs this would entail.[17] Perhaps the government will try to curtail certain private-sector uses of the PIN, such as on credit cards, along the lines of the Canadian parliamentary committee's 1987 recommendations to control the Social Insurance Number.

The commission will also have to come to grips with the fact that the population has developed a remarkable tolerance for the use of the civil registration number (as it is sometimes called). An interview survey in 1984 found that 82 percent of respondents had never found it unpleasant to submit their PIN and had not been bothered by the practice. Only 39 percent had found it unnecessary on occasion to submit the number, and 90 percent had never refused to do so. Unease and refusals occurred in the context of commercial contacts, such as with mail-order firms, but rarely in contacts with government agencies.[18] Thus Swedes are accustomed to living in a surveillance society, reflecting the normative power of the actual. It is also evident that the DIB has had only marginal impact on this surveillance issue.

The National Register of Names and Addresses (SPAR)

One of the most peculiar developments affecting data protection was the creation by the Riksdag in 1976, with the encouragement of the DIB, of a central national register of names and addresses known as SPAR.[19] It was initially maintained by the Computer Center for Administrative Data Processing (DAFA). The idea behind SPAR, from the perspective of the DIB and DALK, was to restrict the proliferation of private registers containing the entire population, to enhance privacy protection, and to reduce the vulnerability of society. For example, DALK referred to restrictions on the use of personal information for direct mail marketing purposes.[20] Paradoxically, this innovation has further enhanced the capabilities of a surveillance society, because it is in effect a national data bank.

Sections 26 though 28 of the revised Data Act regulate SPAR. Public authorities and individuals may use it for "updating, supplementation and checking of data and other personal files, supplementation and checking of data in general, and taking of samples of personal data (sampling)."[21] Personal information included in SPAR can be collected from post office records and state personal files used for national registration, income tax assessments, and assessments for tax on real property.[22] An individual may include a notation in these records that direct mail advertising is not wanted. The idea is that persons seeking certain personal information for legitimate purposes should obtain it from SPAR rather than elsewhere. However, public authorities whose responsibilities are confined to a particular county may use the data bases of the county administrative board instead of SPAR. The government or the DIB, at the direction of the government, "may direct that the personal file of a government authority may be used by another authority" for the "updating, supplementation and checking of data in other personal files."[23] This supplementary provision further illustrates the wide range of data exchange that facilitates surveillance of the population.

SPAR is truly an extraordinary creation in "data protection." It is as unique an innovation as can be imagined for such purposes, because it is in effect a national population register containing for each person such varied data as name, PIN, address, citizenship, marital status, assessed income, taxable capital, and possession of real property, none of which can be kept confidential in Sweden. The creation of SPAR has had few of the intended benefits for the protection of privacy. For example, private concerns can obtain almost any personal data they wish from it. In 1982 the government permitted the insurance company, Skandia, to obtain data from SPAR concerning the age and income of individuals in order to carry out record linkages with its own files for a commercial campaign. The DIB did not want Skandia to have access to information about family relations, income, and real estate ownership.[24] On appeal, the minister of justice agreed with the DIB. However, the government gave Skandia permission to obtain all of the data it requested from SPAR. The only comment attached to the government decision was that the company could use the information and should therefore be given access to it. SPAR even tries to market its information.

SPAR is not what the DIB had in mind when it supported the idea of a national register of names and addresses. It is in effect the kind of data bank long feared in other countries. The data it contains on civil status, for example, reveal whether a married person is living with his or her spouse. The principle of publicity or openness, and the ubiquitous PIN, makes it relatively easy to enhance the data from SPAR with additional linkages. Its accessibility to the private sector is astonishing.

The DIB now claims that it only made small decisions about the creation of SPAR, which was the work of the government.[25] Ironically, SPAR is a symbol of a form of surveillance other Western countries want to avoid; its existence and use also symbolize the limited power of the DIB in the face of a determined government or legislature.

Statistics and Research

Statistics Sweden

Statistics Sweden (SCB) holds a massive amount of personal information for the entire population. It has more than 150 personal registers; 9 include from 100,000 to 1.2 million persons, and 3 cover from 6 to 8.2 million. The latter is the Central Population Register.[26] The DIB under Freese devoted considerable attention to licensing and supervising these registers.[27] In fact, the SCB is the government agency that has perhaps had the most difficulties in its relationship with the DIB. Although harmonious relationships have ultimately prevailed, largely because of the Swedish search for consensus, the SCB was very much surprised to find itself the target of so much attention after the Data Act went into effect. Like its counterparts in other countries, it took the defensible position that a statistical agency uses personal information in ways that do not directly affect a particular individual.[28]

Yet the SCB ran afoul of certain basic ideas or theories that the DIB enunciated strongly during the 1970s, because it seemed to epitomize the proliferation of personal registers—it does collect and store more personal data than any other agency. The DIB favored decentralization of any type of data processing activity. Freese believes that smaller and cheaper computers are easier to control, which led him to advocate at one point the breaking up of the SCB; he also continues to worry about the huge computer memories of the agency.

The unusual record of strife between the DIB and Statistics Sweden reached something of an apogee in 1983, when government-approved plans for a national census of population led to a national debate, not only in the media, but between Freese and Sten Johansson, a Social Democrat, leading sociologist, and the new head of the SCB. The DIB was reluctant to allow substantial linkages of existing registers to take the census, even for statistical purposes.[29] The measures necessary to implement such a census would have further contributed to the country's reputation as a controlled society. Freese also insisted on levels of informed consent from individuals that would have been difficult and expensive to accomplish. The whole debate was inflamed by Johansson's articulation of his long-held view that the DIB was an unnecessary and burden-some luxury. When the entire issue landed in the lap of the government, it finally decided to undertake a more traditional census.

Although the DIB and SCB generally work out a mutual accommodation of their respective responsibilities, some outstanding issues remain. The SCB wants to prolong the time period for which the statistical agency is permitted to keep primary data on individuals on magnetic tapes. The DIB generally seeks anonymization. There are always problems with DIB permissions for sensitive registers held by the SCB. With respect to a register on alcoholics and drug addicts, the government decided to limit the amounts of data collected and then asked the DIB to reconsider its position on specific items, which led to private discussions with the SCB. When the statistical agency merged their existing registers on the "education of the people," the DIB insisted that one-fifth of those included be notified each year of the contents of this statistical register. The SCB argued that such expensive mailings create new risks to privacy. In response to the SCB's appeal, the government decided that the public only needed general notice of the file. The DIB then determined that Statistics Sweden should inform the public through the mass media about the existence of this educational register and of their rights of access to their own records.

The public displays little understanding of the importance of statistics, which is reflected in continued anxieties about mass surveillance. In its 1984 survey, the SCB found that only 52 percent found it reasonable for the agency to keep computerized personal files, 26 percent found it doubtful, and 20 percent found it unjustified.[30] The ratings for national insurance offices, hospitals, and taxation authorities were much higher. In another SCB survey at the end of 1986, 73 percent answered "yes" or "maybe" when asked whether there is a risk of undue disclosure of personal data from Statistics Sweden.[31]

Statistics Sweden has three persons responsible for assuring compliance with the Data Act. They obtain new licenses and regulations and alter existing ones when necessary. The DIB believes that the SCB has tried hardest among all the organizations it regulates to meet the conditions of the Data Act. Although certain major issues still remain to be solved, cooperation between the two agencies has progressed very satisfactorily. For example, the heads of the two agencies meet regularly for discussions. The overlapping membership of their respective boards has also facilitated the SCB-DIB relationship. Finally, it would help to reassure the general public if the DIB would audit data protection practices at the statistical agency. The development of general regulations for research and statistics would also reduce the burdens of compliance.

The SCB has faced a major financial and administrative burden of replying to requests for access from individuals. There were 67,000 such requests during the first four years.[32] One bizarre consequence is that for the first time the SCB had to organize its registers in such a way that a search could be made of all of them for information on a particular person; a statistical agency (unlike an administrative agency) normally has no reason to search for data on a particular person. Moreover, the agency created a new register for persons who made such requests, as indeed happens in other countries. In 1983 the SCB received 8,000 such requests, the peak since 1976, after the newspaper *Expressen* ran a series of request forms on March 7 under a story about using the right of access to control "Big Brother."[33] Most questioners have been surprised at how little information the SCB has about them. People are unnecessarily frightened by its list of registers, since any particular individual is not in most of them. The SCB is developing a system of one-way encryption of PINs into a new number to be used as a statistical number for sensitive registers, which will have the benefit of rendering the information anonymous. The press reported the SCB's request for a DIB ruling on this practice in 1987 as an attempt to deny individuals' access to their own data (which also led to 25,000 more access requests).

The necessity of a functional separation is the key concept for statisticians to promote, since it mandates a total barrier between administrative and statistical uses of personal information. From this perspective, the SCB has a problem, since its data on individuals are subject to subpoena; even though this has never occurred, it is a remaining weakness in statistical legislation. Parliament requested the government to set up a commission of inquiry on this particular question, and it still possible that the law will be strengthened against such releases, which are not possible in most other countries.

Project Metropolitan

The major Swedish longitudinal register, known as Project Metropolitan, poses special problems for data protection.[34] Until 1986, this project at the University of Stockholm charted certain aspects of the careers of a cohort of 15,000 persons born in the Stockholm area in 1953. Around 1980 the DIB encouraged the principal investigator, Professor Carl-Gunnar Janson, to make one single large application for his project, and then approved everything that they possibly could, except for such items as being allowed to link his data to the next census. One major control imposed was that the linked records had to be anonymized, but a code permitting the unscrambling of the same information could be stored in an archive for possible future use. Janson resisted such anonymization, since it would inhibit future linkages and could presage the end of longitudinal research in Sweden. He was also concerned about an individual from his cohort exercising the right to access his or her file, since it could be very damaging to the person to discover information received from a parent or on other sensitive issues. (It does seem peculiar to allow such access to research records.) A linked record of this type might well reveal more than persons know about themselves, again because of the extraordinary range of data accessible for linkage purposes. Fortunately, Janson developed very strict security practices. Data tapes, for example, have to be signed out and to be hand-carried to and from the computer center. Moreover, his entire data tape has now been anonymized at the insistence of the DIB. Since Project Metropolitan involves an extraordinarily detailed "follow-up" study, its licensing by the DIB represents a high degree of tolerance for the linkage of a large amount of sensitive personal information.

There was some hope that the DIB's imprimatur would reassure the general public. Unfortunately, such a view proved optimistic, since a major public debate over Project Metropolitan broke out in the media in February 1986. At one level, it is an example of a controversy about record linkages fanned by an irresponsible and sensationalistic media. Scare stories that began in the Stockholm press spread across North America as front-page items. Newspapers pontificated about the terrible character of this secret research project.[35] Normally well-informed people cited it in public meetings as an outrageous episode.[36] Informed defenses of Project Metropolitan have had limited circulation.[37] Yet anyone familiar with Swedish data protection is aware that Project Metropolitan has been fully subject, some would argue too subject, to the rigors of the Data Act and the meticulous attention of the Data Inspection Board.[38] How then are we to explain such outbreaks? Political goals, including an irrational and ill-informed resistance to the development of the social sciences, inspired at least some of the negative attention in the media.

Yet one must also acknowledge that Project Metropolitan does raise some significant privacy problems and illustrates the extent of surveillance that is possible in Swedish society. There are very serious problems of obtaining and then maintaining informed consent in such a long-term project, since the researchers do not want to lose members of the sample. The existence of Personal Identification Numbers and the principle of publicity made possible the collection and linkage of an enormous amount of sensitive personal data on the members of this particular cohort. Whatever the quality of data protection that is in place, it is astonishing that one can actually retrieve information on persons booked at police stations who had needle marks in their arms, thus indicating some degree of drug abuse. Such a project would hardly be possible in a country outside Scandinavia. Those born in 1953, who suddenly realized that they belonged to this particular club (including some journalists), were upset. Finally, the debate identified how negatively people in the sample felt about having so much data about them in existence. Freese was quoted in the press to the effect that these people were being "treated like rats in a cage." The public's lack of appreciation of such positivistic research underlay all of these problems.

The controversy over Project Metropolitan suggests that research has its limitations, however desirable in the long term, and that it may no longer be possible to undertake certain kinds of longitudinal or epidemiological research because of the sensitivities of the public. At the very least, decisions about permissible research should not be made solely by researchers or in the media. The hard work of balancing the benefits of such intrusive research versus intrusions on personal privacy needs to be made in the legislative arena with statisticians, researchers, and data protectors advancing their respective points of view. Mats Börjesson emphasizes that researchers have to be open about what they are doing and to explain their work. The DIB is preparing a brochure on how data protection applies to this field.

The huge debate over Project Metropolitan well illustrates the problem of competing social values, which is an on-going aspect of the clash between the preservation of privacy and the automation of information systems. Researchers and statistical agencies have a responsibility to the public to work cooperatively with any data protection agency to increase public awareness, understanding, and protection.

Chapter *12*

Responding to Privacy and Surveillance Problems

This chapter assesses various problems that the Data Inspection Board (DIB) has had with the implementation of the Data Act and discusses how to revise the law to meet the contemporary realities of power relationships and governmental surveillance.

The Achievements and Adequacies of Implementation

The DIB has scored a series of major successes in the implementation of the Data Act. The overall impression within the country is that the DIB has done a good job. It has positively influenced record-keeping practices and has also had a large impact on major public information systems through its licensing activities. Jan Freese claims that data processors have adopted a new philosophy of data processing, not simply a series of new techniques for control. He believes that they now ask themselves why they should collect information and what they should store. Data custodians are more aware of the Data Act and of their own internal need to protect the confidentiality and security of personal information. The contrary argument is that there are real problems with public authorities not properly understanding and applying the Data Act in practice. In fact, the DIB is not even sure how many responsible keepers there are. When Mats Börjesson took office in 1986, his public relations campaign concerning the obligation to apply for a license increased the number of registered file keepers from 17,500 to 26,000, yet he can still wonder how many record keepers exist in the country.[1]

The Data Act contains a self-policing mechanism that mandates the continuing duty of responsible keepers to promote implementation. Unfortunately, despite good intentions, the DIB has not yet devoted adequate attention to the supervision and audit of these data custodians. This is a serious deficiency, since inspections are a prime means of ensuring that mechanisms for surveillance control are in fact being followed.

The DIB's prescriptions for improved security have become widely known and have resulted in the creation of security officers at major public systems. The DIB hopes that press stories about hackers will further promote interest in security. The staff asserts that data-processing professionals have basically accepted their role with modest resistance, in part because the DIB needs only

156

one interested person at each authority in order to have an impact and because it has made only a low level of demands.

Even before the 1982 revisions, Freese was arguing that the Swedish Data Act does not diverge very much in practice from laws in other countries. In his view the licensing system had in fact turned out to be mainly a registration and supervising system. This point is truer for the revised Data Act than its predecessor. The current system of requiring license applications from almost everyone forces custodians to think about their practices with personal data. This process of registration demands a self-examination that is lacking in West Germany and the North American systems. As in other countries, the Data Act has played a critical role in bringing issues of information use to the center stage of public debate for interested parties. In all of these instances, the DIB serves as a continuing source of informed commentary, not least for politicians considering the authorization of more intrusive measures.

Freese remains unhappy about the extent of automated data use, even though the DIB serves as a brake on reckless developments. He now advocates licensing in advance for all systems in the public sector, because one cannot really reverse a direction at a later date; this attitude makes sense in a licensing system.

Freese emphasizes that it is always difficult to measure the positive effects of legislation like the Data Act, and he cannot point to any fantastic list of abuses of personal information that have been avoided, although a small list is possible. He is emphatic about the utility of the DIB's contributions as an ombudsman to citizens in difficulty, especially when errors start to spread "like ripples on the water" to other data systems. Surveillance itself is even worse when it is based on erroneous data. According to Freese, the DIB can also point to continuing successes in limiting what data processors propose to do with personal data.[2] He even anticipated the remote possibility of the Data Act becoming obsolete "on some far-off day when humanity has learned to use the new technology on purely human terms—and not from the viewpoint of what is technically and economically feasible."[3] The prospects for such a nirvana seem remote in the late twentieth century, especially in Sweden.

In 1984, Hans Corell of the Ministry of Justice argued that as the public becomes more familiar with computers, they are likely to regard storage of their data with government agencies, employers, and trade unions as "quite harmless," especially if individuals have consented.[4] It is important to be aware that the trends indicate the opposite. Statistics Sweden found that a majority of respondents in 1984, as opposed to a third in 1976, agreed entirely that government agencies keep an unnecessary number of computerized files. There were across-the-board declines in the willingness of people to allow the transfer of data to various types of institutions for record linkages. Finally, and perhaps most discouraging for data protectors, 40 percent of those surveyed thought that their privacy was less protected today than it was five years ago; only 1 percent thought it was more protected.[5]

Thus the evidence suggests that more and more Swedes, including Jan Freese, recognize that they are living in a surveillance society.[6] Other informed persons, including Mats Börjesson, reject this characterization and conclude that their country has simply drawn a different conclusion about the boundaries of the right to be left alone, which has not been reduced to an unacceptable level. He stresses "that the present situation in Sweden has not been forced upon the Swedish people. On the contrary—it is the result of an unbroken development within the frames of a well established democracy." In his view, only the degree of public acceptance indicates whether surveillance has gone too far, since measuring the adequacy of privacy protection is a subjective matter.[7]

It is worth recapitulating the various problems the DIB faces as it struggles to control surveillance. The word struggle is appropriate for how the staff under Freese viewed events, leading the most experienced among them to leave the agency: they were unhappy at fiscal and budgetary restraints and with the effort to turn them into debt collectors. They sensed that these financial pressures were just another way to sabotage their work. Moreover, the staff members have yet to break the "licensing" mold in which they worked for the first decade. They still find themselves swamped with work because of the large number of automated registers in the public and private sectors that still require attention. The ambition of providing more time for staff members to pursue the critical task of audits and inspections has not yet occurred. At issue is whether a staff of thirty-four persons at the DIB can really make data protection an effective force on an ongoing basis in both the public and private sectors. Its former senior technical officer, Gert Persson, concluded in 1986, on the basis of an extensive career in the public and private sectors, "that it is practically *impossible* today to chart the data input, contents, data output and use of all computerized personal registers in Sweden."[8] The DIB illustrates the risk in all countries of the general public receiving only the illusion of strong data protection.

There are real doubts whether data protection can be made financially self-supporting in both the United Kingdom and Sweden, as the respective governments intend. Freese and his colleagues believed that the bureaucratic burden of collecting annual license fees from users detracted from data protection activities. Since the current Social Democratic government is committed to reducing expenditures on data protection, Börjesson's new regime is trying to become more self-financing. Such an effort is politically wise, because it reduces direct conflict on a somewhat peripheral issue between the Ministry of Justice and the DIB.

The highly politicized character of the continuing public debates over specific issues of data protection indicate the sensitivity of surveillance issues. Specific proposals for new record linkages regularly involve clashes between concern for efficiency and privacy. The Social Democratic government has displayed reduced sympathy for the goals of data protection, because of its (supposedly) conflicting goals of "catching economic criminals" involved in tax evasion and fraud. The DIB continues to defend the interests of individuals in the face of various initiatives to (allegedly) save money or reduce fraud. Decisions of the Data Inspection Board are being challenged with increasing frequency by means of appeals to the minister of justice and the Cabinet, especially with respect to new record linkages.

Thus Swedish data protection has lost its novelty and some political support from the highest levels of the current government. Over time, this is a critical problem for all oversight agencies. The political and media climate for carrying out effective data protection remains in flux, especially since Freese has left the DIB. The Social Democrats are in power until at least 1991, with their vision of an ordered society that is at ideological odds with data protection; the Moderate party's conservative vision of individualism and freedom is not by itself an adequate counterweight. The government does not perceive Sweden to be a highly regimented and controlled society nor do many members of the public, long inured to conditions of existence. Thus Freese's lamentations are a minority view. It is clear in retrospect that by 1986 Freese was worn out by his continued battles with major public administrations.

The existence of the DIB has not prevented the emergence of a surveillance society, although it has perhaps curtailed it. Yet the DIB needs to continue to be the aggressive protector of the individual in all kinds of information handling. Professor Peter Seipel of the University of Stockholm describes privacy and data protection as a form of protection for the minority. Perhaps Hans Corell should have the last word with his notion that there are no final solutions to the danger of a "control society" posed by computers; it is a continuing struggle for human rights.[9]

Meeting the Challenge of Revision

The Data Act's minor amendments of 1979 and the more substantial ones of 1982 illustrate the need for periodic revision of such a law to reflect its experimental character and the fast pace of relevant developments in technology and society. But even more significant changes were considered in Sweden; the central issue quickly became how, and in what way, these revisions would occur. The process reveals how the control of surveillance is subject to the political climate and the talents of the data protectors.

From 1976 to 1984 the Parliamentary Commission on Revision of the Data Act (DALK) had primary responsibility for reviewing proposed changes to the Data Act and making recommendations to the government.[10] The years of study by DALK and subsequent consultations undertaken by the government ensured that there was public input into the process of revision. DALK greatly promoted the adjustment of the Data Act to changing realities, because it was a specialized forum of representative legislators who could make candid, informed judgments about the wishes of the DIB and the needs of society. No other country has managed to achieve such a sensitive instrument for considering reform. Having noted this, it is discouraging that irreconcilable differences between the DIB and DALK about further changes to the Data Act necessitated DALK's invitation to the government to dissolve it in 1984. The DIB opposed further changes after 1982, fearing they might weaken the impact of data protection.

The dissolution of DALK also reflected the changed political climate: the interests of the Social Democrats and of data protection clashed. Kurt Hugosson, a Social Democrat, also became the chair of DALK in succession to a leading member of the Conservative party. As a long-time member of the board of the DIB and Statistics Sweden, Hugosson clashed repeatedly with Freese over the years on matters of substantive policy. Thus both DALK and the government were no longer automatic supporters of data protection.

As the DIB tried to adjust to the 1982 legislation, the prospect of more radical changes loomed on the horizon. DIB staff feared efforts to weaken data protection, leading senior personnel to abandon the agency in droves by 1986. The staff believed that the system of licensing and permissions keeps the DIB in general control of the situation in data processing and, hopefully, ensures the continued attention of licensees to privacy interests, but it is doubtful that this would last very long, if the system of requiring licenses were changed. On the other hand, Hugosson, who left the board of the DIB in 1983, was in a strong position to represent the interests of the government through DALK. It can be assumed that conflicting views on record linkages were the reason for the "strong" differences that led DALK to seek its own dismissal in 1984.[11] Future revisions will remain in new hands.

After the demise of DALK, the government appointed a Commission on Data Protection and the Principle of Publicity to consider in particular the use of Personal Identification Numbers. Its chair, Carl Axel Petri, a former Cabinet member and a senior judge, has stated that there is no intention to abolish the numbers but to limit their uses. The commission has also recommended statutory restrictions on the sale of government information to the private sector for commercial purposes. It is also reconsidering the public's right to use open data files subject only to the limitations set down in the Secrecy Act. The existence of this high-level commission, which was expected to report in 1988, is testimony to some Swedish sensitivity to surveillance practices.[12]

Administrative changes hold considerable promise. When Börjesson became director general in 1986, he quickly concluded that it was excessive for the DIB to devote more than 50 percent of its annual resources to checking 2,000 applications and permits for licenses; he is trying to reduce the burden of such activities, so as to permit more inspections. He contemplates standardized and simpler application forms and even the possibility of reducing the need for permits by issuing general regulations and codes of practice for special fields of data collection.[13] These are attractive possibilities for making data protection more effective in controlling surveillance. Proposing revisions to the Data Act is a subject for discussion between the director general and the Ministry of Justice.

One of Börjesson's solutions for reducing the burden of licensing is the development of general data protection rules for such fields as local government, research, statistics, banking, and direct mail marketing. Thus the 284 municipalities should comply with the same basic sectoral rules, which would have the result of covering all welfare data in the country. The DIB can issue such rules as flexible regulations under the Data Act. Börjesson told *Privacy Times* that the definition of a "personal file" in this telecommunications age and the problem of data collection for tax purposes were other pressing issues of statutory revision.[14]

No one believes that the Data Act, or any other data protection law, has achieved real permanence, because various issues remain unresolved, including the question of manual files. DALK did reject a universal statute to cover manual files, but that view seems unlikely to be the last word on the subject, given the experience of other countries. DALK had argued that the principle of open government gave individuals access to such records in the public sector and, according to Hans Corell, that manual records rarely posed the same risks for privacy as automated files.[15] Such a judgment is debatable, if operators of registers choose to use manual records for sensitive data so as to avoid the requirement of authorization.[16] There is no formal evidence as to whether this is occurring, but it seems self-evident that it does.

A major remaining area for close scrutiny concerns the relation between the Data Act and the principle of publicity. The balance between openness and privacy protection is out of control, despite the tradition of an open society. The integration of these competing imperatives is not as well developed in Sweden as in Canada, for example, because of the different stages at which each developed. The principle of publicity makes access to personal data on third parties unconscionably easy. For example, prisoners can obtain information about their guards from open registers. Börjesson is very much aware of the risks of encroachment on the private lives of individuals resulting from an unusually open society. Yet publicity is enshrined in the constitution, whereas the Data Act is simply a statute. Perhaps Swedes need the same constitutional rights to data protection as exist in Germany. Such issues concerning the protection of privacy in an information society are currently being studied by the Commission on Data Protection and the Principle of Publicity. Moreover, the Riksdag has passed a first resolution to add to the constitution a provision giving individuals a safeguard for their privacy when electronic data processing is used.

There is also continuing concern about the regulation of record linkages, which remains the prime data protection problem, and about the need for special legislation for certain sensitive registers. More studies are needed on issues like data quality and error detection and correction, both from a legal and technical perspective. Unfortunately, the demise of DALK means that there is now no general, continuing mechanism for revision of the Data Act.

Public opinion killed nuclear power in Sweden, so one must not underestimate current and prospective resistance to the prevailing surveillance society. Since the climate in society decides what is possible, the government must tread warily.

Part 3

France

Chapter *13*

The French Model

Introduction

The French law of January 6, 1978, on Informatics, Data Banks, and Freedoms is expansive and innovative. In particular, it illustrates the striking tendency for data protection to be expanded to cover a very broad range of societal issues that, from the perspective of English-speaking countries, extend well beyond the protection of the privacy interests of individuals or the control of surveillance. Moreover the National Commission on Informatics and Freedoms (CNIL), the agency set up to implement the legislation, has set up separate subcommissions on freedom to work, research and statistics, local government, and technology and security. French data protectors believe that their mandate includes all of these concerns. One consequence is that their interests have wandered all over the map of contemporary French affairs, and, at least until now, have diluted the effectiveness of their achievements in data protection itself. The French respond that their expansive law is the wave of the future, but it appears to be a dubious mechanism for limiting governmental surveillance, at least as presently implemented.

The CNIL is an independent administrative agency with regulatory power, dominated by a commission. As in Sweden, it makes decisions on the authorization of particular information systems in response to requests from both the public and private sectors.[1] In this sense, the CNIL attempts to balance competing interests itself and to decide difficult cases.

The commission has seventeen members chosen for five-year terms by various official bodies. Although the government itself has direct control of the selection of only three CNIL members, the two most recent presidents of the CNIL were drawn from among appointees of President François Mitterrand. France is a highly politicized society, and the CNIL has taken on similar characteristics in electing a president. This has restricted its effectiveness in resisting governmental surveillance practices, since it appears reluctant to oppose the government.

With respect to the broad themes of this volume, French data protection illustrates a preoccupation with grandiose principles and rhetoric to the neglect of effective implementation, a situation exacerbated by part-time commissioners, weak leadership, and inexperienced staff at the CNIL, especially in the first years. As in Sweden, a very bureaucratic approach to data protection for the public *and* private sectors bogs down in paperwork and the registration of data banks to the neglect of audits, the investigation of complaints, and the conduct of meaningful public relations. France further illustrates the problem of independence that data protectors often face: the unwillingness of the CNIL, for the most part, to confront the government on current and new surveillance practices. The CNIL is as politicized as the society that surrounds and shapes it. Finally, French data protection epitomizes the kinds of problems that arise as data protection becomes a routine activity both for the leadership and the staff of the regulatory agency. The end result is the illusion of protection for a population requiring rescue from data surveillance.

The Development of Legislation

Table 4 outlines the main events in the development of French data protection. On January 6, 1978, President Valéry Giscard d'Estaing signed a law "on informatics, data files, and individual liberties," which created the National Commission on Informatics and Freedoms.[2] Enactment of this data protection law was a considerable achievement, not least because the general legal right of personal privacy in France, as in most Western nations except the United States, is not especially well developed.[3]

A catalyst for the coalescence of inchoate public fears about the surveillance capacities of governments was an article by Philippe Boucher in *Le Monde* on March 21, 1974, entitled "Safari, or the Hunt for Frenchmen."[4] The project known as Safari was comparable to the controversial plans for a national data bank in the United States in the mid-1960s. The French government appeared to be planning to use a unique personal identification number for individuals that would be used in all public registers, records, large data banks, and computer networks.

In the aftermath of the public outcry about Safari, the minister of justice appointed a Commission on Data Processing and Freedom, commonly known as the Tricot Commission after its chief reporter, Bernard Tricot. Its high-powered membership reflected the seriousness with which the government approached the issue. The commission was to propose "measures to ensure that the development of data processing in the semi-public and private sectors will take place in the context of respect for private life, individual liberties, and public liberties."[5] The broad terms of reference led directly to the very expansive 1978 law.

The Tricot Commission's most general conclusion was that preventive action was necessary to reduce the serious potential for abuse of computers: "We believe that the major threat is the increase of social control and the aggravation of unequal relationships within society."[6] Such early recognition of the threat of surveillance was impressive. The *Tricot Report* also focused on the lack of personal self-determination that has resulted from the Information Age: "It is in fact central government, big cities, big business, etc., whose power increases, while every individual feels himself more and more exposed to

Table 4. Chronology of French Data Protection Legislation

April 17, 1974	Ministry of Justice appoints a Commission on Informatics and Liberties (Tricot Commission).
June 27, 1975	Tricot Commission submits its report.
Fall 1976	Government proposes a law on Informatics and Freedoms.
Fall 1977	National Assembly and Senate consider the Law on Informatics and Freedoms.
January 6, 1978	Enactment of the Law on Informatics and Freedoms.
December 5, 1978	Entry into force of the Law on Informatics and Freedoms. Appointment of the first members of the CNIL and election of Pierre Bellet as the first president (resigned July 1979).
November 1979	Jacques Thyraud elected president of the CNIL (served until December 20, 1983).
May 10, 1981	François Mitterrand elected president of France.
December 1983	Five-year terms of office of the members of the CNIL renewed (seven new members).
December 20, 1983	Jean Rosenwald elected president of the CNIL (deceased, June 2, 1984).
June 19, 1984	Jacques Fauvet elected president of the CNIL.
March 16, 1986	Election of a Conservative prime minister.
May 11, 1988	Mitterrand elected president of France for a second term.
June 12, 1988	Restoration of a Socialist government in national elections.
December 1988	Five-year terms of office of the members of the CNIL renewed (six new members).
December 21, 1988	Jacques Fauvet re-elected president of the CNIL.

society, controlled by it, and unable to influence the choices he is invited to participate in." Tricot particularly recommended that all data banks should be openly established and not be allowed to slip into existence: "It should not be tolerated that Ministers take in their stride projects initiated before them and intended to become operational after them, so that people cannot remember anymore when and by whom decisions were taken or that there are half accomplished facts."[7] This is an especially perceptive point of view among the data protection advocates of any country.

The minister of justice's legislative proposals in 1976 were closely modeled on the Tricot Commission's recommendations. The law then became the product of political bargains between the legislature and the government. When the National Assembly and the Senate considered the legislation a year later, considerable modification of the original government proposals took place.

Two main areas of contention pertained to the control of surveillance: the attributes and composition of the CNIL, and the type of licensing system to be created. The legislature determined that the law should cover both the public and private sectors, even though the information systems of the national government were the primary source of concern. Parliament further recognized that extending the coverage of the law to manual as well as automated files had the potential to weaken the overall impact of the law. The compromise was that the basic rules on the collection, recording, and storage of personal data would apply to manual files, but only if a major issue arose.[8] The opposition Socialist party wanted to regulate manual data entirely, but the Ministry of Justice argued that this would dilute the general effectiveness of the CNIL.[9] The Tricot Commission had pointed out the dangers that would arise if manual records were completely exempted from the scope of the legislation; with such a loophole, organizations could set up noncomputerized files of the most sensitive data beyond the reach of the regulatory commission.[10] The legislative compromise helped to obviate this form of surveillance.

Parliament made a very significant deviation from the Tricot recommendations by creating "an independent administrative authority," a first for France, in which the government can only exercise limited advance financial control and has restricted powers of intervention.[11] This crucial degree of statutory independence roughly parallels the situation in most other countries. In adopting the commission model, the legislature was largely influenced by the example of the Swedish Data Inspection Board and by the French preference for a commission rather than a person functioning alone.

Parliament also considerably modified the procedures by which members of the new commission would be selected, essentially removing the power of appointment from the government itself. It is thought that a bargain was reached that the president of the CNIL should be a member of the legislature and not of the government. The vital point is that the CNIL was not intended to be a creature or client of the current government.

Another important trait of the CNIL is its composition. The government of Giscard d'Estaing originally proposed to nominate all twelve of its members, most of whom would thus have been high-ranking civil servants or at least identified with the current government. The Senate insisted on a predominance of legislators on the new commission in order to reinforce its authority and independence.[12] The composition of the CNIL is very similar to the Tricot recommendation of twelve members, plus a president and vice-president, except for the addition of two members from the Court of Accounts (the government audit office), two more data-processing specialists, and one additional person chosen for general expertise.

Under the 1978 law, six public bodies elect two representatives each to the CNIL.[13] The government through the Council of Ministers chooses only three of the seventeen members. The extent to which the government may influence this "miniparliament" is thus structurally limited. Moreover, the Council of State (the powerful central administrative court and independent consultative body), the Supreme Court of Appeal, and the Court of Accounts are independent bodies. Their members come from leading schools of higher education and remain members of these great bodies for the duration of their careers.[14] Although the elite grand corps can hardly be construed as hostile to any incumbent government, their presence reinforces the independence of the commission.

Opening up the membership of the CNIL to members of the Senate and the National Assembly was a major precedent. It resulted in politicians having significant influence on the CNIL and, in practice, turning it into an organization sensitive to political tendencies. An alternative hypothesis is that present or former members of the grand corps in fact control the CNIL. Hence it is hardly surprising that there is some evidence that the CNIL is being run as a political organization rather than as an instrument for forceful implementation of data protection. The effectiveness of the commission model for the control of governmental and private-sector surveillance remains to be demonstrated in France.

Formative Influences

As is true of all the countries studied in this book, the efforts of French data protectors to limit surveillance have been strongly influenced by both current events in the policy process and the more pervasive underlying political culture. First, as in other countries, the law did not really originate in response to any explicit public demands, despite the publicity about Safari. A national survey in 1975 found a very low level of concern about computers and abuses of personal information.[15] The initiative for data protection was largely a response to needs perceived by intellectuals and technocrats; the public only sensed a vague uneasiness about prospective surveillance by great computers. This concern has, however, grown. In 1985, 60 percent thought that informatics posed a threat to liberties; only 25 percent believed the opposite.[16]

Since a high regard for the inherent importance of individual rights is an essential component of concern for privacy, then common knowledge suggests that this concept is a basic part of the French character, as the nation that produced the Declaration of the Rights of Man. On the other hand, French individualism itself has tended to remain latent. Citizens have traditionally trusted the government to protect their interests. The civil liberties movement is weak, and there was no consumer movement until the government created a consumer protection organization in 1970.[17] These societal traits mean that the CNIL has been advancing privacy rights on its own, without significant support from organizations or individuals.

France with its population of 55 million is a highly bureaucratized and centralized state, particularly in governmental terms, which creates further problems for the CNIL in its power relationships. Traditionally, the population expects the government in Paris to act in a paternalistic and bureaucratic fashion. The state controls many major policy fields that touch people's lives directly, such as health and welfare, housing, and education, which in other nations are usually managed to at least some degree by local authorities.[18] The historian Theodore Zeldin highlights "the French habit of accepting government interference in almost every aspect of life, and of seeing the solutions to problems in the granting of state subsidies and the creation of new state institutions."[19]

Alain Peyrefitte, who was minister of justice until 1981, has emphasized the resulting power of the administration: "Not even the Parliament manages to collect enough information to control the bureaucracy. Ministers' answers to questions in Parliament are as vague as courtesy to the nation's representatives allows. In practice, the legislature has no investigative rights, no access to official records, no chance to summon appropriate functionaries as witnesses."[20] The acceptance of centralization and bureaucratization creates significant barriers to controlling surveillance by government information systems.

In comparative terms, France also remains a highly elitist society, which means that political power is shared among very few, and they, including the leadership of the CNIL, have few incentives to challenge the status quo. The leading graduates of the famous schools remain the leaders of society for all of their lives. Simon Nora, a member of this elite group, writes: "Our elite system was a great asset until a decade or so ago. . . . But today France is largely modernized and what is needed is something else, the emergence of a more open and egalitarian society where ordinary people can participate more. The system is now an obstacle to that."[21] Such testimony is particularly significant, since Nora was an early graduate of the National School of Administration (ENA), the most famous of the leading schools, and has spent his career as an inspector of finance, which is an elite core of civil servants. Mitterrand's first government chose Nora to head the ENA itself. Prominent public servants also enjoy considerable prestige. Graduates of leading schools choose government careers much more frequently than their counterparts in other countries.

The cross-appointment of members of the elite to the CNIL has been a source of caution during implementation of the 1978 law. A commissioner from the upper classes is unlikely to be too tough on the other members of the elite who run the large public administrations, since he or she has a continuing relationship with colleagues of similar high status and lifelong careers of leadership. Such persons have no natural inclination to question governmental surveillance practices.

The design and initial implementation of data protection during the seven-year presidency of Giscard d'Estaing was part of his administration's overall concern with the impact of new technology on society.[22] The election of Mitterrand to the presidency on May 10, 1981, with a Socialist majority in the National Assembly, stimulated this positive political climate for data protection, since the Socialists had supported strong legislation in 1977. Around the time of his election, Mitterrand stated: "I will put informatics at the service of men, I will insure its control by an independent system of justice so that no data bank can serve for the manipulation of the spirit of people. I will inaugurate finally a real redistribution of the means of data processing (Informatics), which is the condition for an effective redistribution of power."[23] His government set up a World Center for Personal Computation and Human Development, headed by Jean-Jacques Servan-Schreiber. One of its apparent goals was to provide everyone on earth with a personal computer.[24] It had a substantial annual budget and an international staff of computer experts, until a new conservative government abolished it in 1986.

The government's highly positive attitude toward the promotion of French information technology has an impact on the work of the CNIL, which is reluctant to question or resist its introduction and development.[25] In contrast, German data protectors tend to be more resistant to, and critical of, the dissemination of technology, and they insist on careful evaluation of all such innovations before they are accepted. The technological thrust of the late twentieth century inclines all data protectors to be too respectful of the multiple forms of computerization.

The Socialist party embraces a radical critique of society that perceives government to be the main threat to privacy and other individual liberties. In 1980 Robert Badinter, the minister of justice from 1981 to 1986, joined in criticisms of government plans for national identity cards, which he saw as increasing the possibility for illegal practices by the police.[26] After the election, on September 23, 1981, the daily newspaper, *Les Echos,* which concentrates on business and finance, published an extensive interview with Badinter in which he emphasized that the Socialist government was very aware that any government has a particular tendency to want to use computers to control people. In his view computers should be used for, not against, the general public. The great central administrations should set a good example by not using personal information systems for insidious purposes and by strictly applying the 1978 law. In Badinter's view, since record linkages are a real risk, the government should only conduct those that are strictly necessary, to the exclusion of all ideas of social control, and the CNIL should regulate them.[27] Badinter's views were not pious platitudes, since there was no pressure to make such remarks at the start of a new administration. Ironically, like the Socialists in Sweden, the Socialist government found itself relying on record linkages to solve certain real or alleged societal abuses, such as the tax on great fortunes, which produced a tension with its commitment to data protection. Nevertheless, its overt awareness of the risks of surveillance was impressive.

The new Socialist government's support for data protection, at least until it confronted countervailing values in a specific setting, had an impact on the CNIL. In June 1981, after the election, the CNIL announced some negative decisions on government information systems, which are discussed below in Chapter 17. The press drew a connection between these findings and the results of the election.[28] In September 1981 the Socialist government announced it was abandoning plans for new national identity cards; the irony was that in June 1980 the CNIL had basically accepted the former government's plans for such cards.[29]

The general thrust of the first Mitterrand administration in favor of data protection was clearly established, despite some typical backsliding on specific issues. The government felt bound by the kinds of compromise arrangements worked out between the Parliament and the previous government in 1977–78 and did not seek to change the law to give it more control over the CNIL. This was especially significant since the five-year terms of those first appointed to the CNIL expired on December 5, 1983. However, the prediction that Senator Jacques Thyraud would be replaced as president of the CNIL by a senior official from one of the grand corps indeed occurred.

The Organization of the CNIL

The CNIL is actually run by a commission of seventeen members, who are appointed for terms of five years. Various major public bodies pick twelve of the seventeen members. Only one, the Economic and Social Council, which advises the government, is readily open to government influence. The speakers of the National Assembly and the Senate appoint two additional persons "qualified by their knowledge of data processing applications." The Council of Ministers, which is controlled by the president and prime minister, appoints three additional persons chosen "on account of their authority and competence."[30]

The law provides that the CNIL shall elect from its membership an executive committee composed of the president, two vice-presidents and, recently, one other CNIL member. This central bureau has its own staff, including several high-level technical advisers for legal matters and informatics. In 1984 the CNIL finally acquired internal expertise on informatics in the person of a recruit from another government agency. The president of the CNIL, or by delegation, the deputy vice-president, have considerable power. Together they appoint and control the staff. In addition, the commission may delegate certain powers to the president or the deputy vice-president.[31]

As will be discussed in more detail in Chapter 16, organization was not the strong suit of the CNIL, especially in comparison to the situation in West Germany, until an experienced administrator, Jean Rosenwald, became president at the end of 1983. The organization of the staff remained in a state of flux during the first five years. Rosenwald's important administrative reforms have been continued by his successor, Jacques Fauvet.

The staff is currently organized into three principal bureaus, dealing with legal matters, informatics, and administrative and financial services.[32] The latter is a relatively new component of the central administration, reflecting the fact that such matters were not under strict control during the first years. Louis Joinet, a leading shaper of data protection, served as general director of the staff while he was still at the CNIL but, after he left, no comparable figure took his place until 1984, when, in effect, President Rosenwald took direct control of the staff.[33] In 1985, Pierre-Alain Weill, a judge, became the first secretary-general. One of the current goals is to improve the working relationships of the major staff groupings.

The theory of the CNIL is that the commissioners themselves make the decisions. In practice, requests to the CNIL for an opinion on a particular information system are distributed according to their subject matter among the various staff members. A staff member checks the dossier in question to ensure that the documentation and attachments are correct and complete. He or she can seek further information or clarification from the applicant, even from a government ministry, if necessary. Individual staff members may have as many as one hundred or more requests for an opinion in front of them at any particular moment. If the request is routine, the staff member settles the issue at once, and a notice of the proposed decision is sent to all the commissioners. If there is no concern expressed by a particular commissioner within fifteen days, then the decision stands. Otherwise, the full commission will consider it. If the request for an opinion on an information system covers a large population, such as four to five million persons, then the commission automatically considers the dossier.

The commissioners serve on permanent subcommissions, and at least one member is appointed as the reporter for most major requests for advice. They have also divided among themselves various policy fields, such as health, police, and social welfare records. Specific staff members work in coordination with commissioners responsible for particular fields of activity, especially in the public sector. This may involve preparation of a specific dossier for the full commission or simply continued attention to a particular field of activity. The staff members prepare reports on particular issues and then place several alternatives for decisions before the commission.

As a practical matter, the staff has responsibilities roughly parallel to those of the commissioners, although the burden of work in the first years did not permit specialization. A particular person may have a range of duties as wide as defense, public security, health, and external affairs data, but the detailed responsibilities assigned to each staff member are in no way as structured as those in the Swedish and West German data protection agencies. Moreover, tasks assigned to an individual by the president have changed frequently.

The CNIL has offices for the president and at least the senior vice-president, but otherwise the unpaid commissioners only attend for regular meetings or for consultations with the staff. Thus the staff works alone much of the time. More recently, office space was set aside for the periodic visits of individual commissioners.

The staff of the CNIL had grown to approximately thirty-five employees by the end of 1982. The CNIL's perception of its work load led to an expectation that staff size would continue to increase annually for several more years; there are about forty-five staff members at the time of writing, about half of whom are professionals. However, financial conditions make it unlikely that these numbers will increase substantially in the next few years.

The major institutional change in the structure of the CNIL was the creation by the Socialist prime minister in 1983 of a system of two contact officers in each government ministry, one in the minister's Cabinet and the other at the administrative level. This step acknowledged that the public administration was not quickly absorbing the law. The commission approaches a ministry through these internal contacts (and vice versa), but they play no role in helping the general public, which is an unfortunate departure from the model of several other countries. With the cooperation of the government commissioner at the CNIL, these official contacts approach the commission on behalf of their ministries and, in turn, provide answers to it on relevant matters. They have the advantages of knowing the law and offering the CNIL an entry point for relevant discussions.

Chapter *14*

The Goals of Data Protection

What do data protection laws and data protection agencies seek to accomplish for the control of governmental surveillance? This chapter evaluates the purposes of the French legislation in order to evaluate their relevance for confronting surveillance problems directly and for giving data protectors a clear and specific mandate. In most countries with data protection laws, the goals of the legislation are fairly easy to identify, even if they are not articulated in an adequate manner. However, as this chapter makes clear, the situation in France is that the statute on "Informatics and Freedoms" of January 6, 1978, is clearly much more than a typical data protection act. Although the following pages evaluate the law in terms of its adequacy in dealing with the central concerns about privacy and surveillance that arise in the automated processing of personal information, the ultimate issue is whether its language is a progressive model for the rest of the Western world.

Statutory Objectives

At first glance, the 1978 law has an immediate concern with the regulation of data processing. Article 14 charges the National Commission on Informatics and Freedoms (CNIL) with insuring "that public or private automatic processing of personal data is carried out in accordance with this Act."[1] Although the statute primarily relates to automated data processing, certain provisions contained in articles 25 to 33 also apply "to non-automated or mechanized files, other than those that are removed from the strict exercise of the right of privacy."[2] This last clause of article 45 means that the most ordinary types of manual records, such as a personal address book, would not be regulated. Manual data are primarily subject to such general principles as the requirement that illegal collection of information is forbidden and that people should be informed why personal information is being collected.[3]

Those who formulated the law were primarily concerned with the regulation of major personal information systems in the public sector involving the use of very large computers. Thus one fundamental purpose of the CNIL is to monitor "the application of data processing to personal data," which is a large enough task in itself and has been at the heart of its concerns to the present.[4] It has interpreted the law as expressing the desire of Parliament to have all data-processing activities publicly known and to have more detailed investigations for those in the public sector.[5]

Only a superficial reader of the law would be misled into believing that it deals primarily with data processing, since the scope of its title—informatics, data banks, and freedoms or liberties—and of articles 1 to 3 is considerably more expansive. The CNIL quoted approvingly a definition of "informatique" prepared by the Académie Française in 1966: "The science of rational treatment, notably by automated machines, of information considered as the support of human understanding and of communications in the technical, economic and social fields."[6] Informatics is thus a term used to describe the organization, processing, and transmission of personal information, normally by computers, but it also includes a concern for the implications of information systems for society.

The law is unique in dealing with a great deal more than simply the data protection aspects of computers. The first article specifies that "informatics shall be at the service of every citizen. It shall develop in the context of international cooperation. It shall infringe neither human identity, nor the rights of man, nor private life, nor individual or public liberties."[7] Although President Jacques Fauvet concludes that this philosophical statement is "too general to be of any practical use," President Jacques Thyraud often used the word "liberty" in his speeches, because the CNIL is the guarantor of "freedoms."[8]

Article 2 is equally extraordinary in restricting the scope of decision making on the basis of automated information, noting that no judicial, governmental, or private decision "involving appraisal of human conduct may be based on any automatic processing of data which describes the profile or personality of the person concerned."[9] Article 3 is also unique: "Any person shall be entitled to know and to dispute the data and logic used in automatic processing, the results of which are used against him." Seemingly, this provision means that any administration's decision concerning a particular individual is subject to that person's right to learn both the data and the computer program that were used in reaching it. The commission regards this as applying to a range of data from direct marketing files to medical registers. In 1983 a senior staff member of the CNIL said he knew of no cases in which an individual had exercised this right to contest.[10] Articles 2 and 3 seem to incorporate a fundamental legislative bias against automated data processing, at least to the extent of prohibiting decision making without human intervention. Commentators explain that these articles are designed to ensure that computers are not used blindly for profiling and to promote the transparency or openness of society. Fauvet states that data processing, an irreplaceable aid, should not be making the decisions.[11]

The CNIL itself has not shied away from the implications of the first three articles. Its leaders feel their mandate is to develop these expansive responsibilities, even covering such matters as promoting public access to computers. A 1978 decree by the Council of State instructed the CNIL to keep informed about the uses of informatics and their impact on society.[12] In its first annual report, the CNIL stated its object was not only the regulation of personal information but also maintaining the broadest possible perspective on the relations between data processing and freedom.[13]

The CNIL is conscious of the difficulties inherent in having a variety of ambiguously defined burdens imposed by these articles. Its initial organizational response was the creation of a subcommittee on data processing and freedom of expression, which is concerned with all types of new information technology.[14] The CNIL interprets the tasks of its subcommittee expansively: "Even if in the immediate future, the preponderance of issues studied are not tied directly to the law of January 6, 1978, the issues directly concern citizens, by their need to maintain their cultural heritage, by the need to have access to a wide variety of information, and by the transformation of the conditions of work of the professional categories involved. . . . There is thus the need to proceed to profound reflections on these changes in the means of information, and to work towards the end that informatics will be at the service of each citizen . . . and does not pose a threat to any of their freedoms."[15] As will be discussed further, such broad responsibilities pose a serious threat to the ability of the CNIL to function adequately with respect to the control of surveillance.

It is a tribute to the French preoccupation with fundamental problems, and to their simultaneous isolation from relevant practices in other countries, that they seem to be unaware of the unusual character of articles 1 to 3. The first article imposes a tremendous range of responsibilities on the CNIL, which must somehow ensure that data processing is at the service of every citizen and develops in the context of international cooperation. Thyraud made it clear that the CNIL intended to place more and more emphasis on article 1: "In some respects, it is a sort of declaration of citizen's rights when faced with informatization. The commission has been too often confused with an organization content with recording file declarations. . . . The CNIL's mission is much more vast: that of surveying the development of informatics in relation to the evolution of society. It is only in this respect that it will truly fulfill its role of 'special conscience of the nation.'"[16] Article 1 could justify almost any activity related to computers and data processing, and commissioners or members of the staff are in theory free to put their own interpretation on it. It seems, nevertheless, inevitable that the language of this article will lead to conflicts between the CNIL and those being regulated when questions arise about the appropriate scope of the act.

Perhaps the best example to date of the expansive possibilities of article 1 was the CNIL's creation in 1980 of a permanent subcommission on "Informatics and Freedom to Work." Many experts would find the connection between freedom to work and data protection to be rather weak, suggesting the CNIL was pushing the scope of the law to untenable limits. The CNIL justified its decision as a response to Parliament's desire that the protection of personal liberty from infringement by informatics should be pursued within a very broad frame of reference.[17]

This sweeping statutory focus inevitably presents the implementers of the law with difficulties in application. The civil law tradition requires a continued, close analysis of the meaning of specific statutory provisions. Thus the CNIL constantly evaluates the meaning of specific articles, paragraphs, and words in the law. In this sense a continuous process of interpretation is occurring, although it remains to be seen whether the statute will thereby grow in some organic sense. There is a certain vagueness in various provisions of the law, such as article 5 about the meaning of automated data processing, as well as a perhaps inevitable complexity in understanding the relationship between specific articles.[18] Nevertheless, the CNIL is the primary interpreter and custodian of the meaning of the law, subject to ultimate judicial review by the Council of State.

Philosophical Objectives

The word privacy is not generally known in the French language, even if individuals sometimes refer to "la privacy." It is of course true that many languages have no equivalent for the Anglo-Saxon term *privacy*—which is not to suggest that concern for privacy is in any way lacking in such societies. For example, the Englishman John Ardagh's excellent book on *France in the 1980s* frequently uses the word privacy in discussing certain aspects of life. The French tend to refer expressively to the need for a "private life," which comes close to public concerns about excessive surveillance.

The law addresses questions of privacy only infrequently and then in the specific context of protecting "private life." It may simply be, as is true in other countries, that the overwhelming intent of the law was well known to be privacy protection, and that this basic goal did not need to be articulated in detail in the statute itself. Yet even the concept of protecting "private life" is not usefully defined in the law.[19]

With respect to the meaning of a right to a "private life," Article 1 provides that informatics "shall infringe neither human identity nor the rights of man, nor private life, nor individual or public liberties." One explanation is that the meaning of most of these terms, except for the reference to "human identity," is well recognized in French law. A writer for a 1979 study suggested that "the reference to human identity is a reflection of the concern over the homogenizing effect of data processing: over-generalization may harmfully limit human individuality. A case in point would be the characterization of an individual as a result of a few items of information."[20] More importantly, article 9 of the Civil Code stipulates that "each person has a right to respect for his private life."[21]

An additional problem with understanding the references to privacy or private life in the law is that on several occasions there is an implication that certain types of common data-processing operations "manifestly do not infringe privacy or liberties."[22] Once again, as in other national laws, there is no attempt to define these important terms. The response, as in other countries that rely on the civil law approach, is to argue that the basic law does not burden itself with definitions but relies on jurisprudence to supply precision and appreciation of each term.

Different sectors in society have received these philosophical objectives in different ways. Although the CNIL has not faced a great deal of criticism to date, at least in public, a number of associations, unions, journalists, and academics are observing its activities. They seem to be in favor of expanding and ensuring data protection rather than restricting its scope in any way.

Certain French unions are important pressure groups in favor of strong data protection in a fashion that does not seem to occur in other countries. They have lobbied the CNIL and the public through the media on a variety of issues. They seem to be well aware of the risks of surveillance, especially with respect to the government's plans for new plastic identity cards in 1980. The Democratic Confederation of Labor (CFDT), a group of unions close to the Socialists, began a major initiative against the cards and presented a brief on the subject to the CNIL. The General Confederation of Labor (CGT), the largest labor organization, which is linked with the Communist party, has attacked the CNIL on occasion, specifically by bringing a successful appeal before the Council of State to annul its simplified rule concerning personnel and payment files of private companies.[23]

Only a few academics are interested in data protection as a subject for study, which is roughly comparable to the situation in other Western countries. Some sociologists have looked at the legitimating function of the CNIL in terms of the advice it gives to the government in connection with information systems. They argue that delegating such sensitive matters to it has the negative effect of keeping the debates out of the legislature in France (or in any other country).

Another critical perspective is that the CNIL has been a disappointment to those who expected some strong initiatives in favor of freedom and liberty. They argue that it has not really resisted the technocrats and other advocates of surveillance but has simply warned them. Their cynical view is that the CNIL has the task of keeping the general public quiescent as the technocrats push ahead on all fronts with the building of new information systems and the application of new information technology. Such arguments are equally relevant to other countries. Left-wing critics of the CNIL sometimes dismiss it as being simply interested in the transparence or openness of the central administration, rather than in the fundamental radical goal of restructuring society. Critics dismiss other members of the staff as liberals only concerned with defending society against technocracy.

Information Management Objectives

Perhaps because of the careful work of the Tricot Commission, and also because of Swedish influence, the law contains explicit information management provisions. Article 25 prohibits the acquisition of data "by any fraudulent, dishonest, or illegal means," but with no guidance on what these terms mean. Article 27 specifies that respondents, especially to questionnaires, must be informed whether they have to supply information, the consequences of failure to respond, their rights of access and correction, and the intended recipients of the data. The only exception to these important requirements is the collection of information for purposes of a criminal investigation (one of the most sensitive forms of surveillance).

Article 28 establishes the central principle of the right to be forgotten, one of the most important ideas in the law: "Unless otherwise provided for by law, information may not be stored in personal form beyond the period stated in the application for an opinion or in the declaration, unless such storage is authorized by the Commission."[24] Many data protection laws do not regulate the storage of data in this fashion; the CNIL wisely seeks such limits in all of its decisions. The *Tricot Report* had recommended that personal information in public systems should not be stored indefinitely: compulsory rules should ensure that data are preserved only so long as they serve a necessary purpose, especially when certain data entail risks for the persons concerned.[25] Article 29 imposes a burden on those ordering or carrying out data processing to ensure that all necessary precautions are taken "to protect the data and in particular to prevent these from being distorted, damaged, or disclosed to unauthorized third parties."[26]

The Tricot Commission recommended an absolute prohibition against the collection of a very limited range of information. It argued that the guiding principle "should be that data should be adequate for the purpose [for which it was collected]; such an approach is more fruitful than prohibiting altogether the recording of certain data."[27] Article 30 specifies that "unless otherwise provided for by law, only the jurisdictions and public authorities acting within the scope of their legal powers and, on the favorable opinion of the National Commission, companies managing a public service, may engage in the automatic processing of personal data relating to criminal offenses, convictions, or security [police?] measures." The initial clause, "unless otherwise provided for by law," provides for a legislative override of certain statutory provisions, but such language appears only rarely in the law. Article 31 prohibits the recording or storage in a computer "of personal data which, directly or indirectly, reveal the racial origins or political, philosophical, or religious opinions, or union membership . . . ," without the express consent of the individual. There is an obvious exception for membership data held by churches and religious, philosophical, political, or union organizations, which are otherwise subject to the other statutory requirements.

The sensitivity of regulating surveillance in the areas covered by these articles is further evidenced by the inclusion of another exemption clause at the end of article 31: "For reasons of the public interest, other exceptions may be made to such a prohibition on the Commission's proposal or favorable opinion by a decree made in the Council of State." The requirement of consultation with the CNIL seems like a strong protection, since, as the specialist institution, its point of view should be difficult to resist, but the experience of the DIB in Sweden is not altogether comforting on this score. There is a further qualification in article 33 that articles 30 and 31 do not apply to personal data processing "by press or broadcasting organizations under the laws governing them, if application of those sections would have the effect of restricting freedom of expression." A qualification of this type is fairly common in national data protection laws as part of the standard balancing of competing interests.

In addition to the kinds of specific restrictions on the collection and dissemination of personal information discussed in this section, Professor Herbert Maisl has pointed out that the law ended a certain degree of legal chaos concerning the establishment of government data banks and exchanges of information among them, issues which the CNIL now regulates.[28] Moreover, any perceived illegality may be challenged before administrative tribunals.

Given the extent to which the CNIL could interfere with the routine operation of the civil service, and its tradition of elitist tendencies, there is surprisingly little open conflict between the CNIL and government agencies. The CNIL, on occasion, has advised against certain government proposals for information systems and has regularly recommended modifications in existing and planned information systems in order to protect individual liberties. As is discussed elsewhere in this case study, the CNIL has also faced occasional government dilatoriness with respect to requests for advice in connection with particular information systems, such as those of the Ministry of the Interior. There have also no doubt been conflicts of interpretation between public administrators, accustomed to running their own operations and the CNIL, but these have not yet become visible either in the reports of the CNIL or in interviews. One plausible interpretation is that the CNIL has not yet acted strongly enough against surveillance in any area of the public sector to attract overt opposition. The lack of any major conflicts with the government over data protection is one measure of the CNIL's relative ineffectiveness to date as a watchdog.

Chapter *15*

The Power of the Commission

In order to be effective in limiting governmental surveillance, data protectors require independence, powers of intervention, and the willingness to use them. This chapter sets the scene for evaluating how well the National Commission on Informatics and Freedoms (CNIL) has been functioning in the French political climate. After more than a decade of experience, it is hardly premature to draw measured judgments about the success of the CNIL in regulating information surveillance by government agencies. The judgment of this writer is that it has not been very successful in confronting powerful public administrations, although the effort is ongoing.

Independence

Parliament recognized that independence is crucial if a data protection agency is to accomplish its statutory tasks. The 1978 law specifies that the CNIL "shall be an independent governmental authority," whose members "shall take no orders from any authority in the performance of their duties." Such powers are extraordinary in France. The fact that a member of the executive branch of government cannot be a member of the CNIL further reinforces this expectation of independence.[1] The CNIL has described itself as an "institution of control: . . . A product of the State, its actions are only subject to the control of the Council of State and the Court of Accounts. It should not be compared to a Ministry, a tribunal, or an ordinary public establishment."[2] Since independence is such a fragile reed, the parameters of the CNIL's independence need to be examined in practice, especially since it is so circumscribed by politics.

To begin with the most obvious example of a seeming limitation on the CNIL, the government has direct input into its decision making through its own commissioner. Article 9 specifies that a government commissioner, appointed by the prime minister, shall sit with the commission (without voting) and may call for the reconsideration of a decision within ten days of a discussion. Having such a figure in place is standard practice under traditional administrative law. As is further discussed in Chapter 16, the government commissioner has considerable utility for both sides as the administration's only assured pipeline into the internal deliberations of the commission and as a person officially entitled to represent the government. It is a post of strategic importance for sound implementation of data protection in a commission system and in theory does not limit the commission's independence. The record of rarely asking for reconsideration to date reflects the fact that it is unusual for the CNIL to take decisions against the interests of the government.

As in other countries, the method of achieving the CNIL's budget is central to its independence. Article 7 adopted the *Tricot Report*'s recommendation that the CNIL should be attached to the Ministry of Justice for practical administrative purposes.[3] The Socialist minister of justice, Robert Badinter, publicly acknowledged the independence of the CNIL early in his term of office.[4] There is no advance control of how the CNIL spends its approved budget, as voted by Parliament; only the office of the ombudsman and universities have similar financial independence.[5]

In practice, the CNIL negotiates its budget with the Ministry of Finance, which controls all government expenditures. Since power over budgets leads to influence on policy priorities, these negotiations furnish the government and the Parliament with a means of influencing the CNIL.[6] There were allegations that the failure of the government to furnish adequate financial resources hindered its initial functioning. The government of Giscard d'Estaing may have had lingering dissatisfaction over the legislature's influence on the shape of the CNIL, but the situation improved after the election of the Mitterrand government.

The government could reduce the budget for staff as a way of limiting the CNIL's effectiveness or influencing its decisions, but there is no evidence of such an occurrence to date. This is a practical reality in every country and a significant limitation on the real independence of a data protection agency. The legal adviser to the CNIL, Herbert Maisl, has acknowledged that the budget situation could permit Parliament to put pressure on the CNIL or, he argues, it could be a way for it to support an institution in which a number of its colleagues play a leading role. In his view, the commission, at present, enjoys a certain financial autonomy.[7] It seems likely that serious disputes over budgets will not occur until the CNIL takes decisive stands severely restricting government surveillance, which has not really occurred to date. For his part, President Jean Rosenwald admitted that his budget was small, but he was committed to spending it wisely, especially on inspections, in order to ensure compliance with the law.[8]

The extent to which the CNIL can (and does) act independently of the government is a thorny question. In the first flush of its creation, the CNIL described itself in very independent terms, highlighting the mode of selection of its members and the composition of the commission.[9] However, in its telling phrase, independence does not imply a hostile relationship with the government. Nor, one might add, does the possession of statutory autonomy ensure that any data protection agency will act independently.

The CNIL itself is very proud of its independent status. In a press release celebrating the achievements of the first five years, President Jacques Thyraud stated that "its independence has been perfectly respected since its creation." After reviewing foreign data protection laws, the CNIL's fifth report drew the surprising conclusion that it was the "agent of control with the largest powers and the strongest independent status."[10] Other French observers regard the CNIL as eminently controllable, in part because its large investigative responsibilities, coupled with its limited resources, create a mission impossible.[11]

Decisions of the CNIL are further subject, like those of any other agency of government, to being overruled by the Council of State.[12] For example, its 1982 decision annulled one of the simplified regulations issued by the CNIL, which required 50,000 letters to be reissued.[13] The Council is in some ways a safety valve for government departments against the abuse of power by the CNIL, much like the relationship between the Cabinet/minister of justice and the DIB in Sweden. But the Council of State has been little used to date. Maisl explains that the government has preferred to negotiate the terms of a favorable decision with the CNIL itself rather than turning to the Council.[14] Nevertheless, the latter is in a position to exercise oversight of the CNIL's activities, and there have been some suggestions that this great body regards the new independent administrative agencies with some suspicion. Legal commentator, Jean Frayssinet, concluded that the preconditions for frayed relations exist and that the Council has an important consultative function to perform with respect to the interpretation and application of the data protection law.[15]

A symbolic episode during the presidency of Giscard d'Estaing threatened the independence of the CNIL in a different way. On December 17, 1980, it was announced that Louis Joinet, the head of the staff at the CNIL, was being moved to another job, a decision apparently made by the minister of justice, Alain Peyrefitte. A great deal of press attention ensued, because of concern for the independence of the CNIL and the fact that Joinet was a key figure in data protection circles.[16] In fact, the minister of justice disapproved of Joinet for organizing a union for magistrates. However, it is a testimony to the level of concern for the independence of the CNIL that petitions circulated in the government and in the informatics community seeking his reinstatement; there were fears that the CNIL would lose its credibility as the agent of control for new information technology. After the 1981 election, Joinet became a councillor in the office of the Socialist prime minister.

In the final analysis, the highly politicized nature of government and society makes it almost impossible for the CNIL to operate independently, especially in comparison with its counterparts in other countries. As one of several autonomous administrative agencies, it flies in the face of tradition and reality. In addition to the factors already discussed, the method of selecting the president and members of the CNIL and the presence of active politicians on the commission are further limiting traits.

Although the government can only directly control the selection of three members of the seventeen-member commission and, normally, can further influence the choice of single persons by the president of the National Assembly and of the Senate, various events illustrate the real reach of its partisan power. Senator Thyraud was a candidate for reelection as president after the end of the first terms of most members of the commission. But after President Mitterrand named Jean Rosenwald to the commission, he was quickly elected in place of Thyraud. The press noted the partisan nature of this change, characterizing it as a victory for the new Socialist majority and a defeat for the conservative opposition.[17] Andrew Lloyd of *Transnational Data Report* worried that Rosenwald would bring the CNIL "even closer to being a traditional arm of the French administration—in contradiction with the original intentions of those who planned the legal framework for the CNIL."[18] The selection of Rosenwald could be viewed as an isolated event were it not for his succession by Jacques Fauvet, under similar circumstances, in June 1984.

The reality of the CNIL's "independence" is that almost all its members are politicians in the sense of being well aware, in good French tradition, of the current direction of the political winds. Without any need for direct government meddling, the members selected by various constituent bodies inevitably reflect the current political balance of the society; in fact, the Socialist majority at the commission, if it could even be called that, was evidently slim. Perhaps the majority should be in fact described as being for "the government," reflecting the elite background in state service of many of those selected and their perception, highly limiting to the control of surveillance, that the state needs information in order to carry out its responsibilities.

On the other hand, because of the initial five-year terms, the Socialist government had little early opportunity to have a direct or indirect impact on the membership of the CNIL. After the election of 1981, the National Assembly changed its second representative to a member of the Socialist party. However, most of the first-term commissioners were representative of what was called the "old majority" during the early Socialist years. In a similar vein, because of fixed terms, the right-wing majority government of 1986 could do little to affect those members of the CNIL who were not politicians until the end of 1988. The Socialist's return to power in 1988 further reduced that prospect.

The political tendency at the CNIL has obviously been reinforced by the presence of prominent politicians, such as Senator Thyraud and Raymond Forni; they served as vice-presidents of the CNIL in addition to their legislative responsibilities.[19] The Socialist party was already well represented on the CNIL through Forni. When the CNIL met in 1984 to pick a successor to Rosenwald, it was Forni who nominated Fauvet, the winner.[20] Forni, in opposition until 1981, was eager to have data protectors critical of the government and he generally took public positions in favor of the strict application of the law. But he subsequently argued, in a telling phrase, that the CNIL should not be a countervailing power to the government; his presumption seems to be that the administration should receive what it wants, which, this writer would argue, has been the history of the commission to date.

The reality of data protection contradicts the rhetoric that the commission requires prominent persons and leading politicians in order to be able to oppose the government on major issues; this rarely happens. The point has been made that the Swedish or West German systems could not work in France, since no individual could take on the government alone. One response is that in France, even a commission is unwilling to resist the government of the day (a statement that does a disservice to the CNIL's incremental achievements). Whatever the statutory language, the independence of the CNIL is significantly modified to the extent that it has decided that it needs to coexist with the government. Although an outsider can debate whether this perceived need is real, the sense in France is that it is. The consequences for controlling governmental surveillance are negative.

Powers of Intervention

The CNIL acquired considerable powers of intervention under article 15 of the law, since automated processing of personal information in the public sector can only occur on the basis of its favorable opinion.[21] As in Sweden, the government can issue a decree creating an information system for a particular agency against the advice of the CNIL. However, the French system has an important, additional control in that the government can only act after the Council of State has ruled in favor of the specific application. In effect, as noted earlier, the government is in a legal position to ask the Council to overturn a CNIL decision but has chosen not to do so.[22]

As in other countries, there is a statutory burden on those being regulated to cooperate with the CNIL. Article 21 requires that ministers, public authorities, and other users of personal files "may not oppose action by the commission or its members for any reasons, and instead shall take any step needed to facilitate its work." Decrees in 1978 and 1981 reinforced this requirement and imposed penal sanctions for hindering the CNIL's activities or for refusals to supply information.[23]

Thus the CNIL possesses considerable power to control the surveillance aspects of personal information systems. On the fifth anniversary of the law, Thyraud's press release claimed that successive governments had always acknowledged the CNIL's point of view, even if they had to modify their initial projects. In no case had the government tried to circumvent a decision of his agency. He concluded that such respect for its decisions confirmed the authority and position of the CNIL.[24] Evidently, the CNIL has not yet encountered any closed doors or restricted information as it has gone about its tasks of supervising data processing in the public sector in particular.

The occasional acknowledgments of the CNIL's power are of symbolic importance in a highly politicized society. In the legislature on February 23, 1984, the prime minister explained that a request to create a particular data bank had been sent to the commission, but the system could not be put into operation until the commission gave a favorable decree, and then, only in conformity with its directives.[25] It is also highly symbolic that senior government officials, including the Paris police, have to visit the CNIL when they are seeking approval for a new system.

Unfortunately, the CNIL's resources are not proportionate to its authority. It has a total staff of about forty-five and a limited budget, especially in comparison with the large administrative bodies that it is attempting to regulate.[26] As in other countries, the state is investing considerably more funds in the promotion of informatics and, indeed, in various forms of surveillance than in data protection. Within the sphere of informatics, the commission is a minor operator in contrast with the vast field of industrial activity of the Postes, Telegraphes et Telephones or the promotional work of the Centre d'Etudes des Systèmes d'Information des Administrations (CESIA).[27]

A significant problem in the exercise of power also results from delays in decision making by the CNIL, caused, as in Sweden, by the excessive burden of licensing both the public and private sectors. In 1984 it announced its interest in artificial intelligence expert systems, because of their use of personal information and the relevance of articles 2 and 3 of the law. However, the CNIL intended to wait until an expert system entered into operational service before pursuing close examination.[28] The consequence of a postimplementation approach is that the CNIL is not realistically in a position to stop such "progress" at a later date. It is constantly forced to find ways to accommodate any system that involves a major investment in data collection or technology, especially on the part of the government.[29] In short, the commission often considers cases in which it is not truly free, in any meaningful sense, to roll back what has been accomplished. As in other countries, the problem is to develop a system of early consultation on the surveillance aspects of such undertakings. In its absence, data protectors are simply legitimators of new technology, giving only the illusion of protection to the public.

The main purpose of the government commissioner appears to be to facilitate oversight by the CNIL rather than to hinder it. Madame C. Pitrat, who currently holds this full-time position, oversees the imposition of the law on government agencies. She receives all declarations made to the CNIL and all requests for its advice on government information systems. She or her deputy attends all formal meetings of the CNIL. Although the commissioner does not vote, she obviously has an important voice. Pitrat also functions as a key liaison between the contact persons in each ministry and the commission. In return, the commissioner is asked to assist the CNIL in obtaining relevant information.[30] The problem with this analysis is that it is difficult to learn how the incumbent functions in practice and in private; she may in fact deliver the government's messages to the CNIL on a regular basis.

A Socialist prime minister made the post of government commissioner full-time in order to make the CNIL more effective.[31] Because it seems so peculiar to traditional civil servants to subject certain aspects of their work to external control, the commissioner plays a critical role in promoting the law and making it understood. Maisl has noted that far from regarding themselves as unconditional defenders of the government's wishes in a particular case, the incumbents have viewed their mission as educational in character.[32] At the same time, the post is the sole official voice of the government at the CNIL, although, as noted earlier, most of the commissioners have a good understanding of the government's point of view because of their professional and political backgrounds. The commissioner's main power was exercised on December 11, 1984, probably for the first time, when Pitrat asked the CNIL to reconsider a decision about the use of information on nationality by housing authorities.

The CNIL has done little about record linkages, although it has expressed concern that this is the great problem for the future.[33] Under the law, it should function like the Swedish Data Inspection Board in terms of having to authorize record linkages in specific cases. Because of its admirable emphasis on the principle of finality (personal data should only be used for the purposes for which they were collected), the CNIL is generally hostile to secondary or unintended connections of information. The broad reach of articles 2 and 3 of the law reinforce this concern. But there are fears that this attention is outmoded and/or impossible to maintain in the face of government initiatives. Fortunately for the commission, plans for record linkages between government departments, or even for information exchanges within one agency, are relatively underdeveloped at present in comparison with other countries.

The CNIL did become interested in record linkages because of the data bank on large fortunes created on the basis of the 1981 Socialist law to tax capital accumulation. Laurent Fabius, then minister of finance, visited the CNIL to discuss the issue and responded positively to its desire to review the entire information system of the director-general of taxes.[34] Such a systemic review, regrettably the first of its kind, occurred in 1984. In that year the CNIL also reviewed major proposed matching by the tax authorities in order to combat tax evasion. President Rosenwald studied the issue before his untimely death and was unwilling to give approval without solid guarantees of data protection. President Fauvet, before the decision was announced, stated that the CNIL had to ensure respect for individual liberties but also did not want to appear to be hindering the revolution in informatics.[35]

The Political Climate and the Use of Power

Although the CNIL has significant powers as an institution, some observers have a healthy degree of skepticism about its ability or willingness to oppose the government. The issues are whether the CNIL is willing to exercise real power in confrontations with such a major agency as the Ministry of the Interior, and what its position is when there are major confrontations with the government. One asset of the CNIL is that its political, or even highly visible, elite members are accustomed to operating in the corridors of power, but the evidence to date suggests that, instead of making them more independent, it makes them more tolerant of the surveillance practices of the state.[36]

The exercise of the CNIL's oversight of government agencies is a continuing focus of the following pages. The early relationships between the CNIL and the public administration were not without tensions. When the CNIL was preparing its advice on the creation of an automated system of residency permits for foreigners living in France, its own reporter resigned his functions in this particular instance to protest the apparent plans of the Ministry of the Interior to put the system in operation before the CNIL had an opportunity to give its advice; such an experience illustrates some of the problems the CNIL has in making its authority effective.[37]

In certain cases the CNIL has flexed its muscles. Not by coincidence, several of the stronger stands occurred after the Socialist victory in May 1981. On June 16, 1981, the CNIL rendered an unfavorable decision, perhaps its most famous one, on Project Gamin, a plan to subject all newborns to compulsory physical examinations.[38] On June 9, 1981, it issued a strong decision requiring modifications in the use of the RNIPP (now known as NIR), which is a national identification register.[39] The press suggested that the election had breathed new fire into the CNIL, although staff members emphasize that the CNIL had done all of the preparatory work for these decisions within the previous six months.[40] Although the CNIL's view is that these decisions were not politically motivated, outsiders suggest that the decision on Project Gamin, for example, was made only after it was certain that the new government would oppose the plan.

There is at least one major example of a large data base that was created without the advice of the CNIL. A reform law in December 1982 required the election of administrators of the social security councils. The electorate consisted of 28.5 million persons insured under the system, but there was no easily accessible list. The job of integrating the extant data was given, as a last resort, to IBM France. As Eric Rohde noted in *Le Monde,* the indirect consequence was the creation of the first large, up-to-date, data base on the population; its contents are more complete than the infamous Safari that helped to prompt the law. In fact, the CNIL had originally refused to agree to this system. So the government decided to issue a separate decree for this electoral register.[41] When consultations occurred, the CNIL insisted successfully on the destruction of these registers after the election.

The presence of members of Parliament on the commission highlights the acutely politicized nature of public administration and of data protection in particular. This often comes as a surprise to foreigners, since other countries' agencies do not share these traits to the same extent. No one denies that data protection involves the exercise of political judgment. However, the CNIL has let partisan politics intervene in the organization of its office and in its decision making on such matters as the selection of a president. Having an active politician as president from 1979 to 1983 critically shaped this situation.

Some critics suggest the politicization of the CNIL has produced a deferential attitude on its behalf in relation to the government, as evidenced by the lack of decisions contrary to the interests of the administration or of big business. One premise of this view is that the complex details of data protection are not relevant to the reelection concerns of members of Parliament serving on the CNIL. Senator Thyraud and Vice-President Forni, for example, stand for reelection in less sophisticated communities than Paris. The argument is that it would not be politically advantageous to hinder the government's plan to create surveillance systems for the control of foreign immigration. Consequently, the elected politicians on the CNIL are less likely to advocate a strong use of the CNIL's powers of intervention, especially if their party is in power.

The basic defense of the CNIL's politicization is that France is a very political society and that the CNIL reflects the shifting political spectrum. Before the election of Mitterrand in 1981, the CNIL exhibited a trend toward the right, and it then moved to the left. It is not that the politically affiliated members, who constitute the vast majority, tend to make routine decisions according to party solidarity. The problem is that the commission functions as a form of miniparliament in which political views are known and articulated; rather than concentrating on the articulation of privacy values, it tries to balance the competing interests. Of course, a licensing model of data protection necessitates such internal decision making. The CNIL thus has very different responsibilities from its counterparts in West Germany or Canada. Adherents of the French approach not only emphasize the delicacy of attempting data protection but suggest, in a tentative way, that their federal counterpart in West Germany has not always been adequately political. If the decisions of the CNIL are too much in favor of the government, this is a problem for all countries.

The government's evident ability to influence the choice of a president further curtails the CNIL's power. The administration naturally tries to put in place a friendly person less likely to resist its initiatives on surveillance. The result is the illusion of data protection. The practice in other countries of relying on a more neutral chief executive with civil servant status leads to more effective implementation. President Fauvet, however, seeks to avoid political involvement and to remain neutral.

The functioning of the CNIL raises some critical questions about the proper relationship of an independent data protection agency with the legislature and government. The internal view is that it is inappropriate for the commission to determine that government initiatives on surveillance, such as against terrorism or tax evasion, are not important. It is not the role of such an agency to resist a data base to implement a tax on large fortunes, if the legislature has decided to enact such a measure. The response of this writer is that the task of data protectors is to articulate the interests favoring privacy protection, until the specific battle is over. For the CNIL to do so effectively, it must be willing, upon occasion, to counter government initiatives as an alert watchdog. The departure of Freese from his job in Sweden, however, can be regarded as the consequence of too many such fights. No commissions or commissioners can remain in office if they are constantly challenging the government, but this has never been the situation of the CNIL. To the end of 1986, it had taken only seven negative decisions against the government.

Professor Maisl, an intimate observer of the CNIL, draws an opposite conclusion: "Like other institutions, the CNIL is finally only the reflection of a society at a particular moment and its approach tends logically toward mediation rather than confrontation with the current authorities that would prove to be in vain."[42] He further insists on a model of data protection in which the agency tries to balance the competing interests, or at least does not venture too far in their promotion, rather than simply advancing them. Rosenwald saw his role as balancing privacy interests versus the administrative needs of the government. Similarly, Fauvet seems to have adopted the same perspective in arguing that the indispensable role of the CNIL is to reconcile the rights of society and those of the person, the interests of the individual and those of the state.[43]

Even though the law imposes on the CNIL the responsibility for balancing competing interests in difficult cases, other nations, such as Sweden and Canada, have left this duty to the legislature so as to avoid politicizing and weakening the data protection agency. France placed this power within the CNIL itself to ensure that it was responsive to current public policy trends, but this politicized the agency. The result is that many decisions are partisan, and the CNIL is reluctant to be confrontational. Most important, this leaves no one as advocate solely for privacy and individual rights. In many ways, this is the inevitable result of a licensing system of data protection, where there is no separation of powers.

Chapter 16

The Implementation of Data Protection

Effective implementation is a key factor in the successful conduct of data protection. Thus this core chapter pays extended attention to what has happened since France introduced a data protection law in 1978. What approaches has the National Commission on Informatics and Freedoms (CNIL) used in trying to limit governmental surveillance practices and with what success? Special attention is paid to staffing, since the choice of employees has proved to be so critical to this effort. There is also extensive discussion of the various activities of data protectors as they seek to accomplish their statutory tasks. Finally, the chapter treats how data protection principles have evolved in practice.

The Members and Staff of the CNIL

The President and the Members

The first president of the CNIL, elected on December 5, 1978, was Pierre Bellet, who was also first president of the Court of Cassation. He resigned in July 1979 to be succeeded in November by Senator Jacques Thyraud, who served until 1983. Bellet set the initial pattern of a prominent president with other heavy responsibilities. Thyraud was elected by a vote of eleven to six over Bernard Tricot, the chief reporter of the 1974–75 commission on data protection.[1] Thyraud, a lawyer and municipal magistrate, has been a senator since 1974. He played a leading role in the original debates on data protection and is sensitive to human rights.

Until the mid-1980s, the senator was also the mayor of a small industrial town in the Loire Valley. Thyraud had been mayor since 1959 and, in typical fashion, has seen it as in his community's best interest that he assume higher political office. The French call this enthusiasm for plural office-holding "le cumul des mandats," whereby the more offices you hold, the more power you wield. One critic has pointed out that this practice "has concentrated too much power in too few hands and has given the busy potentate too little time to concentrate properly on any of his duties."[2]

Thyraud was simultaneously a mayor, a senator, and the president of a very busy commission. In retrospect, it is evident that his wide range of responsibilities did not leave adequate time for making data protection truly effective, especially since the tasks are very much full time for his national counterparts.

The majority of the commission that consciously chose a politician as president in 1979 were naively unaware of how much real work was involved. For his part, Thyraud worsened the situation by failing to appoint a strong chief of staff.

Thyraud was initially reelected president by an overwhelming vote in the fall of 1983. However, the renewal of terms for many members of the commission required another election. The celebrations of the CNIL's fifth anniversary in November 1983 became part of his reelection campaign in the face of the ambitions of the Socialist party to take control of the CNIL.[3]

When the CNIL convened in December 1983 to elect a president, a newcomer to the commission, Jean Rosenwald, replaced Thyraud by a bare majority of nine votes after a tie on the first ballot. The press reported the election results as a political victory for the Socialists and a defeat for their conservative opposition.[4] Rosenwald, who had just retired at the age of sixty-nine as first president of the Audit Office, was named to the CNIL by President Mitterrand. He was an experienced public administrator, a long-time member of the Socialist party, and enjoyed a reputation as a defender of human rights, because of his role in the Resistance. Rosenwald, who admitted that he knew nothing about informatics, described himself as among those deeply committed to President Mitterrand. He was also expected to bring better administration to the CNIL.[5] He summarized his program with the formula, "less foreign travel and more missions and inspections in the field."[6] His most important change was to become a daily presence at the CNIL.

Rosenwald died suddenly on June 2, 1984. His replacement, Jacques Fauvet, was elected by a bare majority on the second ballot over Michel Elbel, an adviser to Jacques Chirac, the mayor of Paris, and an obvious representative of the right.[7] Aged seventy, Fauvet had spent the Second World War as a prisoner of war and then joined *Le Monde,* serving as director from 1969 to 1982. In announcing the election, this newspaper added a perceptive comment about the commission: "The mechanism for an essential democratic control, its dynamism depends in large part on the statesmanship of its president."[8] In his first interviews, Fauvet indicated that he was carrying on Rosenwald's initiatives in terms of better administration and careful audits. On December 21, 1988, Fauvet was unanimously reelected to a second five-year term.

There are two vice-presidents of the CNIL. Thyraud was the first incumbent; when he was defeated for the presidency, he became first vice-president. Socialist deputy, Raymond Forni, was a vice-president from 1978 until 1985. During the Socialist regime, his presidency of the Commission on Laws of the National Assembly meant that he too had limited time to devote to the CNIL. Forni did distinguish himself by occasionally taking public positions on issues relevant to the work of the commission. When the new government amended the law on "security and freedom" in 1983, Forni was the only Socialist deputy to oppose an amendment permitting the taking of photographs and fingerprints in certain legal investigations.[9]

These various changes are symptomatic of the extent to which the commission has reflected major political tendencies. The benefits of having politicians in such offices are greater when there is a full-time president in place to supervise the daily work of the agency. The benefits seem to include a greater sensitivity to the needs and wants of the general public, to the implications of decision making affecting the public sector, and to the possibilities of using power in specific cases.

In addition to the three executive officers, the fourteen additional members of the CNIL serve as commissioners. In the first few years, almost one-third of them resigned or were replaced before the completion of their term, suggesting the "weeding out" of persons not particularly committed to informatics and privacy law.[10] Less than one-half of the original members served their full terms. There may have been an initial enthusiasm to accept an appointment to an important and unusual commission, but the work load clearly led to a significant change in membership when the five-year terms expired. Recently, the membership has become more stable. The 1983 newcomers (average age of sixty-one) were from both the left and right in French society. The six newcomers in December 1988 are primarily from the major courts and councils; they may be expected to reflect the fact that the Socialists are again in power.[11]

The commissioners are for the most part an elite group, containing representatives who are senior members of many of the great state bodies, especially the administrative courts. In effect, they represent the highest levels of political and public life, which raises some reasonable concerns about their vulnerability to competing pressures and activities. The Centre d'information et d'initiatives sur l'informatisation (CIII) commented appropriately: "It is certain that the actual sociological composition of the CNIL does not predispose it to strike against the established powers but rather to conciliate them."[12] The high average age of the commissioners is also a factor.[13] While the burden of activities at the CNIL is plausible for a retired member of the Audit Office, for example, the situation is quite different for a person who remains an active member of any major body. One can reasonably question how individuals who are extremely active in professional life or business can also find time to respond to the pressing demands of controlling surveillance. Being a member of the CNIL should not be a sinecure, if data protection is to be made effective.

The statutory requirements for membership on the CNIL exclude individuals from the private sector with current experience in data processing and telecommunications.[14] This has the undesirable consequence of depriving the commission of more technically competent members. Fortunately, the several government commissioners to date have brought with them valuable experience in data processing and informatics.

In any commission model, questions arise about the extent to which the members are free to represent themselves or the organization with which they are affiliated. Although the developing trend appears to be that the members of the commission act upon their personal views, it is natural for members of the great courts, councils, and political parties to reflect the traditions and ideology of their respective identity groups, even though these organizations themselves often lack internal cohesion. This is particularly relevant in a highly politicized society. As in Sweden, the politicians are most tied to their sponsoring agency. It is possible for a party to instruct its members on the CNIL on a particular matter. Thus, far from regarding the presence of politicians on the commission as a guarantee of the CNIL's independence, they are more likely a threat to truly independent action because of their strong, multiple allegiances. Further, the commissioners in general seem to be much less representative of various nongovernmental interest groups than their Swedish counterparts (especially business); the Data Inspection Board has the advantage of being chosen from a wider variety of interest groups than its French counterpart.

The decision-making process of the commission reflects France's predilection for elite accommodation. Normally decisions are taken by the president stating a consensus of the meeting, depending on the particular activity underway, but secret ballots are used several times a year. Although members tend not to be sharply divided on specific issues, the minutes indicate that significant debates occur on particular matters. One essential limitation of the system remains: given the varying backgrounds of the commissioners, it will always be difficult for any president to integrate his or her views into a coherent whole, just as it will always be difficult for an elite group of seventeen persons to reach a consistent series of decisions.

The commission meets for several hours every two weeks except during the holiday season. Occasionally, there are weekly meetings because of the press of business. The type of activities includes giving advice to the public sector, taking decisions for the private sector, and issuing simplified rules. Work on the public sector predominates. The rapidly increasing pace of decision making is also noteworthy. At a meeting on March 23, 1982, for example, there were thirty-five decisions, most of which were routine. On other occasions, such as April 27 or October 5, 1982, only one decision emerged from the meeting. Thus it is rare for the commission as a whole to focus in detail on a specific issue and, even then, only one or two members have prepared the detailed dossier. The issue-by-issue approach also discourages systematic consideration of governmental surveillance practices.

The minutes of the commissioners' meetings now provide some insights into the actual contributions of individual members. Generally, the commissioners work with a very high degree of at least outward unanimity. To date, there is no tradition of recording dissents. Meetings are usually attended by at least three-quarters of the commissioners, but they may not be terribly well prepared. They obtain the dossiers necessary to their decisions, including draft recommendations and a collection of the latest press clippings, five or six days before a meeting. One commissioner estimated in 1984 that he spent five to six days a month at the CNIL, which is in fact considerable for a voluntary activity. The limited amount of time that individual commissioners can devote to their work calls into question the quality of analysis given to the more problematic issues and, indeed, the validity of a large part-time commission.

The *Tricot Report* recommended that the CNIL should not be a court but should have the "character of a collegiate administrative body." The CNIL has since described itself as an "organ of decision making and of thought."[15] The power of decision making rests in theory with the commissioners rather than with the staff. The commissioners want to make decisions themselves and, at least in the early years, claimed to want very little input from the staff on the specific direction a decision should take. In practice, the commissioners are not interested in the innumerable applications for permission to keep information systems; only cases posing problems of principle, that affect a large number of people, or that have a peculiar character, are brought before them.[16] The consequences of this situation for the staff will be discussed in the next section of this chapter.

On major issues, a commissioner and a staff member prepare materials for distribution and for presentation of the essential points at the plenary meeting.[17] This reporter *(rapporteur)* obviously plays a very influential role. For important, specific subjects, he or she becomes the central focus, including the receipt of briefs from interested parties.[18] Reporters sometimes meet with representatives of those being regulated during the course of preparations for major decisions, which typically leads to modifications in the government's plans before the CNIL has to make a decision. The full commission may impose changes in the proposed ruling, or the reporter may be instructed to obtain further information. Although the members become specialists in various sectors, the commission makes the decisions.[19] Lack of coordination between staff and commissioners on a dossier sometimes means that the discussion does not focus on the real issues. The president may invite staff members to be present to clarify situations.

The CNIL initially created three permanent subcommissions to work on specific aspects of its very broad mandate. In 1984 President Rosenwald proposed a new subcommission on local government and assigned each commissioner to at least one, in addition to having a sectoral responsibility. The subcommission on freedom to work is in fact examining the state of personnel records in the public and private sectors. The process apparently began when Peugeot workers complained about an item of illicit information being collected by the company. The CNIL then directed its subcommission to monitor complaints and request information about personnel data. The subcommission has also studied the use of call-monitoring devices on company telephones. One of its chief activities is consultation with major unions.[20]

Eight commissioners are now involved with the subcommission on technology and security (formerly informatics and freedom of expression). Thyraud explained that the CNIL was not using the term freedom of expression in its classical sense: "In previous times freedom of expression was the possibility to say what one wanted to state. . . . Today freedom of expression is the liberty to be oneself and to remain oneself, that is to not permit others to find out your thinking by your attitude, your silence, or your behavior."[21] The concern of this subcommission is the individual's right to keep his or her opinions private in the face of new surveillance technologies.[22] Because few complaints were received, the subcommittee has initiated a number of contacts with relevant companies and professional organizations and has taken the lead by forbidding the introduction of detailed, itemized phone bills. Its goal was to tie freedom of expression to data protection.

The Staff

The *Tricot Report* said that the president of the CNIL should appoint its staff, presumably as part of an effort to ensure the independence of the commission.[23] In practice, the president, a politician, appointed most of the CNIL's employees during its first years. In comparison with other data protection agencies, this staff gave the appearance of being patronage appointees rather than professional civil servants. In the early years many people working at the CNIL had some previous relationship with either the president or one of the commissioners. Charges of nepotism have not disappeared.

The recruitment patterns of the CNIL changed dramatically in 1983–84, when some of those associated with it recognized that a stronger staff was essential to make data protection effective. Rosenwald, with his broad experience in public administration, knew how to provide leadership and how to manage a staff. His candid reaction was that the commission was not functioning in the best traditions of the central administrations. He thought it possible that early recruitment to the CNIL had been too rapid, because of its urgency: "We want to raise the level of competence of our staff. . . . We need to surround ourselves with excellent specialists, whether they are jurists or informaticians."[24] Rosenwald, and Fauvet after him, recruited their senior people from other government agencies.

Rosenwald's "first reaction" on arrival at the CNIL was surprise at the lack of human resources in informatics. Only one of the twelve commissioners had any real background in computers. The recruitment of technically capable staff from inside the civil service had just begun. To supplement a part-time technical adviser on informatics, Rosenwald and Fauvet recruited a high-level computer expert in late 1984.[25]

Beneath the level of senior staff, the *chargés de mission* hold the most important positions. Seven people serve in this capacity at the time of writing; there are also eight attachés, who are mostly newcomers, reflecting the exodus of a number of the most qualified chargés. Almost all of both groups have had a legal education, sometimes coupled with training in data processing and political science. Perhaps one-third have been with the CNIL since 1979. New appointments at this level are now made through open competitions among students at the end of their legal or political studies or by promotion from subordinate positions on the staff. Although there are risks in staffing an agency with inexperienced individuals, the broader public administration experience of recent senior appointees is a counterbalance.

The problem in the long term is the lack of job mobility for those recruited directly into the CNIL. As in other countries, periodic rotation of staff is essential to competent implementation, especially when small numbers are involved. Generally, the staff are not regular civil servants, unless they are on secondment from another government office, in which case they can return to guaranteed positions in their former departments. However, even those staff members hired directly are protected by standard civil service laws and by contracts that are in fact indefinite, unless the government were to terminate their specific position in a future budget. These employment guarantees are crucial to the development of feelings of job security, which are a prerequisite for an aggressive approach to controlling surveillance. Unfortunately, this essential trait has not yet yielded the anticipated results.

Professor Maisl, the part-time legal adviser to the CNIL until the end of 1988, has pointed out that the goal of the CNIL is mediation and conciliation with those being regulated, especially with respect to government agencies.[26] Before rendering an opinion or reaching a decision, it seeks to negotiate an appropriate compromise. One proof of its "success" is that the Council of State first annulled a decision of the CNIL under article 15 in 1987. This situation is also a result of its reluctance to oppose or antagonize the government on an important matter. In analyzing its principal opinions in its second annual report, the CNIL noted that "the position that has been adopted collegially is not always as categorical as some would wish. The CNIL must make a choice between the advantages and the inconveniences, with the hope of establishing sane limits to the concept of the general interest invoked by administrations for which it is the principle of existence. The CNIL has refused projects, but more often it modifies them."[27] This is not the language of a spirited watchdog.

Measures instituted by Prime Minister Pierre Mauroy in 1982 facilitate the process of consultation with central government agencies. Officials in each ministry have the duty to ensure that personnel are aware of the law and of the role of the CNIL. This decision implies that the prior system was not working well. One purpose of the new structure was to indicate that the government wants to set an example of "scrupulous respect" for the law. The staff of the CNIL generally suggest that they have not had any particular difficulties in working with government ministries on requests for opinions. The direct linkage to specific persons with data protection responsibilities at each government office facilitates the evolution of a cooperative attitude and, conversely, deters the development of a confrontational stance between those who implement and those who regulate.[28] This cooperative attitude is also a function of the unique spirit that exists among members of the civil service. Viewing themselves as elites responsible for the functioning of the state, it is not surprising to find a lack of confrontation within the ranks.

Both French and foreign observers have commented on the CNIL's lack of effectiveness, which can be attributed to several factors: the overly broad statutory mandate imposed by the law, the licensing system, and the presence of political representatives on the commission. These result in a completely unmanageable workload, which in turn, demoralizes the staff. The effects of the excessive breadth of the law are evidenced by the copious stacks of files that surround most of the staff members. Simplified standards were introduced in the hope of reducing the paper burden, yet a huge backlog of declarations and requests for opinions built up. The workload was compounded by the lack of local, regional offices of the commission (nor is it thought desirable to have them). Along with their substantial regulatory and licensing duties, the staff also functions as first-level interpreters of the meaning of different articles in the law, to which chargés refer regularly in discussions with those being regulated.

The CNIL is often the victim of a disease common to data protection in most countries—trying to do too many things at once and doing very few of them well.[29] Aside from the implication of this phenomenon for staff morale, the effectiveness of data protection itself is endangered. If the CNIL fails to respond to a request for opinion, its tacit consent is given automatically under the law. This means that a data processor can proceed with a particular surveillance activity without the intervention of the CNIL. Bureaucrats contemplating intrusive practices are likely to be well aware of such possibilities.

The political tendencies of the commission have deeply affected the approaches and attitudes of the staff. Until 1984, when politicians were effectively in control of the agency, no one was really managing the CNIL on a daily basis, with the result that pressing and important work was not being expeditiously completed. The staff, like the commission itself, was more political and politicized than is at least the custom in other Western European countries. Given the potential impact of staff members on the decision-making process, as discussed earlier, the idea that their attitudes and approaches may be based on partisan ideology rather than advocacy of privacy is regrettable.

The modus operandi of the CNIL had a further negative impact on staff attitudes and approaches. Since virtually none of the commissioners were devoting their time solely to data protection, there were problems of effective supervision and cooperation with the staff. There were no consistent administrative procedures between the commissioners and the staff. In an organization in which several persons share the preparation of a dossier, the lack of standard operating procedures and strong central management control can be fatal, both to the overall effectiveness of the system and to the morale of those who must struggle through a haphazardly assembled file. Dossiers are distributed among the motivated and the less motivated. In addition, there was no homogeneity among the members of the commission as to how they actually worked with the staff. Even in an effective commission system, it is difficult for members to ensure that assigned staff members and their own colleagues have prepared a dossier carefully and accurately.

The absence of a full-time, senior administrator to manage the day-to-day burdens of the organization symbolized the CNIL's administrative weaknesses. The addition of a full-time president, a secretary-general, and changes in the staff recruitment process have begun to improve the morale and vigor of the CNIL. Yet the staff has not yet fully understood the problems of data protection in particular government information systems, because it has undertaken so few detailed inspections. This is partly a product of the workload.

Although the revised operating procedures adopted by the commission are designed to simplify the tasks, it is not yet coping very satisfactorily with the resulting flood. The risk is that the CNIL under its current organizational structure is not doing its basic tasks as capably as is necessary. It has not been bureaucratic enough, in the professional sense, to accomplish its work. It is symptomatic that the CNIL did not formally adopt internal rules for its administration until 1987, even though this is normally a first step in the establishment of any agency.[30] The improved level of aspirations since 1984, compared to the work product, further suggests that it will take time for new senior personnel to become thoroughly familiar with their duties.

The Activities of the CNIL

Advising, Supervision, and Inspections

The CNIL's extensive mandate, as dictated by law, includes at least thirteen regulatory duties or missions: issuing deliberations, such as setting up simplified standards or issuing rules on security; rendering advice for the public sector in the form of a law, a decree, or a judgment; making recommendations, such as on the right of access; carrying out inspections; issuing warnings to users; and reporting offenses.[31]

The CNIL adopted the practice in its first five years of always working on a case-by-case basis in response to government requests for new information systems. The bureaucratic character of the law, with its burden of licensing the public and private sectors and its emphasis on responding to requests for advice, has made it difficult for the commission to adopt a systematic, sectoral approach to other public administrations or to control its agenda fully, as is at least somewhat more likely to happen under the advisory systems in West Germany and Canada.[32] This meant that the commission did not receive an overview of the surveillance practices of any particular administration until a comprehensive examination of the tax system in 1984.[33]

Public-sector data processing can only be authorized by a law or regulation of the government "adopted after obtaining the reasoned opinion" of the CNIL. In certain cases processing of personal information has to be authorized by a specific law.[34] If the advice of the CNIL is negative, the government can override it only on the basis of the agreement of the Council of State. Under article 48, existing public-sector data processing only needs to be reported to the CNIL by means of a general declaration (the process normally reserved for the private sector). This has led to one of the greatest limitations of its work, since extant systems in the public sector have not received the same detailed scrutiny as proposals for new systems. It could have chosen to regulate all existing systems of personal information, on the basis of the second section of article 48, but decided not to do so.[35]

Apparently most of the 6,000 personal information systems in the public sector have now been reported to the CNIL.[36] The central public administrations have approximately 5,000 systems containing personal information, but only 1,000 are held at the national level. As further evidence of the extent of public surveillance, there are 15,000 information systems held by local authorities, including 3,200 automated electoral registers.

Articles 16 and 17 of the 1978 law attempted to avoid some of the burdens of the Swedish licensing system by providing for a series of simplified standards "for the most common types of public or private data processing, which manifestly do not infringe private life or liberties." In such a case, only a declaration of conformity with these rules has to be filed with the CNIL. The acknowledgment of the declaration permits the applicant to proceed with data processing, even though the automatic assumption that certain forms of data processing pose no challenges to private life seems misleading. Almost 90 percent of the 150,000 declarations and requests for advice to the end of 1986 are such simple declarations.[37]

The CNIL has produced thirty sets of simplified rules to cover various types of standard data-processing systems, such as personnel work.[38] As in other countries, the process continues of trying to reduce the workload by producing "model" ways of handling a particular type of national surveillance problem.

One of the first simplified rules issued in 1980 concerned government payrolls. The first article contains useful standards for protecting the interests of individuals, but article 3 lists a considerable amount of personal information that can be legitimately collected.[39] This raises the question of whether the CNIL is adequately questioning existing surveillance practices. This is a serious matter because of the reliance on simplified rules for reporting.[40] There is a procedure to follow when the CNIL suspects that a particular information system may not be in conformity with the goals of the simplified rules.[41]

The full commission took approximately fifty formal decisions, forty-one in the form of *avis* or opinions, in the almost fifteen months to the end of 1984.[42] Each dossier on a specific case contains the project proposal, the problem posed for data protection, the personal information to be collected, and its uses. Such a dossier can be ten to fifteen pages in length. The draft decision on the application, which is regularly modified in the course of plenary meetings, follows this same format.

The law specifies in valuable detail (comparable to what is collected in other European countries) the information that applicants for an opinion or those making a declaration must include.[43] Thus the CNIL, like the Data Inspection Board in Sweden, receives very complete information about an enormous number of data processing systems, which gives it an extremely advantageous post from which to understand the extent of surveillance. Any changes in the details or any discontinuance of the activity have to be reported as well.[44] In these circumstances a government agency may have to change the regulation that it issued in compliance with the CNIL's advice.

Decisions are rarely unfavorable: there have been twenty-one in the first ten years of the law. The CNIL believes that such a response to a government request is counterproductive. It is much more common for the CNIL to set forth reservations or qualifications, as happened in 42 percent of such decisions in the first six months of 1987. Jacques Fauvet explained that the commission "prefers dialogue and the search for an agreement with the institutions and organizations whose missions require the development of automated data bases." In fact, Fauvet argued in 1988 that "the government preferred to modify its projects rather than run the risk of an unfavorable decision."[45] Another common response is to press for modification of a proposed project in the course of negotiations with a government agency. The government commissioner plays a critical role by informing herself in advance about a particular dossier and giving advice on data protection measures. Although this conciliatory approach looks appealing, it encourages the government to think that it can introduce almost any form of surveillance, which the CNIL, in the final analysis, will likely accept.

Under article 15, the CNIL has only four months to give its opinion on a request from the public sector, which shall otherwise be deemed to be favorable. There have been 4,759 such requests to the end of 1986, 1,252 in that year alone.[46] Given its burden of work, it is difficult to meet this deadline, and a great many tacit agreements have resulted. Allegations have been made that the commission uses this tactic to avoid delicate matters. Although the CNIL may clarify the conditions for the existence of a particular register at any time, it has not done so to date.

The CNIL distinguishes between giving interpretations of articles of the 1978 law and giving general advice. These are relatively specialized activities in comparison to the decision-making powers of the CNIL in connection with requests for its opinion. The results of these "délibérations" are incorporated in a standard format of several articles, which have the force of law as regulations, unless negated by the government with the concurrence of the Council of State. These regulations provide standards for enforcement purposes if problems arise.

The *Tricot Report* in 1975 strongly urged that data processing in the public sector should be regulated by legal instruments so as to end the legal disorder then existing with respect to various information systems.[47] In essence, the

Tricot Commission found that the legal basis for a number of public-sector information systems could not be established. These lacunas have created an ongoing agenda for the CNIL. It plays a continuing role in advising the government on the data protection aspects of special laws and decrees for particular information systems. In addition, the CNIL can propose to the government statutory or regulatory measures necessary to adapt the protection of freedom to the evolution of the procedures and techniques of data processing.[48]

As new laws and regulations are being passed, they increasingly provide for an advisory role for the CNIL. A 1980 statute creating an automated criminal record system mandates the advice of the CNIL. It had earlier issued its opinion concerning this process of automation and subsequently helped the Ministry of Justice to prepare the decree.[49]

Article 21(3) requires the CNIL to "lay down standard rules for system security as necessary; in exceptional circumstances, it may prescribe security measures, including the destruction of storage media." This responsibility led to its 1981 deliberation on security and information systems.[50] Now that the commission has hired a senior computer specialist, it expects to investigate security matters and to issue standards for security. Article 29 imposes a burden on information processors "to see that all necessary precautions are taken to protect the data and in particular to prevent these from being distorted, damaged or disclosed to unauthorized third parties."

A recent debate over security illustrates the utility of the CNIL. On November 28, 1984, the satirical magazine, *Le Canard Enchaîné,* revealed that it had been able to penetrate the security net around the computers of a service bureau, the Compagnie Internationale de Services en Informatique (CISI), which has the state atomic energy agency (CEA) as its major owner and client. The purpose of the exercise was to test whether security was as impenetrable as CISI had publicly asserted. The magazine claimed to have roamed at will among the data bases of the clients of CISI by usurping the identity of another user currently on the system; it published several columns of data that its agent obtained, taking certain precautions not to reveal the names of persons.

Le Canard claimed that the data bases of CISI were as open to outsiders as a public garden, which created a sensation in the media.[51] The CISI made a complaint to the CNIL against *Le Canard,* because personal data secured in an unauthorized fashion were revealed. Although the apparent lack of security at CISI was in violation of article 29 of the law, article 43 forbids the publication of information that invades personal privacy. The CNIL launched an investigation into the circumstances of the case but with no apparent results. The episode also prompted the CNIL to acknowledge that it had not devoted adequate efforts to promote computer security, especially at service bureaus.

Another major aspect of the general work of the CNIL is to conduct inspections on its own initiative, in response to a complaint, or in order to check compliance with a particular decision.[52] But the Thyraud regime was resistant to such activities: "We are neither policemen nor inquisitors. Our role is intended to take place at a higher level, and our activities are above all preventative." Even Vice-President Forni thought the immensity of the task of inspecting so many data bases meant that only citizens could undertake the task by looking at their own files; the unwanted alternative was to transfer the CNIL into an enormous, quasi-policelike institution.[53] Such inappropriate attitudes for a watchdog betray a complete lack of understanding of how selective audits are used so successfully in other countries.

President Rosenwald, with his auditing background, quickly recognized the need to increase the number of inspections. From only seven in the first eight months of 1983, one hundred had occurred by the end of 1984, and there were forty in 1985, mostly in the private sector.[54] Rosenwald had no illusions about how much actual checking could occur to monitor compliance, but he wanted it firmly known that there was at least a minimum risk in deceiving the commission. President Fauvet is equally enthusiastic about the "dissuasive power" of audits, yet he continues to argue that budgetary constraints explain their minimum number to date.[55] Two audits in April and September 1988 at criminal justice data bases in Nantes and Paris further suggest that the CNIL must learn that they should consist of something more substantial than one-day or several-hour official visits by a few commissioners and staff members.

Article 11 provides that the CNIL may request senior judges to assign a judge, if necessary assisted by experts, to carry out investigations and inspections under its supervision. In 1982 it made use of such senior experts to visit five urban police departments. When a private-sector survey group refused to receive agents of the CNIL in 1984, it decided to send in a magistrate under article 11. However, Maisl has pointed out that magistrates are already heavily burdened with work, which limits the possibilities of using them in this way.[56] They also have no experience in data protection.

The Data Register

Article 22 requires the CNIL to make available to the public a list of data processing activities, specifying in each case the law or the regulation authorizing the establishment of the particular system or the date of its declaration to the CNIL, the name and purpose of the information system, the categories of personal data recorded, and the users or categories of users authorized to receive such information. The CNIL has a register of *automated* personal information systems, which includes data on declarations, follows requests for the opinion of the CNIL, and produces lists of information systems in compliance with article 22.[57] There are at least 160,000 entries in the system, with more than 85 percent from the private sector. Fauvet estimated in 1987 that another 3,000 to 4,000 systems may not have notified the CNIL as required by law, especially because of the proliferation of personal computers.[58]

The register of registers is ostensibly available to the general public, but there has never been a press of users, perhaps because few people know of its existence. The CNIL favors permitting outside access by means of an on-line videotex system operated by a service bureau, rather than the preparation of a printed guide, but such a system is not yet in operation.[59] The Thyraud regime tended to trumpet the virtues of its register, but it is more realistic to note that Rosenwald sought to make it more reliable, in part by hiring a full-time computer specialist.[60] There are also plans to make it easier to search for both the commission and the outside requester. Eventually, the French may find it easier to learn which data banks are watching them.

Individual Access to Data and Complaints

The data protection law emphasizes individuals' right of access to data about them as a means of controlling surveillance. Each application for an opinion or declaration to the CNIL and the regulatory opinion of the CNIL for any public-sector system must specify the department where the right can be exercised.[61] An individual "may require the correction, addition, clarification, up-dating or erasure of data concerning him which are inaccurate, incomplete, ambiguous, outdated or of which the acquisition, use, disclosure or storage is prohibited."[62] A 1981 decree of the Council of State created penal sanctions for opposing an individual's rights of access and correction.[63]

Articles 34 to 37 deal exclusively with the exercise of the right of access to *automated* personal data.[64] The information supplied "shall be in clear language and shall conform to the contents of the records." A person has a right to obtain a copy of his or her record for a charge fixed by agreement with the minister of economy and finance after a decision by the CNIL. If an individual seeking access fears the concealment or disappearance of the personal information, an application may be made to a competent court to order appropriate measures for preventing such acts.[65]

The law lays great stress on accuracy and completeness in record keeping. Article 37 contains an extraordinary provision that "a personal file must be supplemented or corrected even *ex proprio motu* [of its own accord] when the organization keeping it becomes aware of the inaccuracy or incompleteness of a personal item of data in such a file." The intention is to encourage an organization to correct a personal record without waiting for subject access to point out the errors. Moreover, the law provides that if an item of personal data has been sent to a third party, "its correction or deletion must be communicated to such a party unless the commission waives such a proceeding."[66] It would be impressive if articles 37 and 38 were enforced in a meaningful fashion, but there are no criminal sanctions attached to their breach.

Articles 39 and 40 grant an individual an indirect right of access to information systems concerning national security, defense, or public safety. By international standards, guaranteed access to such sensitive files is a very strong protection for civil liberties. An individual applies directly to the CNIL, which nominates one of its members, who is or has been a member of one of the three main administrative courts, to review the entire file and to suppress data that should not have been collected. Unfortunately, fewer than one hundred such requests are made yearly, suggesting a lack of public awareness or, alternately, a surprising lack of concern about surveillance practices in a sensitive area.

An agency in the security and defense field that is directly approached by an applicant should give out information that is communicable and notify the person about the existence of other information. On request, the president of the CNIL then selects a commissioner from one of the major courts to review the relevant information under article 39; this commissioner has the power to decide what is communicable to the individual.[67]

Exercising rights of access on behalf of an individual is a significant area of accomplishment for the CNIL. Commissioners are obtaining full access to the relevant records, follow leads to other files, and, in general, are trying to exercise all of the rights of individuals under the law, but they can only tell the applicants that they proceeded to carry out the necessary verifications. Other remaining problems include how best to gain access to data bases outside Paris, how to ensure the accuracy and reliability of the data when errors are rampant, and how to ensure that the required corrections are in fact made.[68] Senator Thyraud protested to the Ministry of the Interior when it was revealed that the Paris police were requiring candidates for driver's licenses who had been discharged from the military to use their right of access to learn the cause of their discharge.[69] President Fauvet is dissatisfied with the CNIL's role as a counterweight to administrative power in this domain, because it cannot tell an individual what information was canceled, nor whether he or she is actually recorded in a file.[70]

Because France also has a law of July 17, 1978, on access to administrative documents, certain problems arose about coordinating rights of access for individuals under these two 1978 laws.[71] The issue surfaced particularly in connection with decisions of the Administrative Tribunal of Lyons and of the Council of State in 1982–83 in what is known as the Bertin affair. This individual was making both direct and indirect access requests under the two laws. The Council of State decided in 1983 that the data protection law was dominant and that denials of requests for access to personal data in any form must be brought to the attention of the CNIL. Similarly, indirect requests for personal data should also be taken to the CNIL rather than to the Commission d'Accès aux Documents Administratifs (CADA).[72]

The CNIL vehemently contends that the exercise of access rights is the most important means of ensuring compliance with the 1978 law, yet critics argue that the commission is not doing enough to promote knowledge and use of access rights.[73] In 1980 it issued a major opinion on how rights of access should be exercised.[74] An individual does not have to justify such a request, and there are no limits on its use, except for control of abuses. The CNIL subsequently noted that its recommendations have no commanding value or judicial effect, but it expects its advice to have moral force as a practical guide to data holders.[75] Moreover, it tries to play as minor a role as possible in facilitating the process and wants to be approached for assistance to individuals only in the last instance.[76] It is almost as if the CNIL does not want to be responsible for the successful use of the right of access, and thus has adopted a limited role; it only wants to help persons who have been refused access.[77] Nevertheless, in the first ten months of 1984, it received 250 complaints from individuals concerning problems with access requests.[78]

In 1981 the CNIL itself published a small pamphlet on how individuals could exercise their right of access.[79] It informed readers that there are approximately 200,000 automated personal information systems and claimed that every individual is recorded at least 200 times and perhaps as many as 500, if they have children.[80] The focus of the pamphlet is protecting citizens against abusive use of automated information systems.

Acting upon proposals made by the CNIL, the Ministry of the Budget fixed the rates for access at twenty francs for requests to the public sector under article 35 and thirty francs for requests to the private sector.[81] This charge only applies if an individual wants a copy of the data in question. Some observers believe that such costs are very high. The small number of requests is also a strong argument for abolishing charges in order to promote the beneficial exercise of individual rights.

The fact that the right of access is barely being used, as President Thyraud frequently noted and deplored, presents fundamental problems for the successful control of surveillance in that data protection does depend, to at least some extent, upon the individual's right of access creating a "watchdog" climate for data processors.[82] No statistics are collected or published on the number of access requests, such as is common practice in other countries. To a significant extent, the French are not accustomed to exercising such rights. Many persons do not know which organizations include them in their information systems. The consumer movement, which is only modestly developed, has not yet promoted the right of access or the protection of privacy as part of its responsibilities.

There have been some private efforts to promote and test the right of access. In 1982 a number of publications, pressure groups, and unions distributed a sixteen-page publication reviewing the provisions of the law.[83] The publication devoted particular attention to the exercise of the right of access to one's own file and included six form letters that can be used for various types of access. In 1981 the monthly magazine on computer law, *Expertises,* reported, under the headline of the "great inertia," on an individual's testing the right of access to her bank records. There is some evidence that certain organized groups, such as The League for the Rights of Man, have promoted individual requests.[84]

Article 21(5) instructs the CNIL to "receive claims, petitions and complaints." Article 26 adds a seemingly strong ground for complaints: "All persons are entitled to object, for legitimate reasons, to the processing of personal data concerning them." The CNIL has subsequently explained that an individual has no right to object to public-sector data processing, if it is being done under a statute or a regulation issued by the commission.[85] Thus the right to complain about perceived surveillance has its limitations.

The CNIL may simply take notice of a complaint, seek a solution by means of coordination, or send a warning to those involved. It could also report known infractions of the law to the public prosecutor (the *Parquet*) under article 40 of the code of penal procedure.[86] At present, the full commission receives lists of pending complaints and approves appropriate investigations, but it has delegated the general handling of complaints, like the supervision of the exercise of the right of access under article 21(5), to the president and the vice-presidents.

The CNIL has gradually begun to receive more complaints and more precise ones, although it still regards their number as evidence of lack of public interest and knowledge (even though there are now more than 1,000 per year). The complaints commonly concern data processing that has not been declared, refusals of access, communications to third parties, the receipt of unsolicited junk mail, and the collection of sensitive or unnecessary data.[87]

Complaints originate with groups and organizations, such as unions, as well as individuals and the press. In 1981 the Movement against Racism and for Friendship among Peoples accused Interpol of having a copy of a French data bank on Jews created in 1941 (a matter that was then investigated).[88] In 1988 two unions in Alpes-Maritimes complained that information on social services was being delivered to the departmental prefect. The CNIL took a formal decision to instruct the local agency to obey the law and then simply informed the unions that they had done so.

Like its counterparts in other countries, the CNIL is especially dependent on the media to alert it to problems in data protection. It is essential for the media, groups, and individuals to stimulate the CNIL toward the control of surveillance by responding to complaints and by conducting its own investigations.

Annual Reports and Public Relations

Article 23 requires the CNIL to submit a yearly report to the president of the Republic and to Parliament "on the discharge of its duties." Such a report is a novelty, as government organizations tend to operate with a great deal of secrecy or, at least, without much publicity. The CNIL's annual reports are generally well written, well organized, and well argued. Unfortunately, the rhetoric about achievements, at least in some cases, far surpasses the reality.[89]

The CNIL makes various efforts to publicize its annual reports, including a press conference by the president. The tradition of presenting the report to the president of the Republic also seems to be continuing. Although each member of Parliament receives a copy, it is not formally discussed in either house of the legislature.

One purpose of the annual report is to increase public awareness of the agency. The first few generated a notable degree of media attention. Senator Thyraud well articulated the message that the French seemed to be deriving maniacal pleasure from having data banks.[90] In 1983–84, the three successive presidents of the commission held a total of six press conferences. Their use is an exemplary practice and one concrete benefit of having experienced politicians in the leadership of the agency.

The CNIL itself has been pleased with the public attention to its major decisions, arguing that such "opinion has to remain vigilant and to control the use of computers."[91] It also ensures that many of its decisions, even those of a purely local nature, are published in the press. This is as close as the agency has come to a structured campaign of public relations for the general public, such as has been pursued in West Germany or Sweden. In the beginning, the CNIL thought that there was some risk of giving too much information about the law to the public, as it did not have the resources to help people.

One of Thyraud's accomplishments was an extensive interview in *Que Choisir?*, the monthly magazine of the independent consumers' association, the Federal Union of Consumers, with a circulation of 300,000. He acknowledged the problem of publicizing the law: "I perceive the Law is very slow at entering into public awareness. The French are not as much occupied with their liberties as we might have thought. . . . Each person must have the conviction that he must be the defender of the liberty of others, and at the same time of his own."[92] Thyraud also celebrated the fifth anniversary of the CNIL on November 8, 1983. The extensive press coverage was essentially favorable, except for the failure of the agency to prosecute anyone.[93]

There is no objective evidence available about the extent of public knowledge of the 1978 law, because, unfortunately, there have been no surveys on the subject. Press and radio attention to specific issues has raised the level of awareness of the CNIL among the educated public. The public also sees notices about the CNIL and the law on questionnaires. The level of awareness appears to be higher in urban than in rural areas and greater for the public sector than the private. Nevertheless, it is clear that the CNIL has yet to achieve a satisfactory awareness of the law as an element in the control of public surveillance. In fact, there is serious concern about the lack of media interest in its work, as evidenced by a review of its own press clippings for 1986.

The discussion so far in this chapter of the CNIL's efforts to limit governmental surveillance has been generally discouraging. The agency has a politicized commission and a relatively weak staff. It has neglected inspections, does not have a good index of data banks, receives few complaints, and the public is hardly aware of its existence.

Data Protection Principles in Practice

The CNIL does pay continuing attention to the fundamental principles included in the law. Both the commissioners and the staff constantly turn to the text of the statute, rather than to current practices or their own personal views, in order to understand and apply the basic principles involved. In the process, the commission has identified several fundamental ideas about controlling surveillance that are worthy of emulation in other countries.

Perhaps the most basic concern of the CNIL in delivering opinions on data processing by the public sector is the principle of "finality" or end use, which means establishing in advance the ultimate uses of personal information collected for a particular system, including subsequent transfers and communications of data. Fauvet believes that the principle of finality is at the heart of the law.[94] The commission expects that "the nature of the data recorded should correspond well to their ultimate purposes," so that a public body should only collect and process data relevant to, and compatible with, its stated work; nonessential information should not be recorded. In its view, a data base has a particular purpose and no other.

The CNIL early regarded its emphasis on finality as an evolving notion, which has indeed proven to be the case; its strict application has not made sense in certain cases, despite the commission's desire to limit end uses of information as narrowly as possible. The government tends to regard this restrictive inclination as old-fashioned, as more and more systems are created in which the original data will be used for multiple purposes. Thus the commission began to receive requests to approve public information systems with multiple purposes, not all of which could be refused. One result is that "the principle of finality has lost some of its initial rigidity."[95] The CNIL is now allowing "extensions of finality" under certain strict conditions for improving administrative systems and for research and statistics.

A second seminal principle promoted by the CNIL, on the basis of article 28 in particular, is "the right to be forgotten": "The computer, which has a power and a memory so superior to man, must be made to forget."[96] Senator Thyraud claimed in 1983 to have prompted a significant amount of destruction of unnecessary records by the police and the military. In his view, when data are no longer necessary, they ought to disappear.[97] Anonymization is now used as an alternative to destruction of data in certain cases.[98] Nevertheless, this articulation of the right to be forgotten is of inestimable importance for data protection in every country.

The third major set of principles inspiring the work of the commission is an insistence on informed consent for data collection and the general prohibition against collecting and storing certain sensitive data, such as ethnic origins. Respondents must be told about the compulsory or optional nature of data collection and of the consequences of the failure to reply. They must also be told for whom the data are intended and that they have a right of access and correction. The collection of data on racial origins; political, philosophical, or religious opinions; or union membership requires the express written consent of the person.[99] Paragraphs 2 and 3 of article 31, which concern the storing of sensitive information, have caused particular problems for the CNIL in dealing with churches, labor groups, and the Ministries of Defense and the Interior.[100]

The CNIL further continues to clarify the meaning of the important principle of promoting transparency or openness in data processing. Article 26 entitles any person to object to the processing of personal data. The CNIL believes that credit companies are ignoring such measures by using computer profiling in their preparation of credit scores. When one company refused to divulge its plans and computer programs in 1984, the commission held a hearing and launched an investigation, which may lead to new general rules for the credit industry. Since it is unlikely that individuals will know enough to exercise their rights under article 26, the CNIL must play a lead role in implementation.

As the reporter for the data protection bill in the Senate, Jacques Thyraud believed that the wording of article 1 was simply an articulation in practice of the 1789 Declaration of the Rights of Man. This concern with the rights of individuals is a continuing rhetorical thrust of the CNIL itself and, indeed, of French society. In interpreting article 31, which applies limits to the storage of certain types of sensitive personal information, the commission has relied on the Declaration of 1789 and the preamble to the 1958 Constitution of the Fifth Republic, which solemnly proclaims the attachment of the French people to the Rights of Man.[101] In some of its literature the CNIL discusses the right of access to information by an individual as the third generation of the Declaration of the Rights of Man.

Although data protection agencies soon become preoccupied with the problem of translating principles into practices, the CNIL wisely continues to emphasize the basic principles directly derived from the 1978 law, which is much better in this respect than the Swedish model. The commission believes that its reliance on these main principles allows it to adapt the law to new and unexpected situations. This concern can be seen as well in the attitude of the CNIL that the law is a living document that can be expected to evolve over time. The development of its jurisprudence on the statute is only in the first stages. As in the Swedish system, the production of a lengthy series of decisions does not promote coherent jurisprudence. The application of the law requires continuous interpretation, clarification, and fruitful contacts. Fortunately, the commission, as Maisl has pointed out, is able to interpret the new law a great deal faster than the courts.

Turning to less elevated aspects of implementation, the CNIL seems to recognize the centrality of the risks of surveillance posed by linkages among the files of large public administrations. Whenever it evaluates requests for opinions from the public sector, it attempts to evaluate the specific requests in terms of how they fit in with other information systems in the same ministry.[102] After the first election of the Mitterrand government, Jean Querat, a journalist, suggested that the CNIL was especially concerned to prohibit linkages among existing data banks, but that the problem was difficult, especially for technical reasons. He argued that the central administrations have long wanted to centralize their dispersed information systems for purposes of efficiency, but with a Socialist administration, these schemes, he claimed, had little chance to see the light of day. Querat's opinion was that the victory of the left would reinforce the goal of the CNIL. Others point out that it was the minister of the budget in the first Mitterrand government, Laurent Fabius, who in fact automated and linked the data bases of the Ministry of Finance. Maisl suggested some time ago that the paucity of interagency data flows has nothing to do with the legal regime but with rivalries between agencies.[103]

The taxation measures on capital wealth proposed by the Socialist government posed specific questions about record linkages. Illustrating the real limits of its willpower, the CNIL did not want to appear to be standing in the way of new taxation systems proposed by the new government, whatever the terms of the law. It permitted the government to link and verify various individual records of particular persons, but insisted that any person contacted directly should be informed of the methods used to collect and collate the data responsible for the letter in question.[104]

The CNIL has faced an enormous range of problems, because every personal information system in the country held in automated form, and sometimes in manual form, comes under the purview of the act. For example, the CNIL issued a 1981 press release concerning the transfer to Algeria of certain French archives created prior to independence. It drew the attention of the government to the fact that it is necessary to assure the absolute security of identifiable information that directly or indirectly identifies the racial origins; political, philosophical, or religious opinions; and medical information concerning individuals. The CNIL has faced similar issues of perceived surveillance concerning the continued activities of the Mormon church in microfilming copies of historic French church records, and, in 1984, allegations that a census of Muslims who had come to France from Algeria twenty years previously was under way.

Decisions of the Commission and Prosecutions

Even though the CNIL is not a court, it does take decisions in the form of opinions given in response to requests for its advice.[105] An aggrieved individual or company unhappy with one of its decisions can take the CNIL to court, but this seems an unlikely prospect under French law. Under article 15 a public administration can appeal a decision of the CNIL to the Council of State.[106] Especially because the statute is relatively new and important, it would still be difficult for a government department to challenge the authority of the CNIL so directly. Moreover, the CNIL's relatively weak stands on surveillance do not incite agencies to resistance.

In 1982 the General Confederation of Labor (CGT), a trade union close to the Communist party, appealed the alleged illegality of the CNIL's 1980 decision on simplified standards for the personnel files of private companies. The government commissioner pointed out to the Council of State that the CNIL is "a very original institution of French Law" and not simply a consultative body, because it has a specialized regulatory power to control data processing.[107] In preparing the simplified rules, the CNIL had attempted to determine what types of data processing in the personnel field posed no risks to private life or to freedom. After reviewing all of the implications of this particular decision of the CNIL, the government commissioner recommended that it should be annulled.

The availability of strong criminal sanctions buttresses the decision-making power of the CNIL. With respect to the public sector, article 41 provides for fines and/or imprisonment for "whoever engages in the automatic processing of personal data, or has such data so processed, without publication of the official decisions" required from the CNIL. There are comparable punishments under article 42 for recording or storing personal data prohibited under the law. Article 43 contains a particularly strong penal provision:

> Any person who, in connection with recording, filing, transmittal, or any other form of processing, obtains personal data, disclosure of which would impair reputation or standing or invade privacy, and who knowingly and without the authorization of the person concerned discloses such data to any party not authorized to receive them under this or any other Act, shall be imprisoned for two to six months, fined 2,000 to 20,000 francs, or both. Whoever imprudently or negligently discloses or allows disclosures of data described in the preceding paragraph shall be fined 2,000 to 20,000 francs.

Finally, article 44 punishes with a fine and/or imprisonment anyone who uses personal data in the public sector for a purpose other than that specified in the regulation issued by the CNIL. The duty of the CNIL is to report alleged breaches of the law to the public prosecutor, presumably after its own determination that a breach appears to have been committed.

During the first years, the CNIL simply drew public attention to real or alleged instances of noncompliance in the form of general or specific admonishments and warnings. A politicized body like the CNIL was very reluctant to use criminal sanctions until particularly egregious breaches occurred. Its preoccupation has been to try to improve or change a situation rather than to be confrontational or to lay criminal charges. The situation began to change after the failure to use stronger sanctions was one of the few public criticisms of the commission. The CNIL appeared timid rather than simply prudent and judicious, when Thyraud admitted to the press in November 1983 that it had never reported anyone to the public prosecutors. The incredulous press also picked up differences of opinion among the commissioners on the merits of this approach.

Justice Minister Robert Badinter explained to the Senate in 1983 that the particular function of the CNIL was to report infractions to the judicial authorities, who would then decide how to handle the matter. His questioner charged that the commission's failure to do so was weakening enforcement of important legislation.[108] In terms of this exchange, it was evident that the CNIL was unwisely making its own internal decisions on who should or could be prosecuted.

In 1984 President Rosenwald altered the CNIL's course on reporting prosecutions for unauthorized surveillance. While occupying the plant of a French subsidiary of the Swedish conglomerate, SKF Industries, striking workers found a notebook containing highly subjective information on the political views and private lives of applicants for employment. After the press printed excerpts, the CNIL's quick investigation led to its first formal recommendation for prosecution. Rosenwald explained that he had no particular enthusiasm for criminal sanctions, but if errors had occurred, they had to be brought to public notice. His former place of employment, the Audit Office, could not oversee everything, but it had to make occasional examples.[109]

Jacques Fauvet's approach to reporting prosecutions also seems to favor the occasional exemplary case and, in the more normal situation, continued emphasis on dialogue with concerned organizations. In his view, an alleged infraction has to be very serious before the CNIL should report it to the Parquet.[110] When the monthly magazine, *Expertises,* continued its campaign in favor of leaving discretion to prosecute to the prosecutors themselves by reporting more matters to them, Fauvet replied that the commission preferred to separate the process of issuing warnings to suspected offenders from making actual reports to the prosecutors.[111]

By the fall of 1985 Fauvet was issuing much more strident warnings to alleged offenders, leading *Le Monde* to suggest that the period of indulgence was over. The commission lodged a formal complaint, its third, against the nationwide fund for family allowances (MONA), because it had been warned to stop collecting certain sensitive kinds of data.[112] Thus, urged on by media criticisms, the watchdog CNIL was at least beginning to bark. However, the SKF trials became enormously complicated, resulting in at least one conviction, but without any sanctions imposed. Prosecutions are clearly a very inefficient method of promoting implementation, although they do help to publicize the law in the private sector and they demonstrate a serious commitment to the control of surveillance. Fauvet now sees a significant advantage in issuing a solemn warning and then negotiating a solution with the culprit.[113]

Chapter *17*

The Regulation of Surveillance Systems

This chapter examines the impact of data protection on several specific personal information systems, as an illustration of the work of the National Commission on Informatics and Freedoms (CNIL) to date in controlling governmental surveillance. One of the central themes is the piecemeal way in which the commission has approached the regulation of major systems of personal information, because of its own choice, in addition to several characteristics of the law of January 6, 1978. The ultimate goal is to assess the relative success of the data protectors in controlling governmental surveillance. In essence, they have the power to limit, perhaps even to delay, but not to prevent.

The Police and Criminal Information Systems

There are two police forces, the National Police, under the jurisdiction of the Ministry of the Interior, and the gendarmerie, or military police, which is a part of the Ministry of Defense. Both perform the same type of police functions. The creation of national automated police records is the responsibility of the Ministry of Justice. The police have only several automated information systems; some of their most sensitive personal data are held in manual form. Although the degree of automation is largely kept secret, the technocratic imperative is toward automation, led by the specialists of the Ministry of the Interior.[1]

In 1981 *Le Monde* carried a long, critical article by Eric Rohde on police information systems in which he argued that the "problems posed by police data processing are not fundamentally different from those that appeared in 1974," at the time of the debate over Safari.[2] The author suggested that the police computers in the Ministry of the Interior are the most important in the administration. All of the police information systems are operated within the ministry by CEGETI, the electronic center for the collection and processing of information. Since all of the systems originate in the same place, the author argues that their integration is simply a matter of deciding to do so. Rohde suggested that the ministry was seriously delinquent in declaring these systems to the CNIL, "because these data banks effectively contain information for which the [1978] law authorizes neither the collection or storage, much less its processing, whether in automated or manual form." The author claimed that a decree was in preparation that would exempt these particular information systems from the scope of the law, under the provisions of the last paragraph of article 31.

Police record systems are a continuing source of activity for the CNIL, especially in the form of complaints received from people or groups who are naturally suspicious of police surveillance activities.[3] In 1981 the Emergency Committee against the Repression of Homosexuals complained about the recording of homosexuality by the police, despite a letter against the practice from the Ministry of the Interior to the director-general of the National Police. The CNIL assigned Vice-President Forni to investigate the charges, because, according to article 1, it is illegal for anyone to keep such records for the control of homosexuals or for the purpose of verification of identity.

The Ministry of the Interior's automated data base of 230,000 wanted persons is a continuing source of problems. In 1983 it, and the data base on terrorists, were the only two fully automated police systems linked to computer terminals. At least 250 terminals are connected to the data base on wanted persons. Border passport controls can thus check if a traveler is a wanted person. Jacques Thyraud became aroused when a businessman was forced to miss his flight for a fairly minor infraction. The senator was especially incensed at the failure to notify the suspect of the prospect of his temporary incarceration over a small amount and the presence of evident errors in the system, which he described as using a steam-hammer to crush a hazel nut, at least for minor offenses.[4]

There are several surprising aspects to this episode. Ideally, the CNIL should be carrying out regular inspections of the register of wanted persons, given its capacity for surveillance, so as to be fully informed in advance of its contents and operations. It should be concerned about establishing the legitimacy of such uses of personal data at border crossings, according to the license in question, and not simply focusing on such issues as the merits of apprehending individuals there. This is especially true since President Fauvet insists that the CNIL's role is to ensure that the war on crime and terrorism complies with the laws.[5]

One of the continuing problems of the commission's decisions on police records is that they are piecemeal, rather than systematic, in character. In 1984 it was concerned about a proposal for the creation of an automated fingerprint system for the police, especially the retention of noncriminal prints. It agreed to the creation on an experimental basis, submitted the retention issue to the legislature, and agreed to be associated with the Ministries of the Interior and Justice in a study of the broad issues. In 1986 it approved the actual system.[6] The commission also issued a detailed decision on the creation of an automated police system on personal data both known and derived. It took notice of the twin purposes of the system, of the storage of the data for only 400 days, of the desire to ensure accuracy by creating better links between the police and the judicial authorities, and of the restricted dissemination of the data.[7] A decision such as this one seems careful enough when read in its own context, but the problem is that the commission does not adequately examine the totality and interconnections of similar developments in police surveillance.

The gendarmerie, as part of local police work throughout France, maintains files on the local population, which led to one of the most important decisions of the CNIL concerning police data. The issues received a great deal of press attention and led to controversies between the police and the CNIL. The ruling is a good example of how the CNIL dealt with a sensitive matter.

The Commission on Informatics and the League for the Rights of Man informed the CNIL that the gendarmes were collecting and recording data on criminal convictions of individuals.[8] In its 1981 opinion, the commission noted the belief of the gendarmes that the accomplishment of their various tasks required local surveillance. The CNIL had learned that each local unit maintained "very subjective" information, such as notices of convictions and information on morality, in an alphabetical and a chronological file. These data were stored until persons reached the age of eighty. Such indirect collection was against article 25 of the law. Information contrary to the laws on amnesty was also stored. The CNIL concluded that the gendarmes were acting in a spirit adverse to the laws initially mentioned, and that it would consult with the police and the relevant ministries concerning ways in which these information files could be harmonized with the law on informatics and freedom.

The Ministry of Justice is currently creating a single national automated police record system, located in Nantes. The process essentially involves centralizing criminal records from 700 local tribunals, which are now kept in manual form. The very first opinion of the CNIL in 1979 concerned this criminal record system. The commission influenced the ensuing law of January 4, 1980, and the decree concerning the automation of criminal records. It was especially concerned about the use of the National Identification Register for Natural Persons (NIR) and the imposition of adequate security measures.[9] The police record system will be linked to a national registry of the civil status of individuals, so that correct identification can occur.

The creation of a national system of criminal records is a significant step for any society, and one many have resisted. Although the system was created under Giscard d'Estaing, the Socialist government issued the decree.[10] It included security rules as well, which do not appear to be very strong, despite the CNIL's precise advice. Each person using the system will have a unique identifying code, which may not be very useful, depending on the way in which information from the criminal record system is subsequently disseminated by the (presumably) clerical staff that accesses it. Any inclusion or modification of a record in the system has to be confirmed by a second agent. Given the problems that have occurred in such systems in the United States and Canada, these rules are relatively primitive for the ultimate prevention of undue surveillance.

The CNIL has also been involved with other European data protectors in the regulation of the personal information stored on French soil by Interpol, the International Organization of Criminal Police. The CNIL first investigated charges that Interpol had a copy of a data bank on Jews compiled in 1941.[11] Scientologists subsequently tried to use the right of access to obtain their Interpol files.[12] The CNIL then decided that Interpol was indeed subject to the 1978 law, especially articles 16, 24, and 39.

Interpol did not like the prospect of detailed regulation by the CNIL and entered into extensive negotiations with the French government for sovereign immunity. Its secretary-general explained that Interpol functioned to transfer information on criminals from one country to another; these records remain the property of the originating national police force.[13] Interpol handles personal information such as photographs, fingerprints, extradition notices, missing persons, and warning notices. Some of the data are kept on file to answer inquiries and some, excluding names, have already been automated. As yet, it has no automated reference file on individuals.

The international data protection commissioners and the French government approved the idea of a special control commission for Interpol, even though the commissioners expressed some concern about the adequacy of this solution. The agreement became effective in 1984. The five-person commission, only two of whose members are under the direct control of Interpol, has some decision-making powers. It monitors compliance with the standard principles of data protection and with the constitution of Interpol and reports thereon to the executive committee of Interpol.[14] It has a list of personal data bases that is available to nationals of any member country; it will also investigate the contents of individual's files upon requests. The French government named President Fauvet as its representative. The CNIL reports on developments to the international meetings of data protection commissioners.

Negotiating a successful regulatory regime for Interpol was a considerable achievement for the CNIL and the French government, because of the 140 governments involved and the inexorable resistance of the police to outside supervision. However, the battle is not yet over. Some European experts on the data protection aspects of police systems question the ability of the Interpol Commission to carry out the detailed, ongoing auditing required for successful implementation. As Robert Biever of Luxembourg, the commission's first chair, has said, "probably 120 of the 140 member nations in Interpol think that privacy protection is a luxury, not a requirement."[15] There is thus some risk that the CNIL has only achieved a symbolic victory over the surveillance practices of Interpol.

The National Security Agencies

France has separate internal and external security agencies. The Directorate for Surveillance of the Territory handles internal security; the Service for External Documentation and Counterespionage (SDECE) operates security abroad.[16] The 1978 law wisely includes these systems within the purview of the CNIL and even grants a form of indirect access to them for individuals. The security and military authorities still have to seek the opinion of the CNIL and to provide a certain minimum of information. The Council of State, which obviously acts as a kind of conscience for the nation in these matters, stated that there was no necessity to publish certain lists and results of such decision making by the CNIL, but that they could do so. Finally, under articles 1 to 4 of the decree, the prime minister has to be informed of, and to qualify, CNIL agents gaining access to military and defense information, which is similar to the procedure used in West Germany. In practice, two CNIL commissioners and a select staff are responsible for these sensitive areas.

One of the critical issues in the military and security field is determining what kinds of sensitive information can be collected under article 31, which limits certain types of data storage. The CNIL attempts to balance the interests involved by looking at specific applications, such as those pertaining to terrorists or criminals. In 1981 the CNIL determined that certain items in the information systems of the Ministry of Defense should be suppressed on the grounds that individuals have the right to be forgotten, that nothing should be stored on individuals from before the age of sixteen, and that the length of storage should be determined in advance.[17] On September 6, 1988, the CNIL approved an automated data base on terrorists. It required a change about data storage, wanting only direct and not accidental contacts to be recorded by the Ministry of the Interior. These are useful small steps in the control of security surveillance.

There was also one major example in 1982 of a government security initiative that was announced without the prior advice of the CNIL. President Mitterrand responded to terrorist raids on Jewish restaurants and synagogues in Paris by announcing that a central data base on terrorism, created May 24, 1982, was being put into full effect. The automated information system, to be located in the "Police Ministry" in Paris, contains data from international sources and from at least nine agencies dealing with security, including the two main security agencies.[18] Thyraud told a press conference that the CNIL should have been consulted and set forth certain conditions that it would impose on such a data bank.[19] He apparently indicated the opposition of the CNIL to the creation of a data base on all those who could appear as suspects, in order to avoid what he called the German tendency (*"la dérive allemande"*). He seems to favor an archive containing fifteen to twenty thousand files, presumably dealing with known suspects. Any proposed linkages with police files had to be reported to the CNIL.[20]

The plans for a data bank on terrorists were quickly submitted to the CNIL and rapidly approved (with some qualifications and limitations). Taking public issue with the president of the Republic on such a sensitive matter was obviously a strong statement of the CNIL's independence; it was also a useful political stance for the opposition senator. This episode further suggests that all governments tend to forget about the existence of data protectors, when current problems become sensitive.

The critics of the Centre d'information et d'initiatives sur l'informatisation (CIII) use this last episode to illustrate the limits of the commission's power.[21] Its journal, *Terminal 19/84,* also responded to the creation of this new antiterrorist data base. The premise of the author, J. Vetois, is that a democratic state should not transgress democratic principles in the process of defending itself. He suggests that the West German antiterrorist information system, created in 1974, spread a very wide net in monitoring, including apartments with low occupancy rates. The concern is that the type of data base acceptable to the CNIL would not be useful for antiterrorist purposes, and that it would quickly change from an archival to an operational system, without any viable means of monitoring whether or not the opinion of the CNIL was being obeyed. Vetois is plainly skeptical about the ability of the CNIL or anyone else to mount a permanent control over such a system, a skepticism certainly reinforced by American experience with the Federal Bureau of Investigation and the Central Intelligence Agency, and on that basis he feels that a democratic society must reject such an antiterrorist data base.[22] It is likely that *Terminal*'s concern was shared by few others, since the public unwisely believes that such forms of surveillance will never affect them.

In 1982, Louis Joinet, a leading French authority on data protection, agreed that security systems had to be subject to data protection, calling them "the most dangerous to freedoms."[23] Given this expression of concern, it seems surprising that the CNIL devotes little evident attention to security data bases, except for facilitating indirect access for individuals to such records. There is no evidence that the CNIL has systematically examined the personal records maintained by such agencies, but that is hardly surprising, given the power relationships at work in such a delicate situation. The French security agencies continue to be a world unto themselves.

Project AUDASS-ENFANCE: Social Assistance to Children

In 1971 many of the departmental offices of Health and Social Assistance (DDASS) began to automate their systems for furnishing social assistance to children. The integrated system, which could include 700,000 children, became known as AUDASS-ENFANCE. In addition to basic information on the child in question, certain departments included religion, nationality, involvements with the law, marital status of the parents, and drinking habits of the father.[24] At some point in the 1970s, Minister of Health Simone Veil intervened to prohibit the collection of data on religion and the reasons for giving assistance. The Democratic Confederation of Labor (CFDT), a socialist trade union, continued to be exercised by the existence of AUDASS-ENFANCE.

The Ministry of Health had to seek the opinion of the CNIL on AUDASS-ENFANCE. Although the 1980 decision was basically favorable, the CNIL insisted on some important qualifications. The system was limited to data necessary for the administration of social assistance and the preparation of statistics. Data processing could only occur in centers under the direct control of the ministry, and only personnel of the DDASS sworn to professional secrecy could have access to the data. The CNIL successfully insisted that data on individual children should be erased fifteen months after they stopped receiving assistance.[25]

The minister of health quickly instructed the DDASS to stop collecting such data as the nationality and criminal record of the child. The ministry's declaration for the system specified the information to be collected on each recipient, none of which could be described as subjective. Article 4 restricted access to the social workers and data processing specialists of the DDASS. It was also agreed that AUDASS-ENFANCE would not be joined, linked, or released to any other information system.[26]

Criticisms of AUDASS-ENFANCE continued. Such unions as the CFDT argued that this automation threatened the liberties of individuals.[27] *Terminal 19/84* also critically evaluated the CNIL's findings before finally opposing AUDASS-ENFANCE once again. It argued that the system was not necessary for statistics, since a sampling of records would be satisfactory. Such an argument is in fact not very relevant, so long as the data are going to be automated for administrative use in the first place. *Terminal* questioned the need for automating such sensitive records, citing especially the cost and complexity of the operation and the risk of errors. The journal also argued that the privacy of the information in question was not yet assured, because data could be lost in transmission, could be moved to unauthorized computer centers, and, because multiple copies had to exist for security purposes, might not be erased at appropriate times. The CNIL will of course need to do audits to discover such breaches of the law. Finally, *Terminal* argues that the parents are so economically deprived that they will not use their right to access the records.

The *Terminal* critique, which is useful both for the points it makes and for the valuable attention it pays to the work of the CNIL, also illustrates the very difficult situation of the commission in seeking to regulate surveillance systems that a government ministry really wants.[28]

Project GAMIN: The Surveillance of Newborn Children

This episode concerns perhaps the best known decision of the CNIL during the first years of its existence. GAMIN (a word for a young child) has become a very important symbol in the fight against certain implications of the computerization of society; it also involves an important application of the 1978 law. The sociologist Colette Hoffsaes argues that GAMIN is not a monster, nor an aberrant case, but has characteristics typical of many other systems; its autopsy can lead to valuable guidance in a period when automation is such a predominant goal. GAMIN, in her opinion, "is known in social and medical circles as a symbol of the danger of data banks, and in the world of informatics as a model failure to be avoided." Political scientist André Vitalis has termed GAMIN "an especially sensitive system from the point of view of individual liberties. . . . Its development demonstrates a considerable extension of social control."[29]

GAMIN was set in motion by the agency for the Protection of Mothers and Children (PMI), which is a part of the Ministry of Health and is associated in each geographic department with the agency for Health and Social Assistance. As the problem of reducing infant mortality became less central an issue, the PMI began to lose its raison d'être and turned in the late 1960s to the prevention of handicaps, especially among needy children, as an alternative activity. This bureaucratic imperative supports the argument of Hoffsaes and others that GAMIN was primarily a technocratic initiative.

A 1970 law concerning certificates of health created Project GAMIN. All newborn children had to obtain certificates by means of three compulsory physical examinations at set intervals. Physicians had to send the results of the examinations to the PMI, and parents needed certificates to obtain family allowances. In passing this law, Parliament paid no attention to the consequences of accumulating so much information on health certificates, despite the fact that in the same year it strongly resisted the creation of medical information systems during a period of hospital reform.[30]

Nothing was done to implement GAMIN until the Ministry of Health issued several circulars. As an example of what could happen before the CNIL came into existence, the essence of GAMIN appeared in these circulars and not in the 1970 law or subsequent decrees. The 1973 circular for the first time mentioned the possibilities of automation and emphasized identifying "children at risk." The 1974 circular mentioned the concern with the identification of children for priority attention by the PMI and the extension of interest to "social risks."[31]

The main continued proponent of GAMIN was DOMI, the Data Processing Methods Division of the Ministry of Health. It designed and guided the GAMIN information system, but the data were eventually stored at twenty-eight regional computer centers, usually associated with university hospitals. The Ministry of Health could not fully control the process, because the PMI is funded by each department. Thus DOMI only had to interest DDASS in those departments that were already automating their social information systems, as in AUDASS-ENFANCE.[32] No single agency was fully responsible for monitoring the development of Project GAMIN. It went into partial operation in 1974 and by the end of the decade had roots in forty-four departments. The system was designed to handle 2.5 million health certificates per year.[33]

GAMIN gradually attracted considerable criticism from many quarters. As minister of health, Simone Veil was personally opposed to the system, but a report she commissioned was supportive. The proponents' response to criticism was to reshape GAMIN, a process that continues to this day. In one experiment three departments began to use microcomputers in order to keep the data from health certificates locally.[34] Another circular from the Ministry of Health in 1976 spoke about the anonymization of data on children before they reached the age of six and the destruction of the manual registers, which continued in existence despite automation. But there were other discussions of the retention of data until the child reached eighteen, linkages to school information, and possible matching to AUDASS-ENFANCE. Vitalis makes the essential point that GAMIN was never properly regulated by the relevant law and decree.[35]

It then became the responsibility of the CNIL to monitor GAMIN. The law insists that individuals be informed about what will be done with information about them. Vitalis argues that parents did not know what was happening with the data from the health certificates. The problem was especially significant because GAMIN targeted approximately 40 percent of the children born in any particular year as at risk; thus PMI physicians had to make a second selection manually. It also took two months for the automated system to identify a newborn needing particular assistance, which was much too slow for problems needing immediate care.[36] Parents never knew why they had been singled out for special visits by the social workers of the PMI. If it sent a social worker or a physician to see a particular child, additional information, much of it of a social and subjective character, had to be returned to GAMIN. This particular practice attracted considerable opposition from PMI's own social workers, who are sensitive to automated surveillance.[37] The problem was further complicated by the class issue; the newborns most likely to face medical or social risks were largely the progeny of marginal groups.

Vitalis points out that "the collection of information seems to have been the great preoccupation of the promoters of the operation." This technocratic imperative became a real problem when GAMIN ran headlong into the 1974–75 debates about data banks. Hoffsaes says that "it is indisputable that the opposition to GAMIN . . . developed essentially on the theme of the creation of data banks."[38] Moreover, and this is probably the critical issue, the Ministry of Health and its appendages never successfully clarified the goals of GAMIN.[39] As is too often the case in every country, the process was technology-driven without the kind of definition of specific goals that automation usually requires. There were even some doubts about its statistical and epidemiological benefits.[40]

Physicians and their associates were concerned about allowing medical information outside the circle of those bound by medical secrecy. They also resented the bureaucratic implications of having computers giving them detailed instructions about individual patients. Certain physicians passively resisted by failing to fill out forms completely or not returning them to the PMI, especially for the second and third examinations of a particular child. Various physicians concluded that GAMIN did nothing to prevent handicaps or to change the conditions that placed children at risk.[41] GAMIN simply stigmatized the poor.

Terminal 19/84 published a very useful critique of the development of GAMIN in the department of Loire-Atlantique, surrounding the city of

Nantes. A wide variety of motives inspired resistance to GAMIN, many of which had nothing to do with data protection. The opposition in that department came from secretaries at the PMI, unions, social workers, physicians, and the General Council of the department, which finally suspended funds for GAMIN in 1979. A mixed committee, appointed by the General Council to study GAMIN, found considerable concern about the threat posed to "private life."[42] Social workers preferred carrying out systematic visits to newborn children rather than being guided by a computer. They also alleged that the new system reduced their numbers and made it easier for supervisors to control their work. Unions, especially the CFDT, supported social workers in Loire-Atlantique and elsewhere in their criticisms of GAMIN.[43] The General Council there sought unsuccessfully to have the Council of State annul the decree on GAMIN and then complained to the CNIL.

Some of the criticisms of GAMIN reached a very high level of generality. *Terminal* claims a strong resistance to computers in Loire-Atlantique in 1977–79 among members of the General Council, physicians, and social workers. Hoffsaes also argues that GAMIN generally helped to demonstrate the dehumanizing effects of computers, the irrational aspects of automation, the dangers of increasing social control by the state, and the desire to classify people by producing profiles.[44]

The Ministry of Health submitted its request for an opinion on Project GAMIN to the CNIL in 1980. The commission issued an unfavorable decision on the basis of articles 1 and 3.[45] It carried out many consultations with the ministry, unions, and associations of physicians and midwives. However, as Hoffsaes points out, the CNIL never met with the physicians and others at the PMI who favored GAMIN: "The promoters, unconcerned by the breadth of the opposition, had only disdain for 'noisy minorities,' neglected their arguments, and remained persuaded that the CNIL would be content to require only certain modifications." (Such an attitude may be widespread among government departments and agencies.) Unions informed the CNIL that GAMIN was "the first step in a general data bank for the population."[46]

The CNIL had three basic concerns. First, the 1970 law did not specify limits to the use of automated data processing. Second, GAMIN targeted children solely on the basis of automated data and computer programs. Finally, the commission objected that the ultimate purposes of GAMIN were being affected by variations in the submission of the requisite data, so that the system appeared "debatable, useless or unused."

It is not evident why the CNIL decided to take a firm stand on Project GAMIN but not on automated identity cards, AUDASS-ENFANCE, or AUDASS-Aide Sociale. Hoffsaes claims that the commissioners were divided about what to do with GAMIN, and the change of government in 1981 facilitated a strong decision. In her view, which is confirmed by other close observers, the CNIL was reluctant to confront the powerful Ministry of the Interior over identity cards and found an opportunity to assert its independence against what it perceived as a weaker ministry, or a feeble part thereof, in the case of the PMI. The press generally suggested that the Socialist victory had strengthened the will of the CNIL, a point publicly denied by the CNIL.[47]

The CNIL determined that GAMIN could still be used for statistical purposes in anonymous form. In 1982 *Terminal 19/84* noted that the Ministry of Health appeared to be interpreting the negative decision on GAMIN very narrowly.[48] The minister of health asked the CNIL for a further delay in implementing the ruling (which itself permitted a one-year lapse). In granting the delay, the CNIL observed that the ministry had recently requested that the data on children at risk should be destroyed and the computer programs modified. It also accepted the fact that the ministry was engaged in a wide-ranging transfer of its responsibilities to local authorities, which would make the presidents of General Councils responsible for handling all the activities of the PMI.

There are those who now argue that GAMIN has been reconstituted under another name and, more seriously, approved by the CNIL in a 1983 decision. A new dossier on the automation of health certificates for young children reached the commission at the end of 1982; in essence, it broke down the old GAMIN into three subsystems, each requiring a legal decree for implementation. The first decree permitted the old GAMIN to continue to exist for transitional purposes to a new system in thirty-four departments in which it already existed (covering 60 percent of births). The new phase allowed each department to maintain two separate data bases on a minicomputer. The personal data on each infant and its family are for administrative purposes; the second data base of anonymous data on the sociomedical characteristics of each child is for statistical purposes only. Access to and conservation of the data are closely controlled. A third decree created an experimental system of coded data, allowing the linkage of the three health certificates for each child by the responsible physician of the PMI, in order to permit longitudinal research. Such a system can only be created for ten departments for a period of three years. In general, any departmental PMI can refuse to automate, or can create another system, so long as it can furnish the Ministry of Health with the required statistics.[49]

The Ministry of Health obviously learned some lessons from the CNIL's unfavorable decision on GAMIN. Yet *Terminal's* author and a study team from the CFDT union still denounced the 1983 version of GAMIN as a scandal, because of its great technological pretensions, especially in claiming to have reliable data for epidemiological purposes. It also denounced its use for administrative purposes as bureaucratic overkill and remained suspicious of the ultimate motives of the Ministry of Health. *Terminal* bemoaned the fact that public pressure could not be brought to bear on the CNIL before its decision. The greatest irony is that the CNIL continues to trumpet the original GAMIN decision as one of its finest deeds.[50]

In 1987, to bring matters full circle, the CNIL approved general standards for automated systems in departments for evaluating health certificates of newborn children. All identifiable data must be destroyed when the child reaches six years of age or earlier. Each local application requires a review and decision of the CNIL. Generally, users have to use passwords to access the system, medical data are separated from administrative information, links to other systems are forbidden, and dedicated computers are employed.[51] The commission has effectively accepted a modified system of surveillance, because the government wanted it.

Automated Identity Cards

French residents have to carry national identity cards, which are made of paper and are easy to counterfeit. At the end of 1979 the Ministry of the Interior announced plans for a new form of identity card that would be manufactured by computer and encased in plastic. The main goal was more reliable identification papers. Critics, who were not very visible at first, suspected that the main users would be the police for surveillance of the population. The fight against terrorism was also mentioned, especially in the context of an international, or at least European Economic Commission, identity card or passport. But once again the technocratic imperative surfaced, since the proponent of the new cards was Bernard Martinage, director of data processing for the Ministry of the Interior.[52]

The plan was to phase in automated identity cards for 50 million people over a ten-year period. Recipients would be listed in the linked systems of the six computer centers that gave the instructions to make the cards. The card featured an innovative system of using lasers to print the photograph, signature, and the seal of the prefecture. Foreign residents and natives had cards of different colors. The computers could evidently identify individuals solely on the basis of name and date of birth; no identification numbers were to be used.[53]

The new identity card had all the characteristics of a credit card, including the capacity to store information. The card could be made machine-readable, although *Terminal* states that the CNIL managed to suppress this option. But since some optical-scanning devices can read directly from printed characters, as they do in checking the accuracy of manufactured cards, magnetic instructions were not essential for further interconnections and linkages. The conservative *Le Figaro* assured its readers that the cards could be linked to other information systems, such as the register of wanted persons. The Ministry of the Interior sought to assure critics that the data for the cards would not be checked or linked any further in the process of issuing them. But readability by machine meant potential uses of the new cards in optical scanners or computer terminals installed in police cars, as had already occurred in Paris on an experimental basis.[54]

The press debate over the desirability of the new national identity cards intensified at the beginning of 1980. The union of magistrates of the CFDT suggested that the prospect of additional identification procedures conflicted with the principle of individual mobility.[55] There is no requirement for pedestrians in particular to carry identification papers. Existing law also established the limited circumstances under which the police could ask an individual to identify himself. The union suggested that police officers could in fact refuse to carry out the kinds of routine surveillance of individuals that the Interior Ministry intended. Even the police were apparently divided on the desirability of the new system of identification.[56] As is perhaps inevitable in such cases, critics of the identity cards made considerable use of the "slippery-slope" argument. *Terminal* argued for the inalienable right of the subject to falsify papers, in the face of police powers, recalling how this process enabled many French Jews to save their lives during the Nazi occupation.[57]

The CNIL's positive decision on the national identity cards in June 1980 was the first major ruling of the organization, and it tried to emphasize its achievements. As Professor Maisl pointed out at the annual meeting of data protection commissioners in 1980, the CNIL prevented international identity cards, the use of the social security number, and the assignment of a new unique number to card recipients. Its solution was to attach a number to the card and not to the person, so that if a card was lost, the individual received a new number. Maisl claimed that the cards could therefore only be used to prove civil status and that no further identification was possible, based on the card itself or its number. However, the simple name and birth date of the individual would be sufficient for linkages to other information systems.[58]

The government of Giscard d'Estaing moved forward with identity cards, although press criticism continued. There were allegations about secret codes on the cards that machines could read. *Terminal* still opposed the cards: "Giving the state the means of control that are without precedent, thinking that it would not dare to want to use them, is to practice the politics of an ostrich. It is also symptomatic of a desire not to understand the logic of the systems being put in operation."[59]

The election of the Socialists in 1981 was the salvation of opponents of automated identity cards. In an election statement on informatics, François Mitterrand stated that "the creation of computerized identity cards contains a real danger for the liberty of individuals."[60] The Socialists were especially concerned about the challenges to freedom posed by the 1980 laws on "Security and Freedom," which strengthened the hands of law enforcers. The new minister of the interior announced the demise of identity cards. Robert Badinter, the minister of justice from 1981 to 1986, explained that they presented a real danger to individual liberties and private life.[61]

The Socialist decision against such surveillance reflects harshly on the prior (and more recent) decision of the CNIL, which in effect assured the population that automated identity cards did not threaten the values protected by the 1978 law. The episode clearly illustrates just how little power the commission can realistically wield, especially in the face of government intentions. It is difficult for the CNIL, in its current incarnation, to confront a major government initiative on surveillance.

The CNIL receives continuing proposals from the Paris police in particular to find ways of preventing individuals from acquiring multiple paper identity cards. It approved an automated system of checking for fraud in 1984, after receiving assurances on the extent of security safeguards in the police computer. The system matches for different applications for identity cards to the twenty different issuing bureaus in Paris. However, at the end of 1984 the CNIL decided that the Bureau of Social Assistance in Paris had to stop requiring applicants to furnish two copies of their identity cards in order to discourage fraud. The police used the second copy to verify the authenticity of the card in question, but this resulted in the creation of a new register of manual identity cards. The CNIL's main point was that the use of welfare records for this purpose was a deviation from the finality of the register.[62] Fauvet himself served as the reporter on this delicate matter.

The experience with a general plan for automated identity cards made the CNIL more sensitive to their implications for surveillance. Yet when such controversial proposals resurfaced in 1986, under the auspices of the Ministry of the Interior of a new conservative government concerned with terrorism, the CNIL approved such cards, including the requirement of fingerprints on the application form. Jacques Thyraud, the reporter on this dossier, was opposed to their inclusion and storage in manual form, because of the risk of other uses, which occasioned major debates at several meetings.[63] He is not inclined to trust the government in such matters. In effect, the CNIL made only a few qualifications, which the government accepted. For example, individuals are free to establish their identities by any means, so the cards are not mandatory.

The 1987 government decree specifies that identity cards can be used to require the holder to establish his or her identity for purposes established by laws and regulations and to facilitate "the control of identity" by the police, notably at border crossings. The quoted phrase is symbolic, because article 1 of the 1978 law specifies that informatics should not infringe human identity. The major limitation is that the automated system to produce identity cards cannot be linked to any other data bases, nor can data from this register be given to third parties.[64] There will be enormous pressures on the government and the CNIL to approve the use of such data for other surveillance purposes.

When identity cards became available on an experimental basis in one department in 1988, the press reacted adversely.[65] Civil liberties groups are also outraged by the new cards. The critic André Vitalis has denounced them as a control on freedom of movement, an element of an enormous system of control that regards everyone as a potential suspect. However, he acknowledges the CNIL's efforts to act as a countervailing power to the government and to remove the most shocking aspects of the original proposals.[66] What also deserves mention again is that the commission does not have the power, whatever the terms of the law, to stop a major government initiative of this type.

The National Identification Register (NIR)

The National Institute of Statistics and Economic Studies (INSEE), which is under the jurisdiction of the Ministry of Economy and Finance, maintains a National Identification Register (NIR; formerly known as RNIPP), which includes about 50 million persons.[67] This national population register (and the electoral register) have local counterparts in the offices of the mayors. The CNIL rendered a favorable decision on the NIR, proposed by the conservative government, on June 9, 1981.[68]

In 1941 the Vichy government of occupied France instructed its National Statistical Service to assign identity numbers and to create a national population register. When INSEE was established in 1946, the Ministry of the Interior asked for a control system for the electoral registers, so that the population register continued in existence for all practical purposes. For the customary reason of improving efficiency, INSEE began to modernize the system in 1970.

The automated NIR began to function in 1973 from a national center in Nantes, which also operates the electoral register. The thirteen-digit number assigned to all newborn children is for all practical purposes a national identity number.[69] By the late 1970s the NIR had multiple administrative uses. For example, it was employed to assist the mayor's offices in producing the electoral registers. The military, police, and tax authorities also used it to locate persons.

Article 18 of the 1978 law stipulated that the Council of State, with the advice of the CNIL, could authorize the use of the NIR for the processing of personal data. This requirement indicates an awareness that such numbers facilitate surveillance. It was not until the resulting 1982 decree from the Council of State that a proper legal basis existed for this personal identification number.

The CNIL's staff report on the NIR, prepared prior to the issuance of its favorable 1981 opinion, suggested that the system itself posed few problems; the issue was its uses, especially by other government agencies and for purposes of linkage. The commission had already acknowledged that utilizing the NIR was equivalent to using the social security number: how was this process to be controlled? Its staff concluded that the NIR contained very little information on each person. However, there were problems in releasing identifiable individual data to other government users, solely on the basis of internal agreements or an exchange of letters. The staff suggested that the CNIL could accept the use of the NIR for the issuance and correction of national identity numbers, that the data could be made available to public agencies for legitimate purposes, but the CNIL ought to forbid use of the NIR for locating individuals. This report illustrates the influence of the staff on the commissioners, since it largely, but not completely, shaped the final opinion.

The CNIL's forceful decision on the NIR came, not incidentally, just after the Socialist election victory.[70] It began with the obtuse assurance that the NIR "cannot either directly or indirectly threaten private life or liberties." The decision next insisted that maintenance of the NIR should be the sole reason for processing. The CNIL further emphasized that, according to article 18, other uses of the NIR could only be authorized by the Council of State.

The CNIL added several qualifications. The proposed government decree on the NIR should suppress all references to a national identification number, which is either an invitation to an evasive statement or the perpetuation of a legal fiction. However, the CNIL managed to persuade the press of the dubious proposition that it had said that the NIR could not be a national identification number used by all government administrations.[71] One fails to see how the CNIL can make this claim, even though its sensitivity on the subject is understandable, given its own origins in the Safari affair of 1974. The CNIL also wanted precautions taken to destroy the NIR in the case of an invasion or a civil war.

The 1982 government decree stated that the NIR would include only the name of an individual, date and place of birth, sex, and national identification number. The population register had traditionally excluded addresses, marital status, and names of children, although such data are in the adjacent electoral register. The decree also permitted adding date and place of death to the NIR.[72] It also determined that for purposes of exact identification, where necessary, the NIR could include the marital names and the direct line of ancestry of individuals. Neither of these items were mentioned in the CNIL's decision; since the government's decree came from the Council of State, the CNIL was effectively bypassed.[73]

Article 7 of the 1982 decree states that the NIR cannot be used to search for individuals, "unless expressly authorized by law," which is a significant potential loophole, given earlier practices of allowing informal access to NIR. How does this affect, for example, the problem of using the NIR for the national automated criminal record system?[74] Article 9 of the decree further permits INSEE to furnish potential users with information to correct the NIR. Traditionally, many large government agencies, including social security, education, and taxation authorities, have used the national identification number to organize their files. INSEE handled more than 14 million such requests for numbers and their correction in 1978.

The main purpose of the NIR remains the assignment of national identification numbers, even if the CNIL wants them called some other name. It remains unclear just what other surveillance purposes the NIR can and should serve, at least according to the CNIL. Its role as a continuing watchdog is desirable, yet the risk still exists that more and more government agencies will try to use the NIR for various purposes. The question ought at least to be asked whether it is really needed.

At the annual meeting of data protection commissioners in 1982, Commissioner Paul Alba reported on the use of national identifiers in France. He stated that any holder of manual or automated files has to use an identifying code, permitting access to each file. Alba contrasted such an official reference number, which is unique to a single system, and the national identification number, which itself reveals information.[75] The goals of the CNIL are to facilitate accurate data processing and to protect citizens against the risks of linkages. In reviewing the findings of its questionnaire, Alba concluded that "the danger of a unique and common identifier does not exist at this time in France. . . . Although we agree no excessive fear should be felt in this area, the CNIL must remain vigilant in order to prevent the danger of a universal identifying code, which would enable the creation of a gigantic file on all the citizens. On the other hand, we must not encourage a growing number of identifiers which would result in the multiplication of data files." Alba seemed unaware that this was the choice of alternatives.

Thus the CNIL is far from settling the complex problems of unique identifiers, especially for large government information systems. It wonders whether each sector should develop unique numbers, allowing the NIR to be used primarily for social security, or should a shared personal identification number be allowed "for different files for which interconnections would enable a better management of the information available." The preference of government administrations for the NIR is self-evident. Like its counterparts in other countries, the commission is swimming against the tide in its handling of personal identification numbers. The lack of regulation has permitted the widespread use of such identifiers throughout public administrations, and even a requirement of separate systems of identifiers will not prevent record linkages. The CNIL even admits that the existence of article 18, controlling the use of the NIR, is not well enough known or respected.[76]

During the CNIL's tenth anniversary celebrations, Fauvet stated that a fundamental reason for its existence was to avoid a situation in which a person's activities from birth to death are recorded with a unique personal identifier: "This would permit the interconnecting of data banks and enclosing the individual in a network of surveillance, leading to a Surveillance Society."[77]

The commission has to review each proposed use of the NIR. In 1984, for example, it authorized a government financial agency to utilize the NIR to pay state pensions, because no other efficient method was available to attain the same result. In general, the CNIL restricts what it calls *uses* of the NIR data base, but allows it to be *consulted* for other purposes such as to enable a government agency to verify the existence of a person.[78] The CNIL will have to be vigilant to prevent expanding uses for the NIR data base and the national identification numbers themselves, since they are essential tools for surveillance. In 1987 it vetoed a post office plan to automate certain personnel data, because of plans to employ the NIR as the identifier. It also expressed its resistance to building local population registers by vetoing plans of four local communities. The same year, an inspection led the commission to give a national union a year to suppress its unauthorized use of the NIR.

Chapter *18*

Responding to Privacy and Surveillance Problems

This chapter sums up the various problems that the National Commission on Informatics and Freedoms (CNIL) has had with the process of implementation of data protection and considers how to revise the law of January 6, 1978, to meet the contemporary realities of power relationships and governmental surveillance.

The Status of Implementation

Of the agencies treated in this volume, the experience of the CNIL in attempting to control governmental surveillance has been the most disappointing. Those few outsiders with some knowledge of the commission's activities are disillusioned, because of their great hopes for the 1978 law. The pessimists are those who further doubt the prospects for a real revival under the current administration of the agency. Perhaps inevitably, the CNIL has no public sense that such opinions are abroad in the land; it regards itself as a great success.

The CNIL's experience to date is too particularistic and reactive. In its second annual report it claimed that it had not, in fact, had to confront Big Brother: "In the highly centralized current state of France, there is no desire to use data processing as an instrument of social control or of domination. The initiatives are disparate and uncoordinated."[1] Yet, Senator Jacques Thyraud concluded in an early interview: "The CNIL has control power. But it is also true that the administration gives us its projects in little pieces. We need to know the whole situation, because there may be plans afoot to put a vast mosaic in place."[2] In fact, there is little evidence that the commission asked to see the whole picture until the mid-1980s; its power of control will remain a moot point if the information it receives continues to be highly fragmentary. Thyraud has not offered judgments about the extent to which agencies are willing to change their information practices in response to a request by the CNIL. It is able to make significant modifications in government proposals, but the evidence to date is that the latter continues to hold the upper hand in the development of surveillance systems.

Yet the CNIL does exercise some oversight of surveillance practices. In 1982 President Thyraud responded to a question about the extent to which the CNIL had discovered real threats to human interests in data processing during its early experience: "Very honestly, we have never found ourselves confronted with such a menace, but it is a latent possibility. It is clear that the means possessed by the public powers could, if they were used for a bad reason, make possible an unfortunate use of informatics. . . . We learned with surprise that there are in the French administration a certain number of automated data banks that no one knew had been created: the authors had remained totally anonymous."[3] Now, no new information system should be created without consultation with the CNIL.

The decisions, opinions, and advice of the CNIL do seek to breathe life into the law. Thyraud put a very positive face on such developments in 1983, when he was a candidate for reelection as its president. Although he admitted that it was still a "very young" institution, he argued that "it would have been difficult to do better than we have done." Thyraud argued that the commission had been "the conscience of the nation confronted by the phenomenon of informatics" and that it had been a sort of parasite to prevent the administrations and the state from doing what they wanted to do.[4]

A less reverent writer satirized the CNIL's five-year report as follows: "All the world is nice, all the world is fine, and bravo for the CNIL."[5] Critics argue that the CNIL has never taken a tough decision against the government with respect to a proposed new personal information system. It has rarely turned down a government proposal; in part wisely, it tends to negotiate changes during the processing of an application for approval. Even though the commission is independent, its decisions have not been very adventurous.

Thus the CNIL is not yet addressing some of the really fundamental questions in the control of surveillance. As in other licensing regimes, the requests it receives for opinions from the public sector very much shape its work: the tendency is to try to handle the paper flow rather than to set priorities and concentrate on them. Since the CNIL also has to regulate the private sector, it claims not to be in a position to undertake many initiatives on its own. Licensing prevents an appropriate focus on systematic and indeed systemic improvements in data collection activities, because those involved in the process are forever preoccupied with the specifics of any single application or modification thereof. *Terminal 19/84* claims that the general sentiment is that the CNIL has a great deal of difficulty in keeping track of the excessive development of data bases and that both the government and the telecommunications companies are in the habit of presenting it with faits accomplis.[6]

Another critique suggests that the CNIL has not yet taken full advantage of the 1978 law, especially its first several articles. Some suggest that the politicians who tend to dominate the CNIL are acting primarily as politicians and not as independent watchdogs. From this perspective, it would be too risky for politicians to impose the full impact of the law.

One must also consider the argument that the commissioners are in fact perceptive realists when it comes to implementation rather than a group with limited accomplishments. Professor Maisl has advanced the view that the CNIL is not a superadministration to regulate all aspects of computer uses but essentially an agency to listen, watch, and act.[7] Is such a statement a measure of realism or an act of resignation in the face of overwhelming tasks? Any organization has to weigh what it can actually do against its original plans and ambitions, but, at the same time, the essential goals of the relevant legislation need to be addressed as fully as possible.

Although more research is needed on the actual state of relationships between the CNIL and the major central administrations of the government, such empirical work rarely occurs in France. It has taken some time for such ministries to recognize the role and legal responsibilities of the CNIL. The commission faces fundamental problems in trying to regulate the domestic information systems maintained by such powerful agencies as the Ministry of the Interior, which pursues law and order. For example, on April 8, 1981, *Le Monde* drew attention in a "small announcement" to the fact that the Ministry of the Interior had information systems containing data on race and politics, which are illegal unless exempted by the Council of State. Evidently no progress had yet been made on this issue by means of contact with the CNIL or the preparation of a decree.

The four elected politicians on the commission tend to represent the majority at the time of their election. Although this partisan element could be expected to sensitize the CNIL to political realities and even to strengthen its will to take decisive actions against the government when needed, this has not been the normal result to date. The more right-wing deputies and senators chosen after the 1986 elections are in fact less interested in the subject matter than their predecessors, which has contributed to the serious routinization of data protection. The commission lacks both energy to move forward and the strong personalities needed for initiatives. This is in part a product of the fact that the great bodies tend to appoint their retired members to the commission, which is not always beneficial for an activist stance.

Another form of evidence of the commission's relative ineffectiveness is the absence of any significant public conflicts with the government over data protection. While a major confrontation with any government could destroy a small regulatory agency, the lack of such encounters is a negative sign. Instead of judging the politics and policies of the government on surveillance, the CNIL seems to have decided that it cannot do so. The commission lacks the collective will to resist the government on significant issues of information use by large public administrations. It flexed its muscles a little by making the highly unusual number of seven negative decisions in the first six months of 1987, but it almost always acts very cautiously on such matters. Although Jean-Pierre Chamoux and Françoise Chamoux, two informed observers of the commission, suggested in 1984 that it was premature to judge whether it has been strong enough in dealing with large administrative systems and with government decisions, a more critical judgment is possible at the end of a decade of experience.[8]

The record of the CNIL also illustrates the problem of depending on part-time commissioners for strong, affirmative implementation of data protection. Such persons can rarely devote the time necessary to develop appropriate expertise on pending issues. If France were to remove legislators from the CNIL, then it could follow the model of the new National Commission on Communications and Freedom and have a smaller number of full-time members, who could really learn their jobs. The experience since 1982 of the Quebec Commission d'accès à l'information, which has three full-time members, lends strong support for such a model.

Data protection is a difficult and complex task, requiring dedication and commitment. If the Data Inspection Board in Sweden illustrates the reasonably effective functioning of such a commission system, the reverse is true in France. The CNIL was without a full-time president, or even a head of the professional staff, until January 1984. Although President Jacques Fauvet is attempting to reverse this trend, it is an uphill struggle to breathe new life into the CNIL in order to limit surveillance.

The commission has also had major problems in hiring, keeping, and managing competent staff to operate a system requiring universal registration. The fact that 90 percent of registrations come from the private sector means a sizable burden of boring work on routine systems. The two most recent presidents are wisely committed to improving the quality and functioning of the staff, which has undergone a major overhaul. Fauvet has appointed a secretary-general to coordinate staff activities; he is also starting to examine whether decisions of the commission have been implemented in practice.

The risks exist in any country that only the illusion of data protection will be provided, and that data protectors in fact serve as agents of legitimation for new forms and uses of information technology. This risk is greater in France than elsewhere.[9] The rhetoric of the commission is only impressive if one knows little about practical achievements in France and elsewhere. A good example of excessive rhetoric is its assertion, based on an examination of foreign laws, that the French law "is without doubt the most ambitious, and the CNIL [is] the agent of control endowed with the greatest powers and the strongest independent status."[10] The problem is not that the CNIL is different from other countries in its approach to data protection; it simply has not accomplished enough to limit surveillance of the public.

Article 45 has a strong provision empowering the CNIL to recommend to the government the adoption of a decree in the Council of State to provide "that the other provisions of this Act may, in whole or in part, be applied to a file or categories of files which are non-automated or mechanized and which, by themselves or used in combination with a computerized file, threaten civil liberties." This powerful instrument has not yet been used.

In September 1987 the president of the commission, Jacques Fauvet, reacted very negatively to the argument that he and his colleagues should be watchdogs, who should bark and perhaps even bite on occasion. Moreover, he rejects the view that political considerations have had any influence on decision making and argues that negotiations with the regulated have made it unnecessary to take unfavorable decisions.[11] Fortunately, Fauvet has now begun to describe the fundamental role of the CNIL in avoiding the creation of a surveillance society and its function as a watchdog of being more repressive on occasion, if it wishes to be respected.[12]

Despite the several criticisms of the CNIL advanced here, its existence as an oversight and, in this case, regulatory institution has the salutary benefit of providing a forum before which issues of protecting personal privacy in an information society can be debated and resolved in incremental stages. There is no question that the 1978 law is reasonably well suited for the tasks at hand; the problems to date have been inadequate implementation.

Revising the 1978 Law

Socialist Minister of Justice Badinter said in 1981 that Sweden's delay in revising its Data Act was a good example of obtaining experience before redrafting legislation.[13] The Socialists did not attempt to change the law before 1986, in part because opening it to questions in Parliament could lead to a weakening of its force; this attitude continues to dominate the CNIL's own thinking. Some observers now believe that the commission must take the initiative in reform, especially with respect to conducting more audits and lessening the licensing burden. The CNIL regards itself as having the right under the 1978 law to propose any changes necessary for the protection of individual liberties.[14]

It is not yet clear in what ways the law will definitely require amendment. The obligation of making declarations of information systems in the private sector may have to be modified, simply because of the paper burden.[15] The CNIL itself considers that the identification of individuals as suspects occurs too frequently and for too long a period in information systems. In its view, manual files will have to be more fully covered by the law, since they pose more risks than automated ones.[16] The CNIL believes that the general public ought to be informed about the creation of certain data banks, so that it will have an opportunity to react. It argues for the better coordination of the statute with laws and decrees on such matters as research and statistics and the National Identification Register (NIR). The CNIL needs local outlets and assistance for carrying out audits. Finally, it anticipates the need to change the law to respond to developments in data processing and information technology that may make the law obsolete, although it would prefer a process of adaptation via pragmatic solutions.[17]

The CNIL has a mandate to remain abreast of evolving information technology, and this may require statutory revisions. President Fauvet accepts the commission's role as an increasingly essential counterweight to informatics and is concerned about its ability to regulate personal information systems relying on linked minicomputers. He views informatics as leading to the "encirclement of the person. It makes the individual a number."[18] Senator Thyraud claimed that the CNIL is sensitive to surveillance by data linkage: "The consumption of hundreds of pieces of information of this type could permit the knowledge of opinions, private thoughts, and the exercise of influences or of pressure."[19] The commission asserts that its counterparts in other countries are less concerned with the evolution of information technology and its impact on human rights and social life, because foreign laws "are less precise and ambitious than the French law."[20] Other observers believe that the elder statesmen and lawyers who dominate the CNIL are not very knowledgeable about technology, nor interested in it.

Since France is most advanced in the development and application of smart cards (cards with a memory), which incorporate an electronic device in a plastic card, the CNIL has experience with issues at the cutting edge. Smart cards can already store eight kilobits of information, a figure soon expected to reach sixteen. They are in use by financial institutions, the telephone and postal authorities, and even by the medical community as personal data banks.[21] Like any other new form of technology involving the use of personal information, applications of smart cards in both the public and private sectors are subject to various types of regulation by the CNIL. The system in place is to rule on each application on a case-by-case basis. For example, in 1984 the commission heard a presentation about the privacy implications of an experiment with smart cards for the educational records of 8,000 students at the University of Paris-VII. Many local, experimental uses in the health and education fields have now been approved.[22]

The commission tends to regard this type of intelligent card as a portable data bank, which the owner can control through the use of access codes. There is an interesting argument to the effect that this may be the ultimate means for insuring informed consent by the individual. In the CNIL's judgment, smart cards offer improved levels of security to control unauthorized access.[23] The commission recognizes certain potential access problems, if the holder of a smart card used for medical purposes, for example, cannot in fact access certain items of data on his or her file. In a manner typical of expansive French data protectors, the CNIL also expressed its concern that the introduction of this new technology might marginalize sectors of the population which cannot afford payment cards, such as those used to activate telephones.

The magazine *Terminal 19/84* has taken a visible, collective position in favor of major reforms, or at least reorientations, in the 1978 data protection law. It wants to require a positive duty to inform persons about processes of automation concerning them. It also favors the democratization of the commission by including consumers and labor union members and by more openness and publicity for its internal debates and hearings. *Terminal* further encourages using existing organizations of workers and employees to exercise a positive, democratic, collective control over developments in data processing and the choice of information technology.[24] Such admirably democratic instincts are quite far from the current practices of French administration.

One consideration facing the commission and its counterparts in other countries is the risk of proposing changes, since the legislature might weaken the statute in the process of considering specific amendments. This fear tempers efforts by the leadership of the CNIL to tinker with the law, at least until flaws have become significant, self-evident, and intolerable. The return of the Socialists to power in 1988 should reduce the risks of law reform. It is likely that rapid changes in information technology will provide the strongest force for the revision of data protection laws in all countries. If the CNIL does not seize the initiative for proposing revisions—which it is reluctant to do—then Parliament will have to act instead, since the prospect of government efforts to impose stronger controls on its own surveillance practices seems remote in France.

Part 4

Canada

Chapter *19*

The Canadian Model

Introduction

The federal Privacy Act of 1982, a second-generation law, went into effect on July 1, 1983. It supplanted and significantly strengthened the privacy provisions in Part IV of the Canadian Human Rights Act of 1977, which introduced principles of fair information practice in the federal public sector and also created the post of privacy commissioner. The Privacy Act regulates the collection and use of personal information by the federal government. The 1982 law set up a separate office for the privacy commissioner and considerably strengthened its powers of investigation and auditing. Although the Office of the Privacy Commissioner is the only body whose sole activity is data protection, its role is advisory only, and in some ways its oversight is secondary. The balancing of competing interests in difficult cases of governmental surveillance returns to the political arena.

As in West Germany, the advisory system of data protection is well suited to a federal state, although only the two largest provinces, Quebec and Ontario, have equivalent (and somewhat stronger) laws at present. As privacy commissioner since 1983, Dr. John W. Grace has had some significant successes in limiting surveillance, utilizing his particular skills in mediation of disputes and public relations. His independence is promoted by reasonably strong links with the Committee on Justice and Solicitor General of the Canadian House of Commons. In 1987, on the basis of its mandatory review of the implementation of the Privacy Act, the committee made a number of strong recommendations for the control of governmental surveillance, many of which the government has accepted.

The Development of Federal Legislation

As outlined in Table 5, Canada has had two successive federal data protection laws. One of the primary characteristics of this development is that controlling surveillance and protecting privacy has never been a central legislative or public concern but has been subordinate to either human rights or freedom of information laws on both occasions. Data protection was first hidden away in Part IV of the Canadian Human Rights Act; the 1982 Privacy Act is coupled with the Access to Information law in one bill.[1]

The federal government was typical of most Western countries in the early

Table 5. Chronology of Canadian Federal Data Protection Legislation

December 1972	Publication of *Privacy and Computers* by the Task Force on Privacy and Computers.
July 1975	Interdepartmental Committee on Privacy, chaired by the Department of Justice and Department of Communications, produces draft legislation.
July 21, 1975	Liberals introduce Bill C-72 to proscribe discrimination and to protect privacy.
November 29, 1976	Liberals introduce Bill C-25, the Canadian Human Rights Act, a revised version of Bill C-72.
July 14, 1977	Bill C-25, the Canadian Human Rights Act, receives royal assent (passed by the House of Commons on June 2, 1977).
October 1, 1977	Inger Hansen appointed privacy commissioner (served to July 1, 1983).
March 1, 1978	Bill C-25, the Canadian Human Rights Act, proclaimed in force.
May 2, 1980	First reading of Bill C-535, the Privacy Act, 1980, introduced as a private member's bill by Conservative M.P. Perrin Beatty.
July 17, 1980	Liberals introduce Bill C-43, to enact the Access to Information Act and the Privacy Act.
July 7, 1982	Bill C-43 receives royal assent (passed by the House of Commons on June 28, 1982).
June 2, 1983	John Grace appointed privacy commissioner.
July 1, 1983	Access to Information Act and Privacy Act proclaimed in force.

1970s in establishing a major Task Force on Privacy and Computers, which published a number of independent studies and a summary report.[2] Although the report did not suggest an urgent need for legislation, the federal government set up an Interdepartmental Committee on Privacy in order to prepare a law for the federal government.

Public servants produced the policy and draft legislation for data protection, but the government itself decided on appropriate ways of implementation. The concept of the privacy commissioner as an ombudsman was the product of government thinking, not of the few specialists in data protection in the public service, except to the significant extent that the latter began to think of an ombudsman as an alternative model to reliance on judicial review and the creation of a data protection commissioner.[3] The government's approach featured a limited conception of data protection. An ombudsman's role, at least as narrowly defined, is only part of what is necessary for strong data protection. Nevertheless, both Inger Hansen, the first privacy commissioner, and her successor, John Grace, have been much influenced by the ombudsman model.

In 1977 the privacy commissioner was assigned limited tasks that were primarily reactive. The Department of Justice believed that such arrangements could make data protection truly effective in meeting Canadian conditions. Part IV of the Human Rights Act was, in fact, a very modest piece of law-making, especially in comparison with similar laws in West Germany and Sweden. It was conceived as an experiment to find out where the problems really were in data protection. Part IV never attained an independent existence of its own.

When the Progressive Conservative government of Joe Clark came to power in 1979, it put considerable pressure on a committee of public servants from the Department of Justice and the Privy Council Office to produce draft legislation on access to government information. This initiative allowed the revision of Part IV at the same time, largely at the behest of public servants. The plan was to have both access and privacy legislation ready for joint submission to Parliament, but only the former was introduced before the Conservative government fell in December 1979.

Concrete proposals for amending Part IV first came to public attention when two Conservatives, former justice minister, Senator Jacques Flynn, and former Cabinet member, Perrin Beatty, simultaneously introduced private-member bills for a new Privacy Act after the change of government in 1980. Those proposals resurfaced in a Cabinet Discussion Paper prepared by the Department of Justice, dated June 1980, which outlined the key elements of what became the Privacy Act. The amendments proposed for Part IV were separated into those designed to ensure consistency with freedom of information legislation and those designed to improve privacy protection. The government also decided to separate the new legislation from the Human Rights Act, to make the privacy commissioner into an independent official, and to expand the functions of the office and the personal information covered by the law.[4]

Unfortunately, the Standing Committee on Justice and Legal Affairs of the House of Commons devoted almost all of its time to the controversial provisions for access to government information. The entire clause-by-clause review of the Privacy Act occurred in a last-minute, marathon session on June 8, 1982.[5] Thus the privacy provisions of Bill C-43 are primarily those introduced by the government for first reading on July 17, 1980. Fortunately, the Privacy Act significantly improved Part IV by extending privacy protection and reinforcing these rights with procedures for independent, external review by the privacy commissioner and the Federal Court of Canada-Trial Division.

Formative Influences

Public servants knew about the Hessian Data Protection Act of 1970 and the Swedish Data Act of 1973, but such models were not thought to be relevant to the Canadian situation. The influential U.S. Privacy Act downplayed the importance of having an active agency to promote implementation. In 1977, Perrin Beatty, one of the few members of Parliament with a record of serious interest in privacy, did propose the creation of "an information auditor, similar to the Auditor General, who should be charged with reporting to Parliament on how completely departments are complying with the spirit of the act," but his advice went unheeded.[6] Fortunately, representatives of the Department of Justice gradually concluded that European systems of data protection had increasing relevance to the Canadian situation, although they rejected a licensing model because of the administrative difficulties it posed.

Until the Supreme Court of Canada started to make decisions under the 1982 Charter of Rights and Freedoms, the right to personal privacy hardly existed under Canadian law. The Protection of Privacy Act of 1974, which regulates wiretapping, was important primarily because it was the first federal statutory recognition of the right to privacy.[7] In the 1970s the general public knew very little about the challenges to their personal privacy posed by new technology, and consequently there was a low level of public concern about surveillance, even among members of Parliament.[8] The absence of a high-profile public issue, such as occurred in other countries, meant that there was no media spotlight to fan fears of an Orwellian state, except for persistent concern about abuses of Social Insurance Numbers, which are unique personal identifiers.

Some observers suggest that the federalist model of government, with its distribution of powers between the federal and provincial governments, hindered the development of data protection legislation and concern for privacy. Federal data protection was well in advance of any provincial initiatives. Quebec, the first province to act, introduced legislation for the protection of personal information in the public sector in 1982. The other large province, Ontario, which traditionally has more influence than Quebec on provincial legislation, only enacted a similar law in 1987.[9] As discussed in Chapter 23, concern for law and order has also been a primary impediment.

The only significant external influence was the American Privacy Act of 1974. Persons drafting the regulations, directives, and guidelines for Part IV also found some inspiration in the various reports of the U.S. Privacy Protection Study Commission and the U.S. Commission on Federal Paperwork.[10] Fortunately, the Canadian drafters recognized that the U.S. Privacy Act is weak on implementation and created the post of privacy commissioner.

Significant Provisions

There are several progressive characteristics of the Privacy Act of 1982. For example, Canada is the first country to set up so direct a relationship between data protectors and the legislature through a standing committee of Parliament.[11] The potential at least exists for an elected body to engage in continuous monitoring of how data protection is working. There are some weaknesses in parliamentary oversight of data protection, and a better system of consultation with the privacy commissioner on pending legislation is required. The reform of the House of Commons in 1985 helped this situation somewhat by creating a specialist committee that only oversees existing legislation rather than enacting bills.

The most important innovation changed the statutory position of privacy commissioner to a more active role. Instead of having to rely on complaints from individuals, the commissioner is entitled to launch investigations independently.[12] Active use of this oversight capacity is critical to successful control of governmental surveillance. In addition, the Privacy Act now allows the commissioner to investigate the compliance of government institutions with the code of fair information practices in sections 4 to 8 of the act.[13]

The commissioner can further intervene in a number of circumstances. An individual can still appeal a refusal of access to his or her own records by direct complaint to the privacy commissioner, who can also monitor other potential loopholes. For example, the broadest circumstance under which a government agency can disclose personal information is where "in the opinion of the head of the Institution, the public interest in disclosure clearly outweighs any invasion of privacy that could result from the disclosure."[14] Although this provision effectively introduces a balancing test between the public interest and an individual's privacy, the government contends it "is intended to be used only in very limited circumstances. . . . It is felt that some such residual clause is necessary to deal with situations where release is highly desirable but where it is not permitted under any of the other provisions."[15] The head of a government institution has to notify the privacy commissioner in writing of any such disclosures of personal information.[16] The drafters believed that such a requirement would make government institutions reluctant to use the exemption, "except in situations where disclosure is clearly justified."[17]

Judicial review was another critical innovation in 1982. An individual or the privacy commissioner may appeal to the Federal Court-Trial Division after a complaint has been made to the commissioner. Although such review is restricted to denials of access to personal information, this outlet, with the potential to reach the Supreme Court of Canada, gives enforceable rights to individuals. This legislation is an intelligent compromise between the American and European systems.[18] Americans have to rely solely on the courts to enforce access rights under the Privacy Act, whereas Canadians can use the commissioner as a mechanism to avoid the courts except as a last resort.

The Canadian law does emphasize the right of individual access to data as the solution to privacy problems. The 1982 law expanded access rights to cover more institutions, set time limits for action, and provided for judicial review.[19] Such continued confidence in the salutary impact of the right of access is surprising, given its lack of use under Part IV of the Canadian Human Rights Act. However, the number of requests has increased considerably since 1983.

The preparation of regulations, guidelines, and directives by the Administrative Policy Branch of the Treasury Board has substantially influenced the effectiveness of implementation. These guidelines and directives have great influence on government institutions, though only the regulations passed by the governor in council have the actual force of law.[20] Since most of those responsible for implementing data protection in government institutions are not lawyers, they naturally turn to the directives and guidelines of the Treasury Board.

The Privacy Act is fully coordinated with the Access to Information law. For the first time a country has enacted laws on freedom of information and data protection in as coherent a manner as possible. Thus, the term "personal information" has the same meaning in both laws. The drafters consciously sought to avoid a situation where the American Freedom of Information Act has been used to circumvent the provisions in the Privacy Act. In particular, the review procedures followed by the privacy commissioner, the information commissioner, and the Federal Court are identical in both laws.

The Organization of Data Protection

The federal government adopted a complicated system for the implementation of data protection with statutory responsibilities divided among the following: Parliament, the Department of Justice, the president of the Treasury Board, the heads of government institutions, the privacy commissioner, and the Federal Court of Canada.

Just as Parliament had minimal impact on the shaping of the privacy measures, it was slow to exercise active supervision. The new legislation determined that Parliament has the right to establish a committee to undertake a comprehensive review of the provisions and operation of the Privacy Act after a three-year period, to report its findings and any proposed changes to Parliament, and also to review the administration of the Privacy Act on a permanent basis.[21] In 1985 the Standing Committee on Justice and Legal Affairs began its three-year review and released its major report on March 31, 1987.[22]

The Treasury Board has much more direct responsibilities than Parliament, because the president of the Treasury Board is the designated minister for most administrative purposes under the law. On the surface, the duties and functions of the designated minister are significant. He or she shall, for example, "cause to be kept under review the manner in which personal information banks are maintained and managed to ensure compliance with the provisions of this Act." The Treasury Board also has the important function of preparing guidelines and directives for other government institutions.[23]

The statutory powers and responsibilities of the president of the Treasury Board under the Privacy Act make him or her the initial supervisor of government personal information systems. Because the Treasury Board has traditionally played a central role in the annual review of funding for government agencies, much like the Office of Management and the Budget in the U.S., there is a statutory expectation that the Treasury Board will act in a strong manner to ensure that the language of the Privacy Act will become a working reality.[24]

The Administrative Policy Branch of the Treasury Board now coordinates the administration of the Privacy Act through its separate sections on policy development and implementation. The latter section publishes the *Personal Information Index,* a listing of all personal information banks, and reviews the creation of information banks. The Administrative Policy Branch now has eight persons involved in information policy development and five persons working on implementation both for privacy measures and access to information. The Treasury Board continues to be more involved on a daily basis with the Access to Information law than with the Privacy Act, since the former is more risky in a political sense to the interests of the government. The individuals involved in these activities carry considerable weight in the public service because they work closely with the office of the Secretary of the Treasury Board and reflect his or her views. In practice, they emphasize coordination rather than intervention.

The head of each government institution is responsible for administration of the Privacy Act within the organization.[25] A privacy coordinator in each institution handles these responsibilities, which include reporting to the Treasury Board about personal information held by the agency, responding to requests for access, helping to defend decisions to grant or refuse access before the privacy commissioner or the Federal Court, ensuring the appropriate control of personal information, and helping to prepare an annual report to Parliament.[26] The Canadian law is thus very close to other national acts in assigning major responsibilities to the heads of government institutions and coordinators within each government department.

Privacy coordinators almost always serve as access coordinators as well. They report both to the heads of their institutions and to the Administrative Policy Branch of the Treasury Board. A number are brought together by the latter in an Access to Information and Privacy Advisory Committee, which has existed since 1977. Although this committee has some senior officials, the general rank of members is not especially high in the public service hierarchy, which raises questions about their influence as they pursue implementation in their own departments. Grace correctly argues that the coordinators "should become the privacy consciences of their departments, raising their colleagues' consciousness of privacy access and protection principles. To do this, coordinators should be in the mainstream of their organizations. The position of privacy coordinator should be coveted as highly desirable progress, demanding as it does sensitivity and advocacy skills as well as a department-wide knowledge of operating programs and activities."[27] At present, the government is taking steps to ensure such goals.

The Department of Justice is responsible for policy development in the implementation of data protection and for the legal implications of individual cases. It maintains a broad overview of the application of the act in relation to the intentions of the government and the expectations of the public; it advises the designated minister on any administrative questions giving rise to broad policy issues; and it provides legal interpretation and advice, gathering case and precedent information, and coordinating the government's preparation for the parliamentary review of the provisions and operation of the statute.[28] The Department of Justice's Information Law and Privacy unit is the ultimate source of legal advice on the interpretation of the Privacy Act, although heads of government departments or privacy coordinators usually first consult the lawyers in their own organizations.

Both the government and the first privacy commissioner, Inger Hansen, who served from 1977 to 1983, regarded the position as essentially one of acting as an ombudsman responding to complaints from individuals.[29] Hansen did not interpret her functions in an expansive fashion, as was at least theoretically possible. Her experience as a lawyer and as the first ombudsman for federal prisoners, and indeed her personal style, inclined her to operate quietly behind the scenes as much as possible, so as not to interfere with the ability of her office to resolve access complaints satisfactorily and in an informal manner. She does "not believe that the one charged with making findings relating to legal rights between contesting parties can maintain credibility if engaged in partisan advocacy."[30] Her conception was essentially passive, although other data protection specialists recognize that an ombudsman could perform an active monitoring role as well.[31] The style adopted by the people charged with data protection has very important implications for attempts to limit governmental surveillance in every country.

The privacy commissioner does not license or register personal information systems. The 1982 law significantly enhanced the power of the commissioner to monitor and investigate information handling in various areas of government and brought the post closer in character to that of a European data protection commissioner. Advocacy, audit, and supervisory activities now have a clear statutory basis.

Yet despite the expansive title, the privacy commissioner is not fully in charge of implementing federal data protection, as ought to be the case. This was a conscious decision and not an oversight on the part of the government, which determined that it would retain ultimate responsibility under traditions of Cabinet government. This approach is an open invitation to weak implementation. As in other countries, one of the fundamental problems is discovering a way to make the law fully effective in its detailed application.

The privacy commissioner appointed in 1983, John Grace, recognized that the job had changed under the revised legislation. In his view, Parliament had conferred "new status" upon "the value of personal privacy."[32] In fact, the decentralized model of enforcement of data protection has de facto made the privacy commissioner the central catalyst in ensuring effective implementation.

Grace, as a matter of style and personal choice, also adopted an active role from the very beginning.

The information and privacy commissioners share the same office space and certain administrative staff, and it is even possible for one commissioner to occupy both posts. The goal was consistency of statutory interpretation, the avoidance of conflicts between the two commissioners, and the reduction of administrative costs.[33] This system has in fact raised significant internal conflicts of interest within the office. MP Svend Robinson questioned the desirability of having the same persons serving as privacy and information commissioners, since both positions would clearly be full-time jobs.[34] Indeed, it is hard to imagine how one person could effectively articulate and balance the conflicting interests involved in the two statutes. The potential for conflict of interest was also recognized when the Treasury Board set up separate staffs for the commissioners with shared administrative personnel; the offices are separate legal entities and operate independently from shared premises.[35] In 1987 the Justice Committee recommended the separation of the two offices.[36] Although the Cabinet rejected this proposal, de facto separation has occurred anyway.

The Privacy Act determines that "such officers and employees as are necessary to enable the privacy commissioner to perform the duties and functions of the commissioner under this or any other Act of Parliament shall be appointed."[37] The process of selecting staff through the Public Service Commission occupied a great deal of John Grace's initial working time. As of January 1, 1989, he has a separate staff of twenty-nine, including an executive director, a legal adviser, a director of privacy complaints and eight investigators, a director of privacy compliance and seven auditors (including three information system auditors), and a general staff.

If one divides the support staff for management and personnel services proportionately between the information and privacy commissioners, the privacy commissioner has a staff of approximately forty, which is larger than the office of the federal Data Protection Commissioner in West Germany, in a country with more than twice the population of Canada. Yet there remain questions whether the commissioner has adequate staff for the many tasks at hand, which include ensuring the compliance of 375,000 federal government employees with the Privacy Act. As a result of the 1987 parliamentary review of the implementation of the Privacy Act, the office obtained nine new positions in 1988, followed by four more in succeeding years. The extension of the scope of the law to government-owned corporations is largely responsible for the staff increases.

The president of the Treasury Board expected in 1983 that the annual budget of the privacy and information commissioners would be approximately 2.8 million Canadian dollars.[38] The Office of the Privacy Commissioner spent $1.9 million in the 1987–88 fiscal year, if one allocates a proportionate share of general administrative costs to this activity.[39] The government estimates the total costs of implementing both the Access and Privacy Acts across the government departments at about $10 million, roughly the original estimate, with most of the expenditures centered in operating departments.

The problem with the Canadian model of enforcement is finding someone to act in a vigorous manner to make the Privacy Act a meaningful statute. The Standing Committee on Justice and Solicitor General has no permanent staff, so its annual review to date has been limited. The small Information Law and Privacy unit of the Department of Justice primarily furnishes legal interpretations. The Treasury Board continues its traditional coordinating role as its major contribution to the process of implementation. The heads of government institutions and privacy coordinators are preoccupied with the impact of the Access to Information law and with the administration of all requests for access.

The following pages discuss how the Privacy Act is working in practice to limit governmental surveillance and also indicate how the law will be changed if Parliament eventually implements the 1987 proposals of the Justice Committee on revising the act.

Chapter 20

The Goals of Data Protection

What do data protection laws and data protection agencies seek to accomplish for the control of governmental surveillance? This chapter evaluates the purposes of the Privacy Act in order to evaluate their relevance for confronting surveillance problems directly and for giving data protectors a clear and specific mandate.

Since the introduction of computers on a major scale in the early 1960s, federal government institutions have developed many automated personal information systems. However, in contrast to many European data protection laws, neither Part IV of the Canadian Human Rights Act nor the Privacy Act of 1982 restrict their attention to the dangers or risks of automated data processing as such[The Privacy Act applies to all personal information in whatever form.[1] The absence of a precise focus on data processing in the Privacy Act is an intelligent recognition that all forms of personal information can be used in mass surveillance systems. By international standards, such a broad scope for data protection is very innovative.

The actual title of the Privacy Act is an improvement on Part IV of the Canadian Human Rights Act, although Canadians, like Americans, now run the risk of being misled by the broad title into thinking that all privacy problems have been regulated at the federal level. Laypersons attempting to distinguish the Protection of Privacy Act of 1974, which authorizes wiretapping, and the Privacy Act of 1982 will be surprised by the continuing use of similar titles. In fact, the Privacy Act is, at present, a data protection statute. Its purpose "is to extend the present laws of Canada that protect the privacy of individuals with respect to personal information about themselves held by a government institution."[2] The term privacy is not further defined, which is regrettable.

The Privacy Act contains a comprehensive code of fair information practices concerning the collection, retention, disposal, and protection of personal information. This is its most significant contribution to identifying the goals of data protection and, if properly implemented, to restricting the surveillance of citizens. The government decided to strengthen the protections on the use and disclosure of personal information in the 1982 law, noting that these provisions are "what most people have in mind when they refer to privacy protection."[3]

Perhaps the most important new provision is the requirement that "no personal information shall be collected by a government institution unless it relates directly to an operating program or activity of the institution." Wherever possible, such information should be collected directly from the individual, who should be informed about the purpose for which it is being collected.[4] Those interpreting such language in isolation might question its ultimate impact, but public servants reading the directives from the Treasury Board should have no doubts about its intended meaning: "The intent of this provision is to promote the protection of privacy by restricting the collection of personal information by government institutions to those situations in which the information is clearly required for an appropriately authorized operating program or activity. To give effect to this provision, institutions must have parliamentary authority for the program or activity concerned." Additionally, when the collection of personal information is necessary, it "should be restricted to the minimum needed for the program or activity."[5] The Treasury Board notes that the requirement of direct collection "is designed to increase the individual's control over and knowledge of such information and to promote the collection of accurate, up-to-date, and complete information." Moreover, the limiting phrase, wherever possible, "does not permit collection from another source simply because it is easier or less costly to obtain the information in this way than to collect it from the individual to whom it relates."[6]

The Treasury Board further instructs government institutions that the exceptions to direct, informed collection of personal information should be used sparingly, since they are designed primarily for use by investigative bodies. The requirement to inform an individual "recognizes the individual's right to know and understand the purpose for which information about him or her is to be collected, and the use which is to be made of the information. Also, when the individual is not required by law to supply the information, such knowledge and understanding permit the individual to make an informed choice as to whether or not to provide it."[7]

The inherent power of the Treasury Board can be seen in its determination "as a matter of administrative policy," that the above requirement is extended to informing "any individual from whom information about another individual is to be collected of the purpose of collection."[8] Administrative policy also requires government institutions to inform any individual from whom personal information is to be collected whether the response is mandatory or voluntary and the implications of refusal to respond.[9] Such strong instructions could encounter resistance or, more likely, they have been ignored with impunity because of a lack of comprehensive oversight of implementation by either the Treasury Board or the privacy commissioner. On the other hand, informed consent is one area where concerned individuals can help to police the application of the statute.

Section 6 concerns the retention, management, and disposal of personal information. A government institution "shall take all reasonable steps to ensure that personal information that is used for an administrative purpose by the institution is as accurate, up-to-date, and complete as possible." Such information must also be retained for two years in order to give the individual an opportunity to obtain access to it. Otherwise, the disposal of personal information is governed by regulations, directives, and guidelines issued by the Treasury Board.[10] Since one of the goals of data protection is to dispose of unneeded personal information, the unusual retention requirement is somewhat contradictory and reflects an exaggerated emphasis on rights of access. The prevailing argument is that access furnishes any persons with some control over the personal information that the state has about them, which is more dependable than reliance on some disinterested advocate. The optimistic expectation in this case is that access rights will be exercised by the general public. The reality is that retained data can also be reused by the government for surveillance purposes that may not be in the best interests of the individual.

The Treasury Board points out that under section 6(3) any directives or guidelines on the disposal of personal information issued by its president "have the force of law." The first such mandatory principle is very significant: any personal information collected before the Privacy Act came into force on July 1, 1983, that "is not relevant to an authorized operating program or activity of the institution" shall be destroyed. This has led to at least some of the housecleaning of unnecessary personal information that occurred in the United States after the enactment of its Privacy Act. The Treasury Board also mandates disposal of personal information "where further retention . . . might unfairly prejudice the interests of the individual to whom the information relates." Subject to the qualifications above, the Treasury Board wisely directs that "when personal information is no longer required for the purpose for which it was obtained or compiled by the institution, the information shall be disposed of."[11] Again, the difficulty is to ensure that anyone pays attention to such detailed rules in the press of routine business.

Sections 7 and 8 "constitute a code governing the use and disclosure of all personal information under the control of government institutions . . . in recognition of the principle that the right of the individual to privacy includes the right to control the use and disclosure of information about him or herself and, when exceptions to this principle exist, to know what use could be made of the information and to whom and for what purposes the information may be disclosed."[12] The Treasury Board further notes that the code of fair information practices does not take precedence over specific statutory prohibitions in other legislation, that it only permits but does not require the use and disclosure of personal information, and that "it is government policy to balance the requirement for privacy with the need for government institutions to ensure the optimum use of personal information for any purpose permitted by the Privacy Act, in order to promote general efficiency in government operations, eliminate unnecessary collection of information, reduce the response burden on individuals and facilitate the sharing of data for research or statistical purposes."[13] This mingling of goals necessitates careful monitoring of information practices; otherwise, the incentives for surveillance will continue to dominate competing human interests.

Section 8 establishes in considerable detail the thirteen conditions under which a government institution may disclose personal information under its control. (One of the ironies of such "protective" laws is that they devote considerable space to authorizing disclosures.) The first principle is that any individual can consent to such a release.[14] The Treasury Board's administrative policy covers such varied cases as obtaining consent on behalf of minors, incompetents, deceased persons, and representatives of an individual. These careful instructions are more precise than under any other data protection law.

The second major type of permissible disclosure is for a use consistent with the purpose for which the information was obtained or compiled by the institution. Given the abuse of the "routine use" clause in the U.S. Privacy Act, this provision for "consistent uses" poses certain risks, but the Treasury Board made an excellent beginning in defining its meaning.[15] Moreover, if a government agency does not publish its consistent uses in the description of its personal information banks, the privacy commissioner must be notified of any intended use, which can be a very effective device for monitoring personal information practices.

The Treasury Board has also published guidelines and directives concerning the circumstances under which personal information may be disclosed under an act of Parliament or a regulation; in response to subpoenas, warrants, or court orders; to federal investigative bodies; to provinces, foreign states, and international bodies; to members of Parliament; for audit, archival, and research or statistical purposes; for payment of a benefit and collection of a debt; and in the public interest.[16] If properly observed, such rules will further limit government surveillance.

Perhaps the most sensitive condition for disclosure occurs in a situation where, in the opinion of the head of the institution, "the public interest in disclosure clearly outweighs any invasion of privacy that could result from the disclosure." The Treasury Board prescribes an invasion-of-privacy test that must take account of the expectations of the individual, the sensitivity of the information, and the probability of injury.[17] It calls this provision the residual, discretionary clause to cover the inevitable unforeseen situation, in a fashion comparable to "emergency use" under the U.S. Privacy Act. The uses of this statutory exemption need to be carefully monitored by the privacy commissioner, whom government departments must (in theory) inform about such disclosures.

Conflicts over Data Protection

Conflicts over the scope of data protection were not especially evident under Part IV of the Canadian Human Rights Act, nor have any very significant problems emerged to date under the Privacy Act. There are two main reasons for this situation. First, the statute and the administrative policy competently spell out the goals of the legislation, especially with respect to fair information practices and the coverage of all types of personal records, so that the kinds of conflicts that have emerged in West Germany have been largely avoided. The second reason is that the implementation of the Privacy Act has not really been pushed very hard to date by government institutions or the privacy commissioner, especially with respect to sections 4 to 8 of the statute. The emphasis has been on processing an increasing flow of individual requests for access to their own data.[18]

The issues in dispute from within the Privacy Act have been relatively precise, such as the meaning of a Cabinet document or the intent of the drafters with respect to judicial review of exempt banks. To date, most of the internal government disputes have involved the privacy commissioner, the Department of Justice, and the Federal Court having to consider conflicting views of specific issues, such as the denial of an individual's right to see a file or the legitimacy of data in a particular exempt bank. The matters tend to be relatively legalistic, insofar as the general public is concerned.

The privacy commissioner has been very successful to date in avoiding public disputes with the heads of government institutions. John Grace's instinctive approach, like Inger Hansen's, is to avoid controversy and to conciliate. He uses a very direct, personal approach to key people on the other side of any current or prospective issue. In many ways, the promotion of good public relations is one of his many strengths. The prospects for conflict are increasing as Grace's office carries out more targeted audits of the small number of exempt data banks and of the records of disclosure of information in such sensitive fields as law enforcement. His office's new model for risk analysis of government institutions is also leading his auditors into areas of potential conflict over implementation. Grace's distaste for conflict may well be put to the test.

The provinces did not react well to the enactment of the Access to Information Act and the Privacy Act, feeling that they promised open season on access to records flowing to the federal government from the provinces. One of the exemptions made possible under section 19(1) of the Privacy Act permits provinces to claim a blanket exemption from individual access to data received in confidence from the province in question. Unfortunately, the federal-provincial agreements in this area have been tolerating blanket claims to confidentiality, which are contrary to the spirit of the legislation. Grace has taken a strong stand against such practices. There have been some private promises that the provinces, especially Ontario and Alberta, will reconsider their approach in this area. The advent of data protection laws in Quebec and Ontario extends access rights and also facilitates reciprocal transfers of protected personal information.

Parliament paid relatively little critical attention to the Office of the Privacy Commissioner until the three-year review conducted from 1985 to 1987. There has been only limited annual oversight of its workings by a parliamentary committee. No one in the House of Commons has asked the privacy commissioner, the Treasury Board, or the Department of Justice to do more about implementation, because no member of Parliament knows very much about their respective roles and contributions. One main exception is Svend Robinson of the New Democratic party. When a question relating to privacy occurs during question period in the House of Commons, there is no inclination to ask anyone for his views other than the government minister responsible. There has not yet been a development of an expectation that all privacy issues should receive scrutiny from the privacy commissioner, although the 1987 report of the Standing Committee on Justice and Solicitor General sought to encourage this trend.[19]

Chapter 21

The Power of the Privacy Commissioner

In order to be effective in limiting governmental surveillance, data protectors require independence, powers of intervention, and the willingness to use them. This chapter begins the evaluation of how well the privacy commissioner of Canada has been functioning in this regard.

The Issue of Independence

The Privacy Act strengthened the critically important independence of the commissioner. Under the Canadian Human Rights Act, all members of the Human Rights Commission were appointed by the government; the minister of justice, on the recommendation of the chief of the commission, then named one of the members as privacy commissioner.[1] Inger Hansen was thus appointed for a fixed term and held office during good behavior, but Parliament could remove her at any time.[2] She had no special protections for her independence. Hansen was reappointed for a second four-year term on October 1, 1981, but the issue was left hanging in the balance until the last moment, and her concern about the matter contributed to at least theoretical limitations on the independence of the office. Since she was not a regular public servant, she ran the risk of being unemployed if she was not reappointed. Her position was abolished with the proclamation of the Privacy Act on July 1, 1983. Had she not been appointed information commissioner under the Access to Information Act, she would have been without government employment. For someone not as independent in practice as Hansen, such working conditions could have interfered with the operations of her office.

The privacy commissioner now has as much independence as is achievable in a parliamentary system; the commissioner is an officer of Parliament and not a straight political appointment by the Cabinet.[3] In practice, the Privy Council Office and the Prime Minister's Office select a candidate, which still makes the selection process political. Consultation then occurs among leaders of the respective parties in the House of Commons. Although the opposition parties cannot do much to change a government's choice, a Cabinet seeks to avoid political controversy by bringing forward a name that will ensure unanimous approval by the legislature.

The privacy commissioner is responsible only to Parliament, which is a crucial guarantee of independence. The appointment is for seven years, renewable, during good behavior. The incumbent can be removed only after an address made in both Houses of Parliament, which shields the commissioner from the political winds of change and ensures that removal is for good cause.[4] The primary threat to the independence of the commissioner remains concern over eventual reappointment, but there is no obvious solution to this problem. The West German government's decision not to reappoint Hans Peter Bull to a second term shows that such a problem is not idle speculation. Canadian provincial ombudsmen have also been ousted unceremoniously after one term. One advantage of an older incumbent is lack of interest in or need for a second or subsequent term, but the energy required for the post militates against advocating such a choice.

Various provisions in the Privacy Act further support the independence of the commissioner. Section 54(2) establishes the salary of the commissioner as equal to the generous amount paid to an ordinary judge of the Federal Court of Canada. This is designed to reinforce the commissioner's image of independence from the government and the civil service. It is a criminal offense to obstruct the commissioner or any person acting on his or her behalf in the performance of statutory duties and functions. He or she is not subject to a summons in connection with information acquired in the course of normal duties, nor is the incumbent subject to civil or criminal proceedings for anything done in good faith in the exercise or performance of the duties of the position. The annual report of the commissioner is submitted to Parliament. Any special reports to Parliament also have to be transmitted to both houses of the legislature and sent to the Standing Committee on Justice and Solicitor General, which is important in assuring direct access to the legislature.[5] As a practical manifestation of his status, John Grace has in fact recognized his position as a servant of the House of Commons and cultivated contacts with members of Parliament and parliamentary committees.

The Exercise of Power

Under the Privacy Act, the president of the Treasury Board has substantial duties and functions with respect to the use and creation of personal information banks. For example, it has to approve the establishment or substantial modification of such banks.[6] Only Cabinet documents are excluded from these powers. Such responsibilities might better have been given to the Office of the Privacy Commissioner. Yet, in administrative terms, the Treasury Board has greater capacity to exercise such oversight, which the privacy commissioner can then audit.

The serious problem for implementation is to motivate the Treasury Board to make 144 government institutions pay attention to them at the appropriate level and then for the privacy commissioner's office to find the time and resources to monitor compliance with Treasury Board directives. Thus, one key to successful implementation is an active oversight role for the Treasury Board. When the Privacy Act was proclaimed, the Treasury Board president promised to be significantly involved in implementation, but the Board's Secretariat has had limited ambitions for an active role in this regard, in part because of its innumerable responsibilities. The parliamentary review in 1986–87 drew particular attention to this problem.[7]

The privacy commissioner's power remains advisory.[8] The inability to order a government institution to do anything is a significant limitation; the commissioner has to rely on persuasion to be effective.[9] However, the commissioner can now take the initiative in investigating possible breaches of the provisions of the Privacy Act dealing with the collection and use of personal information. In addition, certain specialized disclosures, such as to the police, have special controls whereby the commissioner can carefully scrutinize what has happened. As stated by a former minister of communications, "The Privacy Commissioner can, of course, report to the head of the institution involved, and to Parliament, where he or she finds that a government institution has not complied with the code."[10] The privacy commissioner can also now appeal a disagreement with a government institution over release of information to an individual to the Federal Court.

In testifying before the Standing Committee on Justice and Legal Affairs, Hansen argued in favor of the commissioner not having enforcement power: "When a Commissioner has vast investigatory powers and only the power to recommend, it is easier to gain the knowledge that you need to resolve complaints in an informal way. If the Commissioner functions as a court, there is really no need for the Commissioner. If the Commissioner has power either to discipline administrators or to reverse the decisions, positions will be polarized at too early a stage and thus prevent an easy, early, informal resolution of the problem."[11] Hansen wrote: "Depending on the amount of credibility of the holder of the office, the recommendations may carry a lot of weight or none at all."[12]

John Grace's approach to office coincides with the Hansen conception, except that he has consciously sought a higher profile within government and with the general public. In his view, his position as a creature of Parliament offers considerable power to implement the legislation. Grace has developed a good working relationship with the deputy ministers of government institutions, who are the effective heads of the public service, so that problems can be handled promptly and effectively. His exercise of power is very similar to a West German Data Protection Commissioner with the ultimate sanction being hostile comment in the media and in reports to Parliament. The private threat of such public action has a very salutary effect in resolving differences.

There are also several important statutory mechanisms whereby the privacy commissioner is informed about certain sensitive uses of personal information. This unusual feature permits the commissioner to scrutinize "public interest" and "consistent use" disclosures. The available record indicates that he has not complained about any of the former category of disclosures to date, although he is concerned about the failure of departments to notify him about new uses of data.[13] Such monitoring continues to be a fruitful area of activity for the commissioner.

To date, the commissioners have been deeply committed to relying upon advisory power to achieve results in monitoring the personal information practices of the federal government. This diverges from the structures that are in place in Quebec and Ontario, where the data protection officials have the power to make more decisions about fair information practices. The fact that the two most populous Canadian provinces have moved in a different direction creates a fascinating opportunity to test the advisory model. In terms of experience, however, none of the Canadian data protection laws have been in force long enough to permit definitive judgments about the merits of the advisory versus the regulatory approaches.[14] In the long term, all data protection officials may need at least certain regulatory powers to be truly effective in limiting governmental surveillance.

Chapter 22

The Implementation of Data Protection

Effective implementation is a key factor in the successful conduct of data protection. Thus this core chapter pays extended attention to what has happened since Canada introduced federal data protection legislation in 1977, with a particular focus on the activities of the Office of the Privacy Commissioner. What approaches has it used in trying to limit governmental surveillance practices and with what success? Special attention is paid to staffing, since the choice of employees has proved to be so critical to this effort. There is also extensive discussion of the various activities of data protectors as they seek to accomplish their statutory tasks. Finally, the chapter treats how data protection principles have evolved in practice.

The Office of the Privacy Commissioner

As is true in other countries, the personality of the individual charged with data protection significantly influences the approach taken. Inger Hansen, the first privacy commissioner, interpreted her job as essentially reactive; she was not in a position to influence government policy directly, but she did play an indirect role. She believed that the privacy commissioner was not in a position to give advice to the president of the Treasury Board or to the minister of justice, since in her view it would be a conflict of interest to be both an investigator and a policy adviser, and an ombudsman cannot be too cozy with administrators or legislators. Although Hansen might admit that her job in fact could have been performed in a more activist and policy-oriented fashion, she simply was not comfortable with it. Thus if Hansen had chosen to continue as privacy commissioner, she would have had to reconsider her approach in order to cope with the more activist responsibilities assigned to the commissioner under the 1982 law.

John Grace was appointed as privacy commissioner on June 2, 1983. For twenty years he had been an editorial writer for the *Ottawa Journal* and was editor-in-chief of this independent, but vigorously conservative, newspaper, when it was closed down in 1980. Grace subsequently entered government service as one of the full-time commissioners of the Canadian Radio-television and Telecommunications Commission, working primarily on telecommunications issues. He was an independent commissioner, earning considerable publicity for his dissents from the regulatory agency's major decisions on pay television and the Canadian content of programming. Critics at the time described him variously as an antiregulator opposed to government intervention, a conservative, and a classic nineteenth-century liberal.

There were some initial doubts about the extent of Grace's inclinations as an advocate and an activist, and his appointment as privacy commissioner was thought to reflect a degree of caution on the part of the Liberal government. His previous careers gave him experience in fashioning his decidedly nonconfrontational approach to his work. His staff members take an admirably informal and nonconfrontational approach to the conduct of their investigations and try to avoid decisions based on technicalities. Grace himself determined that their job is to help individuals: "Privacy issues are too important to be decided by technicalities."[1] Having been an observer of the Ottawa political scene for most of his adult life, Grace also has the advantage for this purpose of a wide range of acquaintances in senior government and civil service circles, which facilitates the informal resolution of specific issues. He maintains good contacts with both deputy ministers and members of Parliament.

Grace understands the advocacy and monitoring roles imposed on him by the Privacy Act and has gradually organized and staffed his office in such a way as to undertake such activities in a considered and deliberate fashion. He also recognizes that he has an independent role to play as an agent of Parliament and not of the government.

Grace's speeches and annual reports indicate that he quickly became an activist in this job, willing to take strong stands, as evidenced by his successful warnings about the prospective risks of computer matching. He describes himself as a "specialized ombudsman" and a servant of the Privacy Act, and he is committed to the "primacy of privacy." In his view, his role is to promote privacy interests, to let others articulate competing values on behalf of the state, and to let legislators set the final balance. He is aware of the risks of excessive surveillance of the population. According to Grace, "the Privacy Act is a testimony that Parliament does not want Canadians to be supervised by computers, specifically by government computers, and does not want government trafficking in personal information."[2]

In his first annual report, Grace adopted an important perspective on the basis of claims to privacy: "Respect for privacy is the acknowledgment of respect for human dignity and of the individuality of man. The source for a concern with privacy is an innate respect for personhood."[3] In his second report, the commissioner added a very strong statement on the risks of state surveillance: "The real nightmare of Big Brother . . . is the possibility of becoming a monitored society through the invasive, indiscriminate use of the computer in gathering, storing and comparing the personal information of each individual." Grace even adopted the language of the 1983 decision of the West German constitutional court in emphasizing that "privacy protection begins with the conviction that (1) informational self-determination is essential to human dignity."[4]

Like his predecessor, Grace has had to devote continuing attention to staffing, which again detracts from implementation activities. He has directors for privacy complaints and for privacy compliance [audits], each of whom manages about a half dozen "investigators." To date, they do not specialize by type of information system, which is unfortunate. As happened in the case of Hansen, there were more than 500 applicants for the jobs from within the public service, and appointments were not final until 1985, thus delaying active efforts at implementation.[5] Thereafter, the director of privacy compliance took early retirement, and his counterpart was assigned to intensive French study for an extended period. Thus the senior staffing of the office has been in flux, although the opportunity to replace senior employees has allowed Grace to focus more precisely on the skills needed for auditing work in particular and to promote from within the organization. In 1986 Grace finally decided to hire an executive director for his office, which, as in the French experience, was long overdue.

Activities of the Privacy Commissioner and the Treasury Board

Advising and Auditing

The privacy commissioner has a positive duty to ensure compliance with the code of fair information practices in sections 4 to 8 of the act, which are the very heart of the law. Some observers doubted that the commissioner would exercise these advisory powers, but Grace has gradually made them a central function of his office. He can report noncompliance with these sections to the head of a government institution, including "any recommendations that the Commissioner considers appropriate."[6] Any such report to the head of an institution may also be included in the annual or special reports of the commissioner to Parliament. In practice Grace has continued the Hansen tradition of an informal approach to the commissioner's work, since it leads to discussion and understanding with government institutions: "The Commissioner's investigators operate as informally as possible, reserving formal procedures for only the most difficult cases." However, he does make formal findings after an investigation. To date, his office enjoys "an unfailingly high level of cooperation and support" from the public service.[7]

The commissioner may review records of certain sensitive disclosures either automatically or upon request.[8] Recording communication of personal information to law enforcement bodies requires each government institution to create a unique, personal identification bank, which contains copies of all requests for disclosure from, and all personal information disclosed to, law enforcement bodies. Such a record is particularly useful for effective monitoring of surveillance practices. There is an additional check upon the general disclosure provisions in section 8(2)(m) of the Privacy Act, whereby the commissioner should normally be notified in advance of a pending disclosure and may decide to intervene and recommend against it. The commissioner also has discretion in this instance to notify the individual to whom the information relates.[9]

Section 60 of the Privacy Act permits the minister of justice to refer to the privacy commissioner the conduct or supervision of special studies relating to privacy protection.[10] The commissioner has to communicate such studies to the minister of justice, and such reports must be laid before Parliament within a specified time when either House is sitting. The Justice Committee has recommended that the commissioner be authorized to undertake such studies on his own initiative, because otherwise the government has little incentive to encourage systematic examination of its own surveillance practices.[11] Even if such a change is made, the commissioner would still have to seek additional government funding for any such research efforts. Grace showed admirable initiative in commissioning a consultant's study of the problems of data protection raised by the spread of Acquired Immune Deficiency Syndrome (AIDS) to use as a basis for his own recommendations to government institutions on their handling of AIDS-related personal information.[12]

The statute establishes criteria for the conduct of investigations by the privacy commissioner of complaints received from individuals and of those initiated by his office.[13] The commissioner is further encouraged to carry out audits of information systems, a provision that the government is now committed to making explicit, because of the evident utility of such audits. Grace wisely recognizes his twin roles: a "specialized ombudsman for privacy complaints" and the "auditor of the federal government's personal information handling." The first is better known and uses more resources, but he wisely regards the second to be at least as important.[14]

In fact, the investigation of government compliance was slow to develop, because of delays in staffing. The first actual audit occurred in 1984–85 at the Department of Fisheries and Oceans. It is a small agency with scattered operations, but it allowed the new compliance staff to test and develop appropriate procedures, which were influenced by the practices of the federal Data Protection Commissioner in West Germany. In 1985 the auditors examined several large data banks from among the twenty that were then exempt from access by individuals. Grace recognized that only auditing could justify the exemption of specific, closed banks. His office now conducts audits on its own initiative and with the expectation that the prospect of a compliance investigation should have a salutary effect on government institutions.[15]

The office has an "Audit Guide" and a five-year audit plan, using an internally developed computer model of risk analysis based on a twelve-page "profile questionnaire" completed by all federal institutions. There are twenty-four criteria, each with a valuation function. This system produces a risk listing of high, medium, or low, which then guides the staff in their work. High-risk entities receive intensive audits: the key factors in this category are large amounts of personal data and decentralization. In this exemplary way, a small group of seven auditors can be relatively effective in targeting prospective problems.

The Compliance Branch conducted four major audits of "high-risk" departments in 1987, both at headquarters and in the field, focusing especially on fair information practices.[16] This process helps to sensitize privacy coordinators and staff in the departments to the broad reach of the legislation. More importantly, the auditors identified some serious problems, illustrating the absolute need for such investigations. They generally found that "few employees were aware of the impact of the *Privacy Act* on their day-to-day handling of employee or client personal information." In a regional office of Transport Canada, auditors found "an unofficial 26-volume file containing often sensitive information on all employees, arranged in alphabetical order by name." Correctional Services Canada has twelve series of files containing personal information that are not listed in the *Personal Information Index*. Investigators further found that Agriculture Canada was engaging in improper disclosure of investigation reports to the Royal Canadian Mounted Police (RCMP), Canada Customs, and the U.S. Customs Service through an automated RCMP data base. These disclosures were unrelated to the original collection purpose.[17] Such findings led Grace to conclude that his auditors should not be engaged in basic departmental tasks; rather, they should be reviewing the results of internal audits of departments for compliance with the Privacy Act, which agencies rarely prepare.[18]

Until 1987 the Treasury Board did not enter into the details of implementation of privacy legislation in any energetic or creative way, despite the many contributions of its staff specialists in the Administrative Policy Branch. There has been a large gap between the rhetoric of policy and operational reality. The board regards the head of each government department and the privacy commissioner as having primary responsibility for implementation of the statute. Its role is coordination of administration, but it has limited desire to monitor compliance with the legislation. The Administrative Policy Branch normally handles routine administrative matters, so an aggressive role in implementation is out of character, despite the commitment to privacy protection that continues to exist among its specialists.

The most positive contribution of the Administrative Policy Branch of the Treasury Board under sections 11 and 71 of the Privacy Act was the preparation of interim guidelines, directives, and regulations to breathe life into the statutes. In 1987 the government committed itself to issuing these materials in final form. The addition of access to information problems to its workload has raised the burden; in fact, this topic has priority over privacy issues because of its political sensitivity. The Treasury Board seems content to be a coordinator on behalf of its president. Until recently, it has emphasized such relatively neutral or administrative tasks as publishing the *Personal Information Index* and collecting statistical data from institutions about how the acts are working in practice. These are primarily passive rather than active forms of implementation and amount, in effect, to keeping a scorecard of governmental surveillance practices.

The board assumes, for the most part, that government institutions are enforcing the Privacy Act. The chain of responsibility further devolves as heads of institutions and their privacy coordinators assume that the managers of their information systems are actually implementing sections 4 to 8 of the law as part of a process of husbanding resources. Such a belief is optimistic and naive. The actual activities of managers of specific information systems with respect to forms review and forms clearance need to be studied by the Treasury Board, especially with respect to fair information practices.

In practice, Privacy Act coordinators in departments are a very diverse lot. They often are the best of the records management community, or typical administrators, or people who wanted to become lawyers but never obtained their degrees. One key issue in the initial appointment of privacy coordinators was their sensitivity to issues of access, because of their potential political impact. In 1983 the Treasury Board encouraged deputy ministers to ensure that such coordination was being handled at a high enough level in their respective ministries. This issue is of critical importance if the coordinators are to be reasonably effective in shaping their agency's information practices, and the board is still struggling with this dilemma. Another important problem is significant annual change in the personnel working as privacy coordinators, which represents a serious loss of talent and a weakness in implementation. Learning how to be an effective privacy coordinator is hardly a routine activity, yet there were no formal procedures for training them until 1987, when the government accepted parliamentary recommendations for preparing specialized training packages. This same oversight activity further raised the consciousness of the Treasury Board and individual departments about the relative importance of coordinators.

More than 135 persons work as coordinators of access to information and privacy. If a senior person in an institution serves as privacy coordinator, then he or she has a staff to do the actual work. The largest groups working on privacy coordination, which primarily means responding to access requests, are National Defence, Correctional Services Canada, National Archives, the RCMP, and Employment and Immigration Canada (CEIC). The Treasury Board estimates that 140 person-years are devoted to the work of privacy coordination across the government.[19] These numbers primarily reflect a significant volume of access requests rather than general efforts to implement sections 4 to 8 of the law.

Unfortunately, the Treasury Board remains more concerned with the formal system of access rights than with ensuring that the multiple responsibilities of the designated minister under section 71 of the Privacy Act are carried out in a vigorous fashion. Such an approach also influences the privacy coordinators, who spend their time applying statutory exemptions to access requests rather than promoting sections 4 to 8.

There is no continuing activist mentality on the implementation of data protection at the Treasury Board, especially outside the specialists in the

Administrative Policy Branch. Neither the president of the Treasury Board nor the secretary had, or indeed have, any particular interest in conflicts with their political and public-service colleagues about the protection of privacy. Deputy ministers and their senior assistants are also consensus-oriented, because they could be transferred to another department at any time; thus they have a strong incentive to avoid oversight of one another, even if mandated by the Privacy Act. Data protection can be a time-consuming exercise in the face of other pressing departmental priorities and bureaucratic imperatives.

The Treasury Board is not doing much more than it must under the Privacy Act, and it depends on the privacy commissioner to make the law effective. It would never undertake inspections or audits of personal information systems, because of the nature of its existing relationships with government departments. There would be no parallels for such undertakings in other statutes managed by the board, which might be a good reason to end its administrative role under the Privacy Act at some point in the future and transfer the duties to the commissioner.

In 1987 the Justice Committee made recommendations designed to invigorate the oversight responsibilities of the Treasury Board that are having some impact now that the government has committed itself to improving the administration of the legislation.[20] The review process did give higher priority to the Privacy Act within the board. Indeed, the Information Practices Policy unit has received several additional employees, a public relations budget to publicize the Privacy Act, and a mandate to develop new training programs, including lectures, exercises, and a film. Most fortunately, its nucleus of committed individuals remains intact.

The Personal Information Index

The Privacy Act significantly expanded the requirements of the earlier *Index of Federal Information Banks* to cover all personal information under government control, including descriptions of the purposes, information content, consistent uses, and retention/disposal standards for each bank or class of personal information, in sufficient detail to aid individuals seeking access to personal information about themselves held in government files.[21] The *Personal Information Index 1983* included more than 142 government institutions compared to the 89 covered previously and also included personal information holdings that are not used for decision-making purposes.[22] The current *Index* also has better distribution and sales than its predecessors; 15,000 copies were distributed to public libraries, post offices, and other personal information centers across the country.[23] No other country produces such a helpful guide to governmental surveillance practices.

As noted earlier, the Privacy Act is very expansive by international standards in terms of the amount and character of personal information that has to be included in personal information banks and described in the annual *Index*.

For example, it includes information that "is organized or intended to be retrieved by the name of an individual or by an identifying number, symbol or other particular assigned to an individual." It is especially important that the *Index* must contain "a statement of the purposes for which personal information in the bank was obtained or compiled and a statement of the uses consistent with such purposes for which the information is used or disclosed." Finally, the *Index* includes a description of "all classes of personal information under the control of a government institution that are not contained in personal information banks."[24] This provision is simply a mechanism for access to personal information that is scattered in correspondence or statistical data but not organized for retrieval by individual names.

The *Personal Information Index* is a disturbing indication of the amount of data in the government's personal information banks. The 1988 edition lists a total of 2,700 personal information banks, including 1,104 on the general public and 1,596 federal employee banks.[25] These numbers have grown annually from a total of about 1,500 early in the 1980s. The detailed descriptions of each bank are informative, even if they purvey a sense of orderliness that does not reflect reality in a decentralized bureaucracy. Each edition since the late 1970s significantly improved coverage of information systems, as departments became more familiar with the law and were persuaded to reveal everything they had. In theory, the public should have a fine sense of just how much data are collected about them; in practice, few know that these guides exist and even fewer, outside the public service, have ever seen one.

The Office of the Privacy Commissioner monitors the accuracy and coverage of the *Index* and investigates complaints about alleged deficiencies in the listings. Such activities have included sensitive records of National Defence's Communications Security Establishment and the RCMP's transfer of its Security Service Records to the new Canadian Security Intelligence Service.[26] Departments inform the commissioner of new "consistent uses" of data to be included in the next annual edition of the *Index*. The general contribution of the compliance staff to monitoring and comparison of successive editions of the *Index* and notification of irregularities to government institutions and the Treasury Board is an important contribution to controlling governmental surveillance.[27]

Individual Access to Data and Complaints

From its very inception in 1977, federal data protection legislation has had a particular preoccupation with granting individuals rights of access to their own data, which this writer has sometimes described as "access mania." Each government agency has created a system to deal with the screening and delivery of requests for such access. The concern for access requests has not totally disappeared; the privacy commissioner spoke with pride of the more than 36,000 requests in the first eighteen months of operation of the Privacy Act.[28]

There is general agreement, reinforced by the government in 1987, that informal access is the preferred route for government employees, who make the most such requests.

The general improvement of fair information practices in the 1982 Privacy Act does mean that the right of access has become a less important vehicle for achieving the goals of data protection. All individuals in Canada now have the right of access not only to information about themselves in a personal information bank but also to "any other personal information about the individual under the control of a government institution with respect to which the individual is able to provide sufficiently specific information on the location of the information as to render it reasonably retrievable by the government institution."[29] Although the government may prescribe fees for giving access to personal information, there is no charge in practice for requests under the Privacy Act.[30]

Inger Hansen argued strongly in favor of the importance of the right of access for the protection of privacy, even though the total number of formal requests in the first four years was only 40,620.[31] She believed that this practice exerted considerable control over government information-handling activities, especially since public servants could be held accountable by her office for data in personal files. The threat of an individual having access to his or her own file may have a beneficial effect on the quality of record keeping; moreover, the person in question can best ensure that stored data are accurate. Hansen asserted that when collectors of information are aware of an individual's right of access, "the collectors act more responsibly and fairly. When the authors of reports know that their reports may not be kept confidential, language becomes cautious, derogatory assessments will be supported by examples when the examples only will be cited, leaving the reader to make up his or her own mind. . . . More accurate and open information must take the place of confidential non-accessible records. Unsubstantiated data, save where the safety of others or society is involved, ought not to be stored."[32]

Access requests are a major source of complaints to the privacy commissioner, especially about delays.[33] In 1984–85 only 49 percent of requests were being answered within thirty days, as the act requires, which Grace described as a "flouting" of the statute by National Defence and Correctional Services Canada in particular.[34]

In the investigation of complaints of denials of access, the commissioner's staff may informally question the grounds for claiming exemptions and thus can negotiate the release of information in certain cases. In terms of the number of such exemptions, Grace concludes that only the abuse of section 19(1), concerning information allegedly received in confidence from a province, gives the act a bad name and remains "a major source of frustration to applicants and this office." In particular, "the claim which both Alberta and Ontario have made for total confidentiality shows no sensitivity to fair information principles" and embodies "potential destructiveness to the credibility of the *Privacy*

Act."[35] Grace believes that the situation remains entirely unsatisfactory, because parolees and prisoners are routinely being refused information from their files on the grounds that it was received from a provincial source.[36]

A significant innovation in the Privacy Act permits the Federal Court to review a government institution's decision not to release personal information to an individual.[37] Moreover, the burden of proof is on the government, not the applicant, to make its case. The only precondition is that the privacy commissioner must first review a person's complaint that he or she has been denied access. Court review may occur, even if the privacy commissioner agrees with the institution's position.

The Privacy Act exempts certain personal information banks from access and provides for the privacy commissioner to mediate disputes. Categories of information that the government wanted to keep in absolute confidence included the disclosure of information that might be injurious to federal-provincial affairs, international affairs and defense, law enforcement and investigation, and policing for provinces or municipalities. The argument in favor of such a broad exemption is that "it eliminates the need for detailed review of documents to which access would almost certainly be refused in any case."[38] An entire information bank can be exempted only where the vast majority of the information therein would be exempted under normal circumstances. The law also successfully created a two-tier system of review by the privacy commissioner and the Federal Court of Canada of disputed material placed in exempt banks.[39]

The privacy commissioner has audited exempt banks and reported to the head of a government institution that certain personal files should not be contained therein. If the commissioner decides that the institution's response to advice is "inadequate or inappropriate or will not be taken in a reasonable time," he or she may make an application for judicial review to the Federal Court.[40] To date, only a few cases have gone to the Federal Court, but at least one, the *Ternette* decision, had a major impact in undermining the legitimacy of the remaining exempt banks.[41] Even when there were twenty exempt banks, Grace wisely recognized that their existence results in a loss of credibility for the act on the part of some complainants, in part because "no assurance can be given to individuals that information about them, which may be contained in a closed bank, is accurate and not maliciously or mistakenly compiled."[42]

Grace's auditing efforts have contributed to a substantial reduction in the number of exempt banks. In 1987 the Justice Committee recommended removing the concept of exempt banks from the legislation, since it was essentially redundant, a recommendation that the Progressive Conservative government ignored. Although the government wanted to retain five exempt banks, Grace's auditors have found only one to be properly constituted, that of the Communications Security Establishment. There is also an ongoing factual dispute with the RCMP over the appropriateness of its exempt bank.[43] So, in practice, the concept of exempt banks has almost completely disappeared, since only two remain.

In June 1982, in the final throes of passing the Privacy Act, the Liberal government of Pierre Trudeau amended the legislation so that it did not permit access to most material deemed to be confidences of the Cabinet or its committees.[44] This over-broad exemption is particularly unfortunate, although it has less impact on privacy protection than freedom of information. When there is a request to view personal records held by the Cabinet, the Privy Council Office certifies their exempt status. The Progressive Conservatives promised that they would remove this exemption when they came to power, but this has been forgotten. In 1987 the parliamentary review committee recommended that Cabinet confidences should become a standard exemption under the Privacy Act, reviewable only by the Federal Court rather than the commissioner.[45] The Cabinet rejected this recommendation, because of the tradition of Cabinet solidarity.

The privacy commissioner has a further duty to receive and investigate complaints from individuals who allege that personal information about them held by a government institution has been used or disclosed other than in accordance with section 7 or 8, with respect to the *Personal Information Index,* or any other matter relating to the disposal, retention, use, disclosure, or disposal of personal information by a government institution. The commissioner may also investigate complaints of his own accord when he is satisfied that there are reasonable grounds to do so.[46] In terms of limiting government surveillance, this capacity to initiate investigations is most important, and Grace uses it effectively.

The Office of the Privacy Commissioner has been investigating at least several hundred complaints annually since 1978 and also responding to enquiries and requests for information. The number of complaints continues to grow. For the year ending March 31, 1988, 86 percent of the 661 complaints concerned access problems, including delays. Thus the commissioner is still receiving only a very small number of substantive complaints about implementation of the Privacy Act. As the details in each annual report indicate, the office does an excellent job of handling specific complaints.[47]

The commissioner recognizes that the statistics on numbers of complaints are a two-edged sword; they either indicate that the act is or is not being well used. In his view, the ideal year would mean no complaints, and "the objective should always be to keep complaints to a minimum. Fewer complaints suggest that more applications for personal information are satisfied and fewer persons feel that their privacy rights are being violated."[48] This opinion indicates the continuing preoccupation of the office with access rights to the detriment of encouraging broader grievances about personal information use or the initiation of complaints on the basis of suspected problems.

Fortunately, there are some good examples of general problems that were well handled by the privacy commissioner. A complaint about the distribution of paychecks, open for anyone to see, led to the Treasury Board's decision to place all such checks in window envelopes, which Grace described as "a testimonial to privacy enlightenment at Treasury Board and a model of systemic privacy protection." In another case the commissioner's staff persuaded the Treasury Board to ask Health and Welfare to revise a form for its general physical examination report and to ensure that the agency using these forms should restrict access to them to administrative purposes.[49] In a well-publicized complaint, Grace decided that Revenue Canada Taxation had the right to seek access to personal data held by the city of Kitchener, Ontario.[50]

The commissioner has also done important work in responding to complaints from public service unions about the conflict-of-interest code for public servants, introduced by the Treasury Board in 1986, which mandates collection of sensitive personal information on financial assets and liabilities of individuals.[51] After reviewing and acknowledging the board's right to collect such data, Grace recommended changes in the regulations, because some of the overly broad collection requirements could encompass personal information beyond that needed to detect and prevent situations of real or apparent conflict. The commissioner also persuaded the Treasury Board to agree to resist any efforts to force disclosure of the personal data under the Access to Information Act. He also recommended improvements in physical security for the confidential reports submitted under the code.

One requirement in the Privacy Act is designed to prevent a situation in which a government institution can be surprised by an investigation conducted by the Office of the Privacy Commissioner. Before commencing any investigation, the commissioner has to notify the head of any government institution of his intention to carry out the investigation and also the substance of the complaint. If the commissioner finds that a complaint is well founded, he is required to provide the head of the institution with a report of the findings and recommendations.[52] Deputy ministers have an incentive to work cooperatively with the privacy commissioner to settle disputes, so as to avoid public controversy. Grace also believes that the fact that his recommendations are only advisory promotes results, which his experience to date confirms.

Grace has no statutory power to prescribe or even recommend a civil action against a public servant or government institution that has harmed a complainant in some way or breached a section of the Privacy Act. For example, a city police chief complained that personal information which a detective gave in confidence to a caseworker for use in a parolee's National Parole Board file had then been passed on to the Commission of Inquiry on Habitual Criminals, conducted by Judge Stuart M. Leggatt, which did not have subpoena power. The individual inmate obtained the information. A lengthy investigation concluded that the Parole Board had to bear the ultimate responsibility for a breach of confidence.[53] But the complainant received no compensation, as might properly have been the case. Perhaps the plaintiff could have launched a lawsuit on his own. Another possibility was for the privacy commissioner, acting under section 64(2) of the Privacy Act, to disclose to the attorney general information relating to the commission of an offense against a law of Canada, which could have led to a criminal prosecution against an officer or employee of the National Parole Board.

In 1987 the Justice Committee recommended the addition of criminal sanctions and civil remedies to the act. The government rejected this view on the grounds that public servants who deliberately disclose personal information are subject to administrative sanctions, and it is already a criminal offense to willfully contravene an act of Parliament. The government also concluded that in certain cases damages may now be recoverable on the basis of negligence.[54] This reluctance to add teeth to the law does somewhat weaken the government's watchdog.

Section 74 of the Privacy Act implies that civil or criminal proceedings may be brought against the head of any government institution or any person acting on his behalf or under his direction for the disclosure in bad faith of any personal information or for any consequences that flow from such disclosure. The defense in the case just described would presumably be that the National Parole Board had acted in good faith, even though real or prospective harm occurred to a complainant.

Annual Reports

The privacy commissioner's mandatory annual report to Parliament is a report card on government surveillance practices. The law further provides for special reports at any time, referring to and commenting on any urgent or important matter within the scope of his powers, duties, and functions.[55]

As befits a former journalist, Grace's reports are popularly written and engaging, avoiding at least some of the standard bureaucratic language. He intended his first report in 1984 as "a profession of privacy faith" and an initial statement on his role as commissioner. After gaining more experience, he may attempt "a general statement . . . on the privacy state of the nation."[56] Grace drew important attention to the perils of uncontrolled computer matching, which attracted notice in the press. In his second report, Grace demonstrated a surprising willingness (for a public official) to take strong stands; he did not mince his words in denouncing abuses of section 19(1) of the act and delays in certain large departments in responding to access requests.[57] He has demonstrated two of the most important traits of a data protection commissioner, a capacity to learn and a willingness to be an activist in the best sense of that term.

The head of every government institution has to prepare an annual report on the administration of the Privacy Act for submission to Parliament and referral to the oversight committee.[58] Unfortunately, these reports tend to be primarily statistical in character. Only the better ones contain useful general observations, because there is no reason for a public servant writing such a report to wax eloquent on implementation, even if he or she had the appropriate commitment and level of knowledge. The Standing Committee on Justice and Solicitor General questioned the utility of receiving almost 150 separate reports each year. It recommended that the Treasury Board closely supervise their contents and then prepare a consolidated report on the administration of the act.[59] The government endorsed this recommendation.

Public Relations and Consultation

After several years of effort at public relations through speeches and media contacts, Hansen concluded that Canadians were in general very poorly informed concerning Part IV of the Canadian Human Rights Act and, in fact, had never heard of it. The location of the Office of the Privacy Commissioner within the Canadian Human Rights Commission distorted the public's view of her role and that of her office. Hansen urged the government to undertake a more active role in informing the public.[60]

The creation of a separate Office of the Privacy Commissioner has somewhat enhanced its ability to publicize data protection activities. The rationale for improving public knowledge is simple. It is not easy for anyone to understand the forty-seven pages of text of the current Privacy Act. The office has to play a central role in interpreting the legislation for the general public, although the argument is still heard that the government should be doing the informing. The Justice Committee advocated explicit statutory authorization for public relations work by the Treasury Board and the commissioner, a view that the government accepted.[61] Grace concluded in 1988 that the Privacy Act "probably still remains more unknown than known to Canadians."[62] He then commissioned a study by an outside public relations expert of how his office could help to improve this situation.

Grace is especially good at public relations and at working with the media. His first year in office featured initial attention to the proclamation of the new act, reinforced by the occurrence of Orwell's year. Yet he followed in Hansen's footsteps in complaining that "no mandate exists and no resources are provided for spreading the gospel of privacy" and in asking Parliament to consider giving him the specific mandate to explain and inform the public, as is done for the commissioner of official languages.[63] The reference to lack of resources was surprising, given the budget and personnel already at his disposal. In his second report, Grace asserted that too many are unaware of the protection afforded by the act, but his complaints about lack of use by the public again seemed tied to numbers of access requests.[64]

The Canadian press gives modest but favorable attention to the Privacy Act. The commissioner's annual reports have commanded recurrent publicity, in fact, front-page coverage across the country. Grace has a special capacity to be open and helpful in his media contacts. In particular, he has expressed himself candidly on most issues posed by the press. Grace has encountered little media criticism, certainly less than the information commissioner. In a few cases, the press has suggested that Grace has not been strong enough in supporting individuals' requests for access to their own files, which again reflects a misunderstanding of the essential elements of the legislation and of the fact that Grace himself has to balance competing interests in such cases.

Grace accepts speaking invitations across Canada and makes himself readily available to the media. Even though he has suggested that such activities are only marginally useful, they are a main public relations outlet used by him and his counterparts in other countries.[65] His office also responded to 1,248 inquiries in the 1987–88 fiscal year. One-half were for general information about the Privacy Act and 15 percent concerned Social Insurance Numbers.[66]

Grace is a forceful individual with respect to the issues within his domain. He is consulted on an informal basis about at least some pending bills that have implications for personal privacy, such as the Family Law Reform Act of 1985. He wrote to the Canadian Radio-television and Telecommunications Commission to support the issuance of regulations that came into force on September 25, 1986, on confidentiality of customer records for federally regulated telephone companies.

In his annual reports, Grace has praised the Quebec government's initiatives on data protection and bemoaned the lack of consistent, integrated legislation in the other provinces. He has supported self-regulation in the private sector through active implementation of the Organization for Economic Co-operation and Development's *Guidelines on the Protection of Privacy*. Moreover, he has had wise words on the issue of transborder data flows: "It is ludicrous to worry about what could happen to personal information going outside the country while being less concerned, if not studiously indifferent, to what is happening to the same information in the hands of our federal or provincial governments and our private institutions."[67]

Grace is aware of the risks of co-optation when he is consulted by the framers of legislation about data protection matters, but he also recognizes that this is perhaps his best opportunity to influence the result. Once the government has presented a bill to Parliament, it is much more difficult to achieve a consensus to make changes. Grace may in fact be more effective on an informal basis at the early drafting stages. The task is, in any event, a burdensome one, since so much legislation today has surveillance implications. Grace also has to develop a mechanism in his office to review proposed legislation, in the event that no one in the particular department or the Department of Justice has been willing to consult the privacy commissioner during the drafting stages. Excessive Justice Department secrecy is also an impediment to fruitful consultations.

The Justice Committee recommended the creation of mechanisms to ensure consultation with the commissioner, including notifying his office of proposed developments and the submission of a privacy impact statement in relevant situations. The Cabinet remains committed to informal consultations of this type, although it rejects the formal requirement of an impact statement to accompany each piece of legislation.[68]

Data Protection Principles in Practice

From Principles to Practices

The practice of data protection is primarily a responsibility of the Office of the Privacy Commissioner. It is obvious that his office has spent most of the last six years devising ways to make the data protection law into a living reality. As is also true for the operations of data protection in individual government departments, much of what they have concluded remains hidden from public view. The office, for example, has no need to share its methods for sampling voluminous files with the public, although it is slowly developing practices to follow in such cases. In fact, the principal evidence of "practice" emanating from the privacy commissioner's office is the written report of its first audit at the Department of Fisheries and Oceans, which was sent to the unit in question in August 1985. Its pages indicate the decisions made and the practices followed by the office during its five-month audit in the winter and spring of that year. It is evident from the document that only hands-on experience of this sort has given the investigators a real sense of the problems to be encountered in actual implementation, beyond the simple investigation of a denial of an access request or a complaint about a specific practice.

As noted elsewhere in this book, the practice of mediation remains the favored approach to promoting compliance with data protection, both in advisory and regulatory systems. Starting within government departments, senior managers and privacy coordinators have to mediate conflicts between the Privacy Act and their own data needs and customary practices. One of the powerful instruments of internal privacy advocates is the prospect of "external" review by the Treasury Board or the lawyers at the Department of Justice, or, in the worst case, by the Office of the Privacy Commissioner. A great deal of consultation among the affected parties takes place regularly on specific issues, including the inevitable ones about the actual meaning in practice of the specific language of the statute. In such cases of legalisms, the Information Law and Privacy unit at the Department of Justice plays the lead role, not only because of its accumulated expertise, but because of the residual responsibility of the minister of justice to formulate government policy on privacy and access to information. Of course, conflicts between the two laws are a continuing source of advisory and mediating activity.

Decisions of the Data Protection Agents

In the strict sense of the term, only the Trial Division of the Federal Court of Canada makes decisions under the Privacy Act. The privacy commissioner only gives advice on general or specific matters. But so far as the heads of government institutions are concerned, this is a decision for all practical purposes, since the risks of noncompliance with it are substantial. If it concerns an access request, failure to comply may lead to judicial review and a binding precedent from a judge. Rejection of a general recommendation may lead to censure in the commissioner's annual report to Parliament and then in the media. Until now, John Grace has had a very receptive audience for his recommendations, even for difficult cases of governmental surveillance. The advisory model does facilitate reasonable solutions.

The Federal Court has made very few decisions on access requests under the Privacy Act, because very few litigants, perhaps a dozen, have gone to court. This is of course in line with the goal of the legislation to avoid litigation by relying on an ombudsman. The Federal Court's most significant decision involved judicial assertion of the right to examine material in an allegedly exempt bank in order to ascertain whether the data are legitimately being withheld from an applicant.[69]

The Federal Court is playing a mediating role in disputes over the Privacy Act, despite the fact that it has only limited jurisdiction. Associate Chief Justice James Jerome (a former Speaker of the House of Commons) and Justice Barry Strayer (one of the persons who parented the law at the Justice Department) are handling most of the cases on access to information and privacy. They sometimes use pretrial conferences in chambers to resolve matters outside of the courtroom. Their expansive decisions are also closely tied to implementing the broad goals of the legislation.

Privacy coordinators, specialists at the Treasury Board, government lawyers in individual departments, and the Information Law and Privacy unit at the Department of Justice also regularly make decisions on specific matters, which are only reviewable if an individual applicant for access to his or her data or the Office of the Privacy Commissioner takes exception to them. Since most issues take a legal form, the Department of Justice unit is the key focal point. Its specialists compile an index of their advisory opinions that is not available to the public. Their preoccupation is such matters as the uniform application of exemptions from disclosure across the government. They have little incentive, at least at present, to be on the lookout for invasive practices, although they are sensitive to them in their advisory role.

One of the interesting aspects of the process of decision making is that less than a dozen persons from the Justice Department and the Treasury Board are regularly involved in such matters, with the Office of the Privacy Commissioner serving as an outside source of commentary on the results. In the interim, the specialists offer a running, private commentary on the decisions of the privacy commissioner. As happens whenever human beings try to do similar things together, personalities play a significant role in how well people get along. The good news at present is that the major players—the Justice Department, the Treasury Board, and the privacy commissioner—are working in harmony. This is no small achievement, since the two senior specialists in the Justice Department and Treasury Board left their posts during 1985.

The only continued impediment to even better cooperation among data protection agents is the continuing failure to develop adequate training programs for privacy and access coordinators, as recommended by the parliamentary committee. Fortunately, in 1987 the Canadian Access and Privacy Association began life as the national equivalent to the American Society of Access Professionals and has started to develop and operate training programs. The government is also committing increased resources to this goal.

Chapter 23

The Regulation of Surveillance Systems

This chapter selects several sensitive and important types of personal information in order to evaluate the impact of data protection on various types of national data systems and the nature of continuing privacy and surveillance problems. It also reviews certain continuing issues with respect to the use of Social Insurance Numbers (SINs) and the confidentiality of income tax data. The ultimate goal is to assess the relative success of data protectors in controlling governmental surveillance, in part by illustrating the myriad forms of control over the population.

The Social Insurance Number

The Social Insurance Number was created in the early 1960s for purposes of identifying persons qualifying for unemployment insurance and for tax collection. It has become, in practice, the most common numerical identifier in the country, the equivalent to the Social Security Number in the United States. It is also the most common source of privacy complaints, since, until 1988, there was no general policy on the use of the numbers by the federal government or by any other entity in Canadian society.

The abuse of the Social Insurance Number is the only privacy issue that has regularly commanded the attention of members of the House of Commons in the last twenty years.[1] During his stint as minister of state at the Treasury Board during the Progressive Conservative government in 1979–80, Perrin Beatty planned restrictive legislation. In 1982 he accused the minister of communications of simply omitting the portion that dealt with the abuse of these numbers from the pending Privacy Act. As he stated, "The real issue is whether the government should be encouraging the proliferation of single, identifying numbers and their use in both the private and public sectors considering the consequences it has for personal privacy."[2]

In 1980–81 Inger Hansen, at the government's invitation, prepared a report on the use of the Social Insurance Number. She examined the extent of use of the SIN by various levels of government and concerns about personal identifiers. Her report found that data linkages were not widespread, that the extensive use of the number at the federal level was primarily to identify individuals with the same name, that it had become "a key identifying tool in data processing," and "that much more than the regulation or prohibition of the use of the social insurance number is necessary to prevent the perceived harms."[3]

Much to the disappointment of those concerned about the surveillance problems posed by Personal Identification Numbers, Hansen did not recommend any limitations on the use of the SIN, which was not the conclusion informed observers expected from a privacy commissioner. There was a feeling that Hansen should have taken a stronger stand on restricting the use of the numbers, because of continued public concern. Beatty frankly described the report as disappointing: "It did not address many of the issues which were of concern to people worried about the abuse of social insurance numbers. . . . It was not very reassuring for Canadians who felt that the social insurance number was being abused."[4]

Hansen placed too much reliance on the arguments for efficiency of various levels of government, accepted the inevitability of such unique identifiers, and appeared insensitive to surveillance concerns, in addition to accepting the usual argument that data linkages do not require single identifying numbers. In fact, even today, such numbers remain extremely useful for linkages. Government computers and software programs, except perhaps in the military and national security sectors, are rarely as up-to-date as the products available from manufacturers, because of budgetary restrictions and the difficulties of upgrading an operational system.

Hansen produced a relatively simple proposal to prevent misuse of personal data by advocating the amendment of the Federal Criminal Code to create an offense "against the privacy of another." Such an enactment would "require recipients or collectors of personal data . . . to disclose to the person providing the data all proposed uses of the data not already explicitly provided for or made compulsory by law. The disclosure should be at the time of collection and consent to new uses would be necessary." An "offence against the privacy of another" would "prohibit the wilful undisclosed acquisition, alteration, use, processing, manipulation, transmission or destruction of personal data not otherwise authorized by law, where the personal data are: (a) provided to obtain a benefit or service, (b) provided under compulsion of law, or (c) placed in the custody of another for storage and the exclusive use of the depositor, and where it is expressly or implicitly understood that the data will be kept confidential."[5] Perhaps the greatest advantage of creating such an offense is that its prohibitions would extend at once to both the public and private sectors, including provincial governments.[6]

Although this proposal by the privacy commissioner had the admirable virtue of simplicity, it did not satisfy some of the concerns of those bothered by governmental surveillance, and the government did not act on it. There is a general reluctance to criminalize more activities, especially when the goal is protection of privacy. The minister of justice stated in 1983 that his ministry was engaged in a very serious study of the proposal that a new offense be created for the misuse of personal information. The parliamentary secretary to the minister subsequently noted that there were significant implications for federal-provincial relations in the recommendation of the privacy commissioner, "since the area of data protection outside the federally-regulated sphere to a great extent involves the provinces." He feared that the federal government's use of the criminal law to regulate the use and exposure of personal information "might, without provincial involvement, be viewed by them as intruding on some aspect of their responsibility."[7]

The Department of Justice sought the views of provincial governments on the recommendation of the privacy commissioner. The proposal to create such a criminal offense was being treated as part of the general review of the criminal law: "Some part of the recommendation, as it relates to computerized personal data, may be incorporated as part of the recommendation regarding computer crime."[8] When attacked about real or prospective surveillance issues, Canadian governments routinely respond that the subject is under study or that the division of powers under the constitution requires consultation with the provinces.

The Privacy Act contains no explicit provisions controlling the use of Social Insurance Numbers and, of course, it only applies to federal government data, whereas the public is equally concerned about the uses of the number by provincial governments, municipalities, schools, banks, credit companies, landlords, and other private companies. Thus the uses of the number remain a significant symbol of concern over the preservation of privacy and the threat of excessive surveillance.[9]

Despite using the SIN to berate the Liberals during the late 1970s, the Conservative government showed no interest in acting on this issue until the Justice Committee of the House of Commons tackled the problem in the course of its review of the Privacy Act. It recommended the prohibition of the collection of the numbers unless authorized by federal law, the creation of a statutory prohibition against any denial of services to an individual because of a refusal to provide the number (unless required by law), and the creation of a statutory cause of action for individuals faced with such refusals.[10]

In its most positive response to the reforms proposed by the Justice Committee, the Cabinet accepted the need to place controls on the use of the SIN, because of public concern about its widespread use as a surveillance tool. The government wants to prevent the number from becoming a universal identification number. Its first step in June 1988 was to put its own house in order by prohibiting the new collection and use of the SIN for any administrative purpose without Parliament's express authority. Only seven non-statutory uses of the numbers were approved, eliminating a large number of applications of the SIN, which will be phased out over a five-year period at the estimated cost of 16 million Canadian dollars.[11] For example, SINs will cease to be the principal federal employee identifier and will no longer be the unique identification number for the military. The Treasury Board will also review existing uses by the federal government to ensure that they are in compliance with the Privacy Act.

Government institutions now have to obtain Treasury Board approval for any uses not authorized by statute or regulation and to "justify why the benefits of the SIN's collection and use would outweigh the privacy considerations which would limit its collection and use." The government will also ensure that no right, benefit, or privilege is withheld from, and no penalty imposed on, any individual refusing to disclose a SIN to a government institution, unless disclosure is required by law. Individuals asked for their number will also be informed of the purposes for the request, the voluntary or mandatory nature of the collection, and the consequences of refusal to give it. Such controls may be formulated in a statute at a later date. Moreover, the government will pursue the application of similar rules in the rest of the public and private sectors as part of its campaign to promote compliance with the Organization for Economic Co-operation and Development's *Guidelines on the Protection of Privacy*. Failing the negotiation of satisfactory arrangements with the provinces and territories, the government will explore the legislative alternatives, including an amendment to the Criminal Code to prohibit a request for a SIN that is not authorized by law.[12]

The Canadian government's action to limit and control the use of unique personal identifiers is almost without precedent internationally as an effort to cut back on surveillance of the public. The privacy commissioner hailed the event as "an effective step in preventing governments from assembling profiles of citizens."[13]

Police Information Systems: The RCMP and CPIC

Data protection imposes significant controls on the use of personal information for law enforcement. The Privacy Act has two important exemptions permitting, but not requiring, the disclosure of personal information "to an investigative body specified in the regulations, on the written request of the body, for the purpose of enforcing any law of Canada or a province or carrying out a lawful investigation, if the request specifies the purpose and describes the information to be disclosed."[14] Like other parts of section 8(2), this authorization is discretionary rather than mandatory; "it would still be left to the discretion of the government institution or minister concerned as to whether the information will be disclosed."[15] Such a request has to be written and relatively specific in character. The Cabinet Discussion Paper in 1980 contained extensive argumentation in favor of this particular exemption, reflecting the direct influence of the Royal Canadian Mounted Police (RCMP) with the Department of Justice. It argued that such discretionary disclosure was essential for effective law enforcement by the RCMP and even furnished specific examples. The Cabinet learned that although the RCMP had been cut off from several sources of information within the federal government as a result of Part IV of the Canadian Human Rights Act, "they have been able to tolerate the situation because the existing provision only applies to that personal information which an individual himself or herself provides to the government and only where it is to be used to make decisions about the individual."[16] This would not be the case under Bill C-43, the privacy bill, which would apply to the use and disclosure of all personal information held by the federal government. The Discussion Paper argued that the requirement of specificity and a written format for such requests reflected a similar provision in the U.S. Privacy Act and should prevent the RCMP and other investigative bodies "from embarking on fishing expeditions with respect to personal information." Moreover, the privacy commissioner would be empowered to review such disclosures of information, as is indeed the case under the Privacy Act.[17]

As required under section 8(2)(e) of the Privacy Act, the privacy regulations list seventeen investigative bodies entitled to such disclosures. They represent eleven different government institutions, including the Security and Investigative Services of Canada Post Corporation and the Canadian Forces Military Police. This range is a reminder that disclosing information for law enforcement surveillance does not simply mean giving it to the RCMP and local police forces.[18] The *Interim Policy Guide* of the Treasury Board elucidates the meaning of section 8(2)(e): "Personal information should be disclosed only to aid a specific enforcement or investigative activity and never in response to a vague and indeterminate inquiry."[19] Institutions are provided with a model form and a description of the information that must be included in any such requests, including "a statement of the specific purpose to be served by the disclosure of the particular personal information." Because of the potential impact of this type of disclosure on personal privacy, only the most senior officials in each government institution have the authority to approve such a disclosure to federal investigative bodies. The Treasury Board has to be provided with an annual list, by title, of authorized officials.[20] Government institutions must also develop internal directives to govern such disclosures. These strong measures illustrate the excellent efforts of the Treasury Board Secretariat to breathe life into the provisions of the Privacy Act during the initial process of implementation.

The Treasury Board directives also explain that the records of disclosures for law enforcement purposes have to be retained for a minimum of two years for review by the privacy commissioner. Copies of all requests for disclosure and of all information disclosed have to be maintained in a unique personal information bank set up for this purpose.[21] In 1985 the commissioner's staff began an audit of all such records, which is an important check on unauthorized surveillance. Grace is unhappy that the National Parole Board and Correctional Services Canada are not notifying him of disclosures about parolees and inmates to the RCMP, since they regard them as consistent uses.[22]

Section 8(2)(f) of the Privacy Act makes provision for the disclosure of personal information for law enforcement purposes to provinces, foreign states, and international bodies. This has to occur on the basis of an agreement or arrangement and "for the purpose of administering or enforcing any law or carrying out a lawful investigation." This provision is primarily meant to allow police forces at the domestic and international level to exchange relevant information. The Cabinet Discussion Paper in 1980 argued that "the exchange of information between police forces is the life-blood of effective law enforcement. Thus, it seems desirable that such exchanges not be interfered with in an unnecessary way."[23]

The Treasury Board's *Interim Policy Guide* recognizes that some formalization of existing procedures for disclosure is now required, since many past agreements or arrangements have ranged in nature from formal signed documents to oral commitments.[24] Its recommendations include a set of minimum requirements that should be met in such an agreement in order to ensure consistency of approach among federal government institutions. However, the guidelines acknowledge that "written agreements are sometimes unacceptable to some foreign governments and international organizations when the exchange of information involves law enforcement, intelligence and security matters." A government institution may disclose personal information under an informal arrangement only in such circumstances. Government institutions making any disclosures of this type on the basis of an agreement or arrangement have to report this in the annual *Personal Information Index*.

Regrettably, there are no specific arrangements for record keeping in the Privacy Act to make it easier for the privacy commissioner to monitor law enforcement disclosures. In fact, the federal minister of justice signed substantially similar agreements in 1983 with provincial ministers of justice from across Canada under section 8(2)(f) of the Privacy Act. Some concern exists that these agreements on data sharing do not meet Treasury Board policy as discussed above, since the controls on disclosure contain no safeguards. The RCMP claims these agreements are consistent with the relevant guidelines, including controls on disclosure and use of information.

The agreement entered into on July 20, 1983, between the government of Canada and the government of Ontario illustrates these section 8(2)(f) agreements. The purpose of this specific accord "is to provide for access to, and the use and disclosure of personal information under the control of a government institution to Ontario or a provincial institution with the purpose of administering or enforcing any law or carrying out a lawful investigation pursuant to paragraph 8(2)(f) of the Privacy Act." Canada and Ontario "agree that any personal information disclosed pursuant to this Agreement shall only be used or disclosed for the purpose of administering or enforcing any law or carrying out a lawful investigation or for a subsequent use which is consistent therewith."

There are several problems associated with this statement of purpose and the undertaking, especially the breadth of the definitions. A provincial institution "includes any police force, board, commission or committee of council established pursuant to a Municipal Act or Police Act of Ontario; any municipal or regional government; and any board, commission, corporation, agency, body or office established by or under any Act of Ontario have authority to administer or enforce any law or carry out a lawful investigation." This range is much broader than the terms of the "purpose" clause in the agreement, quoted earlier. Thus an extremely broad range of Ontario organizations can claim access to federal personal information; there is not even a schedule to this specific agreement listing the "provincial institutions" in question. Moreover, "administering or enforcing any law or carrying out a lawful investigation" includes "the investigation, detection, prevention or suppression of crime and other offenses including offenses against the by-laws of a municipality, the preservation of the peace and the gathering of intelligence information for law enforcement purposes." Unlike the careful drafting of the Privacy Act itself, this Ontario agreement seems to have been drafted as loosely as possible in order to cater to the pressure from law enforcement personnel for broad access to personal data.

The 1983 agreement between Canada and Ontario reaches a more desirable level of specificity when it determines that a request made to a federal government institution by Ontario or a provincial institution shall specify the personal information requested, the purpose for the request, and, "wherever practicable," shall be made in writing. Section 5 of the agreement basically excludes the Canadian Police Information Centre (CPIC) from its scope, on the grounds that Ontario and provincial institutions collected the information in CPIC for their own use, and they already have direct access to it. The rules on requests for access do not apply to CPIC, although Ontario and provincial institutions "shall use their best efforts to ensure that the [CPIC] information is only accessed, used, or disclosed in accordance with this Agreement."

The 1983 agreement with Ontario and the schedule to it may be amended at any time by the mutual consent of the parties, effected by means of a simple exchange of letters. The agreement also does not apply to personal information under the control of a federal government institution which may be disclosed: "a) pursuant to any Act of Parliament or any regulation made thereunder, other than the Privacy Act, that authorizes its disclosure; or b) for the purpose of administering or enforcing any law or carrying out a lawful investigation pursuant to any other agreement which meets the requirements of this Agreement." Moreover, "any existing agreements or arrangements between Canada or a government institution and Ontario or a provincial institution will continue in effect to the extent that they are not inconsistent with this Agreement." The effect of this series of clauses is truly mystifying for the uninitiated.

It is obviously very difficult for an outsider to evaluate the overall adequacy of the section 8(2)(f) agreement between the federal government and Ontario. But the generality and looseness of some of the terms at least suggest that the law enforcement community in Ontario has obtained by negotiation what they failed to obtain through direct presentations to the Parliamentary Committee in the hearings on Bill C-43, which are discussed below. The privacy commissioner will have to carry out further research and monitoring on this matter. Fortunately, the introduction of data protection legislation in Ontario in 1988 has facilitated reciprocal protection of personal information and the control of unauthorized surveillance.

The Privacy Act also includes exemptions for law enforcement and investigation, whereby the head of a government institution may refuse to disclose to an individual any personal information obtained or prepared by a federal investigative body with respect to law enforcement, or "the disclosure of which could reasonably be expected to be injurious to the enforcement of any law of Canada or a province or the conduct of lawful investigations." There are similar exemptions permitting but not requiring refusals to disclose any personal information obtained or prepared by the RCMP while performing policing services for provinces or municipalities.[25]

When Bill C-43 was before Parliament, the sections on law enforcement attracted a great deal of critical attention.[26] A twenty-one-page letter written by Attorney General Roy McMurtry of Ontario to Minister of Communications Francis Fox on June 10, 1981, argued that the draft provisions of the Privacy Act "could be construed so as to interfere seriously with the ability of law enforcement authorities to share law enforcement data. . . . Such sharing of information is vitally important, if we are to have effective criminal law enforcement."[27] Further, "access by law enforcement authorities to personal information held in Federal data banks should be as free as possible from restriction. Any possible abuse of access that is perceived can be dealt with by separate legislation or by specific restrictions in this legislation." The Ontario Ministry of the Attorney General rejected the need for a requirement under section 8 of the Privacy Act that disclosures to investigative bodies should be based on a written request or on a formal agreement or arrangement: "Traditionally, data has been shared between all branches of law enforcement agencies, on the understanding that its confidentiality will be respected. Only with such sharing can there be effective law enforcement."[28]

Furthermore, the McMurtry letter argued, in an extraordinary way, that "the Privacy Commissioner's supervisory power should not extend to the law enforcement area. To extend it would seriously impair if not destroy assurances of confidentiality so necessary to effective law enforcement. At the same time it would present significant security risks. . . . The supervision by the staff of the Privacy Commissioner would require that people who have no expertise or commitment to the area of law enforcement make sensitive policy decisions and recommendations."[29] Any such supervision, McMurtry argued, should be internal and conducted by the Minister of Justice and the Solicitor General. Such a series of arguments encapsulates law enforcers' resistance to controls on surveillance.

The McMurtry letter had relatively little influence on the law enforcement sections of the Privacy Act, despite its provocative language. A critique of the letter prepared by Professor T. Murray Rankin for the Canadian Bar Association concluded that "any suggestion in Mr. McMurtry's letter that the free exchange of data between law enforcement agencies in Canada would be hampered seems unsubstantiated."[30]

During the cursory clause-by-clause review of the Privacy Act on June 8, 1982, Svend Robinson of the New Democratic party (NDP) asked Francis Fox a number of questions about the law enforcement provisions. He wanted assurances that there would be a continuation under the Privacy Act of the situation described by the recent Commission of Inquiry into Certain Activities of the RCMP, whereby the RCMP was being denied access "to virtually all personal information possessed by other federal government institutions." Fox responded "that the bill does not grant any new powers to any investigative agency or body of the Government of Canada but establishes a code of conduct for that investigative body, including the Security Service of Canada." The minister refused to offer any categorical undertaking and acknowledged that there were certain types of information not available to the RCMP under Part IV of the Human Rights Act that would be available under the new act.[31]

Robinson returned to the attack during third reading of Bill C-43 and expressed the opinion "that there is no doubt whatsoever that this bill gives sweeping new powers to the heads of government institutions and to the RCMP and to the new civilian security service in particular to intrude into the most confidential and personal aspects of the lives of Canadians."[32] The actual provisions of the Privacy Act and, in particular, the Treasury Board directives and guidelines for the legislation, suggest that there is some exaggeration in this conclusion, with the possible exception of the new Canadian Security Intelligence Service (CSIS). But it is fair to say that no one actually knows how the act is working in practice.

As befits a hierarchical institution, the RCMP set up a special unit to coordinate responses to individual requests for access to information under the central provisions of Part IV of the Canadian Human Rights Act. This secretariat to the departmental privacy coordinator, now known as the Information Access Directorate, handles all privacy and access to information matters. The unit on information access, located at RCMP headquarters in Ottawa, now employs thirty-one persons, which is a large number in comparative terms for the RCMP, and has a high profile within the force. This directorate also handles the descriptions of all of the RCMP's data bases in the published indexes. There are RCMP units spread out across Canada and not all of their records are centralized, so the force has to provide centralized guidance about the processing of requests for access. Since most of the records are investigatory in character, individuals seeking access to their own records have to state where they have been involved with the RCMP, so that the police have some idea where to locate those records.

In trying to make decisions about granting individuals access to their own personal data, the Information Access Directorate uses an "injury test" to determine what personal information is innocuous. The actual record holder may make the initial suggestions as to what will be released. The RCMP has never completely exempted full files of individuals, as they might have done. It has gradually changed its policy on exemptions to release more data to individuals and usually complies with the advice of the privacy commissioner.

In general, the Information Access Directorate did not encounter any problems in persuading members of the RCMP to comply with Part IV, although police forces generally continued to be apprehensive about the impact of the 1982 Privacy Act. Informants point out that the force's perspective on compliance with Part IV reflected prior experience with the control of wiretapping under the Protection of Privacy Act of 1974. The RCMP's reporting and informant systems have not dried up. The argument is that the information received is now more objective and better documented and that members of the RCMP are now phrasing their reports more professionally. Since obtaining objective and well-documented information has been a consistent goal of the RCMP, data protection has helped the force to implement better reporting procedures.

The RCMP's problems have primarily concerned the sharing of information for law enforcement purposes. For example, it no longer obtains uncontrolled access to other departmental information for law enforcement purposes. The RCMP suggested to the Treasury Board that there was a continuing problem with respect to the sharing of information between government institutions, but that "the provisions of the new Privacy Act would remedy the situation by more clearly defining the extent to which government institutions could disclose information to an investigative body named in the regulations, subject to certain conditions."[33] There are no longer any shortcuts in law enforcement within the RCMP nor any doubts about what procedures officers should follow to get access to personal information, especially from a government department.

In a speech delivered at the National Forum on Access to Information and Privacy held in Ottawa on March 7, 1986, Superintendent P. E. J. Banning, the Privacy and Access to Information Coordinator for the RCMP, stated that: "Up to this point, we are not aware that the release of any information under the legislation has jeopardized RCMP operations. . . . Not only is there no evidence that the *Privacy Act* or the *Access to Information Act* has had a negative operational impact on the RCMP; in many ways it has probably made us a more professional organization."[34]

In terms of compliance with privacy legislation, the RCMP has had the advantage of starting with a sound record system that did not need reconstruction. Senior management encouraged compliance. The RCMP is in fact prepared for general audits of its information handling by the Office of the Privacy Commissioner, which has concentrated to date on the RCMP's exempt banks. When RCMP employees do regular audits of its local branches, they watch for potential problems in this area. Moreover, the RCMP does not have a policy of keeping records in perpetuity. Under the Public Archives Act, a records manual governs the disposition policy. The usual retention schedule is three to five years, and a destruction schedule is actually built into the files compiled for investigations.

The privacy commissioners have generally found the RCMP to cooperate readily with data protection requirements. It gives out a great deal of information to requesters and holds back less than other departments. The RCMP gradually improved the scope of its listings in the *Index of Federal Information Banks*. The 1983 *Personal Information Index* listed fourteen banks for the RCMP, excluding those banks dealing with RCMP employees; by 1987 the number was nineteen.[35]

In 1987 the Justice Committee of the House of Commons, recognizing that the nationwide Canadian Police Information Centre was one of the most sensitive tools for public surveillance, recommended that the entire system should be fully subject to the Privacy Act and to the oversight of the privacy commissioner.[36] The committee wanted the commissioner to pay particular attention to the policies and practices of the CPIC system and other comparable automated data bases in the intelligence field, "in order to ensure that the privacy interests of individual Canadians are being adequately protected." The government responded that the commissioner can audit the application of CPIC policy to data under the control of the RCMP, but that it would have to consult further with law enforcement agencies across Canada about handling privacy issues that arise from personal information that they voluntarily provide to the system.[37] Even the recent data protection laws for the two-thirds of the Canadian population that live in Quebec and Ontario do not adequately regulate data from local police forces in CPIC, since they are not subject to the Ontario law. Nevertheless, it is hoped that the several levels of data protection commissioners will start work to improve oversight of CPIC, since it contains data on 10 percent of the population.

The Security Services

One of the most publicized abuses of personal information in Canada in past decades occurred under the aegis of the Security Services of the RCMP. In July 1977 the federal government appointed a Commission of Inquiry Concerning Certain Activities of the RCMP, under the chairmanship of Justice D. C. McDonald. Its major report on *Freedom and Security under the Law* became available in 1981. Among other illegal activities, the RCMP Security Services had access to Social Insurance Numbers and had maintained files on homosexuals in Canada and on tourists who had visited the Soviet Union.[38] Such revelations have made a continuing contribution to fears about governmental surveillance practices.

The McDonald Commission noted that the Security Services maintained files on about 800,000 individual Canadians, that many such dossiers were needlessly opened, and that this amounted to an invasion of privacy.[39] On February 11, 1983, Liberal Solicitor General Robert Kaplan announced procedures for the eventual destruction of many of these files. He agreed with the McDonald Commission's criticisms and noted that a review of Security Service files would begin soon. The guidelines state that files will be destroyed unless they relate to a person who requires a security clearance for employment, there is reason to suspect that the person is a legitimate target for Security Service investigation, or there is reason to believe a person with access to classified information is or may become a security threat by virtue of blackmail, bribery, or indiscretion.[40] The files for possible destruction were to be reviewed by members of the Security Service and officials of the Department of Justice and the Ministry of the Solicitor General.

New Democratic party critic Svend J. Robinson denounced Kaplan's proposed file destruction policy as "full of so many loopholes that, in reality, it is nothing less than a 'Big Brother' privacy invasion policy, written and administered by the RCMP Security Service itself."[41] Kaplan denied these allegations, indicating that tens of thousands and even hundreds of thousands of files would be destroyed: "The policy calls for an independent review by the Privacy Commissioner. I think that will provide an effective safeguard that the privacy of Canadians is being adequately regarded by the Security Service and its file destruction policy." He indicated that the Security Service's criteria for opening new files would be the same as for the destruction of files.[42]

At the end of 1988, the destruction of CSIS records, both old and new, is proceeding again, after a few twists and turns. In February 1985 the government temporarily halted all file destruction after a commission of inquiry into war criminals found its work stymied by earlier efforts. The most satisfactory result is that the Security Intelligence Review Committee (SIRC), an independent civilian oversight body for CSIS, is now overseeing the process as a specialized monitor. The burdened staff of the privacy commissioner can eventually review what has been accomplished and also does not have to become as intimately involved, for the moment, in the work of the security agency as their West German colleagues.

The considerable independence that SIRC has displayed to date encourages confidence in its oversight efforts. Its 1987 report concluded that the countersubversion activities of CSIS were unduly threatening the privacy of Canadians.[43] Acknowledged excesses led to the resignation of the first civilian director of the agency. In addition, SIRC charged that CSIS's countersubversion branch had files on 30,000 persons. The security agency responded that it had records on only 3,867, while the 60,000 files it had inherited from the RCMP's Security Service were scheduled for destruction.[44] In 1988 SIRC confirmed that its original estimate of 30,000 was low; there were 54,000 countersubversion files, of which 3,867 were active. The rest were locked up for review and destruction by CSIS or transferred to special files at the National Archives of Canada. The ending of the moratorium on destruction means that, over a number of years, a similar fate awaits the old files that CSIS inherited from the RCMP. Sixty-seven thousand old files have already been destroyed.

Since January 1988 no new information has been added to any of the above files, and new criteria exist for new countersubversive records.[45]

The governing legislation for CSIS, which Kaplan first introduced in 1983, has some less attractive features than the work of SIRC. The law contains controversial measures concerning the collection and disclosure of information by the Security Service. Section 19, authorizing the disclosure of information, takes precedence over section 8(2) of the Privacy Act, even though the agency is otherwise subject to this law.[46] Moreover, the CSIS act also amended section 9 of the Privacy Act and significantly weakened it, by limiting the requirement that the "head of a government institution shall retain a record of any use by the institution of personal information contained in a personal information bank or any use or purpose for which such information is disclosed by the institution where the use or purpose is not included in the statements of uses and purpose set forth" in the *Personal Information Index* and in other places. This requirement of an audit trail no longer applies to information disclosed for any law enforcement purposes under section 8(2)(e) of the Privacy Act.[47] The CSIS act also amended the Privacy Act to allow the head of a government institution to refuse to disclose any personal information to an individual when it concerns "activities suspected of constituting threats to the security of Canada within the meaning of the Canadian Security Intelligence Service Act."[48]

The debate over legislation to control CSIS also featured one victory for data protectors. Bill C-157 originally contained an extraordinary override provision in section 22(1), whereby "notwithstanding any other law," the Director of the new Security Service could seek a judicial warrant to "obtain any information, document or thing." No other country studied in this volume has a comparable provision.

The media quickly realized, and Kaplan acknowledged, that Bill C-157 would further allow the Security Service access to data from the census of population that is intended to be absolutely confidential.[49] Jill Wallace of the Information Law and Privacy unit at the Department of Justice confirmed the broad reach of this override provision. The Chief Statistician of Canada indicated that such a provision would be contrary to the best interests of Statistics Canada. The McDonald Commission had recommended that census information should remain off limits to the Security Service, under any circumstances. Like many other Canadian newspapers, the *Toronto Star* on June 5, 1983, editorialized against making census data available to the Security Service, on the grounds that it would undermine the accuracy and honesty of responses from individuals to census questions: "1984 is only six months away anyway; Kaplan shouldn't rush it."

Critics of the proposed practice carried their fight to the Cabinet and won. Although an argument can be made that the Security Service would not find access to data at Statistics Canada a very important source of information, the latter does possess, for example, the latest population census, a Personal Income Tax Data Base, an Integrated Vital Statistics Data Base, and specific data bases on 200,000 registered nurses, elementary and secondary teachers (except from Quebec), all university faculty members, and all students currently enrolled in a university.[50] The amount of personal information held by Statistics Canada explains why the secrecy clause of the Statistics Act absolutely prohibits the disclosure of identifiable personal information.[51]

Revenue Canada Taxation

The taxation part of Revenue Canada inevitably collects a great deal of personal information that taxpayers in particular regard as sensitive.[52] It is the second largest user of computers in the federal government and among the top half-dozen users in the entire country. Typical of the kinds of problems that arise was a question directed by former Liberal Cabinet Member John M. Reid to the minister of national revenue in 1983 concerning the fact that everyone's income was appearing on preprinted federal income tax return forms. Reid was concerned that these forms were normally sent to individuals through the mail, where they could be intercepted or lost, and asked what legislative authority the minister had to place information about total income and Social Insurance Numbers on these forms. The minister indicated that the income figures now in use provided for a new income averaging formula for taxpayers who wished to take advantage of it. The justification for the use of the Social Insurance Number was for practical reasons in processing tax returns. Reid responded that the whole process was "an enormous invasion of the privacy of every Canadian."[53] Perrin Beatty supported Reid in questioning the minister of national revenue. Several days later Reid stated that he had been deluged with telephone calls from Canadians "complaining about the amount of information which has been made available on their income tax returns."[54] The practice was subsequently ended. Beatty later became minister of national revenue, which considerably enhanced its sensitivities to surveillance practices.

Revenue Canada Taxation is also a significant user of Social Insurance Numbers. Although the use of the number on certain income reporting slips was not mandatory until 1988, the department encouraged its use because of its significance as a file identifier. The ministry argues that it is in the best practical interests of tax filers to use the SIN to permit positive identification and matching should a form become detached from the return during the assessing process. Revenue Canada claims to maintain the integrity of the confidential personal income tax returns it holds, which are not released except to the tax filer or an authorized representative. This particular statement ends with the surprising claim that "the personal social insurance number, which is not available to the public, is one of the tools used to ensure the privacy of personal tax data."[55] Revenue Canada is, in fact, one of the few legitimate users of the SIN and it had a persuasive argument for requiring its use on more income reporting forms for efficient tax administration and to facilitate legitimate computer verification. The 1988 changes in the SIN reporting requirements for securities and interest-bearing accounts were primarily controversial because individuals first learned about them from their financial institutions, there are penalties for failure to comply, and because the privacy commissioner was not consulted about this particular measure.[56]

Revenue Canada Taxation stands as a compelling attraction to anyone trying to keep track of individuals, since it maintains such data bases as a "taxation taxpayer master file" with information that is directly accessible on more than 17 million residents of Canada. Parliament has recently enacted legislation that requires the release of confidential information in order to help track down spouses who have defied family support or custody orders.[57] A special committee of representatives from the federal and provincial governments drew up the recommendations. The intent of the legislation is to deal with the large number of support and custody orders that are violated by using court orders to obtain access to useful records from immigration, passport, and social insurance for enforcement purposes. A spokesman for the Ontario attorney general explained that the province wants court-ordered release of federal confidential information, because it is such a large and central data source.

Although the original bill proposed that federal taxation records should also be accessible, Revenue Canada Taxation successfully resisted being used for such a tracing function; this is a considerable accomplishment for data protection. Only personal information banks under the control of Health and Welfare Canada and CEIC are accessible under the Family Orders and Agreements Enforcement Assistance Act.

This particular development is a classic example of how two conflicting goals need to be balanced. In this instance, the pressure for increasing access comes from those charged with enforcing custody and support orders. The problem is that such proposals are in an advanced state of development before privacy interests are adequately considered by independent sources. Under an ideal system of data protection, such a legislative proposal would be submitted to the privacy commissioner for his opinion at an early stage in the planning process.

Fortunately, a variety of episodes have made Revenue Canada very sensitive to privacy protection. The most egregious was an employee's theft in 1986 of microfiches containing basic information about 16 million taxpayers. Although the data were quickly recovered, the shock to the public was considerable. The employee was tried and found guilty; at the time of sentencing, the associate chief justice of the Supreme Court of Ontario, William Callahan, concluded that "we live in a very invasive society. The Government can get into our most personal information." The defendant, who pleaded guilty, had perpetrated "a gross insult to the right of privacy which we all have in the information we provide to the Federal Government" and "caused people to question the ability of Government to fulfill its promise of privacy."[58] The privacy commissioner's office, on its own initiative and in full cooperation with the RCMP and the tax authorities, subsequently carried out an independent investigation of the security procedures at Revenue Canada, which resulted in seven recommendations for improvement of training and security procedures.[59]

Revenue Canada seeks to ensure that information on a total of 77 million persons is only used for taxation purposes.[60] The requirements of the Privacy Act are reinforced by section 241 of the Income Tax Act. Any authorized sharing of tax data with other government departments is governed by memoranda of understanding that particularly cover security and auditing procedures. The current concern about drug abuse resulted in 1988 in legislation to amend the Criminal Code concerning the proceeds of crime, authorizing police access to taxpayer information in cases of drug and drug-related investigations. At the urging of the tax authorities, this access was very narrowly defined to major drug offenses and includes court review and authorization. The minister of national revenue may formally object to any such disclosure on various grounds, leading to further judicial review.[61]

The department has developed model training programs to sensitize its 20,000 staff members to the requirements of the Privacy Act and has also instituted reliability checks in accordance with the government's 1986 security policy. The sheer number of employees involved in district offices across Canada offer some sense of how significant these burdens are. Moreover, employees can use terminals to have direct access to 16 million personal records. All of its automated systems employ passwords and other forms of user identification. Audit trails permit management to track usage and take action where there is unauthorized access. The dissemination of information to taxpayers by telephone and in person is an especially sensitive problem, since the need for confidentiality needs to be balanced against the demand for service. The department employs careful identification procedures for this purpose. The agency also uses family allowance records of Health and Welfare Canada to update its address files.

In compliance with the Treasury Board's security policy, Revenue Canada Taxation conducts risk assessments of potential problem areas, either alone or in cooperation with the RCMP, and then introduces necessary preventive measures. Such formal assessments are now a requirement for the introduction of any information technology that handles sensitive information. Revenue Canada should also monitor compliance with the fair information practices incorporated in the Privacy Act as part of its performance review of individual employees. It holds so much sensitive personal data that some Canadians suspect its use for unauthorized purposes.[62] Fortunately, senior management are very sensitive to the issue of data protection, not least because of recent occurrences. Thus Revenue Canada is an example of an institution that takes its responsibility to maintain confidentiality very seriously.

Chapter 24

Responding to Privacy and Surveillance Problems

This chapter sums up various problems that the Office of the Privacy Commissioner has had with the process of implementation of the Privacy Act and considers how to revise the law to meet contemporary realities of power relationships and governmental surveillance.

The Achievements and Adequacies of Implementation

One of the key limitations of Part IV of the Canadian Human Rights Act was that it was almost impossible for anyone to find out if it was indeed working. There was no one responsible for monitoring abuses of personal data within government agencies, except in response to complaints. Retrospective enthusiasm about its effectiveness during the five years of its existence must be limited to its initial impact in the early stages of implementation. The argument could be heard in the early 1980s that there were in fact no controls on government use of personal information for surveillance purposes.

The enhanced roles under the Privacy Act of the privacy commissioner, the president of the Treasury Board, and the head of each government institution have begun to improve this earlier situation. A statement released on June 22, 1983, by Herb Gray, then president of the Treasury Board, announced that as the minister responsible for implementation of the Privacy Act, he would take a definite and direct interest in monitoring its implementation.[1] Following through on this promise might have dramatically improved the quality of data protection at the federal level, but the exigencies of political and public service life made this an unlikely prospect, especially since the Conservative party came to power in 1984. No official body, except for the Office of the Privacy Commissioner, has a strong stake in making data protection effective in order to try to limit government surveillance.

The Privacy Act is a basically sound, second-generation statute, which now requires modernization in response to new surveillance challenges and experience, as recommended by the Justice and Solicitor General Committee of the House of Commons in its 1987 report.[2] At present, no one is likely to propose such a dramatic change as giving the privacy commissioner regulatory power to make final decisions, as is the emerging model in Quebec and Ontario, but such a change may in fact become necessary.

The main federal problem remains lack of implementation within government departments. The structure is in place, but progress is slow. Thus the jury is still out on whether the prime actors, the Office of the Privacy Commissioner, the specialists at the Treasury Board and in the Department of Justice, and the heads of government institutions, can and, indeed, will carry out their assigned tasks under the Privacy Act. The problems of personality, human inertia, funding shortages, competing priorities, and power relationships remain significant impediments to forceful implementation. An optimist will be pleased by what has been accomplished since July 1, 1983; a pessimist may well regard these finite attainments as an unerring reflection of human realities and of the pressures favoring surveillance.

Canada expects to have a third-generation privacy law within the next several years. Although it is too early to pass final judgment on the effectiveness of the office of the commissioner, Canadians have in place a watchdog who is quick to leap into the fray when real or alleged abuses of privacy interests are uncovered. As a result, governmental agencies now tread at least somewhat warily when contemplating increased surveillance of the public.

Revising the Privacy Act

From the point of view of continued improvements in federal data protection, the most important innovation in the Privacy Act is the provision that a standing committee of Parliament had to review the operations of the legislation within a three-year period.[3] But it was not until the Conservative Mulroney government came to power in the fall of 1984 that the government agreed to assign the oversight responsibility to the Standing Committee on Justice and Legal Affairs. It was not a high priority, and the choice among competing committees involved political considerations. Active oversight did not begin until the initiation of the three-year review in the summer of 1985.

One basic need is to provide for meaningful annual monitoring of governmental surveillance practices by building some expertise on the subject in the parliamentary committee. Only one current member of the committee, Svend Robinson of the New Democratic party, was involved in the enactment of the Privacy Act. The new rules for the House of Commons reduce the size of the committee to eleven members, which promotes the development of expertise during the usual four- to five-year life of a Parliament. Arrangements for staff support for the annual review need to be made.[4] The problem of effective annual review is exacerbated by the broad range of controversial issues that comes before this particular committee and the limited attention span of MPs for such a complicated issue as data protection. Moreover, for government members, the likelihood of clashing with the Cabinet over surveillance initiatives is risky, since the inner Cabinet controls future promotions and the distribution of patronage. Opposition members can do little to thwart a majority government, but they can energize the privacy commissioner and the heads of government institutions in their periodic appearances before the committee. Fortunately, when John Grace appeared before the committee in 1987, the members did engage in an impressive exchange of views about his activities.[5]

The more than one hundred recommendations by the Justice and Solicitor General Committee in its 1987 report should play a critical role in promoting implementation of the Privacy Act. In addition to setting the agenda for revision of the Privacy Act for the foreseeable future, the three-year review process had the basic benefit of consciousness-raising about data protection within the federal government by requiring the privacy commissioner, the minister of justice, the president of the Treasury Board, and the heads of selected government institutions, such as the solicitor general, to testify about their department's efforts on implementation.

The government, under the aegis of the Department of Justice, responded to the committee's recommendations within the mandatory period, but it did not fully accept the advice, despite taking significant, positive initiatives to strengthen the administration of the Privacy Act. Most importantly, the government did agree to improve training programs for privacy coordinators and government employees, to extend the coverage of the Privacy Act to crown corporations, to issue new policies on the use of the Social Insurance Number by government institutions and on data matching, and to improve consultation with the privacy commissioner on data protection issues.[6] A number of these initiatives have already borne fruit, and amendments to the Privacy Act are being prepared for Parliament by the Department of Justice.[7]

Unfortunately, the government rejected, ignored, or postponed for further study important committee recommendations concerning exempt banks, electronic surveillance, drug testing, and coverage of the federally regulated private sector. Thus, for the moment, it has rejected the idea of expanding a data protection law into a true "Privacy Act," which addresses many aspects of privacy protection in the society.[8]

The government's acceptance of the need for a policy on data matching is a recognition of the public's concern about this type of retrospective surveillance and of warnings issued by the privacy commissioner and by members of the parliamentary committee. The Treasury Board had already recognized the need to regulate such record linkages in more detail after a survey of matching activities in twelve government institutions. The government's 1989 policy directives to control such projects include requiring certification in each case that an institution is complying with the Privacy Act, requiring consideration of the costs and benefits of each proposed match versus the potential threat to individual privacy, and also stipulating that the privacy commissioner should have a sixty-day advance notice of any proposed match, so that he or she can either recommend against it or inform the public that it is about to take place.[9] Under the government's tough new policy, written ministerial approval is obligatory for data matching, independent verification must be undertaken before decisions based on the results of a match can be made, and individuals must be given the opportunity to refute the information before action is initiated.[10]

The commissioner's office played a crucial role in shaping this major development. Grace concludes that "if the new data-matching and linkage policy is observed in letter and spirit, Canadians for the first time have a reasonable assurance that their privacy will not be systematically breached as the custodians of enormous federal government data banks allow their whirring computers to run free." In his view, the Privacy Act "is the only mechanism Canada has standing in the way of unchecked federal government surveillance by computer."[11]

In 1987 the Justice Committee also drew particular attention to investigating the impact of the use of microcomputers and of the use of information technology in general on individual rights. It recommended explicit amendment of the Privacy Act to give such jurisdiction to the privacy commissioner in consultation with the appropriate government institutions. It also urged the relevant departments, including the commissioner, to develop new policies and practices to cope with the emerging data protection problem posed by personal information held and used in microcomputers. In this instance, it invited the submission of separate reports within eighteen months to Parliament. The government concluded that the commissioner already had sufficient authority to act in this important area.[12]

Until now, the officials in the federal government charged with the implementation of data protection have not paid any particular attention to the surveillance implications of evolving information technology. The specialists at the Treasury Board tend to believe that technology drives the creation of new information systems and that it will be necessary to develop a data policy for information management in the federal government. They also recognize that this process of policy-making is only beginning.

While the initiation of the development of policy will be the initial step toward better control, the sheer size and decentralized nature of the federal government inhibit a coherent approach and the necessary controls. The Department of Communications, for example, promotes applications of new technology, including office automation, everywhere in the federal government, while individual departments are on their own in adopting microcomputers on an ad hoc basis. The result is the multiplication of systems and places for storing personal data, which will eventually make a mockery of the concept of a "personal information bank" contained in the Privacy Act. Again, the gradual development of a capacity to monitor the implications for data protection of ongoing technological developments should be a primary task for the Office of the Privacy Commissioner.

Other informed observers think that new technological innovations, such as encryption, should be studied for their possible contributions to data protection at reasonable cost. Since encryption would be particularly useful for the protection of sensitive data, an agency like the Royal Canadian Mounted Police continues to consider its application in various systems. Fortunately, in 1987 the government undertook a review of its security practices in relation to the protection of personal information, as a result of the theft of microfiches from Revenue Canada Taxation.

In introducing Bill C-43 for third reading in the House on June 28, 1982, Minister of Communications Francis Fox noted that the Privacy Act "paves the way for the next stage in the development of privacy legislation, extension of the principles respecting the protection of personal information to the federally-regulated private sector."[13] This initiative, as recommended by the parliamentary committee, would have particular relevance for federally regulated banks, trust companies, and cable television companies, which hold enormous amounts of personal data.[14]

In June 1984 Canada was one of the last member countries to sign the Organization for Economic Co-operation and Development's *Guidelines on the Protection of Privacy*.[15] This situation was particularly surprising, since Canada successfully pressed for a number of changes in the final draft of the *Guidelines* and was also considerably ahead of a number of other countries that had already signed the *Guidelines* in implementing protective measures in the public sector. The federal government did have to consult with the provinces about the implications of signing the *Guidelines* and, in fact, dragged its feet until November 1986 in terms of informing the private sector of their implications.[16] At present, the government has taken a major step forward in extending privacy protection to the private sector by extending the legislation to crown-owned corporations, including Canadian National Railways and Petro Canada, the national oil company.[17] Thus efforts to control the surveillance practices of the corporate world have finally begun in earnest, even as the implementation burden facing the Office of the Privacy Commissioner continues to grow.

Part 5

The United States

Chapter *25*

The United States Model

Introduction

The United States does not have a data protection agency fully comparable to the other countries, even though the federal Privacy Act of 1974 was innovative and influential in its time. The law incorporates a code of fair information practices for the collection and handling of personal data by the federal government.[1] As in other countries, responsibility for ensuring that the statute works in practice is very broadly diffused, beginning with Privacy Act officers in government agencies and ending with individuals who have to bring a lawsuit to redress a perceived grievance.

Because of opposition to more bureaucracy from President Gerald Ford, among others, the law did not establish a privacy protection commission. Oversight of the Privacy Act was attached to the Office of Management and Budget (OMB), which is part of the Executive Office of the President. This has proven to be an unwise choice for controlling federal surveillance. In practice, the Privacy Act has a relatively low priority in government institutions, because only the Office of Information and Regulatory Affairs of OMB, itself only created in 1980, has any degree of oversight over implementation. OMB has in fact exercised relatively weak leadership in the process of implementation, at least in terms comparable to data protection agencies in Canada and Western Europe. Oversight of the Privacy Act by congressional committees has been limited and episodic.[2]

The United States carries out data protection differently than other countries, and on the whole does it less well, because of the lack of an oversight agency, but it would be misleading to suggest that the Privacy Act is a dead letter. Under its umbrella, and even without the assistance of a data protection commission, the United States has made considerable progress in enacting specialized data protection laws. The latest example is the Computer Matching and Privacy Protection Act of 1988.

Ten American states have enacted data protection laws containing codes of fair information practices.[3] A number of states, notably California, include an explicit right to privacy in their constitutions.[4] But only New York State's Committee on Open Government attempts any oversight under the Personal Privacy Protection Law of 1983. Thus, the political and structural problems of obtaining meaningful control of surveillance at the federal and state levels are similar.[5]

In the United States, the concept of privacy is employed in a wide variety of spheres. In fact, the United States invented the concept of a legal right to privacy.[6] For the last twenty years, federal and state governments have been developing a constitutional right of privacy, which is tested in decisions on subjects as varied as a woman's right to an abortion, the constitutionality of state laws against sodomy, or the right to test student athletes for drug use. Americans are sensitive to foreign ignorance of a long line of court cases protective of personal privacy. They correctly emphasize the complexity and diversity of protections and remedies available to aggrieved citizens.

The United States government is an extraordinarily large institution, which makes it very difficult to view surveillance issues, or even its data protection elements, as a coherent whole.[7] Activities with a significant impact on privacy can take place on many fronts at the same time. For the United States, one has to evaluate the relative effectiveness of the federal system of data protection in terms of the impact of not having a data protection commission, analyze the actual work in implementation of OMB and the individual government institutions, and outline the benefits of the sectoral approach. The provisions on confidentiality in the Tax Reform Act of 1976, for example, are much longer than comparable national data protection laws. The sectoral approach has the advantage of settling one question at a time and is ultimately comparable to the method used in other countries to move beyond general data protection legislation.

One dominant theme of the following pages is evaluating the need for a federal privacy or data protection commission in the United States in the light of the situation in the late 1980s. Further, the progress in fashioning sectoral legislation is also considered, since, as in other countries, this is a major step in achieving meaningful controls on specific forms of surveillance. A third theme is the powerful OMB's lack of political will to act on privacy matters during the Reagan presidency, illustrating once again the importance of the political climate for effective implementation of data protection and limiting surveillance. Reagan rhetoric on privacy contrasted with multiple efforts to control the population through such practices as computer matching. Finally, the U.S. case study demonstrates a noble effort at congressional oversight of surveillance issues by dedicated staff.

The Development of Federal Legislation

The origins of the Privacy Act are directly comparable to contemporaneous English, Swedish, and Canadian developments. Eliot Richardson, the secretary of the Department of Health, Education, and Welfare, created a typical study commission on privacy and computers, which reported in 1973.[8] A central contribution of that advisory committee, chaired by Willis H. Ware of the Rand Corporation, was the articulation of a code of fair information practices, which greatly influenced the Privacy Act and subsequent data protection legislation in other countries.

Table 6. Chronology of United States Federal Data Protection Legislation

1966	Freedom of Information Act enacted.
1970	Fair Credit Reporting Act enacted.
July 1973	Department of Health, Education, and Welfare issues "Records, Computers, and the Rights of Citizens," the report of the Secretary's Advisory Committee on Automated Personal Data Systems.
1974	Major amendments to the Freedom of Information Act.
	Family Educational Rights and Privacy Act regulates government access to personal education records and grants students access to their own records.
May 1, 1974	Senator Samuel J. Ervin, Jr., introduces S. 3418 to create a Federal Privacy Board.
December 31, 1974	President Gerald Ford signs the Privacy Act.
April 8, 1975	Department of Defense creates the Defense Privacy Board.
July 1975	Office of Management and Budget issues guidelines on the implementation of the Privacy Act.
September 27, 1975	Privacy Act enters in force.
1976	Tax Reform Act restricts governmental use of tax information for other purposes.
January 1977	President Carter transfers the responsibilities of the White House's Office of Telecommunications Policy to the National Telecommunications and Information Administration (NTIA), Department of Commerce.
July 1977	Report of the Privacy Protection Study Commission.
November 1978	Right to Financial Privacy Act regulates federal access to individual financial records.
April 2, 1979	President Jimmy Carter proposes privacy legislation on medical, research, and financial records, and news media notes and materials.
April 18, 1979	Office of Management and Budget issues guidelines for the conduct of matching programs.
1980	Paperwork Reduction Act seeks to reduce the government's collection of personal information.
	Privacy Protection Act is designed to control government searches of newsrooms.

(*continued on the following page*)

Table 6. Chronology of United States Federal Data Protection Legislation (*continued*)

January 1980	Office of Management and Budget creates the Office of Information and Regulatory Affairs.
1982	Debt Collection Act regulates the federal government's release of personal information on bad debts to credit agencies.
May 14, 1982	The Office of Management and Budget issues revised supplemental guidelines for conducting computer matching programs.
December 15–16, 1982	Senator William S. Cohen chairs hearings on computer matching.
June 7–8, 1983	Congressman Glenn English chairs the first oversight hearings on the Privacy Act.
1984	Cable Communications Policy Act includes measures to protect the privacy of subscribers to cable television.
1985	Office of Management and Budget issues Circular No. A-130 on "Management of Federal Information Resources."
1986	Office of Technology Assessment issues a report on "Electronic Record Systems and Individual Privacy."
	Electronic Communications Privacy Act prohibits the interception of certain electronic communications and regulates the interception and use of such communications for law enforcement purposes.
September 16, 1986	Senator William S. Cohen chairs hearings on computer matching.
1987	Computer Security Act of 1987 seeks to protect the security of sensitive personal information in federal computer systems.
June 23, 1987	House of Representatives holds hearings on computer matching legislation.
1988	Video Privacy Protection Act protects records of individual borrowers held by video tape rental stores.
October 18, 1988	Computer Matching and Privacy Protection Act enacted to control computer matching.

The Privacy Act created the Privacy Protection Study Commission, which issued an outstanding report in July 1977, primarily concerned with the problems of the private sector.[9] The commission then ceased to exist, having produced thoughtful analyses and recommendations on education, medical, tax, statistics and research, and welfare records held by various levels of government. Its illustrative revision of the Privacy Act was intended to serve as a model for improved data protection.[10]

The recommendations of the Privacy Protection Study Commission had little direct impact on the public or private sectors, except for the considerable number of voluntary improvements that took place as a result of its extensive hearings. These weak results were part of the failure of the Carter administration to settle its own privacy agenda and then to sell it to Congress. The so-called Carter Privacy Initiative, sent to Congress on April 2, 1979, was ill-fated. It proposed four bills providing privacy protection for medical records, federally funded research records, financial records, and news media notes and materials. Although major hearings took place, almost no legislation was enacted before the 1980 electoral defeat of Carter, except for the Right to Financial Privacy Act of 1978.[11]

The federal legislative process is enormously complex, not least because of the separation of powers between the executive and the legislature and the large number of House and Senate committees that can be involved. It is also very difficult to demonstrate need in the commonsense way that Congress requires. This is the particular bane of the sectoral approach to data protection, since it is so hard to document the necessary horror stories without holding full-scale investigations of a particular sector.[12] Congress also insists on a higher threshold of need before legislating for the private sector.

The Reagan administration's approach to privacy was especially ironic, since the protection of the individual from various forms of government intrusion is surely a conservative issue. The administration itself took no positive initiatives on privacy and perceived no need to do so. Although in some quarters there is a perception of the need to establish a data protection commission, the Reaganites were committed to reducing the size of government, not expanding it. One ironic consequence with positive implications for limiting surveillance is that responsibility for both privacy and information management was consolidated at the Office of Management and Budget, and there were limited funds for new information systems. Thus the main consequences for privacy of the Reagan years have been negative, as some of the president's followers have sought to implement their pet schemes to order the country, such as a National Drivers Register or a workers' identity card.[13] Nevertheless, the administration eventually recognized, spurred by high levels of concern for privacy in public opinion polls, that failure to reassure a skeptical public about the civil liberties implications of new information technologies may make it impossible to put promising technological solutions to work.[14]

Especially in the United States, privacy issues are raised in a political climate and need to be sold to the executive and legislative branches. This is an especially telling condition in a data protection system that relies critically on special sectoral legislation to complement the omnibus approach of the Privacy Act. It is also one of the chief limits of such an incremental approach, since coalitions and ripe conditions have to be constructed anew as each need arises. Such specialized legislation also has to be shaped and enacted without the guidance of an official body of privacy specialists, such as exists in other countries. It may be, of course, that this is the only approach possible in such a legalistic society. Moreover, for all the failures to legislate, there have been major successes since the Privacy Act, notably the measures to cover two-way cable television services in the Cable Communications Policy Act of 1984 and the Electronic Communications Privacy Act of 1986, which controls the interception and use of various forms of electronic surveillance, including radio telephones, data transmissions and electronic mail, remote computing services, paging devices, pen registers, and telephone toll records.[15]

The Rejected Models

It is essential to understand why there is no privacy protection commission at the federal level, especially since it is largely a matter of accident or at least of an historic compromise. Senator Samuel J. Ervin, Jr., introduced S. 3418 to create a federal privacy board on May 1, 1974. The Senate Committee on Government Operations also emphasized the need for such an enforcement and oversight mechanism. Its recognition of surveillance issues is especially telling:

> The Committee is convinced that effective legislation must provide standards for and limitations on the information power of government. Providing a right of access and challenge to records, while important, is not sufficient legislative solution to threats to privacy. Contrary to the views of Administration spokesmen[,] it is not enough to tell agencies to gather and keep only data which is reliable by their rights for whatever they determine is their intended use, and then to pit the individual against government, armed only with the power to inspect his file, and the right to challenge it in court if he has the resources and the will to do so.
>
> To leave the situation there is to shirk the duty of Congress to protect freedom from the incursions by the arbitrary exercise of the power of government and to provide for the fair and responsible use of that power.[16]

The Senate committee envisioned the privacy protection commission as "an independent body of experts charged with protecting individual privacy as a value in government and society . . . to help deal in a systematic fashion with a great range of administrative and technological problems throughout the many agencies of the Federal Government."[17]

The Senate committee further emphasized "that Congress, with its limited technical staff and multitude of functions, cannot keep track of these developments in every Federal Agency and for every data bank with the depth of detail required for consistently constructive policy analysis." In addition, "there is an urgent need for a staff of experts somewhere in government which is sensitive both to the privacy interests of citizens and the informational needs of government and which can furnish expert assistance to both the legislative and executive branches."[18] The passage of time has especially demonstrated the relevance of these two points. The Senate report was also most prescient in noting that the proposed commission could "serve the important purposes of raising and resolving privacy questions before government plans are put in operation. . . . Congress and the President need help in identifying those areas in which privacy safeguards are most urgently needed and in drafting legislation specifically tailored to those problem areas."[19] The committee deemed it "absolutely essential" to create an independent body: "One of the principal reasons for establishing a privacy protection commission was to fill the present vacuum in the administrative process for overseeing the establishment of governmental data banks and personal information systems and examining invasions of individual privacy."[20]

The final Senate plan for a privacy protection commission did not include regulatory or ombudsman-like powers for it. However, the qualifications added in the Senate report are particularly relevant to the concerns of this volume: "Those roles may come in time, but they should be the product of specific legislation and come only after efforts to achieve voluntary reforms have failed. Meanwhile, awareness that the Commission might be vested by Congress with regulatory power at some future time should have a salutary effect on those agencies which may be tempted to ignore suggestions, or which fail to give its model guidelines the deference due them."[21]

The Senate committee determined that the proposed commission should be independent. It consciously rejected vesting investigative and advisory functions in either the General Accounting Office (GAO) or the Office of Management and Budget. The committee wanted the privacy protection unit to be available to congressional committees as well as to executive agencies. The Senate report further noted that the Ford administration opposed the creation of a commission, partly for reasons of cost: "It is the Committee's belief, however, that the Commission is vitally needed to promote the quality of legislative and administrative oversight which will provide a privacy bulwark for Americans in the years ahead."[22]

President Ford opposed key parts of S. 3418: "I do not favor establishing a separate Commission or Board bureaucracy empowered to define privacy in its own terms and to second-guess citizens and agencies. I vastly prefer an approach which makes Federal agencies fully and publicly accountable for legally-mandated privacy protections and which gives the individual adequate legal remedies to enforce what he deems to be his own best privacy interests."²³ Several of these assertions are misleading in themselves or have been proven wrong with the passage of time.

The House Committee on Government Operations subsequently issued its report on H.R. 16373, which is the Privacy Act of 1974. Although the House version contained no provision for an oversight body, ten members of the committee were concerned about this omission. In the light of what has happened since 1974, these observations are particularly relevant to the control of surveillance:

> We recognize the fact that some of our colleagues feel it is wiser to wait and see how Federal agencies respond to privacy legislation before establishing any oversight mechanism. No one, however, wants to repeat the experience of the Freedom of Information Act in holding out rights to individuals but providing them only with a costly and cumbersome mechanism of a judicial remedy. Therefore, we would amend the bill to provide for the establishment of an administrative body to mediate conflicts between agencies and individuals, to investigate complaints, hold hearings, and make findings of fact. We would be more than naive if we failed to recognize that individual Federal agencies cannot be expected to take an aggressive role in enforcing privacy legislation. Enforcement of the provisions of this bill will be secondary to each agency's mandate, and will, of necessity, cause additional expense and administrative inconvenience. Only by providing a separate administrative agency with authority for implementing legislation and coordinating the privacy programs of the various Federal agencies can we be assured of uniform, effective enforcement of the rights guaranteed by this bill.²⁴

Experience in Western countries supports the point that it is a contradiction to expect an operating administrative agency to enforce data protection legislation solely on its own, since the interests of surveillance and privacy are so often in conflict.

In debate in the House of Representatives, a number of individuals lamented the absence of a privacy protection commission in the House version of the bill. Congressman Gilbert Gude of Maryland moved an amendment "that would establish a Privacy Commission, which I believe is of vital necessity if the privacy legislation we are enacting is to become a meaningful statute."²⁵ Gude argued that this proposed commission would serve "as a focus of attention for information and privacy issues and will also be a watchdog over agencies which are responsible for implementing the provisions of the act. . . . At a minimum, this Commission should be established to oversee, monitor, and evaluate the newly-legislated safeguard requirements and to offer information and assistance to Federal agencies in their efforts to comply with the act."²⁶

Opponents of the Gude amendment argued that it had been voted down in committee, that it increased costs and bureaucracy, that it impeded civil remedies, that President Ford opposed it, and "finally, if, in this instance, the courts do not do the excellent job they have done under The Freedom of Information Act, then we in Congress can always in the future create a privacy board." Representative Moorhead of Pennsylvania argued further on behalf of the Committee on Government Operations that "vigorous congressional oversight will also help keep the bureaucracy in line. I can assure the Members that our committee will fully exercise such authority."[27] Of course, such vigor has rarely surfaced. Representatives Bella S. Abzug and Edward I. Koch of New York supported the Gude amendment, which was defeated by a vote of twenty-nine to nine. Koch argued that "we must have some kind of a privacy board to regulate what will happen, and the functions of the Federal Privacy Board will be executed probably by OMB. But they will not be able to execute them as well, as efficiently, as ably as a Federal Privacy Board given the powers that the Gude amendment would give to it."[28]

The Senate passed both S. 3418 and H.R. 16373, including in both instances the provisions for a privacy protection commission.[29] Senator Ervin noted the judgment of the Government Operations Committee "that such a Commission is necessary to assist in implementing the bill, to police violations, and to assist both Congress and the executive branch in controlling the Federal Government's incursions of the privacy of Americans."[30] Other prominent senators supported Ervin. Republican Senator Charles Percy pointed out that the "nonregulatory commission . . . will perform two crucial roles, both as an adviser to Federal agencies who must implement this legislation, and as an adviser to Congress, recommending legislative solutions to the chief privacy problems of the private sector. . . . Until the agencies develop and adopt adequate rules and procedures, effective oversight can and must be performed by experts who understand the technology and yet who are sensitive to the basic question of how to protect privacy. This is the central reason for establishing the Commission."[31] Senator Howard Baker stated that "as an advocate of increased congressional and Presidential oversight of Federal intelligence gathering, surveillance, and law enforcement agencies, I believe that an independent Privacy Protection Commission . . . will facilitate legislative and executive oversight through creating a central clearing house for ascertaining the character and existence of all Federal information systems and by bearing a positive responsibility to monitor governmental data system procedures and policies."[32] When Senator Roman Hruska of Nebraska objected to the vast responsibility and supervisory power of the proposed commission, Senator Ervin responded that "this is a very simple bill, with simple features. It is necessary to give the Privacy Commission some power to enforce it; otherwise, it will be just a hollow piece of legislative mockery on the statute books."[33]

As the 1974 session of Congress drew to a close, Senator Ervin accepted a compromise whereby the proposed privacy protection commission was transformed into the Privacy Protection Study Commission and the oversight role for the Privacy Act was assigned to OMB.[34] The compromise was a product of pressures on congressional time, the desire to pass some privacy legislation in the wake of the Watergate affair, the desire to honor Senator Ervin in his last term, resistance to the creation of more bureaucracies, and the risk of a presidential veto. President Ford signed the Privacy Act into law on December 31, 1974, and it became effective on September 27, 1975.

Formative Influences

The problems of surveillance of the public in the United States are comparable to the size and scope of the country. OMB states that "the Federal Government is the largest single producer, consumer, and disseminator of information in the United States."[35] It would probably be fair to extend this characterization to the U.S. government's ranking in the entire world. The federal government is also the largest consumer of computer and information technology. One reason is the huge size and complexity of the federal government and the population of 244 million, easily dwarfing the other countries studied in this volume. Implementing data protection to limit governmental surveillance is thus a formidable task, whatever structural model is adopted. The highly decentralized federal system also guarantees a minimum of automatic data protection, especially with respect to data transfers among government agencies, which are jealous about their prerogatives and sensitive to public outcries about governmental invasions of privacy.

In fact, surveys demonstrate that Americans continue to be concerned about the protection of their personal privacy. A major 1979 public opinion poll showed the public favors a privacy protection commission.[36] The Office of Technology Assessment's recent review of privacy surveys found that "privacy continues to be a significant and enduring value held by the American public, as documented by several public opinion surveys over the last 6 years."[37] Protecting personal privacy, especially in the context of ensuring data protection in personal information systems maintained by government agencies, is a fundamental political issue that unites individuals of varying political persuasions, because of the extent to which it is founded upon concern for individualism and human dignity.

The U.S. federal system of data protection has two important attributes. Despite the absence of a data protection commission, there is a network of people and organizations, inside and outside of government, that attempts to perform similar oversight functions. Most importantly, the House of Representatives' Subcommittee on Government Information, Justice, and Agriculture pays continuing attention to the implementation of the Privacy Act and the Freedom of Information Act. On June 7 and 8, 1983, it held the first oversight hearings on the Privacy Act.[38] The subcommittee's small staff of lawyers performs some of the tasks of a data protection commission by trying to oversee legislative proposals and administrative practices in the executive branch that have an impact on surveillance practices and by prodding OMB to action. The work of this subcommittee is also sometimes matched or supplemented on specific issues by other committees and subcommittees of the House and Senate.

Congress also requests the Office of Technology Assessment (OTA) to carry out various studies of the impact of technology on personal privacy and civil liberties.[39] OTA's reports perform a useful service in drawing attention to specific privacy problems and evaluating policy options. On more specific matters, Congress also obtains research assistance from the Congressional Research Service of the Library of Congress and the General Accounting Office.

Much of the pressure on the federal government to protect privacy comes from lobbying by advocacy groups, such as the Washington office of the American Civil Liberties Union (ACLU); specialist journalists, especially David Burnham, until recently of the *New York Times;* and specialist newsletters, such as the *Privacy Journal* and *Privacy Times.* Ronald L. Plesser, former general counsel to the Privacy Protection Study Commission, is an example of a number of lawyers and lobbyists who pay continuing attention to privacy issues.

Dependence on litigation to enforce significant parts of the Privacy Act reflects the litigiousness of American society. Individuals have to file suit in federal court to enforce rights granted to them under the Privacy Act, because there is no intermediary between the citizen and the government institution. Litigation is expensive and complex, because of the lack of injunctive relief and the high standards developed by the courts for proof of damages for invasion of privacy.

The Organization of Data Protection

The United States is a notable exception to the premise that locating the effective national agent for the implementation of data protection is an easy task. Most important, there is no data protection agency as such. Second, and this is not unusual, the head of each government agency is ultimately responsible for implementation. The Office of Management and Budget, congressional committees, and the courts are expected to exercise limited official oversight of what actually happens.

Basically, OMB, and arguably Congress, want agencies to implement the Privacy Act and related legislation without their direct involvement. OMB emphasized this point most recently in its important 1985 circular on the management of federal information resources.[40] The premise is that each agency has to handle its own information decisions and its own privacy issues. The main way in which outsiders can monitor information handling practices is to review the reports on new and substantially altered information systems that agencies are required to submit to Congress and OMB and to publish in summary form in the *Federal Register* under the Privacy Act. This public notice requirement also applies to disclosures from a system of records pursuant to a routine use and proposals to exempt a system from any provision of the Privacy Act.[41]

OMB is the closest approximation to a data protection agency, although it is artificial to treat it as such, because OMB's current perception of its duties is so passive. Section 6 of the Privacy Act determines that OMB shall "develop guidelines and regulations for the use of agencies in implementing the provisions" of section 3 of the law and "provide continuing assistance to and oversight of the implementation of the provisions of such section by agencies." Under President Carter's Paperwork Reduction Act of 1980, the director of OMB delegated these functions to the newly created Office of Information and Regulatory Affairs (OIRA) within OMB. Except for the fact that it has failed to issue regulations on the specious grounds that OMB only issues nonbinding guidelines, it is at least arguable that OMB is in fact doing all that it is required to do. During the 1983 oversight hearings, Christopher DeMuth, then administrator of OIRA, subtly restated the second part of section 3 to limit its scope, by noting the requirement to oversee the act's "procedural mechanisms to insure that agencies comply with them." He added: "From the outset, we realized that the only way we could insure a successful implementation was to institutionalize the act's requirements, as well as its spirit, in every agency's operation. The guidance we issued initially was designed to give each agency head enough information to develop effective Privacy Act management programs for his or her agency."[42] This conception is similar to the role played by Canada's Treasury Board, except that there is no equivalent to the privacy commissioner of Canada to monitor compliance.

On paper, the Office of Information and Regulatory Affairs plays a major role. Its administrator is appointed by the director of OMB and reports directly to him as the principal adviser on federal information policy.[43] Prior to 1980, a few individuals in OMB's Information Systems Policy Division conducted Privacy Act oversight. The creation of OIRA, with its desk-officer configuration, "made a fundamental change in the way Privacy Act oversight was to be accomplished."[44] James C. Miller III, the first administrator of OIRA and subsequently the director of OMB, made a radical change (and acquired considerable power) by ensuring that his office reviewed all federal regulations prior to publication.

There are about sixty-five desk officers at OIRA, whose responsibilities include oversight of the Privacy Act. Each officer is responsible for overseeing the information resources management activities of one or more agencies. They review submissions from agencies and interact as necessary with their agency counterparts. OMB explains that "while reviews of Privacy Act specific submissions are but a small part of this overall review process (agencies typically submit around 100 reports of new and altered system of records annually), many of the other kinds of reviews have Privacy Act implications." These include submissions on information collection practices, budgets for technology, and proposed regulations. OMB's argument is that "these kinds of reviews complement the reviews that are required by the Privacy Act. They enlarge the oversight process by giving desk officers more comprehensive information about the practices of their agencies."[45]

Desk officer Robert N. Veeder "is the lead Privacy Act expert" in the office and "spends a very large proportion of his time on the Privacy Act." He briefs other desk officers and obtains additional help from the general counsel's office, when necessary. Privacy Act matters can be raised in the staff meetings that occur several times a week. Veeder in effect is the Information Policy branch within OIRA, which has responsibility for developing and issuing Privacy Act policy, reviewing legislative proposals, preparing the president's annual report, issuing guidance to executive agencies, and conducting training sessions.[46]

Until 1986, when she left government service, Assistant General Counsel Cecilia Wirtz of OMB handled legal issues and interpretations for the Privacy Act on a government-wide basis.[47] The Department of Justice plays almost no role in this area; its Office of Information and Privacy concentrates on freedom of information issues. Wirtz fielded legal queries about the law and also did the basic training on behalf of OMB. She was an example of a small number of persons with long experience at OMB who had considerable knowledge of the Privacy Act. Others included Robert Bedell, the deputy administrator of OIRA from 1983 to 1986, who had served in the general counsel's office since 1973, including collaboration with Congress in the drafting of the 1974 law.[48] The only person with similar experience still at OMB is Franklin Reeder.

At present, there is at best one full-time person at OMB overseeing implementation of the Privacy Act. The General Accounting Office's description of thirty-nine key OIRA tasks indicates that only two of them, dealing with information sharing and disclosure, have a direct bearing on privacy and confidentiality.[49] The low priority at OMB of implementation activities concerning the Privacy Act is quite clear.

OMB has been imaginative in selectively delegating its Privacy Act responsibilities throughout the executive branch. As restated in Circular A-130, various duties to give policy guidance are assigned to the Office of Personnel Management, the General Services Administration, the National Bureau of Standards in the Department of Commerce, and the National Archives and Records Administration. The Department of Justice has also issued guidance in the form of several letters.[50] Yet OMB retains its own duty to "review agencies' policies, practices, and programs pertaining to the security, protection, sharing, and disclosure of information, in order to ensure compliance with the Privacy Act and related statutes."[51]

Each federal agency is of course ultimately responsible for its own implementation of the Privacy Act, but this has not meant much over time in terms of the commitment of personnel and resources. Access requests from individuals are frequently handled by Freedom of Information Act personnel. A May 22, 1979, directive from the director of OMB required each agency head to designate an office or official to bear oversight responsibility for the administration of the Privacy Act within that agency; either there was no response or the result is what exists today, where some departments do have Privacy Act, Paperwork Reduction Act, and Freedom of Information Act officers. One trend is to combine these duties into the function of information officers, a process which OMB's 1985 circular on the management of federal information resources might promote.[52] OMB certainly encourages a few people at the general counsel's office of individual agencies to be knowledgeable about the Privacy Act. But most Privacy Act officials are relatively invisible, especially in terms of actually influencing agency policy on surveillance.

A major exception is the Department of Defense, which created its own internal data protection agency, the Defense Privacy Board, on April 8, 1975. It has representation at a very senior level from all parts of the department, its own executive secretary, and four full-time specialists in the Defense Privacy Office.[53] Plesser has described this board as "an institutional home for privacy protection," which can try to "create an atmosphere in which privacy can to a certain extent be an operating goal of that agency. This example exists nowhere else in Government."[54]

Thus, a few federal officials have acquired considerable expertise over time on the Privacy Act and have an unusual impact on its implementation. They constitute an informal network of data protection officials.[55] But, it must be admitted, such individuals have limited power.

In 1983, Plesser drew the following conclusion about agencies' efforts to implement the Privacy Act:

> The agencies by and large find the Privacy Act, in short, to be an annoyance. There is usually a person or two on the General Counsel's staff of most agencies whose job it is to see that the agency or Government department complies with the technical requirements of the Act or, in other words, stays out of trouble. One department, the Department of Health and Human Services, has one Privacy Act officer, outside of the Office of General Counsel, whose job is to be responsible for training, education, policy development and enforcement of the Privacy Act. He is sorely outnumbered. There are at least a thousand employees in the Office of Inspector General of the Department of Health and Human Services alone. . . . That sole individual at HHS in actuality spends most of his time guiding his 'clients' through the maze of the Privacy Act so that they can obtain their goals rather than as a voice for privacy in that massive agency which deals with millions and millions of privacy-related files every day.[56]

The executive branch until recently had another group of privacy specialists, beginning with the Office of Telecommunications Policy under President Gerald Ford. It became the National Telecommunications and Information Administration (NTIA) during the Carter years, when it played an active role.[57] Even in the first few years of the Reagan presidency, NTIA had three or four persons studying various aspects of privacy and information policy, including promotion of American private-sector compliance with the guidelines on protection of privacy of the Organization for Economic Co-operation and Development. When the Reagan administration decided that it had no interest in privacy, NTIA's work was phased out.[58] OMB strongly believes that such "outsiders" are relatively ineffective and that agencies have to handle their own privacy problems. Nevertheless, for a government the size of the United States, the minimal investment in NTIA was surely productive, especially in terms of giving foreign data protectors a contact point for issues of transborder data flow. The initial reliance on the Office of Telecommunications Policy was even better in political terms, because of its location within the Executive Office of the President.

Although the Privacy Act is silent on the matter, OMB perceives itself to share parallel oversight responsibility with subcommittees of Congress.[59] To the limited extent that such oversight has occurred, it has been the work of the Subcommittee on Government Information, Justice, and Agriculture of the House Committee on Government Operations, chaired by Congressman Glenn English of Oklahoma, and the Subcommittee on Oversight of Government Management of the Senate Committee on Governmental Affairs, chaired by Senator William S. Cohen of Maine. In fact, the House Subcommittee does a good job of watching OIRA and individual agencies and encourages OMB to play a more aggressive oversight role under the Privacy Act. Cohen chaired important hearings on oversight of computer matching in 1982 and 1986 (see Chapter 29).

The essential problem of relying on such subcommittees for oversight is that they are political creatures, burdened with all of the usual political concerns of elected representatives, and it is very difficult to persuade them to give sustained attention to any one issue. The saving grace in most cases is that each of these subcommittees has a few talented staff members who perform essential functions. The persistent work of Congressman Don Edwards and his staff in overseeing the development and use of the Federal Bureau of Investigation's National Crime Information Center demonstrates that such congressional oversight can be effective.

In general, Congress demonstrates a predictable lack of interest in a specialized bill that has become a law, even though Senator Ervin recognized that his Senate committee would have to engage in aggressive oversight in order to make up for the failure to create a privacy protection commission.[60] In fact, lack of oversight of this law has been especially true of the Senate, where there has been no center of concern for privacy legislation comparable to the English subcommittee in the House.

Congress does commission various studies of privacy issues from such service groups as the Congressional Research Service, the Office of Technology

Assessment, and the General Accounting Office. OTA has been especially active in the 1980s. GAO has done a number of important reviews of compliance with the Privacy Act by various agencies. Additional studies of such matters as computer matching and agency implementation of the Privacy Act appeared in 1986 and 1987.

Chapter 26

The Goals of Data Protection

This chapter identifies the purposes of the original U.S. Privacy Act in order to obtain some sense of their relevance for confronting surveillance problems directly and for giving data protectors a clear and specific mandate. This is a useful exercise, because Congress began with the ambition of placing some limits on governmental surveillance. It found that "the increasing use of computers and sophisticated information technology, while essential to the efficient operations of the Government, has greatly magnified the harm to individual privacy that can occur from any collection, maintenance, use or dissemination of personal information." In order to "provide certain safeguards for an individual against an invasion of personal privacy," section 2 of the Privacy Act further required federal agencies, "except as otherwise provided by law," to "permit an individual to determine what records pertaining to him are collected, maintained, used, or disseminated by such agencies."[1]

Various public notice requirements are imposed on federal agencies under the act, including explanations to individuals at the point of data collection, advance notice to the public of new or "substantially" altered systems, proposed routine uses, and proposed exempt systems of records, and, until recently, an annual publication listing all agency systems in the *Federal Register*.[2] One of the significant limitations of this otherwise admirable series of requirements is the arcane character of the *Federal Register* as a source of information for the general public. Yet system disclosure is one of the demonstrable, continuing benefits of the Privacy Act in controlling surveillance.

Section 3(a) of the Privacy Act contains several problematic definitions, including the meaning of a "record" and a "system of records." In essence, as encapsulated by John Shattuck of the American Civil Liberties Union, "a record maintained by a federal agency (1) must contain specific information about a person whose name or other particular means of identification appears on the record and (2) must be contained in a system of records from which information can easily be retrieved by the name of the individual or by some other identifying particular." The courts and other commentators have further clarified the meaning of these definitions and identified certain ensuing problems.[3] There is a plausible case for replacing the concept of a system of records by the notion of "any individually identifiable record," so as to spread wider the net of personal data brought under the act.[4]

The Office of Management and Budget's circular on information resources management reinforces the controls on data processing in the Privacy Act by instructing agencies to "create or collect only that information necessary for the proper performance of agency functions and that has practical utility, and only after planning for its processing, transmission, dissemination, use, storage, and disposition." Agencies are also instructed to "limit the collection of individually identifiable information and proprietary information to that which is legally authorized and necessary for the proper performance of agency functions."[5] Such language indicates how governmental surveillance could be better limited, if institutions followed OMB's instructions. Yet this circular only established a framework for action, which remains to be made more effective.

Although the Privacy Act has a clear preoccupation with the data protection aspects of preserving privacy, with Congress finding in section 2 that "the right to privacy is a personal and fundamental right protected by the Constitution of the United States," it typically does not define privacy or privacy interests, beyond including a code of fair information practices in section 3(e). Although it is typical to delegate the development of appropriate, specific standards in such circumstances to a particular agency, Congress failed to do so in the final version of the legislation. Thus the federal courts have largely continued to define the "right to privacy" and the meaning of data protection in discrete cases under the Privacy Act, but this has had little effect on systemic implementation. OMB's policy guidance is only a little more specific than the original legislation. Circular A-130 states that agencies shall "maintain and protect individually identifiable information and proprietary information in a manner that precludes: (a) unwarranted intrusion upon personal privacy . . . ; and (b) violation of confidentiality."[6]

The Privacy Act includes strong language concerning the collection and dissemination of personal data. The purpose clause in section 2(b) requires federal agencies to "collect, maintain, use or disseminate any record of identifiable personal information in a manner that assures that such action is for a necessary and lawful purpose, that the information is current and accurate for its intended use, and that adequate safeguards are provided to prevent misuse of such information." But it was a harbinger of actual agency practices that the first substantive section of the Privacy Act identifies a dozen conditions under which personal information may be disclosed.[7]

Because no external agent actually audits or really questions the information-handling practices of federal agencies, it is impossible to know how the Privacy Act's standards are being applied in practice, although considerable skepticism has been expressed over the years. There is general agreement that the broad limitation on collection is not very effective, because OMB only exerted pressure on this point in the first few years of implementation, and Congress often requires the data collection in the first place. Although the Privacy Protection Study Commission admittedly conducted its review of implementation in the early stages, its 1977 report was fairly harsh about the lack of noticeable effect on agencies of the provisions limiting collection, use, and disclosure.[8] Christopher Vizas, then a staff member of the House Subcommittee on Government Information, Justice, and Agriculture, stated in 1982 that the careful recommendations of the study commission had been ignored and that the government continued to collect massive amounts of personal data in an unregulated fashion.[9]

The debate over the effectiveness of controls on disclosure in the Privacy Act has focused in particular on the concept of routine use. An agency is permitted to disclose a personal record "for a purpose which is compatible with the purpose for which it was collected."[10] Although Congress inserted the provision because of the difficulty of enumerating all of the permitted exceptions to the disclosure restrictions, it is unlikely that it ever intended the extent to which "routine uses" have become a huge loophole rather than a barrier. The standard of compatibility is nowhere defined in the law, and the head of the agency, perhaps supplemented by the courts, is the ultimate arbiter of what it means.

OMB has made a significant effort to provide meaningful policy guidance, but a recent report on the Privacy Act concludes that

even a casual examination of agencies' routine uses suggests that agencies interpret the concept of compatibility to permit uses that are neither functionally or programmatically related to the original collection purpose. In some cases this is due to requirements imposed by statute. . . . In other cases, it is due to a deliberate interpretation on the part of the agency that a particular disclosure would be "necessary and proper" to the operation of a governmental program. This interpretation looks more to the literal definition of compatibility—capable of existing together without discord or disharmony.[11]

OMB actually recommended at the end of 1985 that Congress reconsider this problem of routine uses and provide clearer guidance on routine use disclosures. However, a year later its Circular A-130 seemed to promote data sharing by recommending that agencies shall "seek to satisfy new information needs through legally authorized interagency or intergovernmental sharing of information, or through commercial sources, where appropriate, before creating or collecting new information."[12] Increased reliance on the private sector would further spread the government's surveillance net over the public.

The Privacy Protection Study Commission and the 1983 oversight hearings on the Privacy Act both paid considerable attention to the problem of routine uses.[13] John Shattuck concluded that "the rule limiting disclosure of personal information without the subject's consent has been all but swallowed up by its exceptions, particularly the broad exception for undefined 'routine uses.' . . . In practice this has come to mean any use which an agency deems to be appropriate. So long as a 'notice of routine use' is published in the *Federal Register,* just about anything goes." He especially condemned its use to justify computer matching.[14] Ronald Plesser testified about the routine use notice published by the Federal Bureau of Investigation (FBI) for its general criminal record system, which effectively permits it to disclose anything to anyone it wants: "What they have done is totally legal. . . . They have the freedom and the discretion to release it [records] to the general public, to the press, to other law enforcement agencies, to State and local agencies, where they feel there is a legitimate reason for it. That legitimate reason is essentially unreviewable by courts, certainly unreviewable by other agencies, and essentially the FBI can do with its records what it will. . . . If someone looks at the Privacy Act and thinks that it does, in fact, limit disclosure, I think that person is sorely mistaken." Plesser argued that although the current definition of routine use can and should be interpreted to mean something, it is simply unchallengeable in the courts at present, so that federal agencies are left free to define the term as they want and can use it to justify almost any disclosure.[15]

New York's 1983 Personal Privacy Protection Law wisely included a better definition of the term routine uses. It means, "with respect to the disclosure of a record or personal information, any use of such record or personal information relevant to the purpose for which it was collected, and which use is necessary to the statutory duties of the agency that collected or obtained the record of personal information, or necessary for that agency to operate a program specifically authorized by law."[16]

Chapter 27

The Power of Data Protection Agents

This chapter examines the proficiency of the various actors in the implementation of the Privacy Act to control governmental surveillance. The primary focus on the Office of Information and Regulatory Affairs (OIRA) of the Office of Management and Budget (OMB) is complicated by its multiple responsibilities for other significant governmental activities and its shared or delegated oversight roles with other actors.

Independence

The usual problems of adequately establishing the independence of a data protection agency do not exist with OMB since, as a part of the Executive Office of the President, it is in a very powerful position in the executive branch of government. It is a crosscutting agency with primary responsibility for budgetary and regulatory review throughout the federal government. The major caveat is that OMB is subject to the will of the president. As Ronald Plesser, a privacy advocate and former general counsel to the Privacy Protection Study Commission, testified in 1983, the Reagan administration "is not interested in privacy. . . . There is almost no activity."[1] Absent a conscious exercise in presidential leadership, OMB does nothing more than comply with a minimalist view of its responsibilities in areas that are not perceived as high priority or as politically relevant. If, as under the Reagan administration, OMB is the leader in the attempt to cut back the size and scope of the federal government and to balance the budget, there is no possibility that it will take an expansive view of its responsibilities under section 6 of the Privacy Act. As Plesser further testified, these interests are very important, but in some instances they "conflict with the creation of effective privacy protection."[2]

Compared to the other data protection agencies treated in this volume, OMB has no real independence from the political process that would allow it to stand up for privacy and to make sure that privacy interests are suitably articulated.[3] In the Reagan years, it was much more a proponent of government surveillance over individuals than interested in restricting it.

The Exercise of Intervention

The Office of Information and Regulatory Affairs shares the aura of power that surrounds OMB. Agencies pay attention to its desk officers because of

326 / *The United States*

their influence on the budgetary process and closeness to the White House. As the administrator in 1983 of OIRA then testified, "OMB is the central coordinating and management office in the Government, and if OMB believes that a certain practice or policy of an agency is inconsistent with what the President would want, or with established policies of the administration, or is not justified by the statute, obviously the agencies are going to pay attention."[4] But with respect to the Privacy Act, OMB sees its role as primarily one of giving policy guidance on implementation, as it did most recently in its 1985 circular.[5]

Under Reagan, OMB as an entity (as opposed to individual desk officers) had no interest in trying to limit governmental surveillance. Plesser testified that "OMB serves by answering questions. If there is a question under the Privacy Act, OMB answers that question. There are good, qualified, professional people there who answer the questions that are raised. They do not ask any questions. There is nobody in Government to ask questions about other people in Government."[6] Congressman Glenn English characterized the situation as one in which "OMB is going to get involved in things OMB wants to get involved in and is not going to get involved in things it does not want to get involved in. That is what the bottom line is." English suggested that OIRA "put the Privacy Act down on the list of issues that you are doing too little about. You are doing too little on this particular area."[7]

OMB's record on the implementation of the Privacy Act is especially interesting, because on occasion it does act in a way that illustrates its power to intervene. In 1982 OIRA commented in detail on nineteen system notices from the Department of Labor, which followed its specific recommendations in almost all cases.[8] The last available presidential report on the Privacy Act illustrates the office at work on issues pertaining to the Departments of Justice, Labor, and the Treasury, and the Central Intelligence Agency. The language of the following example is especially interesting, since it was written by OIRA: "OMB in reviewing a proposed Immigration and Naturalization Service (INS) system containing information about the prospective adoptive parents of foreign born orphans objected to the exemption of the system pursuant to sections (k)(1) and (k)(2) of the Privacy Act. After hearing the agency's explanation of the need on occasion to maintain classified information in these files, OMB withdrew its objection to the (k)(1) exemption, but remained firm on the inappropriateness of the (k)(2). INS republished the proposed notice deleting the (k)(2) exemption."[9] The OMB also acts to review specific matters, such as the adequacy of standards for computer security, in the course of its budgetary reviews of requests from specific agencies.[10]

An optimist might see in these examples a model of how OMB could successfully implement data protection if the political will existed to do so. OMB is clearly not reluctant to exercise oversight when it decides that it is important. The final interpretive paragraph of the 1985 circular on the management of federal information resources makes clear that "OMB intends to use existing mechanisms, such as the fiscal budget, information collection budget, and management reviews, to examine agency compliance with the Circular." It offers examples of how management reviews for the most recent budget year had concentrated on five crosscutting information issues.[11] Of course, occasionally giving the Privacy Act similar priority would do a great deal to improve the record of implementation. In the systems of data protection discussed earlier in this volume, the oversight specialists seek to ensure that privacy is given continuing attention; at best, OIRA depends on the commitment of individual desk officers to restricting governmental surveillance.

Unfortunately, the preferred OIRA approach to implementation of the Privacy Act is to let agencies run themselves without its direct and detailed involvement. It views itself as playing a coordinating role for central management and does not become involved in the minutia of program management.[12] For example, during the 1983 oversight hearings, Congressman English and Christopher DeMuth, the administrator of OIRA, discussed how OMB and an agency would determine whether a routine use of personal data was permissible in a particular case. DeMuth emphasized that although discussions might occur, the final decision is up to the agency concerned: "We do not approve or deny routine uses."[13] When the Department of Education initiated a computer match of student loan borrowers in August 1982 but did not publish the notice required by OMB's revised guidelines on matching until December, OIRA responded to a House question with this assertion: "OMB does not routinely monitor the operation of a matching program to ensure the matching guidelines are being followed any more than it monitors an agency's operation of a large automated data base to ensure that the implementing guidelines are being followed. The Privacy Act places responsibility for ensuring agency compliance squarely on the heads of the agencies."[14] In such ways has OMB abdicated real oversight responsibilities under the Privacy Act.

Protecting privacy is a very minor part of OMB's multiple activities. It does have some impact on agency practice with respect to surveillance but will not venture too far into an agency's affairs when such issues are at stake. Unfortunately, none of its surrogates, such as the Office of Personnel Management or the General Services Administration, can begin to match the power of OMB with their sister agencies.

Political power has primarily been used in a negative way in the United States with respect to the implementation of the Privacy Act. At the oversight hearings in 1983, John Shattuck, then national legislative director of the American Civil Liberties Union, correctly asserted that the Reagan administration had emasculated the privacy work of the National Telecommunications and Information Agency and had sharply curtailed enforcement of the Privacy Act by OMB.[15] It has also created a political climate hostile to privacy interests. The result is a power vacuum with respect to controlling governmental surveillance.

Chapter 28

The Implementation of Data Protection

Evaluating the efforts to limit governmental surveillance in the United States does not have the simplicity of focusing on one agency, although the Office of Management and Budget (OMB) will receive primary emphasis in this chapter because of its oversight responsibilities under the Privacy Act. It will also be necessary to examine the implementation of the law by individual agencies and the oversight exercised by Congress.

Supervision, Advising, and Training

Until 1980, responsibility for oversight of the Privacy Act at OMB was in the hands of one or two persons associated with the Information Systems Policy Division. It was not considered a significant activity, and little was done after the issuance of the 1975 guidelines on implementation of the Privacy Act. OMB plays only an advisory role and its advice is not binding on agencies. Its main function was to compile the annual report on the Privacy Act. Little more than a year after the Privacy Act came into effect, Franklin L. Reeder admitted that OMB did not know how it was working. He also offered a well-informed discussion of why it might be necessary at some future date to establish a privacy protection commission.[1]

The important 1975 guidelines on the implementation of the Privacy Act have never been turned into regulations.[2] However, OMB argues that its guidelines have the same effect as regulations. In its 1977 report the Privacy Protection Study Commission referred to "the modest oversight role assigned" to OMB under the Privacy Act and added that neither it, the Privacy Protection Study Commission, nor Congress have "had the staff nor the consolidated expertise necessary to evaluate each report submitted [on new or materially altered record systems]."[3] Such a task should be handled by a data protection agency.

In 1980 the Information Systems Policy Division of OMB issued an eighteen-page publication on the "Administration of the Privacy Act of 1974." It is an effective summary of what OMB was then doing to exercise its responsibilities. Despite the coherence of this particular document, there is little evidence that such procedures had a significant impact on individual agencies. OMB noted that its implementation approach, by minimizing issuance of regulations and detailed procedures, allowed each agency to have discretion in the manner in which it fulfilled its responsibilities under the Privacy Act.[4] It claimed to be closely monitoring administration of the act, calling the attention of agencies to apparent violations, and requesting them to take appropriate corrective action. If OMB had indeed vigorously carried out all of the activities described in this publication, its ongoing oversight would have been much more meaningful.

Section 3503 of President Carter's Paperwork Reduction Act of 1980 created the Office of Information and Regulatory Affairs (OIRA) at OMB. The subsequent reorganization in January 1980 resulted in the assignment of thirty to forty desk officers for each federal agency to handle forms clearance, reports on new information systems, and to review various types of regulations. Each desk officer now has privacy concerns with respect to how information is used and how it is safeguarded. As late as the end of 1981, there was some feeling among congressional staff and at OIRA that the new office would have a real impact on the protection of privacy.

The primary accomplishment of OMB remains the issuance of policy guidelines on the Privacy Act to federal agencies. Although these are nonbinding, they are nontrivial documents in terms of their effect and impact, since an agency normally does not want to incur the wrath of OMB. At present, OIRA is engaged in an effort to rewrite the 1975 guidelines on implementation "to respond to important case law, congressional actions, and Administration initiatives" and to make them more accessible by restructuring their presentation.[5] OIRA has been promising to revise the guidelines since 1983. Another administrator indicated in early 1986 that a comprehensive review was beginning and sought advice from interested parties. This is a significant initiative—not least because it can reawaken interest in the Privacy Act at both OMB and federal agencies—but no results have so far appeared.

In addition to various guidelines on computer matching and debt collection activities, which are discussed below, in 1986–87 OMB prepared guidance on the Privacy Act implications of agency systems (call detail programs) to monitor employees' use of the government's telecommunications system in order to deter unofficial use. Its method is to publish detailed guidance and allow thirty days for comments. This particular episode is a good example of important initiatives that OMB takes on occasion, since it had no imperative reason to become involved in this issue. The General Services Administration had already issued guidance on how to create and operate such a program of call detailing, whereas OMB's guidance "explains the ways in which the Privacy Act of 1974 affects any records generated during the course of call detail programs."[6] The guidance distinguishes between the initial simple record of a telephone call (the call detail report) and the records of administrative, technical, or investigative follow-up of a particular phone call (call detail information or records). Only the latter may specifically identify an individual. OMB cites call detail programs as an example of how "rapid growth in automated data processing and telecommunications technologies has created new and special problems relating to the Federal Government's creation and maintenance of information about individuals. At times, the capabilities of these technologies have appeared to run ahead of statutes designed to manage this kind of information, particularly the Privacy Act."

OMB emphasizes that the use of call detail records to control costs and determine *individual* accountability for telephone calls requires consideration of the Privacy Act. A telephone number linked to a name or some other identifying particular meets the statutory definition of a "record."[7] Using this record as a key to retrieve information from these files creates a statutory "system of records." Agencies are cautioned against using "artificial" means to avoid the effect of the Privacy Act: "By maintaining these records in conformance with the provisions of the Privacy Act, agencies can make certain that legitimate concerns about the implementation of call detail programs (e.g. improper use of the records for surveillance of employees, harassment, unfairness, and record accuracy) are dealt with in a procedural framework that was designed to deal with such concerns." Appendix I of these guidelines includes a model system notice for agencies to use for call detail records. OMB also applies the exceptions from disclosure without consent of the data subject in section (b) of the Privacy Act to call detail records systems and explains how they could be used. Examples of disclosures under section (b)(1) that would not be authorized are "to agency personnel to identify and harass whistle-blowers; to agency personnel who are merely curious to know who is calling whom." However impressive this OMB guidance on call detail programs is, the absence of a data protection agency helps to explain why only four government agencies, and no outsiders, commented on them after they were published in draft form.

OMB has delegated certain responsibilities under the Privacy Act. In particular, the Office of Personnel Management (OPM) oversees government-wide record systems that are physically maintained by an agency but subject to its central control. There are nine such personnel records systems covering more than 70 million individual records. OPM assured Congress in 1983 that this approach has proven to be "extremely effective in providing the tight controls envisioned by the Act to assure the privacy of individuals." In its view, "the types of questions we receive concerning the requirements of the Privacy Act and the dearth of court suits dealing with Privacy Act aspects of Federal personnel record keeping both indicate that the implementation of those requirements is being discharged properly."[8] Unfortunately, these are inadequate criteria to measure whether surveillance of government personnel is under strict control.

In terms of specific oversight activities for systems of records, OIRA continues to engage in forms clearance for personal information collection and reviews reports on new information systems, including proposed routine uses of data. Each year it receives a privacy report from each federal agency and prepares the president's report on the Privacy Act; admittedly, this report is usually several years late. OIRA also comments on proposed legislation.

Advance notices from agencies about proposed new or altered systems of records (RONS) are one of the most important tools at the disposal of OIRA's desk officers, who use checklists of various sorts to ensure compliance. Under section (o) of the Privacy Act, OIRA has to evaluate the probable or potential effect of such a proposal "on the privacy and other personal or property rights of individuals or the disclosure of information relating to such individuals." These systems notices are the only way, under the current system, for OMB to learn what is actually happening in agencies. Most reported systems of records have received some scrutiny under this process since 1975. The agency received 7,000 notices in the first four months after implementation, and in 1982–83 received an average of one hundred per year. This fairly small number indicates a problem with underreporting.[9]

OMB essentially requires agencies to send in reports on new or altered systems sixty days in advance of implementation. The stringent circumstances under which a report is required and its contents (transmittal letter, brief narrative statement, and supporting documentation) are most recently set forth in OMB's 1985 circular.[10] An agency is required to provide "an evaluation of the probable or potential effects of the proposal on the privacy of individuals." OMB reviews each such notice to "determine whether appropriate consideration has been given to personal privacy consistent with the letter, spirit and intent of the Act." The OMB desk officer's review of an agency's report on a new system requires filling out a form containing eighteen questions and preparing summary evaluation and comments.[11]

Various published materials make it possible to illustrate the periodic impact on agencies of OMB's review of new or altered systems. On July 26, 1982, the deputy administrator of OIRA wrote a four-page letter to the Department of Labor commenting in detail on fifteen proposed systems of records. The letter pointed out lack of justification for provisions on retention of data, questioned the basis for and clarified choices of exemptions, and restrained and narrowed proposed routine uses and sought to establish their purposes in order to bring them into conformance with the requirements of the Privacy Act. With respect to a system of Freedom of Information Act (FOIA) and Privacy Act records, OIRA stated that "we are dubious about your attempt to assert for this system whatever exemptions apply to the systems from which subject records come. We think this is a questionable practice." Even though it took the Department six months to reply, it almost totally followed OMB's suggestions for revisions.[12] The report on the Privacy Act for 1982–83 offers eight specific examples of OMB's commenting usefully on agencies' systems notices.[13]

Unfortunately, the General Accounting Office (GAO) reviewed fifty-three Privacy Act notices in 1987 and found twenty-nine to be deficient, leading Representative Glenn English to inform the director of OMB of this lack of agency compliance with the Privacy Act and urging remedial action. English said that many of the errors, "both major and minor, could have been easily corrected if responsible officials assigned even a low priority to meeting the Privacy Act's requirements."[14]

A second major area for OIRA's Information Policy branch and desk officers is scrutiny of agencies' proposed disclosures of personal information as a routine use exemption under section (b)(3) of the Privacy Act. Each agency submitting a new or altered system notice has to explain to OIRA "how each proposed [new] routine use satisfies the compatibility requirement of subsection (a)(7) of the Act."[15] Problems of definition and scope of the application of the concept of routine use go back to the earliest days of implementation.[16] OMB's latest proposed guidelines on call detail programs emphasize (with specific illustrations) that the central concept of compatibility to justify a routine use comprises both "functionally equivalent uses" and other "uses that are necessary and proper."[17] In this connection the "proposed model system notice for call details records" listed seven specific routine uses of records maintained in the system. Although the list seems expansive, it is an indication of how many such uses can be anticipated with enough forethought.

OIRA does regularly review routine use notices and occasionally calls a halt to a particular exaggerated practice. In 1980 OMB reviewed a report on a Department of Housing and Urban Development (HUD) system and "noted an apparent discrepancy between the stated effects the system will have on personal privacy and the routine uses listed in the system notice." It questioned the compatibility of such uses. The departmental Privacy Act officer quickly replied that HUD had deleted the blanket routine uses from the system notice.[18] OMB has had continuing interactions with the Central Intelligence Agency (CIA) concerning its proposed 1982 blanket routine use provision for all of its systems. Both OMB and the chairman of the House Subcommittee on Government Information, Justice, and Agriculture "expressed concerns about the extremely broad, open-ended nature of this disclosure provision," even though OMB did not comment on it at the time it was proposed. Subsequently, there have been meetings on the issue at the staff and general counsel's level. Although no solution has been achieved, the general counsel of the CIA agreed in a letter sent to OMB in 1983 to discuss "all reasonable alternatives to meet the various concerns expressed."[19]

As discussed in Chapter 27, the main problem with routine uses is that OMB can only try to persuade agencies, which have the final power of decision under the Privacy Act. OMB, however, can be very persuasive, because of its control of the federal purse strings, when a political will to act exists. There is no way at present for OMB to know for sure whether agencies are submitting the requisite notices. A similar problem has been documented in Canada, where government institutions are failing to notify the privacy commissioner of new consistent uses of personal data under section 9(3) of the federal Privacy Act. The Office of Technology Assessment (OTA) recently concluded that the routine use exemption "has been used for such a large number of information exchanges and for so many types that it now appears to mean that all uses of Federal records are permitted except those that are expressly prohibited."[20]

OIRA does meet with groups from federal agencies to conduct general or specific training on the Privacy Act. For example, its personnel participate in seminars conducted by the Justice Department's Legal Education Institute.[21] OMB's Circular A-130 also requires the head of each agency to "review annually agency training practices in order to ensure that all agency personnel are familiar with the requirements of the Act, with the agency's implementing regulation, and with any special requirements that their specific jobs entail."[22]

The only department that has attempted systematic training on the Privacy Act is Defense. Its Privacy Office, with assistance from the Privacy Act office at DHHS, created a two-day introductory training course on the law in 1981–82, at a time when the cadre of officials who had first implemented the law was dispersing. The three-person professional staff of this office have given this course all over the United States as part of an effort to train local managers to do their own training. The Defense Privacy Board has also distributed training materials on request to other federal agencies and, in 1988, issued a half-hour training film on the Privacy Act.[23] A certain amount of training on the Privacy Act and FOIA is also carried out by the American Society of Access Professionals, which is primarily made up of persons involved in various issues included under both laws.

A wide variety of individuals in the federal government becomes involved in activities related to the Privacy Act. The select group of desk officers at OIRA are in place, although the history of OMB's involvement with implementation of the statute assures that it does not have a high priority on their agenda. During the Reagan administration OMB was even more uninterested in privacy issues, since it is so attuned to the views of the White House. It does not see the issue as one of concern to many persons, noting in particular the few advocates in the Senate.

The Office of Management and Budget has never done any effective monitoring of the implementation and impact of the Privacy Act that can be compared to the work of the data protection agencies treated earlier in this volume. It has not even made the investment in human resources that characterizes the Department of Justice's effort to serve a policy role under the Freedom of Information Act through its Office of Information and Privacy.[24] OMB does not carry out inspections, audits, investigations, or handle complaints; in fact, it dislikes activities unrelated to the federal budget. At various times in the last several years OMB has indicated its awareness that there has been a complete lack of interest in the privacy issue, as reflected in both the House and the Senate. The absence of privacy advocates has meant that OMB's low profile on the Privacy Act has gone unchallenged, at least until the 1982 hearings on computer matching held by Senator Cohen and the oversight hearings held by the House Subcommittee on Government Information, Justice, and Agriculture in 1983.

OMB is not doing much more than it has ever done to provide useful oversight of the Privacy Act. It is evident that OIRA is almost out of the Privacy Act oversight business, except for the dedicated efforts of its Information Policy branch, which is essentially a one-man operation.[25] This type of information management was not of interest to the Reagan administration, despite the language of Circular A-130. The Privacy Act is regarded as a records management statute only and, in addition, a "liberal reform," despite the fact that protecting privacy can serve the stated conservative goal of keeping government out of private lives. Deregulation has become the predominant concern of OIRA, and various desk officers are now spending a considerable amount of time reviewing and checking for "onerous" regulations. With the exception of slowly revising various policy guidelines, OMB is doing next to nothing to implement the policy side of the Privacy Act.

OMB views its role under the Privacy Act as one of balancing the interests of privacy and the needs of government, which is a very limiting factor from the perspective of protecting privacy; someone in government has to articulate privacy interests on a continuing basis. OMB is hardly an impartial arm of the executive branch, nor is it an independent administrative agency.

One of the defenses available to OMB is that agencies are ultimately responsible for compliance with the Privacy Act. Especially with the publication of Circular A-130, OMB has not been shy about assigning specific review and reporting requirements to the head of each agency and requiring him or her to "be prepared to report to the Director, OMB, the results of such reviews and the corrective action taken to resolve problems uncovered." According to OMB, the head of each agency shall: annually review agency record keeping and disposal policies and practices; review every three years the routine use disclosures associated with each system of records; review every three years the exemption rules promulgated for each system of records; review annually each matching program in which the agency has participated either as a source or as a matching agency; and review annually each system of records notice to ensure that it accurately describes the system.[26] If all agencies complied faithfully with these requirements, the implementation of the Privacy Act would take a quantum leap forward.

Within federal agencies, implementation of the Privacy Act is a highly routinized activity in which ambitious personnel do not want to be involved. Given the low level of implementation and low morale, there is no incentive to be involved in such routine work as processing access requests. No senior administrator of an agency likes the Privacy Act or FOIA in practice, because they tend to interfere with daily work, and there is no outside agency pushing them to a more activist stance. Again, the Defense Privacy Board is a continuing exception to such generalizations, and there are no doubt pockets of active compliance within departments. The availability of the routine-use exception for data transfers and disclosures does take the pressure off operating agencies.

The experience of the Department of Health, Education, and Welfare's (now DHHS) Fair Information Practices unit in the first year of implementation was prophetic. Its initial communication on implementation to the major components of the department drew no responses. The bosses gave the new tasks to busy people, who were already overworked. The welfare division of the agency also had little sympathy with fair information practices, because it regarded its mission as reducing welfare fraud in the program of Aid to Families with Dependent Children by tracking down absent parents. This had led to the enactment of the Parent Locator Service in 1974 at the same time that Congress was passing the Privacy Act.[27] The welfare component was run by accountants and managers, who regarded welfare recipients as deserving intensive surveillance.

The president's annual report has generally done a good job of describing agencies' activities to comply with the Privacy Act and the various OMB guidelines. The general situation is one in which 80 percent of all federal agencies show little activity under the act, since they have few systems of personal information. The activities of seventeen agencies constitute over 80 percent of the government's total, including the largest holders of systems of records: the Department of Defense, the Department of Health and Human Services, and the Department of the Treasury. These three have had major successes since 1975 in deleting or consolidating systems of records. OMB explains that the "Department of Defense in recent years has conducted a program to better define and control personal record keeping within the Department. This effort has resulted in a substantial reduction in total systems."[28] All agencies put identifiable personal data in systems of records, claim exemptions to permit disclosure, and process requests from individuals for access to their data. They are clearly much more careful now than before 1975 in how they handle personal information and in emphasizing reliance on relevant information in decision making. They have also destroyed significant amounts of unnecessary data.[29]

Thus no one wants to deny that the Privacy Act has had an impact. In 1982 the Department of Labor, in what may have been a unique event, decided on its own to undertake a thorough review of all of its systems of records on a component-by-component basis. The purpose was to find any unreported systems of records, to identify systems for deletion or merger, and to determine if existing systems needed amendment, if existing routine uses were still needed and proper, and if appropriate exemptions had been published. This process did lead to a republication notice for all of its revised systems, which, as noted above, then created temporary trouble for the department with OIRA.[30] In the late 1980s a small number of other federal agencies undertook such systematic reviews on their own initiative.

Unfortunately, the federal norm is better represented in OTA's recent finding in a survey of federal agencies that

> 67 percent of agencies responding reported one (34 agencies) or less than one (33 agencies) full-time equivalent (FTE) staff assigned to Privacy Act matters. . . . Only 7 percent of agency components (7 out of 100) responding reported having 10 or more FTEs assigned to Privacy Act matters. Five of these components were located in the Department of Justice and included the Drug Enforcement Agency, Immigration and Naturalization Service, Federal Bureau of Investigation [the largest num-

336 / The United States

ber, 65], and Criminal Division. The other agencies with more than 10 FTEs assigned to the Privacy Act were the Social Security Administration and the Office of the Secretary in the Department of Commerce.[31]

Most of these persons spend their time processing access requests. OTA also found that few agencies had prepared their own internal guidelines on implementation of the Privacy Act or conducted quality audits of their information-handling practices.[32]

As noted above, the Defense Privacy Board is an exception to a record of relative inactivity by agencies: "The Board today continues to serve as the principal policy maker for the Defense Privacy Program and the focal point for implementation on privacy matters for the Department of Defense."[33] It is chaired by the deputy assistant secretary of defense for administration. The full-time executive secretary, William T. Cavaney, also serves as a member and directs the Defense Privacy Office, which provides support for the board. It has met on average about eight times a year. The board had working groups to assist it in the early days of implementation. Now it only has a Legal Committee, which meets about four times a year, and has issued at least fifty-five formal opinions with the assistance of the general counsel's office. These decisions, which have been published in a pamphlet by the Department of the Army, cover a whole series of broad topics and are not narrowly legal.[34] They attempt to ensure consistent application of the law.

The Department of Defense set up its Privacy Board to ensure consistent application of the law by its seventeen components, which have 3.5 million civilian and military employees. It has contacts in each agency. The board is concerned with giving advice on policy issues only, not the details of implementation. It estimates that perhaps one-half of the persons processing records have not had Privacy Act training, which explains the continued emphasis on education.

The House Subcommittee on Government Information, Justice, and Agriculture is the only one in Congress that regularly becomes involved in implementation of the Privacy Act. The vehicle is the requirement under section (o) of the law that each agency send new and altered system reports to the President of the Senate and the Speaker of the House of Representatives as well as to OMB. Robert Gellman, subcommittee staff director, reads all such notices, paying particular attention to routine uses. About one out of fifteen notices prompts him to make inquiries of the agency. Chairman Glenn English then sends complaints to the agency and to OIRA, if necessary. The president's annual report on the Privacy Act regularly notes that this House subcommittee has questioned an agency's practices. In the years 1982–83, these interventions involved the Departments of Health and Human Services, Interior, Justice, Labor, Treasury, the Veterans Administration, and the CIA.[35]

In 1984 the House subcommittee requested the General Accounting Office to conduct a selective audit of departmental compliance with the Privacy Act. The result is a devastating analysis of the weaknesses of implementation.

GAO concluded that "the role and functions of agency Privacy Act officers are less than needed to effectively coordinate and oversee the implementation of the act." Significant functions under the law are not assigned to these officers, all mid-level managers, who lack the requisite resources: "10 of the 14 Privacy Act officers spent less than half their time on privacy matters; two were full time. Five had no staff. Nine had staff but for seven of these officers, their staffs spent less than one full staff year on Privacy Act matters." GAO found that the risk assessments to ensure the security and confidentiality of records, as required by the law, were not being carried out.[36]

GAO learned that systematic reviews of compliance with the Privacy Act were not occurring in the sampled agencies. Privacy Act officers were able to identify only five reviews relating to the law's operations in four of the six agencies since 1980. GAO also found that little systematic attention was being paid to OMB's 1985 Circular A-130. The auditors concluded that "Privacy Act operations need a cohesive, articulated program aimed at assuring that such activities are conducted in full compliance with OMB guidance and the act's provisions. In our opinion, without more active involvement and monitoring by both OMB and agencies, there will be less than full assurance that Privacy Act functions are carried out in a manner that protects the privacy rights of individuals and balances these rights with the information needs of federal agencies." GAO urged the director of OMB to oversee actively the implementation of the law.[37]

Inventories of Federal Personal Data Systems

The Privacy Act requires two types of publication by agencies concerning the systems of records in their possession. Section (e)(4) requires each agency to publish a notice of the existence and character of a system of records upon establishment or revision.[38] Section (f) requires each agency to promulgate rules to facilitate individual access to each system of records. The Office of the Federal Register annually compiles and publishes the agency notices and access rules.[39] The utility of publishing such an annual compilation of all agency systems in its present form is questionable, since the volumes are unknown to, and certainly unused by, the general public for the purposes of understanding governmental surveillance.

Under section (p) of the Privacy Act, OMB published its own 200-page inventory of agencies' systems of records in annual reports on the Privacy Act from 1975 to 1978. From 1979 to 1981, OIRA continued to maintain this automated inventory of federal personal data systems but did not publish it for reasons of economy. Copies were available from OIRA, but no requests were received, which suggests the extent of outside oversight of the Privacy Act. When the Congressional Reports Elimination Act altered the reporting requirements for OMB in 1982, it ceased to maintain this inventory.[40]

Various proposals have been made to improve the availability to the general public of pertinent, easy-to-use information about federal personal data systems. OIRA told Congress in 1983 that neither the publication in the daily *Federal Register* nor the annual compilation volume gave the public adequate notice. Since the compilations sell so poorly, even the Government Printing Office has refused to stock them. OIRA feels that the annual, updated publication requirement is still necessary as a source of information to the public, an agency itself, and the oversight agency. It urged Congress to amend section (f) of the law to give the Office of the Federal Register the authority "to develop a version of the present compilation that is less costly to produce but contains the essential information of the present version." It understood that such a streamlined version with fewer data was under consideration. It also urged the issuance of a regulation to require any agency to make available to any requester the full text of any system notice. The Defense Privacy Board also urged the House Subcommittee to require the annual publication of basic information about each system of records.[41]

In a 1986 study, the Office of Technology Assessment concluded that "in an age of electronic record systems, it is difficult for an agency to keep an accurate catalog of all record systems, both because of the number of systems and because of the continual electronic changes and manipulations." Moreover, the large number of agencies that retain personal data and "the intricacies of their uses and disclosures of information are such that it appears almost impossible for most individuals to monitor how information is being used."[42] Such collective ignorance facilitates a tolerant milieu for governmental surveillance.

Individual Access to Data and Complaints

In order to provide safeguards for an individual against unfair information practices, the Privacy Act "permits an individual to gain access to information pertaining to him in Federal agency records, to have a copy made of all or any portion thereof, and to correct or amend such records." The law further states the rules for how agencies are to facilitate the exercise of access and correction rights.[43]

There are various problems in measuring the use of access rights under the Privacy Act, because of overlap with FOIA, the practice of informal access, and differences in counting procedures. Agencies only began to report the number of access requests to OMB in 1977, and over two million were recorded to June 1983. OIRA estimated then that there were several hundred thousand requests each year to federal agencies, of which over 96 percent were granted. Under conditions specified in section (k) of the statute, certain systems of records may be exempt from individual access. About 14 percent of the 4,700 systems of records are exempt; these are almost all maintained by twelve agencies. They received 73,776 access requests in 1982, and just over 1 percent of them were totally denied.[44] Some agencies only seem to count the number of requests to such exempt systems. For example, the Veterans Administration created its first exempt system in 1983 and reported 44,867 requests for access versus none the previous year. It further "noted that it typically receives and processes annually over 100,000 requests that are subject to the Privacy Act" but, in line with OMB directives, it only reports the number of those requests that cite the statute.[45]

Most agencies with major holdings of records report declining figures for access requests, at least on the basis of the restrictive OMB definition. Defense typically explains that it encourages individuals and its own employees to seek informal access. According to OMB, the law has had an effect in opening up materials "in the area of records the agencies would traditionally not have disclosed because of law enforcement, intelligence, security, or other similar concerns. Here, the record is encouraging. During the reporting period, agencies denied in their entirety only a very small number of requests; most requesters were given *some* information." At the same time, the number of requests to amend records in 1983 was only 2 percent of the number of total requests; of these only 5 percent were totally denied. OMB believes that agencies have informal systems to amend records that parallel informal and customary access practices.[46]

Reports to OMB by a few agencies, such as the Department of Justice and the CIA, suggest that processing and adjudicating access requests is a significant burden.[47] There are also temporary surges in numbers, such as at the Department of Transportation in 1982–83 because of air traffic controllers seeking records before and after their strike, and Coast Guard members seeking access to personnel records because of publicity about computerized matching programs for debt collection. The Department suggested that these activities "increased both military and civilian awareness of access rights under both the Freedom of Information Act and the Privacy Act."[48] More importantly, these episodes indicate the public's desire to use access rights when they have reason to believe that they are under surveillance, but the U.S. system of data protection makes this level of awareness unusual.

In a recent study, OTA determined that "it is nearly impossible for individuals to learn about, let alone seek redress for, misuse of their records. . . . The increased exchanges and uses of information by Federal agencies make it more difficult to determine what information is maintained and how it is used; therefore it is harder for an individual to correct or amend records."[49] These deficiencies are especially serious for the monitoring of surveillance practices.

There is no particular mechanism under the Privacy Act by which an individual may complain about information practices that are perceived as intrusive, and little is known about the number or nature of complaints received by individual agencies. OMB reported in a 1980 publication how it handled the situation: "Complaints about a particular agency's practices are usually answered by providing individuals with information on their rights and agency responsibilities under the Act and then referring the complaint to the responsible agency. Follow-up action with the agency is initiated only in those cases where the agency does not appear to be fulfilling its responsibilities under the Act."⁵⁰ At present, OMB itself receives very occasional complaints but knows nothing about complaints made to agencies.

In arguing in favor of congressional action to improve oversight of the Privacy Act, OTA described how "if an individual has a question about agency practices and procedures, it is difficult for him or her to find the appropriate person to contact in a Federal agency. If an individual wishes to challenge an agency use of personal information, he or she will not have clearly defined or effective recourse because of the problems with the damage remedies of the Privacy Act."⁵¹ Such conditions facilitate the institutionalization of surveillance societies.

Biennial Activity Reports

At the end of 1988, the Computer Matching and Privacy Protection Act amended the Privacy Act to require a biennial, rather than annual, report by the president concerning the administration of the law.⁵² Section (p) of the Privacy Act originally required the president to submit a consolidated report on behalf of all federal agencies that primarily emphasized the number of exempt record systems. OMB's first four reports averaged 300 pages in length, until it decided not to print its inventory of personal data systems, which helped to shrink the size of the next three reports to an average of only 25 pages.⁵³ In 1982 the Congressional Reports Elimination Act substantially broadened the reporting requirements to include describing the actions of the director of OMB to exercise oversight under section 6; describing the exercise of individual rights of access and amendment under section 3; "identifying changes in or additions to systems of records," and "containing such other information concerning administration of this section as may be necessary or useful to the Congress in reviewing the effectiveness of this section [3] in carrying out the purposes of the Privacy Act of 1974."⁵⁴ The House rejected an OMB and Senate effort to remove the requirement of an annual report from the law. OMB then argued that Congress was never commenting on the annual reports it was preparing, and agencies were simply replicating the previous year's data. At the 1983 hearings, Christopher DeMuth stated that he had no objection to the kind of reporting then called for under the law.⁵⁵

The first "annual" report that has appeared since the above covered 1982 and 1983 in 145 pages. It appeared at the end of 1985. The next report, which will also cover several years, has not yet appeared. The president's 1982–83 report is a considerable improvement over its predecessors, despite the optimistic conclusion of OMB's director that "agencies are continuing to implement the Act in a responsible way." The president's covering letter to the Senate and House is somewhat more temperate: "By all evidence, the agencies are implementing the Act with care and diligence and are conducting their activities in conformance with its provisions." In particular, the latest report contains insights into what OMB does to exercise oversight, the legislative priorities of the administration that have improved or were proposed to improve privacy protection, and a discussion of the areas of the act that may need administrative or legislative attention.[56]

The former version of section (p) of the Privacy Act implied that OMB needed to receive reports from agencies in order to produce a consolidated report. Although this language is no longer in the revised section, OIRA still requires such information in substantial amounts. The latest instructions in Circular A-130 require nine minimum sets of data from each agency.[57] The most novel include requests for public comments received on implementation activities and the number and description of matching programs participated in either as a source or a matching agency. In 1986 OMB asked departments for reports on automation of systems of records and also on training programs. Thus each agency prepares an annual report to OIRA, which is not published.[58] Thus the preconditions exist for OIRA to produce a biennial scorecard of government surveillance practices, if the political will existed for them to do so.

Public Relations

The Privacy Act is relatively unknown to the general public, and no one in the federal government does anything to publicize its existence. Only avid consumers of the *Federal Register* would benefit from the public notice requirements of the law. Moreover, anyone reading the Privacy Act would find it relatively incomprehensible at first glance, a situation, of course, that is true for the same laws in other countries. The annual number of known access requests is surprisingly small for a population of 244 million and further indicates lack of public awareness. The mammoth Department of Health and Human Services, with all of its social welfare data, received only 14,000 access requests in 1983, at least according to the OMB definition.[59]

Within the federal government, OMB does not publish a newsletter, even for federal agencies, on the Privacy Act but relies on repetitive telephone communications. OIRA should strengthen the resources of the Information Policy branch in order to facilitate the preparation of such a newsletter, following the model of the Canadian Treasury Board and the Department of Justice.

Shaping New Laws and Regulations

It is customary for data protection agents to play a significant role in shaping new laws and regulations that have an impact on personal privacy. Although Congress has passed at least nine acts since 1974 that have protected information privacy in one way or another, OMB was only involved to a significant extent in the Debt Collection Act of 1982.[60] Such successes as the Cable Communications Policy Act of 1984 and the Electronic Communications

Privacy Act of 1986 are the product of coalitions built around the staff of congressional committees, the privacy experts of the American Civil Liberties Union (ACLU), and lobbyists for the affected industries and trade associations. The Justice Department plays the key role for the administration in such cases.[61]

At the end of the Carter administration, OMB could still describe its role in the consideration of privacy in the legislative review process, especially for the legislative program of the executive branch.[62] That role has changed since 1980, since the Reagan administration has been more likely to try to invade privacy than to protect it. OIRA influenced the Debt Collection Act, the Deficit Reduction Act of 1984, and the proposed Payment Integrity Act amendments in 1986, which introduced and expanded the uses of computer matching of federal, state, and local data in order to conduct eligibility verification procedures for certain program applicants.[63] All three measures necessitate massive amounts of data sharing for surveillance purposes.

OMB reviewed these bills, because it sees all of the legislation being developed by the White House and Congress. OIRA raised a number of concerns about certain privacy implications of procedures for eligibility verification in particular. The Debt Collection Act added section (b)(12) to the Privacy Act, permitting agencies to disclose bad debt information to credit bureaus. OIRA apparently helped to shape additional measures requiring agencies, in advance of such a disclosure, to "validate the debt and the fact that it is overdue, contact the debtor and ask for payment, and offer him or her the right to challenge the validity of the debt." It is a measure of the Reagan administration's limited level of commitment to privacy protection that the president's annual report could trumpet this fact as the first of several "significant legislative initiatives to improve privacy."[64]

OMB did produce guidelines in 1983 on the relationship between the Privacy Act and the Debt Collection Act.[65] In fact, these complicated guidelines primarily illustrate the extraordinary extent to which the statute weakens some of the basic principles of the Privacy Act, mute testimony to the powerful pressures behind the effort for better debt collection by the federal government. The law not only created the (b)(12) exemption for disclosure but short-circuited the already weak controls on routine uses and created statutory authority for agencies to collect Social Security Numbers in certain federal programs. The guidelines further explain how even the Internal Revenue Service is required to release taxpayers' mailing addresses for purposes of the Debt Collection Act. During the Reagan years, as noted earlier, OMB's role in influencing legislation was more apt to encourage surveillance than to limit it.

The Privacy Act in the Courts

Individuals have to bring lawsuits to enforce their rights under the Privacy Act. Some observers still believe that the threat of such litigation is very useful in making progress with an agency, but the prevailing view is that section (g)(1) of the act is unenforceable in the courts. OMB reported in 1980 that 210 suits were filed in 1976–77 under the Privacy Act and that 101 were unresolved at the end of 1978.[66] OTA recognized in 1986 that the time and cost involved to sue is often prohibitive and quoted Richard Ehlke's study of litigation trends on the factors militating against the success of such cases.[67] Ronald Plesser, a practitioner in this field, is even more adamant: "The Privacy Act, to a large extent, is unenforceable by an individual," because courts have decided that it contains no injunctive relief, the plaintiff has to show that the government acted in a willful or intentional manner, the plaintiff may have to prove substantial physical injury, and the act's exemptions are overly broad.[68] John Shattuck of the ACLU essentially confirmed Plesser's negative judgment.

The Privacy Act also includes criminal sanctions in section (i)(1) that can be imposed against any officer or employee of an agency for willful disclosure of individually identifiable information or for willfully maintaining a system of records without meeting the public notice requirements. Fines of up to $5,000 can also be incurred by any person who knowingly and willfully requests or obtains any record from an agency under false pretenses. Few prosecutions have been brought under the act, so that if the criminal sanctions were an initial incentive for federal compliance, as some federal employees have publicly claimed, their absence has considerably lessened sensitivities on this score.[69]

Chapter 29

The Regulation of Computer Matching

This chapter essentially examines how the U.S. system of data protection has worked to date with respect to one of the most vexing privacy issues of the 1980s, record linkages, or what Americans call computer matching. It can be one of the most virulent forms of surveillance practiced by any government. The chapter traces the development of matching programs in the federal government and shows how the Office of Management and Budget tried to develop appropriate regulatory mechanisms in the form of guidelines on how the Privacy Act should be applied. Finally, the chapter identifies the challenges posed to personal privacy by various aspects of matching and describes the new controls created by the Computer Matching and Privacy Protection Act of 1988. The emphasis throughout is on the implications of computer matching for personal privacy and surveillance rather than on other grounds on which the practice can be challenged.

Matching programs originated during the administration of President Carter with the Department of Health, Education, and Welfare's (HEW) "Project Match" in 1977.[1] The Carter and Reagan administrations thus shared the specific goals of attempting to remove fraud, waste, and abuse from government programs. To illustrate the scope of the perceived problem, Inspector General Richard P. Kusserow of the Department of Health and Human Services (DHHS; the reformed HEW) noted in 1982 that his department had 5,000 computerized information systems, over 400 programs, and an annual budget in the neighborhood of $280 billion. He has a staff of 1,000 to pursue the mission of ending fraud, waste, and abuse.[2] A number of goals of the "community" of inspectors general are identical to the aims of good data protection, such as the use of computer matching as an editing and auditing function to remove inaccurate data from personal information systems. Kusserow in fact prefers to discuss "computer auditing" rather than computer matching.

The President's Council on Integrity and Efficiency in government (PCIE), composed of sixteen inspectors general, among others, has been the strongest proponent of computer matching as a management tool. It also reflected to a considerable extent the goals of the Reagan administration. PCIE has developed some good practices for matching programs that are in compliance with fair information rules, such as prohibiting any secret matches. Kusserow and his associates are not insensitive to issues of personal privacy. PCIE's working group on matching wanted from the very beginning to concentrate on the linkage of records at the time someone applies for a benefit (which is known as front-end verification), to publicize the practice because of its deterrent effect, and to use matching for both the underprivileged and elite groups.

Even under the umbrella of the Privacy Act and the OMB guidelines on the conduct of matching programs, PCIE alone is incapable of adequately balancing the sometimes conflicting interests of protecting the personal privacy of Americans versus such competing goals as reducing fraud. Such values as respecting the privacy of individuals and encouraging the efficiency of government have to compete on a more equal footing in order to achieve a satisfactory balance. What happened in the early 1980s is that the people with a special mission to end fraud and waste by surveillance were in the awkward position of simultaneously trying to protect privacy interests.

The current enthusiasm for matching programs is a typical search for a simple panacea for large problems that in some ways are almost hopeless; the enthusiasm is even greater, at least for a time, because the "fix" is technological. Placing too great an emphasis on matching programs to solve the problems of the Social Security Administration, for example, is to slight the more fundamental problems that this particular agency is facing.[3]

Although individuals will willingly give up a certain amount of personal privacy in return for obvious benefits, it is unwise to suggest, as some have done, that more than a few individuals will completely sacrifice their personal privacy. At the same time, the general public is heavily dependent upon existing laws and specialized advocacy groups to ensure the protection of their privacy interests in the process of increased and novel record linkages. One cannot reasonably expect an avalanche of public opinion to stimulate Congress and civil libertarians to vigilance in such specific, technical cases. In countries where data protection agencies exist, the legislature and the public can depend upon this specialized bureaucracy to exercise continuing oversight of surveillance practices, but OMB is not adequately playing this role in the U.S.

Even if alarmist views about omniscient and omnipresent computers are avoided, one cannot ignore the common situation in which the privacy implications of the use of a new technology, such as computer matching, are traditionally neglected in the rush toward some new form of "progress." New information technology usually is associated with the promotion of efficiency, which is clearly a very attractive goal for any government today. Yet the pursuit of efficiency and the suppression of fraud does not leave much room for consideration of such human values as privacy and confidentiality or for placing limitations on government conduct. This situation is independent of the rationale or the motivations prompting the development of such practices as matching programs; that the resulting capacity for surveillance is inadvertent does not mitigate the threat to the privacy interests of citizens.

Those seeking to justify matching programs have looked to the letter, rather than to the spirit, of the Privacy Act. Some even argue that they have ignored the letter of the law. Computer matching directly challenges congressional findings about the need to protect personal privacy set forth in section 2(a) of the Privacy Act, and the spirit, if not the letter, of computer matching is directly contrary to the intentions and aspirations of Congress set forth in the legislative history of the Privacy Act. The need for privacy safeguards holds true today with respect to the practice of computer matching.

The OMB Guidelines on Matching Programs

The OMB guidelines on matching programs of May 11, 1982, are expressly designed to be used in conjunction with its 1975 guidelines on implementation of the Privacy Act. Since the current guidelines seek to justify the transfer or release of personal information for matching purposes from one agency to another under the "routine use" provision of the Privacy Act, it is illuminating that the original guidelines stated that "one of the primary objectives of the Act is to restrict the use of information to the purposes for which it was collected."[4] The 1975 guidelines recognize that there are "corollary purposes . . . that are appropriate and necessary for the efficient conduct of government and in the best interest of both the individual and the public." Examples given in the guidelines of routine uses, as drawn from the *Congressional Record,* are described as "housekeeping measures." It is of course highly debatable whether the massive data transfers necessary for many matching programs fall under such an innocuous category. Furthermore, the 1975 OMB guidelines determine that "a 'routine use' must be not only compatible with, but related to, the purpose for which the record is maintained." Finally, the guidelines note that the requirement of advance public notice for routine uses is intended "to deter promiscuous use of this concept."[5]

In response to pressing demands from the Carter administration for guidance on computer matching, OMB produced draft guidelines on matching programs dated August 2, 1978, and a final version on March 30, 1979.[6] Jake Kirchner of *Computerworld* has described the frantic efforts made by administration lawyers, and even participants in the Carter Privacy Initiative, to find a justification for HEW's Project Match.[7]

Almost all of the privacy arguments still advanced against computer matching were acknowledged, at least in broad outline, by various government agencies and the Carter administration in the 1977–79 period. OMB itself clearly recognized in its memorandum accompanying the 1978 draft guidelines "that matching programs present the potential for significant invasions of personal privacy."[8] The relevance of this statement lies in the fact that in later editions of its matching guidelines OMB seems to have lost sight of this central worry about surveillance.

President Carter treated the guidelines on matching programs of March 30, 1979, as part of his Privacy Initiative. In submitting his legislative proposals to Congress, he made a statement about matching that is no less important today: "Safeguards are needed to protect the privacy of the innocent and to ensure that the use of 'matching' is properly limited."[9]

In various specific ways the 1979 OMB guidelines on matching programs acknowledged the threat to personal privacy inherent in matching programs. Section 1 stated that "these guidelines are intended to aid agencies in balancing the government's need to maintain the integrity of Federal programs with the individual's right to personal privacy." This of course remains the central issue facing agencies that are ultimately responsible for complying with the Privacy Act. The OMB's guidelines are only advisory and do not replace the need to comply with the terms of the statute itself. The 1979 guidelines also explicitly recognized the threat to privacy inherent in matching programs by making their utilization conditional upon a showing that "alternative means . . . would present a greater threat to personal privacy."[10] In each of the two instances cited here, the actual language disappeared from the 1982 version of the guidelines.

The Carter administration ultimately relied on the "routine use" provision of the Privacy Act to legitimize computer matching, a process that Kirchner aptly called "clever manipulation of [the] terminology of the law." Kirchner also stated that "the government had known for years that use of the loophole for matching was, if not technically illegal, at least contrary to the spirit of the privacy law and the intent of its congressional sponsors."[11] The contrary argument is that the case for matching can be made on the basis of compatibility, as defined in section (a)(7).

Various agencies at least initially balked at making their records available for Project Match. General Counsel Carl F. Goodman informed the acting deputy inspector general of HEW that "it is evident that this information on employees was not collected with a view toward detecting welfare abuses." He added that at the matching stage, "there is no indication whatsoever that a violation or potential violation of law has occurred." When the Department of Defense finally decided that complying with Project Match could be construed as a new routine use, Representative Richardson Preyer, chairman of the House Subcommittee on Government Information and Individual Rights, strongly protested to the defense secretary.[12] John Shattuck of the American Civil Liberties Union later noted how Goodman's "candid and reasonable interpretation of the Privacy Act soon gave way to a succession of strained readings seeking to square computer-matching with the Act's prohibition on uses of personal records except for purposes compatible with the purposes for which they were collected."[13]

The 1978 OMB guidelines included some useful controls for the protection of privacy, which are unfortunately missing from the 1979 version, including a requirement that "the matching program should minimize the number and extent of the disclosures of information which pertain to identifiable individuals," and that all routine uses permitting disclosures for matching programs should be as specific and limited as possible. Kirchner's summary judgment is apt: "The intent of the guidelines, no doubt, was to forbid any computer matching program that could not be completely justified under the privacy law. The practical result of the guidelines, however, was in effect to authorize all manner of record disclosures for whatever reason [that] might be conveniently labeled 'routine uses' by any agency wanting to perform a matching operation."[14]

On May 11, 1982, OMB published "Revised Supplemental Guidelines for Conducting Matching Programs" that were half as long as the 1979 edition. The stated purpose of the revision was updating, simplification, the reflection of experience, and the incorporation of agency recommendations for clarifications and changes.[15] In practice, the inspectors general did not like the old guidelines, because they regarded them as cumbersome and as allowing OMB too much scope for intervention, especially in terms of requiring a cost-benefit analysis in advance. The new guidelines reduced the oversight role of OMB and generally reflected the goals of the Reagan administration.

In addition to the criticisms of such guidelines on matching previously advanced, the 1982 version seems to place federal agencies in an almost impossible legal situation. Matching is to be done in compliance with the provisions of the various OMB guidelines and the Privacy Act. But it is impossible for an agency to release data for matching programs to another agency (absent another statute) and still comply with the Privacy Act: "Complying with these Guidelines . . . does not relieve a Federal agency of the obligation to comply with the provisions of the Privacy Act, including any provisions not cited in these Guidelines."[16] There is no certain mechanism whereby a federal agency can ascertain whether it is in compliance with the Privacy Act, short of responding to a criminal prosecution or a civil suit for engaging in a matching program.

The 1982 guidelines provide that an agency can release personal information for matching programs to another agency, "if the agency is satisfied that disclosure of the records would not violate its responsibilities under the Privacy Act."[17] Internal dialogue within any such agency is almost inevitably much too one-sided for the adequate identification and protection of the privacy interests of the individuals thereby affected. Only the Defense Department has a data protection office that can knowledgeably contribute in such instances. Moreover, compliance with the Privacy Act itself may ultimately be insufficient to control surveillance in a satisfactory manner, even if any one agency can hardly be held responsible for the deficiencies of this statute.

The 1982 guidelines place federal agencies in an ambiguous position in terms of compliance with the Privacy Act and protecting personal privacy in an acceptable manner. The articulation of privacy concerns in many parts of the guidelines appears largely to be pious language, although no more so than in other parts of the Privacy Act itself. For example, a source federal agency faces the burden of deciding whether to disclose personal records to another federal agency "to make sure they meet the necessary Privacy Act disclosure provisions."[18] Furthermore, disclosure of records to a matching agency and disclosure of hits by a matching or source agency has to be done in accordance with the conditions of disclosure set out in paragraph (b) of the Privacy Act (which is a large, general paragraph).

This situation clearly indicates the consequences of the lack of an agency charged with monitoring compliance with the Privacy Act itself. OMB has no role under the 1982 matching guidelines, even through its Office of Information and Regulatory Affairs (OIRA). Even if any part of OMB was actively involved in measures for controlling surveillance in a meaningful fashion, this executive agency is too tied to the current political goals of any administration to be an ideal location for balancing privacy interests against other values favoring surveillance.

Conclusions about the Guidelines on Matching Programs

As noted earlier, certain of the aims of matching programs are in conformity with the customary goals of good data protection, such as reducing the amount of personal information collected and ensuring its accuracy. The 1982 OMB guidelines on matching also include some good practical protections for personal privacy, including the requirements that only the minimum information necessary for a match should be disclosed, that there should be written agreements on data use, that there should be controls on the disposition and return of records, and that notices must be sent to the OMB and to Congress concerning the creation of new systems of records.[19] Finally, there is little basis for questioning a match or audit that occurs in close proximity to the filing of an application for a benefit, since the person can be informed and should expect that such an audit will normally take place.[20] The problem is to control the range of data bases that can be searched for such surveillance purposes. The current guidelines only cover interagency matches, not those internal to an agency.[21] Given the huge size of the seventeen federal agencies that are most involved with the Privacy Act, it is presumptuous to suggest that internal matching programs do not pose challenges to privacy.

One of the fundamental issues with federal matching programs is that the sole measure of concern for privacy is the Privacy Act and the 1975 OMB guidelines for its implementation rather than a more general conception and articulation of the privacy interests of Americans.[22] The key question for all inspectors general is whether they have ever violated the privacy of individuals as opposed to violating the Privacy Act. Richard Kusserow of DHHS stated during a November 1982 meeting of the American Society of Access Professionals (ASAP) that his office was not invading anyone's privacy. What seems to have received insufficient consideration from PCIE and the inspectors general is the broad interests and values that are at stake when one is seeking to limit surveillance of the population. The "we are not breaking the Privacy Act" syndrome is not reassuring.

The reliance on routine use to legitimize matching programs is clearly contrary to the spirit and the guiding principles of the Privacy Act. At that same 1982 session, Ronald L. Plesser, formerly general counsel of the Privacy Protection Study Commission, expressed his own doubts that Congress had ever intended such interpretations of routine use as those currently being employed. His additional point that the Privacy Act is almost unenforceable has direct relevance to an evaluation of the adequacy of the prospects for enforcement. A federal employee releasing records for a matching program to another agency might be subject to criminal penalties or a civil suit for failure to comply with the Privacy Act.[23] Yet another participant in the ASAP session remarked that the initial sensitivities of federal civil servants to the possibility of a prosecution or a lawsuit were greatly reduced after the passage of time demonstrated that such prospects were very unlikely.

A number of witnesses at the computer matching hearings also criticized the reliance on the routine use clause of the Privacy Act to justify computer matching and argued that it needed amendment.[24] Since all of these witnesses testified from a civil libertarian perspective, it is important that former Inspector General Thomas F. McBride also noted his sense of "bafflement" by what seems to be a "somewhat illusory protection, the routine use clause of the Privacy Act," and questioned whether there has been some distortion of the intent of the legislation: "Basically what those conducting matches have done . . . is to publish notice and add the match as a routine use, even though it did not seem to have a clear nexus to the purpose for which the data was originally collected."[25]

A final inadequacy of current matching programs and practices is that there was no established mechanism or forum where the conflicting interests inherent in such activities can be debated and balanced. PCIE, for example, is an inappropriate setting for such deliberations, because of its central goals of surveillance. It is equally questionable that OMB or any single federal agency is suitably informed to balance fully such competing interests as efficiency and privacy, especially in light of the vigorous efforts of inspectors general and the Reagan administration to end as much fraud and waste as possible.

Persons familiar with both matching programs and the Privacy Act argue that they want to allow the use of new technology and at the same time protect individual rights.[26] The question is how to achieve such laudable balance. There is probably little disagreement that computer matching should be carried out in such a manner as to pose as little challenge as possible to the privacy interests of citizens, but the issue remains of how best to do this. If one agrees that the indiscriminate use of matching is in no one's best interests, who is going to set the appropriate limits? These issues will be considered again below.

The Monitoring of Matching Programs

OMB has the main responsibility for oversight of matching programs, even though each agency is itself liable for compliance with the Privacy Act. Its most recent statement of agency responsibilities includes a requirement for each agency to review annually "each ongoing matching program in which the agency has participated during the year, either as a source or as a matching agency, in order to ensure that the requirements of the Act, the OMB Matching Guidelines, and the OMB Model Control System and Checklist have been met." For purposes of its annual report, OMB also collects data on the number and description of matching programs.[27] The 1982 guidelines also require an agency to publish a notice of an intended match and to furnish a copy to Congress and OMB, but since they are guidelines rather than in the act itself, the notice provisions are not binding on agencies. Thus the Department of Education initiated a match of student loan borrowers in August 1982 but did not publish the required notice until December.[28] The publication of notice requirements is a weak form of control on government surveillance unless it is actually enforced.

In the 1983 oversight hearings on the Privacy Act, Christopher DeMuth, then the administrator of the Office of Information and Regulatory Affairs at OMB, described computer matching as a very powerful administrative tool for eliminating fraud in a variety of government programs that has to be "conducted within the parameters laid down by the Act." He saw no evidence that matching was "running roughshod over the policies of the Privacy Act."[29] When, in the aftermath of these hearings, the House Subcommittee on Government Information asked the General Accounting Office (GAO) to review agencies' implementation of the Privacy Act, its auditors concluded that federal institutions "(1) did not have current, complete data on the extent of matching programs, (2) did not always follow OMB's matching guidelines, and (3) differed in interpretation of the matching guidelines as to whether programs needed to be reported to OMB." The General Accounting Office concluded that: "Overall, the agencies participated in more matching programs than they reported to OMB and the Congress."[30]

At present, OIRA desk officers review agencies' reports of matching programs on a regular basis. They reviewed seven reports from agencies in 1982 and six in 1983. The published descriptions of each of sixteen matches suggest that OIRA had no comments or criticisms to offer of any of them.[31] Nine agencies undertook matches, with the Department of Labor and Veterans Affairs the leaders with four apiece. Eight federal agencies and two nonfederal, the United Auto Workers and the Virginia Employment Commission, served as sources of matching data, thus illustrating that data from the states and the private sector are used for matching by federal agencies. Various data from the Office of Personnel Management were used four times. The only federal source agencies that were not themselves conducting matches were the Tennessee Valley Authority and the Coast Guard. Although the descriptions published by OIRA are fairly innocuous, because of the lack of detail, they offer a sense of just how far afield an agency may go: DHHS's Office of Child Support Enforcement matches its records with those of the Selective Service System in order to determine the addresses of absent parents.[32]

The public notice system under the Privacy Act is working very poorly. For example, in 1982 the Office of the Assistant Secretary for Personnel Administration published a routine use for its payroll systems permitting disclosure to "a State or local agency for the purpose of conducting computer matching programs designed to reduce fraud, waste and abuse in Federal, State, and local public assistance programs and operations." The only comment received by DHHS was from the American Federation of Government Employees, which claimed that federal employees were being singled out for scrutiny and that the use was not compatible with the system's purpose. DHHS rejected this assertion, since one purpose of the system is to report wage information to state and local governments for tax purposes and for other child support programs.[33] DHHS was the only one of nine separate agencies notifying OMB about matches in 1982–83 to receive public comments about them. Department after department informed OMB that it received no response to these publication activities, which indicates lack of public awareness of surveillance practices.

In a recent review of computer matching, the Office of Technology Assessment (OTA) described several data banks created solely for matching purposes, including the proposed Internal Revenue Service Debtor Master File containing the names of all delinquent federal borrowers to match against tax returns. OTA's own survey of federal agencies reported a total of approximately 700 matches from 1980 to April 1985, with the number of matches tripling over time. OTA concluded that "welfare recipients and Federal Employees were most often the targets." In its view, which is sensitive to the risks of excessive surveillance, "the linking of systems in computer matching can be regarded as moving towards a *de facto* national data center or national recipient system."[34]

OTA found that "there are numerous procedural guidelines for computer matching, but little or no oversight, follow-up, or explicit consideration of privacy implications." Internal agency checks and guidelines do not exist. In its view, "neither the source agency, the matching agency, nor OMB is accountable for the decision whether or not to disclose records for a matching program."[35] Although there are differences between matching and front-end verification and computer profiling, OTA's conclusions to its excellent discussions of these related topics are quite similar.[36]

The Challenge of Matching Programs to Personal Privacy

Despite the instinctive resistance of civil libertarians to matching programs, their objective threat to such values as personal privacy must be evaluated in concrete terms so as to avoid a Luddite or an Orwellian mentality. The fundamental issue is identifying exactly what privacy interests need to be protected in the process of computer surveillance. This is never an easy matter. One can reasonably ask whether a person's privacy is in fact invaded in any meaningful way if his or her record in a federal information system is simply checked along with millions of others for compliance with a particular requirement. The standard fair information practice is that an invasion of privacy certainly occurs if the data were not collected from individuals with such a purpose in mind.

The development of matching programs will more fully reveal their surveillance potential, but these should be anticipated as much as possible in advance. What privacy interests are involved if matching occurs within a single system of records? Are different challenges posed by matching programs that are recurring as opposed to single operations? Is the latter type of operation more likely to resemble an ill-conceived fishing expedition among personal records?

Individual expectations of personal privacy are generally based upon claims of personal autonomy and freedom from surveillance, as opposed to an expectation based solely on constitutional and legislated rights to privacy. Protecting privacy in other words should not simply be a question of law. In pursuing practical controls on such surveillance, one can initially be guided by the code of fair information practices in the Privacy Act. Equally germane are the general principles highlighted in the 1977 report of the Privacy Protection Study Commission, two of which are especially appropriate to a consideration of matching: minimizing intrusiveness in individual lives, and giving persons a legitimate expectation of confidentiality when they give up information about themselves to the government for a particular purpose.[37]

One basic premise set out in section 2(b)(2) of the Privacy Act is that an individual should be able "to prevent records pertaining to him obtained by such agencies for a particular purpose from being used or made available for another purpose without his consent." Thus real privacy problems emerge when federal information systems are used for purposes that were in no way anticipated or announced at the time of data collection. Privacy advocate Robert Belair has stated with respect to intraagency data transfers that "this type of sharing threatens privacy interests by permitting the non-consensual sharing of subject information without notice to the subject." He further identified a subject's interest in prohibiting disclosures of data for compatible purposes: "First, from a conceptual standpoint, it is not logical to conclude that because personal information is used for a purpose compatible with the purpose for which it was developed or collected, record subjects have no interest in contesting disclosure. . . . The disclosure of information to a new party, the passage of time, and changes in circumstances may all have the effect of making a 'compatible' disclosure harmful to a subject's interests."[38] Thus informed consent should be a basic tool to restrict governmental surveillance.

Probably the most invasive aspect of matching programs is the follow-up of individuals who are identified by the matching process as "hits."[39] If one argues that manipulation of a million automated records is only a minimal challenge to privacy, the harsh reality in terms of surveillance is that the process ultimately leads to the targeting of specific persons for further contacts. This practice reveals one of the flaws in the PCIE argument that "computers are much less intrusive with regard to individual privacy than people."[40] Such an assertion tells only part of the story.

A whole series of questions needs to be answered from a privacy perspective about the treatment of hits. How is the process handled? At what point is the individual singled out actually approached? Is the approach done over the telephone or in person? Is the target summoned impersonally to present himself or herself at a government office? Is the procedure accusatory or sensitive to individual rights? What are the emotional and psychological burdens for an individual of being identified by means of a hit as a target in a government investigation for fraud? How often is such an investigation inspired by an error, such as in a Social Security Number, that is no fault of the data subject? Could such a process unfairly jeopardize a subject by means such as investigative calls to an employer? In its recent survey, OTA found that "for the majority of matches reported to OTA, information on hits verified was either unknown or unavailable."[41]

There is not enough public evidence about matching experience to furnish adequate answers to these questions. The basic fact, however, as PCIE has indicated, is that "raw hits have to be verified." It is not clear whether the entire process depends upon direct contact with the target, or whether further analysis of secondary data can be undertaken initially. The pursuit of hits that prove to be invalid or erroneous subjects individuals to unnecessary surveillance in a very direct way. PCIE inadvertently makes this point in the following statement: "It should first of all be recalled that people who need assistance and legitimately apply for help are not the targets of matching and will not show up on match lists unless through error."[42] Some fundamental questions remain unanswered about the quality of personal data in federal information systems, especially in terms of accuracy and timeliness; Swedish experience suggests that such problems as achieving "correct" information systems are serious.

Further information about how the process is intended to work appeared in a *Federal Register* announcement of a proposed matching program between the Department of the Army and the City of New York. Readers are informed that "only the 'hits' will be turned over to personnel from the City of New York." There is no indication of whether these are raw hits or those that have been initially investigated. The latter may be implied from the additional statement that "in those situations where there is any question as to eligibility, the recipient will be personally contacted to resolve the issue."[43]

The investigation of hits necessitates direct contact with the individuals thought to be concerned. In 1982 Massachusetts matched private bank and welfare records in order to target welfare recipients with more assets than the law permitted. The state issued termination notices to 1,600 persons without any advance contact with them. After an appeal rate six times higher than normal, it was found that 15 percent of the 1,600 were targeted on the basis of erroneous Social Security Numbers. Other valid explanations included money held in trust or in joint accounts and money held for legal purposes, such as paying funeral expenses.[44]

Publications of the Office of the Inspector General for DHHS demonstrate how certain matches and follow-ups involve especially sensitive matters. For the purpose of finding "illogical billing situations" involving physicians or health care providers, the inspector general's office reviewed billing files on abortions and sterilizations. DHHS designed a computer application to identify billings for an abortion procedure where more than one claim was processed within a short period of time: "The program was run in one location. The results were turned over to program administrators for follow-up." With respect to sterilization procedures, the goal was to ensure that claims were not processed for persons under twenty-one, since the individual has to have reached that age to obtain a government payment for this purpose. The computer application identified claims for sterilization and related services, which obviously included all persons for whom billings had been submitted. The result was that "five hundred sterilization and related service claims were identified," and "claims totaling over $300,000 were referred to program administrators for follow-up."[45] One does not need to know much about the details of these particular matching programs to realize that very sensitive interests of young persons are involved.

Another of the critical issues associated with the regulation of computer matching is how to prevent its uncontrolled growth. The practice raises nascent fears about the creation of a dossier society in which legitimate expectations of privacy are difficult to achieve.

Matching programs may lead to the creation of large new information systems. The Reagan administration had a plan for a National Recipient Information System in DHHS that would have included 25 million welfare recipients in an automated data base.[46] PCIE has issued assurances that no great master file in the hands of the government will result from computer matching.[47] But Richard Kusserow stated at an ASAP meeting in 1982 that Veterans Affairs was creating a national file of deceased individuals. Unless one accepts the unpalatable notion that dead persons have no further claims to personal privacy, as is indeed the law under the Privacy Act, the creation of such a large national data bank is a direct result of matching programs. Some matches also involve the use of the entire federal payroll. PCIE has further stated that "no permanent files identifying [hit] individuals result [from computer matching,] and therefore no master file can develop over time."[48] The same political pressures inspiring matching programs may also lead to a master file of "welfare cheats," so that they can be kept under surveillance more easily.

PCIE has made the surprising claim that matching programs reduce the threat of government invasion of privacy, because the process uses "large, separate and disparate data bases and files."[49] In fact, it is the use of such disparate information systems that creates one of the most significant challenges to personal privacy. Massive amounts of personal information are involved. For example, the Social Security Administration matched its Title 2 Retirement, Survivors, and Disability file, involving 350 reels of computer tape, with a list of all persons that had died in previous months (obtained from the Health Care Financing Administration).[50]

The preoccupation with government efficiency is leading to the national data bank mentality that Congress rejected with such enthusiasm during the mid-1960s.[51] A national data bank might be very efficient, but it would also further encourage the kind of surveillance society that Orwell warned against. In fact, many of the initial concerns about matching programs evoked images of a national data bank and the advent of Big Brother. In 1978 the Carter administration recognized the risk that the public would begin to fear such a creation.[52] A spokesman for the Department of Defense stated in 1980 that he was philosophically opposed to the use of computer matching to facilitate registration for Selective Service, because of the "Big Brother" tone of matching programs. Inspector General Kusserow has publicly stated that he is anxious to avoid bringing on "Big Brother."[53] Yet matching is now a major government activity, which has resulted, for example, in a single data base of all federal government employees that is used for linkages. Its existence can only encourage new uses.

What are the acceptable and tolerable limits of computer matching? The process of government would indeed be more efficient if we were all subject to detailed surveillance. The federal government could furnish everyone with a unique personal identifier, perhaps including a photograph and digitized fingerprints, that would not suffer from the limitations of Social Security Numbers. It could encourage every federal agency to build one central personal information system in order to facilitate matching programs.

One approaches the core values associated with personal privacy in reflecting on why some of these proposals seem unpalatable in American society. But how does one draw the line, and who should do so? How far afield can a federal agency legitimately venture in testing for compliance with the eligibility requirements of a particular program? Should constraints exist against the matching of all records associated with any individual applying to the government for a benefit or payment? Should there be no restrictions on access to data from the Internal Revenue Service or the Bureau of the Census? Should the government have access to individual bank accounts for matching purposes in order to reduce fraud, abuse, and waste? A concern for privacy interests, among others, explains the fundamental resistance to uncontrolled matching operations. Some routine uses of matching may be legitimate, such as for front-end verification, but most of us do not want to encourage the creation of total profiles for individuals, even within the confines of a particular agency, because of the risks of a surveillance society.

The Computer Matching and Privacy Protection Act

The Privacy Act has been in considerable need of revision to reflect more fully the challenges posed to personal privacy by new forms of information technology, including computer matching. Until 1988 the mechanisms for regulating such record linkages were inadequate. OTA found that "the Privacy Act as presently interpreted by the courts and OMB guidelines offers little protection to individuals who are the subjects of computer matching."⁵⁴ The revised Privacy Act will seek to regulate and control matching programs and has set up a permanent mechanism for the identification and protection of privacy interests in the form of Data Integrity Boards.

Following the tradition of sectoral legislation, Congress sought specific statutory solutions for computer matching, which are, in fact, significant amendments to the Privacy Act. In 1986 and 1987, Senator William Cohen introduced bills to control computer matching that the Senate subsequently passed without dissent. The House enacted its own version of the proposed law in July 1988. On October 18 President Reagan signed a compromise measure into law.⁵⁵

The Computer Matching and Privacy Protection Act has a limited scope, applying only to the "computerized comparison of records for the purpose of (i) establishing or verifying eligibility for a Federal benefit program, or (ii) recouping payments or delinquent debts under such programs." It does not apply to matches performed for statistical, research, law enforcement, foreign counterintelligence, security screening, and tax purposes. Nevertheless, the Privacy Act, which presented only a few "easily overcome" procedural barriers to matching, now has new controls.⁵⁶ The informative House report on its bill notes that, although the goals of computer matching programs are admirable, "the results are less certain. Matching has been criticized as unproven and ineffective, as well as illegal and violative of private rights."⁵⁷ The new law emphasizes due process and administrative goals, including analysis of costs and benefits, rather than concentrating on privacy and surveillance issues. This reflects a shrewd political assessment of how best to persuade Congress to act.

The House report made the important judgment that computer matching was a major uncontrolled federal activity: "Guidance issued by OMB has been largely ignored by agencies and unenforced by OMB. There is no meaningful oversight of computer matching in the Executive Branch."⁵⁸ The matching law requires the agencies involved to create written agreements concerning their use of matching records. Citizens must be given prior notice in the *Federal Register* of proposed matches. Agencies must also provide "adequate advance notice" of any proposal "to establish or make a significant change in a system of records or a matching program" to OMB, and, more importantly, the oversight committees in the House and Senate.⁵⁹ Agencies cannot take steps to deny or cut off a benefit to a person on the basis of adverse data uncovered, unless they have validated their accuracy and offered the individual an opportunity to contest the findings.

To ensure that matching procedures are followed, agencies that conduct or participate in matches are required to create Data Integrity Boards, made up of an agency's own senior officials, to oversee and approve matches. Each board must ensure compliance with all relevant statutes, regulations, and guidelines; conduct cost-benefit analyses; and make available an annual report on matching activities. If a board disapproves a proposed match, any party to the agreement may appeal to the director of OMB and notify the congressional oversight committees. The director makes the final decision. For the first three years, OMB has to prepare a consolidated annual report on matching activities.[60] OMB, which generally supported the new law, will issue guidelines on implementation before the act becomes fully effective in 1989.

At the House hearings on the matching bill in June 1987, representatives of the American Civil Liberties Union and the American Bar Association warned of the risk of the de facto creation of a national data bank and of the need to provide for injunctive relief for the individual against government agencies. The 1988 law prohibits "the establishment or maintenance by any agency of a national data bank that combines, merges, or links information on individuals maintained in systems of records by other Federal agencies." The law further outlines the functions that OMB should perform in overseeing the implementation of the controls on matching.[61]

Chapter *30*

Responding to Privacy and Surveillance Problems

This chapter considers further changes that are necessary in the Privacy Act, so that a variety of problems in data protection can be dealt with satisfactorily. Before looking at some general and specific proposals for revisions of the law, the chapter briefly reviews the achievements and adequacies of implementing the Privacy Act and also how problems of evolving information technology are being handled at present.

The fundamental argument of the U.S. case study is that the United States increasingly risks becoming a surveillance society, so long as it does not create a federal data protection agency. In the past it has been possible to argue that English-speaking countries did not follow European models of data protection. But developments in Canada and the United Kingdom severely limit the salience of this argument. Although there is no need (as yet) for a European-style registration system, the British initiative in creating a Data Registrar under its Data Protection Act of 1984 increases the international pressure on the U.S. to develop an oversight mechanism for ensuring more effective controls on governmental surveillance.

The current U.S. federal system for data protection is seriously deficient, because it lacks an adequate monitoring mechanism to ensure that the Privacy Act of 1974 is properly enforced and privacy interests adequately articulated. Admittedly, the Data Integrity Boards mandated for agencies by the Computer Matching and Privacy Protection Act of 1988 are a major step in the right direction. Although the focus of this case study is directed to the problems of protecting personal privacy at the federal level and in the public sector, the findings can be applied by analogy to the public sector at the state level and to private-sector problems with privacy.

The Adequacies of Implementation

A number of significant accomplishments followed from the introduction of the Privacy Act of 1974, and it continues to be of value in some respects. It has been most influential as a records management act, including the implementation of fair information practices and control of the management and design of personal information systems. The Privacy Act had a considerable initial impact, so far as the bureaucracy was concerned. In fact, the act has changed agency behavior in ways that need to be remembered: for example, personal information is not publicly disclosed as it might have been in the past.

The U.S. experience shows that the operation of a large administrative program does not stimulate a high level of concern for the privacy interests of those being serviced, unless management makes it a very high priority, as has rarely been the case under the Privacy Act. The busy individuals in administrative agencies are already overworked. Moreover, those persons working on welfare issues, for example, remain more concerned about achieving surveillance of target populations than protecting anyone's privacy. Although there are coordinators for the Privacy Act in each federal agency, their role has been very limited. In some agencies administration of the Privacy Act has become a political football, due sometimes to rivalries and bickering, so that privacy coordinators have often lacked internal support. In a large agency like the Department of Health and Human Services, concern for the protection of privacy has not been among the leading objectives of senior management during the past decade. However, even if it is understandable that the Privacy Act does not bring joy to the hearts of busy administrators, this does not mean that the interests the law was designed to serve should be neglected; other countries are doing a much better job in this area.

The differences of opinion in the United States about the effectiveness of the Privacy Act are really quite extraordinary, if one looks at them in comparison with the relative consensus that exists in other countries (with the possible exception of France). President Reagan's covering letter to Congress for the latest report on the Privacy Act is quite positive.[1] At the 1983 oversight hearings, the administrator of the Office of Information and Regulatory Affairs (OIRA) stated: "We believe that the Act is working well for the most part. It is largely accomplishing the goals the Congress set for it. If changes are needed, they are more in the nature of administrative clarification than major substantive amendments."

The chairman of the Defense Privacy Board made a more compelling case, at least for the Defense Department: "In summary, the Privacy Act works because we work hard at it. I believe its effects are important and lasting. . . . At the practical level, it has not imposed a significant burden—at least for us. The excitement which accompanied its enactment may be gone but the benefits of the Act continue. . . . I can assure you that in our department the Privacy Act is alive and well."[2]

All of the testimony by nongovernment persons at the 1983 oversight hearings was highly critical of the implementation of the Privacy Act by the Office of Management and Budget (OMB) and federal agencies. John Shattuck stated that "unfortunately, the Privacy Act in reality has fallen far short of its promise." Ronald Plesser concluded that the act "is overly complex, over bureaucratic, and contains really no effective enforcement mechanism. It has become almost totally unavailable to most citizens because of the cumbersome and frustrating nature of its enforcement remedies."[3] None of this would have surprised the father of the Privacy Act, Senator Sam Ervin, Jr. He told David Burnham in 1982 that "the Privacy Act, if enforced, . . . would be a pretty good thing. But the government doesn't like it. . . . There are mighty few laws they cannot nullify."[4]

In a fashion typical of legislative parents, Congress did not pay much attention to the Privacy Act after assisting at its birth. There has been little leadership from Congress or the OMB with respect to implementing and improving the Privacy Act. When Senator Ervin accepted the 1974 compromise whereby no privacy protection commission would be created, he stated that the Senate Committee on Government Operations would have to engage in "aggressive oversight."[5] This has not occurred, except to the extent that the staff of the House Subcommittee on Government Information, Justice, and Agriculture has played a continuing role as a watchdog for privacy. Such oversight has been a useful, small-scale form of outside effort toward the control of surveillance.

Press attention to the Privacy Act is at best episodic, especially in a political climate where protection of privacy is not perceived as an issue. David Burnham of the *New York Times* was until 1987 the only reporter for a major newspaper who made a specialty of information policy issues, including privacy. Robert Ellis Smith, an experienced journalist, concludes that the press's diminished interest in privacy has helped to detract attention from the issue and discouraged the creation of a constituency to promote revisions of the Privacy Act. Journalists are only interested in horror stories and do not want to have to dig too hard to find them. Perhaps the diminishing privacy of such public figures as Robert Bork and Gary Hart in 1987 will force the media to reconsider its interest in privacy protection, but it is also evident that this goal is contrary to the best interests of the press. At present, the media includes only limited reporting on the surveillance capacity of personal information systems.

The Need for a Privacy Protection Commission

The only real resemblance between the Privacy Protection Study Commission and the original privacy protection commission proposed by the Senate in 1974 was in their names. The study commission made an important recommendation in its final report for "an independent entity within the Federal Government" that would "oversee, regulate, and enforce compliance with certain of the Commission's recommendations."[6]

Some of the actual recommendations of the study commission necessitate a data protection agency along the lines intended in the 1974 Senate proposals for a privacy protection commission. These are reviewed in some detail here, because they are as timely as when they were first written. The implementation strategy of the study commission required that privacy issues be kept in proper focus: "This requires continuing attention from a broad public-policy perspective—a need that is not fulfilled today even within the scope of the Privacy Act.

A means must be found to provide continued public awareness of what is clearly a continuing and pivotal concern, and to assure ongoing attention to develop and refine understanding of specific and emerging problems."[7] The study commission further concluded that "improving the capability of the individual to protect himself can be an inadequate tool for resolving major systemic problems. The Commission sees a need for some influential 'prodding' structure, some sustained oversight over the actual implementation of the protection it recommends. The Federal agency experience under the Privacy Act . . . attests to the need as it has arisen within the Federal government."[8] The study commission regarded its proposed federal entity as essential to interpret both law and policy on privacy in all areas of the public sector. It could provide an efficient means of arriving at common solutions to the shared privacy protection problems of federal agencies.[9]

The study commission recommended that the independent entity to be created by the federal government should have a monitoring and evaluation function with respect to the implementation of any statutes and regulations enacted upon the commission's recommendation. It should also have "the authority to formally participate in any Federal administrative proceeding or process where the action being considered by another agency would have a material effect on the protection of personal privacy, either as a result of direct government action or as a result of government regulation of others."[10] The independent entity could continue to study and investigate areas of privacy concern. It also should have the power to issue interpretative rules that must be followed by federal agencies in implementing the Privacy Act. Finally, as the study commission proposed, the independent entity should be empowered to advise the President, Congress, and government agencies regarding the privacy implications of proposed federal or state statutes or regulations. The study commission referred to the independent unit as a federal privacy board; it recommended that its only enforcement authority "be in connection with the implementation by Federal agencies of the Privacy Act itself."[11]

Reviewing some of the detailed recommendations in the final report of the Privacy Protection Study Commission reveals a number of areas in which the inadequacies of the Privacy Act could be remedied in considerable measure by the creation of a data protection agency. The report concluded "that the Privacy Act needs significant modification and change if it is to accomplish its objectives within the Federal government."[12] It noted that federal agencies have taken advantage of the flexibility of the Privacy Act to contravene its spirit, a situation that could be monitored by a data protection agency. The study commission sought to preserve "the essential autonomy of each agency to decide how best to comply with each requirement" of the Privacy Act, but again that could be fulfilled under the general oversight of a data protection agency.[13] The commission agreed that data protection provisions should be specifically incorporated in detailed federal legislation, when appropriate;

again, ensuring such an inclusion and helping to shape it is an appropriate task for a data protection agency.

In discussing the eight basic principles in the Privacy Act, the commission noted the accountability principle, whereby an agency was responsible for its privacy practices. Without a data protection agency, it can be argued, an individual citizen, the courts, or the Office of Management and the Budget are not in a good position to monitor or respond to relevant developments. A data protection agency could further keep track of variations that the commission noted in broad versus narrow agency interpretations of routine uses under the Privacy Act. The commission wanted Congress to review all statutes that authorized incompatible uses and disclosures of personal information in order to determine which it wished to retain. This is the kind of task for which Congress could usefully depend on the assistance of a privacy protection commission.[14]

The study commission determined that the staffs of federal agencies require guidance as to what constitutes an unwarranted invasion of privacy: "One of the primary functions of the entity recommended by the Commission . . . would be to assist agencies in developing policy to assist agency employees in making such determinations." It also pointed out that there had been no adequate monitoring of federal agency compliance with the Privacy Act's information-management principle and no specific, consistently applied criteria had been established.[15] From the perspective of this volume, the findings of the commission read like a list of functions that should be given to a privacy protection commission.

The study commission generally found that those federal agencies "that have established formal, structured approaches and mechanisms to implement the Privacy Act are the most successful in their implementation of the Act." In order to promote compliance, it recommended that "the head of each agency should designate one official with authority to oversee implementation of the Act," since "the Act's individual enforcement model is simply ineffective on a broad scale."[16] This practice is in general conformity with how the French and West German public sector assists in implementing data protection. Finally, the commission noted that "attention to information policy issues is not usually a priority concern of agency personnel. While many employees view the Privacy Act and the issues it raises as important, a sizable number still see the Act as a nuisance and an impediment to the performance of their agency's missions and functions."[17] It can be argued that this statement encapsulates a rule of life applicable to all bureaucracies, thus furnishing an additional argument in favor of creating a data protection agency.

The tragedy, of course, is that the very sound recommendations of the Privacy Protection Study Commission for a desirable type of data protection agency have not been implemented. President Carter is reported to have made a conscious decision not to create a new agency in the form of a federal privacy board because of his desire to reduce government bureaucracy.[18] Senior government officials, including leading Cabinet members, who reviewed the findings of the Privacy Protection Study Commission, were not enthusiastic about creating an additional oversight board, this time for the protection of privacy interests, which might interfere with their prerogatives and routine activities. Experience in all countries demonstrates that bureaucracies initially resist data protection, and that only legislative bodies can impose such controls upon them.

In 1982 hearings, Senator William S. Cohen described the situation with respect to lack of enforcement of the Privacy Act: "I can't find anybody in this administration or any other administration that's terribly concerned about these kinds of issues [the lack of a centralized monitoring authority]. OMB wants out. Inspectors General certainly are not going to be the ones to be concerned about treading upon the sensitivities of people's rights of privacy. There isn't really anybody within the Government structure that is too concerned about it."[19] In agreeing with this assessment about the lack of controls on computer matching, Professor David F. Linowes, formerly chairman of the Privacy Protection Study Commission, pointed out that the Privacy Act "needs substantial review and some limited modification, in particular, concerning the enforcement mechanism and some of the vagueness in the language and some penalty provisions, which we do not have." He reminded the hearing that the study commission had recommended an "Office of Privacy Protection, not a regulatory agency." It could be set up by executive order in the White House to carry out such a monitoring function, although Linowes thought that it would be better if Congress created an agency by statute.[20]

In the same hearings, Ronald Plesser, who served as general counsel to the study commission, emphasized the need for administrative oversight under the Privacy Act, a point with which Senator Cohen agreed. Plesser pointed out the tragedy "that there is no one in the government with the role of enforcing or even overseeing the privacy standards. The privacy officers in agencies stand as lonely voices. Only the Department of Defense has institutionalized privacy protection with its Defense Privacy Board staffed by high-level civilians and military officers. The OMB has some responsibilities; however, their prime mission is elimination of fraud and abuse and not privacy protection."[21]

The Office of Technology Assessment's (OTA) 1986 study of *Electronic Record Systems and Individual Privacy* strongly supported the need for a privacy protection commission. It seriously faulted OMB's oversight of the Privacy Act and noted the lack of a federal forum in which the conflicting values at stake in the development of federal electronic record systems could be fully debated and resolved. OTA concluded that congressional action was necessary, because "Federal agency use of new information technologies in processing personal information has eroded the protections of the 1974 Privacy Act."[22] The OTA study concluded with a positive assessment of the type of data protection agency discussed in this chapter.[23] When it was released, Senator Cohen and Representative Don Edwards welcomed its findings concerning problems with the Privacy Act but warned of political resistance to the creation of a new oversight board.[24] In fact, when Congressman Glenn English introduced a bill to create such a data protection board after his subcommittee had held oversight hearings in 1983, the political judgment was that there was a lack of support for such an initiative.

Without a privacy protection commission, it will be of dubious utility to continue to rely on individuals protecting their privacy through their own initiative in the courts and on shaping data protection legislation on a sector-by-sector basis. The processes are simply too expensive and complicated to be accomplished without continuing input by the specialists working for a data protection agency. A privacy protection commission would facilitate the design, justification, and implementation of sector-by-sector legislation for data protection. Moreover, the sector-by-sector approach to the protection of privacy prevalent in the U.S. is not as unique as is sometimes suggested.

A privacy protection commission would have a great deal of work to do in terms of current issues that have implications for personal privacy, especially at the initial stage of thinking about new information systems or information practices. A commission could engage in oversight of, and contribute to the resolution of the privacy implications of, many sensitive issues of surveillance. Examples include computer matching programs, national identity cards, the National Drivers Register, the national missing persons index, immigration controls, the Social Security Number, the Secret Service's use of the Federal Bureau of Investigation's National Crime Information Center, the use of tax records for draft registration, the use of smart cards instead of food stamps, and the establishment of security standards for personal information.

The crucial role of a privacy protection commission would be in furnishing leadership in the federal public sector by serving as a catalyst for protecting personal privacy and by articulating privacy interests in every relevant situation. This is not an argument that privacy interests should always be predominant but simply that they should always be considered during development of legislation and administrative practices. The current federal situation is marked by confusion of jurisdiction and relative inaction, as evidenced by the debate over computer matching programs. It might be sufficient for the proposed privacy protection commission to have advisory powers only, since such a system has worked well in other countries. Others may believe that it is too late for such an organization to function without regulatory power, at least for the areas recommended by the Privacy Protection Study Commission in 1977.[25]

A privacy protection commission in the United States should have the following responsibilities and functions:

1. Articulating privacy concerns in every relevant situation, functioning essentially as an alarm system for the protection of personal privacy.
2. Carrying out oversight to protect the privacy interests of individuals in all federal information-handling activities.

3. Implementing statutory duties under a revised Privacy Act.

4. Conducting investigations and audits of information systems to monitor compliance with the provisions of a revised Privacy Act.

5. Developing and monitoring the implementation of appropriate security guidelines and practices for the protection of personal information in federal hands.

6. Advising and developing regulations appropriate for specific types of personal information systems. Staff members of the proposed privacy protection commission could thus become specialists in different types of information systems and information flows.

7. Monitoring and evaluating developments in information technology with respect to their implications for personal privacy.

8. Conducting research and reporting on all types of privacy issues in the United States.

A well-designed privacy protection commission should have a statutory mandate and specified goals for the protection of personal privacy. It should be headed by a commission and an executive director. The commission should have as much independence of the executive and legislative branches of government as is constitutionally possible. The commission should seek to function by way of consensus, mediation, and cooperation with federal agencies with respect to their information-handling activities. Its creation should further contribute to the shaping of information policies for U.S. society.

The lack of a data protection agency in the United States is especially striking in light of the vast array of other regulatory agencies in existence. There has admittedly been too great a tendency in the past for governments to create new regulatory bodies. But surely one can now demonstrate that general problems of surveillance exist. How much is the protection of privacy worth in comparative terms? The Nuclear Regulatory Agency has a staff of 3,000. The Justice Department has a Wildlife section that tries to control the illegal trade in animals, plants, and skins. John Shattuck testified in favor of a privacy protection commission similar in size and functions to the U.S. Civil Rights Commission, an independent advisory agency created in 1957 to monitor the enforcement of civil rights laws.[26] A model for the head of such a commission would be the comptroller general of the United States, who is the head of the General Accounting Office. He is appointed by Congress for a single, fifteen-year term and then retires at full pay, which is an excellent method of achieving independence.[27]

There are thus many precedents, some of them bad, for the creation of such an independent commission. Some federal models are alleged to be impotent, isolated, lacking in power, and staffed with weak people. (The contrast is usually with OMB, which suffers from none of these deficiencies, except the will to act under the Privacy Act.) The European precedent for data protection commissions indicates that such real problems can largely be avoided, at least during the first years. The experience of the new Data Integrity Boards will be instructive in this regard.

Some have argued that such a federal privacy protection commission lacks a constituency, such as a consumer movement, to support it. One response is that it has been the legislatures in other countries, such as France and West Germany, that have recognized the need for strong, independent data protection agencies; there has never been a mass popular uprising in favor of such innovative legislation. In the right political climate, a single congressional subcommittee should be able to persuade senators and representatives of the need to act, as has happened so often with sectoral privacy legislation.

The reasons advanced in the past for the creation of a privacy protection commission remain totally persuasive today. It was a fundamental error, especially when viewed from the perspective of more than a decade's experience, not to create such a commission in 1974.

Revising the Privacy Act

The Privacy Act needs to be revised in both general and specific terms, since the current system is simply not working satisfactorily. A case can easily be made that the law has failed in its primary goal, even if it has succeeded to varying degrees with its secondary goals.

A basic problem with the Privacy Act is its title; it has given the general public the mistaken impression that all federal privacy problems have been properly handled.[28] In fact, the existing law does not address many of the most fundamental problems of protecting personal privacy that have emerged since 1974. If there is a law called the Privacy Act, the assumption of politicians and the media is that privacy is being protected. The lack of interest in, or evidence of, the enforcement and impact of the Privacy Act has also discouraged its revision, unlike the situation in other Western countries where first-generation data protection laws have been or are being revised. The several hearings on computer matching in the 1980s performed a valuable service by indicating that real surveillance issues exist at the federal level, and that the Privacy Act was ineffective in handling them. Congress then revised the Privacy Act to deal directly with computer matching.

The Privacy Act must also reflect more fully the challenges posed to personal privacy by new forms or applications of information technology. Robert Gellman states that the central issue is its failure to provide any kind of meaningful controls over information technology. The Office of Technology Assessment, especially through its Communications and Information Technologies Program, does perform a very useful function in conducting studies at the behest of congressional committees of the societal impact of technology. OTA has developed a formula of using advisory panels, workshops, and reports by contractors to assure that wide consultation occurs during the conduct of its studies. Its publications are useful to committees of Congress and receive good coverage in the media. OTA is also the only place in the federal government where a qualified research staff exists for the serious examination of these issues. The problem at present is that Congress is not following up OTA reports with appropriate legislative solutions.

Earlier parts of this case study have regularly referred to OTA's 1986 examination of *Electronic Record Systems and Individual Privacy,* which specifically addressed the impact on individual rights of new technological advances. The study observed that "computer and telecommunication capabilities have expanded the interests of Federal agencies in personal information and enhanced their ability to process it. These capabilities have also overshadowed the ability of individuals to use the mechanisms available in the Privacy Act because, in general, it is more difficult for them to follow what occurs during the information-handling process." An OTA survey of federal agencies also documented the occurrence of increased automation, computer networking via telecommunications systems, and the explosive growth in the number of microcomputers to over 100,000 in 1985.[29] OTA pointed out the negative implications of these developments for personal privacy. The implications for surveillance are self-evident.

Dramatic changes have occurred in the federal government's use of information technology for surveillance purposes in the years since the Privacy Act was enacted, and the process of change is quickening rather than slackening. The committee report on the Senate version of the Privacy Act in 1974 expressed its intent "to require strict reporting by agencies and departments and meaningful congressional and executive branch review of any proposed use of information technology."[30] The law was written for the classic mainframe computers, which are rapidly being supplemented by an enormous number of microcomputers. The ease with which agencies can link automated data systems to create temporary or permanent systems of records is a good example of how surveillance technology has overtaken the law.

At the oversight hearings in 1983, the Defense Privacy Board expressed its concern about "the impact of information technology on record-keeping practices and privacy protection. The trend toward mini and micro computers with larger capabilities makes the development of adequate workable privacy safeguards or controls extremely difficult."[31] At the end of 1985, the Office of Information and Regulatory Affairs identified the effect of automation as a key Privacy Act issue requiring further study:

> The Act was drafted at a time when the government was at the beginning of the computer revolution. At that time, 80% of all systems of records consisted of paper records. . . . Today we have governmental anti-fraud and abuse programs that match huge quantities of records about individuals, a process made possible on such a large scale only by automation. Automated profiling techniques designed to be used with

matching programs are coming into use. Moreover, we are about to reach a point when ordinary government workers will have micro computers on their desks tied into a network by sophisticated telecommunications. One element in OMB's rewrite of the implementing guidelines will be a careful examination of how the Act works in this automated age and whether its provisions, its definitions, and its checks and balances are adequate.[32]

In June 1987 the deputy director of OMB instructed his Office of Information and Regulatory Affairs to conclude a review of the Privacy Act by the end of 1987, but there have been no results to date.[33] Although an initiative like the OMB guidelines on "call detail programs" and privacy protection are admirable, OIRA in its present configuration does not have the political will or resources to do all of the tasks already assigned to it and also monitor the implications of new technology for privacy. It has now acquired significant new duties under the Computer Matching Act. Moreover, the fundamental thrust of OMB's 1985 circular is to promote the effective use of available technology for federal information management, which has surveillance of the relevant public as a basic purpose.[34]

Given the pace of developments in informatics in the last decade, it is hardly a radical notion to argue that it is time to revise the Privacy Act in many ways. The option of doing nothing hardly bears discussion. Although concern continues to be expressed about the impact of new technology on civil liberties, no comprehensive oversight is taking place by either the executive branch or Congress.

Basically, the Privacy Act needs to be completely rewritten to comply with the needs of the present and to remedy its current deficiencies. Few members of the current House of Representatives were in Congress at the time of the enactment of the Privacy Act, and the time should be ripe for revisions. It also would be foolish at any point to rely solely on a privacy protection board to achieve implementation, given the huge, decentralized structure of the United States government. The current infrastructure should remain in place and be strengthened in a variety of ways to limit governmental intrusiveness.

Because of its statutory responsibilities under section 6 of the Privacy Act, OMB is currently the key to successful implementation. Its Office of Information Policy in OIRA needs to be strengthened in its resolve to act and in staff resources. In the absence of action to create a general oversight board, it would be at least desirable to have an Office of Privacy Policy within OIRA. Consideration must also be given to issuing the various OMB guidelines under the law in the form of regulations, thereby assuring that agencies have to comply.[35] OMB likes to think that its guidelines have the effect of regulations but that is not always the case at present.

There is also nothing wrong with the model of having each agency responsible for compliance with the Privacy Act; the same model is successfully followed in West Germany and Canada, for example. What is necessary is for each of the seventeen departments and agencies that are responsible for 80 percent of activity under the law to follow the model of the holder of the most systems of records, the Department of Defense, and create both a formal Privacy Board and a Privacy Office in each unit. Such offices should have explicit responsibility for implementation of the Privacy Act within their domains and not just process requests for access to personal information or fill out forms for OIRA. This would have the additional benefit of raising the visibility and esteem of Privacy Act officers, who are primarily invisible today within the huge departments that employ them. OTA makes the additional point that the number and training of privacy officials needs to be strengthened.[36]

The Data Integrity Boards created under the 1988 computer matching law for each department are an important first step. The deputy director of OMB has suggested that, at some future time, the role of the boards might be expanded to make them an integral part of each agency's Privacy Act implementation activities. This would be a very useful development.[37]

The need to strengthen congressional oversight of governmental surveillance activities is also self-evident. While it is plausible to bemoan the jurisdictional structure of committees as an impediment to the protection of individual rights, that is not an adequate defense. It took eight years for the first oversight hearings to occur; the response to computer matching was somewhat more timely. Despite the admirable efforts of the House Subcommittee on Government Information, Justice, and Agriculture, more needs to be done. In particular, OIRA should be called to testify after their biennial report on the law has been submitted to Congress. OTA has also suggested that "if committees with crosscutting privacy jurisdiction were established in both Houses, either as permanent committees, new subcommittees, or select committees, and all bills having privacy implications were referred jointly or sequentially to those committees, privacy issues could be debated and resolved in a more deliberate and focused manner."[38] Unfortunately, this recommendation flies in the face of congressional practice and the realities of U.S. lawmaking.

A number of specific suggestions for revision of the Privacy Act have been canvassed at various points in this case study, and a brief recapitulation here may be useful. OMB's own list of needed reforms includes examining the effectiveness of the public notice process, clarifying the definition of a routine use, adding two needed exceptions for disclosure to section (b), permitting the exemption of information made classified by statute under section (k), and meshing the disclosure and exemption provisions of the Freedom of Information Act and the Privacy Act.[39] The Office of Personnel Management and the Defense Privacy Board have also advanced very specific suggestions for matters requiring attention.[40] The Office of Technology Assessment has recently emphasized the need to review the basic principles of the Privacy Act, to create audit trails for data use, and to regulate the ease of data transfers.[41] Thus, the directions are at hand that would further strengthen controls on governmental surveillance in the United States, but it may require a privacy disaster for major congressional action to occur.

Controlling Surveillance

These conclusions draw together the main themes that emerge from the separate treatments of the operation of data protection laws and agencies. The goal is to provide a critique of data protection laws and agencies as vehicles for limiting surveillance of the population. The conclusions are shaped as a series of propositions for controlling surveillance in the public sector, including discussion of the supporting arguments that emerge from the case studies. The report card for data control is both positive and negative, and we may salute the progress of the data protectors yet remain concerned for the future of this important initiative. Although the preceding pages have recognized the shaping role of differing national historical traditions and constitutional practices, the main findings confirm the comparability of problems and solutions in privacy protection and surveillance control from country to country.

In order to keep governmental surveillance of the population under reasonable control, data protection laws and agencies are essential in Western industrial societies. These laws should define privacy interests as carefully as possible in order to facilitate implementation and in order to confront surveillance practices more directly than they do at present. The agencies or agents essential for implementing these laws should concentrate on data protection rather than developing other aspects of information policy in any given society.

The most important conclusion concerns the need to inspire data protectors to vigorous efforts as watchdogs over surveillance activities. Data protectors must be active and committed individuals who are very independent in the exercise of controlling power in order to serve as a countervailing force to excessive and intrusive surveillance practices. It is an open question whether advisory powers are adequate for this purpose; perhaps all data protectors need some regulatory power in order to play a more meaningful role in the control of surveillance. In particular, to be effective, data protectors must pursue audits with vigor in order to monitor compliance with fair information practices. In this connection, these conclusions also discuss the limits of data protection agencies in their work to date, since there is continuing evidence that the public is receiving only the illusion of surveillance control.

The Necessity of Data Protection Laws

Protecting privacy by limiting governmental surveillance is a vital activity, since individuals can no longer do it entirely for themselves in the face of massive changes in information-handling activities and in surveillance techniques. In the late twentieth century, the assistance of laws and regulatory authorities is essential. Data protection laws are thus absolutely indispensable for limiting the collection and use of personal information in the public sector. More than a dozen countries, the latest being Australia and Ireland in 1988, have enacted data protection laws on the basis of reasoned decisions of national and state legislatures. Eight countries have ratified the Council of Europe's Convention for the protection of personal information, while another ten have indicated their intention to legislate so as to eventually ratify the agreement.[1] These actions and, more importantly, the experience of such countries with the implementation of data protection in the public sector over a considerable period of time, lend strong support to the general argument for the necessity of such laws.

Most advanced industrial nations that do not have data protection laws are in the process of developing them, including Greece, Italy, Japan, the Netherlands, Portugal, Spain, and Switzerland. The addition of such countries is a necessary and elementary form of progress. The difficulties of drafting a law in accordance with national traditions, the need to incorporate the experience of other countries, the economic climate of the early 1980s, and generally crowded legislative calendars seem to explain failures to enact such laws before now.

A critical issue of coordination of legislation occurs in federal states, where the ideal is data protection laws and mechanisms for implementation that are integrated between the federal and state levels. Thus the West German federal and state governments have coordinated systems for data protection in the public sector, but this is not the case to date in the United States or Canada, beyond a shared reliance on a code of fair information practices. In Canada the federal privacy commissioner has a somewhat different set of powers and responsibilities than the Quebec Commission d'accès à l'information, which follows the French and Swedish models in the use of regulatory power. In 1987 Ontario enacted a law that is closer to the federal model than to Quebec's, but at the same time it grants more regulatory power to its information and privacy commissioner than is exercised by the twin federal commissioners. The risk of public confusion is perhaps offset by opportunities for experimentation.

The data protection movements of the 1970s in Western Europe and North America were shaped more by a common response to common problems than by national differences. The late Paul Sieghart, a leading British authority on data protection, advanced the proposition that whatever the model adopted, data protection has to fit comfortably into the existing legal and constitutional framework of a nation.[2] It should not be, he seemed to be suggesting, an alien creature. Professor Spiros Simitis, the Hesse Data Protection Commissioner, argued that Sieghart was advancing an attractive but dangerous notion for countries currently without data protection laws, since one result could be no data protection at all. Simitis perceives that data protection problems have a common origin in industrializing societies and require common solutions. It is evident from the case studies that data protection agencies or agents do face similar problems with excessive surveillance and that the practical methods they have adopted to combat it have more commonality than the national legislation has differences.

Data protection laws originated in response to actual, perceived, and even paranoid public fears about the surveillance capacity of computers.[3] Given the real concerns about surveillance in the face of automation, it has been relatively easy to persuade legislatures of the need for action. Even if such fears are mildly irrational on occasion, the enactment of a protective law has the decided benefit of helping to calm public anxieties and of providing a safety valve for the expression of continued concerns about the future of personal privacy and the control of surveillance. The general public debate over the proposed censuses of population in West Germany in 1983 and 1987 indicates that the existence of a regulatory scheme does not end or discourage public anxieties about the confidentiality of information, nor does it end symbolic resistance to data collection, but it does furnish a level of assurance that someone is overseeing data-handling practices in the public sector. Data protectors participated openly in this West German debate and served as a prime source for the media of factual information about confidentiality.

The evidence of the importance of data protection presented in this book should dispel any notion that data protection is simply a Quixotic cause pursued by privacy and human rights advocates, civil libertarians, and politicians clamoring for attention. Although enthusiasm for deregulation currently exists in most countries, data protection is not an appropriate area for the exercise of such sentiments; this is one issue where governmental intervention is manifestly necessary. In fact, the critical issue is how best to strengthen data protection in the face of strong, sustained, countervailing pressures for surveillance.

"Horror stories" of excessive surveillance should be unnecessary to justify the enactment of privacy protection laws, however appealing they may be to politicians and the media. In part, it is very difficult to uncover such episodes, because governments and the private sector have every incentive to cover them up. It requires subpoena power and a staff of trained investigators to discover what is really happening, which is one reason that privacy advocates so often refer to the extraordinary abuses of personal privacy uncovered by the Krever Commission of Inquiry into the Confidentiality of Health Information in Ontario.[4] The failure of data protectors to uncover atrocious examples of data abuse does not vitiate the need for data protection. In fact, specialists have their own favorite horror stories of surveillance that was nipped in the bud, as the case studies above illustrate. The particular deterrent benefit of having data protectors in place has been the discouragement and prevention of such abuses by the continued oversight of information practices.

European data protection laws include the hidden agenda of discouraging a recurrence of the Nazi and Gestapo efforts to control the population, and so seek to prevent the reappearance of an oppressive bureaucracy that might use existing data for nefarious purposes. This concern is such a vital foundation of current legislation that it is rarely expressed in formal discussions. This helps to explain the general European preference for strict licensing systems of data protection, and West Germany itself has established a strict legal regime for all data collection activities, reinforced now by the 1983 census decision of the Federal Constitutional Court. Thus European legislators have reflected a real fear of Big Brother based on common experience of the potential destructiveness of surveillance through record keeping. None wish to repeat the experiences endured under the Nazis during the Second World War.[5]

Privacy protection can further be justified as good housekeeping. Governments need data for legitimate purposes and must have fair information practices in place to govern its collection and use, or they risk noncompliance and negative publicity that jeopardizes the successful conduct of various initiatives. The public are very inclined to put the worst possible interpretation on the information practices of large institutions. Yet even once "outlandish" notions, such as the idea of a single national data bank, have become more and more achievable.

The debate over the coverage of all manual personal information systems in data protection laws must be reoriented to surveillance concerns. On merit, the argument for extending data protection to manual records is strong in that it would reduce incentives for leaving sensitive personal data in manual form. The pragmatic argument against wholesale coverage of manual systems, especially in a licensing or registration system, is simply related to the amount of work involved, such as under the 1984 Data Protection Act of the United Kingdom. It would indeed be contrary to the best interests of data protection to build up a large enough bureaucracy to regulate all manual files in such systems, but that is an argument against licensing and registration.

The Organization for Economic Co-operation and Development's *Guidelines* are wisely designed to "apply to personal data, whether in the public or private sectors, which, because of their nature or the context in which they are used, pose a danger to privacy and individual liberties."[6] The Canadian and U.S. Privacy Acts prudently cover all types of personal records. The Scandinavian notion of particularly sensitive information includes racial, religious, political, criminal, and sexual matters, health information, and the use of intoxicants.[7] The 1978 French law includes certain sensitive manual files.[8] Articles 30 and 31 of the French law specify types of information similar to what the Scandinavians have deemed sensitive, and the National Commission on Informatics and Freedoms (CNIL) has been especially rigorous in regulating their collection.

Although no overall consensus exists on what is sensitive information, the most relevant consideration is that any data can be risky for purposes of surveillance, given appropriate (or inappropriate) associations with other information. This was the conclusion of the West German Federal Constitutional

Court in its census decision. Thus the actual coverage of data protection should at least extend to manual records used for sensitive purposes, including linkages with automated registers, even if problems of definition are not easy to solve, since the utility of manual registers for surveillance cannot be underestimated.[9]

The pressures for the automation of personal data are almost irresistible from whatever perspective one chooses to evaluate them, and they create considerable pressure on data protection activities. The traditional time lag between the development of a new form of technology and its implementation is rapidly disappearing. The data bases of the public and private sectors are more intertwined in Sweden than in any other country outside Scandinavia, and the capacity for integrating public and private data resources exists elsewhere as well. Continued public anxiety on this score reflects credible fears about the creation or indeed existence of massive, linked personal information systems that can be Orwellian in every sense of that infamous adjective. It is the role of data protectors to thwart this tendency.

One also needs data protection laws to control the impact of various bureaucratic impulses of governments that engender increased surveillance. Austerity measures often lead to more intrusive procedures, since attempts to reduce welfare dependency or fraud require automated monitoring systems for implementation. For example, the 1983 restrictions on foreign spending announced by the Mitterrand government necessitated measures to monitor the monetary transactions and spending practices of French citizens through banks and credit card companies.[10] Even if the purpose of a system is to perform a required administrative task, as is the case in most such instances, the implications for eroding the privacy of the individual by facilitating surveillance are considerable. The French government, for example, had to create a system that monitored who traveled abroad and whether for business or recreational purposes. Since the press suggested that 90 percent of the population does not vacation abroad, the government thereby collected detailed information on an elite and/or potentially troublesome population. The essential point is that economic controls at a time of financial crisis for the state had negative implications for personal privacy; only data protectors and their allies in the media can make governments give such matters due advance consideration.

Government agencies are the leading invaders of the personal privacy of citizens, since they maintain systems with the largest scope and most numerous records. Even a system for the seemingly innocuous purpose of paying a benefit can be subverted for surveillance of a particular person, when the need arises. The fundamental premise, indeed the bureaucratic imperative, is that new uses for automated information systems will always develop, once they are in existence; hence the essential need for enhanced data protection for the ultimate purpose of protecting the personal privacy of individuals to the fullest extent possible in a democratic society. The necessity for data protection laws (and control agencies) thus seems fully established, even if the problems of controlling governmental surveillance are never going to be easy.

The nature of the political process in liberal pluralistic democracies also requires the creation of laws and agencies for data protection. Citizens need protection against legislative whims and excesses, however "democratic" the process that produces them. If one aspect of the right to privacy receives statutory recognition in the form of a data protection law, then it is much more difficult for changes in government moods and the public temper to challenge successfully this aspect of fundamental human rights. Just as individuals differ in their degree of concern for their own privacy, so various political parties in any country inevitably differ in their evaluation of the importance of continuing to restrict surveillance of citizens versus their other priorities, especially in the heat of the moment. A legislative form of data protection at least encourages a less hasty reordering of priorities, because external consultation with data protection authorities is necessary. The public is also more likely to react if a new government proposes to change or abolish a data protection act.

Data protection in every country obviously has to function in a changing political climate. A supportive environment has a lot to do with promoting or resolving conflicts between data protectors and government ministries. Contrasting attitudes of political parties can also be found in all countries. Opposition parties are generally in favor of data protection, which becomes another weapon against the government; once in power, they sometimes chafe under the controls imposed by data protection, since they appear to interfere with other priorities of the moment.

For politicians, support for privacy protection should have the advantage of being a relatively manageable issue in contrast to such seemingly intractable problems as controlling the spread of nuclear weapons and managing the economy; moreover, concern for privacy is an issue that the public can readily understand and appreciate. Unfortunately, many politicians tend to regard data protection in practice as quite arcane, boring, and suspiciously civil libertarian. They display little inclination to value personal privacy when searching for a solution to a perceived problem, such as drug use, tax evasion, or threats to national security.

The ultimate protection for the individual is the constitutional entrenchment of rights to privacy and data protection. One can make a strong argument, even in the context of primarily seeking to promote data protection, that having an explicit entrenched constitutional right to personal privacy is a desirable goal in any Western society that has a written constitution and a bill of rights. The purpose of creating a constitutional right to privacy is not to leave data protection solely to the courts, except for the interpretation of the necessary statutes in cases of conflict, but to allow individuals to assert privacy claims that extend beyond the act. A Canadian parliamentary committee reviewing the Privacy Act suggested the amendment of the Canadian Charter of Rights and Freedoms to establish a basic right to privacy.[11] In Sweden a government committee recommended the inclusion of protection against undue infringement on privacy by means of electronic data processing in the constitutional catalogue of rights and liberties, and the Riksdag has now taken the first step toward implementation.

All Western societies require constitutional standing for both data protection and informational self-determination in accord with the census decision of the German Federal Constitutional Court. As Simitis has written: "Since this ruling at the latest, it has been an established fact in this country that the Constitution gives the individual the right to decide when and under what circumstances his personal data may be processed."[12]

The practical evidence of the need for data protection laws has appeared repeatedly in the case studies. The evidence of surveillance problems facing all of us is concrete. The negative consequences of not having data protection laws are suggested by the positive experiences of countries that have them. However, the enactment of general data protection laws does not end surveillance of the populace. Even if it were true that the vast majority of isolated information systems, in the private sector in particular (for example, payroll systems), pose no practical challenges to the privacy of the individual, the remaining sensitive systems or risky uses of innocuous systems furnish plenty of scope for the activities of data protectors for the remainder of this century; perhaps by then the limits of automation may be apparent, or we may have been forced to submit to a fully controlled maximum-security society. The existence of data protection laws gives some hope that the twenty-first century will not be a world in which personal privacy has been fully eroded by the forces promoting surveillance.

Defining Privacy Interests to Limit Surveillance

Two fundamental criticisms emerge from a comparative study of data protection laws as a means of controlling surveillance. The first is that there is a failure in some cases to distinguish between the broad need for the protection of all aspects of personal privacy and the need for data protection. This situation primarily exists in North America, where data protection laws usually bear the misleading title of Privacy Acts.[13] The understanding and protection of privacy requires conceptual principles; the conduct of data protection is more operational in character. The British were wise to call their statute a Data Protection Act; in fact, the word "privacy" does not appear anywhere in it.[14]

The second, more important criticism is that most national legislation neither adequately defines the privacy interests of the individual that need to be protected nor the data protection principles that need to be implemented in order to limit surveillance. More successful efforts at identifying precise privacy interests should refocus the attention of data protectors to the threat of excessive surveillance, as is accomplished admirably in Schedule 1 to the U.K.'s Data Protection Act. Data protectors need to be encouraged to confront surveillance practices more directly.

The vague language in first-generation laws was a conscious response to real problems of definition. Political scientists acknowledge the desirable principle of specificity in setting statutory standards but recognize that legislators like to create loosely worded mandates, as opposed to specific goals, in order to avoid hard decisions about definitions and to permit the legislation to respond to experience.[15] The generality of the early laws was also a deliberate effort to make their scope broad enough to permit intervention in the maximum number of cases.

There are conflicting views about the desirability and possibility of greater precision in data laws. One perception is that general language promotes flexibility in implementation. However, it is difficult to understand, for example, why Swedes should be so resistant to the identification of statutory objectives that move beyond the vague goal of preventing unwarranted invasions of privacy. The need for adequate definitions is especially important for guiding specialists in data processing in their work. While agreeing that all European data protection laws lack a precise definition of privacy, Herbert Burkert, a leading German commentator, suggests that this reluctance stems from the newness of laws dealing with technology. Such an excuse is less applicable to second-generation laws, since experience can be codified. Other informed observers think that the standards in all privacy legislation are necessarily vague.[16] Existing research on the meaning of personal privacy is an admittedly inadequate guide to legislators in any country.[17]

One response to the abortive efforts to define privacy interests is to hold up the European approach as an example. French civil law, for example, does not encourage extensive efforts at definition, because of risks of obsolescence, preferring to let jurisprudence develop definitions over time. Although this point may have general validity, it is less relevant to a situation where data protection laws in countries with either civil or common law traditions share the same inadequacies in spelling out privacy interests.

The ideal data protection law should strive for as much explicitness as possible in the identification of privacy interests in order to facilitate, guide, and inform the process of limiting surveillance. It is sometimes argued that the changing nature of challenges to privacy discourages such efforts. Yet, at present, there is a core element of well-defined privacy interests that stands the test of time and is not fully susceptible to changes in technology, ideology, age, income, or social developments. The core of privacy interests remains essentially the same in Western nations, while surveillance threats continue to escalate.[18]

The problem is to encapsulate in acceptable and enforceable terms what each of us thinks and feels about his or her own interests in a value like privacy, even if it is no easier than articulating the meaning of freedom and related human rights. Alan F. Westin's influential study of *Privacy and Freedom* wisely suggested that there is a link between the two values.[19] Controversies over how the law should protect privacy have their counterpart in debates over the appropriate legal guarantees of liberty and equality. In fact, a number of issues now subsumed into privacy used to be treated in English common law under the rubric of the liberties of the subject. The literature on other human rights has similarly amorphous characteristics as the writings on privacy. Because values such as privacy are so important and pervasive in preserving essential aspects of human existence, they are difficult to define, especially in legal terms.[20]

Some preliminary qualifications are necessary in the process of identifying the relevant interests in information-handling activities. Our focus is on data protection in the contemporary, liberal, democratic and pluralistic societies in the West rather than in totalitarian or tyrannical regimes. Protection of privacy should also remain largely a nonlegal activity in most areas of human existence, meaning that even when data protection laws exist, individuals have to rely to a considerable extent on their own efforts, such as refusing to give out personal information, in order to limit unwanted surveillance.[21] As a basic goal, the movement to protect privacy in the face of computer-based technology must raise individual consciousness about the dangers. People have to become more aware of the risks involved in disclosing information about themselves. Simitis has written: "As long as data processing is not carried out under conditions of transparency, especially for the data subject, data protection will remain illusory."[22] Again under the auspices of data protectors, similar consciousness-raising is needed for the persons who design and operate systems of social control.

The appropriate model for controlling surveillance requires a balancing of competing interests and values by individuals and societies. The human claim to privacy is one critical factor in this balancing test; it must compete with the government's right to obtain and use personal information for legitimate purposes, subject to fair information practices. Neither has absolute primacy over the other, although the experience of the 1980s suggests that data protection is normally less of a legislative priority than efficient government. Perhaps most importantly, the claims of individuals to avoid intrusive surveillance need to be balanced against the interests of others and of society.[23] When guided by more precise statutory standards, data protection agencies should play an even more effective role in this process.

Data protection laws must do more than state that something called privacy is desirable and that its infringement should be discouraged, as is too frequently the case at present. Fortunately, current laws are more successful in identifying the standards and fair information practices in the administration of personal information systems that will ultimately protect the privacy interests of the individual. Table 7 presents a listing based upon an analysis of existing statutes in the several countries. These are the important interests of the individual that need to be protected and indeed have been protected during the 1970s. Referring to them as "data protection principles or practices" seems more appropriate than oblique references to "a code of fair information practices," because one can then more logically connect privacy, data protection, and the control of surveillance. Data protection is thus one way in which the law can make an explicit commitment to the protection of personal privacy.[24]

The principles for the control of surveillance in Table 7 do not require detailed discussion here, since their application has been discussed and illustrated in the individual case studies. Paul Sieghart summarized them succinctly in the aphorism that the right person should get the right information for the right purposes.[25] One might also emphasize the fundamental importance of principle three, which places the highest significance on reducing data collection to the fullest extent possible in the first instance and then retaining personal data in identifiable form only as long as necessary.

Table 7. Data Protection Principles and Practices for Government Personal Information Systems

---

1. The principles of publicity and transparency (openness) concerning government personal information systems (no secret data banks).

2. The principles of necessity and relevance governing the collection and storage of personal information.

3. The principle of reducing the collection, use, and storage of personal information to the maximum extent possible.

4. The principle of finality (the purpose and ultimate administrative uses for personal information need to be established in advance).

5. The principle of establishing and requiring responsible keepers for personal information systems.

6. The principle of controlling linkages, transfers, and interconnections involving personal information.

7. The principle of requiring informed consent for the collection of personal information.

8. The principle of requiring accuracy and completeness in personal information systems.

9. The principle of data trespass, including civil and criminal penalties for unlawful abuses of personal information.

10. The requirement of special rules for protecting sensitive personal information.

11. The right of access to, and correction of, personal information systems.

12. The right to be forgotten, including the ultimate anonymization or destruction of almost all personal information.

The Need for Data Protection Agencies

Perhaps the most important conclusion of this volume is that it is not enough simply to pass a data protection law in order to control surveillance; an agency charged with implementation is essential to make the law work in practice.[26] A statute by itself is an insufficient countervailing force to the ideological and political pressures for efficiency and monitoring of the population that are at work in Western society. Sociologist Arnold Simmel argued a generation ago that effective mechanisms were essential to prevent the encroachments upon privacy made possible by social and technological developments. Moreover, "the chances that these methods will be used are vastly increased if ideologies are at hand to legitimate such use."[27] Data protection agencies are a manifestation of a counterideology that suggests that the unfettered use of information technology for social control is illegitimate.

The fundamental task of such a mechanism in the public sector is to protect citizens from excessive governmental surveillance. Unfortunately, as Hans Peter Bull of West Germany has emphasized, every administration thinks it is acting in the best interests of the citizens or at least the collectivity, no matter what it is attempting to do. That is one reason why it has usually been the legislature and not the executive branch of government that has recognized the essential need for a data protection agent; legislatures have at least occasionally acknowledged that they too cannot always be trusted to act in favor of personal interests. Yet such insights are often fleeting—a "window of opportunity"—in the continuing process of lawmaking. Thereafter, legislators have had much less reason to support data protection or to monitor implementation, especially when it appears to interfere with other priorities.[28] Legislative bodies are as capable as governments of supporting measures that directly or indirectly encourage surveillance, because they tend to look only at the basic purpose of a particular measure and are inclined to value efficiency and controlling costs very highly.

Governments and government bodies do not have the expertise, the time, or the inclination to make the requisite detailed decisions for effective data protection. The creation of a specialized bureaucracy to accomplish these tasks avoids most of the worst problems identified by students of the implementation process. Without such a mechanism, the most obvious result is the relatively unrestricted collection and transfer of personal data by government agencies, excessive monitoring of the private lives of the citizenry, and only limited adherence to a data protection law. In many ways, this has been the experience in the U.S. federal system.

Experience under the U.S. Privacy Act demonstrates the inadequacies of the courts as a primary vehicle for the implementation of an important statute. The development of a monitoring agency would facilitate the rapid application and interpretation of the relevant law. Oversight by ordinary civil servants is too weak, since they are so subject to political considerations, as was the case at the

Office of Management and Budget during the Reagan era, nor have individual citizens managed to breathe continued life into the Privacy Act. Unless a federal data protection agency is created in the United States, the federal system for articulating privacy interests in a systematic fashion is woefully inadequate. A data protection agency could have at least struggled, for example, against the almost uncontrolled process of computer matching. The subsequent outcry over such linkages led eventually to congressional intervention but, as is customarily the case at the federal level, this required the creation of yet another temporary, ad hoc coalition of privacy advocates, in the absence of a statutory body charged with such responsibilities. While such alliances will always be essential to confront major governmental initiatives toward increased surveillance in any country, they are incapable of routine, detailed implementation.

In evaluating the need for a protective agency, it cannot be emphasized too strongly that the incentives for the government and the bureaucracy are in the direction of invading, or at least ignoring or neglecting, privacy interests rather than protecting them. Most measures that are perceived as "necessary" to cope with a societal problem involve surveillance through data collection. Especially in difficult economic times, the predominant goals are to improve efficiency, to reduce fraud, to cut expenditures on programs and staff, and to step up monitoring of the target population. Few bureaucracies are inherently sympathetic to the privacy interests of their clientele. Public servants do not like to acknowledge that they often invade privacy, yet their goals are usually at odds with such values. The fact that greater sensitivity now exists in many countries is a tribute to consciousness-raising by data protectors.

A data protection agency is also essential because bureaucratic resistance to data protection is predictable.[29] The tendency is to resist strongly any new and continuing forms of external oversight that intrude into its control of its own domain. Unlike the introduction of an ombudsman in New Zealand, who did not pose any apparent threat to other actors in the political system, data protection impinges on every agency of government.[30]

Initial resistance to the whole idea of limiting surveillance does not end with a law's enactment. Data protectors have had to remind the regulated in a forceful manner of the existence of their offices, because bureaucracies attempt to ignore its statutory role as much as possible. Two reasons that West Germany has had reasonable success in implementation are that the law-driven character of the society encourages civil servants to adhere to such laws of their own accord, and data collection activity must be controlled by special laws incorporating protective principles. In France and Canada, both the CNIL and the Canadian privacy commissioner have had to make strong efforts to remind the government and its departments of their existence. Failure to consult with the Canadian commissioner has been one of the major weaknesses of implementation to date.[31]

The problem of controlling surveillance is exacerbated by the fact that data protection further requires significant behavioral change on the part of those being regulated. As one observer has written, "the lesser the distance between the required behavior and existing behavior patterns, the greater the likelihood that a statutory mandate will be self-enforcing, that is, the bulk of the affected population will adhere to the law without the deployment of any special enforcement resources."[32] For the most part, this has not been the case with data protection, because it requires significant modifications in information-handling practices. The self-interest of the agency in improving the efficiency and public acceptability of data-handling activities is secondary to what it perceives as its basic tasks. A ministry that previously followed sound informa-tion practices has fewer problems than a less accomplished organization. Data protectors have all had serious problems with one agency or another and have depended for the most part on promoting appropriate behavioral changes in the target population on an incremental basis.

Perhaps the strongest argument in favor of data protection agencies is the multiple benefits that have accrued to the public in those countries that have them. Even if their records of achievement are imperfect, the evidence of their specific successes in limiting surveillance is extensive. They have reduced the risks of the actual "death of privacy" or the "end of private life." In West Germany, conservative government ministers still blame data protection for hindering security activities in particular. Yet the federal Data Protection Com-missioner has proven to be very necessary and effective in practice; it has been an exemplary data protection agency. Spokesmen in the Bundestag have subse-quently admitted that its creation was essential.

In essence, data protection commissioners or agencies are an alarm system for the protection of privacy. They exercise continuing oversight of surveillance practices and review compliance with the stated goals of legislation through audits and security checks. They regulate specific national information systems in appropriate ways, largely through a process of mediation and the balancing of interests. They monitor and evaluate new technological developments in data processing and telecommunications. Each agency has specialists in various types of information systems and data flows who can speak intelligently about data protection and security with the operators of government information systems.

Data protection agencies are essential if one seeks to limit surveillance of the populace. Every government agency has to be monitored in order to control its insatiable demands for personal information. Moreover, it is a complex matter, for example, to supervise the police and security agencies effectively, so that they do not achieve uncontrolled access to all existing sources of personal information. Simitis writes that institutionalized control agencies "have the necessary knowledge enabling them to analyze the structure of public and private agencies and to trace step by step their information pro-cedures. They can therefore detect deficiencies and propose adequate remedies. What data protection really means depends thus on their activity."[33]

Limiting surveillance is a difficult activity, because of the balancing of interests that is involved; it cannot be self-activating and successful. Data protectors are specialists in articulating privacy interests on a systematic basis on behalf of the public and in applying fair information practices. Neither legislatures nor courts are as capable of performing the same essential tasks. Moreover, data protectors try to ensure that data protection is not only for good economic times but is applied on a consistent basis for the protection of individuals. This issue has arisen in all countries with national data protection laws.

There are accompanying risks in creating data protection agencies. The most basic is that they will fail. They may simply become agents for legitimating information-collecting activities and new information technology, because of the scope of problems of regulation and enforcement. The existence of data protection can have the effect of bestowing a seal of approval on any mass surveillance system, which is a further reason to resist pro forma implementation.

At present, data protection agencies are in many ways functioning as legitimators of new technology. For the most part, their licensing and advisory functions have not prevented the introduction of threatening new technologies, such as machine-readable identity cards or innumerable forms of enhanced data banks; they act rather as shapers of marginal changes in the operating rules for such instruments of public surveillance. They lose such battles (or are ignored), as often as they win them. If the protectors appear to have participated fully in the discussion, yet lack the power, the ability, or the will to regulate certain invasive aspects of these innovations, the public may wrongly infer that its privacy interests have been safeguarded.

Data protection agencies risk isolation as agents of legitimation versus their fundamental role of questioning the need to create new surveillance systems and to expand existing ones. In many cases, specific innovations and improvements may be justified, but once in existence they are open to potential use and abuse. If a data protection authority simply acquiesces to most such changes, as is too often the case, it risks simply becoming an agent of legitimation for whatever the government chooses to do.

The public's perception of the efficacy of data protection leaves something to be desired as well. The central fact is that the public no longer believes in grandiose promises of confidentiality. Who can blame them in the light of such episodes as the theft of identifiable tax records on 16 million Canadians from a Toronto office of Revenue Canada Taxation in 1986, an event that John Grace, the privacy commissioner of Canada, aptly called "a Chernobyl for data protection"?[34] Close scrutiny of the work of 600,000 West German census enumerators in 1987 confirmed the practical problems of ensuring compliance with the detailed rules of data protection in such a massive undertaking. Moreover, the world is full of technocrats who enjoy detailing the imperfections of computer security when they are not promoting the application of the latest wizardry. The effect on public confidence in data protection is unsettling.

Who can blame the public for fearing computer matching, when data protectors have been able to do so little, in practice, to prevent them, despite their best efforts? Controlling record linkages for purposes of surveillance remains, in theory and in reality, the central problem of data protection in all Western countries. Data protection agencies are currently struggling with the problem of matching programs, and it is never a foregone conclusion that they will prevail against other societal forces favoring surveillance, including the legislature.

The public is being lulled into a false sense of security about the protection of their privacy by their official protectors, who often lack the will and energy to resist successfully the diverse initiatives of what Jan Freese has aptly termed the "information athletes" in our respective societies. Thus, for example, West German data protectors, despite their admirable efforts, had only a marginal impact on the law for the 1987 census, nor could their explicit and implicit support for the integrity of the law prevent significant public resistance and controversy.

Data protection agencies pose a fundamental question. Are we witnessing the emergence of the toothless and blind watchdog? In terms of sheer size, not to speak of power, what prospects do thirty to fifty data protectors have against large and powerful government ministries with many thousands of employees? These are not minimal problems in making data protection effective.[35]

The Effective Conduct of Data Protection

Despite the constraints of various constitutional, legal, and administrative traditions, it is possible to advance an ideal model for operating a data protection agency. In order to be effective watchdogs over public administrations, data protectors have to adopt a functional, expansive, and empirical, rather than a formal and legalistic, approach to their statutory tasks. Their efforts must be to understand what is happening in practice—and what might happen—in each type of personal information system. The staff has to understand government administration and information technology in order to achieve appropriate controls on surveillance. It must work to understand the needs of the agencies being regulated, in order to promote efficient implementation. The desirable approach, as illustrated by Bull and Simitis in West Germany, Freese in Sweden, and Grace in Canada, involves an expansive policy outlook, followed by careful legal and technocratic application of the law.

A data protector has to be able to learn from experience, to be adaptable, and to be able to transmit an understanding of data protection to the clientele. An important educative function also has to be performed. The stance should be one of negotiation and, as far as possible, the avoidance of public confrontations with those being regulated. Simitis argues as well for a gradualist or incremental approach to data protection, involving cooperation, a process of learning, and a search for consensus.[36] In his judgment, the job of being a data protector is highly political, a view that is acceptable only so long as the goal of limiting intrusiveness is not sacrificed by what are traditionally regarded as political compromises, such as too often has been the case in France.

The case studies demonstrate that the general similarities of approaches among the various existing data protection agencies are greater than the differences, although there are some significant variations in the relative success of implementation to date. The practical details of how data protectors are selected, organized, and motivated make a great deal of difference in results, even after data protection has achieved a certain level of maturity, as in West Germany, Sweden, and Canada. The example of the CNIL in its early years is a vivid reminder that data protection staff members must be talented and professional in order to handle complicated tasks.

The issue of whether a commission or a commissioner is a better way of controlling surveillance remains something of an open question, even if the relative effectiveness of data protection in West Germany and Canada argues persuasively for the commissioner model. Yet the choice of a commissioner as opposed to a commission system may not make much difference in the control of surveillance, since the weaknesses tend to have the same roots. Neither model has been functioning perfectly. It may be easier for the government or the civil service to resist or attack a single commissioner rather than a representative commission, but then the former seems more effective in achieving results based on experience to date. The actual model adopted seems to depend most on the political and constitutional traditions of the country in question.

The advantages to date have rested with single commissioners. Although head of the Swedish Data Inspection Board, Freese essentially acted as a data protection commissioner. His dynamism considerably reduced the role of the governing board in specific activities. The use of politicians to be the executive heads of agencies, such as occurred in France in the early years, is a less successful model. Trying to achieve data protection is a full-time job, requiring considerable commitment to leadership. Politicians bring considerable experience to collective decision making, but they are less effective at implementation on a day-to-day basis, because of their competing obligations and rival (usually elective) interests.

In his pioneering study of ombudsmen, Walter Gellhorn concluded that "the mere existence of their offices means little. The men in the offices are what counts." Implementation of any law requires committed and talented personnel, possessing the political and managerial skills to use available resources for the pursuit of statutory objectives. As political scientists Paul Sabatier and Daniel Mazmanian point out, political skills refer "to the ability to develop good working relationships with sovereigns in the agency's subsystems, to convince opponents and target groups that they are being treated fairly, to mobilize support among latent supportive constituencies, to adroitly present the agency's case through the mass media, and so on."[37] This is an excellent list of qualifications for a data protection leader.

Despite the risk of discussions of leadership resulting in prescriptions for appointing supermen or superwomen, the ideal data protection commissioner is self-confident, perceptive, experienced, well-connected, reasonable but firm, has a strong presence, and is politically astute. He or she must have an awareness of the multiplicity of implementation games and the devices available to counteract them.[38] An essential but very difficult task of leadership is to build a constituency to support limits on surveillance practices, especially when tough choices have to be made.

The selection of a leader and senior staff for a data protection agency is thus a critical step.[39] The personality and beliefs of the commissioner substantially influence whether the office develops a broad policy outlook on data protection as opposed to paying attention only to limited legal responsibilities. What such a person thinks about the relative importance of individual rights in a democratic society also makes a considerable difference. The central point is that the application of any data protection law inevitably bears the imprint, for both good and bad, of the personalities and philosophies of the leading individuals involved.

The goals of data protection are of considerable significance for the societies in which we live, much more so than for many other regulatory agencies today. Controlling surveillance is of comparable importance to the regulation of nuclear power and environmental protection. That point is at least worth asserting, because it encapsulates the view that implementing data protection must be regarded by its proponents as a vital activity.

The watchdog must have both a bark and a bite. Successful implementation of data protection requires active, energetic leadership and dedicated, trained staffs. They have to establish a tone of ethical and moral concern for the control of surveillance. Unfortunately, in several countries the process of implementation has already reached the phase of routinization and formalization, or what the French with their customary expressiveness term *banalisation*. The initial era of good feelings, of enthusiasm for newness, of what we may term "the honeymoon phase," has passed.

The historical experience of regulatory agencies in every country is, of course, not encouraging about the prospects for preventing the weakening of the implementation process over time. Data protection agencies have for the most part been highly motivated by the novelty and societal significance of the issues they are confronting. The long-term prospects are for the disintegration of this level of initiative. Mazmanian and Sabatier have hypothesized that "in general, the commitment of agency officials to statutory objectives, and the consequent probability of their successful implementation, will be highest in a new agency with high visibility that was created after an intense political campaign. After the initial period, however, the degree of commitment will probably decline over time as the most committed people become burned out and disillusioned with bureaucratic routine, to be replaced by officials much more interested in security than in taking risks to attain policy goals."[40] They predict such declines in enthusiasm as occurring over a five- to seven-year period; not surprisingly, data protectors are not immune to such forces.

The leaders of the first generation of the 1970s have left the data protection scene: Simitis is the only one still in harness. These men and women were especially vigorous leaders with significant profiles in the media. Their successors face a considerable challenge in surpassing the standards set by them. Moreover, and more seriously, the leaders of the first generation have been largely replaced with more traditional public servants whose approaches conform more closely with the low-profile approach of normal regulation.[41] (One particular strength of the newcomers of the mid-1980s is that many of them are accomplished, professional administrators, while others have strong backgrounds for dealing with the media.) It would be surprising if data protection commissioners were equally good at every aspect of their tasks, including public relations. Freese in Sweden had unique skills as a publicist, as does Grace in Canada.

In terms of future leadership for data protection, there is considerable risk that less vigorous officials will be appointed, as governments tire of their persistent (and necessary) interventions on behalf of privacy interests. Walter Gellhorn cited an opposition politician's claim in Sweden in the early 1960s that no special mechanisms were needed to control the ombudsman, because no one is chosen who will make trouble for the government and its ministers; an appointee has to share the established outlook.[42] Unfortunately, this type of problem is becoming more evident in the choice of data protection commissioners, as certain governments display less inclination to be sensitive to the need to limit surveillance by choosing strong leaders.[43] The nature of democratic societies makes it unlikely that an institutional solution can be found for such a problem.

Data protection has also become more politicized in a partisan sense in connection with these changes of leadership. It is, of course, a counsel of wisdom to acknowledge that data protection is indeed a political activity, in the sense of the need to weigh conflicting societal values and interests. These tiny bureaucracies, faced with such overwhelming regulatory tasks, should not to any considerable extent reflect partisan politics in the society at large by shifting their positions in response to political trends. Such bending with the political wind may be a recipe for a comfortable existence for data protectors, but it is unlikely to be the way to assuage public anxieties about surveillance or to solve complex problems of data protection.

The argument is not that the implementation of data protection should be dominated by fanatics. Such an approach would be as counterproductive as a solely technocratic or bureaucratic perspective. A strong commitment to data protection, a talent for public administration, and an understanding of technocracy and technology must be mutually balanced. In one informant's view, for example, data protection is only one interest at stake in public administration, and the job of data protectors is to search for solutions. For example, although the staff members of the German federal commissioner advocate individual rights, they are aware of the competing interests of the government, the Bundestag, and the public. The same informant believes that the federal commissioner's office should not be the judge in establishing the particular balance but should be prepared to fight for its point of view, if necessary. Its success depends upon the quality of its arguments, a view that is a very sound, if somewhat idealistic, approach to the control of surveillance, since it neglects considerations of power. The matter of whether the actual balancing of interests should be done within a data protection agency or by others is a matter for continuing debate, which we will return to below.

In terms of its development and application, data protection is an issue for specialists, given the complex character of most data banks and information technology. Yet, like nuclear or environmental regulation, the control of surveillance is no less important and worthy an object for action. The solution is to entrust basic implementation to a cadre of specialists. Some staff members of data protection agencies are clearly better than others at achieving their statutory goals. The key factors are strong senior management, training, and prior experience in public administration. The CNIL, for example, tried to function for too long without a strong staff director. The quality of the staff is an important factor in the achievements of the Swedish Data Inspection Board, the German federal Data Protection Commissioner's office, and the office of the Hesse Data Protection Commissioner. The same offices have been successful in avoiding such traditional bureaucratic tendencies as large staffs, excessive regulation, trivialization of the subject, and high costs.[44] Simitis has emphasized the importance of avoiding bureaucracy: "This means that from the very beginning the number of people involved must be limited. Limited in the sense that you need people who are able to discuss problems together, to formulate new ideas together, to develop together new initiatives. . . . The moment a Data Commissioner becomes a bureaucratic institution, nobody will ever again believe in the necessity of such an institution."[45] Data protection does create more bureaucratic burden for operators of systems. The most comforting aspect of this inevitable result is that the existing data protection agencies have been reasonably successful in avoiding such bureaucratic characteristics, at least to the extent permitted by their statutes. Ironically, the current issue is whether such authorities have the staff and resources to accomplish their goals.

More importantly, the commitment to a nonbureaucratic approach and a small staff must not result in an overworked and overcommitted staff that provides only the illusion of data protection. Ironically, the situation in Hesse has led to some problems in this regard, since Simitis works only part-time and, until 1986, functioned with an especially small staff.[46] The admirable anti-bureaucratic thrust that has kept staff sizes relatively small can mean inadequate data protection in practice. Neglect of inspections, for example, is a universal trait of data protection to date.

One of the classic conditions leading to noncompliance with a particular statutory policy is lack of funds, talent, time, or energy at the agency charged with implementation.[47] Norwegian experience has illustrated at least certain characteristics of such resource-based noncompliance, when a tiny staff could not handle the avalanche of paper from universal licensing activities. However, data protectors have for the most part been fortunate in the staff and funds available to carry out their assigned tasks. Moreover, the costs of data protection are infinitesimally small compared to the costs of running other human rights agencies or the amounts of direct and indirect subsidies furnished by all governments for the promotion of various forms of information technology.[48] The public has no reason for concern about the costs of data protection, except perhaps to argue that the resources committed to this essential activity are too limited.

Eugene Bardach has noted staff turnover as another relevant blockage to successful implementation, because it removes experience. This issue has two sides: there can be too little and then too much turnover, as happened in Sweden. Freese kept the same staff intact for too long, and then most of them left about the same time. As Gellhorn noted, "the theoretical enhancement of independence that flows from security in office must be weighed against the possibility that a critic may lose verve and flexibility if too long involved in the same work."[49] A staff, for example, may become frozen in size and stagnant in permanent positions, suggesting a considerable advantage in the rotation of staff with other government departments, such as occurs in West Germany, where an employee can return to the parent unit, the federal Ministry of the Interior. Security is often coupled with limited opportunities for career advancement in a small agency.

Some staff members, especially those with considerable experience, are finding themselves bored by the data protection issue, which they describe as a very narrow field of specialization. They sometimes say that all issues look the same to them at a certain point. The staff does need to build up considerable expertise and collective experience over time, but it is important to rotate personnel on a recurring basis. The lack of staff mobility at any moment is often reflective of the economic situation.

Data protection should probably not be a lifetime career, yet it must attract people with a commitment to the importance of what they are doing. This problem touches all the professional staff and with predictably mixed results. The CNIL has not yet achieved much stability. The 1986 changes at the Swedish Data Inspection Board have in fact reinvigorated the data protection initiative by bringing in a fresh approach.

If data protection laws fully articulate the privacy interests that a legislature wants to protect, the agencies of implementation should not have excessive discretion in the application of the law and the interpretation of its principles, such as seems to exist in Sweden and France. The government and the legislature are, in broad terms, in a better position than such an agency to balance general societal values, at least in terms of framing appropriate statutory language, although there will continue to be situations in which the protection agency will have to warn both the executive and the legislature against the implications of certain practices for surveillance. Privacy should not be threatened more than it is likely to be by fleeting enthusiasms for panaceas or by ideological shifts.

In seeking to promote a balance between privacy and other competing values, the protection agency's primary role is to continue to articulate the interests requiring defense. This applies in particular to such a pressing issue as preserving individual rights during the fight against terrorism or in record linkages. The data protection agency should not be a miniparliament that seeks to settle the appropriate balance internally, nor should it concentrate solely on presenting a balanced perspective of the competing interests to the external master, be it the government or the legislature. Its emphasis should be on the antisurveillance side of the balance, since the forces allied against privacy, or at least in favor of efficient surveillance, are generally so powerful.

The argument of this volume is that data protectors should concentrate on the articulation and advancement of privacy interests to control surveillance, since they are the primary group in government that has the responsibility and capacity to do so. Balancing the competing interests in difficult cases should be left largely to the legislature, with the caveat that the privacy protectors must find a way to convey their views forcefully. However, if the cabinet, government, or legislature ultimately has to settle a dispute between a protection agency and a government department, there are further risks of compromising data protection interests. The best systems of data protection, such as in West Germany, Sweden, and Canada, are those in which privacy interests are being most strongly articulated. This necessarily includes effective efforts to communicate concerns to the government and legislature.

Independence and the Exercise of Power

As described in the case studies, data protection agencies exercise a degree of independence in the performance of their tasks that is relatively unusual among governmental institutions. Observers and practitioners agree that data protection agencies require as much independence as is constitutionally possible, subject to the most appropriate type of governmental, legislative, administrative, or judicial review, since independence must be balanced with some form of accountability.[50] Simitis emphasizes that a data protection agency relies on its guaranteed independence for authority in dealing with institutions under its control.[51] Most of the West German commissioners do not yet have the maximum of independence outside the normal hierarchy of government, and they are chosen by a process that is not independent from party politics.

In practice, government control of budgets is a considerable threat to the successful exercise of data protection, whatever the relevant law may say about independence and the necessity of furnishing an agency with the means to do its task. The effectiveness of a data protection agency is dependent in large measure on its financial resources to support, train, and recruit personnel. Its independence is obviously affected, whatever the legal assurances, because the government ultimately determines the budget. The government's problem is to furnish the watchdog with adequate funding without totally circumventing the established budgetary process for a small agency. Adequate resources are essential to competence and credibility for a data protection authority, yet all governments have carefully controlled expenditures in the 1980s. Dr. Ulrich Dammann of West Germany stated in 1983 that in practice governments find it hard to cut data protection budgets: "Governments are well aware that cuts in the budget of a controlling office would not be accepted by the media and the public. So, no [West German] government up to now has tried to do that."[52] Even if such cutbacks can be avoided, data protectors usually require increasing resources: for example, the size of the systems they oversee increases, yet they have little independence in practice in obtaining approval for their budgets. After *Le Monde* stated in December 1988 that the CNIL had not yet rendered its advice on the Ministry of the Interior's announcement of a single criminal information system for the National Police, the secretary general of the CNIL responded that no such request had been received and added that his agency needed more resources to carry out the many tasks assigned to it.[53] Indeed, all data protectors face hard questions about whether their budget and staff sizes are adequate for the important tasks at hand.

The issue is how to protect the budget (and independence) of a data protection agency once it becomes a thorn in the side of various ministries as it carries out its assigned tasks. Any government or legislature will only tolerate so much opposition from a data protection agency, whatever its statutory degree of independence. The problem is to create a necessary system of governmental oversight for a data protection agency that is compatible with the legitimate exercise of its responsibilities. The history of data protection to date does not give cause for significant alarm on this score, although the prospects for problems with independence have increased as data protectors successfully challenge other interests of governments. The Canadian privacy commissioner would be unemployed if his term were not renewed, whereas the director general of the DIB has a guaranteed pension at the end of one term.

Legislative review of the work of a data protection agency on an annual or at least continuing basis seems to be a most appropriate mechanism for exercising oversight of its practice of independence. Regrettably, legislative interest declines once the novelty and political attractiveness of data protection wears off; there has to be a structural method to ensure continued attention. The Canadian Privacy Act of 1982 wisely requires formal review of the functioning of the act by a parliamentary committee within a three-year period and continuing annual oversight by the same committee.[54] It is essential for the legislature in each country to play such an ongoing role, if there is to be a real balance between independence and effective controls on surveillance.

A vehicle must be designed for implementing data protection that will act independently and vigorously but not recklessly, because its own performance is being regularly monitored. The interaction between data protectors and legislatures should be symbiotic. As part of cultivating better public relations in order to strengthen their hand at implementation, data protectors need to nurture their links to the legislature and its committees, since this is their ultimate guarantee of independence and influence in the political process.

A legislature can in theory always change the law if it does not approve of the implementation of data protection or the activities of a data protection authority. To this point, legislatures have remained largely supportive of the goals of data protection, at least during the process of revising an existing law. But the examples of legislatures weakening the force of data protection in North Rhine–Westphalia, Baden-Württemberg, and Norway in the early 1980s should not be forgotten. Even the vaguest threat of such revision can curtail the authority's effective operation. A data protection agency is of course not "a state within a state" and has to accept the authority of the legislature.

A discussion of independence must devote coherent attention to questions of power relations in the control of government surveillance. There are important concerns about the relative weakness of any data protection agency in its relationship with the government. Given the typical association of bureaucratic power with such factors as the number of employees and the size of budgets, data protection agencies are minor players, even though their mandate extends across the entire spectrum of governmental activity. Since its legislative mandate and independence are sometimes coupled with advisory powers only, the authority has an uphill fight to make its voice heard successfully.

The struggle of any data protection agency to promote compliance is ongoing, because its authority raises considerable issues about competition for power. As Bardach has written, "all parties in the implementation process are involved, in some degree, both in trying to control others and in trying to avoid being controlled by them." Data protectors in particular need to cope with a full range of implementation games, including efforts to trim back or distort the original statutory objectives. The process is both political and involves politics.[55] A small data protection authority has particular problems in relating to large administrative agencies for regulatory purposes. As well, any administrative agency normally assigns low priority to data protection, because of its other direct responsibilities. Thus data protectors must work to win the cooperation of the regulated.

The harsh reality is that data protectors run the risk of being only a tiny force of irregulars equipped with pitchforks and hoes waging battle against large technocratic and bureaucratic forces equipped with lasers and nuclear weapons. This is especially true for their essential work in the public sector, where they are not simply a part of the government, but the primary protector of citizens in their relations with the government itself.

The issue is essentially one of power. As an internal conflict over power relations, those administrative agencies that are most involved in the types of data processing that promote surveillance are often those most resistant to any interference with their complicated and sometimes covert operations. Often such agencies also command the lion's share of the public purse and hence have the strongest voice in the policy process. When the government is faced with a critical choice between surveillance of the populace and data protection, it is not surprising to find a lack of support for privacy protection among these major players. Thus data protection leaders experience, to a degree even greater than most civil servants, the tensions between the fulfillment of agency goals—which often challenge the government—and the desire to retain a job. Data protectors who seek continued employment are more likely to avoid controversy, given the fate of some of their predecessors.

In terms of external conflicts over power relations, data protection agencies are squeezed between power holders and the powerless in trying to foster public support for their goals. In lean economic times, efficiency is the god of politics: if that god demands surveillance in the name of more rational and more cost-effective public policy, there is little effective resistance, since the power holders remain relatively unaffected and the powerless have little influence on public decision making. This is especially true if the target group(s) are among the more marginal members of society, such as welfare recipients, people living in subsidized housing, or prisoners. There are clear limits to the power of a data protection authority if a government is determined to introduce a practice that may be, at least in part, highly invasive of personal privacy.

Data protection offices thus face major problems of independence and authority, despite the careful efforts in most laws to give them as much independence as possible. Budgetary restraints and political pressures to select less challenging data protection leaders are but two examples of current realities that are unlikely to disappear in the future. How much independence do data protectors actually have to accomplish what should be done? They are not insensitive to, or unaware of, such problems; what is more necessary is mutual reflection on the extent to which they are all captives of such considerations. The main solutions lie in the realm of personnel selection and public relations.

The Adequacy of Advisory Powers

In this volume I have been critical of the licensing approach embodied in the Swedish and French legislation, because it is an excessively bureaucratic mode of controlling surveillance. Although arguments can be made for a system of licensing and regulation, this approach seems too formalistic and burdensome for the problems at hand. Licensing agencies are burdened with huge registration tasks for the public and private sectors that hinder necessary attention to audits. Data protection for the public sector is more effective in Germany and Canada than in France or Sweden, simply because the former countries do not dilute their agencies' efforts by asking them to engage in detailed regulation of the private sector.

In general, data protection agencies can function with advisory powers only for automated personal information systems in the public sector and for all manual files used for sensitive purposes. But advisory powers may increasingly be judged inadequate for the responsibilities that data protectors face in controlling powerful legislative and administrative initiatives in governmental surveillance.

Agencies in West Germany and Canada have performed well with only advisory powers. Burkert suggests that advisory functions are crucial to the current success of data protection agencies: "When conflicts arise, they seem to prefer bargaining to prohibitive measures."[56] Otherwise, in his view, in the face of actual regulatory power, the information flows to an agency, which are necessary for efficient and effective operations, may be shut off, leading to wrong decisions because of lack of cooperation and information from those being regulated.

Reliance on advisory powers fits well with the conciliatory approach to implementation that a data protection agency normally uses to overcome bureaucratic resistance and noncompliance. Data protectors have to act in a flexible and pragmatic fashion, responding as much as possible to experience and learning from their mistakes. In practice, even licensing agencies tend to function in this manner. Data protection is a control system with a great deal of discretion at the disposal of those responsible for implementation. The interpretation and use of this power can be well managed by a small advisory agency. Moreover, an advisory system allows an agency to structure its own workload in order to focus to maximum advantage on critical problems of excessive surveillance.[57]

Licensing information systems increases paperwork, costs, and bureaucratic burden. Sweden and Norway revised their laws to reduce these pressures.[58] They could not cope in a meaningful way with the avalanche of paper work. As a Swiss participant wisely observed at a 1982 conference, "it is impossible to control everything; it is therefore necessary to curtail or to concentrate institutional control on the crucial problems," such as in the area of the police and security services. An individual from the private sector warned that licensing and registration only leads to form-filling and token compliance.[59]

The preoccupation with licensing means the neglect of such central tasks as audits. In France the flow of declarations to the CNIL from the private sector in particular overran the resources of the agency and delayed the full implementation of other critical aspects of data protection. Fears of a similar result under the registration scheme in the United Kingdom are being realized.

At the same time, there is a real question whether data protection agencies can continue to rely on powers of persuasion to achieve their statutory objectives. West German and Canadian data protectors can be ignored or spurned, while their Swedish and French counterparts are often reluctant to take strong stands for fear of offending the government and other powerful interests. Access to the press, public opinion, and the legislature have so far provided sufficient weapons to promote implementation when needed. But what happens to a data protection organization if, as is sometimes alleged for the DIB under Freese, the government stops listening, or tires of listening, to warnings of danger from enhanced data processing or record linkages? If such agencies regularly have to temper their findings to what is politically acceptable, then the control of surveillance will be weak, as has been the case in France.

Some new data protection laws point to the future in granting certain decision-making powers to the data protection commissioner without creating a full "licensing" or "permission" system. The latest model is the information and privacy commissioner established under Ontario's 1987 law on Freedom of Information and Protection of Personal Privacy. The commissioner has the ultimate power to order a government institution to grant access to a personal record or to correct it.[60]

Recently, certain ombudsmen have faced considerable difficulties in persuading government departments and the legislature to adopt their specific advice, especially in some Canadian provinces. Dr. Karl A. Friedmann, the activist first ombudsman of British Columbia, was not reappointed when his first term ended; the Ontario government regularly rejects some major recommendations of its ombudsman. Since some data protectors, like ombudsmen, have to rely on moral suasion and public support to enforce their advisory opinions, they have encountered and will face similar problems, especially given the pervasiveness of surveillance issues. Good advice that is ignored by a government or a legislature is not very effective.

There is some evidence of declining public support for specific data protection initiatives in the face of other compelling societal interests. Some of this is due to the fact that data protection has become more faceless for the public, owing to the appointment of data protectors with less interest in, or capacity for, public relations. The ultimate success of the enterprise is highly dependent on continued public support, especially from the media, in the face of limited resources and power. Events in Canada, West Germany, and Sweden demonstrate a latent and overt prospect of strong public support for data protection, but its continued cultivation is highly essential. Outbreaks of aroused public concern create a positive climate for the implementation of data protection. Yet most of the routine issues of surveillance are necessarily handled in private consultations, in which the participants recognize that privacy protectors are in no position to turn to the media too frequently.

The inadequacy of statutory sanctions further reduces the effectiveness of reliance on advisory powers. Bardach has correctly pointed out that a fundamental hindrance to implementation of any law is that "society has not yet developed an array of workable legitimate sanctions that public agencies could impose on each other in the event of less than full compliance." His conclusions are directly relevant to the successful application of data protection: "The principal social mechanism for enforcing agreements is a recognition on the part of participating parties that failure to comply would jeopardize a long-term relationship of value to all those concerned. . . . To the extent that [public-sector] parties can be relied upon to fulfill their agreements—and, more important, to the extent that they are perceived by others as reliable—the reasons exist largely in the mutual desire, or necessity, to perpetuate good relations."[61]

Although most data protection laws permit criminal sanctions against public servants for breaches of the law, their practical influence on implementation seems minimal, since they are unlikely to be used, except in the most sensational cases. Criminal sanctions are selectively applied to individuals and organizations as a warning to others, but the prospects for, or desirability of, their widespread application are remote. Louis Joinet, the French expert, agrees that the need for such criminal sanctions was overestimated: in reality, the truly effective sanction comes from publicizing the decisions of an agency like the CNIL. If a French government ministry does not accept a decision, at least on a significant issue of surveillance, it gives the general public the impression of not respecting rights and liberties.[62] Yet, as a Canadian parliamentary committee recommended in 1987, legislation like the Privacy Act should include criminal sanctions, since the privacy commissioner is otherwise reduced to recommending only wrist-slapping measures when egregious breaches of the law are discovered. The Canadian government's rejection of this recommendation typifies the resistance to the use of criminal sanctions in an era of decriminalization. Fortunately, other sanctions, including dismissal of an employee, are used when serious breaches of confidentiality occur.

The Primacy of Data Protection Concerns

An argument exists about how far data protection agencies should stray from the control of surveillance.[63] Bull and Freese both stated that data protection is only intended for the protection of privacy, whereas others worry that it can be used to affect other unrelated interests. Bull made the point that data protection should not be used as a vehicle to support a national or European computer industry by unnecessarily restricting transborder flows of personal data. One sees a similar risk of the CNIL's being used to promote various governmental and industrial interests, because of its statutory responsibility for transborder data flows. In such domains, concern for privacy is only a minor aspect of competing economic and intellectual interests. Freese saw fit to comment on the unfairness and intrusiveness of the tax system, because of its implications for privacy. This is a good example of how a data protector has to become involved, on occasion, in matters affecting surveillance that appear to lie outside the normal sphere of activities. Some speakers in the Bundestag have thought that the federal Data Protection Commissioner has strayed too far on occasion from the primary interest in data protection, but such an attitude betrays a fundamental lack of understanding of the broad sweep of efforts to limit surveillance in society.

Legislatures and prominent data protectors have expressed views at least somewhat supportive of a very broad role for data protectors. Paul Sieghart argued that the objective of data protection is to defend a whole series of rights and freedoms, "and *in particular* the right to privacy." Simitis believes that data protection should be only a part of an overall policy covering the distribution of information in a society; it should not be isolated, but situated within "the larger frame of circulation of information." He wisely advises that "data protection is essentially a part of a general information policy," but the essence of the argument of this volume is that data protectors should limit their contributions to policy formulation to efforts to control surveillance. Thus data protection is primarily about the reinforcement of the traditional rights of individuals among themselves and with respect to groups, a view that Sieghart ultimately accepts.[64]

More than any other national legislation, the French law is not simply a data protection act. Its expansive concerns about many aspects of an information policy for society may even be the perceptive wave of the future. Senator Jacques Thyraud, former president of the CNIL, asserted that it would "survey the development of informatics in relation to the evolution of society."[65] At least as so starkly stated, this ambition is both too expansive a task in itself, since no tiny institution can manage to oversee so broad a topic, and an impossible activity for the CNIL, which already has burdensome duties to accomplish for both the public and private sectors. It is possible that, like the language of certain articles of the law, Thyraud was merely being hyperbolic.

Some of the confusion over the appropriate scope of data protection derives from the fact that the preservation of personal privacy should be an essential component of general information law and policy for any society. Most Western nations are struggling to formulate such a policy, but the coherent achievements to date are rare.[66] The Swedish government, for example, is visibly concerned to develop an overall information and data policy for the society. This may include a possible role for the DIB, which has staff members in close touch with such developments. Such laws have to coexist with statutes on confidentiality, access to government information, protection of reputation and personality, freedom of expression and of the press, the unrestricted flow of information, and various media laws. Significant problems of integration and operation exist in each country, as the difficult task of shaping an information policy goes forward.

In terms of crafting the statutory mandate of a data protection agency, it is possible to distinguish between promoting a broad information policy for a society and evolving a more narrow policy for personal data; the latter might better fit into the responsibilities of such agencies. Since they have been established and are generally deemed to be successful, the temptation to give them additional work is great. Developing an information policy for a society is desirable, but assuring data protection is only a part of the problem. Data protectors *should* concentrate on data protection, because of the importance of their tasks and the risk that the administrative burdens will otherwise become impossible for tiny units. They can contribute to the debate on formulating an information policy without taking over full responsibility for it. Data protectors have specialized expertise on such related areas as access to government information, secrecy and statistical laws, data security, and archival issues. The DIB's simultaneous responsibility for credit information and debt recovery laws suggests a model for such an agency implementing special laws directly related to data protection or, eventually, all laws related to the various aspects of protection of personal privacy.

Although the Privacy Act in Canada is oriented to data protection, the privacy commissioner has become a wailing wall for all sorts of privacy problems. There are good reasons why the commissioner should oversee the Protection of Privacy Act, which in fact regulates wiretapping, and also other general privacy issues, such as the use of electronic monitoring and drug testing. The Canadian parliamentary committee reviewing the Privacy Act supported the idea of making the privacy commissioner ultimately responsible for all aspects of privacy protection.[67] When New York state passed a data protection law in 1983, it assigned this related task to the existing office for the coordination of access to government information, the Committee on Open Government. This type of coordination of data protection and freedom of information by commissioner(s) working from the same office already exists in Canada at the federal level and in the provinces of Quebec and Ontario.

The range of possible new tasks for data protectors is large. What about certain data protection principles that Table 7 excludes? There is room for skepticism about the ultimate merit of the Data Inspection Board's insistence on the decentralization of automated record systems maintained by governments as an essential measure to ensure data protection; nor is the vulnerability of computers an issue directly related to personal privacy and the control of surveillance. Norwegians earlier engaged in the analysis of privacy interests by focusing on the specific sensitivity of various types of personal information. Since this approach has not proved productive, there is a similar skeptical response to continuing Norwegian efforts at such analysis.[68] Although the search for specification is admirable, the Scandinavian model requires separate privacy and data protection categories. In particular, the interest model seems to go too far afield into matters that do not seem to be legitimate concerns of data protection, such as the right to a friendly administration or the right to prevent misuse of power.[69]

At present, the implementation of data protection by very small agencies is a burdensome, complicated, and unfinished business. Despite the developing expertise that could justify a legislative decision to impose the formulation of information law and policy as an additional set of tasks, the time is not yet ripe for such a step, since data protectors still have so much to accomplish, and governmental enthusiasm for surveillance shows few signs of abating. The assignment of additional financial resources and personnel for enlarged tasks carries too great a risk that an essential set of duties will be diluted and even corrupted. Data protectors should for the moment resist efforts to expand their mandate beyond privacy and data protection issues. Working to limit governmental intrusiveness is itself a significant, continuing contribution to a co-herent information policy.

Complaints, Audits, and Access Rights

Citizens who feel that they are subject to unjust surveillance can seek redress of their grievances. Responding to complaints and inquiries from groups and individuals and conducting self-initiated audits of information systems are two of the most important functions of a data protection agency. The ombudsman-like function of handling complaints acts as a safety valve for the concerned public and helps to set the agency's priorities for inspections. Complaints guide the agency to sensitive matters. Their number and quality also appears to grow as knowledge of the existence of data protection agencies increases.[70]

Data protection commissioners are a form of highly specialized ombuds-men with a more active part to play than the classical role of responding to individual complaints.[71] It is not enough to respond to repeated similar griev-ances from a changing cast of individuals. The staff has to pursue general systemic improvements in information-handling practices by using a variety of methods.

The conduct of audits is one of the most important and least developed aspects of controlling surveillance. The federal experience in West Germany and Canada demonstrates their centrality for the pursuit of statutory objectives. Both countries have created separate units for inspections to assist staff mem-bers who specialize in particular types of systems.[72] In Canada, Grace encour-ages government departments to undertake internal audits of their compliance with the Privacy Act, which his investigators can then audit. The Swedish Data Act was revised to allow the staff of the DIB to concentrate on inspections, thus making data holders aware of the risks of discovery, but this has not occurred, because of the continued burden of routine licensing. The situation at the CNIL is similar.

Audits are crucial to an activist, aggressive stance. Their neglect means that offenders against fair information practices do not have the sense that someone is looking over their shoulders; given the minuscule size of data protection offices relative to the organizations they monitor, it is necessary to create an atmosphere of prior restraint for prospective privacy offenders. They have to worry about a lawsuit or a criminal prosecution. Government officials who handle personal information have to fear a privacy audit as much as most of us dread a tax audit (with the obvious benefits for compliance in both instances). The same bureaucrats have to accept the model of internal auditors who are unable to check every financial transaction; but the idea that the auditors may find errors and problems leads to a desire to promote such goals as accuracy and compliance. However amicable the approach, government agencies dislike either detailed scrutiny, negative publicity, or direct intervention by data protectors, if it can be avoided.

Bardach identifies an "implementation game" that may help explain the reluctance of data protectors to undertake audits: "Most civil servants do not earn particularly handsome salaries and wages, and many feel entitled to take additional compensation by tailoring their work environment to suit themselves as much as possible."[73] It requires some effort to leave Bonn, Stockholm, Paris, and Ottawa in order to visit the outlying locations of government information systems. Thus, there is a tendency in Sweden to conduct a great deal of audit activity by telephone, which, whatever the arguments in its favor, does not have the flavor or potential benefits of an on-site inspection.

If data protectors generally agree on the utility of complaints and audits, outsiders have some doubts about the emphasis on the right of access by individuals to their own records in government data banks, because of the burdens and costs it imposes on the bureaucracy and, more importantly, the failure of the public to make use of the right of access. Such access does help to alleviate the concerns of individuals about surveillance and encourages accuracy in the maintenance of personal files, but one can be skeptical of the German and French argument that it is the "ultimate means of data protection."

Excessive emphasis on the right of access is a considerable waste of time and resources, especially for second-generation data protection acts, since more fundamental aspects of fair information practices need to be addressed, such as whether data should be collected in the first place.[74] On the other hand, a civil servant's knowledge that an individual file is in fact accessible has a practical influence on promoting the accuracy and relevance of data. Allowing individual access to administrative records, which normally have to be retrievable by name anyway, imposes few additional costs on a government unit. Reliance on informal access procedures, especially for government employees, also reduces costs. Sieghart made the pragmatic argument that the right of access "is a means rather than an end, because the end is to get the information system right, and if you give the data subject the right of access it is much more likely to be right."[75]

At the Bellagio conference in 1984, there was strong consensus on the importance of the right of individual access to personal information as a meaningful mechanism for data protection. Many conferees stressed the continuing relevance of maintaining and strengthening access and correction rights and urged that other data protection problems not be allowed to diminish their importance. The salutary effect that the mere existence of access rights is likely to have on record keepers, the importance of such rights to persons who are concerned or suspicious at the possible content of government records concerning themselves, and the importance of access rights to those who are the subjects of administrative decisions were viewed as rationales for continuing emphasis on this aspect of data protection. The existence of access rights is also likely to have a substantial impact in encouraging agencies to provide informal access to personal data as a matter of course. Finally, the need for access rights is more understandable to politicians considering the need for a data protection law than some of the more challenging aspects of this activity. Individuals also perceive the acquisition of a right of access to their own data as a positive control on surveillance practices.

Monitoring Surveillance Technology

Public concerns about the advent of large computers in government data-processing systems led to the creation of data protection agencies, which should play a special role as monitors of developments in information technology. New surveillance practices are constantly arising as by-products of technological innovation or new applications of information technology. The major forces are a dramatic drop in the cost of large and small computers and a corresponding rise in the speed and ease of data storage and communication. The spread of the microcomputer is of particular concern to data protectors, because it facilitates data transfers and increases problems of auditing and control.

A primary purpose of data protection laws is to control, or at least regulate, the technological imperatives associated with the dynamic and largely positive developments surrounding computers, silicon chips, fiber optics, satellites, and associated storage, transmission, and telecommunications devices. Data protection is not inherently hostile to new forms of information technology, nor is it intended to place unnecessary hindrances on information-handling activities that are related to legitimate government programs or private-sector activities. Without data protection, technological innovations could quickly overcome current practical barriers to the collection, manipulation, storage, and transmission of personal information in both the public and private sectors. The innovations that are described on a daily basis in the press, frequently brought about by government initiatives and sponsorship, increase the need for data protection measures where none currently exist. For either a well-meaning or a malevolent regime, there are no technical limits to electronic surveillance and social control at the present time.

Technological imperatives further suggest that the various pressures and demands affecting information handling by government bureaucracies will tend dramatically toward ever more automation, as is already happening in the most advanced countries. The career rewards for personnel continue to be for the promotion of computers for the advancement of departmental activities, to cut program costs, and to reduce fraud and waste; there are no career benefits for turning down a proposed new form of automation or of record linkage for whatever reasons. The recent enthusiasm for computer matching in North America is an example. One can even envision a future in which manual files of personal data will no longer exist for any significant purpose (except the most sinister), given the emergence of word processors and personal computers. Important systems of personal information will not remain in manual form in either the public or private sectors, except perhaps as a means of evading data protection.

Data protectors in all societies are confronting fabulous technological developments affecting large, powerful institutions.[76] These include the continued and voracious expansion of the public and private sectors' appetite for more and more refined and integrated personal data at the expense of personal space and individual autonomy. There is no trend to reduce significantly the collection, storage, and use of personal data, despite the supervisory and controlling efforts of data protectors.

As discussed in the introduction, various technological innovations facilitate surveillance and make data protection more difficult. Simitis has further drawn attention to the emergence of decentralized data processing, which makes it laborious to carry out careful inspections, at least as compared to an audit of an information system in a central location.[77] This is a particular problem in federal states. With distributed data processing, there is no central storage of personal information, which means that data are assembled as needed rather than being permanently stored in a specific data bank at one site; a computer can now seek data anywhere on request. New data protection controls have to be devised as distributed data processing becomes more common. In Canada, for example, the concept of discrete "personal information banks" under the Privacy Act will become an even more artificial concept, in terms of the realities of data storage and use, than it already is.

On a more positive note, system designers now incorporate data protection routines as standard procedures, as awareness of fair information practices spreads. They also resist more and more linkages to a system, because of the risks of a breakdown and errors, which indirectly limits surveillance. Thus some technological innovations can have direct benefits for fair information practices, especially if data protectors have engaged in the appropriate amount of consciousness-raising. They are more and more reliant on specialists in informatics to mobilize technological expertise for protective purposes.

Fears are sometimes expressed that the existence of data protection agencies will in some way inhibit or prevent progress and innovation in information technology. Burkert suggests that this fear has existed in the United States in particular.[78] Experience to date with data protection indicates that there is little basis for such concern. The opposite fear is more credible—that data protection agencies will function simply as legitimators of new forms of technology. In one sense the warnings issued by such an agency about the need to protect personal information can shield the innovators from unexpected hostile responses from consumers, who suddenly become aware of the actual implications for surveillance of a particular device. The manufacturers and promoters of new forms of information technology are normally the last ones to consider the protection of personal privacy, as evidenced by their expressions of surprise when surveillance concerns are brought to their attention. Moreover, governments are much more concerned for the promotion of information technologies and communications than for limiting their uses in any way. The European Economic Community, for example, has undertaken a modest effort for the harmonization of data protection laws within member states, but these efforts pale into insignificance in comparison with the community's special efforts to promote new information technology by allowing major European companies to work together on robotics, silicon chips, word processors, and microcomputers.[79]

Thus one role of data protection agencies is to perform assessments of the potential impact of new forms of information technology, so that their implications for surveillance can be dealt with at the planning and development stages. The enormous complexity of large processing systems makes it essential that such problems be recognized at an early point. Since hardware and software have to work together, a minor change may affect the whole process.[80] Data protectors need to articulate privacy interests in the initial and ongoing evaluation of all technological innovations, since their sponsors and systems designers are so engrossed in the technology as to be sometimes insensitive to its social implications.

Data protectors face a continuing need to develop greater expertise on, and understanding of, surveillance technology in order to monitor such critical developments. To put it bluntly, most offices have lacked an appropriate level of understanding of the latest innovations in computers, telecommunications, and security, which is a further barrier to effective implementation. More specialists in informatics are now needed where lawyers once dominated, since technology is changing the nature of the control function. Each office needs to develop some additional research capacity to monitor relevant trends. Many data protectors are indeed taking steps to increase the capabilities of their staff through training and the addition of technical specialists. In fact, the annual meeting of data protection commissioners is a vehicle that should promote mutual understanding of new technology and its implications for surveillance through joint research and educational efforts, since this aspect of data protection ineluctably transcends national legal traditions and boundaries.

Strengthening Data Protection Legislation

The kinds of real and potential problems discussed in this volume have not been adequately addressed to date in most revised data protection laws, nor have the relevant agencies given sufficient attention to them. Unfortunately, the annual international meeting of data protectors has done little to focus attention on such central matters. Individual data protection agencies are simply very busy with existing tasks.

Data protection agencies seek to implement data protection principles in all specialized legislation and regulations dealing with personal information systems. The process of promoting such sectoral legislation is of vital importance. It permits general data protection principles to be shaped in precise, statutory form to suit a particular type of problem and in order to grant specific enforceable rights to individuals. In an ideal constitutional situation, such as the Federal Republic of Germany after the 1983 census decision of the Federal Constitutional Court, efforts at sectoral legislation can promote the implementation of highly desirable constitutional rights to data protection. Yet it is symptomatic of the general data protection scene that, even in West Germany, the process of complying with the 1983 decision is moving at a snail's pace, because of basic resistance. Sectoral legislation should be in place for every type of personal information system in every country by the year 2000.

Specialized legislation for each sector, as is especially well practiced in the United States, can also tailor the principles of fair information practice to an appropriate format for the personal information in question. The dichotomy alleged to exist between the omnibus and sectoral approaches to data protection is false; in practice, all agencies ultimately seek specific data protection solutions in legislation that governs the use of personal information. The data protection agency can facilitate such ameliorative solutions by preparing its own evaluations of the potential impact on personal privacy of proposed legislation and information systems. Having the protection agency prepare, or at least review, such plans will hopefully prevent them from simply becoming routine documents churned out by the administrative bureaucracy. It is important that small data protection agencies encourage the main government departments to prepare their own initial reviews of the impact of new technology, preferably in the form of "privacy impact statements," since the departments or ministries are legally responsible for implementation of data protection laws in most countries, and there is a serious risk that data protectors in oversight bodies will be swamped if they have to carry out all such evaluations of surveillance risks themselves.

Quebec's 1982 legislation on the protection of personal information is especially interesting in the context of ensuring specialized data protection. Article 168 determines that its provisions "prevail over any contrary provision of a subsequent general law or special Act, unless the latter Act expressly states that it applies notwithstanding this Act."[81] This measure has the effect of giving data protection strong underpinnings in Quebec law, which already has (in Article 5 of its provincial Charter of Human Rights and Freedoms) guarantees that "every person has a right to respect for his private life."[82] This innovative Quebec proviso also ensures that data protection has to be almost automatically considered for inclusion in any new legislation affecting personal information. Finally, Article 169 of the Quebec law determined that any general laws, special acts, or regulations inconsistent with the 1982 data protection law ceased to have effect in 1987. Strong pressures thus existed to revise conflicting dispositions within a specific time period.

One possible future scenario for data protection agencies is that once they have built data protection principles into every piece of legislation and administrative practice dealing with personal information, they can then will themselves out of existence. The more likely prospect is that the risks of surveillance will increase at such a pace for the foreseeable future that societal needs for data protection will necessitate continued monitoring and intervention by the data protection authorities. Nevertheless, agencies should reduce their future burdens by ensuring that data protection is incorporated in new systems, practices, and laws from the start of planning, which is of course much easier and cheaper than trying to incorporate technical and legal protections after the fact.

A universal system of Personal Identification Numbers (PINs) is the key to a successful surveillance society, so data protectors need to resist their introduction and proliferation for multiple purposes or must at least achieve the strictest controls on their use beyond the original intent. Unfortunately, controlling the use of PINs is a difficult task, as experience in Sweden, Canada, and the United States illustrates. Having a PIN makes it almost impossible for anyone to escape total surveillance. For example, a Swedish woman cannot escape an ex-husband, because it is impossible to change a PIN assigned at birth under any circumstances, so he can always locate her from public sources. The 1987 Australian decision to drop government plans for a national identity card, on the basis of large-scale public concern, is a further example of resistance to various forms of identification.

It is an auspicious sign of the law attempting to keep pace with technological change that Hesse, the originator of general data protection, has enacted a new Data Protection Act, and that a parliamentary committee has proposed significant revisions to the 1982 Canadian Privacy Act, many of which the government has accepted.[83]

Even more importantly, Canada and the United States, in particular, need to confront the basic issue of whether they can continue to function without general data protection laws or data protection agencies with some degree of jurisdiction over the private sector. This is clearly an area where the Swedish, French, and British experiences in various forms of regulation for the private sector are well in advance of other countries. The Justice Committee of the Canadian House of Commons and a Quebec research group have recommended important regulatory initiatives in this sphere.[84] The German situation illustrates the limitations of relying essentially on the government, rather than the data protection commissioners, to control surveillance in the private sector. Although this book deals with the public sector only, I am persuaded that statutory data protection is also essential for the private sector.[85] The long-term goal must be to ensure individual rights in all spheres of human existence.

How will data protection authorities look by the year 2000? There is a real risk that they will be looked back upon as a rather quaint, failed effort to cope with an overpowering technological tide rather than as a fruitful, successful exercise in promoting the coexistence of competing human and societal values. Both scenarios are possible. The central thrust will clearly be the technological imperative of integrated communications devices and computers. The combination of technological change and governments' need for data will produce a continuing series of challenges to privacy interests, in response to which data protection agencies will have to be vigilant, articulate, and resourceful in fashioning acceptable solutions in the public interest.

As an optimist and an overall admirer of their track record to date, it is my judgment that the existing model of having a data protection agency to articulate privacy interests on a continuing basis will have long-term validity for the control of surveillance, despite the problems discussed in this volume. The ultimate success of data protection as a means to promote bureaucratic accountability and limit government surveillance depends on the extent to which data protection continues to be a significant political issue.

Notes

Introduction

1. The latter phrase is an apt way to characterize a society dependent on information exchanges through the use of computers and telecommunication devices. I am using surveillance to mean "any systematic attention to a person's life aimed at exerting influence over it." See James B. Rule, D. McAdam, L. Stearns, and D. Uglow, "Documentary Identification and Mass Surveillance in the United States," *Social Problems* 31 (December 1983): 223.

2. See David H. Flaherty, *Protecting Privacy in Two-Way Electronic Services* (London, 1985).

3. David H. Flaherty, "Protecting Privacy in Police Information Systems: Data Protection in the Canadian Police Information Centre (CPIC)," *University of Toronto Law Journal* 26 (1986): 126. See also Diana R. Gordon, "The Electronic Panopticon: A Case Study of the Development of the National Criminal Records System," *Politics and Society* 15 (1986–87): 483–511.

4. *Privacy Journal* 14 (May 1988): 5.

5. Joel Brinkley, "Latest Israeli Weapon: Bureaucracy," *New York Times,* May 11, 1988, p. A3. See also Thomas L. Friedman, "Report Sees 'Big Brother' in Israeli Data on Arabs," ibid., September 12, 1987, p. 3.

6. American Express's new image processing billing system "presents almost limitless possibilities . . . for identifying target groups of customers and marketing new products and services"; John Markoff, "American Express Goes High-Tech," *New York Times,* July 31, 1988, sec. 3, pp. F1, F6. This company's global data processing system uses more than 120 mainframe computers, 170 minicomputers, and 46,000 individual work stations.

7. *The Economist,* February 18, 1989, p. 26.

8. See the informative review in U.S. Congress, Office of Technology Assessment, *Criminal Justice, New Technologies, and the Constitution,* OTA-CIT-366 (Washington, D.C., May 1988), pp. 33–37.

9. Jonathan Chevreau, "Optical storage system unveiled for mainframes," *Globe and Mail* (Toronto), September 23, 1983, p. B16; John Markoff, "The PC's Broad New Potential," *New York Times,* November 30, 1988, pp. 27, 44.

10. David E. Sanger, "4-Megabit Chip Set by I. B. M.," *New York Times,* February 26, 1987, p. 29.

11. *Privacy Journal* 15 (November 1988): 7.

12. U.S. Congress, Office of Technology Assessment, *Electronic Delivery of Public Assistance Benefits: Technology Options and Policy Issues,* OTA-BP-CIT-47 (Washington, D.C., April 1988), p. 15. The same study discusses recent debates on the creation of identity cards (pp. 14–15).

13. Rule et al., "Documentary Identification and Mass Surveillance," p. 232; Gerald Messadie, *La fin de la vie privée* (Paris, 1974).

14. See U.S. Congress, Office of Technology Assessment, *The Electronic Supervisor: New Technology, New Tensions,* OTA-CIT-333 (Washington, D.C., 1987).

15. See John Markoff, "A New Breed of Snoopier Computers," *New York Times,* June 5, 1988, p. E32.

16. The details are from Bob Woodward, *Veil: The Secret Wars of the CIA, 1981–1987* (New York, 1987), pp. 415–16, 448–50, 457.

17. Peter Wright, *Spycatcher: The Candid Autobiography of a Senior Intelligence Officer* (Toronto, 1987), p. 360; Data Protection Act 1984, c. 35, section 27. The legal framework that then shaped the confidentiality rules for the Department of Health and Social Security is discussed in David H. Flaherty, *Privacy and Government Data Banks* (London, 1979), pp. 74–77.

18. Bill 34, Freedom of Information and Protection of Privacy Act, *Statutes of Ontario,* 1987, c. 25.

19. This description of Sweden is not designed to be an attack on a society that is widely regarded as immensely successful in so many ways, nor am I criticizing the right of the Swedish people and their elected representatives to fashion exactly the kind of society that a majority wish to live in. In particular, while I am questioning the amount of privacy that can be enjoyed in that country, I am not explicitly arguing that Swedes somehow enjoy less freedom than the rest of us.

20. See Alan F. Westin, *Privacy and Freedom* (New York, 1967).

21. For comparable British efforts to create a surveillance society, based on private-sector use of the Electoral Register, see Duncan Campbell, "Secret Society. 1. The databank dossier," *New Statesman,* April 24, 1987, pp. 8–9.

22. This happened in the 1980s to both Sten Johansson, the director since 1983, and Edmund Rapaport, his interim predecessor.

23. Jan Freese, "The Future of Data Protection," in *Seminar on Opennness and Protection of Privacy in the Information Society: Proceedings,* (Embassy of Sweden and Netherlands Central Bureau of Statistics, Voorburg, Netherlands, 1987), p. 108.

24. Gert Persson, "Computerised Personal Registers and the Protection of Privacy," *Current Sweden* 344 (February 1986): 4. Ample documentation for my thesis about Sweden can be found in this informed assessment by the former senior technical officer for the Data Inspection Board.

25. Details will be found below in chapter 11.

26. See the compelling study by Kenneth C. Laudon, *Dossier Society: Value Choices in the Design of National Information Systems* (New York, 1986).

27. *Privacy Journal* 6 (November 1979): 3; ibid., 10 (December 1983): 1, 5.

28. Neil J. Vidmar, *Privacy and Two-Way Cable Television: A Study of Canadian Public Opinion* (Downsview, Ont.: Ontario Ministry of Transportation and Communications, May 1983), pp. 15–16, 27, 37, 43; Vidmar and David H. Flaherty, "Concern for Personal Privacy in an Electronic Age," *Journal of Communication* 35 (1985): 91–103. These findings for Ontario residents were confirmed by two polls conducted by Decima Research in 1987 and 1988: 94 percent thought that it was important or very important to protect their personal information held by the government, and 77 percent were of the opinion that the storage of data on computers means no guarantees of privacy. See Sidney B. Linden, "Emerging Privacy Issues," Presentation to a Conference on Privacy and Information Access, Toronto, November 23, 1988.

29. See Westin, *Privacy and Freedom,* p. 7; and Council of Europe, *Legislation and Data Protection: Proceedings of the Rome Conference on Problems Relating to the Development and Application of Legislation on Data Protection* (Rome, 1983), p. 81.

30. Ruth Gavison, "Privacy and the Limits of the Law," *Yale Law Journal* 89 (1980): 428.

31. Arnold Simmel, "Privacy," *International Encyclopedia of the Social Sciences* 12 (1968): 480, 482, 485; and Edward J. Bloustein, "Privacy as an Aspect of Human Dignity: An Answer to Dean Prosser," *New York University Law Review* 39 (1964): 962–1007.

32. Simmel, "Privacy," pp. 481, 486.

33. Hans Zetterberg, a sociologist and editor-in-chief of *Svenska Dagbladet*, argues that Swedes are developing a changed and more complex conception of their own identity, which leads them to resist giving out information about themselves, and to "problematic identities." See *Statistics and Privacy: Report from a Conference in Stockholm, Sweden, 24–26 June, 1987* (Stockholm, 1988), pp. 32–33. Perhaps this trend is a specific response to a surveillance society that has not yet become as apparent in other countries.

34. David Burnham, *The Rise of the Computer State* (New York, 1983), pp. 38, 47.

35. Ibid., p. 9.

36. Burnham, "U.S. to Urge Census Bureau to Share its Personal Data," *New York Times,* November 20, 1983, p. 1; Burnham, "White House Kills Plan to Share Census Data," ibid., November 24, 1983, p. A16.

37. See David Burnham, "'74 Privacy Law out of Date, Many Groups Assert," *New York Times,* December 26, 1984, pp. B1 and B11.

38. *New York Times,* December 20, 1987, p. E18.

39. Organization for Economic Co-operation and Development, *Guidelines on the Protection of Privacy and Transborder Flows of Personal Data* (Paris, 1981); Council of Europe, *Explanatory Report on the Convention for the Protection of Individuals with Regard to Automatic Processing of Personal Data* (Strasbourg, 1981).

40. The chain of accountability may be complex. It is perhaps fairer to say that elected government officials are responsible to the legislature and that unfavorable reports on data protection create difficulties for them, with repercussions on their civil servants. However, there are elements of direct accountability in most countries, because data protectors communicate directly with the relevant civil servants on particular issues, normally through officials who have specific internal responsibility for data protection and act as a liaison with the data protection agency. See the informed discussion of bureaucratic resistance to mechanisms to promote accountability in Priscilla M. Regan, "Personal Information Policies in the United States and Britain: The Dilemma of Implementation Considerations," *Journal of Public Policy* 4 (1984): 19–38.

41. The types of systems selected for study in each country have depended upon the degree of centralization of records at the national level, the practical results of data protection, and the finite resources of this research project.

42. See David H. Flaherty, "Final Report of the Bellagio Conference on Current and Future Problems of Data Protection: Nineteen Eighty-Four and After," *Government Information Quarterly* 1 (1984): 431–41.

Chapter 1

1. The German text of the BDSG, passed in 1977, can be found in "Gesetz zum Schutz vor Missbrauch personenbezogener Daten bei der Datenverarbeitung (Bundesdatenschutzgesetz)," January 27, 1977, *Bundesgesetzblatt* 1: s. 201. An English text prepared by the OECD is in Ulrich Dammann, Otto Mallmann, and Spiros Simitis,

eds., *Data Protection Legislation: An International Documentation* (Frankfurt am Main, West Germany, 1977), pp. 70–107; and in Rein Turn, ed., *Transborder Data Flows,* vol. 2, *Supporting Documents* (Arlington, Va., 1979). Henceforth in this section reference will be made only to the English version.

2. *Der Spiegel,* June 7, 1976, pp. 110-15.

3. In 1983, the Federal Constitutional Court interpreted these articles as creating a general right of personality, which can include a right to privacy.

4. Hans Peter Bull, "The Federal Commissioner for Data Protection" (typescript) (Bonn, 1981), p. 2.

5. As is true in most of the continental European countries, with the notable exception of France, the implementation of data protection largely involves jurists dealing with one another in the context of a commitment to the primacy of law and a common bond of language forged in legal education and public administration.

6. *Frankfurter Allgemeine Zeitung,* April 22, 1976; Spiros Simitis, "Reviewing Privacy in an Information Society," *University of Pennsylvania Law Review* 135 (1987): 724-25.

7. See Hans Peter Bull, "The Principles of Data Protection: International Agreements and German Legislation" (Address to a Symposium on Computer Security and Privacy, Monte Carlo, January 26, 1981), p. 7.

8. BDSG, sections 19(1), 19(2).

9. Spiros Simitis, Ulrich Dammann, Otto Mallmann, and Hans-Joachim Reh, *Kommentar zum Bundesdatenschutzgesetz,* 3d ed. (Baden-Baden, 1981), p. 597.

10. Bull, "Federal Commissioner," p. 6.

11. Bull, "Principles of Data Protection," p. 7.

12. Bull, "Federal Commissioner," p. 3.

13. The federal Ministry of the Interior (BMI) has approximately 1,400 staff members, excluding any of the numerous operating agencies that it ultimately supervises, such as the police or security agencies.

14. See generally, Werner Ruckriegel, "Private Sector Data Protection Control in Germany," *Transnational Data Report* 5 (March 1982): 95–96.

Chapter 2

1. See the English text of the BDSG in Ulrich Dammann, Otto Mallmann, and Spiros Simitis, eds., *Data Protection Legislation: An International Documentation* (Frankfurt am Main, West Germany, 1977), pp. 70–107; and in Rein Turn, ed., *Transborder Data Flows,* vol. 2, *Supporting Documents* (Arlington, Va., 1979).

2. See E. J. Cohn, *Manual of German Law* (London, 1968), pp. 1, 6.

3. Spiros Simitis, "Reviewing Privacy in an Information Society," *University of Pennsylvania Law Review* 135 (1987): 730.

4. Section 2 defines a data file as "a collection of data which is assembled on a uniform basis and can be recorded and arranged according to specific features and rearranged and evaluated according to other specific features, irrespective of the methods used. This shall not include files and collections of files unless they can be rearranged and evaluated by automatic means."

5. *Bulletin* (Press and Information Office of the Federal Republic, Bonn, January 11, 1980), p. 3. The office of the federal Data Protection Commissioner prepared this material.

6. Council of Europe, *Legislation and Data Protection* (Rome, 1983), p. 32.

7. Hans Peter Bull, "The Federal Commissioner for Data Protection" (typescript) (Bonn, 1981), p. 1.

8. *The Week in Germany,* July 6, 1984, p. 6.

9. Heinz Tutt, "Data Protection," *Cologne Stadt-Anzeiger,* January 6, 1984, quoted in *German Tribune,* January 22, 1984, p. 15.

10. The *Bulletin* published by the federal government in January 1980 on data protection noted that the BDSG, partly because of the problems of definition and of determining its scope, had left certain important problems of information and communications policy unregulated: "For example, how may information on the involved persons be assembled? Which questions may the public administration direct to the citizen? Which methods of secret collection of data can be looked on as legitimate?"

11. See Council of Europe, *Legislation and Data Protection,* pp. 31, 65.

12. Der Bundesbeauftragte für den Datenschutz (The Federal Data Protection Commissioner), *Dritter Tätigkeitsbericht des Bundesbeauftragten für den Datenschutz* (Third Activity Report of the BfD) (Bonn, 1980, p. 4. The titles of these annual reports are hereafter cited in English, and "Der Bundesbeauftragte für den Datenschutz" is cited as BfD.

13. Hans Peter Bull, "The Principles of Data Protection: International Agreements and German Legislation" (Address to a Symposium on Computer Security and Privacy, Monte Carlo, January 26, 1981), p. 13.

14. Ibid., p. 1; see also Bull, "Federal Commissioner," p. 1.

15. *Bulletin,* Bonn, January 11, 1980, p. 3.

16. *What Does the Data Protection Law Do for You?* Information for citizens published by the BfD, Bonn, September 1978, p. 1. The brackets appear in the BfD's English version.

17. Ibid., section 1.1.

18. Alan F. Westin, *Privacy and Freedom* (New York, 1967), p. 7.

19. See H. Burkert, "Institutions of Data Protection: An Attempt at a Functional Explanation of European National Data Protection Laws," *Computer Law Journal* 3 (1981): 187; and *Fifth Activity Report of the BfD* (Bonn, 1983), section 1.2.

20. BDSG, sections 9(1), 10.

21. *Third Activity Report of the BfD,* section 3.11.1.1.

22. Bull, "Federal Commissioner," pp. 1–2.

23. BDSG, section 10(11).

24. Ibid., section 11.

25. *Third Activity Report of the BfD,* section 3.11.1.1.

26. The U.S. Privacy Protection Study Commission wisely recommended the preparation of a privacy impact statement for each piece of federal legislation. However, there is a great danger that such an activity will become routinized and expensive. See Charles Peters and Michael Nelson, eds., *The Culture of Bureaucracy* (New York, 1979), pp. 4–8.

27. This material is derived from an article in the *Kieler Nachrichten,* November 20, 1979, quoted in *German Tribune,* December 2, 1979.

28. See *Vorschriften zum Datenschutz in Nordrhein-Westfalen* (Dusseldorf, 1981), p. 12, paragraph 26.

Chapter 3

1. See the English text of the BDSG in Ulrich Dammann, Otto Mallmann, and Spiros Simitis, eds., *Data Protection Legislation: An International Documentation* (Frank-

414 / Notes to Pages 40–45

furt am Main, West Germany, 1977), pp. 70–107; and in Rein Turn, ed., *Transborder Data Flows,* vol. 2, *Supporting Documents* (Arlington, Va., 1979). See in particular sections 17(1), 17(4), and 17(5).

2. Hans Peter Bull, "The Federal Commissioner for Data Protection" (typescript) (Bonn, 1981), pp. 4–5.

3. Ibid., p. 5. The same minister is responsible for the fulfillment of the commissioner's duties as a public officer, which only means that the BMI has to pay his salary and care for his personal rights. The ministry could admonish him if he did not fulfil his tasks, for example, by taking extended holidays, or could "take legal proceedings against him if he should commit an act which, in case of a judge, would give reason for dismissal."

4. See *Bremer Nachrichten,* December 23, 1977, quoted in the *German Tribune,* January 15, 1978, p. 5.

5. One of the several matters that regularly distracts data protectors in every country from antisurveillance activities is staff recruiting, facilities, and the fight for budget share.

6. *Transnational Data and Communications Report* 9 (December 1986): 29.

7. The government is obliged by law to provide the commissioner with the necessary staff and financial resources by means of a special chapter in the budget of the Ministry of the Interior; Bull, "Federal Commissioner," p. 5.

8. Council of Europe, *Legislation and Data Protection* (Rome, 1983), p. 119.

9. *Transnational Data and Communications Report* 10 (April 1987): 25–26.

10. He was a close colleague of the late Franz Josef Strauss, the conservative head of the Bavarian-based Christian Socialist Union (CSU). *Time* described Zimmermann as "a conservative long known for his anti-immigration and anti-environmentalist views" and noted that a wide range of left-wing groups had protested his appointment; *Time,* October 18, 1982, p. 36.

11. *Die Welt,* October 27, 1982, p. 1.

12. A delicious irony is that in 1988 Bull became the Minister of the Interior in the state of Schleswig-Holstein. He will now oversee data protection as one of his duties and will consult regularly with the federal minister of the interior who effectively fired him. Bull announced a revision of the data protection law for his state in line with the other recent second generation acts promoted by Social Democratic governments.

13. *Transnational Data and Communications Report* 10 (November 1987): 9; Spiros Simitis, ed., *Data Protection Act of the State of Hesse* (Wiesbaden, 1987), p. 35. One of the impressive practical guarantees of the independence of Bull and Simitis is that each retained a university professorship.

14. Bull, "Federal Commissioner," pp. 7–8.

15. BfD Press Release, January 18, 1982.

16. Council of Europe, *Legislation and Data Protection,* p. 86; Simitis, *Data Protection Act of the State of Hesse,* pp. 35–40.

17. Bull regards the situation in which a ministry has to decide whether to follow his advice on a particular matter as a completely normal distribution of power in German society.

18. On this and a number of other points, I am particularly indebted to extensive discussions with Herbert Burkert.

19. Bull, "Federal Commissioner," p. 4.

20. Quoted in Peter Dippoldsmann, "Census and Judgement of the Constitutional Court in the FRG: Some Principles and Consequences," *Information Age* 7 (October 1985): 206.

21. Dr. Dammann of the federal DPC has pointed out that when the legislature in Baden-Württemberg became unhappy with aspects of Dr. Ruth Leuze's data protection work, it did not cut back her budget, for fear of bad public relations, but simply changed the law.

22. Jost Schindel, "Germany Declares Self-Determination over Personal Data," *Transnational Data Report* 7 (August–September 1984): 359.

23. BFD Press Statement on the Occasion of the Submission of the 6th Report on the Activities of the Federal Data Protection Commissioner on 24 January 1984.

24. Ibid. See especially Dippoldsmann, "Census and Judgement of the Constitutional Court," 203–14.

25. See Eibe H. Riedel, "New Bearings in German Data Protection. Census Act 1983 Partially Unconstitutional," *Human Rights Law Journal* 5 (1984): 67–75. The English text of the court's decision appears in ibid., 94–115.

Chapter 4

1. For example, see *Bremer Nachrichten*, December 23, 1977, quoted in *German Tribune*, January 15, 1978, p. 5. See section 18(2) of the BDSG in Ulrich Dammann, Otto Mallmann, and Spiros Simitis, eds., *Data Protection Legislation: An International Documentation* (Frankfurt am Main, West Germany, 1977), pp. 84–85; or in Rein Turn, ed., *Transborder Data Flows*, vol. 2, *Supporting Documents* (Arlington, Va., 1979).

2. *Fifth Activity Report of the BfD* (Bonn, 1983), section 1.2.

3. *Transnational Data and Communications Report* 11 (November 1988): 26.

4. Weyer's career in various aspects of public administration is typical of most of those engaged in data protection. He did not have any significant prior interest in data protection or computers. From 1970 to 1979 he was a political civil servant in Bonn for the state of Berlin, dealing with federal-state matters.

5. Weyer's successor, Hans Maier-Bode, is also a civil servant.

6. Spiros Simitis, ed., *Data Protection Act of the State of Hesse* (Wiesbaden, 1987), p. 35.

7. BDSG, section 19(3).

8. See Chapter 29.

9. Council of Europe, *Legislation and Data Protection* (Rome, 1983), p. 118.

10. See *Frankfurter Allgemeine Zeitung*, February 24, 1981; and *Fifth Activity Report of the BfD*, sections 1.8 and 1.9.

11. See Thomas K. McGraw, "Regulation in America: A Review Article," *Business History Review* 49 (Summer 1975): 162–64.

12. BDSG, section 19.

13. These events can be followed in the annual activity reports of the BfD under the heading of general experiences with the law.

14. Council of Europe, *Legislation and Data Protection*, p. 117.

15. *First Activity Report of the BfD* (Bonn, 1979), section 3; *Second Activity Report of the BfD* (Bonn, 1980), section 2; *Third Activity Report of the BfD* (Bonn, 1981), section 3; and *Fourth Activity Report of the BfD* (Bonn, 1982), sections 2 and 3.

16. BDSG, section 19(3); *Third Activity Report of the BfD*, section 1.3.

17. See Ulrich Dammann, "Auditing Data Protection," *Transnational Data Report* 6 (April–May 1983): 161–63.

18. Council of Europe, *Legislation and Data Protection*, p. 126.

19. Costs are a frequent explanation for lack of existing security. Section 25 of the

Sixth Activity Report of the BfD (Bonn, 1984) discussed security in detail for the first time.

20. Ibid., and *Third Activity Report of the BfD*, section 1.8. The *Bundesanzeiger* is an official publication, appearing on a quarterly basis, which can be consulted in public libraries, county courts, and local administrative offices.

21. Council of Europe, *Legislation and Data Protection*, p. 120, and also pp. 105, 123.

22. *Third Activity Report of the BfD*, section 1.7.

23. Ibid., section 3.2.1.2.

24. Council of Europe, *Legislation and Data Protection*, pp. 54–56, 109.

25. Simitis, *Data Protection Act of the State of Hesse*, pp. 9–11, 14, 31–33, 47.

26. BDSG, section 21.

27. Hans Peter Bull, "The Federal Commissioner for Data Protection" (typescript) (Bonn, 1981), pp. 7, 10–11.

28. *Fifth Activity Report of the BfD*, section 1.10.

29. Bull, "Federal Commissioner," p. 12.

30. The commissioner has the right to be present on the government benches, but not to speak; however, he or she may respond to questions in committees. Section 3 of each report includes detailed information on the state of data protection in selected areas of public administration, further evidence of a systematic approach.

31. *Fifth Activity Report of the BfD*, sections 1.2, 1.3.4, and 1.6.

32. Simitis, *Data Protection Act of the State of Hesse*, p. 39.

33. Herbert Burkert, "Organization and Method of Operation of the Data Protection Authorities," *Study on Data Security and Confidentiality*, section 2, Final Report to the Commission of the European Communities, July, 1980, p. 185.

34. Representative examples include: BfD, *Der Bürger und seine Daten. Eine Information zum Datenschutz* (The Citizen and His Data. Information on Data Protection) (Bonn, 1980); BfD, *Bürgerfibel Datenschutz* (A Citizen's Guide to Data Protection) (Bonn, 1982); and BfD, *Der Bürger und seine Daten im Netz der sozialen Sicherung* (The Citizen and His Data in the Social Security Network) (Bonn, 1984).

35. Friedrich Karl Fromme, "Data Protection: An Expensive Toy," *Frankfurter Allgemeine Zeitung*, February 10, 1981; and Bull's response in ibid., February 24, 1981.

36. Hans Peter Bull, letter to author, November 16, 1984.

37. *Frankfurter Allgemeine Zeitung*, October 30, 1986, and Baumann's reply in ibid., November 11, 1986.

38. See the coverage of her 1987 report in ibid., January 9, 1988.

39. For the range of matters considered, see *Fifth Activity Report of the BfD*, section 1.4.

40. See BfD Press Release, January 18, 1982, section 10; and *Sixth Activity Report of the BfD*, section 4.1.

41. See Herbert Burkert, "Institutions of Data Protection: An Attempt at a Functional Explanation of European National Data Protection Laws," *Computer Law Journal* 3 (1981): 184–86.

42. The law, for example, does not forbid the storage of occupation data or the serial number of personal identification and passports.

43. The general findings of a DPC site visit to a particular organization can also take the form of an official complaint.

44. See BfD Press Release, January 18, 1982, section 3.

45. Ibid., section 4.

46. BDSG, section 20; and *Fifth Activity Report of the BfD*, section 1.3.4.

47. On this point, see Peter Gola, "The Development of Data Protection Law in 1981," *Neue Juristische Wochenschenschrift* 28 (1982): 1498–1505. Gola and Klaus Hümmerich regularly publish articles reviewing annual developments, paying particular attention to litigation.

48. BDSG, section 41.

49. Burkert, "Institutions of Data Protection," pp. 186–87.

Chapter 5

1. See the description of social administration systems in Hans Peter Bull, *Datenschutz oder Die Angst vor dem Computer* (Munich, 1984), pp. 277–81.

2. *Third Activity Report of the BfD* (Bonn, 1981), section 3.10.1.

3. However, for some examples of specific, continuing problems in social security, see Spiros Simitis, "Reviewing Privacy in an Information Society," *University of Pennsylvania Law Review* 135 (1987): 716.

4. The following is based on *Third Activity Report of the BfD*.

5. BfD Press Release, January 18, 1982, section 5.

6. *Third Activity Report of the BfD*, section 1.2.

7. Ibid., section 3.10.5.2.

8. George Wiesel, "INPOL: The West German Police Information System," *Police Studies* 4 (1980): 22.

9. Ibid., pp. 23–24, 27; descriptive details of the INPOL system can be found in ibid., pp. 22–35 and in *Transnational Data and Communications Report* 11 (April 1988): 25.

10. Wiesel, "INPOL," p. 33. PIOS stands for persons, institutions, locations, and objects.

11. *Third Activity Report of the BfD*, English Summary, February 4, 1981, p. 2.

12. See Wiesel, "INPOL," p. 24.

13. See *Deutscher Bundestag*, February 12, 1981, pp. 907–9. There are detailed discussions of data protection provisions for INPOL in the *Third Activity Report of the BfD*, sections 3.11.2.1 and 3.11.2.2, and in the *Fourth Activity Report of the BfD* (Bonn, 1982).

14. *Frankfurter Allgemeine Zeitung*, November 11, 1986.

15. See Bull, *Datenschutz*, pp. 244 and 237–48.

16. A full report of a clash between Professor Bull and Dr. Herold in the fall of 1979 appears in the *Kieler Nachrichten*, November 20, 1979, republished in *German Tribune*, December 2, 1979.

17. See the quotation of Professor Bull by a West German journalist in *Transnational Data Report* 4 (September 1981): 26: "If in the Federal Republic of Germany a more authoritarian disposition should prevail, then privacy protection will diminish."

18. See sections 12(2) and 13(2) of the BDSG in Ulrich Dammann, Otto Mallmann, and Spiros Simitis, eds., *Data Protection Legislation: An International Documentation* (Frankfurt am Main, West Germany, 1977), pp. 79–81; or in Rein Turn, ed., *Transborder Data Flows*, vol. 2, *Supplementary Documents* (Arlington, Va., 1979).

19. Ibid., section 19(3), last sentence.

20. *Third Activity Report of the BfD*, English Summary, February 4, 1981, p. 2; *Bulletin*, Bonn, January 11, 1980, p. 8; Hans Peter Bull, "The Federal Commissioner for Data Protection" (typescript) (Bonn, 1981), p. 11.

21. Bull, "Federal Commissioner," p. 11.

22. *Third Activity Report of the BfD*, section 3.11.1.3.

23. Press Release on the Fourth Activity Report, January 19, 1982, section 3; *Bulletin*, Bonn, January 11, 1980, p. 9.

24. Press Release on the Fourth Activity Report, January 18, 1982, section 3.

25. *Third Activity Report of the BfD*, section 1.1.

26. See the detailed and complex discussion in ibid., section 3.11.1.1.

27. *Transnational Data and Communications Report* 11 (March 1988): 25.

28. See the Fromme article, *Frankfurter Allgemeine Zeitung*, February 24, 1981; and *Kieler Nachrichten*, November 20, 1979, quoted in *German Tribune*, December 2, 1979.

29. Bull was quoting from a speech by Chancellor Schmidt at the Federal Office for the Protection of the Constitution in 1979 (Press Release, Fourth Activity Report for 1981, January 18, 1982).

30. See Hermann Borgs-Maciejewski and Frank Ebert, *Das Recht der Geheimdienste* (Security Law) (Stuttgart, 1986).

31. See Note [Eckhart K. Gouras], "The Reform of West German Data Protection Law as a Necessary Correlate to Improving Domestic Security," *Columbia Journal of Transnational Law* 24 (1986): 597–621.

32. See David H. Flaherty, *Privacy and Government Data Banks* (London, 1979), pp. 145–47.

33. Ibid, p. 162.

34. See the summary in *Bulletin*, Bonn, January 11, 1980.

35. Ibid., p. 11.

36. These include given name and surname, address, date and place of birth, religious affiliation of the individual and of his spouse, citizenship, date of entry into the country, principal and additional residence, family status, income bracket, tax exempt allowances, legal status, relationship to children, and address of foster parents and stepparents.

37. Bull, *Datenschutz*, pp. 195–96.

38. See the excellent discussion in *Bulletin*, Bonn, January 11, 1980, pp. 10–11.

39. See *Third Activity Report of the BfD*, section 2.3.

40. Bull, *Datenschutz*, p. 195 and, in general, pp. 190–98.

41. See Peter Dippoldsmann, "Census and Judgement of the Constitutional Court in the FRG: Some Principles and Consequences," *Information Age* 7 (October 1985): 207–11.

42. *Time* (International Edition), March 31, 1986; *Week in Germany*, March 7, 1987, p. 2.

43. The *Ninth Activity Report of the BfD* (Bonn, 1987) contains an assessment of the plusses and minuses of the identity card legislation, showing that the office is still willing to criticize parliamentary decisions.

44. *International Herald Tribune*, March 28, 1983, p. 2.

45. Frank Kuitenbrouwer, "German Census Postponed on Court Order," in *Transnational Data Report* 6 (1983): 182. As I wrote in 1979: "Observers of other countries might expect the use of census data by the Gemeinden [local communities] to become a source of public controversy. . . ." (*Privacy and Government Data Banks*, p. 146.)

46. *First Activity Report of the BfD* (Bonn, 1979), section 3.3.5.

47. Even in the light of the Court's decision, representatives of the Federal Statistical Office continued to argue for the old practice. See J. Werner and E. Südfeld, "Protection of Privacy, Automatic Data Processing and Progress in Statistical Documen-

tation in the Federal Republic of Germany," Eurostat News-Special Edition, *Protection of Privacy, Automatic Data Processing and Progress in Statistical Documentation* (Luxembourg, 1986), pp. 110–11.

48. See Bull, *Datenschutz,* pp. 308–16.

49. Further details and informed discussion can be found in Kuitenbrouwer, "German Census Postponed on Court Order," 182–83; and Jost Schindel, "Germany Declares Self-Determination over Personal Data," ibid., 7 (August–September 1984): 359–61.

50. See Eibe H. Riedel, "New Bearings in German Data Protection. Census Act 1983 Partially Unconstitutional," *Human Rights Law Journal* 5 (1984): 67–75.

51. "Bad Grade for the Census," *Frankfurter Allgemeine Zeitung,* March 19, 1988.

52. See Werner and Südfeld, "Protection of Privacy," pp. 108–25.

53. *Sixth Activity Report of the BfD* (Bonn, 1984), section 9.1.

54. Bull, *Datenschutz,* pp. 315–16.

55. *Third Activity Report of the BfD,* sections 2.6, 3.4, 3.4.1.

56. See James M. Markham, "Germans Stand Up Not to Be Counted," *New York Times,* May 10, 1987; and Klaus Pokatzky and Michael Sontheimer, "Zähler und Gezählte," *Die Zeit,* June 12, 1987, pp. 33, 35.

Chapter 6

1. Hans Peter Bull, "The Federal Commissioner for Data Protection" (typescript) (Bonn, 1981), p. 12.

2. *Third Activity Report of the BfD* (Bonn, 1981), section 1.1. See also *Fifth Activity Report of the BfD* (Bonn, 1983), section 1.1.

3. *Third Activity Report of the BfD,* section 1.1.

4. Council of Europe, *Legislation and Data Protection* (Rome, 1983), pp. 20, 30, 173–75.

5. Spiros Simitis, ed., *Data Protection Act of the State of Hesse* (Wiesbaden, 1987), p. 7.

6. S. Simitis, "Data Protection: New Developments, New Challenges," *Transnational Data Report* 8 (March 1985): 95.

7. See *Bulletin,* Bonn, January 11, 1980, p. 5.

8. Simitis, *Data Protection Act of the State of Hesse,* p. 6. For this and the preceding paragraph, see generally ibid., pp. 5–15.

9. The text is in *Gesetz- und Verordnungsblatt für das Land Nordrhein-Westfalen,* no. 15 (April 22, 1988), pp. 160–69.

10. See Hans Gliss, "German Data Protection Revisions Proposed," *Transnational Data Report* 6 (October–November 1983): 355–56.

11. BfD Press Statement on the Occasion of the Submission of the 6th Report on the Activities of the Federal Data Protection Commissioner on 24 January 1984, pp. 2, 3.

12. See Eibe H. Riedel, "New Bearings in German Data Protection," *Human Rights Law Journal* 5 (1984): 71, 73.

13. By 1988 only Bremen, Hesse, and North Rhine–Westphalia had revised their data protection laws to comply with the Karlsruhe decision.

14. *Transnational Data and Communications Report* 11 (February 1988): 25.

15. R. Baumann, Report to the Annual Meeting of Data Protection Commissioners, Quebec, September, 1987.

16. *Transnational Data and Communications Report* 11 (March 1988): 25.

Chapter 7

1. Data Act as amended with effect from July 1, 1983, section 2. The original version of the act is found in *Svensk Författningssamling* (*SFS;* Swedish Code of Statutes) 1973:289; the amended version is in *SFS* 1982:446. Subsequent references will be to the amended version unless otherwise noted.

2. Ibid., sections 6, 7–14, 20–25.

3. Ibid., section 2a.

4. His valedictory is Jan Freese, *Den Maktfullkomliga Oförmågan* (The Power of Incompetence) (Stockholm, 1987).

5. Jan Freese, "More than Seven Years of Swedish Legislation—Analysis of Impact and Trends for the Future" (Address to a Symposium on Computer Security and Privacy, Monte Carlo, January 26, 1981), pp. 3–4.

6. Ibid., p. 8.

7. Data Protection Act 1984, c. 35 (U.K.).

8. Data Act, section 15.

9. Jan Freese, "The Swedish Data Act," *Current Sweden* 294 (September 1982): 8.

10. Council of Europe, *Legislation and Data Protection* (Rome, 1983), p. 121.

11. Hans Corell, "Technological Development and Its Consequences for Data Protection," in Council of Europe, *Beyond 1984: The Law and Information Technology in Tomorrow's Society* (Strasbourg, 1985), p. 53.

12. Ibid., p. 56.

13. Freese, "More than Seven Years of Swedish Legislation," p. 4. The Riksdag amended both the Credit Information Act and the Debt Recovery Act in 1981.

14. These two acts are described at some length in Jan Freese, "Protection of Privacy: A Swedish Model," a paper delivered to the International Conference on the Future of Public Administration, Quebec, Canada, May 28, 1979, published in *Conference Proceedings* 9 (1979): 1969–1974.

15. Freese, "More than Seven Years of Swedish Legislation," p. 4.

16. Freese, "Protection of Privacy," p. 1973.

17. Ibid., pp. 1968–70.

18. See Richard F. Tomasson, *Sweden: Prototype of Modern Society* (New York, 1970), chap. 1.

19. Freese, "Protection of Privacy," p. 1961. One author simply argues that life is better with computers: see Hans De Geer, *Bättre Eller Sämre med Datorer?* (Better or Worse with Computers?) (Stockholm, 1982).

20. Jan Freese, "The Future of Data Protection," in *Seminar on Openness and Protection of Privacy in the Information Society. Proceedings* (Embassy of Sweden and Netherlands Central Bureau of Statistics, Voorburg, Netherlands, 1987), p. 108.

21. See David H. Flaherty, *Privacy and Government Data Banks* (London, 1979), pp. 105–6, 109; and Gert Persson, "Computerised Personal Registers and the Protection of Privacy," *Current Sweden* 344 (February 1986): 1–10.

22. Freese, "Swedish Data Act," p. 3.

23. Freese, "More than Seven Years of Swedish Legislation," p. 3; and Freese, "The Swedish Data Act," pp. 2–3.

24. Jan Freese, "The Right to be Alone in Sweden," *Transnational Data Report* 6 (December 1983): 447. See, generally, Gustaf Petren, "Access to Government-Held Information in Sweden," in Norman S. Marsh, ed., *Public Access to Government-Held Information: A Comparative Symposium* (London, 1987), pp. 35–54.

25. The Secrecy Act, as amended March 20, 1980, further establishes significant

limitations on the principle of openness in a relatively complex way and reinforces data protection interests. See Chapter 8.

26. Marquis W. Childs, *Sweden: The Middle Way on Trial* (New Haven, Conn., 1980), pp. 23, 42.

27. Corell, "Technological Development," p. 47.

28. Freese, "More than Seven Years of Swedish Legislation," pp. 4–5.

29. All data are from Statistics Sweden, "Statistics Sweden and the General Public," January 16, 1985 (mimeographed press release). A brief summary appeared in *Transnational Data Report* 8 (March 1985): 69–70.

30. The foregoing paragraph is based in part on Commission nationale de l'informatique et des libertés (CNIL), *Premier Rapport au président de la République et au Parlement 1978–1980* (Paris, 1980), pp. 203, S118.

31. This information is derived from ibid., p. 207; and Herbert Burkert, "Organization and Method of Operation of the Data Protection Authorities," *Study on Data Security and Confidentiality*, section 2, Final Report to the Commission of the European Communities, July 1980, p. 159.

32. Freese, "Right to Be Alone in Sweden," p. 447.

33. Freese, "Protection of Privacy," p. 1962. In both Norway and Denmark the director of the agency is not a member of the governing board. In the latter, the director has the power under Danish administrative law to take "principled cases" to his council, which meets only seven times a year.

34. Normally the board meets approximately once a month; eight to ten such meetings occur each year.

35. Sten Markgren, *Datainspektionen och skyddet av den personliga integriteten* (The Data Inspection Board and the Protection of Personal Privacy) (Lund, Sweden, 1984); Annette Kavaleff, *God personregistersed? En undersökning av datainspektionens styrelsebeslut* (Fair Practices in Personal Data Registers? A Study of Data Inspection Board Decisions) (Stockholm: Law and Informatics Research Institute, 1983).

Chapter 8

1. Data Act, section 1. The original version of the act is found in *Svensk Författningssamling* (*SFS;* Swedish Code of Statutes) 1973:289; the amended version is in *SFS* 1982:446. Subsequent references will be to the amended version unless otherwise noted.

2. Jan Freese, "More than Seven Years of Swedish Legislation—Analysis of Impact and Trends for the Future" (Address to a Symposium on Computer Security and Privacy, Monte Carlo, January 26, 1981), p. 1.

3. Ibid., pp. 2, 9. See also the DALK Report on Revision of the Data Act, *Statens offentliga utredningar* 1978: 54, p. 339; hereafter cited as DALK 1978.

4. Data Act, section 3; comparable language appears in sections 6, 9, and 15.

5. See Jan Freese, "The Right to Be Alone in Sweden," *Transnational Data Report* 6 (December 1983): 448.

6. A legitimate defense for the original Data Act is the customary practice of clarifying in detail the purposes for legislation in the preparatory works for it. This is a stylized process in Sweden, although it may lead to weak definitions in the law itself, such as happened with the Data Act; see Stig Strömholm, ed., *An Introduction to Swedish Law* (Stockholm, 1981), p. 37.

7. The DALK report on the revision of the Data Act affirmed Freese's conclusion (DALK 1978, p. 340).

8. P. G. Vinge, *Swedish Data Act* (Stockholm, 1973).

9. This is a central argument of Alan F. Westin, *Privacy and Freedom* (New York, 1967). On the demographic variables, see Statistics Sweden, "Statistics Sweden and the General Public," January 16, 1985 (mimeographed press release).

10. Data Act, section 3.

11. Two Scandinavian researchers, Annette Kavaleff and Sten Markgren, have been unable to identify coherent bases for decision making in the body of DIB decisions. See Sten Markgren, *Datainspektionen och skyddet av den personliga integriteten* (The Data Inspection Board and the Protection of Personal Privacy) (Lund, Sweden, 1984); Annette Kavaleff, *God personregistersed? En undersökning av datainspektionens styrelsebeslut* (Fair Practices in Personal Data Registers? A Study of Data Inspection Board Decisions) (Stockholm: Law and Informatics Research Institute, 1983).

12. Jan Freese, "Protection of Privacy: A Swedish Model," a paper delivered to the International Conference on the Future of Public Administration, Quebec, Canada, May 28, 1979, published in *Conference Proceedings* 9 (1979): 1955.

13. Freese, "More than Seven Years of Swedish Legislation," p. 4.

14. DALK 1978, p. 341.

15. Flaherty, *Privacy and Government Data Banks* (London, 1979), p. 127; and Statistics Sweden, "Statistics Sweden and the General Public."

16. Data Act, section 3.

17. Ibid., section 3a.

18. The 1982 revisions added race and sexual life to this list (ibid., section 4).

19. Flaherty, *Privacy and Government Data Banks,* p. 116.

20. Data Act, section 8.

21. Ibid., sections 8, 15.

22. Ibid., section 13.

23. Ibid., section 13, paragraph 2.

24. DALK 1978, p. 53.

25. Data Act, section 6.

26. Ibid., section 11, paragraph 2.

27. Ibid., sections 6 and 26, last paragraph. There is a similar provision concerning the use of the government personal and address file known as SPAR.

28. Secrecy Act, March 20, 1980, chapter 7, sections 1, 4, 7, 17–18; see Flaherty, *Privacy and Government Data Banks,* pp. 102–5. The 1980 Act was amended again in 1982. It is a comprehensive document with sixteen chapters and 129 sections; the English translation is one hundred pages long.

29. Ulf Lundvik, "New Secrecy Act in Sweden," *Transnational Data Report* 3 (September 1980): 6.

30. Ibid.; Secrecy Act, 1980, chapter 1, sections 3, 5; chapter 13, section 1.

31. Despite this tolerance for record linkages, the labor unions were opposed to the 1982 revisions to the Data Act, which in their view weakened data protection, because they were worried about private companies using surveillance to the detriment of employees.

32. See Flaherty, *Privacy and Government Data Banks,* part 2.

Chapter 9

1. Jan Freese, "More than Seven Years of Swedish Legislation—Analysis of Impact and Trends for the Future" (Address to a Symposium on Computer Security and Privacy, Monte Carlo, January 26, 1981), p. 5.

2. Commission nationale de l'informatique et des libertés (CNIL), *Premier Rapport au président de la République et au Parlement 1978–1980* (Paris, 1980), p. 206.

3. Olof Ehrenkrona, "The Swedish Model in a New Light," *Svenska Dagbladet*, October 9, 1987.

4. Freese, "The Swedish Data Act," *Current Sweden* 294 (September 1982): 4.

5. Data Act, section 2. The original version of the act is found in *Svensk Författningssamling (SFS;* Swedish Code of Statutes) 1973:289; the amended version is in *SFS* 1982:446. Subsequent references will be to the amended version unless otherwise noted.

6. Ibid.

7. Council of Europe, *Legislation and Data Protection* (Rome, 1983), p. 28.

8. Section 2a also permits associations, doctors and dentists, and public authorities offering health, medical, and social services to maintain files in accord with their statutory responsibilities. Previously, the Data Act did not include such standard authorizations.

9. David H. Flaherty, *Privacy and Government Data Banks* (London, 1979), p. 117.

10. Mats Börjesson, "Swedish Data Protection in Practice," in *Seminar on Openness and Protection of Privacy in the Information Society: Proceedings* (Embassy of Sweden and Netherlands Central Bureau of Statistics, Voorburg, Netherlands, 1987), p. 76.

11. Data Act, section 6a.

12. Ibid., section 18.

13. DALK Report on Revision of the Data Act, *Statens offentliga utredningar* 1978: 54, pp. 340, 341.

14. Ibid., p. 341.

15. Flaherty, *Privacy and Government Data Banks,* p. 112. There have been some private members' bills to have decisions of the DIB reviewed by the ordinary courts rather than by the government.

16. Jan Freese, "The Swedish Data Act," p. 9. Critics point out that this is the normal way of doing business for a regulatory agency.

17. See the discussion of pending appeals in Jan Freese, "The Right to be Alone in Sweden," *Transnational Data Report* 6 (December 1983): 449. By 1987, there had been about 140 government decisions in such appeals.

18. Flaherty, *Privacy and Government Data Banks,* pp. 117–19.

19. Ibid.

20. Data Act, section 21.

21. *Svenska Dagbladet,* September 11, 1982.

22. This section was successfully used in the decision of the Ängelholm court in December 1981, which is discussed in Chapter 10.

23. Freese, "The Swedish Data Act," p. 7.

24. Hans Corell, "Technological Development and Its Consequences for Data Protection," in Council of Europe, *Beyond 1984: The Law and Information Technology in Tomorrow's Society* (Strasbourg, 1985), p. 54.

25. Mats Börjesson, "Swedish Data Protection in Practice," p. 76; and Jan Freese, "Freedom of Information and Privacy Protection in Sweden," in Pierre Trudel, ed., *Accès à l'information et protection des renseignements personnels* (Montreal, 1984), p. 16.

26. It is not clear from the Swedish use of the word "control" in English, whether the DIB is referring to front-end verification or matching at a period of time substantially later than the time of a particular transaction.

27. *Privacy Times,* April 11, 1988, p. 6.

28. Ibid., pp. 22–23.

29. John Wicklein, *Electronic Nightmare: The New Communications and Freedom* (New York, 1981), pp. 204–5.

30. Ibid., pp. 203–4.

31. Flaherty, *Privacy and Government Data Banks,* p. 122.

32. This primarily refers to the underground economy and such white-collar crimes by business concerns as tax evasion, fraudulent bankruptcies, and evasion of customs duties and value-added taxes.

33. Council of Europe, *Legislation and Data Protection,* pp. 28–29. See also Lena Berke, "Economic Crime in Sweden," *Current Sweden* 322 (August 1984).

34. Corell, "Technological Development," p. 49.

35. Ibid., pp. 60–61.

36. Ibid., p. 63.

Chapter 10

1. See David H. Flaherty, *Privacy and Government Data Banks* (London, 1979), pp. 113–14.

2. Freese, "The Swedish Data Act," *Current Sweden* 294 (September 1982): 9. In this writer's view, the concept of privacy cannot be lost or abolished in this sense; it can only be severely curtailed, as in the Orwellian scenario.

3. Jan Freese, "Privacy Protection and International Data Flow," January 14, 1982; hereafter cited as Freese, January 1982.

4. John Wicklein, *Electronic Nightmare: The New Communications and Freedom* (New York, 1981), pp. 201–2.

5. Ibid., p. 205.

6. An example of Freese at work appeared in an article in *Expressen,* March 1, 1983. He is quoted to the effect that Sweden is moving toward a society characterized by control of the population. However, he expresses optimism for the future because the system of trying to control all citizens will break down by itself.

7. This information is derived from Commission nationale de l'informatique et des libertés (CNIL), *Premier Rapport au président de la République et au Parlement 1978–1980* (Paris, 1980), p. 206.

8. Jan Freese, "More than Seven Years of Swedish Legislation—Analysis of Impact and Trends for the Future" (Address to a Symposium on Computer Security and Privacy, Monte Carlo, January 26, 1981), p. 6.

9. DALK Report on Revision of the Data Act, *Statens offentliga utredningar* 1978: 54, pp. 351, 360, 361; hereafter cited as DALK 1978.

10. Speech Notes, Nils Rydén, Deputy Director, DIB, September 11, 1981.

11. Freese, "More than Seven Years of Swedish Legislation," p. 8.

12. DALK 1978, p. 351.

13. Supplementary terms of reference of the Committee on Data Legislation, decision at Cabinet meeting on December 4, 1980, p. 1. The revisions are discussed in *Transnational Data Report* 5 (April–May 1982): 130.

14. Data Act, section 2.

15. Ibid., section 1.

16. The process of identifying a responsible keeper is not as clear-cut as it might seem, since several organizations may be involved in maintaining a single register; alternately, a large institution, such as Stockholm University, may have many registers under its single umbrella of responsible keeper, and it may be difficult for a user to find out which files are kept by the organization.

17. Data Act, section 12.

18. Ibid., sections 5–6, 7, 63.

19. See Freese, "The Right to be Alone in Sweden," *Transnational Data Report* 6 (December 1983): 448.

20. Data Act, section 17.

21. Thomas Osvald, "Regulations Concerning Data Security," *Information Privacy* [now *Information Age*] 1 (November 1978): 90.

22. Thomas Osvald, "The Data Act and Documentation Requirements," (mimeographed report, DIB, April 20, 1983), pp. 2–3.

23. Data Act, section 16.

24. Ibid.

25. The stories appeared in *Dagens Nyheter,* January 27, 1983, and *Svenska Dagbladet,* February 12, 1983.

26. A personal computer used solely for personal purposes does not need to be licensed, but it is not excluded from the rules of the Data Act.

27. Mats Börjesson, "Swedish Data Protection in Practice," in *Seminar on Openness and Protection of Privacy in the Information Society: Proceedings* (Embassy of Sweden and Netherlands Central Bureau of Statistics, Voorburg, Netherlands, 1987), pp. 77, 85.

28. This has yet to occur; see Jan Freese, "Protection of Privacy: A Swedish Model," a paper delivered to the International Conference on the Future of Public Administration, Quebec, Canada, May 28, 1979, published in *Conference Proceedings* 9 (1979): 1959.

29. Datainspektionen, *Personregister I Sverige* (Personal Registers in Sweden) (Data Inspection Board, Stockholm, August 1982).

30. Council of Europe, *Legislation and Data Protection* (Rome, 1983), p. 122; see also the discussion, pp. 115–16.

31. Such a list has to include the license number received from the DIB, the name and purpose of every personal file, the location of the data processing, and whether any personal data are disseminated for processing abroad. See Simon Corell and Jens Danielsson, "The Swedish Data Act and Health Care Data Usage," in J. H. Van Bemmel, Marion J. Ball, and Ove Wigertz, eds., *Medinfo 83: Proceedings of the Fourth World Conference on Medical Informatics, Amsterdam, August 22–27, 1983,* 2 vols. (Amsterdam, 1983), pp. 973–76.

32. Wicklein, *Electronic Nightmare,* pp. 202–3.

33. Data Act, section 10, paragraph 3.

34. Ibid.

35. Flaherty, *Privacy and Government Data Banks,* p. 121; Statistics Sweden, "Statistics Sweden and the General Public," (mimeographed press release, Stockholm, January 16, 1985), pp. 3, 6, 7.

36. Freese, "The Swedish Data Act," *Current Sweden* 294 (September 1982): 6; and Wicklein, *Electronic Nightmare,* p. 203. Hans Corell, formerly senior legal advisor of the Ministry of Justice, suggests that the individual's ability to access a file has a real impact on the civil service, which also risk exposure in the process for misuse or poor use of their powers (Council of Europe, *Legislation and Data Protection,* p. 99).

37. See Wicklein, *Electronic Nightmare,* pp. 198–99, 203.

38. Freese, "Protection of Privacy," p. 1965; Jan Freese's essay in Pierre Trudel, ed., *Accès à l'information et protection des renseignements personnels* (Montreal, 1984), pp. 22, 26; and Freese, "Swedish Data Act," p. 7.

39. Freese, "More than Seven Years of Swedish Legislation," p. 5.

40. All the words quoted are from the statement of claim in the text of the judgment of the court.

41. This is based upon an English translation of the judgment of the court, which has also been reported in brief in *Transnational Data Report* 5 (January–February 1982): 12. An appeals court overturned this decision, and the Supreme Court refused to review it, so the couple did not obtain damages.

42. Hans Corell, "Technological Development and Its Consequences for Data Protection," in Council of Europe, *Beyond 1984: The Law and Information Technology in Tomorrow's Society* (Strasbourg, 1985), p. 54.

43. Speech Notes, Nils Rydén, 1981.

44. CNIL, *Premier Rapport au président de la République et au Parlement,* pp. 212–13.

45. This paragraph is based on ibid., p. 205.

46. Ibid., p. 213.

47. The DIB did produce a ten-year review in 1983. See Datainspektionen, *Rätten att få vara ifred—tio år med datainspektionen* (The Right to be Left Alone—Ten Years with the Data Inspection Board) (Stockholm, 1983).

48. See *Datainspektionens årsbok 1986/87* (Stockholm, 1987).

49. *Svenska Dagbladet,* January 29, 1983.

50. DALK 1978, pp. 342–44.

51. Ibid., p. 343.

52. Ibid.

53. Ibid., p. 349.

54. Ibid.

55. Ibid., pp. 350–51.

56. Ibid.

Chapter 11

1. Data on a particular person are stored until he or she reaches the age of eighty, but no information on a specific person can be given out after the slate has been clean for a decade.

2. John Wicklein, *Electronic Nightmare: The New Communications and Freedom* (New York, 1981), p. 199.

3. Some problems about the DIB's right to regulate security work done by the Police Board were settled so the DIB has access to the relevant security files. Compared to West Germany, data protectors in Sweden seem to treat national security issues with kid gloves. The records and information systems of national security agencies are subject to the Data Act. Freese has pointed out that this is quite appropriate, since intelligence service files are the most important ones (ibid.). In theory the DIB has the power to direct the security agencies to control the information they collect and use on individuals. But these security agencies are part of the Swedish military organization, which creates some difficulties for the DIB in accomplishing anything, even if it had a real will to act. Moreover, the government created the data bases in this field, so the DIB in practice can only have a limited impact on their use for surveillance.

4. The long-unsolved murder of Prime Minister Olaf Palme on February 28, 1986, has had an impact on public confidence in the police. See Richard Reeves, "The Palme Obsession," *New York Times Magazine,* March 1, 1987, p. 20.

5. There were also predictions that he would be sued for damages by the lodger; *Transnational Data Report* 7 (August–September 1984): 298.

6. These paragraphs are derived from Eric Hallman, "The Swedish Enforcement

System—A Case Study," (mimeographed report, The National Tax Board, Solna, Sweden, September 22, 1981).

7. These include the central tax file (tax refunds), the regional social insurance office (employment status), the courts (possession of real estate), and the communes' registers of social welfare cases (ability to pay debts).

8. Tax Auditing (Electronic Data Processing) Act, *Svensk Författningssamling* (*SFS;* Swedish Code of Statutes) 1987:1231, section 2.

9. *Globe and Mail* (Toronto), November 24, 1988, p. B19.

10. Quoted in Wicklein, *Electronic Nightmare,* p. 206.

11. DALK Report on Revision of the Data Act, *Statens offentliga utredningar* 1978: 54, p. 344; hereafter cited as DALK 1978.

12. Ibid., pp. 344–45.

13. Ibid., p. 345.

14. Ibid.

15. Ibid., p. 346.

16. See the strong attack on the PIN by Alf Thoor, the political editor of *Expressen,* in *Transnational Data Report* 7 (April–May 1984): 139.

17. Edmund Rapaport of Statistics Sweden writes that the PIN is "an absolutely necessary instrument in its work. Were the personal identity number system to be abolished, the result, for Statistics Sweden, would be the widespread disruption of the work carried out"; see Rapaport, "Statistics and Privacy—The Official Production of Statistics at a Crossroads," in Eurostat News, Special Edition, *Protection of privacy, automatic data processing and progress in statistical documentation* (Luxembourg, 1986), Theme 9, Series C, p. 81. Rapaport is an expert for the Commission on Data Protection and the Principle of Publicity.

18. Statistics Sweden, "Statistics Sweden and the General Public," (mimeographed press release, January 16, 1985), pp. 1, 10.

19. Flaherty, *Privacy and Government Data Banks* (London, 1979), p. 116.

20. DALK 1978, pp. 346–49, 354–55.

21. Data Act, section 26. The original version of the act is found in *SFS* 1973: 289; the amended version is in *SFS* 1982: 446. Subsequent references will be to the amended version unless otherwise noted.

22. Ibid., section 27.

23. Ibid., section 28.

24. This account is from "Skandia is Permitted to Link Records," *Svenska Dagbladet,* May 19, 1982.

25. A one-member SPAR committee oversees its use.

26. Datainspektionen, *Personregister I Sverige* (Data Inspection Board, Stockholm, August 1982), pp. 36–38.

27. See Flaherty, *Privacy and Government Data Banks,* pp. 116–19 and, generally, ibid., Part 2.

28. There is an informative discussion of the SCB's sensitivity to, and problems with, data protection issues in its excellent report: Statistics Sweden, *Statistics and Privacy: Report from a conference in Stockholm, Sweden, 24–26 June, 1987* (Stockholm, 1988). More detail on matters discussed in these pages can be found therein. In 1978 DALK ruled against the automatic exemption of statistical registers from the licensing provisions of the Data Act, although there are continuing proposals to reduce the burden of data protection on statistical activities; DALK 1978, pp. 352–54.

29. In response to public resistance to censuses of population, certain governments would like to take a census, without bothering the public, by simply linking

existing data bases. At present this is only feasible in certain countries like Denmark. Making possible integrated searches in this way seems more intrusive and supportive of widespread surveillance than the standard census itself.

30. Statistics Sweden, "Statistics Sweden and the General Public," p. 2.

31. Statistics Sweden, *SCBs Image 1986—en enkätundersökning* (SCB's Image 1986— A Public Opinion Survey) (Stockholm, April, 1987), p. 6.

32. Flaherty, *Privacy and Government Data Banks,* p. 118.

33. In North America and the United Kingdom, data collected by a central statistical agency are normally exempted from the subject access provisions of data protection, because they are used only for statistical purposes.

34. See Carl Gunnar Janson, *Project Metropolitan 21: A Longitudinal Study of a Stockholm Cohort* (Stockholm, 1984).

35. See the news reports in *Globe and Mail,* February 11, 1986, p. 1; *New York Times,* March 11, 1986, p. 1; and the editorial in *Montreal Gazette,* February 19, 1986.

36. The press was unaware of the numerous scholarly publications issued by Project Metropolitan since 1975. See a partial listing in David H. Flaherty, Edward H. Hanis, and S. Paula Mitchell, eds., *Privacy and Access to Government Data for Research: An International Bibliography* (London, 1979), p. 83. There is also a description of the project in Flaherty, *Privacy and Government Data Banks,* pp. 135–36.

37. See, for example, Ulf Himmelstrand, "The Data Fetish," *New Society,* January 16, 1987, pp. 21–22.

38. The Swedish Ombudsman determined in 1987 that the Project was in full compliance with the relevant laws (*Dagens Nyheter,* June 26, 1987).

Chapter 12

1. Mats Börjesson, "Swedish Data Protection in Practice," in *Seminar on Openness and Protection of Privacy in the Information Society: Proceedings* (Embassy of Sweden and Netherlands Central Bureau of Statistics, Voorburg, Netherlands, 1987), p. 74.

2. Jan Freese, "Seven Years of Swedish Data Legislation—Analysis of Impact and Trends for the Future," in *Informatique et protection de la personnalité: Universités de Berne, Fribourg, Genève, Lausanne, et Neuchâtel. Enseignement de 3e cycle de Droit 1980* (Fribourg, Switzerland, 1981), p. 72.

3. Jan Freese, "The Swedish Data Act," *Current Sweden* 294 (September 1982): 9.

4. Hans Corell, "Technological Development and Its Consequences for Data Protection," in Council of Europe, *Beyond 1984: The Law and Information Technology in Tomorrow's Society* (Strasbourg, 1985), p. 59.

5. Statistics Sweden, "Statistics Sweden and the General Public," (mimeographed press release, January 16, 1985), pp. 3, 4, 16.

6. See "The Swedish Model in a New Light," *Svenska Dagbladet,* October 9, 1987.

7. Commentary, Data Protection Commissioners' meeting, Quebec, September 1987.

8. Gert Persson, "Computerised Personal Registers and the Protection of Privacy," *Current Sweden* 344 (February 1986): 6.

9. Corell, "Technological Development," pp. 62, 63.

10. DALK Report on Revision of the Data Act, *Statens offentliga utredningar* 1978: 54, p. 337; hereafter cited as DALK 1978.

11. Corell, "Technological Development," p. 57.

12. Carl Axel Petri, "The Conflict between Openness and the Right to Be Let

Alone," in *Seminar on Openness and Protection of Privacy in the Information Society: Proceedings* (Embassy of Sweden and Netherlands Central Bureau of Statistics, Voorburg, Netherlands, 1987), pp. 42–44.

13. Mats Börjesson, "Swedish Data Protection in Practice," in ibid, p. 76.

14. *Privacy Times,* April 11, 1988, p. 6.

15. Corell, "Technological Development," p. 57.

16. On the other hand, it is more difficult to link manual data, so that manual storage does reduce the risk of unauthorized computer matching and of sensitive information being transferred to third parties.

Chapter 13

1. This study generally slights the important work of the CNIL in the private sector, except to the extent that it impinges upon the general tasks and organization of the agency.

2. Loi No. 78-17 du 6 janvier 1978 relative à l'informatique, aux fichiers et aux libertés, *Journal Officiel de la République Française,* January 7, 1978 (hereafter, Law of January 6, 1978). The most convenient edition is CNIL, *Informatique et Libertés: Textes et documents,* 8th ed. *Journal Officiel de la République Française,* no. 1473 (Paris, 1986), pp. 19–34. I have relied for the most part on the translation circulated by the Organization for Economic Co-operation and Development on March 5, 1979. Most other translations in the case study are my own.

3. However, a law of July 17, 1970, had added a new part to the introduction to the French Civil Code, which created a statutory recognition of the right to personal privacy in the sense that everyone has the right to respect for his or her private life (Law 70-643, 17 July 1970, article 9). See André Vitalis, *Informatique, pouvoir et libertés,* 2d ed. (Paris, 1988), pp. 145–58. A recent study is Pierre Kayser, *La Protection de la vie privée,* vol. 1, *Protection du secret de la vie privée* (Paris, 1984).

4. See Vitalis, *Informatique,* pp. 77–90.

5. *Rapport de la Commission Informatique et Libertés,* 2 vols. (Paris, 1975), p. 7; hereafter these volumes will be cited as *Tricot Report.* I have used the Council of Europe's translation of the first volume: *Report of the Committee "Informatics and Liberties"* (Strasbourg, June 10, 1976).

6. Ibid., p. 17.

7. Ibid., p. 61.

8. Law of January 6, 1978, article 4.

9. On these and related points, see the excellent commentary on the 1978 law by Herbert Maisl, "La Maîtrise d'une interdépendance: Commentaire de la loi du 6 janvier 1978 relative à l'informatique aux fichiers et aux libertés," *La Semaine Juridique* 52, no. 2891 (March 8 1978): 7.

10. *Tricot Report,* p. 30.

11. Law of January 6, 1978, articles 6, 8, 13.

12. See Maisl, "La Maîtrise," pp. 7, 39, 40. According to one commentator, the Senate wanted to inspire the institution by including members of a different outlook and to establish sociopolitical control of the administration. See Jean Frayssinet, "Les Rapports entre les protections non juridictionelle et juridictionelle des administrés: Le Cas de l'accès à l'information administrative," *La Revue Administrative* (November–December 1983): 566.

13. The groups are the National Assembly, the Senate, the Economic and Social

Council, the Council of State, the Supreme Court of Appeal, and the Court of Accounts.

14. If they serve in a particular government ministry, enter politics, or serve on the CNIL, for example, they continue to be salaried by their corps and can always return to it. See John Ardagh, *France in the 1980s* (London, 1982), pp. 84–86.

15. See Françoise Gallouédec-Genuys and Herbert Maisl, *Le Secret des Fichiers* (Paris, 1976), pp. 316–25. A 1976 survey in Nantes also found low levels of concern for privacy. Only 23 percent of the sample of 596 persons regarded the use of computers as threatening the private life of individuals. See André Vitalis, "L'Informatique et son image dans l'opinion nantaise," *Revue INSEE* 24 (March 1977): 44.

16. Agence de l'Informatique, *L'Etat d'informatisation de la France* (Paris, 1986), p. 200.

17. Ardagh, *France in the 1980s,* pp. 405–7.

18. Ibid., p. 189.

19. Theodore Zeldin, *The French* (London, 1983), p. 169.

20. Alain Peyrefitte, *The Trouble with France,* trans. William R. Byron (New York, 1981), p. 169.

21. Nora, as quoted in Ardagh, *France in the 1980s,* pp. 24, 90.

22. The Nora-Minc report and the extraordinary international colloquium in 1979 on Informatics and Society evidence this concern. See Simon Nora and Alain Minc, *The Computerization of Society: A Report to the President of France* (Cambridge, Mass., 1980); *Actes du Colloque International Informatique et Societé,* 5 vols. (Paris, 1980).

23. *01-Informatique Hebdo,* May 18, 1981. See also Rex Malik, "France's Social Agenda for *Le Computer*," *Computerworld* 17, no. 19 (May 9, 1983): In Depth, pp. 1–22.

24. See *Globe and Mail,* November 20, 1981, p. 12.

25. On technology generally, see the report by the Agence de l'Informatique, *L'Etat d'informatisation de la France,* especially pp. 116–19, 195–97.

26. *Le Matin,* March 21, 1980.

27. *Les Echos,* September 23, 1981, p. 12.

28. See, for example, Jean Querat, "Des fichiers par centaines de milliers," *Le Figaro,* July 3, 1981.

29. See *01-Informatique Hebdo,* September 21, 1981.

30. Law of January 6, 1978, article 8.

31. Law of January 6, 1978, article 10.

32. CNIL, *7e Rapport d'activité au président de la République et au Parlement, 1986* (Paris, 1987), pp. 298–300.

33. The original proposal for a data protection law included a secretary-general to direct the staff of the agency. Senator Thyraud discouraged the idea in the Senate, because he was hostile to a commission with weak commissioners who mainly ratified staff decisions. Once he became involved with the CNIL, he resisted having a staff director in place. Ironically, failures in administration became one of the chief weaknesses of the CNIL during his presidency.

Chapter 14

1. The law determines that "the automatic processing of personal data means any series of operations effected by automatic means, involving the collection, recording, preparation, modification, storage and destruction of personal data, as well as any series of such operations relating to the use of files or data bases, including interconnections or comparisons, consultation or communication of personal data." (Loi No. 78-17 du 6

janvier 1978 relative à l'informatique, aux fichiers et aux libertés, *Journal Officiel de la République Française,* January 7, 1978 [hereafter, Law of January 6, 1978].) Article 4 defines personal data as "data which permit, in any form, directly or indirectly, the identification of the persons to which they relate."

2. Ibid., article 45.

3. Ibid., articles 25, 27.

4. Ibid., article 6.

5. CNIL, *2e Rapport d'activité au président de la République et au Parlement 1980–1981* (Paris, 1982), p. 52. All reports of the commission are hereafter cited by years as CNIL, *Rpt.;* the publication date is always the subsequent year.

6. CNIL, *Rpt., 1978–80,* p. 7.

7. This is in accord with the significant recommendation of the *Tricot Report* that the scope of the CNIL should include "liberties in general and not only the protection of private life." See *Rapport de la Commission Informatique et Libertés,* 2 vols. (Paris, 1975), p. 71; hereafter cited as *Tricot Report.*

8. J. Fauvet, "The Activities of the French National Commission of Data Processing and Freedom," in *Data Privacy and Security. State of the Art Report. 13:6* (Oxford, 1985), p. 34; *Le Quotidien de Paris,* November 11, 1983.

9. Law of January 6, 1978, article 2.

10. Council of Europe, *Legislation and Data Protection* (Rome, 1983), pp. 90–91.

11. Interview with J. Fauvet, *L'Ordinateur individuel* 100 (February 1988).

12. CNIL, *Informatique et Libertés: Textes et documents,* 8th ed. (Paris, 1986), p. 47.

13. CNIL, *Rpt., 1978–80,* p. 9.

14. See CNIL, *Rpt., 1978–80,* p. 16; and CNIL, *Rpt., 1980–1981,* pp. 119–29.

15. CNIL, *Rpt., 1980–1981,* pp. 128–29.

16. Interview with *Temps Réel,* summarized in *Transnational Data Report* 5 (January–February 1982): 13.

17. CNIL, *Rpt., 1980–1981,* p. 11.

18. See, for example, Law of January 6, 1978, article 45.

19. The *Tricot Report,* pp. 19–20, stated that "the protection of private life in the face of the collection, processing, and harmful dissemination of certain information has been one of our dominant preoccupations. But we have not had to try to define what private life means, because our mission did not stop at its frontiers."

20. LINK Resources Corporation and Transnational Data Reporting Service, Inc., *Data Protection/Privacy Compliance Guide* (New York, 1979), p. 87.

21. I am indebted to Madame Françoise Chamoux for this point.

22. Law of January 6, 1978, article 17.

23. See *Expertises* 28 (March 1981): 12.

24. Law of January 6, 1978, article 28.

25. *Tricot Report,* pp. 49–50.

26. Article 42 provides criminal sanctions in the form of imprisonment and/or fines for breach of this provision.

27. *Tricot Report,* p. 46; also pp. 15–17, 45–49.

28. H. Maisl, "Legal Aspects of Data Flows between Public Agencies in France," *Computer Networks* 3 (1979): 201.

Chapter 15

1. Loi No. 78-17 du 6 janvier 1978 relative à l'informatique, aux fichiers et aux libertés, *Journal Officiel de la République Française,* January 7, 1978 (hereafter, Law of January 6, 1978), articles 8, 13.

2. CNIL, *Premier rapport au président de la République et au Parlement 1978–80* (Paris, 1980), p. 15. All reports of the commission are hereafter cited by year as CNIL, *Rpt.;* after this first report, the publication date is always the subsequent year.

3. *Rapport de la Commission Informatique et Libertés,* 2 vols. (Paris, 1975), p. 75; hereafter cited as *Tricot Report.*

4. *Les Echos,* September 23, 1981, p. 1. See also CNIL, *Rpt., 1983–84,* pp. 268–69.

5. Its accounts are subject to standard auditing after the fact by the Court of Accounts; see CNIL, *Rpt., 1978–1980,* p. 16.

6. See Alain Peyrefitte, *The Trouble with France,* trans. William R. Byron (New York, 1981), p. 182.

7. Herbert Maisl, "Informatique et libertés," *Techniques de l'ingénieur,* 6–1985, no. H 500, p. 6.

8. Interview with Jean Rosenwald, *Ordinateur,* April 23, 1984.

9. CNIL, *Rpt., 1978–80,* pp. 15–16. See also Council of Europe, *Legislation and Data Protection* (Rome, 1983), pp. 101–2.

10. CNIL, *Rpt., 1983–84,* p. 172. For comparable claims, see Fauvet, "La CNIL," in Claude-Albert Colliard and Gérard Timsit, eds., *Les Autorités administratives indépendantes* (Paris, 1988), pp. 145–46.

11. See Michel A. Calvo, "Les Pouvoirs d'investigation de la Commission nationale de l'informatique et des libertés," *La Semaine Juridique* 14, no. 13748 (April 8, 1982): 174.

12. This provision is in accord with the recommendations of the Tricot Commission; see *Tricot Report,* p. 73. See also the discussion in H. Maisl, "La Maîtrise d'une interdépendance," *La Semaine Juridique,* 52, no. 2891 (March 8, 1978).

13. See *L'Actualité Juridique Droit Administratif* 9 (September 20, 1982): 541–44; this issue is discussed below in Chapter 16.

14. Maisl, "Informatique et libertés," p. 7.

15. J. Frayssinet, "Les rapports entre les protections non juridictionnelle et juridictionnelle des administrés: Le Cas de l'accès à l'information administrative," *La Revue Administrative* (November–December 1983): 568.

16. See *Le Monde,* December 24, 1980; January 14 and 17, 1981.

17. Ibid., December 21 and December 22, 1983; *Le Quotidien de Paris,* December 21, 1983; *Libération,* December 22, 1983.

18. *Transnational Data Report* 7 (March 1984): 63.

19. Forni was also president of the powerful Law Commission, which controls the flow of proposed new legislation to the National Assembly and the Senate. He left the CNIL in August 1985 for a senior post with a regulatory body but returned after his reelection in 1988.

20. *Le Quotidien de Paris,* June 20, 1984.

21. Only the Council of State can overturn an unfavorable opinion, a view confirmed by the minister of justice in 1981; see *Les Echos,* September 23, 1981, p. 12, and CNIL, *Rpt., 1980–1981,* p. 92.

22. CNIL, *Informatique et Libertés: Textes et documents,* 8th ed. (Paris, 1986), pp. 51–52.

23. Ibid., pp. 51, 57–58.

24. Jacques Thyraud, "Un Exemple de Contre-Pouvoir," press release, November 7, 1983.

25. CNIL, *Rpt., 1983–1984,* pp. 261–62.

26. The budget of the CNIL was 3.1 million francs in 1979, 7.4 million in 1980,

13.3 million in 1984, and 14.7 million for 1988. See CNIL, *Rpt., 1980–81,* p. 12; *Rpt., 1981–82,* p. 12; *Rpt., 1983–84,* p. 14; and *Rpt., 1988,* p. 11.

27. See Rex Malik, "France's Social Agenda for Le Computer," *Computerworld* 17, no. 19 (May 9, 1983): In Depth, pp. 10, 11, 19, 20. CESIA, which the article describes as a small agency, has a budget more than seven times greater than the CNIL.

28. CNIL, *Rpt., 1983–84,* pp. 133, 151.

29. At an early stage in the CNIL's history, André Vitalis perceptively commented that, in effect, the CNIL could not terminate the numerous systems of personal information that are operated by most public administrations and large private organizations, but can only assure a legal framework for their administration. As a consequence, it can give a false sense of security to a public anxious about the development of data banks and offers a type of social legitimation to systems that might better be ended because of their illegality; *Informatique, pouvoir et libertés* (Paris, 1981), p. 204.

30. See CNIL, *Rpt., 1980–81,* pp. 10–11.

31. Council of Europe, *Legislation and Data Protection,* pp. 112–14.

32. Maisl, "Informatique et libertés," p. 6.

33. See the article in *Le Figaro,* November 11, 1983.

34. CNIL, *Rpt., 1981–82,* pp. 25, 29.

35. Bertrand Le Gendre, "Les projets de M. Jacques Fauvet," *Le Monde,* October 3, 1984.

36. Maisl argues that the powers of influence and persuasion of the "public men" on the commission should not be underestimated; see "Informatique et libertés," p. 7.

37. CNIL, *Rpt., 1980–81,* p. 20.

38. Ibid., pp. 28–29; see Chapter 17 below.

39. On October 6, 1981, the president of the CNIL noted a lack of action with respect to the decree and asked the government commissioner to investigate the delay. The decree appeared on January 22, 1982, and seems to have complied with the recommendations of the CNIL; ibid., p. 27.

40. The commissioners applied something of a brake to decision making during the period of political indecision surrounding the elections, not least because a number were directly involved in the election itself.

41. Eric Rohde, "La Préparation des élections à la sécurité sociale," *Le Monde,* May 4, 1983.

42. Maisl, "Informatique et libertés," p. 5.

43. CNIL, *Rpt., 1983–84,* p. 5.

Chapter 16

1. *Transnational Data Report* 2, No. 6 (1980): 9.

2. John Ardagh, *France in the 1980s* (New York, 1982), pp. 191, 192, 201.

3. See the discussions in *Le Monde,* October 14, 1983; *Le Quotidien de Paris,* November 11, 1983; and *Libération,* November 9, 1983.

4. See for December 21, 1983, *Le Figaro, Le Monde, Le Quotidien de Paris, Bulletin Quotidien;* see also *Libération,* December 22, 1983.

5. See *Le Monde,* December 22, 1983; and Andrew Lloyd, "New Head for French Data Protection Board," *Transnational Data Report* 7 (March 1984): 63.

6. Interview with J. Rosenwald, *Ordinateur,* April 23, 1984.

7. *Le Monde* and *Le Quotidien,* June 20, 1984.

8. *Le Monde,* June 20, 1984.

9. See *Le Monde,* February 10–11, 1980 and December 19, 1980; and the interview with Forni in *Le Matin,* April 23, 1983.

10. See CNIL, *Premier rapport au président de la République et au Parlement 1978–80* (Paris, 1981), pp. 121–22. All reports of the commission are hereafter cited by years as CNIL, *Rpt.;* the publication date is always the subsequent year.

11. For a discussion of the newcomers, see *01-Informatique Hebdo,* December 26, 1983; *Expertises des systèmes d'information* (hereafter *Expertises*) 58 (January 1984): 1–2; and ibid., 112 (December 1988), p. 417.

12. "CNIL: Un Premier bilan," *Terminal 19/84* 13 (March 1983): 27. The Centre d'information et d'initiatives sur l'informatisation (CIII), created in 1979, is made up of leftist computer experts and members of the Democratic Confederation of Labor (CFDT).

13. Professor Herbert Maisl wrote revealingly in 1985: "It is incontestable that politics plays an inevitable role at the CNIL, that the average age there is quite high, which makes the commission more an assembly of wise people than a grouping of young pioneers of new technology, and, in addition, that technicians serve only a modest role there"; see "Informatique et libertés," *Techniques de l'ingénieur,* 6–1985, no. H 500, p. 6.

14. Article 8 prohibits from membership "anyone holding office or an interest in a firm involved in the manufacture of equipment used in data processing or telecommunications, or in the provision of data-processing or telecommunications services."

15. *Rapport de la Commission Informatique et Libertés,* 2 vols., (Paris, 1975), p. 73; hereafter cited as *Tricot Report;* and CNIL, *Rpt., 1978–80,* p. 19.

16. Maisl, "Informatique et libertés," p. 8.

17. In the fourteen and one-half months to the end of 1984, at least fifteen different commissioners served as reporters, averaging two dossiers each. Seven took only one case, three took two cases, three (including vice-presidents Thyraud and Forni) took three cases, one took four cases, and another handled five; see CNIL, *Rpt., 1983–84,* pp. 195–260. One newcomer, Michel Elbel, handled four dossiers. Of course, one cannot quantify the relative burden of individual cases.

18. In its June 1980 decision in favor of national identity cards, the CNIL did not follow the advice of Raymond Forni, its reporter on the subject, but this is likely to remain a rare event; *Le Monde,* June 4, 1980.

19. See CNIL, *Rpt., 1978–80,* p. 19, and CNIL, *Rpt., 1980–81,* p. 114. It is unusual for the CNIL as a whole to hear direct representations from the regulated; the reporter and the government commissioner handle such matters.

20. See CNIL, *Rpt., 1983–84,* pp. 99–114.

21. *Que Choisir?,* March 1982, p. 25.

22. CNIL, *Rpt., 1980–81,* pp. 119–29; also *Rpt., 1981–82,* pp. 132–36; *Rpt., 1987,* pp. 174–75.

23. *Tricot Report,* p. 75.

24. Interview with J. Rosenwald, *Ordinateur,* April 23, 1984.

25. Paragraph based on interview with J. Rosenwald, ibid.; interview with J. Fauvet, *01-Informatique Hebdo,* December 3, 1984; and CNIL, *Rpt., 1983–84,* p. 14.

26. Maisl advises the president on legal questions, attends meetings of the president's office, conducts studies on particular issues, represents the CNIL in litigation and at outside events, and attends commission meetings.

27. CNIL, *Rpt., 1980–81,* pp. 17–18. Such modifications do not appear in the text

of the CNIL's opinion, so it is often necessary to review the minutes of an actual plenary session to learn what the CNIL has actually accomplished.

28. Interview with Gérald Flon, *01-Informatique Hebdo,* December 10, 1984.

29. The corollary is simply engaging in crisis management.

30. The rules are in CNIL, *Rpt., 1987,* pp. 178–88.

31. Law of January 6, 1978, articles 6, 14; see the listing of duties in CNIL, *Rpt., 1978–80,* pp. 16–17.

32. In the eight years to the end of 1987, there were 170,472 registrations of information systems in the form of declarations and requests for advice; CNIL, *Rpt., 1987,* p. 15. The numbers offer some evidence of how much time the staff devotes to the manipulation of paper. The only comforting fact is that the annual figure for new registrations has stabilized at about 20,000.

33. The CNIL's discussion of its overview of the systems of the director-general of taxes is quite impressive. Among other things, it offered the commission an opportunity to discuss the reconciliation of such competing interests as controlling surveillance and ending tax fraud. See CNIL, *Rpt., 1983–84,* pp. 6, 17, 63 and, especially, 41–64.

34. Law of January 6, 1978, article 15.

35. The issue is discussed in Pierre Kayser, *La Protection de la vie privée,* 2 vols. (Paris, 1984), 1:299–301.

36. *Transnational Data Report* 4 (January–February 1982): 13.

37. Law of January 6, 1978, article 17; CNIL, *Rpt, 1986,* p. 19.

38. See CNIL, *Informatique et Libertés: Textes et documents,* 8th ed. (Paris, 1986), pp. 79–192.

39. Ibid., pp. 107–9.

40. Thus, for example, the CNIL surprisingly accepted a simple declaration, rather than a request for its opinion, in connection with the National Driver's License register; CNIL, *Rpt., 1980–81,* pp. 15, 100.

41. CNIL, *Informatique et Libertés,* p. 59.

42. Thirty-six of these decisions are printed in CNIL, *Rpt., 1983–84,* pp. 188–260.

43. Law of January 6, 1978, article 19.

44. However, there are some surprising exceptions: "Applications for opinions relating to the automatic processing of personal data affecting national security, defense or public safety" may omit some of the details required by article 19. The Council of State may also decree that such regulatory acts of the CNIL "relating to certain processing affecting national security, defense and public safety shall not be published"; Law of January 6, 1978, articles 19 and 20.

45. See CNIL, *Rpt., 1983–84,* pp. 214–26, 256; and Jacques Fauvet, "Informatique et Libertés," *Le Journal du Parlement,* November 15–30, 1984; Fauvet, "La CNIL," in Claude-Albert Colliard and Gérard Timsit, eds., *Les Autorités administratives indépendantes* (Paris, 1988), p. 146.

46. CNIL, *Rpt., 1986,* p. 19.

47. *Tricot Report,* p. 32.

48. It bases this expansive claim on the final paragraph of article 1 of the Decree of July 17, 1978, which essentially incorporates the first sentence of article 1; CNIL, *Rpt., 1980–81,* p. 56; CNIL, *Informatique et Libertés,* p. 53.

49. CNIL, *Rpt., 1980–81,* pp. 39, 41.

50. See CNIL, *Informatique et Libertés,* pp. 99–100; and CNIL, *Rpt., 1980–81,* pp. 138–42.

51. See *Le Canard Enchaîné,* November 28, 1984; *Le Monde,* November 29 and 30, 1984; December 6, 1984; *L'Express,* December 14–20, 1984, pp. 51–3; and, especially, Jean-Pierre Chamoux, *Menaces sur l'ordinateur* (Paris, 1986), pp. 187–90.

52. Law of January 6, 1978, article 21(2); CNIL, *Rpt., 1980–81,* pp. 83–87.

53. See Brigitte Kantor, "La CNIL contre Big Brother," *Le Matin,* December 12–13, 1983; and Pierre-Yves Le Priol, "Contre Big Brother," *La Croix,* November 9, 1983.

54. See CNIL, *Rpt., 1983–84,* p. 29; *Rpt., 1985,* pp. 40–50.

55. Interview with J. Rosenwald, *Ordinateur,* April 23, 1984; interview with J. Fauvet, *01-Informatique Hebdo,* December 3, 1984. Details about inspections can be found in an interview with G. Flon, *01-Informatique Hebdo,* December 10, 1984, and in CNIL, *Rpt., 1987,* pp. 14, 187.

56. For details of the inspections it carried out in 1982, see CNIL, *Rpt., 1981–82,* pp. 81–91, 265–73; CNIL, "Minutes," November 27, 1984; Maisl, "Informatique et Libertés," p. 7.

57. By government decree of December 28, 1979, even the existence of the information systems of the Ministry of Defense cannot be published; CNIL, *Rpt., 1980–81,* p. 17.

58. *Transnational Data and Communications Report* 11 (February 1988): 10.

59. Maisl, "Informatique et Libertés," pp. 8, 11.

60. See Council of Europe, *Legislation and Data Protection,* p. 90, and *Expertises* 63 (June 1984): 1.

61. Law of January 6, 1978, article 19.

62. Ibid., article 36.

63. CNIL, *Informatique et Libertés,* pp. 57–58.

64. Law of January 6, 1978, article 34. Article 45 extends the right of access to *manual* files for personal data that should not be collected in the first place, such as information on race or religion, or information that an individual suspects has been acquired by illegal or dishonest means. This complicated article needs to be consulted in its entirety in order to understand the conditions under which an individual can obtain access to manual files.

65. Ibid., article 35.

66. Ibid., article 38.

67. CNIL, *Informatique et Libertés,* pp. 55–56, 198–99.

68. CNIL, *Rpt., 1983–84,* pp. 85–88.

69. See CNIL, *Rpt., 1980–81,* p. 55.

70. J. Fauvet, "The Activities of the French National Commission of Data Processing and Freedom," in *Data Privacy and Security: State of the Art Report 13:6* (Oxford, 1985), p. 37.

71. See, generally, Roger Errera, "Access to Administrative Documents in France: Reflexions on a Reform," in Norman S. Marsh, ed., *Public Access to Government-Held Information: A Comparative Symposium* (London, 1987), pp. 87–121.

72. See the response to a parliamentary question printed in CNIL, *Rpt., 1983–84,* pp. 274–75 and 27; and Herbert Maisl and Céline Wiener, "Conseil d'Etat," *Recueil Dalloz Sirey* 38 (November 17, 1983): 546–49.

73. See generally CNIL, *Rpt., 1980–81,* pp. 52–65, and *Rpt., 1982,* pp. 58–70.

74. CNIL, *Informatique et Libertés,* pp. 85–89.

75. CNIL, *Rpt., 1980–81,* p. 57.

76. Ibid.

77. CNIL, *Informatique et Libertés,* p. 86.

78. CNIL, *Rpt., 1980–81,* p. 64; interview with G. Flon, *01-Informatique Hebdo,* December 10, 1984.

79. The first and second editions of this pamphlet totalled 150,000 copies; CNIL, *Rpt., 1980–81,* p. 59.

80. Critics suggest that these data are totally speculative.

81. CNIL, *Informatique et Libertés,* p. 69; CNIL, *Rpt., 1980–81,* p. 56.

82. See the interview with Thyraud in *Que Choisir?,* March 1982, p. 25.

83. A copy was included in *Terminal 19/84* 8 (1982): i–xvi.

84. *Expertises* 32 (August 1981): 2–6; Council of Europe, *Legislation and Data Protection,* pp. 89–90.

85. CNIL, *Rpt., 1980–81,* pp. 54–55.

86. Ibid., p. 66.

87. See the discussions in each annual report, including CNIL, *Rpt., 1986,* pp. 34–53.

88. The CNIL did a major investigation over several years of claims that the police were still using certain files on French Jews from the Second World War. See CNIL, *Rpt., 1981–82,* pp. 88–89, 275–98.

89. The volume published on the tenth anniversary of the 1978 law further demonstrated the CNIL's capacity for self-advertisement. Despite its preparation by outsiders and publication by a commercial press, the contents are almost totally descriptive and uncritical. See CNIL, *Dix ans d'informatique et libertés* (Paris, 1988).

90. See Bernard Delthil, "La France en fiches," *Le Quotidien de Paris,* February 12, 1981.

91. CNIL, *Rpt., 1980–81,* p. 53.

92. *Que Choisir?,* March 1982, p. 24; Ardagh, *France in the 1980s,* p. 406.

93. See, for example, *Le Figaro,* November 7, 1983; *Libération,* November 9, 1983; and *La Croix,* November 9, 1983.

94. Interview with J. Fauvet, *Le Temps,* June 10, 1985.

95. See the early discussion of finality in CNIL, *Rpt., 1980–81,* pp. 80–82, 102, and of the evolving scene in CNIL, *Rpt., 1983–84,* pp. 5–6, 128.

96. See CNIL, *Rpt., 1980–81,* p. 98.

97. Kantor, "La CNIL contre Big Brother."

98. See the discussion in Maisl, "Informatique et libertés," p. 10.

99. Jacques Fauvet, "Informatique et Liberté," *Le Journal du Parlement,* November 15–30, 1984.

100. See CNIL, *Rpt., 1978–80,* pp. 25–30; *Rpt., 1980–81,* pp. 88–100; *Rpt., 1987,* pp. 17–23.

101. See CNIL, *Rpt., 1980–81,* p. 95.

102. Ibid., pp. 17, 53.

103. Jean Querat, "Des fichiers par centaines de milliers," *Le Figaro,* July 3, 1981; Maisl, "Legal Aspects of Data Flows between Public Agencies in France," *Computer Networks* 3 (1979): 200–201.

104. See the explanation offered by Noëlle Lenoir, then a senior staff member of the CNIL, in Council of Europe, *Legislation and Data Protection,* pp. 90–91; and CNIL, *Rpt., 1983–84,* pp. 41–64.

105. Between its slow beginnings in 1979 and September 1988, the CNIL has made approximately 900 decisions. As of 1988, the full texts are available in an on-line data base. See CNIL, *Rpt., 1987,* p. 12.

106. For an assessment of a 1987 decision in which a member of a public administration contested the CNIL's right to authorize two data bases, see Jean Frayssinet,

"Le Conseil d'Etat et le contrôle de la légalité d'un traitement automatisé de données nominatives créé pour le compte de l'état," *Expertises* 106 (June 1988): 178–89.

107. The decision of the Council of State is reported in *L'Actualité Juridique Droit Administratif,* September 20, 1982, pp. 541–44. Most of the conclusions are presented by the commissioner for the government, who is in fact a member of the council; this person's recommendations for solutions are regarded as essential. See also CNIL, *Rpt., 1981-82,* pp. 124–31.

108. See Law of January 6, 1978, article 21(4); the exchange in CNIL, *Rpt., 1983-84,* pp. 268–69; and the commentary in *Expertises* 56 (November 1983): 229, 264.

109. Interview with J. Rosenwald, *Ordinateur,* April 23, 1984.

110. Interview with J. Fauvet, *01-Informatique Hebdo,* December 3, 1984.

111. *Expertises* 68 (December 1984): 313–14, and ibid., 69 (February 1985): 12. Jean Frayssinet has analyzed various decisions in prosecutions for *Expertises:* see 83 (1986): 101–8; 92 (1987): 41–47; and 101 (1987): 444–53.

112. *Transnational Data and Communications Report* 9 (February 1986): 29.

113. Ibid., 10 (November 1987): 24; Colliard and Timsit, *Les Autorités administratives indépendantes,* pp. 297–98.

Chapter 17

1. For introductory information about recordkeeping by the Ministry of Justice and the Ministry of the Interior, see CNIL, *Dix ans d'informatique et libertés* (Paris, 1988), pp. 131–46, 149–52; certain privacy implications are discussed in CNIL, *10e Rapport au président de la République et au Parlement, 1987* (Paris, 1988), pp. 241–48. All reports of the commission are hereafter cited by years as CNIL, *Rpt.;* the publication date is always the subsequent year.

2. Eric Rohde, "L'après-Safari," *Le Monde,* March 22, 1981.

3. See CNIL, *Rpt., 1980-81,* pp. 70–72.

4. See Bertrand Le Gendre, "Blocages aux frontières," *Le Monde,* May 20, 1983. The gendarmes are proceeding with plans to make their data base of wanted persons accessible by terminals in police cars; *Le Figaro,* June 1, 1984.

5. Interview with J. Fauvet, *L'Etudiant,* March 1986.

6. CNIL, *Rpt., 1983-84,* pp. 71–74; *Rpt., 1986,* pp. 108–12.

7. CNIL, *Rpt., 1983-84,* pp. 221–22.

8. See CNIL, *Rpt., 1980-81,* p. 92; *Rpt., 1981-82,* pp. 74–76, 265–73.

9. CNIL, *Informatique et Libertés: Textes et documents,* 8th ed. (Paris, 1986) pp. 41–44, 74–78; see CNIL, *Rpt., 1980-81,* pp. 39–41.

10. Decree 81-1003, *Journal Officiel de la République Française,* November 11, 1981.

11. See *La Croix,* May 13, 1981; *Le Monde,* May 9, 1981.

12. CNIL, *Rpt., 1980-81,* pp. 62–64; *Le Monde,* May 22, 1981.

13. The constitution of Interpol stipulates that it is to promote mutual assistance among police forces in the spirit of the U.N. Declaration on Human Rights. It forbids the organization "to undertake any intervention or activities of a political, military, religious or racial character." Thus Interpol refuses to disseminate information on all of these matters or for administrative purposes.

14. For further details, see G. Russell Pipe, "Interpol Forms Personal Records Control Commission," *Transnational Data Report* 5 (December 1982): 377; CNIL, *Rpt., 1981-82,* pp. 193–97, and *Rpt., 1983-84,* pp. 157, 174–75.

15. *Privacy Journal* 14 (November 1987): 4.

16. Alain Peyrefitte, *The Trouble with France,* trans. William R. Byron (New York, 1981), p. 198.

17. CNIL, *Rpt., 1980–81,* pp. 95–98.

18. *Computerworld* 16, no. 34 (August 23, 1982): 2.

19. *Transnational Data Report* 5 (September 1982): 292; *Terminal 19/84* 11 (October 1982): 7–8.

20. *Terminal 19/84* 11 (October 1982): 8.

21. Ibid., 13 (March 1983): 28.

22. J. Vetois, "Lutte anti-terroriste: Retour du fichage?" in ibid., 11 (October 1982): 7–8.

23. Council of Europe, *Legislation and Data Protection* (Rome, 1983), p. 58.

24. Bertrand Le Gendre, "Les Prudences d'AUDASS," *Le Monde,* December 5, 1980; see also CNIL, *Rpt., 1980–81,* pp. 18–19, 206–8.

25. Ministry of Health and Social Security, Declaration on the System AUDASS-ENFANCE, January 21, 1981, *Journal Officiel de la République Française,* March 10, 1981, pp. 2431–32, article 3.

26. *Le Monde,* December 5, 1980; Ministry of Health and Social Security, Declaration on the System AUDASS-ENFANCE, articles 2a, 4, 7.

27. *Le Monde,* December 5, 1980.

28. *Terminal 19/84* 4 (March 1, 1981): 25–26. The CNIL on June 29, 1982, published a favorable opinion on AUDASS-Aide Sociale, a sister-system to AUDASS-ENFANCE, with the same integrated and automated characteristics. It covers social assistance to the ill, the elderly, the blind, and families; see CNIL, *Rpt., 1981–82,* pp. 35–39.

29. C. Hoffsaes, "Le Système GAMIN: Erreur technocratique ou premier pas vers un fichage généralisé?" *Esprit. Changer la culture et la politique* 5 (May 1982): 22; A. Vitalis, *Informatique, pouvoir et libertés,* 2d ed. (Paris, 1988), p. 91.

30. Hoffsaes, "Le Système GAMIN," p. 23; Vitalis, *Informatique,* p. 95.

31. Hoffsaes, "Le Système GAMIN," p. 24; Vitalis, *Informatique,* pp. 92–93.

32. Hoffsaes, "Le Système GAMIN," pp. 25, 26; Vitalis, *Informatique,* p. 97.

33. Vitalis, *Informatique,* p. 95; *Le Matin,* July 30, 1980.

34. Hoffsaes, "Le Système GAMIN," pp. 25, 30.

35. The Ministry of Health's circular of 1973, for example, went far beyond the simple application of the law; Vitalis, *Informatique,* pp. 92, 93, also 96, 100, 103.

36. Ibid., pp. 94, 95–96, 99.

37. Hoffsaes, "Le Système GAMIN," p. 29.

38. Vitalis, *Informatique,* pp. 101, 102; Hoffsaes, "Le Système GAMIN," p. 33.

39. Hoffsaes, "Le Système GAMIN," pp. 26–27.

40. See Vitalis, *Informatique,* p. 98.

41. Hoffsaes, "Le Système GAMIN," pp. 29, 35; Vitalis, *Informatique,* p. 98.

42. *Terminal 19/84* 2/3 (1981): 11.

43. For much more detail on the criticisms of GAMIN by social workers and unions, see ibid., 13; Hoffsaes, "Le Système GAMIN," pp. 28, 36–37; Vitalis, *Informatique,* pp. 99–100.

44. *Terminal 19/84* 2/3 (1981): 12–23; see Hoffsaes, "Le Système GAMIN," pp. 38–41.

45. See CNIL, *Rpt., 1980–81,* pp. 28–31, 226–30.

46. The national secretary of the CFDT wrote a brief against the scheme for the CNIL's reporter. One newspaper printed sections of this brief on the day the CNIL was

supposed to announce its decision. The same paper also called the commissioner's report to the CNIL on Project GAMIN relatively moderate, whereas, the journalist claimed, other members of the CNIL were more critical. See Hoffsaes, "Le Système GAMIN," pp. 30–31; Bernard Delthil, "Quand l'ordinateur se mêle de ce qui ne le regarde pas," *Le Quotidien de Paris,* April 7, 1981.

47. Hoffsaes, "Le Système GAMIN," p. 31; Bertrand Le Gendre, "La Lutte contre le fichage," *Le Monde,* June 25, 1981.

48. *Terminal 19/84* 10 (1982): 26.

49. This paragraph is based on Pierre Benoît, "EX-GAMIN: La CNIL se déjuge-t-elle?" *Terminal 19/84* 15 (July 1983): 25; CNIL, *Rpt., 1982–83,* pp. 271–72.

50. See Herbert Maisl, "Informatique et libertés," *Techniques de l'ingénieur,* 6–1985, no. H 500, p. 13.

51. The commission put a positive gloss on these developments in a review of GAMIN in CNIL, *Rpt., 1986,* pp. 174–81.

52. See *Terminal 19/84* 4 (March 1981): 4; and the interview with Martinage in *Informatique et Gestion,* No. 122 (March 1981).

53. Details are from *Terminal 19/84,* 2/3 (1981): 20–21.

54. *Terminal 19/84* 2/3 (1981): 21–22; Jean-Charles Reix, "Bientôt, la carte d'identité magnétique," *Le Figaro,* May 7, 1980, p. 11; *Le Monde,* June 25, 1980.

55. See *Terminal 19/84* 2/3 (1981): 18–19.

56. *Le Figaro,* May 7, 1980, p. 11.

57. *Terminal 19/84* 2/3 (1981): 20.

58. CNIL, *Rpt., 1978–80,* pp. 48–52, 130–33.

59. *Terminal 19/84* 4 (March 1981): 4.

60. *01-Informatique Hebdo,* May 18, 1981.

61. *Les Echos,* September 23, 1981, p. 12.

62. CNIL, *Rpt., 1983–84,* p. 26.

63. See the review and discussion in CNIL, *Rpt., 1986,* pp. 97–108, and Thyraud's interview in *La Croix,* November 20, 1986. Thyraud and a staff member had only a month to prepare the CNIL's report on identity cards, including thirty-two interviews and trips to Bonn and Berlin.

64. Decree No. 87-178 of March 19, 1987, *Journal Officiel de la République Française,* March 20, 1987.

65. *Libération,* April 6, 1988, p. 1; *Le Monde,* April 8, 1988. The conservative *Le Figaro,* April 6, 1988, p. 1, and ibid., April 7, 1988, was more favorable.

66. See *Terminal 19/84* 29 (July–August 1986): 16–18; ibid., 30 (October–November 1986): 3–5.

67. The national electoral register, with which it is closely connected, covers 30 million persons; CNIL, *Rpt., 1980–81,* p. 17.

68. CNIL, Déliberation No. 81-68; Decree, *Journal Officiel,* January 29, 1982.

69. The digits indicate sex, year and month of birth, birth department, and place of birth. Two digits are usually added to the NIR for it to serve as the social security number. See Pierre Kayser, *La Protection de la vie privée,* 2 vols. (Paris, 1984), 1:132. One journalist described the social security number as a "veritable record of the socio-economic activity of the country"; Querat, "Des fichiers par centaines de milliers."

70. CNIL, *Rpt., 1980–81,* pp. 25–27, 223–25.

71. Bertrand Le Gendre, "La Lutte contre le fichage."

72. The data for the NIR continue to come from birth and death notices from the mayor's offices.

73. Council of State Decree, articles 3, 4, 5, *Journal Officiel*, January 29, 1982; CNIL, Délibération 81-68, articles 5, 8. Individuals have a right of access to their files.

74. See CNIL, *Rpt., 1980–81*, pp. 39–41.

75. Continued decreases in the costs of data storage should reduce the need for unique identifying numbers for retrieval purposes, since any up-to-date system should be able to distinguish most individuals on the basis of data stored about them. Any unique number facilitates linkages but again existing, or at least emerging, technology negates the real need for numbers for such purposes.

76. CNIL, *Rpt., 1983–84*, p. 24. See also the critique of NIR in *Terminal 19/84* 29 (July–August 1986): 25–6.

77. Aimé Savard, "Les Puces qui nous gouvernent . . . ," *La Vie*, No. 2213, January 28, 1988.

78. See the general discussions in CNIL, *Rpt., 1983–84*, pp. 65–70; and *Rpt., 1986*, pp. 61–66.

Chapter 18

1. CNIL, *2e Rapport au président de la République et au Parlement, 1980–1981* (Paris, 1982), p. 171. All reports of the commission are hereafter cited by years as CNIL, *Rpt.;* the publication date is always the subsequent year.

2. *Le Point*, August 11, 1980.

3. *Que Choisir?*, March 1982, p. 25.

4. Interview with J. Thyraud, *Le Quotidien de Paris*, November 11, 1983.

5. Béatrice Vallaeys, "La Commission Informatique et Libertés est contente d'elle," *Libération*, November 9, 1983. A similarly critical tone appeared in Andrew Lloyd's summary remarks in *Transnational Data Report* 7 (March 1984): 63.

6. *Terminal 19/84* 25 (September–October 1985): 30. Earlier evaluations can be found in ibid., 13 (March 1983): 25–30.

7. Opening statement, Conference on Data Protection, Nanterre, June 1981.

8. Jean-Pierre Chamoux and Françoise Chamoux, "French Data Protection: The First Five Years," *Transnational Data Report* 7 (April–May 1984): 164, 166.

9. The study group that publishes *Terminal 19/84* describes the CNIL as playing a double role: "The existence of the commission legitimizes informatics, because it limits excesses and in the process contributes to its development." See *Terminal 19/84* 13 (March 1983): 28; and ibid., 15 (July 1983): 27.

10. CNIL, *Rpt., 1983–84*, p. 172.

11. Jacques Fauvet, "A propos de l'allocution de Monsieur Flaherty," CNIL, Paris, September 7, 1987, a commentary on the keynote address by this writer at the 1987 annual meeting of the data protection commissioners in Quebec. See David H. Flaherty, "Vers l'an 2000: L'Emergence des sociétés de surveillance dans le monde occidental," in CREIS (Centre de Coordination pour la recherche et l'enseignement en informatique et société), *Bulletin de liaison* 5 (June 1988): 3–13.

12. Aimé Savard, "Les puces qui nous gouvernent . . . ," *La Vie*, no. 2213, January 28, 1988, and CNIL, *Dix ans d'informatique et libertés* (Paris, 1988), p. 8. See also the critique of the CNIL's work in "CNIL: Une Crédibilité à soutenir: Un Chien de garde édenté?" *Le Monde Informatique*, January 18, 1988.

13. *Les Echos*, September 23, 1981, p. 12.

14. CNIL, *Rpt., 1980–81*, p. 56.

15. See Chamoux and Chamoux, "French Data Protection," pp. 163–66.

16. A 1987 high court decision has emphasized this need, because it annulled a conviction of the manager of a private company for maintaining an unregistered data base on the grounds that the paper files were not covered by the law. See Jean Frayssinet, "La Cour de cassation et la loi informatique, fichiers et libertés, ou comment amputer une loi tout en raffermissant son application," *La Semaine Juridique*, no. 11 (March 16, 1988), no. 3323.

17. See, generally, CNIL, *Rpt., 1983–84*, pp. 153–56; and Herbert Maisl, "Informatique et libertés," *Techniques de l'ingénieur*, 6–1985, no. H 500, pp. 7, 14.

18. CNIL, *Rpt., 1983–84*, p. 5; interview with J. Fauvet, *Le Temps*, June 10, 1985. Monitoring such developments is the particular concern of the CNIL's subcommission on technology and security. See *CNIL, Rpt., 1983–84*, pp. 145–53.

19. *Que Choisir?*, March 1982, p. 25.

20. CNIL, *Rpt., 1983–84*, pp. 172–73. The Scandinavians are viewed as an exception.

21. A description of the technology of smart cards can be found in Agence de l'Informatique, *L'Etat d'informatisation de la France* (Paris, 1986), pp. 276–79.

22. CNIL, *Rpt., 1986*, pp. 184–91, 199–203.

23. CNIL, "Présentation de la carte à mémoire. Intervention de Monsieur Vié," (September 10, 1984) to the annual meeting of Data Protection Commissioners in Vienna.

24. *Terminal 19/84* 13 (March 1983): 28.

Chapter 19

1. Privacy Act, *Revised Statutes of Canada*, 1985, c. P-21. The most useful edition is Privacy Commissioner of Canada, *The Privacy Act: An Office Consolidation and Index. 1987 Edition* (Ottawa, 1987).

2. Department of Communications and Department of Justice, *Privacy and Computers: A Report of a Task Force* (Ottawa, 1972).

3. The government decided to create a number of ombudsmen, including one for privacy, and to associate them with the Canadian Human Rights Commission; Minister of Justice, news release, "Basford Announces Federal Ombudsman Legislation," Ottawa, December 19, 1977.

4. The Minister of Justice and Attorney General, "Privacy Legislation: Cabinet Discussion Paper" (mimeographed, Ottawa, June 1980), pp. 4, 8; hereafter cited as Cabinet Discussion Paper, 1980. This was several months after the Liberals under Pierre Trudeau returned to power.

5. House of Commons, *Minutes of Proceedings and Evidence of the Standing Committee on Justice and Legal Affairs*, Issue No. 94, June 8, 1982, pp. 94:171–258.

6. House of Commons, *Debates*, February 24, 1977.

7. The Supreme Court has most importantly recognized an individual's right to a "reasonable expectation of privacy against governmental encroachments" in its decisions in *Hunter* v. *Southam*, 2 *Supreme Court Reports* 2 (1984): 159–60; and *Queen* v. *Dyment*, December 8, 1988. Protection of Privacy Act, 1974, *Statutes of Canada*, *1973–74*, c. 50.

8. The London, Ontario, privacy survey in 1982 did find high levels of concern. See Neil Vidmar and David H. Flaherty, "Concern for Personal Privacy in an Electronic Age," *Journal of Communication* 35 (1985): 91–103.

9. An Act Respecting Access to Documents Held by Public Bodies and the

Protection of Personal Information, *Revised Statutes of Quebec,* c. A-2.1 and *Statutes of Quebec, 1982,* c. 30; Freedom of Information and Protection of Privacy Act, *Statutes of Ontario,* 1987, c. 25.

10. Peter Hicks, Treasury Board, private communication to author, May 12, 1978. The drafters made use of the model for revising the Privacy Act proposed by the Privacy Protection Study Commission. See Cabinet Discussion Paper, 1980, p. 10.

11. Privacy Act, sections 40(2), 75(1).

12. Ibid., section 29(3).

13. Ibid., section 37(1).

14. Ibid., section 8(2)(m).

15. Cabinet Discussion Paper, 1980, p. 14; see also Treasury Board Canada, *Interim Policy Guide: Access to Information Act and the Privacy Act* (Ottawa, June 1983), pt. 3, pp. 48–50.

16. Privacy Act, section 8(5).

17. Cabinet Discussion Paper, 1980, p. 14.

18. See Privacy Act, section 41; and *Annual Report, Privacy Commissioner, 1983–84* (Ottawa, 1984), p. 2.

19. See Privacy Act, sections 2, 12–18, and *Annual Report, Privacy Commissioner, 1983–84,* pp. 6–7.

20. Treasury Board Canada, *Administrative Policy Manual,* December 1978, chaps. 410, 415, 420, 425; and Treasury Board's *Interim Policy Guide.* The privacy regulations appear in ibid., pt. 3, Appendix B.

21. Privacy Act, sections 75(1) and 75(2).

22. House of Commons, *Open and Shut: Enhancing the Right to Know and the Right to Privacy. Report of the Standing Committee on Justice and Solicitor General on the Review of the Access to Information Act and the Privacy Act* (Ottawa, 1987); hereafter cited as *Open and Shut.* The committee acquired its present name when new parliamentary rules went into effect in 1986.

23. Privacy Act, sections 71(1)(a) and (d).

24. Under the Financial Administration Act, the Treasury Board "may act on all matters relating to administrative policy in the Public Service of Canada," which gives it some authority throughout the government; Treasury Board, *Interim Policy Guide,* pt. 3, p. 2.

25. Ibid., p. 5.

26. Ibid., pp. 5–6.

27. *Annual Report, Privacy Commissioner, 1983–84,* p. 9.

28. Press release on the proclamation of the Access to Information and Privacy Acts, June 22, 1983, pp. 3–4.

29. See Minister of Justice, "The Canadian Human Rights Bill. Background Notes" (mimeographed, 1977), p. 9; and *Annual Report of the Privacy Commissioner, 1981* (Ottawa, 1982), p. 127.

30. See Cabinet Discussion Paper, 1980, p. 145. Hansen's reference to partisan advocacy refers to the "legal gymnastics that lawyers enjoy."

31. According to Hansen: "While an ombudsman finds facts, he must be objective; if the facts show that the complainant did not get that to which he is entitled, by all means let the ombudsman be an advocate. When complaints cannot be justified in law or fact, but the ombudsman finds that law or policy ought to be changed, he or she must speak up. The roles are compatible, so long as you do not take the side of the complainant until you are satisfied he or she has suffered a wrong." Private communication, Inger Hansen to David H. Flaherty, August 5, 1982.

32. *Annual Report, Privacy Commissioner, 1983–84,* pp. 6, 7.

33. Cabinet Discussion Paper, p. 17.

34. House of Commons, *Minutes of Proceedings and Evidence of the Standing Committee on Justice and Legal Affairs,* Issue No. 94, June 8, 1982, pp. 94:248–49.

35. *Annual Report, Privacy Commissioner, 1983–84,* p. 9.

36. *Open and Shut,* pp. 37–38.

37. Privacy Act, section 50(8).

38. House of Commons, *Debates,* June 23, 1983, p. 26719.

39. *Annual Report, Privacy Commissioner, 1987–88* (Ottawa, 1988), p. 47.

Chapter 20

1. Section 3 defines personal information as information "recorded in any form," including photographs and sound recordings pertaining to identifiable individuals; Privacy Act, *Revised Statutes of Canada,* 1985, c. P-21.

2. Ibid., section 2.

3. The Minister of Justice and Attorney General, "Privacy Legislation. Cabinet Discussion Paper, 1980" (mimeographed, Ottawa, June 1980), p. 9.

4. Privacy Act, sections 4, 5.

5. Treasury Board Canada, *Interim Policy Guide: Access to Information Act and the Privacy Act* (Ottawa, 1983), pt. 3, pp. 14–15.

6. Ibid., p. 15.

7. Ibid., pp. 16–17; Privacy Act, section 5(3).

8. Treasury Board, *Interim Policy Guide,* pt. 3, p. 17.

9. Ibid., p. 18.

10. Privacy Act, sections 6(1), (2), (3). Sections 4 and 7 of the Privacy Act regulations and the Treasury Board's *Interim Policy Guide,* pt. 3, pp. 20–24, deal with these matters.

11. Treasury Board, *Interim Policy Guide,* pt. 3, pp. 21–23.

12. Ibid., p. 25.

13. Ibid., pp. 25–26.

14. Privacy Act, section 8(1); Treasury Board, *Interim Policy Guide,* pt. 3, pp. 28–32.

15. Privacy Act, section 8(2)(a); Treasury Board, *Interim Policy Guide,* pt. 3, pp. 32–35.

16. See Treasury Board, *Interim Policy Guide,* pt. 3, pp. 35–59.

17. Privacy Act, section 8(2)(m); Treasury Board, *Interim Policy Guide,* pt. 3, pp. 49–50.

18. Internal disputes over the meaning of the provisions in the Privacy Act have also been avoided because of the success in coordinating it with the Access to Information Act.

19. See House of Commons, *Open and Shut: Enhancing the Right to Know and the Right to Privacy. Report of the Standing Committee on Justice and Solicitor General on the Review of the Access to Information Act and the Privacy Act* (Ottawa, 1987), pp. 51–53.

Chapter 21

1. Canadian Human Rights Act, *Statutes of Canada* 1976–77, c. 33, sections 21(1), 57. Given the diverse statutory responsibilities for implementation, a discussion of

independence should perhaps treat more actors than the privacy commissioner. But, for example, one can hardly question the independence of the president of the Treasury Board, a leading Cabinet member, with respect to the exercise of his duties and functions under the Privacy Act, and the Federal Court is obviously independent in its limited function of reviewing denials of access to records.

2. Ibid., section 21(4).

3. Following a resolution of the Senate and House of Commons, the governor in council fills the position by commission under the Great Seal; Privacy Act, *Revised Statutes of Canada,* 1985, c. P-21, section 53(1).

4. Ibid., section 53(2), (3).

5. Ibid., sections 58(2), 68(1), 66, 67, 38, 40(1).

6. Ibid., section 71(3)(4).

7. See House of Commons, *Open and Shut: Enhancing the Right to Know and the Right to Privacy. Report of the Standing Committee on Justice and Solicitor General on the Review of the Access to Information Act and the Privacy Act* (Ottawa, 1987), pp. 41–42; hereafter cited as *Open and Shut.*

8. See the Minister of Justice and Attorney General, "Privacy Legislation. Cabinet Discussion Paper, 1980" (mimeographed, Ottawa, June 1980), p. 2.

9. The privacy commissioner is empowered to disclose to the attorney general of Canada evidence "of an offence against any law of Canada or a province on the part of any officer or employee of a government institution," but, in practice, such reporting will occur very infrequently and is not part of the regular exercise of power by the office; Privacy Act, section 64(2).

10. House of Commons, *Debates,* June 28, 1982, p. 18854.

11. House of Commons, *Minutes of Proceedings and Evidence of the Standing Committee on Justice and Legal Affairs,* Issue No. 18, March 12, 1981, p. 18:5.

12. Inger Hansen, "The Canadian Human Rights Act, Part IV," in John D. McCamus, ed., *Freedom of Information: Canadian Perspectives* (Toronto, 1981), p. 254.

13. See Privacy Act, sections 8(3), 8(4); *Annual Report, Privacy Commissioner, 1984–85* (Ottawa, 1985), pp. 40–42; *Annual Report, Privacy Commissioner, 1987–88* (Ottawa, 1988), p. 44; and *Open and Shut,* pp. 56–57.

14. See, however, Commission d'accès à l'information, *Rapport annuel 1987–1988* (Quebec, 1988).

Chapter 22

1. *Annual Report, Privacy Commissioner, 1983–84* (Ottawa, 1984), p. 3.

2. Ibid., p. 4.

3. Ibid., pp. 2–3, 5.

4. *Annual Report, Privacy Commissioner, 1984–85* (Ottawa, 1985), p. 3.

5. Although the office has to comply with government hiring rules, which largely means recruiting competitively from within the existing public service, it remains unclear whether Grace's staff will, in practice, enjoy job mobility within the same group.

6. Privacy Act, *Revised Statutes of Canada,* 1985, c. P-21, section 37(3).

7. *Annual Report, Privacy Commissioner, 1984–85,* pp. 6, 9, 25.

8. Privacy Act, sections 8(4), 8(5), 9(3), 37(1).

9. Ibid., section 8(5); and Treasury Board Canada, *Interim Policy Guide: Access to Information Act and the Privacy Act* (Ottawa, 1983), pt. 3, pp. 39–40, 53.

10. Privacy Act, section 60(1). Grace has received no such referrals to date.

446 / Notes to Pages 266-72

11. See House of Commons, *Open and Shut: Enhancing the Right to Know and the Right to Privacy. Report of the Standing Committee on Justice and Solicitor General on the Review of the Access to Information Act and the Privacy Act* (Ottawa, 1987), p. 78; hereafter cited as *Open and Shut*.

12. Privacy Commissioner of Canada, *AIDS and the Privacy Act* (Ottawa, 1989).

13. Privacy Act, sections 31-37.

14. *Annual Report, Privacy Commissioner, 1984-85,* p. 13. See also *Annual Report, Privacy Commissioner, 1983-84,* pp. 2, 3, 7.

15. *Annual Report, Privacy Commissioner, 1984-85,* pp. 8, 13, 43-44, and *Annual Report, Privacy Commissioner, 1983-84,* p. 7.

16. Detailed reports on audits are in *Annual Report, Privacy Commissioner, 1987-88* (Ottawa, 1988), pp. 38-43.

17. Ibid., pp. 39, 41-43.

18. Ibid., p. 9.

19. Sample staff totals for 1987-88 are as follows: National Defence, thirty-one; RCMP, thirty-one; Correctional Services, sixteen; CEIC, eleven; and National Archives, nine. These institutions had the most Privacy Act requests in the five years to March 31, 1988.

20. *Open and Shut,* pp. 41-42.

21. Treasury Board, Memorandum, Bill C-43: Privacy Index Publication, September 23, 1982.

22. Government of Canada, *Privacy Act: Personal Information Index 1983* (Ottawa, 1983). Any interim changes are recorded in the periodic Access to Information and Privacy *Implementation Reports,* prepared by the Treasury Board, and intended for the general guidance of access and privacy coordinators.

23. Treasury Board, Bill C-43 (Privacy Act). Personal Information Index Reporting Package (September 1982), p. 1.

24. See Privacy Act, sections 10(1)(b), 11(1)(a)(iv), 11(1)(b).

25. Canada, *Personal Information Index 1988* (Ottawa, 1988). These figures are based on an actual count by the Privacy Commissioner's Office.

26. *Annual Report, Privacy Commissioner, 1984-85,* pp. 37, 38.

27. See ibid., pp. 41, 43; *Annual Report, Privacy Commissioner, 1987-88,* p. 16.

28. There were 159,835 formal requests from July 1, 1983 to December 31, 1987: 65 percent led to full disclosure; 22 percent, partial disclosure; while only 1 percent received no personal information; *Transnational Data and Communications Report* 11 (August-September 1988): 24.

29. Privacy Act, section 12; Privacy Act Extension Order No. 2, *Canada Gazette,* pt. 1, October 29, 1988.

30. *Privacy Act,* section 77(1)(j).

31. The total annual figures for formal requests for access from 1978 to 1982 respectively were as follows: 13,081, 6,636, 10,370, and 10,533.

32. Inger Hansen, Notes for Panel Discussion, Data Processing Institute, Ottawa, March 18, 1982, pp. 13-14.

33. See Privacy Act, sections 15, 16, 29(1)(b)-(f).

34. See *Annual Report, Privacy Commissioner, 1984-85,* pp. 5-6, 22-23, and 32-34.

35. Ibid., pp. 8-9, 17.

36. *Annual Report, Privacy Commissioner, 1987-88,* p. 11.

37. Privacy Act, section 41.

38. See Minister of Justice and Attorney General, "Privacy Legislation: Cabinet

Discussion Paper," (mimeographed, Ottawa, June 1980), pp. 2, 15; hereafter cited as Cabinet Discussion Paper, 1980.

39. See ibid., p. 16.

40. Privacy Act, section 36(1).

41. *Annual Report, Privacy Commissioner, 1984–85*, pp. 45–47.

42. Ibid., pp. 8, 44, and *Annual Report, Privacy Commissioner, 1983–84*, pp. 10–11.

43. See *Open and Shut*, pp. 46–49; and *Annual Report, Privacy Commissioner, 1987–88*, p. 21.

44. Privacy Act, section 70.

45. *Open and Shut*, pp. 29–33.

46. Privacy Act, sections 29(1)(a), (g), (h), 29(3).

47. See, for example, *Annual Report, Privacy Commissioner, 1987–88*, pp. 22–36.

48. *Annual Report, Privacy Commissioner, 1984–85*, pp. 6–7.

49. Ibid., p. 22; and *Annual Report, Privacy Commissioner, 1983–84*, p. 17.

50. See *Annual Report, Privacy Commissioner, 1984–85*, pp. 19–21.

51. "Report of the Privacy Commissioner of Canada concerning the Conflict of Interest and Post-Employment Code for the Federal Public Service" (mimeographed, Ottawa, Febuary 1987).

52. Privacy Act, sections 31, 35.

53. *Annual Report, Privacy Commissioner, 1984–85*, p. 21.

54. *Open and Shut*, pp. 49–51; and Department of Justice, *Access and Privacy: The Steps Ahead* (Ottawa, 1987), pp. 16–17.

55. Privacy Act, sections 38, 39, 59(1)(b). There have been no special reports to date.

56. *Annual Report, Privacy Commissioner, 1983–84*, p. 2.

57. *Annual Report, Privacy Commissioner, 1984–85*, pp. 6, 8–9.

58. Privacy Act, section 72. The Treasury Board determines the form and contents of such reports; Privacy Act, section 71(1)(3).

59. *Open and Shut*, pp. 94–95.

60. See House of Commons, *Minutes of Proceedings and Evidence of the Standing Committee on Justice and Legal Affairs*, Issue No. 18, March 12, 1981, pp. 18:12–13; *Annual Report of the Privacy Commissioner, 1981* (Ottawa, 1982), p. 145; *Annual Report of the Privacy Commissioner, 1982* (Ottawa, 1983), p. 49.

61. *Open and Shut*, pp. 7–8.

62. *Annual Report, Privacy Commissioner, 1987–88*, p. 8.

63. *Annual Report, Privacy Commissioner, 1984–85*, pp. 9, 10.

64. Ibid., pp. 2, 5.

65. Ibid., p. 24, and *Annual Report, Privacy Commissioner, 1983–84*, p. 10.

66. *Annual Report, Privacy Commissioner, 1987–88*, p. 46.

67. Ibid., pp. 11–12, 14–15, 18.

68. *Open and Shut*, pp. 51–53; Department of Justice, *Access and Privacy*, pp. 19–20.

69. *Re Ternette and Solicitor General of Canada, Dominion Law Reports* 10, 4th ser. (1984): 587.

Chapter 23

1. See David H. Flaherty, *The Origins and Development of Social Insurance Numbers in Canada* (Ottawa, 1981).

2. Beatty failed in a series of motions to restrict the use of the Social Insurance Number; see House of Commons, *Debates,* June 28, 1982, pp. 18865, 18866–67.

3. Privacy Commissioner of Canada, *Report of the Privacy Commissioner on the Use of the Social Insurance Number* (Ottawa, 1981), pp. 3, 82, 162.

4. House of Commons, *Debates,* June 28, 1982, pp. 18865–66. The reported authorized uses of the more than 23 million entries in the "Social Insurance Number Registration" bank still seem very expansive. It remains the closest Canadian equivalent of a national data bank for administrative purposes. See *Annual Report of the Privacy Commissioner, 1981* (Ottawa, 1982), pp. 112–17, and Canada, *Personal Information Index 1987* (Ottawa, 1987), chap. 8, pp. 29–30.

5. Canada, *Report of the Privacy Commissioner,* p. 214.

6. Ibid., pp. 215–17.

7. House of Commons, *Debates,* January 25, 1983, p. 22190; ibid., January 27, 1983, p. 22312.

8. Ibid., January 27, 1983, p. 22312.

9. See David H. Flaherty and Peter J. Harte, "Social Insurance Number," in James H. Marsh, ed., *The Canadian Encyclopedia* (Edmonton, 1985), p. 1720.

10. House of Commons, *Open and Shut: Enhancing the Right to Know and the Right to Privacy. Report of the Standing Committee on Justice and Solicitor General on the Review of the Access to Information Act and the Privacy Act* (Ottawa, 1987), pp. 44–46; hereafter cited as *Open and Shut.*

11. Ten federal institutions abandoned twenty specific applications of the numbers. Their use is still authorized by fifteen statutes and regulations, many of which cover large segments of the total population (pensions, student loans, family allowances, income tax, and unemployment insurance).

12. See, generally, Department of Justice, *Access and Privacy: The Steps Ahead* (Ottawa, 1987), pp. 4–7; and Treasury Board Canada, "Federal Government Restricts Use of Social Insurance Number," press release, June 8, 1988.

13. Privacy Commissioner, "Saying No to SIN," news release, June 9, 1988.

14. Privacy Act, *Revised Statutes of Canada,* 1985, c. P-21, section 8(2)(e).

15. The Minister of Justice and Attorney General, "Privacy Legislation: Cabinet Discussion Paper" (mimeographed, Ottawa, June 1980), p. 12; hereafter cited as Cabinet Discussion Paper, 1980.

16. Ibid., p. 13.

17. Ibid.; Privacy Act, section 8(4).

18. Privacy Regulations, schedules 2 and 3 in Treasury Board Canada, *Interim Policy Guide: Access to Information Act and the Privacy Act* (Ottawa, 1983), pt. 3, Appendix B.

19. Ibid., p. 37.

20. Ibid., p. 38.

21. Ibid., p. 39.

22. *Annual Report, Privacy Commissioner, 1987–88* (Ottawa, 1988), pp. 16–17.

23. Cabinet Discussion Paper, 1980, p. 14.

24. Treasury Board, *Interim Policy Guide,* pt. 3, p. 41.

25. Privacy Act, sections 22(1) and 22(2). The RCMP says that additional exemptions require it to refuse to disclose any personal information obtained or prepared by it, while providing policing services for provinces or municipalities, when the federal government has, on the request of the province or municipality, agreed not to disclose such information. This is a serious problem, since the RCMP plays a major role in offering such policing services for about one-third of the population.

26. See House of Commons, *Standing Committee on Justice and Legal Affairs,* Issue No. 17, March 10, 1981, p. 17:8.

27. Letter from Attorney General Roy McMurtry to Minister of Communications Francis Fox, p. 12.

28. Ibid., pp. 12, 13.

29. Ibid., pp. 18–19.

30. T. Murray Rankin, *Freedom of Information and the McMurtry Letter: A Response to Provincial Concerns* (Canadian Bar Association, April 1982), p. 56.

31. *Standing Committee on Justice and Legal Affairs,* Issue No. 94, June 8, 1982, pp. 94:196–200.

32. House of Commons, *Debates,* June 28, 1982, p. 18860.

33. Treasury Board Canada, Secretariat, *Report to the President of the Treasury Board on the Operation of Part IV of the Canadian Human Rights Act (April 1, 1981 to March 31, 1982)* (Ottawa, 1983), p. 4.

34. P. E. J. Banning, "The RCMP Perspective on the Access to Information and Privacy Acts," National Forum on Access to Information and Privacy, Ottawa, March 7, 1986, pp. 8, 10.

35. Canada, *Personal Information Index 1983* (Ottawa, 1983), pp. 204–8; *Personal Information Index 1987* (Ottawa, 1987), chap. 92.

36. See the general review of CPIC in David H. Flaherty, "Protecting Privacy: Data Protection in the Canadian Police Information Centre," *University of Toronto Law Journal* 35 (1986): 116–48.

37. *Open and Shut,* pp. 53–55; *Access and Privacy: The Steps Ahead,* pp. 20–21.

38. Commission of Inquiry Concerning Certain Activities of the Royal Canadian Mounted Police, *Freedom and Security under the Law,* Second Report, 2 vols. (Ottawa, August 1981), 1:518, 583; 2:795.

39. Ibid., 1:518–21.

40. *Globe and Mail,* February 12, 1983, p. 12.

41. House of Commons, *Debates,* February 14, 1983, p. 22808.

42. Ibid.

43. Jeff Sallot, "CSIS Unduly Invading Citizens' Privacy, Report Says," *Globe and Mail,* June 30, 1987, p. A3. See Security Intelligence Review Committee, *Annual Report, 1986–87* (Ottawa, 1987), p. 37.

44. See *Globe and Mail,* July 4, 1987, p. A5.

45. SIRC, *Annual Report, 1987–88* (Ottawa, 1988), p. 14.

46. Canadian Security Intelligence Service Act, *Revised Statutes of Canada,* 1985, c. C-23, sections 19, 71(2).

47. Ibid., section 89; Privacy Act, section 9(1.1).

48. CSIS Act, section 90; Privacy Act, section 22(1)(a)(iii).

49. Bill C-157, section 22(1); Jeff Sallot, "Spy Agency to See Secret Census Data," *Globe and Mail,* June 3, 1983, pp. 1–2.

50. Canada, *Personal Information Index 1983,* pp. 215–18.

51. See David H. Flaherty, *Privacy and Government Data Banks* (London, 1979), pp. 178, 191–99.

52. See Canada, *Personal Information Index 1983,* pp. 86–89.

53. House of Commons, *Debates,* February 11, 1983, p. 22748–49.

54. Ibid., February 14, 1983, p. 22809.

55. Revenue Canada Taxation, "Use of the Social Insurance Number," Information Circular 82-2, February 8, 1982, pp. 1–2.

56. *Privacy Times* 8 (October 26, 1988): 5–6.

57. Family Orders and Agreements Enforcement Assistance Act, *Statutes of Canada,* 1986, c. 5.

58. The judge sentenced the accused to twenty-four months in a provincial reformatory; *Queen* v. *Andreas Hackner,* Supreme Court of Ontario, Toronto, December 14, 1987; *Weekly Criminal Bulletin,* 2d ser., 4 (June 23, 1988): 73.

59. "Report of the Privacy Commissioner of Canada concerning the Security of Microforms containing Personal Information held by Revenue Canada (The Toronto and Saskatoon incidents)" (mimeographed, May 1987).

60. This paragraph is based on a discussion at a meeting of the Minister of National Revenue's Advisory Council on Tax Administration in Calgary, June 8, 1987. This writer has served on this panel since 1984.

61. *Statutes of Canada,* 1988, c. 51, section 420.28.

62. Polls commissioned in 1987 by Revenue Canada Taxation indicate that 67 percent of respondents thought that the department kept tax returns confidential, 14 percent disagreed, and 19 percent did not know. The confidence level had gradually improved from 58 percent in 1978.

Chapter 24

1. President of the Treasury Board, "Notes for a Statement," June 22, 1983, p. 4.

2. House of Commons, *Open and Shut: Enhancing the Right to Know and the Right to Privacy. Report of the Standing Committee on Justice and Solicitor General on the Review of the Access to Information Act and the Privacy Act* (Ottawa, 1987), pp. 43–44; hereafter cited as *Open and Shut.*

3. See the statement by the minister of communications, House of Commons, *Debates,* June 28, 1981, p. 18854; Privacy Act, *Revised Statutes of Canada,* 1985, c. P-21, section 75.

4. Since the Standing Committee on Justice and Solicitor General has no permanent staff beyond a clerk, it retained two academic specialists in 1985 to assist in the special three-year review. This writer drafted the material on privacy protection as a consultant to the committee.

5. See House of Commons, *Minutes of Proceedings and Evidence of the Standing Committee on Justice and Solicitor General,* Issue No. 15, May 5, 1987.

6. See, generally, Department of Justice, *Access and Privacy: The Steps Ahead* (Ottawa, 1987).

7. Governmental secrecy is still so excessive that the drafters of amendments do not consult with the privacy commissioner before submitting the proposed revisions to the Cabinet. At this stage and thereafter, it is much harder to make changes.

8. The privacy commissioner himself favors self-regulation for the private sector. See *Annual Report, Privacy Commissioner, 1987–88* (Ottawa, 1988), pp. 7–8.

9. *Open and Shut,* pp. 43–44; Department of Justice, *Access and Privacy: The Steps Ahead,* pp. 7–9.

10. See *Annual Report, Privacy Commissioner, 1987–88,* p. 14.

11. Ibid., pp. 5, 6.

12. See *Open and Shut,* pp. 77–79; and Department of Justice, *Access and Privacy: The Steps Ahead,* pp. 9, 21.

13. House of Commons, *Debates,* June 28, 1982, p. 18854.

14. See *Open and Shut,* pp. 74–77.

15. OECD, *Guidelines on the Protection of Privacy and Transborder Flows of Personal Data* (Paris, 1982).

16. See Department of Justice, *OECD Guidelines on the Protection of Privacy and Transborder Flows of Personal Data: Implications for Canada* (Ottawa, 1985); and *Open and Shut,* pp. 73–74.

17. As of July 31, 1987, 54 parent crown corporations, which are publicly owned, and 114 wholly-owned subsidiaries employ almost 183,000 persons.

Chapter 25

1. The original Public Law 93-579 has been codified, including amendments, at chapter 552a of title 5 of the *United States Code.*

2. See Hearings before a Subcommittee of the House Committee on Government Operations, June 7–8, 1983, *Oversight of the Privacy Act of 1974* (Washington, D.C., 1983).

3. See Robert Ellis Smith, *Compilation of State and Federal Privacy Laws 1988* (Washington, D.C., 1988), pp. 14–16, 28–29.

4. "All people are by nature free and independent, and have certain inalienable rights, among which are those of enjoying and defending life and liberty; acquiring, possessing and protecting property; and pursuing and obtaining safety, happiness, and privacy"; California Constitution, article 1, section 1, November 1972.

5. See Personal Privacy Protection Law, 1983 *New York Laws,* c. 652; *Privacy Law in the States,* appendix 1 to *Personal Privacy in an Information Society: The Report of the Privacy Protection Study Commission* (Washington, D.C., 1977), and Robert Ellis Smith, *Report on Data Protection and Privacy in Seven Selected States* (OTA, Washington, D.C., 1985).

6. See Samuel D. Warren and Louis D. Brandeis, "The Right to Privacy," *Harvard Law Review* 4 (1890): 193–220. The American literature on privacy is richer than for any other country. See David H. Flaherty, ed., *Privacy and Data Protection: An International Bibliography* (White Plains, N.Y., 1984).

7. The complexity and richness of American data protection laws is a persuasive theme of Robert Aldrich, *Privacy Protection Law in the United States* (NTIA Report 82-98, Washington, D.C., May 1982). This document is reprinted in *Oversight of the Privacy Act of 1974,* pp. 481–583.

8. Department of Health, Education, and Welfare, *Records, Computers, and the Rights of Citizens: Report of the Secretary's Advisory Committee on Automated Personal Data Systems* (Washington, D.C., 1973).

9. *Personal Privacy in an Information Society: The Report of the Privacy Protection Study Commission* (Washington, D.C., 1977). Five appendices were published separately.

10. *The Privacy Act of 1974: An Assessment,* appendix 4 to *The Report of the Privacy Protection Study Commission,* pp. 153–73.

11. The references to the House hearings in 1979–80 on insurance and health records can be found in Flaherty, *Privacy and Data Protection,* p. 62. The Privacy Protection Act of 1980, designed to control government searches of newsrooms, was not a product of the Privacy Protection Study Commission.

12. However, after a reporter obtained unauthorized access to the video rental list of the family of Robert Bork during his nomination hearings in 1987, the Video Privacy Protection Act of 1988 was quickly passed.

13. See Joseph W. Eaton, *Card-Carrying Americans: Privacy, Security, and the National ID Card Debate* (Totowa, N.J., 1986).

14. OMB, *Management of the United States Government: Fiscal Year 1988* (Washington, D.C., 1987), pp. 60–61.

15. The genesis of the "cable privacy" legislation is discussed in David H. Flaherty, *Protecting Privacy in Two-Way Electronic Services* (White Plains, N.Y., 1985), chap. 5. The Computer Security Act of 1987 (Public Law 100-235), which mandates the creation of a Computer System Security and Privacy Advisory Board within the Department of Commerce, is concerned with the privacy of sensitive personal information in federal computer systems.

16. See Senate Committee on Government Operations and House Committee on Government Operations (Subcommittee on Government Information and Individual Rights), *Legislative History of the Privacy Act of 1974: S. 3418. (Public Law 93-579)* (Washington, D.C., 1976), p. 169.

17. Ibid., p. 179.

18. Ibid., p. 180.

19. Ibid., pp. 186, 187.

20. Ibid.

21. Ibid., p. 179.

22. Ibid., pp. 179–80.

23. Ibid., p. 956.

24. Ibid., pp. 330–31. An amendment to the bill on the floor of the House failed.

25. Ibid., p. 893; the amendment is on pp. 945–47.

26. Ibid., p. 948.

27. Ibid., p. 949.

28. Ibid., pp. 951–52.

29. Ibid., pp. 334–47, 396–409.

30. Ibid., pp. 770, 773.

31. Ibid., pp. 779, 786.

32. Ibid., p. 834.

33. Ibid., pp. 808–9, 813.

34. Ibid., pp. 846, 865.

35. OMB, Circular No. A-130, "Management of Federal Information Resources," section 7(a), *Federal Register* 50 (December 24, 1985): 52736. A 1985 compilation indicated that there are 3,700 civilian record systems; see *Privacy Times,* December 24, 1987, p. 7.

36. Louis Harris and Associates, Inc., and Alan F. Westin, *The Dimensions of Privacy: A National Opinion Research Survey of Attitudes towards Privacy* (Stevens Point, Wis., 1979).

37. OTA, *Electronic Record Systems and Individual Privacy* (Washington, D.C., 1986), pp. 26–29.

38. House Committee on Government Operations (Subcommittee on Government Information, Justice, and Agriculture), *Who Cares About Privacy? Oversight of the Privacy Act of 1974 by the Office of Management and Budget and by the Congress* (Washington, D.C., 1983).

39. Its latest and most relevant series of reports are: OTA, *Electronic Surveillance and Civil Liberties* (Washington, D.C., 1985); *Management, Security, and Congressional Oversight* (Washington, D.C., 1986); and *Electronic Record Systems and Individual Privacy* (Washington, D.C., 1986).

40. OMB, Circular No. A-130, "Management of Federal Information Resources," pp. 52733–34, 52739.

41. OMB, Information Systems Policy Division, "Administration of the Privacy

Act of 1974," (January 4, 1980), printed in *Oversight of the Privacy Act of 1974,* pp. 616–17; and *The President's Annual Report on the Agencies' Implementation of the Privacy Act of 1974 CY 1982–1983* (mimeographed, Washington, D.C., 1985), pp. 117–18.

42. Ibid., pp. 57, 67. See also OMB, "Administration of the Privacy Act," p. 608.

43. The director delegated the authority to administer all functions under the Paperwork Act and the Privacy Act to the administrator, although he is still responsible for the administration of such functions (44 *United States Code* 3503). There have been at least four administrators of this office since 1980, which does not contribute to an encouraging environment for implementation of the Privacy Act.

44. Testimony of Christopher DeMuth, Administrator, OIRA, in *Oversight of the Privacy Act,* pp. 58, 69.

45. *President's Annual Report 1982–1983,* pp. 4–5.

46. *Oversight of the Privacy Act,* pp. 59, 71, 78–80. The administrator of OIRA in 1983 testified that he occasionally spent a half-day on the Privacy Act, especially in connection with computer matching issues (p. 78).

47. Ibid., p. 81.

48. Ibid., pp. 55–56.

49. See ibid., pp. 478–80.

50. See OMB, "Administration of the Privacy Act," pp. 610–14; and OMB, Circular No. A-130, "Management of Federal Information Resources," p. 52739.

51. OMB, Circular No. A-130, "Management of Federal Information Resources," p. 52748.

52. Ibid., pp. 52730–51.

53. This organization will be described in detail in Chapter 28. See *Oversight of the Privacy Act,* pp. 142–45.

54. Ibid., pp. 224, 239.

55. For example, Lois Alexander, a lawyer with the Office of Research and Statistics of the Social Security Administration, has served for at least a decade as a liaison on data protection matters in the large Social Security Administration within the enormous Department of Health and Human Services (DHHS).

56. *Oversight of the Privacy Act,* pp. 237–38. The official in question at DHHS has since left government service.

57. Carter dismantled the Office of Telecommunications Policy in January 1977, and transferred ultimate responsibility for implementing the Privacy Protection Study Commission's report to the National Telecommunications and Information Administration, a part of the Department of Commerce.

58. *Oversight of the Privacy Act,* p. 227.

59. See ibid., pp. 57, 62.

60. *Legislative History of the Privacy Act,* p. 867.

Chapter 26

1. The Privacy Act of 1974, Public Law 93-579, codified at chapter 552a of title 5 of the *United States Code;* see section 2. Detailed discussion of the matters treated in this chapter will be found in *The Privacy Act of 1974: An Assessment,* appendix 4 to *Personal Privacy in an Information Society: The Report of the Privacy Protection Study Commission* (Washington, D.C., 1977).

2. *The President's Annual Report on the Agencies' Implementation of the Privacy Act of 1974 CY 1982–1983* (mimeographed, Washington, D.C., 1985), pp. 117–18.

3. Privacy Act, sections (a)(4) and (a)(5). See Hearings before a Subcommittee of the House Committee on Government Operations, June 7–8, 1983, *Oversight of the Privacy Act of 1974* (Washington, D.C., 1983), pp. 274–76; and Richard Ehlke, "Litigation Trends under the Privacy Act," in ibid., pp. 445–49.

4. See *Personal Privacy in an Information Society: The Report of the Privacy Protection Study Commission* (Washington, D.C., 1977), pp. 503–5; and *Oversight of the Privacy Act,* pp. 276, 449.

5. OMB, Circular No. A-130, "Management of Federal Information Resources," *Federal Register* 50 (December 24, 1985): 52736.

6. Ibid.

7. Privacy Act, section (b). The Debt Collection Act of 1982 (Public Law 97-452) added a twelfth condition permitting disclosure of bad debt information to credit bureaus.

8. *Personal Privacy in an Information Society,* pp. 513–21, 532, 536.

9. Panel discussion, American Society of Access Professionals, Washington, D.C., November 19, 1982.

10. Privacy Act, sections (a)(7), (b)(3).

11. *President's Annual Report 1982–1983,* pp. 120–21 and, generally, pp. 118–21.

12. OMB, Circular No. A-130, "Management of Federal Information Resources," p. 52736.

13. See *Personal Privacy in an Information Society,* pp. 516–21.

14. *Oversight of the Privacy Act,* p. 273, also pp. 276–79.

15. Ibid., pp. 224, 253.

16. 1983 *New York Laws,* c. 652, section 92 (10).

Chapter 27

1. Hearings before a Subcommittee of the House Committee on Government Operations, June 7–8, 1983, *Oversight of the Privacy Act of 1974* (Washington, D.C., 1983), p. 256.

2. Ibid., p. 240.

3. See Testimony of David H. Flaherty, ibid., p. 182.

4. Ibid., p. 114.

5. OMB, Circular No. A-130, "Management of Federal Information Resources," section 7(a), *Federal Register* 50 (December 24, 1985): 52738–41, appendix 1.

6. *Oversight of the Privacy Act,* p. 256; see also p. 236.

7. Ibid., pp. 116, 117.

8. Ibid., pp. 95–112; for similar examples in 1979–80, see pp. 621–39.

9. *The President's Annual Report on the Agencies' Implementation of the Privacy Act of 1974 CY 1982–1983* (mimeographed, Washington, D.C., 1985), p. 68. The other examples cited are on pp. 74, 91–92, 97.

10. See *Oversight of the Privacy Act,* pp. 601–2.

11. OMB, Circular No. A-130, "Management of Federal Information Resources," p. 52751.

12. *Oversight of the Privacy Act,* p. 116.

13. Ibid., pp. 90–94, 113–14.

14. Ibid., p. 598.

15. Ibid., p. 271.

Chapter 28

1. Franklin Reeder, "Coordination of the Federal Privacy Act," in Steven E. Aufrecht, ed., *Expanding the Right to Privacy: Research and Legislative Initiatives for the Future: Final Conference Proceedings* (Los Angeles, 1976), pp. 32–33, 34–37. My comments depend in part on notes I took during Reeder's presentation.

2. The guidelines can be found in Senate Committee on Government Operations and House Committee on Government Operations (Subcommittee on Government Information and Individual Rights), *Legislative History of the Privacy Act of 1974: S. 3418. (Public Law 93–579)* (Washington, D.C., 1976), pp. 1015–1133; hereafter cited as *Legislative History of the Privacy Act*. OMB's emphasis on nonbinding guidelines spreads to its surrogates, such as the Office of Personnel Management.

3. *Personal Privacy in an Information Society: The Report of the Privacy Protection Study Commission* (Washington, D.C., 1977), p. 531.

4. OMB, Information Systems Policy Division, "Administration of the Privacy Act of 1974," January 4, 1980, p. 5. This document is reprinted in Hearings before a Subcommittee of the House Committee on Government Operations, June 7–8, 1983, *Oversight of the Privacy Act of 1974* (Washington, D.C., 1983), pp. 604–20.

5. *The President's Annual Report on the Agencies' Implementation of the Privacy Act of 1974 CY 1982–1983* (mimeographed, Washington, D.C., 1985), p. 12.

6. This paragraph is based on OMB, "Privacy Act of 1974; Guidance on the Privacy Act Implications of 'Call Detail' Programs to Manage Employees' Use of the Government's Telecommunications Systems," *Federal Register* 52 (April 20, 1987): 12990–93.

7. Ibid.

8. *Oversight of the Privacy Act*, pp. 470–71.

9. Ibid., pp. 58, 68; *President's Annual Report 1982–1983*, p. 6.

10. OMB, Circular No. A-130, "Management of Federal Information Resources," *Federal Register* 50 (December 24, 1985): 52740.

11. *Oversight of the Privacy Act*, pp. 616–17, 652–54.

12. This correspondence is printed in ibid., pp. 95–112. This major notice was the product of the department's thorough review of all of its systems of records; see *President's Annual Report 1982–1983*, p. 74.

13. *President's Annual Report 1982–1983*, pp. 68–69, 74, 91–92, 97.

14. *Privacy Times*, December 24, 1987, p. 7.

15. The Privacy Act of 1974, Public Law 93-579, codified at chapter 552a of title 5 of the *United States Code;* see sections (a)(7), (e)(4)(d); OMB, "Management of Federal Information Resources," p. 52740.

16. OMB tried to respond to President Carter's 1979 directive to control such practices, but supplementary guidelines were never issued, although a draft was circulated to agencies; see *Oversight of the Privacy Act*, pp. 124, 125.

17. OMB, "Proposed Guidance on the Privacy Act Implications of 'Call Detail' Programs to Manage Employees' Use of the Government's Telecommunications Systems," *Federal Register* 51 (May 23, 1986): 18985.

18. *Oversight of the Privacy Act*, pp. 621–27.

19. Ibid., pp. 118–19; *President's Annual Report 1982–83*, p. 97.

20. OTA, *Electronic Record Systems and Individual Privacy* (Washington, D.C., 1986), p. 103.

21. *President's Annual Report 1982-1983*, p. 8.

22. OMB, Circular No. A-130, "Management of Federal Information Resources," p. 52739.

23. *Oversight of the Privacy Act,* pp. 149–51.
24. This office has a staff of thirty-three, including seventeen attorneys.
25. The branch itself has six staff members; OIRA employs seventy.
26. The original language and other assignments can be reviewed in OMB, Circular No. A-130, "Management of Federal Information Resources," p. 52739.
27. See David H. Flaherty, *Privacy and Government Data Banks* (London, 1979), pp. 281, 285.
28. See *President's Annual Report 1982–83,* p. 19 and pp. 13–115 for a description of each major agency.
29. William Cavaney, the executive secretary of the Defense Privacy Board, stated at a meeting of the American Society of Access Professionals in Washington on November 19, 1982, that he was aware of the destruction of personal information.
30. *President's Annual Report 1982–83,* p. 74.
31. OTA, *Electronic Record Systems and Individual Privacy,* pp. 25, 117.
32. Ibid., p. 26.
33. *Oversight of the Privacy Act,* p. 144 and, generally, pp. 142–45, 153.
34. This pamphlet and the Defense Privacy Board's Decision Memorandum 83-1, dated June 7, 1983, are printed in ibid., pp. 155–78. See also Department of Defense, *Privacy Program* (DoD 5400.11-R, Washington, D.C., August 1983); and Department of Defense, *Training Manual: Privacy Act of 1974* (Washington, D.C., January 1988 edition).
35. *President's Annual Report 1982–83,* pp. 51–52, 63, 68, 74, 91–92, 97, and 114.
36. General Accounting Office, *Privacy Act: Federal Agencies' Implementation Can Be Improved* (GAO/GGD-86-107, Washington, D.C., August 1986), pp. 20, 24–27, 46–47.
37. Ibid., pp. 41–44, 47–48.
38. The Congressional Reports Elimination Act of 1982 (P.L. 97-375) removed the requirement that agencies publish yearly the full text of all their systems of records in the *Federal Register.* OMB claims that this action saved over $1 million.
39. Office of the Federal Register, *Privacy Act Issuances, 1980 Compilation,* vol. 1: *Systems of Records, Agency Rules* (Washington, D.C., 1981). A combined volume for 1982–83 was published in 1984; there was also a 1984 edition.
40. *Oversight of the Privacy Act,* pp. 89–90, 614–15.
41. Ibid., pp. 596–97, 146–49.
42. OTA, *Electronic Record Systems and Individual Privacy,* pp. 102, 107, 114.
43. Privacy Act, sections 2(b)(3) and 3(d)(f). See also OMB, Circular No. A-130, "Management of Federal Information Resources," section 8(5), p. 52736.
44. *Oversight of the Privacy Act,* pp. 60, 72, 74.
45. *President's Annual Report 1982–83,* p. 115.
46. Ibid., pp. 20–21, 53.
47. See the reports in ibid., pp. 69, 97–98.
48. Ibid., p. 85.
49. OTA, *Electronic Record Systems and Individual Privacy,* pp. 102, 103.
50. *Oversight of the Privacy Act,* p. 619.
51. OTA, *Electronic Record Systems and Individual Privacy,* p. 107.
52. Computer Matching and Privacy Protection Act of 1988, Public Law 100-503, section 8.
53. The titles are listed in David H. Flaherty, ed., *Privacy and Data Protection: An International Bibliography* (White Plains, N.Y., 1984), pp. 108–9.
54. Privacy Act, section (p).

55. *Oversight of the Privacy Act,* p. 88.

56. *President's Annual Report 1982–83,* p. 19 and passim.

57. OMB, Circular No. A-130, "Management of Federal Information Resources," p. 52740. OMB's instructions to agencies for the 1982 report were exceptionally detailed. See *Oversight of the Privacy Act,* pp. 615, 646–51.

58. See, for example, *The 1980 Annual Report to OMB for the Department of Health and Human Services for the Privacy Act of 1974* (mimeographed, Washington, D.C., April 1981).

59. *President's Annual Report 1982–83,* p. 49.

60. See the valuable table of "statutes providing protection for information privacy," in OTA, *Electronic Record Systems and Individual Privacy,* p. 15.

61. See Linda Greenhouse, "The Wiretapping Law Needs Some Renovation," *New York Times,* June 1, 1986, p. E4.

62. See the 1980 publication in *Oversight of the Privacy Act,* p. 618.

63. See the description of the first two acts in OTA, *Electronic Records Systems and Individual Privacy,* pp. 44–46 and, in particular, pp. 147–49, the "summary of final rules for income and eligibility verification required under the Deficit Reduction Act of 1984."

64. *President's Annual Report 1982–83,* p. 116. The other two initiatives, the Intelligence Identities Protection Act of 1982 and proposed amendments to the Freedom of Information Act, are also very peculiar examples of initiatives to improve the "privacy" of individuals.

65. These are published in ibid., pp. 133–44, and *Oversight of the Privacy Act,* pp. 414–25.

66. *Oversight of the Privacy Act,* p. 614.

67. See ibid., pp. 464–69, and OTA, *Electronic Record Systems and Individual Privacy,* p. 21.

68. *Oversight of the Privacy Act,* pp. 240–42.

69. One federal official in Louisiana was prosecuted for releasing administrative information on an identifiable individual; see *Privacy Journal,* 3 (February 1977): 1. In St. Louis in 1982 four detectives and one private investigator pleaded guilty under the Privacy Act to obtaining personal records from the Federal Bureau of Investigation under false pretenses and selling them; see *Privacy Times,* October 6, 1982, p. 1.

Chapter 29

1. An earlier draft of this chapter appeared in Hearings before the Senate Subcommittee on Oversight of Government Affairs, December 15–16, 1982, *Oversight of Computer Matching to Detect Fraud and Mismanagement in Government Programs* (Washington, D.C., 1983), pp. 472–89.

2. American Society of Access Professionals (ASAP), Washington, November 18, 1982. The inspectors general originated during the Carter administration. A second statutory enactment made them presidential appointments intended to be an auditing branch in each department.

3. See Michael J. Boskin, *Too Many Promises: The Uncertain Future of Social Security* (Homewood, Ill., 1986).

4. OMB, "Privacy Act Guidelines," *Federal Register* 40 (July 9, 1975): 28953.

5. Ibid.

6. OMB, "Privacy Act of 1974: Supplemental Guidance for Matching Programs,"

(draft, August 2, 1978); OMB, "Guidelines for the Conduct of Matching Programs," (March 30, 1979), *Federal Register* 44 (March 30, 1979): 23138.

7. Jake Kirchner, "Privacy. A History of Computer Matching in the Federal Government," *Computerworld,* December 14, 1981, p. 2.

8. OMB, "Supplemental Guidelines for Matching Programs" (draft, August 2, 1978), p. 2.

9. Quoted in Kirchner, "Privacy," p. 13.

10. OMB "Guidelines for the Conduct of Matching Programs" (March 30, 1979), p. 23139.

11. Kirchner, "Privacy," pp. 3, 6.

12. Goodman and Preyer are cited in ibid., pp. 6–7.

13. See Hearings before a Subcommittee of the House Committee on Government Operations, June 7–8, 1983, *Oversight of the Privacy Act of 1974* (Washington, D.C., 1983), pp. 278–79, and especially the 1977 correspondence of Goodman and Shattuck on pp. 284–90.

14. Kirchner, "Privacy," p. 15.

15. See *Oversight of the Privacy Act,* p. 597.

16. OMB, "Revised Supplemental Guidance for Conducting Matching Programs," memorandum, May 11, 1982, *Federal Register* 47 (May 19, 1982): 21656–57.

17. Ibid., p. 21657.

18. Ibid.

19. Ibid., pp. 21657–58.

20. In fact, the OMB guidelines state that such front-end verification is not a "matching program"; ibid., p. 21657.

21. A point made by Hugh V. O'Neill, then of the Department of Health and Human Services, at a session on computer matching, American Society of Access Professionals, Washington, D.C., November 18, 1982.

22. For example, the questions and answers about computer matching issued by PCIE on July 1, 1982, discuss the protection of personal privacy solely in such terms; PCIE, "Questions on Computer Matching," July 1, 1982, question 11.

23. The Privacy Act of 1974, Public Law 93-579, codified at chapter 552a of title 5 of the *United States Code* (5 *U.S.C.* 552a); see sections (i)(1) and (g)(D).

24. The speakers included leading privacy advocates John Shattuck, Ronald Plesser, and Robert Ellis Smith. See *Oversight of Computer Matching,* pp. 79, 80–81, 84, 104, 120, 127, 143, 156–57.

25. Ibid., p. 24.

26. Hugh V. O'Neill, DHHS, in an ASAP presentation, November 18, 1982.

27. OMB, Circular No. A-130, "Management of Federal Information Resources," section 7(a), *Federal Register* 50 (December 24, 1985): 52739–40. OMB and PCIE have developed a *Model Control System for Conducting Computer Matching Projects Involving Individual Privacy Data* (Washington, D.C., 1983), and a *Computer Match Checklist* (Washington, D.C., 1983).

28. *Oversight of the Privacy Act,* p. 598.

29. Ibid., pp. 117–18.

30. GAO, *Privacy Act: Federal Agencies' Implementation Can Be Improved* (GAO/GGD-86-107, Washington, D.C., August 1986), pp. 31–32, 47.

31. *The President's Annual Report on the Agencies' Implementation of the Privacy Act of 1974 CY 1982–1983* (mimeographed, Washington, D.C., 1985), pp. 6–8. The total number of matches reported to OMB continues to be impossibly small. Six matches

were reported in 1983 and thirteen in 1984; see OTA, *Electronic Record Systems and Individual Privacy* (Washington, D.C., 1986), p. 49.

32. *President's Annual Report 1982–1983,* p. 8.

33. Ibid., p. 51.

34. OTA, *Electronic Record Systems and Individual Privacy,* pp. 39, 40, 49, 58.

35. Ibid., pp. 53, 54.

36. See ibid., pp. 81–83, 94–95.

37. *Personal Privacy in an Information Society: The Report of the Privacy Protection Study Commission* (Washington, D.C., 1977), pp. 15–21.

38. Robert R. Belair, "Information Privacy," in Helen A. Shaw, ed., *Issues in Information Policy,* NTIA-SP-80-9 (Washington, D.C., 1981), pp. 44, 48.

39. The 1982 OMB guidelines define a "hit" as "the identification, through a matching program, of a specific individual"; see OMB, "Revised Supplemental Guidance for Conducting Matching Programs," p. 21657.

40. PCIE, "Questions on Computer Matching," July 1, 1982, question 13.

41. OTA, *Electronic Record Systems and Individual Privacy,* p. 53.

42. PCIE, "Questions on Computer Matching," July 1, 1982, questions 6 and 10.

43. *Federal Register* 47 (June 21, 1982): 26686.

44. This paragraph is based on House Committee on Government Operations, *Computer Matching and Privacy Protection Act of 1988,* Report 100-802 (Washington, D.C., 1988), p. 6.

45. DHHS, Office of Inspector General, *Computer Applications,* vol. 1, *Health Provider Fraud and Abuse* (Washington, D.C., June 1982), pp. 40–41.

46. See *Computerworld,* May 11, 1981, pp. 1, 6; and *Privacy Journal* 7 (April 1981): 1–2.

47. PCIE, "Questions about Matching," July 1, 1982, question 12.

48. Ibid.

49. Ibid., question 13.

50. *Computerworld,* March 8, 1982, p. 35.

51. See the up-to-date discussion in House Committee on Government Operations, *Computer Matching and Privacy Protection Act of 1988.*

52. See Kirchner, "Privacy," p. 14.

53. *Computerworld,* February 4, 1980, p. 5. Kusserow spoke at an ASAP meeting, Washington, D.C., November 18, 1982.

54. OTA, *Electronic Record Systems and Individual Privacy,* p. 57. See also GAO, *Computer Matching: Assessing Its Costs and Benefits,* GAO/PEMD-87-2 (Washington, D.C., November 1986), and GAO, *Computer Matching: Factors Influencing the Agency Decision-making Process,* GAO/PEMD-87-3BR (Washington, D.C., November 1986).

55. See Hearings before the Subcommittee on Oversight of Government Management of the Senate Committee on Governmental Affairs, *Computer Matching and Privacy Protection Act of 1986* (Washington, D.C., 1986); and Hearings before a Subcommittee of the House Committee on Government Operations, June 23, 1987, *Computer Matching and Privacy Protection Act of 1987* (Washington, D.C., 1987).

56. House Committee on Government Operations, *Computer Matching and Privacy Protection Act of 1988,* pp. 1, 5, 21–22.

57. Ibid., pp. 3, 5.

58. Ibid., p. 11.

59. Computer Matching and Privacy Protection Act of 1988, 5 U.S.C. 552a, sections 2 and 3.

60. Ibid., section 4. The key legislative concepts of "matching programs," "matching agreements," and "Data Integrity Boards" are discussed in detail in House Committee on Government Operations, *Computer Matching and Privacy Protection Act of 1988*, pp. 22–36.

61. Computer Matching and Privacy Protection Act, sections 6 and 9.

Chapter 30

1. *The President's Annual Report on the Agencies' Implementation of the Privacy Act of 1974 CY 1982–1983* (mimeographed, Washington, D.C., 1985).

2. Hearings before a Subcommittee of the House Committee on Government Operations, *Oversight of the Privacy Act* (Washington, D.C., 1983), pp. 73, 151. The Defense Privacy Board listed the following specific accomplishments under the Privacy Act: (1) outlawing secret personal files (unofficial files of convenience); (2) giving individuals a proprietorship in their records; (3) making "records managers aware that they are trustees for the person who is the subject of a record as well as for the government"; (4) reducing the proliferation of forms of marginal necessity; (5) a significant reduction in the number of systems of records; and (6) "a trend towards maintaining only that information that is both relevant and necessary for a system manager"; see pp. 145–46, 151.

3. Ibid., pp. 224, 273.

4. David Burnham, *The Rise of the Computer State* (New York, 1983), p. 224.

5. Senate Committee on Government Operations and House Committee on Government Operations (Subcommittee on Government Information and Individual Rights), *Legislative History of the Privacy Act of 1974: S. 3418. (Public Law 93-579)* (Washington, D.C., 1976), p. 867.

6. *Personal Privacy in an Information Society: The Report of the Privacy Protection Study Commission* (Washington, D.C., July, 1977), pp. 35–37.

7. Ibid.

8. Ibid., p. 35.

9. Ibid., p. 36.

10. Ibid., p. 37.

11. Ibid.

12. Ibid.

13. Ibid., p. 499. I disagree with the view "that each agency is in the best position to judge what is best, reasonable, or appropriate for it" under the Privacy Act (p. 523).

14. Ibid., pp. 499, 502, 517, 519.

15. Ibid., pp. 521–22.

16. Ibid., pp. 523, 532.

17. Ibid., p. 532.

18. John Wicklein, *Electronic Nightmare* (New York, 1981), pp. 212–13.

19. Hearings before the Senate Subcommittee on Oversight of Government Affairs, December 15–16, 1982, *Oversight of Computer Matching to Detect Fraud and Mismanagement in Government Programs* (Washington, D.C., 1983), p. 253.

20. Ibid., pp. 253–54.

21. Ibid., pp. 94–95.

22. OTA, *Electronic Record Systems and Individual Privacy* (Washington, D.C., 1986), pp. 104–7.

23. Ibid., pp. 118–22.

24. *New York Times,* July 3, 1986, p. 14.

25. See *Personal Privacy in an Information Society,* p. 37.

26. *Oversight of the Privacy Act,* p. 283.

27. I owe this suggestion to David F. Linowes.

28. For an excellent review of many of the deficiencies of the Privacy Act, see Robert R. Belair, "Information Privacy," in Helen A. Shaw, ed., *Issues in Information Policy,* NTIA-SP-80-9 (Washington, D.C., 1981), pp. 37–52.

29. OTA, *Electronic Record Systems and Individual Privacy,* pp. 13, 22–25.

30. *Legislative History of the Privacy Act,* p. 168.

31. *Oversight of the Privacy Act,* p. 146.

32. *President's Annual Report 1982–1983,* p. 117.

33. Hearing before a Subcommittee of the House Committee on Government Operations, June 23, 1987, *Computer Matching and Privacy Protection Act of 1987* (Washington, D.C., 1987), pp. 17–18, 25.

34. See OMB, "Proposed Guidance on the Privacy Act Implications of 'Call Detail' Programs to Manage Employees' Use of the Government's Telecommunications Systems," *Federal Register* 51 (May 23, 1986): 18982; and OMB, Circular No. A-130, "Management of Federal Information Resources," *Federal Register* 50 (December 24, 1985): 52730.

35. See the agreement concerning the need to strengthen the role of OMB in OTA, *Electronic Record Systems and Individual Privacy,* pp. 115–17.

36. Ibid., p. 117.

37. Hearing before a Subcommittee of the House Committee on Government Operations, *Computer Matching and Privacy Protection Act of 1987,* pp. 17–18, 25.

38. OTA, *Electronic Record Systems and Individual Privacy,* p. 118.

39. *President's Annual Report 1982–1983,* pp. 117–23. OMB indicated a somewhat different list of needed reforms in *Oversight of the Privacy Act,* pp. 61–62, 75–76.

40. See *Oversight of the Privacy Act,* pp. 146–49, 470–74.

41. OTA, *Electronic Record Systems and Individual Privacy,* pp. 102–4.

Conclusion

1. See *Transnational Data and Communications Report* 11 (March 1988): 29; and Council of Europe, *Explanatory Report on the Convention for the Protection of Individuals with Regard to Automatic Processing of Personal Data* (Strasbourg, 1981), hereafter cited as Council of Europe, *Convention.*

2. Council of Europe, *Legislation and Data Protection* (Rome, 1983), p. 51.

3. It is not essential to settle the relative contribution to the origins of data protection laws of any bureaucracy's insatiable need for data, since the need to protect personal privacy in the face of such encroachments seems self-evidently important as an impetus to reform. See James Rule et al., *The Politics of Privacy* (New York, 1980).

4. Ontario, *Report of the Commission of Inquiry into the Confidentiality of Health Information,* 3 vols. (Toronto, 1980). Justice Horace Krever chaired the commission.

5. I owe this point to discussions initiated by Jean-Pierre Chamoux of France, supported by Hans Peter Bull of West Germany, at the Bellagio conference. See David H. Flaherty, "Final Report of the Bellagio Conference on Current and Future Problems of Data Protection," *Government Information Quarterly* 1 (1984): 431–42.

6. OECD, *Guidelines on the Protection of Privacy and Transborder Flows of Personal Data* (Paris, 1981), pp. 9, 24–25, 26–27.

7. Jon Bing, "Personal Data Systems—A Comparative Perspective on a Basic Concept in Privacy Legislation," *Information Privacy* [now *Information Age*] 2 (January 1980): 30.

8. Although other countries have usually failed to accept this persuasive French position, there is no ready evidence that the focus of a data protection law solely on automated records has stopped or reversed the computerization of manual records.

9. There are helpful discussions of criteria for sensitivity in the explanatory memorandum accompanying the OECD, *Guidelines,* pp. 27, 29; Council of Europe, *Convention,* pp. 17, 32; and Council of Europe, *Legislation and Data Protection,* pp. 16–17, 38, 42, 53, 64, 65.

10. The system is described in critical detail in *Le Monde,* March 30, 1983, pp. 2, 10.

11. Canada, House of Commons, Standing Committee on Justice and Solicitor General, *Open and Shut: Enhancing the Right to Know and the Right to Privacy* (Ottawa, 1987), p. 91.

12. Wolfgang Hoffman, "Controversy over Banks' Role as Suppliers of Customer Information," *Die Zeit,* January 20, 1984, as republished in *The German Tribune,* January 29, 1984, p. 8.

13. The Council of Europe focused its efforts on data protection, which it defines as "the legal protection of individuals with regard to automatic processing of personal information relating to them"; Council of Europe, *Convention,* pp. 5, 29.

14. Data Protection Act 1984, c. 35, in *Halsbury's Statutes of England and Wales,* 4th ed. (London, 1985), 6:831.

15. See Nelson Rosenbaum, "Statutory Structure and Policy Implementation: The Case of Wetlands Regulation," in Daniel A. Mazmanian and Paul A. Sabatier, eds., *Effective Policy Implementation* (Lexington, Mass., and Toronto, 1981), p. 64.

16. Herbert Burkert, "Institutions of Data Protection: An Attempt at a Functional Explanation of European National Data Protection Laws," *Computer Law Journal* 3 (1981): 169n, 172. Herbert Auernhammer, the official in the Ministry of the Interior who continued to oversee the development of the data protection law in West Germany until 1985, claims that privacy cannot be defined once and for all. Simitis also believes that privacy interests cannot be defined more precisely in today's laws. In my view, the search for precision in general laws has to continue, leading to appropriate care in sectoral applications of the principles of data protection. See Council of Europe, *Legislation and Data Protection,* pp. x, 31, 37–38.

17. See W. A. Parent, "Recent Work on the Concept of Privacy," *American Philosophical Quarterly* 20 (1983): 341–55.

18. I reject the view that the battle to protect privacy has been lost already and that persons simply have to adjust to less privacy in an information age. The primary changes over time are in the particular balance of values, such as privacy, that individuals and societies choose for themselves. Examples of inventions and social changes that have affected this balance include the telegraph, the telephone, urbanization, and now the computer.

19. Alan F. Westin, *Privacy and Freedom* (New York, 1967), p. 67.

20. For a successful attack on reductionists, such as William Prosser and Richard Posner, who do not see any privacy interests as such for the law to protect but only subordinate values such as reputation, see Ruth Gavison, "Privacy and the Limits of the Law," *The Yale Law Journal* 89 (1980): 421–71.

21. Refering to privacy claims as nonlegal simply acknowledges that the search for privacy is influenced by such varied areas as the architecture of homes, town planning, the character of family, neighborhood, and community life, communications and

correspondence, institutional life affecting individuals, and the entire role of governments, law enforcers, and courts in human existence. For such a broad portrayal of concern for privacy in a preindustrial society, see Flaherty, *Privacy in Colonial New England* (Charlottesville, Va., 1972).

22. Spiros Simitis, ed., *Data Protection Act of the State of Hesse* (Wiesbaden, 1987), p. 8.

23. One also takes for granted the right to disclose all information about oneself and to place no value on personal privacy.

24. See Gavison, "Privacy and the Limits of the Law," p. 459.

25. Council of Europe, *Legislation and Data Protection*, p. 16.

26. The OECD *Guidelines* recommend that "countries should establish legal, administrative or other procedures or institutions for the protection of privacy," but, unwisely in my view, permit "different approaches to the issue of control mechanisms," using the establishment of special supervisory bodies as simply one alternative; see *Guidelines*, pp. 12, 34–35. The Explanatory Report of the Council of Europe notes that "most countries having a data protection law also have a special protection authority," but "this does not mean that the convention requires each State to have a data protection authority"; Council of Europe, *Convention*, p. 23.

27. Arnold Simmel, "Privacy," *International Encyclopedia of the Social Sciences* 12 (1968): 482.

28. See Lawrence Baum, "Comparing the Implementation of Legislative and Judicial Policies," in Mazmanian and Sabatier, *Effective Policy Implementation*, p. 47.

29. It is natural to encounter resistance to explicit, institutionalized efforts to control behavior administratively. See Eugene Bardach, *The Implementation Game: What Happens After a Bill Becomes a Law* (Cambridge, Mass., 1977), p. 66.

30. Larry B. Hill, *The Model Ombudsman: Institutionalizing New Zealand's Democratic Experiment* (Princeton, N.J., 1976), p. 75.

31. See *Annual Report, Privacy Commissioner, 1985–86* (Ottawa, 1986), pp. 16–20.

32. Rosenbaum, "Statutory Structure and Policy Implementation," pp. 64–65.

33. Simitis, "Data Protection—A Few Critical Remarks," in Council of Europe, *Legislation and Data Protection*, p. 177.

34. *Annual Report, Privacy Commissioner, 1986–87* (Ottawa, 1987) pp. 2–3.

35. See the initial assessment in David H. Flaherty, "Governmental Surveillance and Bureaucratic Accountability: Data Protection Agencies in Western Societies," *Science, Technology & Human Values* 11 (1986): 7–18; and the discussion in Flaherty, "Final Report of the Bellagio Conference," pp. 440–41.

36. See Council of Europe, *Legislation and Data Protection*, pp. 20, 30.

37. Walter Gellhorn, *Ombudsmen and Others* (Cambridge, Mass., 1967), p. 438; and Paul A. Sabatier and Daniel A. Mazmanian, "The Implementation of Public Policy: A Framework of Analysis," in Mazmanian and Sabatier, *Effective Policy Implementation*, p. 20.

38. See generally Bardach, *The Implementation Game*.

39. Although I emphasize the importance of personnel for effective implementation, I do not wish to deny the force of sociologist Gary Marx's point that appropriate structures for data protection have to be in place if such people are to act. In fact, a sound structure may permit an agency to survive the appointment of a weak commissioner.

40. Sabatier and Mazmanian, "The Implementation of Public Policy," pp. 20, 22.

41. There is a strong argument, of course, for rotating people through such leadership positions over time in order to hinder stagnation.

42. Gellhorn, *Ombudsmen and Others*, p. 204.

43. Except perhaps in France, data protection agencies have to date avoided another implementation game, whereby hostile interests seek to appoint sympathetic personnel or to reeducate them to their point of view once in office. See Bardach, *The Implementation Game.*

44. If data protection becomes only a debate on the meaning of legal terms, it runs the risk of encouraging the excessive legalization and even trivialization of the process of data protection. The real goals of this crucial activity can be lost in a controversy among lawyers over the meaning of the law, as has happened to some extent in West Germany.

45. Council of Europe, *Legislation and Data Protection,* pp. 118, and also 41–42, 51, 121.

46. Some critics believe that Hesse needs a full-time DPC. Simitis' involvement with the office varies from one to two days a week during the first half of the calendar year to a full-time presence as the time for his annual report draws near. Hesse is in fact the only jurisdiction anywhere in which the DPC tries to function on a part-time basis.

47. Fred S. Coombs, "The Bases of Noncompliance with a Policy," in John G. Grumm and Stephen L. Wasby, eds., *The Analysis of Policy Impact* (Lexington, Mass., 1981), pp. 53–61; Bardach, *The Implementation Game,* p. 187.

48. Comparing the costs of data protection among the respective agencies studied in this volume would be very difficult. The cost of the different factors of production vary widely and often in a manner that is hard to explain. The expenses of a data protection authority are also to a high degree related to a country's administrative system and the distribution of roles between authorities. Even the fixing of charges does not have only economic grounds. (I am grateful to Edmund Rapaport of Statistics Sweden for discussions on this point.)

49. Bardach, *The Implementation Game,* p. 128; Gellhorn, *Ombudsmen and Others,* p. 423.

50. See Council of Europe, *Legislation and Data Protection,* pp. 101–3, 118–19, 123, 131–32.

51. Simitis, "Data Protection—A Few Critical Remarks," in ibid., p. 177.

52. Ibid., pp. 85, 87, 93–94, 108, 123.

53. "L'Ordinateur mène l'enquête," *Le Monde,* December 9, 1988, pp. 1, 14; and December 10, 1988, p. 13.

54. Unfortunately, from 1983 to 1987, there was no meaningful annual oversight by the relevant committee. In many ways, the conduct of the three-year review from 1985–87 served this function.

55. Bardach, *The Implementation Game,* p. 312; see also pp. 85, 278.

56. Burkert, "Institutions of Data Protection," p. 181.

57. See Council of Europe, *Legislation and Data Protection,* p. 107.

58. See the discussion in ibid., pp. 84, 92–93, 115–16, 121.

59. Ibid., pp. 105, 109–10.

60. Bill 34, Freedom of Information and Protection of Privacy Act, 1987, *Statutes of Ontario,* 1987, c. 25, sections 50 and 54.

61. Bardach, *The Implementation Game,* pp. 121, 225–26.

62. Council of Europe, *Legislation and Data Protection,* pp. 44–45.

63. For a valuable review of the scope of existing laws, see Bing, "Personal Data Systems—A Comparative Perspective," *Information Privacy* 2, no. 1 (1980): 28–33.

64. Council of Europe, *Legislation and Data Protection,* pp. 19–23, 51–52; and Simitis, "Data Protection—A Few Critical Remarks," p. 93.

65. *Transnational Data Report* 5 (January–February 1982): 13.

66. A good beginning is Department of Science, *A National Information Policy for Australia: Discussion Paper* (Canberra, December 1985).

67. *Open and Shut,* pp. 71–73.

68. See Jon Bing, "Classification of Personal Information with Respect to the Sensitivity Aspect," in *Data Banks and Society* (Oslo, 1972), pp. 98–141.

69. See Arve Fóyen, "Experiences with Implementation of the Norwegian Personal Registers Act," in Council of Europe, *Legislation and Data Protection,* pp. 212–14 and, generally, pp. 81–83.

70. A single complaint may in fact require a good deal of staff time to resolve, thus making raw counts of the number of complaints of little utility for comparative purposes.

71. Larry Hill concluded in New Zealand that "the Ombudsman's mere existence as a wailing wall for the expression of grievances is therapeutic for citizens." He described the great bulk of the clients in question as "competent, responsible, ordinary New Zealanders with very real problems"; see *Model Ombudsman,* pp. 127, 129, 194. Unfortunately, there is no systematic information about who actually complains to data protectors.

72. Such staff specialization in types of information systems seems essential to promoting systemic reforms.

73. *The Implementation Game,* p. 76.

74. On a related issue, only Canada publishes a detailed guide to personal information systems, so that a person may learn about the existence of various data banks and the surveillance practices associated with them. This aspect of informing the public is not well handled in other countries.

75. Council of Europe, *Legislation and Data Protection,* p. 111.

76. See Hans-Peter Gebhardt, "Data Protection in Telecommunications Services," *Transnational Data and Communications Report* 11 (June–July 1988): 18–23.

77. Council of Europe, *Legislation and Data Protection,* pp. 117–18.

78. Burkert, "Institutions of Data Protection," p. 169.

79. See *International Herald Tribune,* March 28, 1983.

80. Data protectors must be especially prepared for influencing the redesign of major government information systems, as the time, funds, and skilled programmers become available. The likelihood that such redesigns will make greater use of standard, as opposed to custom-designed, software systems makes it easier for data protection to be built into the system from the beginning, since it is not a difficult problem and creates only marginally more work over time.

81. Quebec, An Act Respecting Access to Documents Held by Public Bodies and the Protection of Personal Information, *Revised Statutes of Quebec,* c. A-2.1; *Statutes of Quebec,* 1982, c. 30.

82. H. Patrick Glenn, "The Right to Privacy in Quebec Law," in Dale Gibson, ed., *Aspects of Privacy Law* (Toronto, 1980), p. 42.

83. See Simitis, *Data Protection Act of the State of Hesse; Open and Shut;* and Department of Justice, *Access and Privacy: The Steps Ahead* (Ottawa, 1987).

84. See *Open and Shut,* pp. 74–77; and Groupe de recherche informatique et droit, *L'Identité piratée: Etude sur la situation des bases de données à caractère personnel dans le secteur privé au Québec et sur leur réglementation en droit comparé et international* (Quebec, 1986).

85. My views are developed in David H. Flaherty, *Protecting Privacy in Two-Way Electronic Services* (White Plains, N.Y., 1985), especially chaps. 5–7.

Index

impact of, 26, 107, 134, 151, 156–59, 202, 236; independence of, 46, 112–15, 117, 392; use of power by, 66, 102, 115–20, 122–25, 140, 141–42; licensing power of, 67, 93, 94, 102, 116, 134, 156–57; appeals to government from, 93, 109, 395; and revision of Data Act, 95; board of, 98, 101, 103, 112; advocates individual rights, 99; constituency for, 99; expectations of, 100; compared to CNIL, 101, 102, 112, 165, 190–91, 211; staffing of, 102, 115, 128–30, 142, 160, 389, 390; role of director general, 102, 126–28; attitude toward computerization, 104; defines privacy, 105, 106, 107; balances interests, 109, 140; conciliatory approach of, 110, 145; and government ministries, 110–11; budget of, 113, 114, 115, 123, 158; and Ministry of Justice, 113, 114, 158; and exempt files, 116, 132; and Statistics Sweden, 119, 151–53; prosecutions by, 119; resists record linkages, 120–22, 123, 124–25, 139, 188; articulates privacy interests, 122, 140; and changing political climate, 124, 195; dominated by Freese, 128; bureaucratic tendencies of, 130–31; statutory duties of, 131–35; inspections by, 133–35, 400–401; complaints to, 136–37, 142, 148–49; reporting by, 138; shapes new laws and regulations, 141; encourages SPAR, 149–50; and Project Metropolitan, 153–55; relations with DALK, 160; and information policy, 398–99. *See also* Data protection—Sweden

Data Integrity Boards, 357–59, 367, 370

Data linkages. *See* Record linkages

Data Ordinance (Sweden), 116

Data processing, regulation of, 393, 403; Federal Republic of Germany, 27, 30–31, 33, 35, 47, 56, 90; Sweden, 95, 114, 132, 133, 151; France, 175, 176–77, 178, 180, 202–3, 207–8; Canada, 253; United States, 321–22, 329–30. *See also* Informatics

Data Processing Methods Division (DOMI), 222

Data protection: defined, xiii–xiv, 462 (n. 13); as political issue, 10; purpose of, 11, 334, 397–99; effectiveness of, 13, 391, 399; opponents of, 14–15, 239; and competing interests, 15, 16, 190, 312, 365, 379, 388–89; models of, 17, 94, 200, 369, 386, 396, 405; legislative role in, 24; and political climate, 46, 124, 376, 396; constitutional entrenchment of, 46–47, 376–77; origins of, 80; and balance of interests, 85, 122, 154–55, 334, 345; routinization of, 85, 128, 130, 159, 166, 235, 387; and new technology, 86, 122–23, 171, 402–4; licensing systems of, 94, 95, 131, 191,

234, 374, 394–95; role of conflict in, 123; importance of leadership of, 128, 250, 263, 371, 386; benefits of, 144; illusion of, 158, 389; politicization of, 165–66, 169, 189–91, 199, 234–35; academic interest in, 179; and staff rotation, 198; and individual access to data, 207; principles of, 210–11; and public relations, 277; and mediation, 278; bureaucratic resistance to, 364, 382, 391; coordinated systems for, 372; as non-legal activity, 379; neglect of auditing in, 389, 400–401; costs of, 389–92, 464 (n. 48); power relationships in, 393–94; and information policy, 398–400; and private sector, 406

—Canada, 100, 359, 391, 395; absence of, 4; and freedom of information, 98, 161, 243, 248; index of data banks, 135, 269–70; compared to France, 190–91; and influence of foreign laws, 245–46; parliamentary oversight of, 246–47, 299; costs of, 251–52; federal-provincial problems of, 257, 271–72, 283; regulatory power in, 262, 297. *See also* Ontario; Quebec

—Federal Republic of Germany, 391; constitutional basis of, 22, 34, 46–47, 86, 88, 89, 161; media role in, 22, 63–64; issues of power in, 24–25; complexity of, 27; officers for, 27; role of Ministries of the Interior in, 28; relation to federal and state laws, 28, 89; varying approaches to, 32; conflicts over, 32, 37–39, 57, 85, 111, 257; opponents of, 32–33, 36, 64; resistance to, 35, 45, 85, 383; budgets for, 41–42, 83; staffing of, 50–51, 102; costs of, 55, 64; role of courts in, 61, 67–68; public awareness of, 63; as cooperative effort, 66; impact of, 70, 76, 82, 84–86, 395; critics of, 76; need for licensing of, 90; compared to France, 190–91

—France: bureaucratic approach of, 94; Swedish influence on, 94, 168; and freedom of information, 98; and mass media, 111; routinization of, 123, 235; formative influences on, 169–72; political climate for, 171, 182, 386; and freedom of expression, 196–97

—Hesse: origins of, 22; and definition of privacy interests, 34; independence of commissioner in, 42–44; data registers in, 60; access to data, 61. *See also* Simitis, Spiros

—North Rhine–Westphalia, 393; constitutional basis of, 38; data registers in, 60

—Sweden, 391; origins of, 94, 143; legislative involvement in, 95; costs of, 95, 114–15, 130, 134; creation of DIB, 96; and freedom of information, 98, 161; and surveillance, 100; conflicts over, 110, 124; and balancing interests, 117, 125, 130, 147,